EVERYDAY LIFE

OF

THE GREEKS AND ROMANS

E. GUHL and W. KONER

CRESCENT BOOKS
NEW YORK

This 1989 edition published by Crescent Books,
distributed by Crown Publishers, Inc., 225 Park Avenue South,
New York, New York 10003.

Printed and bound in Finland

ISBN 0-517-68633-3

h g f e d c b a

CONTENTS.

THE GREEKS.

THE ROMANS.

TRANSLATOR'S NOTE.

In order to make the present volume more acceptable to the English reader the letterpress has been considerably shortened, partly by means of condensation, such as the more concise character of our language, in comparison with the German, permits of, partly by the occasional omission of details which seemed to lie somewhat beyond the scope of the work. Nothing of importance, however, has been left out, and it is hoped that this English version will fulfil, no less perfectly than the original, the task of rendering a comprehensive account of the life and manners of the two great antique nations, founded on the latest results of modern research, and illustrated by the careful reproduction of Greek and Roman monuments. It ought to be added that after the decease of one of the authors—Professor E. Guhl, in 1862—Professor W. Koner, of the University Library, Berlin, has brought out two revised and considerably augmented editions of their common work.

THE GREEKS.

1. In undertaking to describe the life of the Greeks in its distinct external appearance, we have first of all to direct our attention to the products of architecture. For of all the creations designed by man's ingenuity and executed by his hand, these produce the grandest and most powerful impression and give the most distinguishable character to the life of a nation.

Originated by the free creative phantasy of man, they have to serve at the same time certain purposes and demands of life. They therefore open a view into the genius of their creators, giving at the same time a picture of the real existence in which these creators moved. If this is true of nations in general, it is particularly the case with the Greeks, because they were enabled and gifted more than any other nation to render the innermost nature of their genius in external works of art. It being the task of all investigations of antique Greece to make us understand the spirit and mode of thinking and living of this people, we shall scarcely be able to attain this aim without considering, together with the creations of their poetry and philosophy, with the legal institutions of the State and the doctrines of their religion, also the numerous and variegated productions of their architecture. In these, no less than in the others, Greek genius and Greek culture find their expression, with all the greater distinctness as these introduce us into the varied phases of real existence, and tend to show a distinct character common to all their different peculiarities.

For whatever part of Greek life we may consider—be it public acts of religion or social intercourse, public feasts and games, or the more quiet scenes of home and family—we find that for all these their ingenious mind has created works of architecture, which, through being regulated by these various demands, give us a much more vivid idea of this life than the mostly isolated written testimonials in our possession are able to. Indeed, the materials which these latter offer to our investigation can only be completed and invested with full life by an accurate knowledge of the monuments.

To do this in a manner as complete and comprehensive of all the phases of life as possible is the task of "the architectural remnants of the Greeks," with which we begin our description of antique life. It is not our intention to give an æsthetical reason for the forms, or a history of their development, which belong to a different science. We only wish to show how the Greeks supplied the various demands of religion, and of public and private life, in their edifices. For this reason also our division of the abundant material cannot but be a purely practical one; beginning, quite in accordance with Greek notions, with a description of the temples, and adding afterwards the various kinds of profane buildings. For it was the custom of the Greeks to begin with divine things even in the works of daily life, and of all their creations none are so apt to bring home to us this connection between the celestial and terrestrial as those belonging to the domain of the fine arts.

Poetry begins simultaneously with the narration of human feats of valour and the praise of the immortal gods. The fine arts are developed from the ornamentation of the various appliances of daily life, combined with the desire of giving distinct form to the image of the deity. In this manner architecture serves a material want in affording shelter to human beings, but no less it meets the ideal want of the religious mind in erecting the temple as the protecting dwelling of the divine image. A firm house was prepared for the god to testify his protecting presence, and a centre was created, round which the exercises of various arts grouped themselves. In building and adorning temples architecture has become a fine art, and the images of the gods dwelling therein, combined with the symbolical representation of their deeds and history, have raised sculpture to its highest perfection. Moreover, in the same manner, as within the holy precinct the peace-offering was celebrated, the temple became likewise the centre of festival and dignified events which were so frequent in the life of the Greeks, and endowed it throughout with an artistically beautiful and harmonious impression. In front of the temples were heard the songs of the god-inspired poet; it was there that the processions of Greek virgins moved in measured grace, that the powerful beauty of youths strengthened by athletic sports showed itself. In the shadow of the temples walked the sages and leaders of the people, and round them gathered the wide circle of free and honest citizens, rejoicing in the enjoyment of a life ennobled by art and culture, and justly proud in the consciousness of being Greeks. In this way the temple became the rallying-point of everything good, noble, and beautiful, which we still consider as the glory of Greek culture and refinement. To the temple, therefore, we must first of all devote our attention in order to revive our consciousness of the spirit and essence of classical antiquity.

2. But not at all times were there amongst the Greeks such temples connected with the veneration of certain gods. Not to speak of the earliest periods of Greek history, during which the gods were adored as nameless and impersonal powers, as, for instance, by the Pelasgi, it also happened at much later times that the divine principle was considered as present in certain phenomena of nature. Fountains and trees, caves and mountains, were considered as seats of the gods, and revered accordingly, even without being changed into divine habitations by the art of man. So it happened that offerings and gifts were devoted to certain trees believed to be the symbols and seats of certain gods; nay, sometimes such trees were adorned with garlands, and altars were erected in front of them. Representations from later periods testify this in various ways. Fig. 1, for instance, shows a sacred pine, to which are attached peculiarly tied wreaths and sounding brasses (κρόταλον), as they were used in the service of Dionysos, the altar in front being destined for the reception of offerings.

Fig. 1.

Amongst mountains, particularly Parnassos and Olympos were considered as favourite seats of the gods. We also find not unfrequently that certain religious rites were connected with natural caves; these being naturally considered as the seats of superhuman powers because of the strong impression made by

their mysterious darkness on the human mind. Pausanias, for instance, tells us that a cave in a cliff near Bura in Achaia was dedicated to the Herakles Buraïkos, and that in it there was an oracle which disclosed the future by means of dice. Recent travellers believe that they have rediscovered this oracu-

Fig. 2.

lar cave of Herakles in the cliff represented by Fig. 2. They allege that the natural rock has been shaped purposely into a certain form, and that, at the top of the rock, the rudely worked likeness of a head is recognisable.

These and other similar usages point back to a time when the gods were considered in the light of indefinite powers; the want of temples, properly speaking, seems to have become more urgent only when the gods began to be imagined and represented under distinct human forms. Only then it became of importance to find for the representative image of the god a certain protected dwelling-place. But here again it was originally the custom to make use of natural objects which were considered as connected

with the nature of the god, and the same places which formerly were considered as the habitations of divine beings now were in reality used or prepared for the reception of the idol. We know, for instance, that the oldest image of Artemis, at Ephesos, was placed in the hollow stem of an elm-tree: even Pausanias saw in his own time the image of Artemis Kedreatis in a large cedar at Orchomenos. Later sculptors often show divine images of smaller size placed

Fig. 3.

on the stem or branches of protecting trees, as is the case in a relief (Fig. 3).

3. The above-mentioned appliances for the protection of

divine images may be considered as preparatory stages of the temple properly so called. In the same degree as architecture in its attempts at constructing and securing human dwellings became more and more developed (see § 21), the desire became apparent of procuring to the god a dwelling at once firm and lasting in accordance with his eternal nature. With the progress of architecture, which made this possible, the development of sculpture went hand in hand ; and as, in the poems of the Greeks, the gods become more and more humanised, we notice in the same degree a change in the fine arts from the bare and simple outline to a more and more perfect human representation of the gods. And the nearer god approached man, the closer also the primitive protection of the image began to resemble the house. A lucky accident has preserved in Euboea several specimens of the oldest temple-buildings in the shape of simple stone houses. In this island, not far from the town of Karystos, rises the steep mountain of Ocha (called at present Hagios Elias). At a considerable height there is a narrow plateau, to which there is only one access, and over which the rock rises still a little higher. On this plateau modern travellers (first Hawkins) have discovered

a stone house, from which there is a splendid view over the sea and the island (see Fig. 4). According to the measurement of Ulrich, it forms an oblong from west to east of forty feet in outer length, by twenty-four in width.

Fig. 4.

The walls, four feet deep and formed of irregular pieces of slate, rise to seven feet in the interior. In the southern wall there is a gate covered with a slab thirteen feet long by one and a half feet thick, and two small windows which remind one of the gates in old Kyklopic or Pelasgic walls (see § 18). The roof of this house consists of hewn stone slabs, which, resting on the thickness of the wall, are pushed one over the other towards the inside—a mode of covering which has also been used in the buildings of the earliest period of Greek archi-

tecture, as, for instance, in the treasure-houses of the old royal
palaces. It ought also to be noticed, that in the middle of the
roof there has been left an opening nineteen feet long by

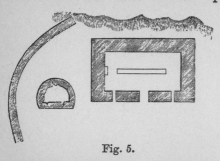

one and a half wide, the
first beginning of the *hypæthral* formation (see plan,
Fig. 5, and interior, Fig.
6). In the interior there
protrudes from the western
wall a stone, which most
likely was destined for the
reception of the idol or of

Fig. 5.

other holy objects. In the
temples of later periods the
holy statues also stood generally nearest to the western
wall, looking to the east,
where the entrance usually
was. That this is not the
case here is explained by
the situation of the holy
edifice, for close to the
eastern wall the rock falls
steep into the sea. For this

Fig. 6.

reason the gate could be placed only on the southern side, up to
which winds the rocky path which forms the only approach. To the
west of the temple there are remnants of a wall which either served
as an enclosure (peribolos), or may also have belonged to a treasure-
house. Notwithstanding the objections of some archæologists, we
are entitled to consider this building as a temple, perhaps dedicated to Hera, who was particularly worshipped in the island of
Eubœa. This opinion is further confirmed by the myth, that, on
this very Mount Ocha, the goddess celebrated her wedding with
Zeus; we may indeed assume, almost with certainty, that the
described temple was erected in commemoration of that mythical
event, on the very spot where it was said to have taken place. Of
similar construction are three other stone buildings in Eubœa
lying close to each other north-east of the village of Stura, two of
which are oblong, while the third and middle one is a square in

form, covered with a hypæthral roof like a cupola, formed by protruding slabs.

4. From the simple form of the quadrangular house surrounded by smooth walls, as we have seen it in the just-mentioned primitive temple, there took place a gradual progress towards more beautiful and varied formations. These embellishments consisted chiefly in the addition of columns. Columns are isolated props used to carry the ceiling and the roof, and applied in a particular artistic form and order. Such props are mentioned in the Homeric poems; they were used chiefly in the interiors of the royal palaces described therein, where, for instance, the courts are surrounded by colonnades, and where the ceilings of the lordly halls are supported by columns. All the later forms of Greek temples arose from the connection of these props with the holy edifice, and from their different uses in the exteriors and interiors.

Before we describe the temples we have to consider the different kinds of columns. Not to speak of the gradual transformation which the column underwent in the course of time, the consideration of which belongs to the history of art, we have to distinguish two chief kinds, the knowledge of which is required in order to form a notion of the different species of the temples themselves.

These two species of columns, which are generally denominated the orders of columns, are the Doric and Ionic. A third, the Corinthian order, belongs to a later period of Greek art. The Doric column has its name from the Greek tribe of the Dorians, by whom it was invented and most frequently used, and with whose serious and dignified character its whole formation corresponds. It is divided into two parts, the shaft and the capital. The shaft consists of a stem of circular form, which up to a third of its height slightly increases in circumference (ἔντασις), and decreases again more or less towards the top. The bottom part rests immediately on the stereobaton or base of the temple. Only in rare cases the column was monolithic, usually it consisted of several pieces or "drums" (σπόνδυλοι), composed without mortar, which were fastened to each other by dowels of cedar wood, such as have been discovered on the columns of the Parthenon and the temple of Theseus at Athens. Lengthways the shaft was broken

by parallel indentures (ῥάβδωσις), now called flutings, the edges
of which formed sharp angles, and which, as we can see from
several unfinished temples, were chiselled into the columns after
they had been put into their places.   On the shaft rests the
second part of the column, the head or capital, which the Greeks,
in analogy to the human head, called κεφάλαιον, the Romans
capitulum.   The capital of the Doric order consists of three parts.

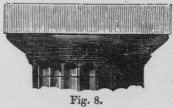

The first is called ὑποτρα-
χήλιον, neck, and forms
the continuation of the
shaft, from which it is
separated by one or more
indentures. In its upper

Fig. 8.

part it widens, and is
generally adorned by several horizontal stripes called
by the Romans rings, *annuli.*   After this follows
the chief portion of the capital, a ledge also, of circular formation, and strongly projecting all round.
It was called by the Greeks ἐχῖνος, and comprised
the supporting power of the column, under the
weight of the beams and the roof resting on it.
The third part consists of a square piece with square
edges, which is called the bearer (ἄβαξ, whence the
Latin *abacus*), and is destined for the reception of the
chief beam or architrave (ἐπιστύλιον) resting on the
column (see page 12).

Fig. 7.

The artistic (æsthetic and static) import of all
these parts must not occupy us here, any more than
the changes which they underwent in the gradual
development of Greek art.   We must confine ourselves to the
general remark, that the older the building, the heavier and
more compressed is the formation of the whole column, as is particularly shown by the few still-existing columns of a temple at
Korinth, which perhaps belongs to the sixth century B.C. As an
example of the most beautiful form, we add (Fig. 7) the reproduction of a column of the Parthenon belonging to the acme of
Greek architecture; its capital is shown on a larger scale in
Fig. 8.

The Doric order expresses artistically the spirit and the

serious tendency of the Doric tribe; the lighter and more versatile mind of the Ionic tribe finds its expression in the more ornamental order of columns called after it. About the time of its origin we will say nothing here. May it suffice to state, that as early as

Fig. 9.

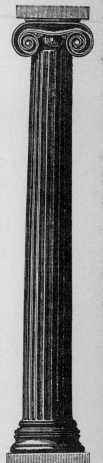

the thirtieth Olympiad (656 B.C.) the Ionic order of columns was in use, together with the Doric. At that time Myron, tyrant of Sikyon, is said to have devoted to the gods a treasure-house at Olympia which contained two rooms, one of them showing the Doric, the other the Ionic, order of columns.

The Ionic column differed from the Doric first of all by its greater slenderness. Its height in the average was equal to eight diameters at the bottom of the column, while the Doric column amounted usually only to four or five. The column is divided into three parts, a foot or base being added to the shaft and capital. The base consists of several prominences (*torus*) like bolsters, separated from each other by indentures (τρόχιλος) which rest on a square slab (πλίνθος), and in a manner raise the column from the earth. The

Fig. 10.

shaft shows the same cylindric form as that of the Doric column but the decrease in size towards the upper part is less considerable, and the fluting also differs from the Doric in so far as the deep parts are more excavated, and between them there are small flat parts called ridges (*scamillus*). The capital shows, instead of a simple and severe formation, a greater variety and elegance of form. The neck is embellished by sculptural ornaments, the echinus is less prominent, and shows a sculptural ornament called ovolo. The richest and most striking characteristic of the Ionic capital is the part which, somewhat like the abacus of the Doric capital, droops, as it were, under the weight of the architrave, and leans in an elastic curvature over the echinus; both in front and at the back it shows a double spiral ornamentation usually called the volute; at the sides it forms a bolster called by the Romans *pulvinar*. Above this lies a small slab, also adorned with sculptures, and destined to receive the beam. Fig. 10 shows a simple Ionic column which belonged to the no longer existing temple on the Ilissos at Athens; Fig. 9, a rich capital from the Erechtheion at Athens.

The third or Korinthian order of columns (the independent development of which does not seem to date back before the end of the fourth century B.C.) resembles, in the formation of the basis and the shaft, the Ionic order. The capital, on the other hand, has the form of an open chalice formed of acanthus leaves, over which rises from the same basis a second higher row of leaves. In the interstices of this mass of leaves we see stems, with smaller

Fig. 11.

chalices at their tops, rising upwards, and from the tops of these there are again developed stalks divided into two, the tops of which are bent like volutes under the weight of the abacus, which in a manner rests on them. The beams are generally borrowed from the Ionic order. Vitruvius (iv. 1, 9) tells a pretty story, according to which the celebrated architect and engraver (το-ρευτής) Kallimachos, of Athens, was the inventor of this capital; perhaps he was the first to use it artistically. In any case, the perfection of the Korinthian capital (as we know it from

its simplest beginnings in the temple of Apollo at Phigalia, up to
its noblest development in the capitals of the temple of the Didy-
maic Apollo near Miletos, and in those of the mausoleum of Halikarnassos, and on the choragic monument of Lysikrates at
Athens, Fig. 11 (see Fig. 152), belongs to the time after Perikles.
Perhaps the first attempts at an ornamentation which was
taken from plants, and might easily be reproduced in clay, were
made at Korinth, the seat of clay potteries, and in that case the
Korinthian capital would have received its name from its first
home.

5. The simplest and most natural way of connecting the
columns with the temple itself, was to leave out the smallest
of the four walls in which the entrance was placed, and to erect
instead of it two columns, which thus formed a stately and
beautiful ingress, and also carried the beams and the roof of the
temple. The Greeks called a temple of this kind ἐν παράστασιν,
the Romans a *templum in antis*, because in it the columns were
placed between the front pillars of the side walls, which latter
were called by the Greeks παράσταδες, and by the Romans *antæ*.
But this change of design could not be made without consequences
for the arrangement of the temple itself. By opening in this way
the temple on the one—generally the eastern—side, there was
certainly gained an appropriate ornamentation of the chief
façade; but, on the other hand, the regard for the holiness of the
image required a further seclusion of the room in which it was
placed: for the house of the god was sacred, separated from the
profane world, and accessible only after a previous purification.
In consequence, the space of the temple-cella was divided by a
wall into two parts, of which the one, the νάος proper, contained
the image of the god, the other
being used as an outer court or
outer temple, and therefore called
by the Greeks πρόναος or πρόδομος.

An example of this most primitive and simple design is preserved in a small temple at Rham-

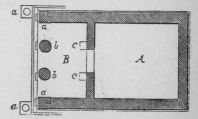

Fig. 12.

nos, in Attika, which is generally designated as the temple of
Themis. Its plan (see Fig. 12) shows an oblong form similar to

that of the temple on Mount Ocha, but that on the east side the wall has been omitted, and between the two ends of the side walls or *antæ* (*a a*) two columns (*b b*) have been erected. Passing through these columns we enter the pronaos (*B*), against the back wall of which, built of polygonal stones, stand two marble chairs (*c c*), dedicated the one to Nemesis, the other to Themis, as the inscriptions on them indicate (see Fig. 13). Perhaps they contained originally the statues of these goddesses; the statue of one goddess at least, in an antiquated style, has been discovered in the pronaos. The temple is small, and stands in a very irregular position by the side of a larger one, which is usually considered as that of Nemesis. For this was the goddess particularly venerated by the inhabitants of Rhamnos, and her affinity to Themis, the goddess of justice, the violations of which Nemesis had to revenge, would account for the close vicinity of the two temples; their irregular position with regard to each other finds its explanation in the circumstance of the different dates of their erection. For the temple of Nemesis belongs to the time of Kimon, while that of Themis was erected at an ante-Persian period, most likely contemporaneously with the building of the ante-Persian Parthenon and the ante-Persian Propylæa, as is shown by the polygonal structure of the walls of the cella and the use of the porous stone for the columns and antæ.

Fig. 13.

The façade which shows us the further peculiarities of the Doric order we see, Fig. 13. We observe, first of all, that the temple rests on some steps, as was the universal custom amongst the Greeks. The columns of the Doric order, as described in the last paragraph, carry, together with the two antæ, the upper part of the whole building, generally called the beams. The beams of the Doric order are divided into three parts—architrave, frieze, and cornice. The architrave consists of four-edged, smoothly hewn stone beams, which are placed from column to column (hence the Greek

name ἐπιστύλιον, *i.e.* on the columns), and are equally continued
beyond the wall of the temple. Over this follows a second layer of
a similar kind, but that here certain prominent parts, adorned with
vertical stripes and called triglyphs (τρίγλυφος), occur alternately
with square pieces called by the Greeks μέτωπον, and usually
adorned with images, *i.e.* reliefs. After these representations
(ζῶα) the Greeks called this part of the beams ζωφόρος. The
completion of the beams was formed by the cornice called by the
Greeks γεῖσον, and consisting of a prominent rafter cut obliquely
downwards. Over these beams rises on the two smaller sides of
the temple a pediment, *i.e.* a triangular structure, as necessitated by
the sloping position of the roof; it was formed by a stone wall
and surrounded by a cornice similar to the geison of the beams.
The Greeks called this gable ἀετός or ἀέτωμα, perhaps owing to
its similarity to an eagle with extended wings. The gable front
surrounded by the cornice was called by the
Greeks τύμπανον ; it was generally adorned with
sculptures, such as we shall see on several of
the larger Greek temples. The ridge of the
roof as well as the corners of the gable were
provided in most of the temples with ornaments
(ἀκρωτήριον), which generally, similar to those
on the sarcophagi and στῆλαι, were formed like
anthemia (Fig. 14). Instead of these we also
find not unfrequently on the corners of the ætos pedestals,
destined to carry statues or holy implements like tripods and
vases.

Fig. 14.

6. There is still another kind of the *templum in antis*
described in our last chapter, which seems not to have been called
by the Greeks by a separate name, neither is it mentioned separately by Vitruvius, to whom we owe the classification of the
different forms of the temple. Nevertheless it deserves our particular attention, as showing the strictly logical process followed
by the Greeks in this matter.

For, after the one smaller side of the temple had received
columns instead of a wall, it was natural to do the same on the
opposite side. This was indeed only in accordance with the
feeling of symmetry shown by the Greeks, to which we shall
have to refer in considering another form of the temple.

A beautiful example of this form of the *templum in antis* we find in a temple discovered at Eleusis, of which Fig. 15 shows the plan. It was dedicated to Artemis Propylæa, and the position of the ruins close by the propylæa of the sacred precinct of the

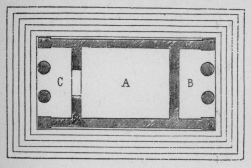

Fig. 15.

temple at Eleusis shows beyond doubt that it is really the temple seen, and called by that name, by Pausanias; it is indeed one of the rare cases where the name of a Greek temple can be proved with certainty. The temple, of which little more than the foundations remain, but which can be easily reconstructed with the help of these foundations and of some fragments of Pentelic marble,* is divided into three parts, of which the cella (A) and the pronaos (C) are formed exactly as we have seen in the temple of Themis.

Beyond the back wall of the cella the side walls of the temple have been continued, and between their antæ two columns have been erected; in this way a space (B) has been formed, which, although perhaps not equal in dimension, corresponds exactly with the pronaos or prodomos, and is therefore called by the Greeks ὀπισθόδομος. In the same way as the pronaos was the front hall, the opisthodomos was the back hall, of the temple, and therefore by the Romans appropriately called a posticum.

This arrangement assists us in understanding the use of the spaces thus gained in front and back of the cella; for they must be considered not only as casual extensions of the temple, but they have a distinct significance for the religious service and its usages, as it was always the habit of the Greeks to combine artistic and religious considerations. The openness of both spaces indicates sufficiently that they were not properly holy or conse-

---

* This was the case at least at the time of the first investigation. At present the ruins found at that time have (with the exception of a few almost unrecognisable remnants) disappeared, that is, they have been used for the houses of the insignificant modern Eleusis.

crated places. They were, on the contrary, as Bötticher justly remarks of the pronaos, "show-rooms." The pronaos, which formed the entrance and as it were preparation hall of the holy room, was furnished accordingly. Sculptures and other ornaments alluded to the god and his myths; in the temple of Themis we recognised the two chairs as being most likely the seats of divine images. There were also implements placed here to prepare for the entrance into the sacred room proper. The basin with conse-crated water had its place here, with which everybody sprinkled himself or was sprinkled by the priest, before entering into the immediate presence of the god, whose image always stood fronting the entrance-door. These rooms were frequently secured and closed by railings, traces of which are preserved in several temples, and in this way, although open to the eye, they could be used for the reception of the treasures with which pious custom richly endowed the temples, as is distinctly told us of the festive temples at Athens, Delphi, Olympia, and elsewhere.

A similar ornamentation, by means of statues referring to the god of the temple, or anathemata devoted to him, must have been in the opisthodomos. It must, however, be added that in some temples the opisthodomos occurs as a separate chamber behind the cella. In that case it was used for the keeping of that property of the god which was not shown in public, such as old sacred implements or perhaps old images; in some cases also money and public or private documents were kept in it because of the greater security of the place. This, for instance, was done at the Parthenon, where even a list of objects kept in the opistho-domos has been discovered. In this case the back hall of the temple (posticum) remained the show-room, adorned with sculp-tures, anathemes, and pictures in a similar manner as the pronaos on the opposite side of the temple.

7. In his sketch of the different forms of the temple Vitruvius mentions after the antæ-temple the prostylos. This name already indicates a temple in which the columns (στῦλοι) protrude on one side, and which naturally forms in this way a further step in the development of the temple. In the antæ-temple the columns as it were replaced the one smaller wall of the temple-house, which had been omitted in order to give the outer part of the temple a certain public character. But after this significance of the column

as a separate and "room-opening" (Bötticher) prop had once been recognised, it became impossible to abide by this form, and it is quite in accordance with the steady and gradual progress always observable in Greek art that the columns were also advanced quite independently on the open side of the temple which required ornamentation. The general design was not modified hereby, and could remain exactly the same as in the antæ-temple.

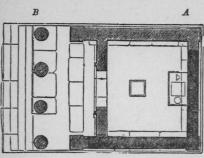

Fig. 16.

An example of this design is offered by the small Ionic temple near the large temple at Selinus (see Fig. 16). Selinus, on the south-western coast of Sicily, was a colony of the Doric town of Megara, by whose inhabitants a great many towns were founded. Their attention was particularly directed towards Sicily, where, after founding several other colonies, they built, about the thirty-seventh Olympiad, the town of Selinus, perhaps on the site of an old Phœnician colony. The fertility of the soil and the favourable situation of the town made it soon a considerable emporium, and with its growing wealth was combined an artistic culture to which we owe several still-existing ruins in the Doric style. Besides these ruins of the Doric order (see Figs. 21, 23, 33), there has been discovered a small sanctuary which shows a peculiar combination of the Doric and Ionic styles, and has lately been reproduced and described at great length as the temple of Empedokles, with the restoration of its original colours. On a base of steps about 2½ feet in height rises the little temple about 15 feet high and resembling in its design exactly the temple of Themis. We have the cella (A) and the pronaos (B), with the only difference that the columns adorning the latter stand, not between the antæ, but protrude beyond them. The columns grow considerably slighter upwards, in analogy to the Doric order, but they have a base and an Ionic capital; their flutings resemble more the Doric than the Ionic order. The beams also are in the Doric order; on the architrave three layers are indicated by colours; the frieze has triglyphs and metopa, which were also painted; the pediment shows the form we have met with in the temple of Themis.

The connection of the portico with the cella is brought about by a continuation of the architrave from the pillar of the antæ to the column, by means of which the beams and the roof in front form a strong projection carried by the columns. This is an evident gain for the design of the temple; for in this way both the portico and the pronaos are increased in size, and the column now fulfils much better its task as an independent and " room-opening " prop.

8. Although the prostylos marks a progress in the develop-ment of the column-edifice, it cannot be denied that it shows a certain want of symmetry and proportion in its design. The back part does not correspond with the façade, indeed the strong projection carried by the columns seems to require a similar arrangement on the opposite side of the temple. There is some-thing imperfect in the look of such a temple, particularly if one imagines its position open on all sides. This want could not but become apparent to the Greeks, who in almost all their artistic doings have shown a particular predilection for symmetrical proportions. Greek orators weighed carefully the measure of their periods, and symmetry was the principle of strophe and antistrophe in their lyrical poetry. The same care has been noticed in the plastic or pictorial ornamentation of rooms and of certain objects, in which the Greek artists always tried to carry out a perfect symmetry and parallelism of the grouping. This feeling it could not satisfy to see the front part of the temple developed in such a striking manner, and it was only natural that the Greeks should have added before long a portico to the opposite side of the temple. From this as we have seen quite natural and essentially Greek proceeding arose a new form, called by the Greeks very appropriately ναὸς ἀμφιπρόστυλος, *i.e.* a temple with projecting porticoes on both sides. The amphiprostylos is, indeed, the necessary supplement or rather completion of the prostylos, a completion which was the more natural as through the double antæ-temple (see § 6) (which might appropriately be designated as *amphiparastatic*) one was accustomed to an opistho-domos or posticum, corresponding with the pronaos. The posticum, which was wanting in the prostylos, is gained in the amphi-

prostylos by means of the back hall, and became available in the same manner as we have seen in the developed form of the antæ-temple (see § 6). Altogether the amphiprostylos stands in the same relation to the prostylos as the double to the single antæ-temple, and we notice here again the steady and equal progress which has given to all Greek creations their harmony and organic necessity, or, which is essentially the same, their beauty. As an example of this not very frequent form of the temple, of which Vitruvius does not name an instance, we mention the temple of Nike Apteros, the wingless goddess of victory, in the Akropolis at Athens* (see Fig. 17). This elegant Ionic structure crowns, like a votive offering, the front part of the wall which Kimon had erceted as at once a protection and ornament of the Akropolis.

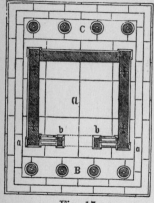

Fig. 17.

It was taken off by the Turks and used for the building of a bastion, but was restored to its original form from the remnants found in the destroyed bastion, during the first decennium of the revived kingdom of Greece (see the sketch of the side view; Fig. 18). From the right-hand side of the great staircase, which leads up to the propylæa, a small flight of steps ascends to the temple of Nike Apteros. It stands pretty close to the right wing of the propylæa, and is for this reason shorter than in other cases, for instance in the temple on the Ilissos, which other-wise corresponds with it exactly. It is said that its dedication to the wingless goddess of victory signified the retaining of victory for Athens; according to earlier statements it was erected by Kimon after the completion of the above-mentioned wall in order to commemorate his double victory over the Persians on the Eurymedon (Ol. 77, 3 = 470 B.C.); Bursian, on the other hand, places its completion, or at least that of its upper parts, in the time of Perikles. The dimensions of the temple are but small

* Of temples of this class without colonnades we also mention one, the ruins of which have been discovered by Stuart on the Ilissos, not far from Athens. The amphiprostylos is more frequently applied where the cella is surrounded by a colonnade. (See § 9, *d.*)

(18¼ feet in width, 27 feet in length), but its style is beautiful and elegant. It consists of a simple cella A (Fig. 17), with an outer hall B on the eastern side towards the propylæa, and a postico C, on the western side towards the staircase. The opening of the cella towards the east is not, as in most cases, effected by a door in the

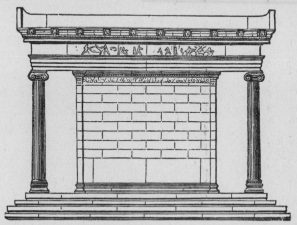

Fig. 18.

wall, but by two slender pillars (*b b*) between the antæ (*a a*), which afford an open view of the interior and of the statue placed therein. Against the outer hall the cella was as usual closed by means of railings, the fastenings of which are still observable on the pillars and antæ.

The columns have bases and beautiful capitals in the form of volutes; their slightly heavy proportions remind one of the Doric order; the beams, on the other hand, are strictly Ionic. Accordingly, the architrave (which in the Doric order (see § 5) consists of a simple smooth stone) is divided into three horizontal stripes (*fasciæ*), over the uppermost of which there is a thin ledge. The frieze no more exhibits the division into metopa and triglyphs, but consists of an uninterrupted plane, equal in height to the architrave, and adorned with bas-reliefs which represent battles between Greeks and Persians. After this follows the cornice (γεῖσον), which, unlike the simplicity and heaviness of the Doric cornice, consists of several pieces composed in an easy and graceful manner.

The pediments both at the back and in front are similar to those of the Doric temple, but that they rise a little higher, and the cornices round them correspond with the geison of the beams. Fig. 19

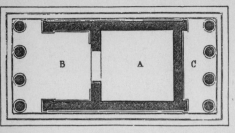

shows the plan of the above-mentioned temple, which Stuart has discovered on the southern bank of the Ilissos, not far from the well Enneakrunos; this temple was used in Stuart's time as a Christian church, but has now entirely disappeared. It was an amphiprostylos

Fig. 19.

of the Ionic order, the division of which into cella A, pronaos B, and posticum C, agrees exactly with the above-stated principles. It was 40½ feet in length, by 19½ in width.

9. The most extensive use of the columns takes place, when they are placed not only before and behind the temple, as in the amphiprostylos, but when they are ranged round the four sides of the building.

This is the last and most perfect form to which the combination of the columns with the temple-house could lead, and it must be considered as the necessary development of the different preparatory stages mentioned in the above.* Here we have, at last, a temple-house surrounded by columns on all sides, beautifully variegated, and yet not wanting in organic unity. In consequence, this form was used by the Greeks more frequently than any other, and most of the remaining temples, particularly those of the Doric style, belong to it.

Concerning the mode of its erection, we must imagine that the columns were placed at equal distances round the cella, so that one might walk round it, barring such cases where statues or partition walls prevented it. For the distance of the columns from the wall of the cella there is no certain rule ; on the longer sides it was generally equal to the distance of the columns from

---

* An historic proof of this gradual growth cannot be given, seeing that already the oldest monuments known to us show the complete surrounding by columns. With the sole exception of that on Mount Ocha, the above-mentioned temples must not be considered as actually older than those to be described in the following pages. They are only specimens of a pre-historic period of architecture, the single forms and stages of which were continued even after the completion of the peripteral temple.

each other, in front and at the back (*i.e.*, on the two smaller sides)
it was considerably larger than this. The beams rested on the
columns (see Figs. 13 and 18) as in the prostylos and amphiprostylos ; they surrounded the cella in an uninterrupted line,
the walls of the former being built up to an equal height, and
afterwards connected with the beams by means of cross-beams
made of stone. Stone slabs adorned with so-called caskets, that
is, square indentures (*lacunaria*), were placed on these cross-beams
and formed the so-called lacunaria-ceiling. In this way a protecting roof was gained for the colonnade, and at the same time
the organic unity of the temple was obtained by means of the
connection of the columns with the cella. Fig. 20, showing the
section of a temple of this kind, will serve to illustrate this
arrangement. A signifies the interior of the cella, B the colon-

B   A   B

Fig. 20.

nades on both sides, *a b* the columns, *b c* the beams, connected with
the wall of the cella by means of the lacunaria-ceiling. (About
the interior, see Fig. 30.) The ceiling of the colonnade protruding
in this way from the cella to right and left was called by the
Greeks (in analogy with the name of the gable ἀετός, as mentioned above) πτερόν, wing, and from this expression the name
ναὸς περίπτερος was derived, viz., a temple surrounded on all sides
by a protruding wing of this kind. In the same way as this

name refers to the ceiling of the colonnade, another is taken from the columns themselves, and according to the latter a temple of this kind is called a ναός or οἶκος περίστυλος, that is, a temple surrounded by columns, the colonnade itself being called τὸ περίστυλον. The name peripteros was always, and has remained, the most common one.

After having described the structure of the peripteros so as to give a distinct notion of the pteron, and of the construction of this kind of temple in general, we must now turn to the consideration of the plan in order to learn the division and arrangement of the different rooms. This division is more complicated in the peripteros than in any other class of temples; we find indeed the different kinds of divisions as numerous as the classes of temples we have hitherto met with. It will be remembered

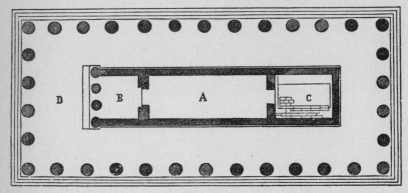

Fig. 21.

that in these latter there was only one arrangement of the interior peculiar to each; but as it is the chief purpose of the peripteros to surround the temple-house with a colonnade, this house itself may have any of the described forms; it may be, in other words, an antæ-temple, a prostylos, or an amphiprostylos. These possible variations in the plan of the peripteros have hitherto, perhaps, not been sufficiently noticed. Vitruvius does not mention them, and the rules laid down by him comprise only the smallest portion of the preserved monuments.

a. The temple-house surrounded by the colonnade may first be an antæ-temple, as described by us in § 4. An example of this design is offered by one of the older temples at Selinus (see

Fig. 21). It is situated, with two other similar ones, on a hill, in the western part of the town; the colonnade D is formed by six columns on the small, and thirteen on the long, sides; the cella is an antæ-temple with two columns between the walls, which latter do not end in common antæ, but take the form of columns. Through these columns one ascends the pronaos (B) on two steps; after it follows, raised again by one step, the cella proper (A), from which a staircase of five steps leads into the opistho-domos (C); this is walled in on all sides, and forms a completely closed room, inaccessible except from the cella.

b. The antæ-temple might also have columns between the antæ of the two small sides, as, for instance, in the temple of Artemis Propylæa at Eleusis (Fig. 15). This kind of temple-house may also become the centre of a peripteros by being surrounded by columns. This is the case in the Theseion, one of the finest and best-preserved temples of Athens (Fig. 22).

This temple lies on a small hill north-west of the Akropolis, and is, in all probability, identical with that devoted by the Athenians to the memory of their national hero Theseus, to whose appearance in the battle of Marathon they owed the victory. In memory of this event they afterwards resolved to

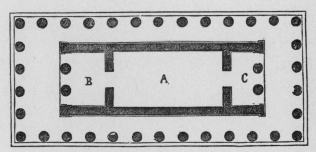

Fig. 22.

transfer the remains of Theseus from the island of Skyros (con-quered by Kimon) to Athens, and to bury them in a manner worthy of the hero. This was done by Kimon, the son of Miltiades, Olympiad 76, 1 (476 B.C.), and on the same occasion our temple was erected, and called, after the hero, Theseion.* The building is of Pentelic marble; thirty-four columns, in the most

* More recently it has also been declared to be a temple of Ares.

beautiful Doric style, in its freer and more elegant Attic modification, surround the temple-house, so that six columns stand on each of the small, and thirteen on each of the large sides. The temple-house itself has the form of a double antæ-temple ; in the middle lies the cella proper A,* joined on the eastern side by the pronaos B, on the western by the opisthodomos C, the latter forming, like the pronaos, an open hall. Beams and ceiling of the peristylos show traces of rich polychromatic painting. The temple, formerly richly decorated with statues on the gable and the metopa, has for a long time being used as a church of St. George, to which circumstance its good preservation is most likely due. At present the antique remnants found at Athens are kept in it.

c. In another form of the peripteros, the temple-house consists of a prostylos surrounded by columns. It is, however, rarely met with, the just-mentioned arrangement (b) being the most usual. As an example of this third style, we mention one of the older temples on the western hill of the town of Selinunt, in Sicily (see Fig. 23). Inside of the colonnade lies the oblong temple-house, which shows a portico of four columns. It contains, besides the cella proper (A), a peculiarly shaped pronaos (B), and an opisthodomos (C), the latter being walled in on all sides.

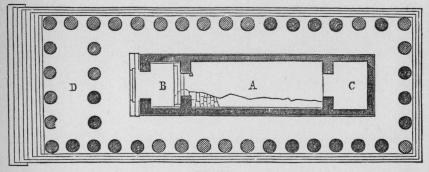

Fig. 23.

d. The highest development of the peripteros is reached when the cella is formed by an amphiprostylos (the complement of the

* The width of the interior of the cella is 20 ft. 4 in. (English measure).

prostylos, see § 8), being at the same time surrounded by a colonnade.

As an example we quote the temple of Athene Parthenos in the Akropolis of Athens, which altogether must be considered as one of the most perfect, if not *the* most perfect, monument of Greek architecture.* Being dedicated to the highest protecting goddess of Athens and of the Attic country, it occupied the most important site of the Akropolis, and evinced, both by the grandeur of its dimensions and its artistic splendour, the culture of the nation itself, which, under Perikles, had reached the acme of its power. On the same spot, where had stood the older Athene-temple, destroyed by the Persians, Perikles erected this new one. The two architects, Iktinos and Kallikrates, completed the gigantic work in about ten years, in 438 B.C. The sculptural decoration of the gables and metopa was supervised and no doubt partly executed by Phidias, an intimate friend of Perikles, and equally supreme in art as the other in politics. On a strong base of Piræic stonework, surrounded by three high steps of Pentelic marble (the upper one being $101\frac{1}{4}$ ft. wide by 228 ft. long), rose the peripteros, formed by forty-six Doric columns, of which eight stood on each of the smaller, and seventeen on each of the longer sides (see plan, Fig. 24, and view, Fig. 25). The architrave was adorned with golden shields and inscriptions, while the metopa of the frieze showed the more lasting ornamentations of reliefs, representing the myths of Athene and the heroes renowned in her service. On the gables were enthroned the sublime forms, by means of which Phidias and his disciples had celebrated two important events from the cycle of myths relating to Athene. The one showed the first appearance of the goddess amongst the Olympians after her birth from the head of Zeus; the other represented the contest in which the victorious goddess had gained the supremacy of the Attic land from Poseidon. Everywhere the splendour of the Pentelic marble (of which the columns, the beams, the walls of the cella, and even the tiles of the roof, were made) was discreetly modified by the application of colours.

During the Middle Ages it was transformed into a Christian church, of which Spon and Wheler have seen as late as 1676, and afterwards described, the altar-niche on the east side and the

* See the plan of the Akropolis, Fig. 52, B.

whole interior arrangement;* and, owing to this circumstance, the Parthenon, like the temple of Theseus, had been well preserved, until the siege of Athens by the Venetians under Morosini, in 1687, caused the deplorable destruction of this unique building. The besieged had placed a powder magazine in the cella, and when this was hit by a shell of the besieging artillery, a dreadful explosion took place, which destroyed almost the whole building, with the exception of the two pediments.

It must be considered as a fortunate circumstance in this disaster that the ruins, although poor and scanty, if compared with the former splendour of the building, still are sufficient to allow of a tolerably accurate reconstruction of its general features. Moreover the very ruins show a dignity and beauty of form which baffle description: a proof of the excellence of Greek architecture, which even without the passing splendour of outer ornaments, and deprived of the imposing effect of the whole building, still preserves its overpowering impression.

The design of the temple, with regard to its principal rooms, does not now seem doubtful; the previous investigations of architects and archæologists concerning the cella and the opisthodomos seem completed by the excavations in the Acropolis of C. Bötticher, during the early summer of 1862.

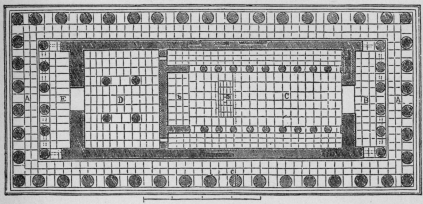

Fig. 24.

Fig. 24 shows the plan of the Parthenon after the design of Using, which is founded on a thorough investigation of the

* The bottom part of this niche exists still at the present time.

different opinions; we are not prepared to vouch for *all* its details, neither can we enter upon our own notions with regard to single parts, gained by personal study of the remnants. Passing through the columns of the colonnade (A), one encounters a second row of six columns, forming the portico of the pronaos (B). The pronaos is raised by two steps over the level of the peristylos, and was used for the keeping of the precious offerings, which were brought from far and near to celebrate the holiness of the temple and of its protecting goddess. They were kept safely behind iron railings, and carefully locked up by the Tamiai,* but might be seen from the outside. In an inscription, a list of the objects kept here has been preserved to us. The entrance to the pronaos, which formerly had been blocked up by the 6 ft. thick wall of the apsis of the church built into the Parthenon, was re-opened by Bötticher.

Fig. 25.

These parts of the building were also decorated with sculptures. Beginning from the portico, the frieze round the whole cella was covered with the marvellous representation of the festive procession of the Panathenæa, or, according to Bötticher's opinion, the preparations for this procession. These reliefs, 3 ft. 4 in. in height, extended originally over 528 ft.; 456 ft. have since been recovered from the ruins, and transferred to England, with a great many other sculptures from the Akropolis,

* The holes for fastening these railings were discovered by Bötticher, from bottom to capital, in all the columns of the pronaos and posticum.

by Lord Elgin. At present they are in the British Museum, but other parts of the frieze, found later, have been kept at Athens. Over the entrance to the pronaos, and therefore to the cella proper, there is an ingenious representation of an assembly of the gods looking at the approaching processions of youths and maidens. They are seated in arm-chairs, simply and beautifully grouped, and amongst them the forms of the god Poseidon, of the hero Erechtheus, and of the goddess Aphrodite with Peitho and Eros, are recognisable. A large door in the back wall of the pronaos forms the entrance to the cella proper (C), which is a hundred feet long, and therefore called hekatompedon. Two rows of columns, each nine in number, divided this room into three naves, and above these there was a second row of Doric columns forming an upper story, up to which led staircases from the side naves. At the end of the middle stoa, which we must imagine as hypæthral, stood, closed in by a bar and protected by a canopy, the chryselephantine Agalma of Pallas (*b*); in front of it was the daïs of the prœdria (*a*), the site of which is still recognisable by a piece of Piræic stone pavement in the middle of the marble floor. Concerning the masterly statue of Athene by Phidias, we can only say a few words illustrating its artistic arrangement. The base on which the figure stood was ornamented by a representation of the birth of Pandora, and by the forms of twenty gods. On this pedestal stood the statue of the goddess herself, in a simple but majestic posture, 26 yards* in height; face, neck, arms, hands, and feet were made of ivory; the drapery (which Phidias had fortunately made removable) was of pure gold, which noble metal also prevailed in the other parts of the figure. Combined with the splendour of the material and the imposing impression of the whole figure, the careful ornamental treatment of the details added to the total effect. There were, for instance, the helmet with a sphinx and other ornaments, and the shield standing at the feet of the goddess with a battle of the Amazons on the outer side; nay, even the edges of the high sandals showed a Kentauromachia with numerous figures, amongst which, it is said, there were portraits of Perikles and Phidias, the last-mentioned being afterwards made the grounds of accusa-

---

* German *Ellen*. The measurements are throughout on the German scale unless stated otherwise.

tions of impiety against the great statesman and his artistic friend.

Behind the cella with the statue in it, was the opisthodomos, a closed room connected with the cella by means of two little doors at the northern and southern ends of the intervening wall. Remnants of these doors, destined only for the business purposes of the treasure officials, were also found amongst the ruins in 1862. The ceiling of the opisthodomos was carried by four columns; many articles of value, documents, and anathemata not meant for public exhibition, were here kept by certain officials, who had to render strict account of them. From the opisthodomos another door, secured by a double railing, led into the back hall, similar in form to the pronaos, and used, like it, for placing works of art and pious offerings (E).

10. After the description of the ναὸς περίπτερος, which we have now considered in all its varieties, we pass over to the pseudo-peripteros treated by Vitruvius, together with the peripteros. As the name indicated (ψεῦδος, deception, appearance), this temple is not in reality surrounded by a pteron, but only appears to be. A pteron, as we have seen, consists of the wing-like protrusion of beams and ceiling, supported by separate columns. If the idea of the pteron is done away with, the beams and ceiling may remain, but they no more form an independent protrusion round the cella; that is, they are no more supported by independent columns, but by a firm wall, which on its part may supply the columns by semi-columns or pilasters. This form is very rare in Greek architecture, which was founded on truth, but the Romans have applied it more frequently (see § 63). It is true that one Greek specimen of the pseudo-peripteros is known to us, but in it the purpose of producing the illusion of columns has evidently been absent, the arrangement having become necessary by the large dimensions of the building and the nature of its material. This temple was at Akragas. Akragas "the splendour-loving noble city, of all the most beautiful," as Pindar calls it, was founded at the beginning of the sixth century by Gela, a Doric colony on the south coast of Sicily, and, by its favourable position and fertile soil, had acquired considerable wealth. The numerous remnants of its former artistic splendour are, together with those of Selinus, amongst the finest specimens

of the older Doric style. Not far from the well-preserved
so-called temples of Juno and Concordia the foundations have
been discovered of an enormous temple dedicated to Zeus, and
finished, all but the roof, after the victory of the Carthaginians
over the Agrigentines (Ol. 93, 3 = 406 B.C.). Diodor, who
gives a detailed description of the temple with measurements,
admired, after so many centuries, the grandeur of its remnants.
According to later measurements the length of the temple, steps
included, is 359 ft., its width 175½ ft. ; its height must have been
120 to the top of the gable, as may be calculated from the
remaining fragments of the beams and columns : its site was
therefore almost three times as large as that of the Parthenon.
The columns, being almost 62 ft. in height, stood so widely apart,
that, to cover the intervening spaces by means of free architraves,
slabs of stone almost 26 ft. long, and over 10 ft. thick, would
have been required. But the use of such the nature of the
material would not permit, the buildings of Agrigent being not
of marble but of a soft crumbling kind of chalk (*Muschelkalk*),
which grows firmer in the course of time, but is wholly unavailable for the covering of open spaces of considerable extension.
In consequence, the Agrigentines were obliged to erect solid walls
between the columns as high as the beams, and to place on them
an architrave and frieze of single smaller blocks of stone. Instead
of a free colonnade, the temple-house was therefore surrounded by
a solid wall, with columns protruding by one-half of their
circumference on the outer side, the corresponding places on the
inner side being marked by pilasters. Whether the lighting of
the building was hypæthral, or (as some archæologists have rather
rashly conjectured) was effected by means of windows in the
upper part of the wall between the half-columns, must be left
undecided. The cella is long and narrow, as is frequent in
Sicilian monuments (see Figs. 21 and 23), and its walls were also
adorned by pilasters. The place of the door is difficult to define,
because of the quite unusual uneven number of seven columns at
the façade. Kockerell thinks there must have been two doors, one
on each side of the façade ; a native archæologist, Politi, on the other
hand, accepts one large door in the middle, but this divided into
two entrances by the colossal statue of a giant instead of a pillar.*

* This statue is still in existence ; it consists of several enormous blocks of stone,

11. In our description of the Parthenon (see page 28) we noticed that the middle part of the cella was entirely open to the sky. This leads to a new form of the temple often used in larger designs, and called by Vitruvius the hypæthros. His description (leaving alone the prescriptions for the numbers of columns and other arrangements, which in this, as in most cases, by no means tally with the Greek monuments) is couched in the following terms :—" In the inside (of the cella) there are colonnades, with double rows of columns, separate from the walls, so that one may walk round them just as in the outer colonnades. Only the middle nave is open to the sky, and there are doors at both ends leading to the back house and front house. Specimens of this kind there are none in Rome, but at Athens there are the eight-columned temple of Minerva, and the ten-columned one of the Olympian Jupiter." The former of these is none other than the Parthenon; the latter we shall refer to in our description of Roman temples.

We cannot enter upon the literary feud about the existence or non-existence of the hypæthral temple, considering (with Bötticher) the question settled in the affirmative. For not even to mention the opinion that the services of certain gods required uncovered rooms, it seems natural that large buildings without windows, or even large doors, for lighting purposes, had an open space in the middle, which, moreover, was quite in accordance with the open court of the dwelling-house. Analogies between these two were frequent. In this way architectural necessity tallies perfectly with the statement of Vitruvius, which, moreover, is confirmed by a thorough investigation of genuine Greek monuments. There are distinguishable even several species of the hypæthros, which show that it had become necessary by the conditions of peculiar rites at an early period, and that its form and size might be modified in various ways. The simplest form of the hypæthros we have seen in the small temple on Mount Ocha (Fig. 6), where the small opening in the roof was most

which have been found amongst the ruins, and arranged on the ground, forming a complete figure. It is generally supposed that a whole row of such statues used to carry the ceiling of the cella. But in that case most likely other fragments would have been found, which, at least during my own prolonged stay at Girgenti, has not been the case.

likely required by the nature of Zeus and Hera, as divinities of the ether and sky. Amongst the peripteros-temples the examples of hypæthral cellæ are not unfrequent.* We mention first the temple of Apollo Epikurios, near the town of Phigalia in Arkadia. On the side of one of the mountain ranges which surround Phigalia in a wide circle, lies the village of Bassæ. Here, near the summit of Mount Kotilios, we find the ruins of a temple, which, barring a slight difference in the distances and the nature of the material, seems to agree perfectly with the description in Pausanias of a sanctuary of Apollo Epikurios. According to him the temple was built by Iktinos, the architect of the Parthenon, and was surpassed in beauty amongst the temples of the Peloponnesos only by that of Athene Alea, near Tegea; a remark which is the more important as Pausanias only in rare cases mentions the artistic value of a building. The remnants of the temple, which have been examined carefully for the first time in 1818, fully confirm this opinion, although a great part of the building had been purposely destroyed, most likely in order to obtain the bronze rivets joining the stones to each other. The original plan is, however, easily recognisable. The design (Fig. 26) shows a colonnade of thirty-eight columns (AA); six on each of the narrow, and fifteen on each of the long, sides (inclusive of the corner columns of the façades); all of these are preserved standing erect. The pronaos (B) is formed by the walls of the cella and two columns *in antis*. The cella is divided into a covered space (D) and an uncovered one (C), the latter enclosed by strongly projecting pilasters. The fronts of the pilasters resemble Ionic half-columns, and show above the capitals a frieze representing battles of the Amazons in excellent bas-reliefs. The middle part of the space was open, and formed as it were a court surrounded by niches, adapted for the keeping of votive offerings by the frieze which protected their contents. The back part of the cella (D) was covered by a ceiling carried by two of the above-mentioned pilasters, which protruded obliquely from the wall of the cella, and besides by a single column, the latter serving at the

* For the same reason we mention the hypæthros here, differing in this from the arrangement of Vitruvius, who goes by the position of the outer columns. But the nature of a great number of peristylos-temples cannot be clearly understood without a previous knowledge of the hypæthros.

same time as a specimen of the Korinthian order in its most simple form. Behind this was placed, according to Blouet's opinion, the statue of a god (*b*). There seems to have been a door in the back wall of the cella; possibly there may have been a door in the place marked *c* leading to the colonnade at the side. Behind the cella follows the opistho-domos (E), enclosed by the wall of the former and two columns *in antis*. As a peculiarity of this temple, caused most likely by its locality, it is mentioned that the chief façade looked almost due north, instead of east, as was usually the case.

One of the remaining temples at Pæstum corresponds still more exactly with Vitruvius's description. Amongst the remnants there, which represent the severity and noble simplicity of the early Doric style, one temple is prominent, which, because of its size, is considered as the chief temple of the town; and, for the same reason, is generally supposed to have been dedicated to the protecting deity, Poseidon. It consists of a peripteros of six columns on each of the narrow, and fourteen on each of the long,

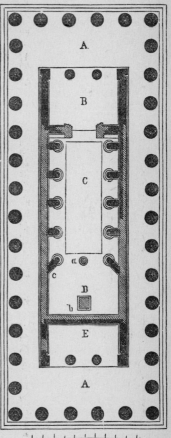

Fig. 26.

sides; the cella, surrounded by colonnades, has both in front and at the back two columns *in antis*. Through the pronaos one enters the cella, both sides of which show double rows of columns, as described by Vitruvius. On the back wall of the cella there are staircases, which can be distinctly recognised, nay even used, at the present day. They lead to the hyperoon or upper gallery, and between them is the entrance-door to the opisthodomos. Fig. 27 shows the interior of the temple in its present condition. It is 193 feet long by 81½ wide.

To conclude, we mention the temple of Zeus at Olympia. Amongst the ruins of this sacred place (situated in the plain of

Fig. 27.

the Alpheios and forming a brilliant centre of Greek national life), for some time remnants had been noticed which showed a better material than the bricks commonly used. After the liberation of Greece from the Turks a French exploring expedition closely investigated the place, and came to the conclusion that amongst these ruins the remnants of the celebrated temple of Zeus Olympios were preserved; nay, it was even found possible to form from these a sufficiently clear notion of the sacred edifice which once enclosed the most sublime image of the father of the gods, the pride and joy of Greece. We shall have to consider further on the splendid festivities celebrated by the nation, as it were in the presence of the god; here we must limit ourselves to the temple itself, which, next to the Parthenon, may be considered as the climax of artistic perfection, in the same way as in the statue of the god, by Phidias, it possessed the only work of sculpture which rivalled and in some respects surpassed the excellence of Athene Parthenos. " The style of the temple," Pausanias says, in his simple description (V. 10), "is Doric; with regard to the exterior, it is a peristylos. The material is porous stone found on the spot. Its height, up to the top of the gable, is 68 feet, its width 95 feet, its length 230 feet. The architect was a local man named Libon. The tiles of the roof are not of burnt clay, but of Pentelic marble, resembling bricks in their shape. At the two corners of the gable there are gilt receptacles, and on the top of each of them there is a gilt figure of Nike." The occasion of building the temple was a victory of the Olympians over the inhabitants of the neighbouring city of Pisa (Ol. 52); but the completion of the sculptures on the metopa and gables, by Phidias and his pupils, did not take place till Olympiad 86. Of the

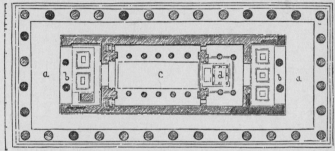

Fig. 28.

surrounding colonnade *a* (see Fig. 28) only nine columns have been found in different places, besides parts of the wall of the cella with the antæ, between the latter of which there were two columns both in front and at the back. In the pronaos *b* there has been found, underneath a Roman pavement which consists of marble and oriental alabaster, a roughly composed mosaic of pebbles, such as are found in the Alpheios, which represents sea-gods and goddesses, and which undoubtedly was the original floor. Close by this was the base of a statue, also mentioned by Pausanias, such as are frequently met with in the entrance-halls of temples. The cella was divided into different parts, the middle one (*e*) being uncovered and surrounded by two colonnades in two stories; in connection with it there was a smaller covered compartment (*d*), which contained the statue of the god. Zeus was represented as sitting on a throne, which is described as an elaborate structure of cedar wood, laid in with ebony and richly adorned with valuable stones and sculptures. The base was also richly decorated in accordance with the figure itself. The face, the chest, the naked upper part of the body, and the feet were of ivory; the eyes consisted of brilliant stones. The waving hair and beard were of solid gold, as was also the figure of Nike which the god held in his extended right hand; the sceptre in his other hand was composed of different precious metals. The drapery covering the lower part of the body was also of gold, with flowers in a kind of enamel. But all this splendour of valuable materials was as nothing compared with the grandeur of the divine form. In this Phidias had embodied the description of those wonderful lines of the Iliad (I. 528) which lived in the memory of every Greek—

Ἦ, καὶ κυανέῃσιν επ’ ὀφρύσι νεῦσε Κρονίων·
ἀμβρόσιαι δ’ ἄρα χαῖται ἐπερρώσαντο ἄνακτος
κρατὸς ἀπ’ ἀθανάτοιο· μέγαν δ’ ἐλέλιξεν Ὄλυμπον.

So he sat, sublime and inapproachable, and yet mildly inclining towards the spectator, perhaps the most perfect realisation of the Greek ideal of godhead, and therefore the goal of every one's

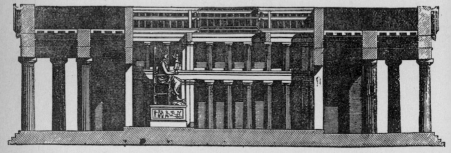

Fig. 29.

longing; not to have seen the Olympian Zeus was considered as a misfortune. The height of the statue was 40 feet, almost too colossal, in proportion to the surrounding architecture, so that the Greeks themselves used to say that if the god rose from his seat he would knock in the roof overhead. On both sides of the room containing the statue there were steps leading to the upper gallery and most likely open to the spectators for a closer view of the statue and the single ornaments. In front of the statue a piece of black marble pavement has been discovered, which quite

Fig. 30.

tallies with a statement of Pausanias; for, according to him, a piece of the floor immediately before the statue was paved with black marble, instead of white stone; this piece was surrounded with an enclosure of white Parian marble, and into it oil was poured so as to preserve the statue from the dampness of the soil, in the same way as the evaporation of water was considered beneficial to the statue of Athene in the dry atmosphere of the Akropolis. Behind the back wall of the cella was the opisthodomos, which again, through the columns between the antæ, opened into the peristylos. Fig. 29 shows the length, Fig. 30, on a little larger scale, the width, of the temple.

12. The peripteros, *i.e.* the temple-house wholly surrounded by columns, marks the ultimate completion of Greek architecture. There were certainly a great many varieties of the form so gained, as, for instance, the formation of the cella as antæ-temple, pro-stylos, and amphiprostylos, and many modifications of the interior arrangement; still, the idea of a temple-house surrounded by colonnades is common to all of them. But this idea itself might be enlarged by adding to the first row of columns a second one, so as to form a double colonnade or pteron. This temple was

called by the Greeks, very appropriately, a ναὸς δίπτερος,* *i.e.* a temple with a double pteron. "The dipteros," Vitruvius says, "has eight columns both in front and at the back, but round the cella it has a double colonnade. Of this order are the Doric temple of Quirinus, and the Ionic one of Diana built by Ktesiphon."

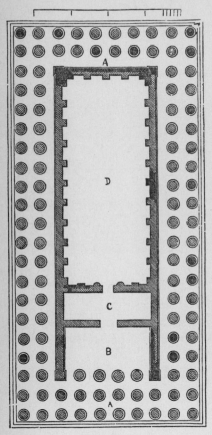

This rule of Vitruvius does, as is often the case, not tally with the remaining monuments, the number of the columns in the façades being occasionally ten, instead of eight as prescribed by him. Of the two mentioned specimens, the temple of Quirinus was at Rome, erected by Augustus; the other one is one of the most brilliant examples of this order, which seems to have been used chiefly by the luxurious Greeks of the colonies in Asia Minor. The temple of Artemis at Ephesos (see § 2) was built at a very early period, and always considered as the earliest and at the same time one of the grandest and most perfect specimens of the Ionic style (see § 4). It was afterwards considerably enlarged, but the original plan was not essentially modified. For a long time it was mentioned as the absolute perfection of the rich Ionic

Fig. 31.

style, and counted by the ancients themselves amongst the seven

---

* To be quite complete we ought to add, that denominations of this kind were also derived from the number of the columns of the façades. A temple, the façade of which had four columns, was called a tetrastylos (see Figs. 16—19); one with six was called a hexastylos (see Figs. 21—23); the Parthenon with its eight columns was an oktastylos (see Figs. 24, 25); the ten-columned temple of Apollo of Miletos (Fig. 31) a dekastylos; and the votive temple at Eleusis a dodekastylos, because of the twelve columns of its portico (see Fig. 39).

wonders of the world. Remnants of the building have quite lately been discovered by English excavations, but accounts have not yet been published; we, therefore, cannot enter into a detailed description, although the plan of the temple may be guessed with tolerable certainty from the accounts of the ancients themselves. We add, instead, the design of a temple (Fig. 31), which, with regard to both size and splendour, might vie with that of Artemis, and which must be considered as an equally important specimen of the dipteros. It is the temple of Apollo Didymæos at Miletos. Miletos was one of the richest and most important colonies of the Ionians on the coast of Asia Minor. According to tradition, it had been originally inhabited by the Karians, from whom it was taken by the Kretans; afterwards the Ionians chose it as a colony; they increased it and raised it to one of the most important commercial cities, whose ships sailed to all parts of the Mediterranean and beyond the Columns of Herkules, and, on the other side, carried their wares into the Pontus Euxinus. The names of the philosophers Thales and Anaximander, and of the historians Kadmos and Hekatæos, prove the existence of scientific culture combined with commercial industry. The same may be said of the fine arts, and particularly of architecture, the high development of which is shown in the remnants of the once-celebrated temple of Apollo.

Connected with an oracle revered in this place ever since the time of the Kretan colony there had been built, at an early date, a temple of Apollo, the service in which had been, also for a long time, in the family of the Branchides. This older temple disappeared in the general destruction of Miletos by the Persians (Olympiad 71, 3), but after the independence of the city was restored, in more splendid style, by the Milesian architects Pæonios and Daphnis; it seems, however, never to have been quite finished. The plan was on the grandest scale; the façade, consisting of ten columns, was longer almost by two-thirds than that of the Parthenon of Athens; the columns were $6\frac{1}{4}$ feet in diameter by 63 feet in height, and were slenderer than those of the Artemisin at Ephesos and of other Ionic temples. Accordingly, the beams were lighter and weaker, as is shown in the design of the façade (Fig. 32). Through the double colonnade (Fig. 31, A) one enters, first, the pronaos B, which was bounded

towards the peristylos by four columns *in antis*, and the walls of
which were adorned by pilasters with very rich Korinthian

Fig. 32.

capitals.   Through a small room (C), destined either for the
keeping of treasures or for staircases, one entered the cella (D),
most likely open in the middle, and enclosed at the sides by colonnades.   There seems to have been no opisthodomos surrounded
by walls.

13. The dipteros, as we have seen, was only an enlargement
of the peripteros; the pseudo-dipteros, on the other hand (the last
temple with a square cella in the list of Vitruvius), is a kind of
medium between peripteros and dipteros, and is, therefore, mentioned by Vitruvius between the two.   The explanation of the
name is similar to that of the pseudo-peripteros; it means a temple
which has the appearance of a dipteros without being one in
reality, *i.e.* the pseudo-dipteros seems to have two colonnades
without having them; or, to say the same in different words, its
external plan is exactly like that of a dipteros, but that the
second row of columns between the exterior one and the wall of
the cella has been omitted.   "Pseudo-dipteros," Vitruvius says,
"is called a temple which has eight columns in front and at the
back, there being fifteen columns on each of the longer sides
inclusive of the corner columns.   But the walls of the cella, both
in front and at the back, are exactly opposite the four middle
columns.   The interval between the exterior columns and the
walls is, therefore, all round, equal to two interstices and one
diameter of the bottom part of a column."   Evidently this order,

which is approved of by Vitruvius on account of its picturesqueness and of the saving of the interior colonnade, is a thing between a dipteros and a peripteros. With the latter it has in common the one colonnade round the whole cella; with the former the circumstance of this colonnade being wide enough to give room for an imaginary interior row of columns. It is said to have been invented by Hermogenes about the time of Alexander the Great, but one does not see why it should not have occurred before. At Selinus, at least, the largest of the temples on the eastern hill of the city is built in this style. It is, like the other buildings of that city, in the Doric style, but approaching the Attic by the gracefulness of its proportions. Fig. 33 shows the plan of this temple. The colonnade *A* surrounding the temple has exactly the width of two interstices and one bottom diameter of the columns. The pronaos B is formed by the projecting

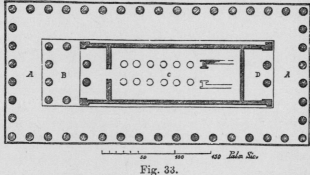

Fig. 33.

antæ-walls and six detached columns. The cella (C) seems to have been open and surrounded by colonnades; behind it follows the opisthodomos D.

There were several Ionic temples of this order; Hermogenes, named by Vitruvius as its inventor, is indeed the architect who for the first time treated the Ionic style according to a scientific system, in opposition to the Doric style, to which he objects on the ground of several irregularities. The temple of Artemis Leukophryne at Magnesia on the Mæandros, cited by Vitruvius, was, to judge from the discovered remnants, of the Ionic order, as was also, most probably, the temple of Apollo at Alabanda, the native city of Hermogenes, also mentioned by Vitruvius.

We quote, as an example of the Ionic pseudo-dipteros, the temple at Aphrodisias in Karia, which was built in the early times of the empire, and the ruins of which are exceptionally well preserved. The protecting goddess of Aphrodisias was Aphrodite, as indicated by this name being substituted for the original Ninoë, and her service was celebrated with a splendour evidently influenced by the worship of similar Asiatic deities. This was often the case in Asia Minor. For these reasons it is not unlikely that the mentioned temple was dedicated to Aphrodite. It is of large dimensions and easy, graceful proportions, quite in accordance with the nature of the goddess and her service.

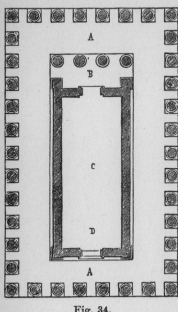

Fig. 34.

Fig. 34 shows the plan* of the temple divided into the colonnade (A), the pronaos (B), and the cella (C, D); Fig. 35 represents a sketch of the façade,

Fig. 35.

elegant and graceful in its proportions.   Peculiar to it are the

---

* The width of the inside of the cella is about 22 ft. 6 in. English measure.

little tablets on the shafts of the columns with Greek votive inscriptions, which interrupt the flutings.

14. Hitherto we have discovered as the fundamental idea of the most widely different temples, the oblong square cella, the house of the god, surrounded by columns in various ways, and divided for the purposes of the service into pronaos, cella, and opisthodomos. This was, indeed, the prevalent form of all Greek sacred edifices, even of the chapels (ναΐσκοι).

There are, however, some exceptions to this rule. First, with regard to shape, there are the round temples. But, besides this, there may be different arrangements of the interior, or even of the whole plan of the building, caused by the peculiar requirements of the service. A specimen of the former variation was the double temple; one of the latter, the votive temple.

a. The round-temple we can mention but briefly. Vitruvius, it is true, mentions it in his list of different temples, but without reference to Greek specimens, as has been the case with regard to those hitherto considered. The only specimen of the round temple in existence is, as far as my knowledge goes, the tholos of Polykleitos, in the hieron of Asklepios near Epidauros; the foundation walls, together with some remnants of the geison, are preserved. There are, however, some analogous buildings mentioned in the records of the ancients. In the agora of Sparta, not far from the Skias, stood a circular building containing the statues of Zeus and Aphrodite, surnamed the "Olympian" (Paus. III. 12, 11). The expression, tholos (Θόλος), applied by Pausanias to the building near the Buleuterion at Athens, where the prytanes used to sacrifice, also seems to indicate a circular form. Small figures of silver, and the statues of the heroes presiding over the single tribes (φύλαι), were placed in them. Some temples at Platææ and Delphi seem also to have been of a round form; we know, however, nothing else about their plans. A round house, οἴκημα περιφερές, stood in the Altis grove at Olympia. It was erected by Philip, king of the Makedonians, after the battle of Chæronea (Ol. 110, 3), and was called, after him, the Philippeum. It was made of burnt bricks, there were columns round it (peripteros), and on the top there was a brass decoration in the form of a poppy-head, which served, at the same time, to fasten the beams of the roof. In the interior were placed the statues of Philip, his father Amyntas, his son Alexander the Great, and those of Olympia and Eurydike, wrought in gold and ivory by Leochares. Whether or not the

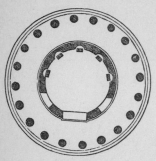

Fig. 36.

Philippeum had the significance of a temple, it may, in any case, be considered as analogous to the round temple, for which reason we have added (Fig. 36) the original plan of the building as designed by Hirt.

That form of the round temple which Vitruvius designates as monopteros, consisting of an open circle of columns with beams and a roof placed on them, is specified by the analogous Choragic monument of Lysikrates at Athens. To this we shall have to return in speaking of profane architecture (§ 24, Fig. 152).

b. The double temple. Several temples are mentioned by the ancients in which two deities were adored, each in a separate room. In this case the cella had to be divided, whence the expression ναὸς διπλοῦς; and this seems to have been done in various ways. The one least in use seems to have been that of putting the rooms of the different gods one on the top of the other. Of this, Pausanias knows only one example, viz., an old temple at Sparta dedicated to the "armed Aphrodite," whose image was placed in it. This temple had an upper story dedicated to Morpho. Morpho, however, was, according to Pausanias, only a surname of Aphrodite. Her image in the upper temple was, unlike the other, without arms. The goddess was represented with her feet in fetters and veiled, most likely in allusion to her significance as the goddess of death.

More frequent was the division of the cella into two level rooms, one by the side or at the back of the other. The separation of the cella by a wall built parallel to the length of the temple (such as it might be found in an Egyptian temple at Ombos) seems not to have been used by the Greeks. The double temple of Asklepios and Leto at Mantinea, cited by Hirt as a specimen of this division, may (according to the statement of Pausanias, VIII. 9, 1) just as well have been divided by a cross-wall right in the middle of the cella.

The last-mentioned division of the cella is proved by several other temples. At Sikyon, for instance, Hypnos, the god of sleep, and Apollo, surnamed Karneios, were adored in a double temple. The image of Hypnos was in the front compartment, while the interior was dedicated to Apollo; the latter, only priests were allowed to enter (Pausanias, II. 10, 2).

Another double temple at Mantinea was dedicated to Aphrodite and Ares. Pausanias remarks that the entrance to the room of Aphrodite was on the eastern, that to the apartment of Ares on the western, side.

Of a partition of the temple by a cross-wall we have an instructive example in the sanctuary of the old Attic deities Athene Polias, Poseidon and Erechtheus, and the daughter of Kekrops, Pandrosos, situated in the Akropolis of Athens, and called promiscuously temple of Athene Polias, Erechtheion, or Pandroseion. At a very early period there was, opposite the long northern side of the Parthenon, a temple which, according to Herodot, was dedicated jointly to Athene Polias and the Attic hero, Erechtheus. (Ol. 68, 1.) King Kleomenes, of Sparta, who had expelled Klisthenes from Athens, was refused the entrance into this temple because in it were placed the national deities of the Athenians (Ol. 75, 1); this temple was destroyed by fire while the Persians held the city. Not unlikely the rebuilding of the Erechtheion was begun by Perikles together with that of the other destroyed temples of the Akropolis; but as it was not finished by him, it is generally not mentioned amongst his works. From the fourth year of Olympiad 92 we have a special account of the state of the building. From a public document, in which the architects give an account of their work, we gather that, at that time the walls and columns of the temple were finished, only the roof and the working out of details remaining undone. This temple was renowned amongst the ancients as one of the most beautiful and perfect in existence, and seems to have remained almost intact down to the time of the Turks. The siege of Athens by the Venetians in 1687 seems to have been fatal to the Erechtheion, as it was to the Parthenon. Stuart found the walls and columns still erect, but part of the architrave, half of the frieze, and almost the whole cornice were destroyed; stones, rubbish, and the ruins of the roof covered the floor; in the northern entrance-hall was a powder magazine. At present the temple has been restored as far as possible.

The plan of this building, which represents the Attic-Ionic style in its highest development, is, for various reasons connected with the divine service, one of the most complicated we know of during the Greek period (Fig. 37*). The chief part of it we must

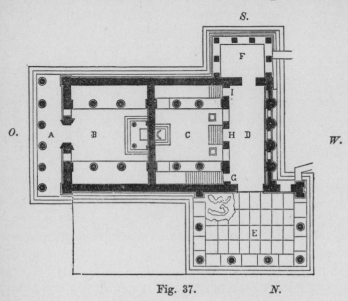

Fig. 37.

consider as a cella stretching from west to east; the masonry is 73 feet in length by 37 in width; on the eastern side a pronaos is formed by a portico of six Ionic columns. A door led from this pronaos into the cella (B) dedicated to Athene Polias, which could be entered only from this eastern side; it was separated from the cella (C) of Poseidon Erechtheus by an uninterrupted cross-wall. Another wall, interrupted by three entrances (I H G), separated the Erechtheion proper from the cella of Pandrosos—a small apartment, not unlike a corridor (D), which finished the building towards the west. The western outer wall was adorned with columns, between the intercolumnia of which there were windows, but it had no entrance corresponding to that on the eastern side. The entrance into the Pandroseion—

* Compare the plan of the Akropolis, Fig. 52, B.

and through it into the middle room of the Erechtheion—consisted of a pronaos (E) carried by six slender and richly decorated Ionic columns (compare Fig. 10), and situated at the western end of the northern long side; from it a beautiful and still-preserved door led into the sanctuary. Corresponding to this pronaos we discover, at the western end of the southern long side, a small graceful hall (F), the ceiling of which is carried, instead of columns, by six caryatides, representing Athenian maidens (compare Fig. 214); a small postern led from this hall down into the Pandroseion. Thus much about the plan and arrangement of the interior of the temple, as gathered from Bötticher's clever researches. A conjectural reconstruction of this beautiful edifice is shown, Fig. 38; it is the more authentic as the remaining portions, although partly displaced and damaged, still give a distinct notion of the former state, even with regard to ornamental details.

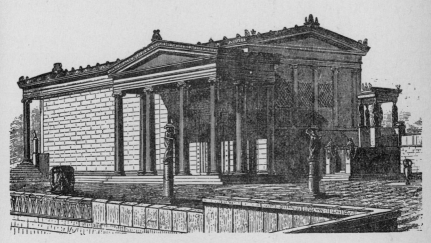

Fig. 38.

c. We will conclude our survey of the exceptional forms of Greek temples with a description of the great votive temple at Eleusis. The sanctuaries hitherto considered were habitations of the deity represented by its image. Greek temples, as a rule, were not destined for the reception of crowds with a view to common religious ceremonies. Individuals might enter to pray and offer, or to gaze at the divine images; but the great religious festivities took place outside the temple. There were, however, a few holy edifices for the purpose of common prayer; which, therefore, were not only houses of the gods but also places for religious meetings. These were the so-called votive temples (τελεστήρια, μέγαρα), destined for the celebration of mysteries; and, therefore, constructed on an entirely different plan from other temples. The great importance of the mysteries for antique life is well known; they date from early Pelasgic times, but their symbolic celebration, relating to the divinities of the earth and its culture, was in the acme of Greek development combined with artistic energy of every kind. The original import of their mystical doctrine was rendered in mimico-dramatic representations, and formed at the same time the subject of choral hymns. For this purpose large rooms were required, and the only building of this kind known to us, viz., the Megaron at Eleusis, is indeed unique in its arrangements. It has at present disappeared almost tracelessly, but former excavations throw a sufficiently distinct light on various important points of its interior arrangements (Fig. 39). The temple was quadrangular in form, from 212 to 216 feet long by 178 wide; in front was a portico of twelve columns which formed the pronaos (A). The second compartment, which one entered by a door from the pronaos, formed an almost perfect square; it was divided into five parallel naves by four rows of columns. The columns, some of which have been found, carried galleries, as in the hypæthral temple, but that in this case they were broader, and rested on two rows of columns respectively (C and D). The space in the middle (B) extended through both stories, and formed a kind of central nave of increased height. Plutarch mentions the history of the building in his life of Perikles, its originator.

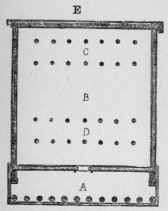

Fig. 39.

According to him, Koroibos, most likely under the supervision of Iktinos, began the Telesterium; he also erected the columns of the first story, and covered them with their architraves. After his death, Metagenes added the frieze and erected the upper columns (*i.e.*, the

columns of the upper story) ; the opening over the anaktoron
(viz. the centre nave B) was covered by Xenokles. Underneath
the floor was a kind of crypt, supported by short cylindrical props
(*Cylinderspitzen*), and used, perhaps, for preparing the above-
mentioned mimical representations. On the side opposite the
entrance a raised terrace was added to
the temple, to which led, through a
narrow square courtyard, an entrance
decorated with columns. Most likely
there was a door also on this side, destined for the conductors of the mysteries (mystagogoi), while the large door
in the façade gave entrance to the
initiated, into the holy chambers. Fig.

Fig. 40.

40 shows a rich Corinthian capital of a pilaster found amongst
the ruins, and belonging, most likely, to the decorations of the
pronaos.

15. In looking back on the interior arrangements and the
surroundings of the temples, we are struck again by their rich and
solemn appearance. Wherever the situation made it possible, the
temple was secluded from the current of profane life ; it stood in
a peribolos, which, at the same time, served to receive the votive
offerings less appropriate for the interior. Here were symbols of
the gods, trees, rocks, and fountains, frequently with holy traditions attaching to them; here were statues sometimes wholly
exposed to the air, or else protected by elegant small roofs ; heroa,
or small chapels (ναΐσκοι), and altars used for the reception of
offerings, and often dedicated to several deities; nay, even groves
and gardens were comprised in these enclosures.

The most important were the altars (βωμός, θυτήριον) on
which burnt-offerings were devoted to the deity of the temple.
Burnt-offerings of the flesh of living creatures did not take
place in the interior of the temple (see § 59). They were
performed on the thymele before the pronaos, the doors being
open at the time so that the image of the god celebrated could
look on the altar. It need not be mentioned that in large temples
these altars were decorated with great splendour. Originally they
were only natural hillocks which gradually increased in size
by the ashes and horns of the burnt animals, and soon became

capable of architectural and sculptural development. Pausanias
describes (V. 13) the altar of the Olympian Zeus as an artificial
structure, the base (κρηπίς or πρόθυσις) of which was 125 feet in
circumference.   On this stood the altar proper, 22 feet in height ;
stone steps led to the prothysis, and thence to the uppermost
platform of the altar, to which women had no access.   The altar,
Pausanias adds, consisted of the ashes of the thighs of the killed
animals, as was also the case with an altar of Hera of Samos ; the
altars of the Olympian Hera, of the Olympian Gaia, and of Apollo
Spodios at Thebes, also consisted of ashes ; while an altar near the
large temple of Apollo Didymæos, at Miletos, was composed of
the blood of the slaughtered animals.   We also hear of altars of
wood ; at Olympia there was one of unburnt tiles which once
every Olympiad was rubbed with chalk.   For the greater part,
however, the larger and more elaborate altars were made of stone,
the inside being possibly filled up with earth.   An altar at
Pergamon is distinctly stated to have consisted of marble ; the
shape was usually quadrangular.   Pausanias (V. 14, 5) calls the

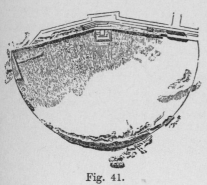

Fig. 41.

altar of Artemis of Olympia
square, and gradually rising upwards ; square was, also, the
colossal altar at Parion, said
to have been one stadium (600
feet) in length and width.   A
specimen of an altar in the
form of a terrace we have in
that devoted to Zeus Hypatos,
or Hypistos, at Athens (Fig. 41).
It was cut from the living rock
and formed, partly by nature,
partly by the hand of man, into a terrace, visible from afar, up
to which led steps and well-constructed paths.   Professor E. Curtius
has proved this structure to be an altar, and not the Pnyx, or
place of public assembly, as was formerly supposed.   It was one
of those places of oldest Athenian worship, connected with the
" highest Jove ; " which, with the increase of the city, was raised
and enlarged proportionally.   (See the perspective view, Fig. 42.)

Facing the altar for burnt-offerings rises the façade of the
temple, consisting of beautiful marble ; or, if made of lesser

material, clad with delicate stucco, discreetly coloured, a modification of the glaring whiteness, also occasionally applied to the protruding details of a marble erection. Now and then votive offerings are fastened to the façade, in addition to the sculptures of the frieze and pediment. Tripods and statues crown the top of the gable, golden tripods or other statuary ornaments are placed on its edges, and golden shields were often hung up on the architrave, as, for instance, in the Parthenon. Statues of priests and priestesses stand at the sides of the entrance ; the number and value of the offerings and statues increase on entering the pronaos; frequently valuable plate was kept here, partly for the purposes of the service, as, for instance, basins for washing, partly with a view to alluding to sacred events, as in the case of the

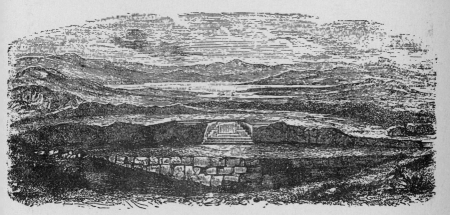

Fig. 42.

couch of Hera in the pronaos of the Heræon, near Mykenæ ; in its vicinity was also placed, as an anathema, the shield which Menelaos had snatched from Euphorbos before Troy. The cella was fitted up in a similar but still more splendid style. The divine image is enthroned in a carefully secluded space, frequently in a separate niche, but always under a shelter from above. The images of friendly deities (ἀρεδροι) were frequently placed in its vicinity, surrounded at a greater distance by statues and offerings of various kinds. Very important was the oblation-table (ἱερὰ or θυωρὸς τράπεζα) placed before the image, and corresponding to the burnt-offering altar outside, but destined only for bloodless offerings.

Even in their homes the Greeks had such sacred tables, near or on which were placed statues of the gods, and dishes with the first portions of the food. Where one and the same cella was devoted to several divinities, each of them had a separate τράπεζα inside, and an altar of burnt-offerings outside, of the temple. The thymele in front of the pronaos and the trapeza before the image are the chief criteria of what Bötticher calls the *cultus*-temple, *i.e.* of a temple which served for the performance of *sacra* and other devotional acts of the people represented by the priests. Both were wanting in another class of temples, viz. the agonal or festive temples. In these the trapeza was supplanted by the bema, from the top of which the prizes gained in the agon were distributed. Although occasionally portable, the altars were generally made of stone. Some of them are known from pictures, others have been rediscovered. On an earthen vessel found at Athens an altar is depicted with a fire burning on it in honour of Zeus, whom we discover standing by the side of it, together with Nike. On a low pedestal is raised a small erection with ornaments like volutes (Fig. 43). Stuart has found, at Athens, an octagonal altar adorned with garlands, skulls of bulls, and knives (Fig. 44). A round altar of white marble, with similar ornaments, and a small erection, have been found in the island of Delos (Fig. 45). Valuable implements of the service, like candlesticks, basins, or small votive offerings, were placed on tables, as is shown, for instance, in a terra-cotta reproduction (see Fig. 46).

Fig. 43.

Fig. 44.

16. The highest splendour of Greek architecture was shown where several temples were placed together in one particular

space devoted to the gods. Of such centres of Greek life and
religious worship several are known to us; as, for instance, the
grove Altis, at Olympia, where an abundance of architectural
monuments were crowded together, and where the agility and
beauty displayed by the youth in the games, celebrated in honour
of Zeus, offered plentiful suggestions to the sculptor. At other
places competitions in music and poetry were added to the display
of gymnastic skill, which formed the prominent feature of
Olympian festivals. But even where no such games took place,
several sanctuaries were frequently built together. At Girgenti,
even at the present day, a row of temples is discoverable on a

Fig. 45.

Fig. 46.

height overlooking the sea; at Selinunt there are two groups of
buildings on two hills, and the remaining three ruins of temples
at Pæstum seem also to have belonged to a group.

The entrances to such holy enclosures were always decorated
with a splendour corresponding to their sanctity and beauty; the
largeness and beauty of the entrance-gate, or portal, indeed,
seemed to indicate in advance the corresponding importance of the
place. The simplest kind consisted of a gate rising in command-
ing dimensions over the wall of the peribolos. Perhaps an
entrance-portal of this kind must be recognised in a separate gate
of beautiful stone which has been discovered standing erect in

the small island of Palatia, near Naxos (Fig. 47) ; its inner width
is 3,45 metres. Palatia was connected with the larger Naxos by
means of a bridge, and had a temple, near which the mentioned
portal has been found ; it consists of a threshold, which origin-

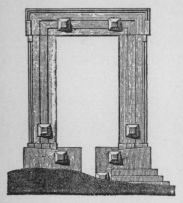

ally seems to have been level with
the ground, over which it is raised
at the present time ; it is also possible that there were steps leading
up to it ; the posts and the lintel
are divided into three parallel stripes
like an Ionic architrave, and surrounded with a simple cornice.

Where the entrance-structure was
developed more richly it was natural
to conform its appearance to the chief
model of Greek architecture, the
temple itself. The simplest kind of
this conformity is displayed in the

Fig. 47.

beautiful portal leading to the peribolos of the temple of Athene,
at Sunion, on the southern point of Attika. To this building
(see the plan, Fig. 48) the name propylæa may be applied,
which was the general denomination of portal-erections. The
propylæa of Sunion resemble in their design a temple with

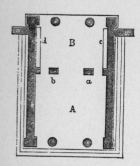

two columns *in antis* on the two small sides,
and with the cross-wall of the cella left
out. When the plan of this building was
first made public, it was thought that in
the space covered by the roof no cross-wall
had been intended, but Blouet has since
discovered that the actual gates, formed
by two pillars (*a b*), were in this cross-wall.
These pillars, or shall we call it a broken
wall, divided the whole space into two
halves, of which the outer one (A) forms a

Fig. 48.

kind of portico, while the second division (B) is turned towards
the inside of the peribolos and the temple itself. In the latter
stood marble benches (*cd*) against both the side walls.

Richer forms and developments are shown by the propylæa
of the two temple-enclosures best known to us, viz. at Eleusis

and in the Åkropolis of Athens.   The former was destined to
enclose the large votive temple described above (§ 14, Fig. 39).
In the plan (Fig. 49) the walls of both an outer (A) and inner

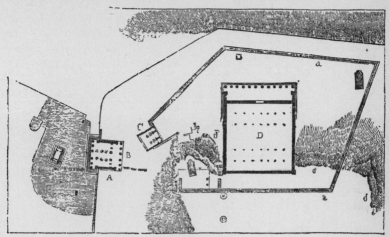

Fig. 49.

(*a a*) peribolos are recognisable.   The entrance is formed by the
large propylæa (B), near which the above-mentioned temple of
Artemis Propylæa is situated (see Fig. 15).   These propylæa

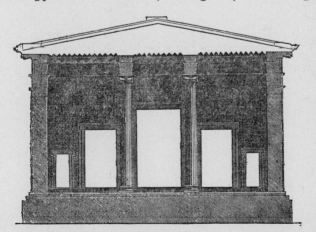

Fig. 50.

form a square space, enclosed by a wall on each side, and by a
portico of six Doric columns, both in front and at the back.
Inside, there is a cross-wall (Fig. 50), interrupted by five doors

corresponding to the intercolumnia of the portico ; it divides the whole space into two compartments, in the larger of which there are two rows of three Ionic columns each. The same arrangement we shall have to mention again in the propylæa of Athens, after which those of Eleusis were fashioned. On entering the outer peribolos, through this beautiful building, one encounters a second smaller erection of propylæa (C), which leads into the inner peribolos. The latter lies higher than the other parts, and is also surrounded by a wall (*aa*). It surrounds the votive temple (D) at a moderate distance. The plan of the smaller propylæa is shown, Fig. 51. They also are enclosed by walls on the two long

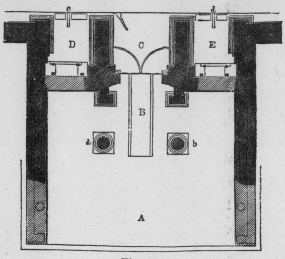

Fig. 51.

sides ; a cross-wall divides the whole space into two halves. The side where the entrance lay was open in front, and had columns which supported the roof. By the walls, to right and left, are raised steps (*ab*) ; the part in front of the columns (A) had an even pavement, while in part B the pavement rises gradually to the amount of about sixteen inches. Into the well-preserved floor grooves have been cut, seemingly destined for the wheels of vehicles, or for rollers. The small inner space (C) was separated from the last-mentioned one by a door, the leaves of which opened inside, as is still recognisable by marks on the floor. On the right and left sides, the passage (C) is joined towards the interior by two smaller rooms, like niches, in which, most likely, statues were placed; in front of these are some holes (*cd*), carefully worked out, and evidently connected with the exhibitions which here took place. Altogether, the mentioned details seem to indicate that this entrance was used to prepare the visitors for the ceremonies in the votive temple, by arrangements or exhibitions of some kind.

The greatest splendour of antique art, however, was displayed in the propylæa which formed the entrance to the Athenian Akropolis. The Akropolis is situated on a table-land 1,150 feet in length, and 500 broad in the widest places; being 160 feet high, and of steep ascent except where it slopes towards the town. The Akropolis, in a manner, marks the beginning of Athens, both as a state and a city, having been, at a very early period, surrounded by walls, and containing the oldest national sacred monuments. The old temples were destroyed by fire during the Persian occupation, but when liberty and prosperity were restored they once more rose from their ashes with renewed splendour (see plan of the Akropolis, Fig. 52); the temple of the Wingless Nike (Figs. 17, 18, and 52, D) was erected here, so as to attach the goddess of victory to Athens; here rose in majestic severity the Parthenon (A), and the graceful structure devoted to Athene Polias and Erechtheus (B), while between both stood the imposing form of Athene Promachos (E) as in defence of the castle. Numerous holy statues, altars, architectural groups, and other ornaments, stood around these splendid monuments; and it was but natural that the entrance to this beautiful and hallowed spot should be adorned with splendour. For this purpose the propylæa (C) were erected by Mnesikles on the side looking towards the city; the building of it took from 437 till 432 (B.C.), and the expense amounted to 2,012 talents. The chief part of the building consisted of a large square, enclosed by walls on the right and left, but opening towards both the city and the Akropolis by means of porticoes. Nearest to the inner portico, which was slightly raised, a wall went right across the space, being interrupted by five doors corresponding to the intercolumnia of the former (see Fig. 50); these doors formed the entrance proper. Between this wall and the outer portico lay a space of not inconsiderable dimensions, which was divided into three naves by means of two rows of Ionic columns, each row consisting of three columns.

The unevenness of the soil was equalised by means of steps, but between the mentioned centre columns a gently ascending road was hewn into the rock, so as to effect a commodious entrance for the carts laden with the splendid peplos of Athene, which formed a feature of the procession of the Panathenæa. The whole space was covered with slender marble cross-pieces, which spanned the naves and carried a rich and graceful casket-work (*Cassetten-werk*). Two lower side-wings with porticoes joined the chief

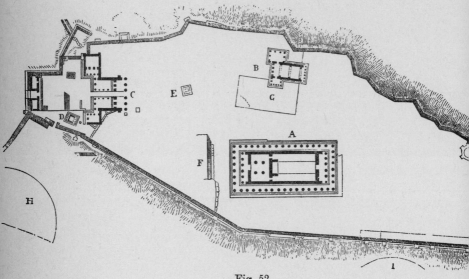

Fig. 52.

A. Parthenon.	D. Temple of Nike Apteros.	G. Terrace of Polygons.
B. Erechtheion.	E. Pedestal of Athene Promachos.	H. Theatre of Herodes.
C. Propylæa.	F. Steps in the rock.	I. Theatre of Dionysos.

façade, so as to add to its impression. The northern one, which is still well preserved, contained in its interior the celebrated paintings by Polygnotos from the Iliad and Odyssey ; and even at the present day its walls are covered with the smooth marble slabs which once served as the frames of these pictures. The other wing was of similar construction, but of lesser width; during the Middle Ages the materials of this building have been used for a watch-tower of the castle, which was inhabited by the Franconian dukes of Athens. Between these two buildings, which were in beautiful proportion with the great façade of the propylæa, ended the splendid marble steps placed in the slanting rock of the Akropolis; their length was equal to the width of the propylæa; some of the steps are still in existence. Between these steps lay a wide carriage-road, paved with large slabs of marble, into which grooves had been chiselled for the wheels of the above-mentioned vehicle. Recent excavations have discovered the lower part of the steps, and the entrance-gate between two towers; the gate, however, is of Roman origin.

17. After having discussed the Greek buildings supplying the ideal demands of the adoration of the gods, we now must turn to those which served the material purposes of life.

Amongst these the walls ought to be mentioned first. We have noticed the habit of the Greeks of enclosing the precincts of their temples with walls, and the same feature we find repeated in the oldest specimens of their settlements. This is proved by the numerous remnants of old cities, both in Hellas and the Peloponnesos, which tend to show that wall-enclosures were amongst the very earliest productions of Greek architecture. The Greeks themselves ascribed these colossal structures to the Cyclops, a mythical race of giants, who are said to have come from Lykia, and to have taken a prominent part in building the walls of Tiryns. Nowadays these structures are generally called Pelasgic, owing to the opinion of their being built by the tribe of that name. This opinion seems to be confirmed by the fact that these monuments are generally found in places originally possessed by the Pelasgi. At Athens, the oldest parts of the fortifications of the Akropolis were called Pelasgic walls, and their erection was ascribed to the Pelasgi, who once had a settlement there (Paus. I., 28, 3). A third name applied to these walls refers to the mode of their construction. In the more ancient walls of this kind it consists in the piling on each other of rough, many-edged stones, and is therefore called polygonal building. Amongst the remaining monuments, the walls of Tiryns are most remarkable, which consist of large blocks of stone heaped on each other, the intervals being filled up by smaller stones. " Of the town," Pausanias says (II., 25, 8), "no remnants exist but the walls, which are the work of the Cyclops. They consist of rough stones,

each one of which is so large that the smallest of them could not
have been carried by a yoke of mules. At an early period smaller

Fig. 53.

stones have been placed
between, so as to join
the large ones together."
In another place (IX.,
36, 5) he calls them quite
as admirable as the pyra-
mids of Egypt, both by
the grandeur of their
dimensions and the diffi-
culty of the work required in erecting them.

The walls of Tiryns seem to be, at the present time, in the
same state as when Pausanias saw them. They have been
examined by Gell, after whose drawing a fragment is reproduced
in Fig. 53 (scale = 10 feet English measure). A second kind of
these very old monuments show the stones still in their irregular
polygonal form, but with some traces of workmanship upon them.
The stones have been worked into the polygonal form nearest to
their natural shape, and afterwards carefully joined together, so
that the wall presents a firm uninterrupted surface. The finest
specimens are found in the walls of the very ancient town of
Mykenæ, in Argolis (Fig. 54). They are of considerable thick-

Fig. 54.

ness; the two outer
surfaces consist of hewn
and carefully composed
stones, while the space
between is filled up with
small stones and mortar.
This kind of construction
was called by the Greeks
ἔμπλεκτον; it was fur-
ther strengthened by the addition of solid inner cross-walls. The
use of polygonal stones, as applied in the walls of Argos, Platææ,
Ithaka, Koronea, Same, and other places, may result in great
firmness, by means of the stones being put together as in a vaulted
structure. In consequence it was retained occasionally by the
Greeks, even after the freestone construction has been introduced (see Fig. 13); in our own time it has been applied, for

instance, in the terraces which form the base of the Walhalla, at Regensburg, and in the protective walls on the shores of the German Ocean, which Forchhammer has appropriately compared to Cyclopic-Pelasgic walls.

Notwithstanding the advantages of polygonal structures, the desire for regularity led, at an early period, to the use of horizontal and regular layers of stones, as is shown by several old walls. The walls of Argos consist partly of horizontal arrangements of totally irregular stones. In some places, as, for instance, in the remnants found in Ætolia, the layers, although horizontal, are totally irregular with regard to the cross-joints ; while in other places, the transition to the regular freestone style is shown more distinctly by the application of vertical cross-joints. An instance of this are the walls of Psophis, in Arkadia (Fig. 55). A similar arrangement appears in a tower on the wall of Panopeus (Fig. 56), and still more distinctly the regular freestone style is shown in the wall of Chæronea, in Bœotia, which, moreover, has the

Fig. 55.

peculiarity of not being perpendicular, but of showing a decided talus. (Compare the walls of Œniadæ, Figs. 64 and 69.)

The use of regular freestone afterwards became general amongst the Greeks. Not only the walls of temples, but also those of later cities were erected in this way, as is shown, for instance, by the well-preserved walls of Messene (built 371 B.C.), of which we shall give illustrations. As the most solid and, at the same time, most artistic walls, those are mentioned by means of which the Athenians had joined the Piræus harbour to their city. Unfortunately only few remnants, consisting of single large blocks of stone, are preserved.

Fig. 56.

Fig. 57 (scale = 100 yards) shows the plan of the castle of Tiryns, which may serve as a specimen of these ancient fortifications. A signifies a gate, C a tower, and B a road ascending from the lower plain; D is the present entrance. Near E and H are the galleries, to which we shall have to return; near F is another

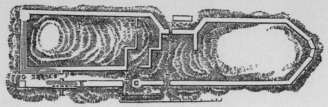

Fig. 57.

gate, up to which leads the road G. Near I a cistern has been found, and near K is another smaller gate.

18. Concerning gates we have to add that, where the top of a mountain was transformed into a castle by means of walls, there was generally but one gate. There are, however, examples of such castles having several gates; as, for instance, the above-mentioned Akropolis of Mykenæ. A town, on the other hand, as the centre of commerce, required numerous entrances; and it was considered a particular honour to a city to have many gates, the fortified safeness of which symbolized, in a manner, its importance. The importance and size of the gates naturally depended on the importance of the roads which led to the city. In consequence we have to distinguish between gates and posterns (πύλαι and πυλίδες, Pforten), the most important amongst the former being called the large gate (μεγάλαι πύλαι). Such was the dipylon at Athens, where met the roads from Eleusis and Megara, the large harbour road, and the roads from the Academy and the Kolonos; while, inside, these were joined by the High and Market Street of the city; in this way an enormous amount of traffic was concentrated in this one point.

Originally the gates were of the simplest construction. Where the stones of the walls were left in a rough state, the gates were constructed in a similar manner. The single blocks were pushed gradually towards each other till, at last, they touched, and in this way formed a simple arch. This primitive mode of construction is shown in a postern at Tiryns (Fig. 58), where, as we have seen, the walls were of an equally simple kind. In the same manner the arched openings of a gallery have been constructed, which is built into the wall of the same castle. The gallery itself likewise consists of layers of stone pushed towards each other, as is shown by the view of the interior (Fig. 59, compare Fig. 57,

Fig. 58.

Fig. 59.

Fig. 60.

H). The same construction also appears in the passages within the wall, of which Fig. 60 represents a section.

The construction of the gates improves in proportion to that of the walls. They may be constructed by over-laying the stones, or by the placing of a long straight block across the two side-posts. A simple specimen of the former method we see in some small posterns at Phigalia (Fig. 61) and Messene (Fig. 62); the latter is specified by a small door in the Akropolis of Mykenæ (Fig. 63), and a gate at Œniadæ, in Akarnania (Fig.

Fig. 61.

64). One of the oldest and most curious examples of such gates

Fig. 62.

Fig. 63.

Fig. 64.

is the so-called lions' gate at Mykenæ (Fig. 65). It stands

between a natural prominence of the rock and an artificial projection of the wall, and is formed by two strong and well-smoothed blocks of stone, which serve as side posts, and incline towards each other, so as to diminish the space to be covered. On them rests, horizontally, an enormous block of stone, 15 feet long, which forms the lintel, and in this way

finishes the gate. The wall itself is much higher than the gate ; in order to weaken the pressure of the upper stones on the lintel, and to prevent it from breaking, a triangular opening has been left above it, in which, afterwards, a thinner slab of stone, about 11 feet wide by 10 high, has been placed. On this slab we see two lions in alto-relievo, standing with their fore-paws on a broad base, which supports a column growing thinner

Fig. 65.

at the lower end. Göttling recognises in these lions, with the Phallic symbol between them, the protecting image of the castle of Mykenæ. In any case the group is interesting as the oldest specimen of Greek sculpture in existence.

Both the larger gates and the smaller sally-ports were, as much

as possible, protected by projecting parts of the wall. We have already mentioned this fact in speaking of the gate of Mykenæ ; we add a gate at Orchomenos (Fig. 66), in which the projection of the wall on the right-hand side of the entrance may still be distinctly recognised.

Fig. 66.

A gate at Messene, showing both firmness of structure and artistic proportions, is still in existence. This city, founded and raised to the capital of Messenia by Epaminondas, was, next to Korinth, considered as the safest stronghold of the whole Peloponnesos, owing to the solidity of its walls ; the above-mentioned gate quite tallies with this statement, found repeatedly in ancient authors. The design (Fig. 67) and the section (Fig. 68, scale = 100 feet English measure) show that it was a double gate with an outer (*a*) and inner (*b*) door. It is situated in a kind of tower, destined to increase the strength of the wall, inside of which there is a circular space like a courtyard. The two gates lie opposite each other in this courtyard, the one marked *a* on the outward side, that marked *b* being turned towards the town.

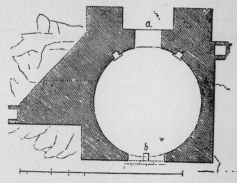

As remarkable we have still to mention the occurrence of vaulted gates in Akarnania, quite lately discovered by Heuzey. Generally speaking, the use of arches does not occur in Greece

Fig. 67.

Fig. 68.

Fig. 69.

before the time of the Makedonians; but in Akarnania there are found, in old polygonal fortifications, gates, the outer walls of which show a vault, while the inside part is still covered by horizontal pieces of stone (see Fig. 69).

19. The description of the gates leads us to that of the towers, which were almost universally used to increase the firmness and defensive conveniences of the walls. The gates naturally required a great deal of protection, and by this means, as Curtius has pointed out, the art of fortification itself was considerably developed. It seems, indeed, that the tower itself was only a development of the projection of the wall which is usually found to the right of the gate, as a favourable point of attack on the storming forces.

The simplest form seems to have consisted of a mere jutting

out of the wall, repeated at certain intervals, by means of which the besieged could direct their defence to different points easier than would have been possible from a straight wall. Such tower-like projections we find in the old Pelasgic walls of Phigalia, in Arkadia (Fig. 70); they are partly quadrangular,. partly semicircular.

We also find towers on single rocks, or prominences, the natural strength of which had to be increased by fortifications; they

Fig. 70.

were used to reconnoitre the surrounding country, which, for instance, was the purpose of a tower in the Akropolis of Orchomenos in Bœotia (Fig. 71).

At Aktor a tower of two stories has been preserved. It stands

on a point where the walls of the town meet at an obtuse angle. It has been preserved so well that the two stories are distinctly recognisable; but no traces of a staircase have been found. Most likely it consisted of wood, like the ceiling of the first story, so as to be easily removable, if necessary, in

Fig. 71.

case of an attack. The entrances to the tower were two small gates, approachable from the top of the wall; on the three sides turned outward there were windows, which, like the embrasures of mediæval castles, are very small towards the outer side, but increase considerably in size towards the inside.

Of similar construction are the towers found on the walls of Messene, both as a protection and an ornament. A round tower, amongst others, stands where the walls meet at an obtuse angle (see the plan Fig. 72, scale = 10 metres, and the view, Fig. 73); another tower, in good preservation, illustrates the kind of entrance from the top of the wall; Fig. 74 (scale = 9 metres) gives a side-view of it. The stones are placed on each other in layers, but the cross-joints are mostly oblique and irregular; the former are hewn

Fig. 72.

Fig. 73.

Fig. 74.

so that the front side projects slightly from the surface of the wall (a style called by the Italians, Rustico); the tower, as well as the walls, are crowned by battlements, which are still distinctly recognisable; the small windows converge in an acute angle towards the outside, the inside part widening in the form of a pointed arch. The door, approachable from the top of the wall (see Fig. 74), closes in a straight line.

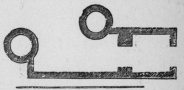

Fig. 75.

Two round towers, standing almost separate, protect the gate of Mantinea (see plan, Fig. 75, scale = 30 metres).

Single towers were often built on the sea-shore, particularly on islands, both as watch-towers against pirates and as places of refuge for the inhabitants. (Similar strongholds built by the Venetians, against the landing of the infidels, are found on many

points of the Greek coast.)   The most important structure of this
kind has been preserved in the isle of Keos.   It rises, in four
stories, straight from the ground, and is crowned with battlements,
and surrounded on its four sides by projecting blocks of stone,
which carried an open gallery, perhaps "the only well-preserved
example of the peridromos, so important in antique fortification."
(Ross, "*Inselreise*," I. p. 132.)

Of similar construction, but round in shape, is a tower in
Andros (Fig. 76), built most likely for the protection of the
neighbouring iron mines.   It is remarkable by winding stairs in

Fig. 76.

Fig. 77.

Fig. 78.

the interior, and by a circular chamber in the lower story, which,
like the treasure-houses (see § 21), grows smaller towards the
top by the overlaying of the stones ; the ceiling is formed by
radiating slabs of stone (Fig. 77).

To detached towers, courts surrounded by masonry were
sometimes added, as places of refuge for the inhabitants of the
neighbouring country and their goods.   Fig. 78 shows the plan
of such a combination, situated in the island of Tenos, where
the court, connected with the tower and enclosed by a strong
wall, is nearly 84 feet long.

20. After the buildings of protection follow those of utility.
Amongst these we must consider particularly aqueducts, harbours,
roads, and bridges ; of all of which considerable remains have been

preserved. Curtius ("On the Waterworks in Greek Cities" in *Archæologische Zeitung*, 1847, p. 19, ss.) has laid down, as the leading principle of Greek aqueducts, their accommodation to the natural conditions of the soil, widely different in this respect from the waterworks of the Romans, "who, in their imperial manner, made the fountains follow one straight line from their origin to the capital; and in this way accomplished marvellous edifices entirely independent of the conditions of the soil." The oldest epoch of town waterworks is undoubtedly marked by the cistern, which became necessary where the dryness of the soil required the collection of rain-water, or where the wells became insufficient for the increasing population. They are mostly perpendicular, gradually widening shafts, hewn into the living rock, and covered with slabs; one descended into them on steps. Such cisterns are frequently found in Delos, at Iulis in Keos, at Old-Thuria in Messenia, and at Athens in the southern parts of the city, and on the stony backs of the hills which slope towards the sea; while in the eastern and northern parts of the city we find numerous remains of wells, often connected by subterraneous channels. To a later epoch, mostly to the time of the Tyrannis, belong the waterworks, by means of which the fountains rising on the neighbouring mountains are led (in communications hewn in the rock, or enclosed by walls) into reservoirs, and distributed thence over the town by a system of canals. By a system of this kind the springs of the Hymettos, Pentelikon, and Parnes were conducted into Athens; and, in a similar manner, several villages in the dry plains of Attika were supplied with water by subterraneous aqueducts, partly still in use. Of other waterworks we mention an aqueduct seven stadia long, dug through a mountain by Eupalinos; a system of works supplying the castle of Thebes with water; and the underground aqueducts of Syrakusæ, the latter of which are still in use. The remains of these, as well as of other aqueducts near Argos, Mykenæ, Demetrias, and Pharsalos, prove sufficiently the care taken by the Greeks in this important branch of architecture.

Although natural harbours were frequent on the Greek coast, many of them required additional arrangements for the safety of the ships at anchor. We possess, for instance, the remains of a stone jetty, built for the protection of the excellent harbour of

Pylos, on the west coast of Messenia.   It is built, like the walls of the town, in the Pelasgic manner, horizontal layers being the rule,

and extends considerably into the sea, so as to protect the harbour against storms and currents. Fig. 79 illustrates a bird's-eye view of the remnants of the breakwater.

Fig. 79.

More extensive were the works in the harbour of Methone, or Mothone (the modern Modon), to the south of Pylos. To the line of cliffs, which naturally protects the harbour, a wall has been added, extending into the sea in the shape of a repeatedly broken bow, and surrounds the harbour proper on three sides in connection with the equally secured shore; Fig. 80 shows the plan of the har-

bour, which is still in frequent use. A and B mark the points where remnants of the old masonry are still in existence. Other harbours were on a still larger scale, and supplied with arsenals, lighthouses, temples, and works of art ; of these, the Korinthian harbour at Kenchreæ and the Piræus are the most remarkable.

Fig. 80.

The harbour proper consisted in the latter also in natural bays, turned to account and further protected by walls built into the sea on both sides of the entrance, so as to defend the inner space against both waves and enemies. No less complicated was the harbour of Rhodes ; according to Ross, it retains, at the present day, the original constructions ; which, by turning to account the natural bays, made it one of the most important stations for commercial and war purposes. Fig. 81 shows the design ; *a*, *b*, *c*, signify respectively the harbours for boats, commercial and war vessels ; *d* is the exterior harbour, *e* the site of the town.

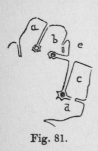

Fig. 81.

Concerning the roads of the Greeks we certainly have written evidence of carefully paved roads and streets, particularly in connection with the festive processions to the great national places of worship; but little is said about the method of the Greeks in these structures, and only few remnants remain to enlighten us as to the way in which they were made even, or paved. In low, boggy places the want of level and secure roads was naturally felt first; their earliest form seems to have been that of dams (χώματα, γέφυραι). According to Curtius, a dam led from Kopai, in Bœotia, to the opposite shore of the Kopaic bog. It is 22 feet wide, propped by stone walls, and supplied with a bridge, so as to give an outlet to the water of the Kephissos. Like the choma, which led through the marshes of the Alphæos, and formed the border-line between the dominions of the Tegeatai and Pallantioi, it served at the same time both as a protection of the arable land against the waves and as a means of communication. Sometimes canals were connected with such dams, an example of which is offered by Phenea.

Roads led up to the old lordly castles " as they are found at Orchomenos and other places." (Curtius's "History of the Building of Roads amongst the Greeks," 1855, p. 9). In later historic times, however, the chief purposes of road-building were commercial traffic and festive processions. "It is the worship of the gods which here again has given rise to art, and the holy ways were the first artistically constructed roads amongst the Greeks" (p. 11), connecting tribes and countries for the purpose of common celebration. Still, at the present time Greece is crossed by roads on which the grooves for wheels are hewn into the rocky ground. On these the holy vehicles, with the statues of the gods and the implements of worship, could be moved conveniently. Between these tracks the road was levelled by means of sand or pebbles. Where there were no two pair of grooves, arrangements were made to avoid collisions.

We know a little more about the construction of bridges amongst the Greeks. In most cases bridges across rivers and ravines were made of wood; as an example of a very firm, long bridge made of wood we mention that across the Euripus, between Aulis and Chalkis, in the island of Eubœa, built during the Peloponnesian war, and, perhaps, afterwards superseded by a dam-structure, remnants of which are still in existence. There are, however, found in Greece bridges wholly made of stone; but

their dimensions can have been but small before the arch-vaulting
principle came into use.   Gell mentions a bridge of this kind
near Mykenæ, and another similar one near Phlius the coverings
of which consisted of blocks of stone.

Wider rivers were crossed by a mode of structure which we
have mentioned in connection with the openings of gates and
walls.   The layers of stones were pushed gradually towards each
other from both sides, and when the space between was thus
sufficiently diminished it was covered by slabs of stone, or rafters,
laid across.   This system is used in a bridge between Pylos and

Methone, near the village
of Metaxidi, in Messenia
(Fig. 82).   Only the lower
layers are antique; the
arch is of later date.

A complicated and
well-calculated structure
is the bridge across the
river Pamisos in Messenia.
It is placed where a
smaller river falls into the

Fig. 82.

river Pamisos, and consists of three parts, one of which lies
towards Messene, the second towards Megalopolis, and the third
towards Franco Eclissia (Andania). (See plan, Fig. 83, and view,
Fig. 84)   The front parts of the pillars of the two branches

Fig. 83.   Fig. 84.

crossing the two rivers are pointed, so as to break the force of the
waves.   The piece *a* in Fig. 83 is illustrated by Fig. 85; it shows
one smaller opening which is covered with straight pieces of stone,
while the larger opening shows the gradual approach of the layers.

This is shown by the remaining old layers, to which, later, an arch has been added.

The same form of covering is found in a bridge across the Eurotas, near Sparta (see design, Fig. 86). In looking at Fig.

Fig. 85.

Fig. 86.   Fig. 87.

87 it ought to be remembered that the pointed arch of the vault is a later addition. (About a peculiar kind of waterworks, viz., the fountain-houses, see § 21, Figs. 90 and 91.)

21. After the buildings destined to protect man against man, we have to consider those which shelter him against the influences of nature, viz., the human habitation. The first human habitations, not to mention caves, were amongst the Greeks, as amongst other primitive nations, huts, constructed differently according to the nature of the country. They were said to have been invented by Pelasgos, the progenitor of the Pelasgic tribe in Arkadia. Of such huts and similar more or less primitive dwellings we possess neither descriptions nor actual specimens. The stages of development from the hut to the regular dwelling-house, as described in the Homeric poems, are likewise conjectural; the arrangements, however, of the dwellings of the old Greek royal families, which evidently are described as actually seen by that poet, can be understood, at least, in their chief features. This applies particularly to the description of the palace of Odysseus, which, together with partial descriptions of those of Alkinoos, Priamos, and of the house-like tent of Achilles, conveys a sufficiently clear notion of the royal mansion of the time.

According to these descriptions the royal palace was divided

into three parts, the distinction of which is recognisable in Homer.
The same division, with such modifications as were necessitated by
the more limited space, applied, undoubtedly, also to the more
important private houses. The first division was intended for
every-day life and intercourse; it consisted of the courtyard (called
αὐλή by Homer), into which one entered from the street, through
a door of two leaves (τὰ πρόθυρα, θύραι δίκλιδες). In the middle
of this courtyard stood the statue of Zeus, the protector of
dwellings (Ζεὺς ἐρκεῖος). It was surrounded by outhouses
destined for the keeping of stores, for handmills, bedrooms of the
male servants, and stables for horses and cattle, unless the latter
were kept in separate farms. Opposite the gate of the yard was
the frontage of the dwelling-house (δῶμα or δόμος) of the family
of the Anax; in front of the entrance-gate was a covered portico
(αἴθουσα δώματος), corresponding to a similar one on both sides of
the yard (αἴθουσα αὐλῆς). This portico in front of the house
must have been of considerable size as, according to Homer, it
was occasionally used by the princes as the place of their assemblies. Through it one entered the forehouse, or πρόδομος, which
is to be considered either as a kind of entrance-hall to the house
proper, running along its frontage, or as the innermost part of the
αἴθουσα δώματος, in which case it was, perhaps, closed by a wall.
In this place the couches of the guests were prepared for the
night.

The dwelling-house (δῶμα) of the Anax and his family, which
follows after the πρόδομος, comprises the hall of the men, the
women's rooms, the connubial chamber, the armoury, and the
treasury. The hall of the men (τὸ μέγαρον) was the chief room
of the palace; according to Homer it was a large room resting on
columns. Perhaps, in contrast to the light and airy prodomos, it
is described as shady (σκιόεις), the light entering only through
windows at the sides, or through an opening in the smoky ceiling,
which served also to let out the smoke. Near the back wall of
the megaron, and opposite the door which led to the women's
chambers, stood the hearth (ἐσχάρη), on which the meal of the
revellers in the hall was prepared. The floor was of stone,
perhaps varied in colour, and the walls were covered with large
pieces of polished metal. It is true that the megaron of Odysseus,
the ruler of a poor, rocky island, was bare of these ornaments; but

the palaces of richer kings, like, for instance, that of Menelaos, undoubtedly showed this favourite old wall-decoration, not to speak of the perhaps fictitious description of the splendid hall of Alkinoos. The question about the nature of the μεσόδμαι, mentioned by Homer, we do not wish to decide definitively ; some modern archæologists, like Rumpf and Winckler,* the one following the other's investigations, consider them to be two galleries, placed at the end of the megaron, on both sides of the entrance to the women's chambers : older commentators believe the mesodmai to be niches between the pilasters, or these pilasters themselves. We ourselves incline to the latter opinion, because such a gallery would be quite adapted to the hall of a hostelry, used as a women's room in the daytime and a sleeping-room for the men at night, but in the megaron of a palace it seems strangely out of place.

The third division was devoted to the smaller family circle ; its collective name was originally θάλαμοι, afterwards changed into γυναικωνῖτις. A small corridor (πρόθυρον) led to these rooms, the largest of which was a hall on the ground-floor, belonging to the female members of the family and their handmaidens. Smaller chambers, being the bedrooms of the maidservants, fifty in number, in the house of Odysseus, might be found by the side of this hall, while the upper story (ὑπερῷον) contained separate sleeping and sitting rooms for the members of the king's family. The connubial chamber, or thalamos proper, of the king and queen was, perhaps, in the lower story, at the end of the large hall of the women ; it seems, at least, that Odysseus placed his bedroom there from the fact of his cutting the top off an olive-tree in his yard, and using the stem as a post of his connubial couch. Near it, most likely, was the armoury, although certain archæologists have placed it, like the connubial chamber, in the upper story.

Thus much about the house of the Anax in Homer's time. Many conjectures as to the situation of the staircases to the upper story, the place and destination of the tholos, of the corridors of the spear-stand, &c., we have purposely omitted. In Homer's time such palaces, varying according to the locality and the owner's wealth, were scattered all over Greece. Many theories as to details, mostly founded on vague conjectures, have, for the

* A. Winckler, "The Dwelling-houses of the Greeks." Berlin, 1868, p. 31—55.

greater part, been exploded by Hercher (in his meritorious paper "Homer and Ithaka, as it was in reality," in "Hermes," vol. i., p. 263, ss.)

As an important part of the fortified palace we have still to mention the treasury (θησαυρός), the firm construction of which guaranteed the safety of its valuable contents, as is proved by several vaults still in existence. Amongst these we mention particularly the treasure-house of Atreus, remains of which are found amongst the above-mentioned Cyclopic remnants at Mykenæ. This thesauros, which is expressly mentioned by Pausanias, has been re-discovered and repeatedly described by modern scholars. It consists of a round chamber lying on the slope of a hill. (See plan, Fig. 88, and section, Fig. 89.) The entrance is through a space enclosed by walls (A); the gate (B) is formed by horizontal layers of stone, and covered with an

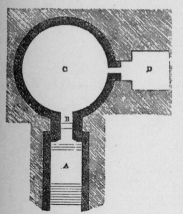

Fig. 88.   Fig. 89.

enormous slab of stone, over which, as in the lion's gate (see Fig. 65), a triangular opening has been left so as to protect it from the weight of the upper stones. Through this door, on which the traces of nails are still observable (destined evidently to fix a metal coating), one enters the chief apartment (C), which is joined at the side by another chamber (D). The latter is cut into the rock, while the walls of the chief apartment consist of horizontal layers of stones arranged in a circular form. These layers approach each other towards the top, which produces the appearance of a cupola, closed at the top by a larger stone (Fig. 89).

Pausanias mentions several thesauroi, the convenient arrangement of which is exemplified by the one described above. At Mykenæ he mentions, besides the treasure-house of Atreus, those of his sons, of which also remnants are still in existence. At Orchomenos, in Bœotia, he mentions the thesauros of Minyas as a wonderful work, unsurpassed by any monument in Greece or elsewhere (Pausanias, 9, 38, 1). His description tallies perfectly with the construction of the treasure-house at Mykenæ, but for thé size, the latter being only 48 feet in diameter, against 70 of the Orchomenos thesauros.

The same principle of forming the vaults by overlaying has been applied to other buildings, as tombs of heroes, fountain-houses, and religious treasure-houses, at an early period. Ross has discovered a fountain-house in the island of Kos, in which the tholos principle has been applied in a similar manner. About one and a half hour's walk from the city of Kos on the slope of Mount Oromedon, lies the well Burinna, which supplies the town

with water. In order to keep it quite cold and pure a circular chamber (2,85 metres in diameter, and 7 metres in height, up to the round opening in the vault) has been erected, into which the water runs, and from which it issues through a subterraneous canal 35 metres in length, and of an average height of 2 metres. Fig. 90 shows the mouth of the canal (A), the chamber (B), and the cleft in the rock (C) whence the water issues; between this and the chamber there is a door. The chamber (see Fig. 91, D) is built like the treasure-house at Mykenæ, and opens at the top by means of a

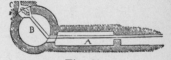

Fig. 90.

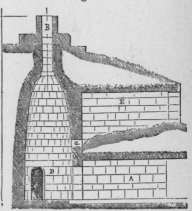

Fig. 91.

shaft (B) 3 metres high, which leads through the mountain in order to connect the water with the open air. Above the roof of the canal (A) (which consists partly of large horizontal blocks of stone, partly of long, narrow pieces of freestone) a small chamber (E) has been discovered, the entrance to which lies on the slope of the mountain, between the mouth of the canal and the opening of the shaft. It is connected by a small window (A) with the principal chamber, and may have been the sanctuary of the nymphs of the fountain, or the watchman's dwelling, besides letting in fresh air to the fountain in addition to the shaft (B).

22. About the historic dwelling-house of the Greeks our information is almost as scanty as about the Homeric palace. Remaining specimens are totally wanting, perhaps with *one* exception; and a systematic description of the Greek house by Vitruvius seems to relate more to the splendid mansions of post-Alexandrine times than to the houses of the common citizens. His account, moreover, is not easily understood; so that about this most important feature of Greek domestic life little is to be ascertained.

In comparing the historic Greek house with that of the Homeric poems, we find, as an important deviation, that in the latter the women's chamber was always in the upper story; while in the former men's and women's apartments, although separated, lay generally on the same flat. This rule, however, is not without exceptions with regard to both cases.

Both the Homeric and the historic houses have, in common, the important feature of a courtyard. In both it is surrounded by columns, and forms, as it were, the centre round which the other parts of the house are grouped equally, and into which the single rooms open. The historic house, however, was much inferior in size and splendour to that described by Homer, as was natural, seeing that it was inhabited by simple citizens instead of kings and rulers of the people. Homer never even mentions private dwellings. Moreover, it was a peculiarity of the Greeks, in their best times, to concentrate all their splendour and luxury in the adornment of temples and other public edifices, while their private dwellings were small and modest, not to say mean. The homes of the Greeks were their public places, their Stoas and Agoras; on these they looked with pride and joy; only in the Makedonian period, when Greek freedom and greatness had vanished, luxurious private houses became the fashion; while at the same time begin the complaints of both religious and civic buildings being more and more neglected. But even then buildings of large size and

great splendour were more common in the country seats of the
rich than in the towns, where the limits of space and the regular
lines of the streets precluded a too great extension.

Hence one yard only was the rule for town-houses. The
descriptions by Vitruvius of numerous splendid rooms, &c.,
evidently refer to the palace-like buildings of the time after
Alexander ; still these descriptions are of great importance to us.
For in that part of the house first described by him, which he
calls gynaikonitis, the original nucleus of an old Greek dwelling
seems preserved ; while the second part, called andronitis,
contains the additions of increased and more refined luxury. We
must try first to recognise the old simple house in his description.

" On entering* the door," Vitruvius says, " one comes into a
rather narrow passage, called by the Greeks θυρωρεῖον." It
corresponds to our modern passage. To right and left of it are
rooms for domestic purposes. Vitruvius mentions on the one
side stables, and on the other, the porters' rooms. Through the
passage, which is also called θυρών or πυλών, one enters the
περιστύλιον. The peristylion is an open yard surrounded by
colonnades, also described as αὐλή or τόπος περικίων. "This
peristylion," Vitruvius continues, " has colonnades on three sides.
But on the southern side are two antæ (*i.e.* front and wall pillars),
which stand at a considerable distance from each other, and carry
a beam. They form the entrance to a room, the depth of which
is equal to two-thirds of the interval between the antæ. This
place is called by some προστάς, by others παραστάς ;" it is,
therefore, a room which, on its broad side, opens into the yard ;
an open hall, in fact, to which, most likely, the not uncommon
expression παστάς may also be applied.

" Further towards the interior," Vitruvius concludes, " are
large rooms, where the lady of the house sits with the maids at
their wheels. To the right and left of the prostas are bedrooms
(cubicula), one of which is called thalamus, the other amphitha-
lamus. All round the yard, under the colonnades, are rooms for
domestic purposes, such as eating-rooms, bedrooms, and small
rooms for the servants. This part of the house is called gynaikonitis." In this gynaikonitis, as we said before, we recognise the

---

* We omit the references to the Roman house contained in his description, as to
this we shall have to return hereafter.

old Greek house. The husband, whose life passed in public, possessed only the smaller outer part of it ; while in the interior

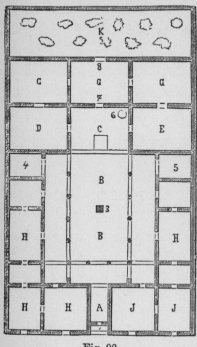

Fig. 92.

the housewife, with her maids, was in command. Fig. 92 is meant to illustrate the plan of an old Greek dwelling on this basis.

The above-mentioned chief parts are easily recognisable. A is the small passage, B the open courtyard surrounded by colonnades, C the open hall (προστάς, παραστάς, παστάς), to which are joined the bedroom of the master of the house (D) (the thalamos) ; and on the other side the amphithalamos, perhaps the bedroom of the daughters. At the back of these are good-sized rooms for the maids (G), working under the supervision of their mistress. Round the yard, and opening into the colonnades, lie other rooms for domestic purposes, such as storerooms, bedrooms (H), &c., some of which, on both sides of the street-door and looking towards the street, were frequently used as shops or workshops (I). Behind the house, and more or less shut in by the neighbouring houses, might be a garden (K), frequently mentioned by ancient writers.

The street-door leading into the passage was mostly in a line with the façade. The expressions πρόθυρον and προπύλαιον, however, seem to indicate that in some houses there must have been a small space in front of the door, which might be adorned with antæ, or, as is proved by the still-existing remains of a private house, with columns (see Fig. 92). By the propylaion stood frequently, if not generally, the image of Apollo Aggieus (2) ; perhaps at some distance from the house was placed the symbol of

---

* A street-door is illustrated in Gerhard's "Goblets of the Royal Museum of Berlin." Table XXVII.

Hermes as the protecting god of roads and traffic. It consisted merely of a column or pillar.

In the yard usually stood an altar, separate and visible from every side, and dedicated to Zeus Herkeios, as the supreme protector of the family. This circumstance is already mentioned in Homer. According to Petersen's opinion, the sanctuaries of the θεοὶ κτήσιοι (the gods giving possession) and of the θεοὶ πατρᾷοι (the gods of families or generations) were placed in the *alœ* (4 and 5), a less accessible part of the house, but connected with the colonnade. From the courtyard one entered the open hall which, as it were, formed the boundary between the public and the private life of the family, and therefore was most adapted for the gatherings of the family at religious offerings and common meals. It is therefore here that the hearth, the holy place of the house, devoted to Hestia, the all-preserving goddess, must most likely be placed. Originally it was no doubt used for cooking, but even later, when a separate kitchen had become necessary, the hearth remained the centre of the house, and on this altar all the events of domestic life were celebrated by religious acts.* "A particular occasion," says Petersen, " for worshipping Hestia was offered by all important changes in the family, such as a departure, a return from a journey, or a reception into the family, even of slaves, who always took part in the domestic worship of Hestia. Birth, giving of a name, wedding, or death, were celebrated in like manner. This altar was also holy as an asylum; to it flew the slave to escape punishment, on it the stranger, nay, even the enemy of the house, found protection ; for the worship of Hestia united all the inhabitants of the house, free-born or slaves, nay, even strangers." For this important function of the altar, the place assigned to it by us seems the most appropriate.

To the right and left of the prostas were the thalamos and amphithalamos, in the former of which were placed the sanctuaries of the connubial deities; in the back wall of the prostas was a door, which is frequently mentioned by ancient authors as particularly important for the arrangement of the Greek house. It is called μέταυλος, to distinguish it from the door leading into the

* See Petersen, "The Domestic Worship of the Greeks," in *Zeitschrift für Alterthumswissenschaft.* 1851. p. 199. Petersen places the altar in the large hall of the men, which, according to him, separates the two yards.

yard from the outside, the θύρα αὔλειος, "because it lies opposite
the αὔλειος, *beyond* or *behind* the αὐλή." * In case it was closed,
the maid-servants, who seem to have been employed in the workrooms, and slept on the floor above (πύργοι), were secluded from the
other parts of the house,—a circumstance repeatedly mentioned by
Greek authors. Where there was a garden, it was connected
with the house by a door (8), called θύρα κηπαία (garden-door).

So much about the older Greek house with one court. The
numerous descriptions of the enlarged house differ in so many points
that a new attempt at an analysis may seem desirable ; it will be

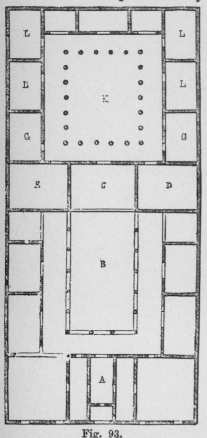

based entirely on the practical considerations which must have led
to the addition of a second yard.
In the towns, at least, this change
must at first have been applied
to buildings already in existence.
The increase of luxury made a
more commodious enlargement of
the houses of the wealthy desirable. This extension had to be
directed towards the back, the
frontage being fixed by the line
of the street ; while, on the other
hand, the frequently occurring
gardens might be conveniently
used for the introduction of a
second yard. In consequence,
the whole first part of the house
has remained unchanged (see
Fig. 93) ; the only innovation
being that from the metaulos
(Fig. 92, 7) one gets immediately
into the second yard (K), instead of into one of the large
workrooms. These workrooms

Fig. 93.

(G), together with other apart-
ments (L), were arranged in a manner which, with regard to size
and position, must have varied greatly, according to circumstances.

* See Becker "Charikles." 2nd edition. II., p. 88.

The additional space so gained was appropriated by the narrower family circle, while the first part became the scene of the more public intercourse. The metaulos remains the boundary between the two parts, from which circumstance alone its hitherto unexplained second name μέσαυλος can be derived. The metaulos (door *behind* the first yard) becomes in this way a mesaulos (door *between* two yards). The prostas, in the back wall of which this door lies, retains its importance, derived from the sacred hearth. This arrangement becomes still more likely from its analogy with the *tablinum* in the Roman house, which, as we shall show, was most likely an imitation of the prostas.*

It need not be added that the above description is intended only to convey a very general notion of the Greek dwelling-house.

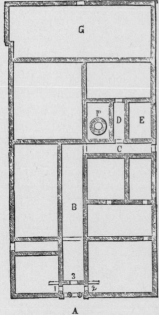

A
Fig. 94.

Fig. 95.

The rule was naturally modified by the nature of the locality, the requirements of individual families, &c., in the same way as this may be observed in the houses of Pompeii, which illustrate the construction of the Roman house in manifold varieties, or in modern dwelling-houses. The only preserved specimen, indeed, of a Greek private house shows many deviations even from the important features

---

* We call the reader's attention to Winckler's comprehensive researches ("The Dwelling-houses of the Greeks," Berlin, 1868, p. 133, *ss.*), from whom, however, we differ in several points.

of our plan. We are speaking of a building which has been discovered in the isle of Delos (Fig. 94). It shows a very beautiful vestibule (προπύλαιον), which lies on the narrow side towards the street, and consists of two Ionic columns between two graceful antæ (Fig. 95). To right and left small doors (Fig. 94, 1 and 2) lead into side-rooms, while the large door (3) leads into a narrow passage (B). The aula (C) to which this passage leads is very short and narrow, and seems to have been without columns. Unfortunately, the rooms adjoining the passage and the yard have not been described by the archæologists who investigated the building; they only tell us of the existence of a cistern (F). The room D, open on both sides, may perhaps be considered as a very small prostas, in which case the room to the right of it (E) would be the thalamos; G would then be the second yard, but here also no columns seem to have been found. The editors believe the building to have been a public bath—which, however, seems unlikely from its moderate dimensions. The cistern, which seems to have given rise to this idea, may just as well have belonged to a private house. The Greeks were just as anxious to have a water-reservoir in their houses as we are at the present day. Parts of the important building in Delos have, as Ross complains, been destroyed to gain stones and mortar for new buildings. But for this barbarous custom, whole quarters of the town might still be in existence. Under many, perhaps most, of the houses cisterns were dug, partly (according to their width) spanned by small arches, partly covered with long pieces of granite.

23. From the dwelling of living individuals we now turn to the abode of the dead, from the house to the grave. The piety of the Hellenic people made the latter of great importance; hence the astonishing variety of their forms. We will divide them into groups according to the different modes of their construction. Graves, therefore, may be heaps of earth, they may be hewn into the rock, or they may be detached buildings, according to the conditions of the locality, or the mode of burying. Within these divisions there are, again, many varieties of size, form, and construction.

In places where stone was scarce, mounds were made of earth; where stones were found in the ground, these were heaped on each other; where the soil was rocky, natural caves were used, or artificial ones dug. Such are the oldest forms of graves; only later, when civilisation was more advanced, separate monuments were more commonly erected.

a. Tombs consisting of earth-mounds, as the oldest and simplest form of graves, were common to the Caucasian race, as is shown by numerous remains from east to west. Greece also is rich in such primitive structures, which in a small chamber contain the remains of the dead, and, by their imposing forms, serve at the same time as monuments. Owing to the primitive mode of their structure their appearance resembles more the works of nature than that of human hands; they were called by the Greeks κολωνοί (hills), another expression, χώματα (heaps), being derived from their kind of construction. Of this kind are the enormous mounds of earth which are still to be seen on the shores of the Hellespont, and which, according to old Greek traditions, contain the remains of Homeric heroes, like Achilles, Patroklos, Aias, and Protesilaos. Tombs of the same kind were erected by the Athenians in the Marathonian plain to those fallen in the great battle; the largest

Fig. 96.   Fig. 97.

of these was originally 30 feet high (see Fig. 96). Smaller tumuli are numerous in the Attic plain; of a similar kind are also the large burial hills of the Bosphoranian kings which are found at Pantikapaion, on the Kimmeric Bosphorus (see Fig. 97).

In order to add to the firmness of these mounds, and to avoid the sliding down of the earth, they were frequently surrounded by a stone enclosure, as for instance was the case with the tombs of Æpytos at Pheneos, in Arkadia, and of Œnomaos at Olympia. There still exists in the island of Syme a tumulus which exactly answers to the description of Pausanias. Its diameter is 19 metres; it is quite surrounded by a stone wall (κρηπίς or θριγκός) 1·25—2·19 metres in height, which consists of polygonal stones (λίθοι ἀγροί, λογάδες) (see Figs. 98 and 99). The conical mound has been destroyed almost entirely.

Fig. 98.   Fig. 99.

Mounds of this kind were also made of stone, as for instance the tomb of Laïos, near Daulis, mentioned by Pausanias, to which kind we shall have to return.

Fig. 100.

Fig. 101.

b. Another kind of primitive tombs were caves in rocks, either natural or artificial, and decorated by art. Of these also we have to distinguish various kinds. A natural cavern may have been extended and used as a tomb; or the rocky soil may have been hollowed into a subterraneous chamber; or, lastly, a more or less separate piece of rock may have been excavated and decorated externally. The caves and galleries of quarries must have led to the idea of subterraneous graves in rocks at a very early period. Structures of this kind (the name of which, Kyklopeia, denotes their great age) are found near Nauplia. Similar caverns of irregular formation may be seen near Gortyna, in the isle of Crete; more

regularity is shown in the Nekropolis of Syrakuse, which also
seems to have been occasioned by quarries. Simple shafts of
great depth, ending in a burial chamber, are found amongst
the above-mentioned royal tombs of Pantikapaion (see Figs. 97

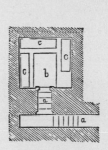

Fig. 102.   Fig. 103.

and 100), where a tunnel, erected of blocks of stone, has also been
discovered (see Fig. 101).

The burial caverns of both old and more modern dates found in
the islands are still more numerous and important than those of the
Greek peninsula. Some of them are cut into the rock in such a
manner that the ceiling requires no additional props, as is the
case, for instance, in a tomb in the island of Ægina, of which
Figs. 102 and 103 show the plan and section. A narrow staircase
(*a*) leads to the entrance, which has the form of an arch (*b*), and
through it into the burial-chamber. The latter contains three

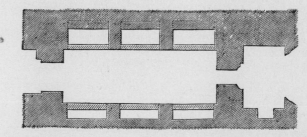

Fig. 104.

sarcophagi, which are constructed of simple slabs of stone, with
a cover of the same material. They occupy three sides of the
chamber.

A grave in the isle of Melos contains three sarcophagi on each

side, which stand in semicircular niches, as is shown by the plan
(Fig. 104) and the section (Fig. 105, scale = 10 metres).

In other tombs the ceiling has been propped by pillars and
cross-walls, by means of which the interior is at the same time
divided into several separate chambers. A burial-chamber in

Fig. 105.

Delos shows two pillars (*a*) on each of the two side-walls, between
which lie small niches (*b*) (see plan, Fig. 106). In each of these
niches are two sarcophagi, placed one on the top of the other.
The height of the grave is 2·30 metres. The ceiling consists of
stone slabs joined closely together (see Fig. 107).

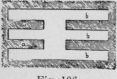

Fig. 106.

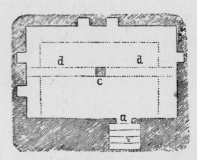

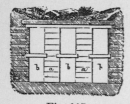

Fig. 107.   Fig. 108.

A subterraneous grave in the isle of Chalke shows a different
arrangement (Fig. 108). A narrow staircase (*b*) leads to the
entrance-door (*a*). Inside the chamber (14½ feet long) is a pillar
(*c*), from which two strong stone beams (*d d*) extend towards the
two smaller walls of the chamber. They carry the ceiling, consisting of slabs of stone, and lying only a few feet under the

surface. All round the room by the wall are the couches of the dead, resembling stone benches. Ross, on discovering them, found them empty. In the walls are square niches, for the reception of jugs and other objects, which it was the custom to leave with the dead. This custom (see § 35) is exemplified by the numerous graves in the small island of Chilidromia. These are not cut into the rock, but built of chalk-stone in a simple manner, not very much below the surface. Fig. 109 shows one of them, opened by Fiedler, in which the skeletons and the offerings to the dead were found in their original position. The grave itself consists of a square hollow sufficiently large to receive the body, and surrounded by stones, the two longer walls being built of carefully fitted chalk-stones without mortar, while the two shorter sides are formed by large slabs. The body was placed with its head towards the south. Two small drinking-vessels and two copper coins were found in the same chamber, which was covered with three large stone slabs. At the foot-end of the body was another smaller room, enclosed and covered in a similar manner, and, like a store-room, containing a number of objects, all destined for the dead. Amongst these were one large and several smaller cans, an oil-pitcher, several vases for offerings, and various drink-

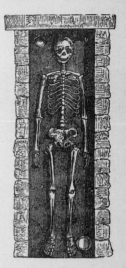

Fig. 109.

ing-cups, all made of burnt clay ; there was also a bronze mirror. An earthen lamp showed distinct traces of having been used.

The same custom was observed when the dead were buried in coffins (σοροί). Several coffins of burnt clay have been found at Athens. Fig. 110 shows a coffin covered with three slabs ; Fig. 111 is an open dead-box, filled with vessels of various kinds. Another kind of graves in rocks consisted in chambers cut into the slope of a rock, the surface near the entrance being arranged architecturally. Grave-façades of this kind are very frequent in

Phrygia and Lykia; they indicate a civilisation originally foreign
to the Greeks, but imitated
by them even during their
historic times, from which
many of these monuments
date.

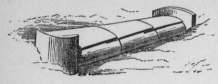

Fig. 110.

The Lykian graves display
a most curious imitation of
wood-architecture, carried into the minutest details. Usually the
façade is divided into several parts by means of beams protruding
from the surface (see Fig. 112). Our illustration shows a grave
in a steep slope of a rock at Xanthos; the imitation of wood is
carried even to the copying of nails and pegs to join the different beams; it resembles the frontage of a house solidly built of
timber, with a ceiling of unhewn trunks of trees, such as the huts

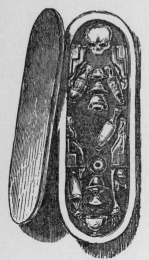

Fig. 111.

Fig. 112.

of Lykian peasants have at the present day. A perpendicular
beam in the middle divides the façade into two deepened partitions.
Sometimes the cross-beams quite protrude from the surface, in
which case a kind of porch is formed in front of the façade. This
arrangement is found, for instance, in a grave at Myra (see
Fig. 113), which, moreover, is decorated with excellent paintings
both by the side of the façade and inside the entrance-hall. A

grave at Telmessos (Fig. 114) shows a complete façade in the Ionic style. Two Ionic columns between two antæ carry a pediment adorned with acroteria, and forming in this way the portico; in the back wall is the entrance to the burial-chamber.

Graves with façades of this kind are also frequently found on the Greek continent—more frequently, indeed, it seems than in the islands; sometimes artificial constructions have been added to increase the natural firmness of the rock. In a grave in the island of Thera, discovered by Ross, the chamber is formed by

Fig. 113.

a natural cleft in the rock; but the walls have been propped by masonry, and the ceiling consists of slabs of stone. Another grave in the slope of a hill, discovered by the same scholar in the island of Kos, consists of a small forecourt, which leads to the entrance-door, decorated in the best Ionic style, remnants of which have been preserved in a chapel close by. The grave itself (see plan, Fig. 115, and section, Fig. 116) consists of a vaulted chamber, 6 metres in

Fig. 114.

length (*a*), on both sides of which are the couches of the dead (*b b*), 2·50 metres long by 66 centimetres wide. Fragments in the best Ionic style found near it most likely belonged to the separate porch of this grave-chamber, which, according to an inscription, was the heroon of Charmylos and his family.

A grave at Lindos, in the isle of Rhodes, is entirely worked into the rock. It is one of the most perfect specimens of this style, imitated most likely from the monuments of the opposite Lykian coast. Instead of the above-mentioned Lykian wood-imitations we here, however, find the forms of Greek architecture in the decoration of the façade. Fig. 117 gives an illustration of the grave, which unfortunately is in a very decayed condition. The façade resembles a Greek portico, with Doric columns, an architrave, frieze, and cornice. Of these columns, originally twelve in number, four are said to have been detached, while the others protruded from the surface of the wall by halves or a little more. Larger structures of the kind have been discovered in Cyprus. The one discovered by Ross shows the form of a court surrounded by columns (see view, Fig. 118, and the plan, Fig. 119).

Fig. 115.

Fig. 116.

Fig. 117.

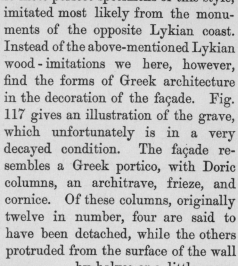

Finally, we mention the beautiful graves at Kyrene, on the north coast of Africa.

Fig. 118.

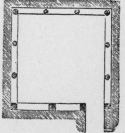

Fig. 119.

The rocky ground near the city has been worked into terraces,

in which the graves are situated. The graves themselves mostly
consist of small chambers cut into the rock, and are for the

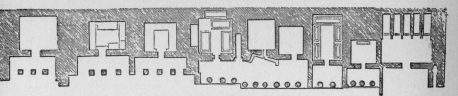

Fig. 120.

Fig. 121.

greater part adorned with porticoes, which give them a most
picturesque appearance. Fig. 120 shows the plan, Fig. 121 the
perspective view, of a terrace adorned with a long row of grave-
façades; Fig. 122 shows the dwellings of the living in the close
vicinity of the city of the dead at Kyrene.

Fig. 122.

c. In and on graves of this kind are found many objects, either
for the purpose of adorning them or for that of indicating the

identity of the body. Of vessels and other utensils intended for the use of the dead, we have spoken before. When the buried person began to be considered as a hero, the grave required an altar. (Graves were commonly called heroa, even if not in the form of temples.) Such altars, in the shape of dice, with the name of the dead inscribed on them, are numerous in Bœotia, round the Helicon. Others, round in shape, and either smooth, with only an inscription (like one at Delos, Fig. 123), or adorned with sculptures, mostly of garlands and skulls of bulls, belong principally to the Greek islands (see Figs. 44 and 45) ; on others

Fig. 123.   Fig. 124.

figures are represented. An altar found in a grave at Delos (Fig. 124) shows the representation of an offering in bas-relief, besides the inscription—

ΠΑΥΣΑΝΙΑΣ ΜΕΙΔΟΝΟΣ ΧΑΙΡΕ.

The gravestones discovered by Ross in the isle of Kasos are of very extraordinary appearance. They consist of semi-globes of blue marble, about 8—10 inches in diameter, in the smooth front side of which the name of the deceased has been chiselled in several lines of letters, belonging to the third or fourth century B.C.

The most common kind of above-ground monuments for the dead all over Greece till far into Asia, are the old Attic stelai (στήλη). They are narrow, slender slabs of stone, gently tapering towards the top ; they stand erect, fastened in the ground, or on a bema, and have the name of the deceased inscribed on them.

They are crowned with anthemia, *i.e.* ornaments of flowers and
leaves, either in relief or painted, sometimes also with pediments adorned with rosettes ; sometimes the stele shows
representations, relating to the life of the deceased, in bas-
relief. In the times of the Makedonians and Romans the
stele becomes shorter and broader, with a pediment at the
top. Fig. 125 shows a stele, found at Athens, with a
palmetto-ornament.

Peculiar to Attica are the grave columns of blue
Hymettic marble, with inscriptions on them, round which
were wound ribbons and wreaths in memory of the dead.
Figs. 126 and 127, both taken from Athenian earthen
vessels, illustrate these columns, one of them being flat at
the top, the other adorned with a capital of acanthus-
leaves. Other stelai show the form of small chapel-like
buildings (heroa), between the surrounding columns of
which the forms of the dead are represented in relief. Fig. 128 shows
a monument of this kind, found in a grave in the isle of Delos ;

Fig. 125.

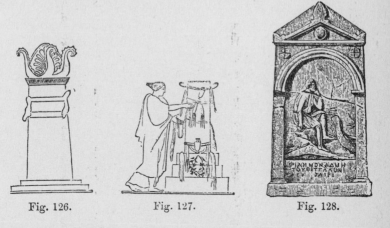

Fig. 126.   Fig. 127.   Fig. 128.

Fig. 129, a similar one dug out at Athens, the bas-relief of which
shows the taking-leave of the deceased, called "Phrasykleia," from
the surrounding friends, a favourite subject during the best period
of Greek art. Portrait-statues, in full or half figure, were, during
the Makedonian and Roman times, frequently placed on the
graves, or, if space permitted it, inside the heroa ; this was the
custom particularly in the islands. Fragments of such statues

from the graves of the Telesikratides, the ruling noble family of Anaphe, have been found in that island; Ross conjectures that the roof-like covers of sarcophagi found in the isle of Rhenæa also used to carry statues of this kind.

Frequently detached coffins, or sarcophagi, wrought of stone, are found in the grave-chambers, in which the bodies were deposited. These are numerous in Lykia, but in Greece they have been found only in a few cases at Platææ, and in the islands of Thera, Karpathos, and Anaphe.

Fig. 129.

24. In the constructions of Greek tombs above the earth, two technical divisions must be made.

a. The first consists of graves cut from the rock, but transformed into real buildings by means of outside and inside

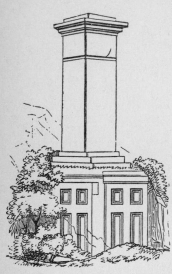

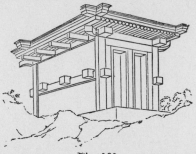

Fig. 131.

arrangements and decorations. Of this kind the most numerous and varied examples are naturally found in the rocky Lykia, dating not only from the old Lykian, but also from the Greek times. The simplest form consists of a square stout pillar

Fig. 130.

resting on steps, and crowned with a simple cornice. A specimen of this form, found at Tlos, is seen Fig. 130. A second form is that of the imitation of a complete wooden house, of which the above-mentioned graves only gave the façade (Fig. 131). Trunks of trees joined together seem to form the roof, which protrudes considerably on all sides, and is both finished and

crowned by a horizontal cornice, formed by the crossing each
other of beams. In a third kind of grave the roof, instead of
being flat, shows a pointed arch, somewhat like our pointed roofs
(*Walmdächer*) (Fig. 132); sometimes
skulls of bulls, also wrought in
stone, adorn their fronts. Fig. 133
shows a roof of this kind, cut from
the rock in the manner of a relief; it
is found at Pinara. In Greece, also,
graves of this kind were in use, as is
shown by several specimens in the isle
of Rhodes; the monuments of the coast
of Lykia, lying opposite, may have
been the models. Ross found near
the village of Liana a rock rolled
from the height, the interior of which
contained a complete grave-chamber,
with three couches for the dead; the
exterior showed two niches, one on
each side of the entrance (Fig. 134).

Fig. 132.

Grander than, and very different from, the Lykian graves, is
another monument found by Ross in the isle of Rhodes. It
consists of a large block of sandstone the lower part of which has
been hewn into a square form with vertical walls. Each of the
long sides measures 27·81 metres, and contains twenty-one semi-

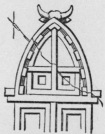

Fig. 133.   Fig. 134.

columns about 5 metres in height, which, standing on three steps,
were evidently destined to carry a cornice; this, however, has been
destroyed by the upper parts falling on it. Whether the top
consisted of a stone pyramid, or of a hill planted with shrubs and

trees, cannot now be distinguished. On the northern side, which is the best preserved (see Fig. 135), between the fifth and sixth columns of the western corner (see plan, Fig. 136; scale = 15 metres), lies a door (*a*), through which one enters the grave-chambers. The first compartment is an entrance-hall (*b*),

Fig. 135.

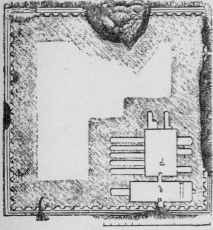

Fig. 136.

9·20 metres wide by 3 metres deep, in the small sides of which there are niches. A second door (*c*) leads into a larger chamber (*d*), (6·70 by 4·40 metres), in the walls of which are unequal niches, with five couches for the dead; these, however, were found empty when the tomb was opened. On the walls of all these chambers (which extend only over a fourth part of the whole basis, and probably were joined by others) a fine coating of stucco has been preserved, with some traces of painting on it. Tombs of this kind, cut into the rock, were not usual in Greece. Detached grave-buildings were evidently the rule, and of the numerous varieties of these we propose to give some specimens.

b. The oldest and simplest buildings of this kind are the developed forms of the above-mentioned earth-mounds. From surrounding these with stone walls one proceeded to building the

Fig. 137.

whole tomb of stone, and in changing the round form for the square a quadrangular pointed stone pyramid was arrived at. Pausanias saw a monument of this kind near Argos, on the road to Epidauros; it was explained to him as the common memorial of those slain in the fight between Proitos and Akrisios. A number of similar monuments have more recently been discovered in Argolis, the most important of which, near

Kenchreai, is a pyramid built of square stones (see Figs. 137-139).
The basis is 48 feet long by 39 feet wide. According to Ross, the
southern corner is rectangular, and here a door, covered by protruding stones in the manner of the Tirynthian galleries, leads
into a narrow passage, at the end of which one enters, by a second
door on the right-hand side, the inner chamber, measuring 10 feet
square. It remains doubt-
ful whether this building
was a tomb or a watch-
tower. Where the round
shape of the earth-mounds
was retained (see, for example, the grave in the isle
of Syme, Fig. 98), with an
additional architectural
arrangement of the sur-
rounding stones, the result
was a handsome round
building resting on a quad-

Fig. 138.

Fig. 139.

rangular base, and frequently used for tombs. Fig. 140 shows a
beautiful specimen of this style found in the nekropolis of Kyrene.

Some of the graves at Mykenæ are old and simple. Like the
megalithic tombs of Western Europe, they consist of roughly hewn
stones, and contain small, low
chambers, covered with large
slabs of stone. Fig. 141 shows
the largest amongst them.

We now come to graves
of a more monumental cha-
racter. Near Delphi one has
been discovered which has

Fig. 140.

exactly the form of a house. It lies amongst graves of various
kinds, and is surrounded by remnants of sarcophagi and other
ruins which indicate the site of the old nekropolis of Delphi.
Thiersch describes it as an "edifice of freestone, which shows the
antiquity of its style by the fact that the sides, the door, and a
window above it, grow narrower towards the top;" he adds that
its destination as a grave cannot be doubted (see Fig. 142).

Some tombs found at Carpuseli, in Asia Minor, are more

elegant in design.   They are square and stand on some steps ;
the walls consist of equal blocks of freestone, showing a base at the
bottom and a cornice at the top.   One of the largest amongst

Fig. 141.

Fig. 142.

them (see Figs. 143 and 144) contains in the interior of the
chamber, the entrance to which is not visible, a strong pillar,
which carries the ceiling, consisting of large beams and slabs of
stone ; on it stood, perhaps, the statue of the deceased.

In the Greek islands tombs are frequently found which, like the
subterraneous chambers, contain several couches for the dead.   They
consist of strong masonry, and their ceilings are vaulted, whence
the name tholaria now commonly applied to them.   The only
specimen we quote (Fig. 145) has been found in the island of
Amorgos.   It comprises three graves, separated from each other

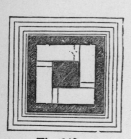

Fig. 143.

Fig. 144.

Fig. 145.

by slabs of stone.   Over each of these is a niche in the wall, containing glass vessels, lamps, &c.   The door is very low; its
threshold consists of a rounded slab of stone.   The tomb itself is
at present covered by alluvial earth, but stood originally above
ground like others of the same kind in the islands of Ikaros,
Kalymnos, Leros, and others; some of these tombs contain from
five to six burial compartments.

Graves of this kind were considered chiefly as safe receptacles of
the remnants of the dead; others were destined at the same time

to preserve the memory of the deceased by means of artistic beauty. In this manner the grave developed into the monument. The dead, according to Greek notions, were considered as heroes, their graves were frequently called heroa, and naturally took the form of holy edifices. The façades of the above-mentioned graves in rocks remind us of those of temples, and, on the same principle, detached tombs (for instance, those in Thera and other islands) were built like temples. A tomb discovered by Fellows at Sidyma in Lykia seems to resemble a temple, with separate standing columns in the façade (see Fig. 146). The same similarity to a temple is shown by a tomb at Kyrene, the façade of which, contrary to rule, contains two doors adjoining each other (see Fig. 147).

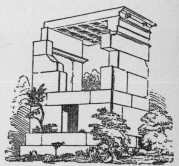

Fig. 146.

The most perfect specimen of this style has been made known by the researches of Fellows near Xanthos in Lykia. It is in a state of almost complete destruction, but from the well-preserved base and from a number of ruins and redis-covered sculptures the plan of the whole may be con-jectured

Fig. 147.

with tolerable certainty. A model, as well as the remains of it, is in the British Museum, in which to each of the single fragments its supposed original position has been assigned. Another reconstruction, differing from the above, has been attempted by Falkener, from which we have borrowed the plan (Fig. 148) and the perspective view (Fig. 149). According to Falkener's conjectures, the monument consisted of a base 10·25 metres in length, 6·90 metres in width, and of almost the same height, adorned with two surrounding stripes of battle-scenes in relief, besides an elegant cornice. On this base rose

an Ionic peripteros, the peristylos of which had four columns
on each of the smaller, and six columns on each of the
longer sides; the cella shows on each side two columns *in antis.*
A richly decorated door leads from the pronaos (*a*) (to which
corresponds the posticum (*b*) on the other side) into the roomy
cella (*c*). The frieze and the pediment were adorned with reliefs ;
on the points of the gables stood statues, as also in the interstices

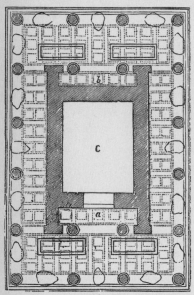

between the rich Ionic columns.
The widely spread use of such
monuments is shown by a beautiful structure found at Cirta,
on the north coast of Africa (the
Constantine of the present day),
and said to be the grave of
King Micipsa, who founded a
Greek colony in this place. A
square structure rises on a base
of steps (as in the grave of
Theron, at Agrigentum) ; there
is a door on each side, worked in
relief. On the top of this structure stands a small Doric temple,
also square in shape, and showing
gables on all sides. The roof
thus formed is carried by eight
columns, again forming a square,

Fig. 148.

which stand perfectly free, and do not enclose a cella (see Fig. 150).

To conclude, we mention one of the most splendid monumental
graves that ever existed, viz., the tomb of Maussollos, King of
Karia, at Halikarnassos.   Unfortunately only ruins remain, which,
by order of the British Government, have been freed from the
surrounding rubbish by Mr. C. T. Newton (1856-59), and carefully measured by the architect of the expedition, Mr. R. P.
Pullan. Pliny ("Hist. Nat.," XXXVI. 5, § 4, ed. Sillig) in his
description of this monument (considered by the ancients as one
of the seven wonders of the world) says, that Artemisia erected it
for her husband Maussollos (ob. Olympiad 167, 352 B.C.).   It
is an oblong, measuring from north to south 63 feet, the front
and back being a little shorter. The circumference of the monu-

ment (*i.e.* of the peribolos) amounts to 411 feet; it rises to a height of 25 cubits (37½ feet), and is surrounded by thirty-six columns. The colonnade round the tomb was called the pteron. The sculptures on the east side were by Skopas, those on the north side by Bryaxis, those on the south side by Timotheos, and those on the west side by Leochares. Above the pteron rises a pyramid corresponding in size to the bottom part, which on twenty-four steps narrows itself into a pointed column. On the top is

Fig. 149.

a quadriga of marble, the work of Pythis, including which the height of the whole monument is 140 feet. From marble steps, pieces of columns, capitals, and some fragments of sculptures, together with Pliny's remarks, the mentioned English scholars have cleverly conjectured the original form of the building. The chief view of the western front is shown in Fig. 151 according to their designs. We prefer Pullan's attempt at a reconstruction to that of Falkener, inserted in our former editions. From fragments of

Fig. 150.

the horses and chariot of the quadriga, its own dimensions, as well as the circumference of the pyramid on which it stood, can be calculated, the height of the latter being definable by the discovered steps, and that of the pteron by the columns, &c. In many places the traces of painting in red and blue have been discovered. Of the above-mentioned reliefs fourteen tablets were found let into the walls of the Turkish citadel of Budrun,

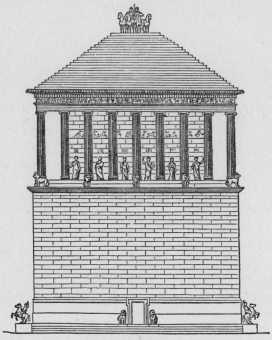

Fig. 151.

built from the ruins of Halikarnassos. In 1846 they were purchased by the English Government for the British Museum. By the Romans the word mausoleum was used as a general term for tombs, reminding by their splendour or design of our monument.

c. In some of the artistic grave-monuments the keeping of the body was quite dispensed with. We are speaking of the so-called kenotaphia, erected to deceased persons whose remains were not in the possession of their friends, or their paternal city, which wished to honour their memory. This leads us to monuments erected in honour of living persons, for instance, of victors in public games, or wrestling competitions. The most beautiful amongst them, and, at the same time, one of the loveliest remnants of Greek antiquity, is the one erected at Athens to commemorate the victory gained by the choragos Lysikrates (334 B.C.). It is called either the choragic monument of Lysikrates, or the lantern of Diogenes (Fig. 152). It is altogether 34 feet high. The base is slender and square in shape; on it rises an elegant little round temple; six Corinthian semi-columns protrude from the circular wall (see Fig. 11) carrying beams, the frieze of which represents an episode from the history of Dionysos, the god of festive games. Above the beams is the roof, wrought in the shape of a flat cupola from a large block of marble; from the middle of it a stone-flower of acanthus-leaves seems to grow. It served to support a tripod, for the legs of which artistically decorated resting-points have been preserved on the cupola.

Fig. 152.

25. Amongst public buildings we mentioned first the gymnasia, which, originating in the requirements of single persons, soon became centre-points of Greek life. Corporeal exercise was of great importance amongst the Greeks, and the games and competitions in the various kinds of bodily skill (to which we shall return) formed a chief feature of their religious feasts. This circumstance reacted on both sculpture and architecture, in supplying the former with models of ideal beauty, and in setting the task to the latter of providing suitable places for these games to be celebrated. For purposes of this kind (as far as public exhibition was not concerned) the palæstrai and gymnasia served. In earlier times these two must be distinguished. In the palæstra (παλαίστρα from πάλη, wrestling) young men practised wrestling

and boxing.   As these arts were gradually developed, larger establishments with separate compartments became necessary. Originally such places were, like the schools of the grammarians, kept by private persons ; sometimes they consisted only of open spaces, if possible near a brook and surrounded by trees.   Soon, however, regular buildings—gymnasia—became necessary. At first they consisted of an uncovered court surrounded by colonnades, adjoining which lay covered spaces, the former being used for running and jumping, the latter for wrestling.   In the same degree as these exercises became more developed, and as grown-up men began to take an interest in these youthful sports, and spent a great part of their day at the gymnasia, these grew in size and splendour. They soon became a necessary of life, and no town could be without them, larger cities often containing several.   Minute descriptions of these establishments by Greek authors we do not possess, but the important parts are known to us from occasional remarks, particularly in the Platonic dialogues.   There we find mentioned the ἐφηβεῖον, where the youths used to practise ; further, the bath (βαλανεῖον), to which belonged a dry sweating bath (πυριατήριον), for the use of both wrestlers and visitors. The ἀποδυτήριον was the room for undressing.   In another room, the ἐλαιοθήσιον, the oil was kept for rubbing the wrestlers, and there possibly this rubbing itself took place ; in the κονιστήριον the wrestlers were sprinkled with sand, so as to give them a firm hold on each other.   The σφαιριστήριον was destined for games at balls, while other passages, open or covered (collectively called δρόμος), were used for practice in running or simply for walking. A particular kind of covered passage were the ξυστοί, which had raised platforms on both sides for the walkers, the lower space between being used by the wrestlers—an arrangement similar to that of the stadia, whence the name of *porticus stadiatæ* applied to them by the Romans.

About the connection of these different parts we receive information by Vitruvius, who, in his fifth book about architecture (chapter xi.), gives a full description of a Greek gymnasion.   He begins his architectural rules (derived from the gymnasia of late Greek times) with the court, which, as in the dwelling-house, is called περιστύλιον, and may be either a perfect square or an oblong ; its whole circumference ought to be 2 stadia = 1,200 feet. It is surrounded by colonnades on all four sides, that towards the south being double, in order to shelter the rooms lying on that side against the weather. Adjoining the single colonnades lay spacious halls (*exedræ*), with seats for philosophers, rhetoricians, and others; behind the double colonnade lay various rooms, the centre one (*ephebeum*) being a large hall with seats, for the young men to practise in. Like the prostas of the older dwelling-house it seems to have been the centre of the whole building. To the right of it were the *coryceum* (for games at balls, κώρυκος), the *conisterium* (see p. 108), and next to it, where the colonnade made an angle, the *frigida lavatio* (cold bath), called by the Greeks λουτρόν. On the other side, in the same order, lay the *elæothesium*, the *frigidarium*, or rather, which is more likely, the *tepidarium* (tepid bath), and the entrance to the *propnigeum* (heating-room), with a sweating-bath near it, to which, on the other side, were joined a *laconicum* and the *calda lavatio*.

In most cases this was the whole of the gymnasion. At a later, more splendour-loving period, these establishments were considerably enlarged, and in some cases a stadion was added to the gymnasion. Vitruvius mentions this extension in his additions to the above description. He says, that beyond this peristylos three porticoes may be added (with remarkable analogy to the addition of a second court to the older dwelling-house): one on the side forming the peristylos (his name for the whole of the buildings just described), and two others to right and left of it. The first-mentioned one, towards the north, ought to be very broad, with a double colonnade; the others, simple, with raised platforms (*margines*), at least 10 feet wide, going round at the side nearest to the wall and columns; the deeper-lying centre, with steps leading to it, being destined for the wrestlers to practise in during the winter, so as not to disturb those walking on the platforms. These, he says, were the ξυστοί of the Greeks. Between these two ξυστοί are to be plantations, gardens, and public walks, called by the Greeks περίδρομίδες, by the Romans *xysti;* on the third side of these grounds lies the stadion, a large space for the accommodation of both spectators and wrestlers.

These precepts, of course, were not carried out in every Greek gymnasion; they only may serve to give a general notion of such establishments. Instead of adding a new one to the many conjectural designs attempted by archæologists, we will give a description of a really existing Greek gymnasion, which, although very simple in design, tallies in the most essential points with the description of Vitruvius. Leake has discovered its remains at Hierapolis in Asia Minor (see plan, Fig. 153, scale = 90 metres). A A are covered passages, B the open colonnade, behind which the chief building is situated. In the latter the ephebeum (D) forms the centre, joined on one side by the coryceum (E), the

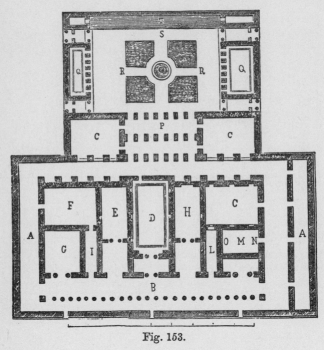

Fig. 153.

consisterium (F) and the cold bath (G), to the latter of which belonged perhaps the room I. In the two rooms opening towards the portico we must recognise the apodyteria, which Vitruvius does not mention at all. Room H would, according to Vitruvius, be the elæothesium, L the tepidarium, and N the entrance to the heating-room and to the warm baths (M O), of which Vitruvius mentions the various divisions. Turning to the back part of the establishment, we notice several rooms (C C), either *exedræ* or rooms for the keepers, between which lies the double portico

(P), turned towards the north, and forming the entrance from the first into the second division. Q Q are the covered passages with single porticoes, the plantation (R R) lies between them, the third side of the quadrangle being occupied by the course (S), with steps (T) for the spectators.

Quite different is the arrangement of the Gymnasion of Ephesos, which was built probably by the Emperor Hadrianus, and is amongst the best preserved ones in existence (see plan, Fig. 154, scale = 100 feet, English measure). The frequent use of the vault proves its Roman origin, while in the arrangement of the chief parts the essential features of Greek construction

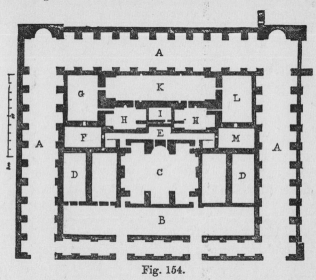

Fig. 154.

remain the same. We find no peristylos, the chief building being, instead of it, surrounded by a portico (*crypto-porticus*, A) joined by numerous exedræ, which, however, are not, as Vitruvius prescribes, *spatiosæ*, but resemble small niches of both round and quadrangular shapes. From the portico one enters an open space, thought to be the palæstra (B), and evidently intended to supply the peristylos. After it follows the ephebeum (C), which here also is the real centre of the building. The rooms D D seem to have had no communication with the ephebeum; they open into the palæstra B, and may be considered as elæothesium and conisterium, unless we take them for the apodyteria. Behind the ephebeum lies a passage (E) leading to the baths, F and G being most likely the situations of the cold, L and M those of the warmer baths. H H are explained by the editors of the "Ionian Antiquities" as the hot or sudatory bath. Near I a staircase leads into a vaulted chamber, still blackened by smoke, which the editors take to be a laconicum. Perhaps it may have been a propnigeum, the room above being in that case the laconicum proper. K, which corresponds to the palæstra B, was most likely the sphæristerium or coryceum.

26. The centre of political and commercial intercourse was the agora. Like the gymnasion, and even earlier than this, it grew into architectural splendour with the increasing culture of the Greeks. In maritime cities it generally lay near the sea; in inland places at the foot of the hill which carried the old feudal castle. Being the oldest part of the city, it naturally became the focus not only of commercial, but also of religious and political life. Here even in Homer's time the citizens assembled in consultation, for which purpose it was supplied with seats; here were the oldest sanctuaries; here were celebrated the first festive games; here centred the roads on which the intercommunication, both religious and commercial, with neighbouring cities and states was carried on; from here started the processions which continually passed between holy places of kindred origin, though locally separated. Although originally all public transactions were carried on in these market-places, special local arrangements for contracting public business soon became necessary in large cities. At Athens, for instance, the gently rising ground of the Philopappos hill, called Pnyx, touching the Agora, was used for political consultations, while most likely, about the time of the Pisistratides, the market of Kerameikos, the oldest seat of Attic industry (lying between the foot of the Akropolis, the Areopagos, and the hill of Theseus), became the agora proper, *i.e.* the centre of Athenian commerce. The described circumstances naturally led to an ornamentation of the market-place. Nevertheless, in old towns the agora was not an artistic whole with a distinct architectural design. Its confines were originally irregular, and the site of temples, and the direction of the streets leading into it, made an alteration of its boundary-line difficult. This was different in cities founded at a later period; the regular

construction of the agora seems indeed to have been initiated by the colonies of Asia Minor. Pausanias says of the market-place of Elis, that it was not built according to the Ionian custom, but in a more ancient style.

Concerning these Ionic market-buildings, we again meet with the form of a quadrangular court surrounded by colonnades. This form, eminently suited to the climate, was frequently used by the Greeks, both in private and public buildings. The description by Vitruvius (" Arch.," V. 1) of an agora, evidently refers to the splendid structures of post-Alexandrine times. According to him it was quadrangular in size, and surrounded by wide double colonnades. The numerous columns carried archi-traves of common stone or of marble, and on the roofs of the porticoes were galleries for walking pur-poses. This, of course, does not apply to all market-places, even of later date ; but, upon the whole, the remaining specimens agree with the description of Vitruvius. Figs. 155 and 156 illustrate the beautiful market-place of Delos. It lies on a terrace near the small harbour of the town, and consists of a quad-

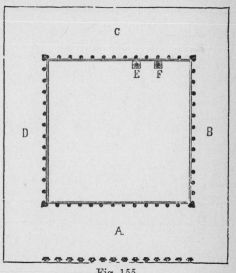

Fig. 155.

rangular court surrounded by a Doric colonnade. The length of the whole is 170 feet (English measure). The western colonnade (A) is the largest, being 40 feet wide ; it has a number of doors through which the entrance from the terrace and the sea into the agora was effected. E and F mark the sites where, most likely, stood altars ; in the centre of the open area was a fountain.

Richer and larger was the agora of Aphrodisias in Karia. It occupied an area of 525 by 213 feet, and the inside of it was adorned with an elegant Ionic colonnade containing marble

benches.   Outside of the enclosing wall was also a colonnade.
Altogether 460 columns stood in this place.

To complete the picture of a Greek agora we mention a
monument which once adorned the market-place of Athens.   It is

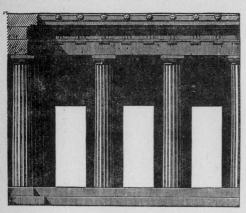

the so-called "Tower of
the Winds," erected
about 50 B.C. by An-
dronikus of Kyrrhos, and
supplying two important
requirements of com-
mercial gatherings.   The
interior contained a
water-clock, and on the
floor (see plan, Fig. 157)
the grooves are still re-
cognisable, the gradual
filling of which with
water from a reservoir
marked the passing time.
On the top of the roof
is a capital, and on it
stands a movable bronze
figure of a Triton (no
more in existence), which,
moved round by the
wind, pointed with its
staff to the different
directions of the winds,
the figures of which, in
bas-relief, adorned the
eight sides of the build-
ing.   Underneath this
frieze the lines of a sun-
dial are chiselled into
the wall.   Two small

Fig. 156.

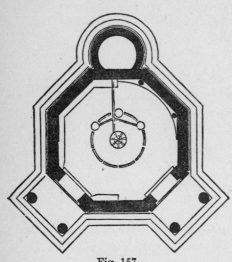

Fig. 157.

porticoes contain each two fluted columns without bases, the
capitals of which remind us of the Corinthian style.   A semicircular building is affixed to the chief edifice, the whole impression of which is extremely graceful (Fig. 158).

27. We have repeatedly mentioned the stoa or colonnade in connection with other buildings; we now have to consider it as a separate artistic erection. Something of the kind we have already seen in the xysti, where wide colonnades were terminated on one side by a wall, on the other by a row of columns. In the same manner the stoa, as an independent building, occurs both as an ornament of streets and squares, and as a convenient locality for

Fig. 158.

walks and public meetings. Its simplest form is that of a colonnade bounded by a wall. This back wall offers a splendid surface for decorations, and is frequently adorned with pictures. A stoa in the market-place of Athens contained illustrations of the battle of Œnoë, of the fight of the Athenians against the

Amazons, of the destruction of Troy, and of the battle of Marathon; hence the name στοὰ ποικίλη.

The progress from this simple form to a further extension is on a principle somewhat analogous to what we have observed in the temple; that is, a row of columns was added on the other side of the wall. The result was a double colonnade, στοὰ διπλῆ, as a specimen of which, Pausanias mentions the Korkyraic stoa near the market-place of Elis. As important we notice Pausanias's remark that this stoa " contained in the middle *not* columns,

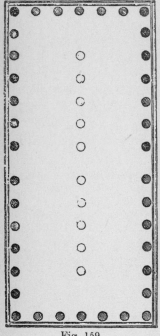

but a wall; " which shows that most of the double colonnades contained columns in the centre as props of the roof. Indeed, such remains as are preserved indicate this arrangement more or less distinctly. This is the case particularly with the so-called basilika of Pæstum. This building, lying to the south of the small temple, looks itself at first sight like a temple, from which, however, it differs considerably on closer investigation. First of all, it has on its smaller sides an uneven number of columns (*viz.* 9), while in the temple the situation of the entrance in the middle necessitated an even number of columns. Inside the colonnade we here find, instead of the walls of the cella, rows of columns, and in the middle between these another row

Fig. 159.

of slightly larger columns, which divide the building into two equal parts, and, like the wall in the Korkyraic monument at Elis, carry the roof.

The design of the colonnade at Thorikos in Attica seems to have been of a similar character (see Fig. 159). It has seven columns in each of the two smaller façades (a little over 48 English feet wide) and fourteen on each of the long sides; a row of columns in the middle (no more in existence) seems to have carried the roof.

In stoas destined for public consultations a further division of the centre space became desirable, and, indeed, we are told that in some of them the interior was divided by rows of columns into three naves. Touching the agora of Elis, towards the south lay a stoa in which the Hellanodikai assembled for common consultations. If was of the Doric order, and divided into three parts by two rows of columns. If we assume that it was surrounded by a wall, instead of a simple row of columns, Fig. 160 will show us the design (scale = 50 feet). A is the centre nave, B B the two side naves, C a semicircular termination to the centre nave analogous to the *exedræ* in the gymnasia ; D is the portico by means of which the building opens towards the agora. In this way we gain the form of a building somewhat similar both to the cella of a temple and to the Roman basilica. Perhaps the στοὰ βασίλειος in the agora of Athens, where the Archon Basileus sat in judgment, was arranged in a similar manner.

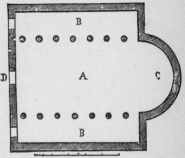

Fig. 160.

28. The arts practised in the gymnasia were publicly displayed at the festivals. The buildings in which these displays took place were modified according to their varieties. The races both on horseback and in chariots took place in the hippodrome (ἱππόδρομος), for the gymnastic games of the pentathlon served the stadion (στάδιον), while for the acme of the festivals, the musical and dramatic performances, theatres were erected.

Hippodromes were originally of very simple design. The heroes before Troy raced in a plain near the sea, the boundaries of which were marked in the most primitive manner ; a dry tree one fathom (*Klafter*) in height, with two white shining stones leaning against it, served as the goal (σῆμα). The spectators took their seats where they could find them on the hills, near which a course was generally chosen with this view.

This regard to the locality, so characteristic of Greek architecture, was even observed when the recurrence of festive games had made more complicated arrangements necessary. This was particularly the case with the hippodrome of Olympia, of which we possess minute descriptions, and which therefore may serve as an

example of Greek race-courses in general. Pausanias says in his
description of this building (if so it may be called), that one side

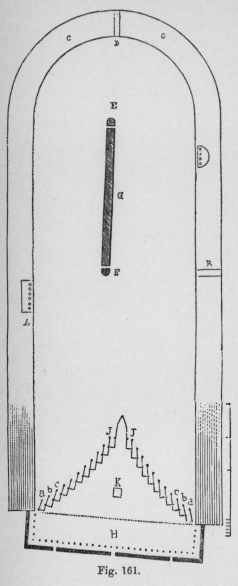

Fig. 161.

of it was formed by a low
range of hills, where the
seats of the spectators were
situated. Perhaps this one
side was sufficient for that
purpose during the first time
after the introduction of
races (Olympiad 25). But
when the multitudes at the
Olympian festivals began to
increase more and more, a
wall of earth ($\chi\hat{\omega}\mu\alpha$) was
erected opposite the hill-
side with more seats. These
two platforms bounded the
course proper on its two
long sides, the wall being
a little longer than the
hill, owing perhaps to
the oblique direction of
the line of starting. It lay
to the left of the hill, and,
being extended as far as
the wall, finished the course
on this side; the architectural boundary of the whole
was formed on the same
side by a portico built by
Agnaptos. On the opposite
side the wall joined the hill
in a semicircle, with an
outlet in the centre, which
on this side finished the
course. Here also was
placed the goal round which
the charioteer had to turn, the most difficult operation of
the whole race. "Here was," says Pausanias, after mentioning

the outlet, " the horror of horses, the taraxippos (ταράξιππος)
It has the form of a round altar, and when the horses pass
it, they are struck, without a visible cause, with great fear,
which produces restiveness and confusion ; the reason why
often the chariots break, and the charioteers are wounded."
A second goal was at the other end of the course ; on it stood
the statue of Hippodameia, and it marked the spot which the
chariots, after rounding the taraxippos, had to reach in order
to gain the victory. The plan of the course is shown by Fig. 161
(scale = 300 feet), according to Hirt's investigations. A is the
slope of the hill, R the rows of seats on the wall, C C the semicircle
joining the hill, D the above-mentioned passage. Opposite this
stands the taraxippos E, F being the second goal with the statue
of Hippodameia. Whether between these two goals the ground
was raised, in analogy to the *spina* of the Roman circus, or whether
the line of separation between the up and down courses was
marked by columns, Pausanias does not say. Some arrangement
of this kind must certainly have been desirable, and has therefore
been conjectured by several archæologists (G). The side of the
Hippodrome lying opposite the curve is closed by the portico of
Agnaptos (H). In front of it was a contrivance which, although
Pausanias describes it with evident gusto, can hardly be recognised
with certainty. It is the ἄφεσις, the start (J J) or barrier, from
which, on a given sign (a bronze eagle thrown into the air by
some mechanical appliance), the horses dragging the chariots set
out on their run. The ἄφεσις protruded into the space of the
course like the prow of a vessel, each of its two sides being about
400 feet long. Inside it were the places for horses and chariots
(οἰκήματα). They were placed with a view to showing perfect
impartiality to all competitors, and were assigned to them by
lot. Each compartment was closed by a rope ; on a sign being
given the rope was first withdrawn from the compartment
nearest the portico (a a) ; when the horses thus released had
reached the compartment (b b), the rope was withdrawn there
and two other chariots (or racing horses) entered the course, and
so forth up to the furthest point of the ἄφεσις.* Between the lists

* On this ἱππάφεσις the inventor of it, Kleœtas, the Athenian sculptor, prided
himself much. The whole arrangement, however, has been doubted as too complicated for the practically minded Greeks. Still the words of Pausanias distinctly

and the portico of Agnaptos lay an open court (K), in which the preparations for the race were made, and where stood the statues of Poseidon Hippios and Here Hippia. Altars and statues were, moreover, placed in various points of the building. Two of the former were respectively dedicated to Ares Hippios and Athene Hippia, as the protecting deities of warlike and chivalrous exercises; others were devoted to the ἀγαθὴ τύχη, to Pan, Aphrodite, and the Nymphs, not to mention several other divinities. Demeter Chamyne had a temple on the top of the hill, most likely above the spectators' seats.

29. Analogous to the design of the hippodrome was that of the stadion (στάδιον). This being originally designed for the running of foot-races, its length-wise shape was also determined.

Fig. 162.

The runners here, however, being men, both the length and width of the course were of smaller dimensions. The usual length of the stadion was 600 feet, a measure which, first decided upon by Herakles for the Stadion of Olympia, afterwards became the unit of the Greek road-measure. Some of the stadia are, however, much longer; the one at Laodikeia being, for instance, 1,000 feet long by only 90 wide (see Fig. 162). Here a natural declivity of the soil had been made available. The games took place in the valley, the spectators being seated on the slope of the hill, which for that purpose had been formed into terraces. Such favourable situations, however, being scarce, generally the sides of the stadion

indicate the gradual releasing of the horses, and also the *two* sides of the startin line.

had to be artificially raised, which was done by surrounding it with a wall of earth.* This arrangement seems to have been the common one amongst the Greeks, and Pausanias mentions several stadia (for instance, at Corinth, Thebes, Athens, Olympia, and Epidauros) consisting of a χῶμα; moreover, he mentions expressly that this was the usual way of their construction. In later times artistic decorations were added, and the seats built of solid stone. The Stadion of Messene is a beautiful example of natural fitness and additional artistic arrangement. Lying in the lower parts of the town its form was determined by the nature of the soil (see Fig. 163, scale = 100 metres). The area, the scene of the competitions (*a a*), lies in a natural hollow through which flows a brook. The hills on both sides were used for seats (*b b*) without any attempts being made at making the two long sides of the stadion parallel. Colonnades were erected on the top of the rising ground, and the semicircular termination of the course was fitted

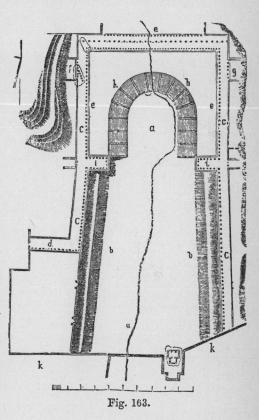

Fig. 163.

with stone seats all round. The colonnade (C) extended on one side to the end of the course, which is there finished by the

---

* Sometimes this was done only on *one* side of the stadion, as was, for instance, the case in that lying, according to Pausanias, behind the theatre of Ægina. Ross says of the Stadion of Delos, that its western side is bounded by a hill, the eastern one being left entirely without seats, with the exception of a kind of *tribune* about forty-five paces in length lying right in the centre, and having contained, as it seems three or four rows of seats.

town wall (*k*) ; on the other it ends in an obtuse angle (*d*), owing
to the slight decline of the ground at that point.   The colonnades
also extend toward the end of the course, where they enclose a
square court, and are joined together by a double portico (*ee*).
This double portico seems to have been the chief entrance, the
wall enclosing this whole part being besides interrupted by two
minor entrances (*f* and *g*).   In the centre of this raised peristyle
lies the semicircular termination of the stadion (*h h*), called by the
Greeks σφενδόνη, or occasionally θέατρον, owing to its similitude to
the place for the spectators of a theatre.   It was reserved for
wrestling-matches, the pankration, and the like.   Here, at Olympia,
the umpires were seated ; at Messene also this space was evidently
reserved for a better class of people : hence the sixteen **rows** of
benches surrounding the area all made of stone.   Two protrusions
of the surrounding colonnade (*i i*) give this space a beautiful
architectural conclusion (see the section of the stadion, Fig. 164,

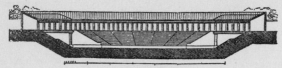

Fig. 164.

scale = 70 metres).   Right opposite, in a curve of the town wall,
lies a building evidently used for religious purposes.   The stadion
of Ephesos was entirely a product of art ; it seems to date from the
later time of the city's splendour under the successors of Alexander
the Great, or even under the Roman emperors.

The barrier from which the runners started was on the same
side as in the hippodrome, the goal, which was not wanting in
the stadion, being placed in or near the curve of the sphendone.
Both starting-point and goal were marked by columns ; a third
column, according to one account, stood between them in the centre
of the stadion.   These three formed the line (perhaps otherwise
marked) dividing the stadion into two halves, an arrangement
necessary for the " double run " and the run against time.   For in
these the runner had to turn round at the goal (νύσσα, τέρμα, &c.)
and run back.   This seems indicated by the inscription written on
the last column, according to the account of the Scholiast (Sophokles, El. 691), of κάμψον (turn !), the words on the two other

columns being ἀρίστευε (be brave !) and σπεῦδε (make haste !) The
stadia with semicircles at both ends
required a different arrangement.
These seem to belong to a later
epoch, and may in many cases have
been imitated from Roman amphitheatres. A beautiful specimen of
this later style is the Stadion of
Aphrodisias in Karia, which is about
895 English feet in length (see
Fig. 165). Here also a natural
declivity of the soil has been turned
to account, and, in order to have
room for rows of seats, the hollow
has been artificially increased. The
whole space is surrounded by a wall
with ornamental arcades (see cross-
section, Fig. 166), through which
fifteen public entrances led into the
interior ; several subterraneous passages opened into the area without
touching the seats of the spectators
(see longitudinal section, Fig. 167).
Such passages seem to have been
common. Pausanias (VI. 20, 8)
mentions one in the stadion of
Olympia through which the competitors and the Hellanodikai used
to enter ; the Olympian stadion at
Athens still shows on its left long-
side the traces of a subterraneous
entrance, cut through the rock.

30. The theatres formed the
climax of festive architecture in
Greece, in accordance with the important position of the drama in
Greek poetry. Their beginnings
were, however, simple, the more

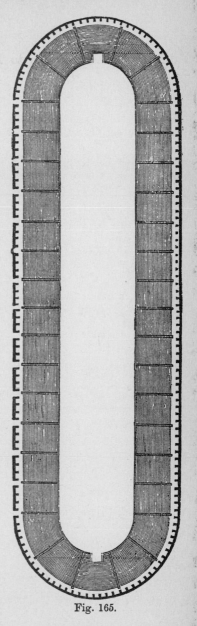

Fig. 165.

so as they were in use before the drama had attained its artistic

development. Originally they were destined for the performance
of the choric dances and songs appertaining to the worship of
Dionysos, but soon they obtained public importance, and became
both a means of artistic culture for youths and maidens and a
source of public enjoyment. Theatres were even used for quite
different purposes. Pageants of all kinds could take place in
them, and at the same time they offered a convenient point for the
communications made to the people on the part of the government.
Regular public meetings were held in theatres, as was, for
instance, commonly the case at Athens in the great theatre of
Dionysos, even after the dramatic performances had reached a high
perfection.

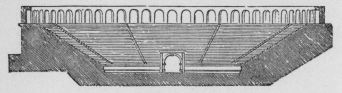

Fig. 166.

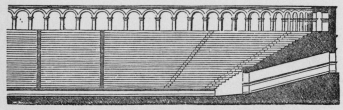

Fig. 167.

The form and construction of the buildings were here again
adapted to local circumstances, natural risings of the ground being
generally chosen for the purpose. Differently from the hippodrome
or stadion, the action here had to be fixed to a certain point,
round which the spectators' seats had to be arranged, so as to
enable them to direct their eyes to this centre of action. Hence
the form of a greater or smaller segment of the circle was chosen
as most convenient.

The oldest theatres consisted of two chief divisions; the stage
for the dancers (χορός, ὀρχήστρα), and the place for the spectators.
The former was levelled in the simplest manner; in the centre

stood the altar of the god to be celebrated, most frequently Dionysos, whose worship was connected with dancing. Round the orchestra rose on the one side the seats of the spectators, in the form of a semicircle or of a large segment, mostly on the slope of a hill. Originally the people sat on the hill itself, afterwards seats (first of wood, later of stone) were put up, where the soil was soft; where it was rocky, concentric rows of seats were cut into it. This custom was not relinquished by the Greeks even after the demands of artistic beauty and perfection were pitched very high, which explains the fact that in Greece proper only one theatre (at Mantinea) has been discovered where the natural height has been supplied by an artificial one, which simply consists of an earth wall propped by surrounding walls of polygonal stones, and covered with rows of seats.

Only in very few cases, however, was the locality naturally quite adapted to the purpose. Generally alterations and enlargements were required, which ultimately, in the splendour-loving cities of Asia Minor, at a post-Alexandrine period, led to the theatre being wholly built of stone.

Other alterations of the original theatres date from a much earlier period. From the original Bacchic chorus the drama had developed into tragedy and comedy; and although these are said to have been performed at first by Thespis on a movable scaffold, they soon were transferred into the standing theatres, the more easily as the drama itself was considered as part of the Dionysos-worship. This circumstance made the erection of a stage necessary. Even in the older theatres a wall had been erected at the back of the orchestra, partly for architectural, partly for acoustic reasons, and this wall now was gradually extended into a separate stage-building. The first theatre erected of stone with a regular stage was that of Athens, which became the model of all others, both in Greece and the colonies. It was dedicated to Dionysos. After the wooden scaffolds, originally used, had broken down during a theatrical performance in which Æschylos and Pratinas appeared as competitors, this theatre was built on the southern slope of the Akropolis (see Fig. 51, J). The hill itself was partly turned to account architecturally. The theatre was begun in Olympiad 70, and finished between 340-30 B.C., under Lykurgos. It had almost entirely disappeared under the rubbish of centuries

when it was restored to light in its whole extent by the celebrated
German architect Strack in 1862 (see Fig. 181).

In the theatre of Athens a common type had been gained,
which, with many local modifications, was reproduced ever after.

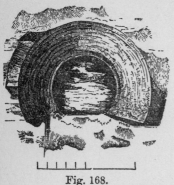

Fig. 168.

The theatre was divided into three
parts—the orchestra, forming almost
a complete circle, the place for the
spectators, and the stage-building.
The place for the spectators (τὸ
κοῖλον, the hollow pit) consisted of
several steps rising round the orchestra in a semicircle or larger segment, and serving the audience as
seats (ἐδώλιον). Towards the stage
the seats were closed by a wall,
which served both
as a prop and a
boundary, and, fol-
lowing the rising
line of the seats,
did not obstruct the
view on to the
stage. The position
of these walls,
standing either in
an obtuse angle to-
wards each other,

Fig. 169.

or in a straight line, was the cause of two different arrangements,
according to which we may divide all the Greek theatres known
to us into two classes. As
an example of the first class,
we may mention the theatre
of Delos (see Fig. 168,
scale = 50 metres). It consists of a natural rising of
the ground, being artificially
brought into a more regular

Fig. 170.

shape, and completed by a solid wall 19 feet thick by 30 long.

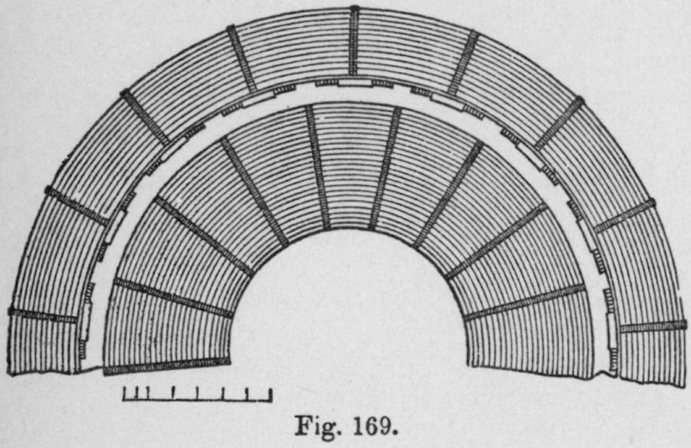

Another example is the theatre of Stratonikeia (see Fig. 169, scale = 60 feet, English measure), built most likely at the time of the Seleukides, and enlarged under the Roman emperors.

Of theatres with a rectangular termination of their seats we mention that of Megalopolis in Arcadia, originally one of the largest and most beautiful in Greece (see Fig. 170). It consists of a hill considerably en-
larged, in consequence of which Pausanias calls it *the* largest theatre. The accounts of its diameter differ from 480 to 600 feet. In its pre-

Fig. 171.

sent ruined condition neither the stage nor the seats are distinctly recognisable.

The same form is shown by the theatre of Segesta, in Sicily, the koilon of which dates from early Greek times; other rows of seats on artificial bases, in addition to the original twenty, have

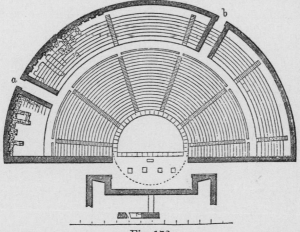

Fig. 172.

later been added. A passage divides the earlier and later parts of the seats. The remnants of the stage belong to later Roman times. Fig. 171 shows the perspective view, Fig. 172 the plan (scale = 140 Sicilian palms).

The interruption of the rows of seats by wider intervals is

frequently found in theatres, particularly in the larger ones. In order to facilitate the ascent to the rows and single seats, these passages (διαζώματα) used to divide the seats into several concentric stripes. *One* diazoma only occurs both in the theatres of Segesta and Stratonikeia (Fig. 169). Others have two, as, for instance, the small theatre of Knidos, which has also been considered as an odeum (see Fig. 173; width of the orchestra = about 65 English feet). Its koilon is enclosed by rectangular walls, most likely owing to the direction of the streets between which the theatre lies.

The theatre at Dramyssos in Epeiros has three diazomata,

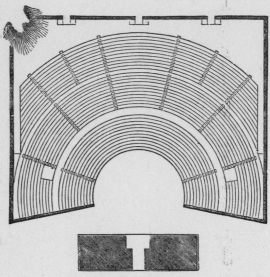

Fig. 173.

two dividing the seats, and one enclosing the whole koilon; it may at the same time serve as an example of the above-mentioned rectangularly closed theatre. The koilon (see Fig. 174; scale = 100 English feet) is well preserved; in the place of the upper third diazoma Donaldson conjectures a colonnade, of which, however, no remnants are now in existence. The diameter of the orchestra is very small compared with that of the spectators' place; *d* and *e* mark steps leading up to the second diazoma. The style of the building is very simple, and it therefore is considered by many as very early and of Greek origin; according to others it belongs to Roman times. Of the stage building no recognisable parts remain.

On the outside the koilon was generally enclosed by a wall, as is shown by the theatre of Dramyssos and others; Vitruvius in his description of the Greek theatre speaks of a colonnade, but of this no authentic traces remain in ruins of the Greek period.

The entrances to the seats were generally between the propping walls and the stage-building; the spectators ascended from the orchestra. In larger theatres other entrances became desirable. In the theatre of Dramyssos stairs on the outside of the propping wall led to the first diazoma. In other theatres, where the locality permitted, entrances to the upper parts of the koilon had been arranged, as, for instance, in the theatre of Segesta, and also in that of Sikyon (see Fig. 175; scale = 60 metres). In the latter, two passages (*a* and *b*) led through the mountain itself into

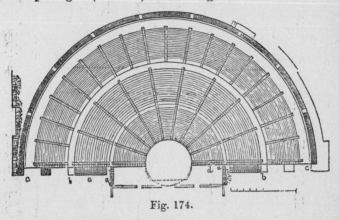

Fig. 174.

the centre of the koilon (see a view of passage *a*, Fig. 176). Moreover, the single rows of seats intercommunicated in all theatres by means of narrow stairs, which, verging like radii towards the centre of the orchestra, divided the koilon into several wedge-like partitions (κερκίδες). In Greek theatres these are generally found in even numbers, varying, according to size and other local conditions, from two to ten. Where several diazomata are found, the mutual position of the stairs has been changed (as at Knidos, Segesta, Stratonikeia), or their number has been doubled (as at Dramyssos). Two of the stair-steps are equal in size to one of the sitting-steps, the latter being so arranged that the spectators had room to sit at ease without being inconvenienced by the feet of those occupying the upper rows. Their height was,

according to Vitruvius, no less than 1 foot, and not more than
1 foot 6 inches, which small measure is accounted for by the
custom of raising the seats by means of bolsters and cushions; the

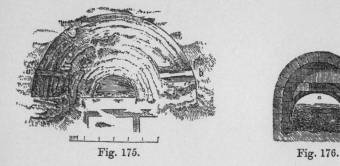

Fig. 175.   Fig. 176.

width of the seats was equal to about twice their height. The
steps are generally simple in design, with a view, however, to convenience and comfort. Frequently they are slightly raised in
front, the lower part at the back being destined for the feet of

Fig. 177.   Fig. 178.

those sitting in the row behind. This is illustrated in the simplest
manner by the sitting-steps of the theatres of Catana (Fig. 177)
and of Akrai (Fig. 178), in Sicily, a being the sitting-steps, b
those of the stairs.

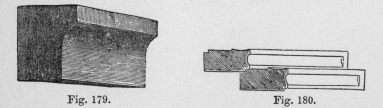

Fig. 179.   Fig. 180.

In other theatres the front side of the steps has been slightly
pushed back or hollowed out, so as to gain room for the feet.
Such is the case in the theatres at Megalopolis (Fig. 179), at

Tauromenium, and at Side in Asia Minor. Particularly comfortable are the steps of the theatre at Sparta, with their seats slightly
hollowed out (Fig. 180); those at Iasos, in Asia Minor, are formed
in the manner of arm-chairs, the seats in front of the diazoma
being real arm-chairs with backs to them, as was also the case
in the theatre of Epidauros, celebrated amongst the ancients.
Particularly interesting with regard to these arm-chairs is the
above-mentioned theatre of Dionysos at Athens, rediscovered in

Fig. 181.

1862. The place for the spectators consists of about one hundred
rows of seats, divided into thirteen kerkides by means of fourteen
stairs, the two last of which lie near the entrances, close by the
side-wall. The height of each step is 0·345 metre, the horizontal depth 0·782 metre; the latter is divided into two parts,
the front one (0·332 metre deep) being used as the seat; the
back one (0·45 metre deep), slightly hollowed, being destined for
the feet of those sitting higher. The width of the stair-steps is

0·70 metre, their height corresponding with that of the sitting steps in this manner, that the stair-step at first is 0·22 metre high, but gradually rises towards the back. In this sloping part grooves have been cut into the step, so as to prevent people from slipping. The lowest row of steps immediately surrounding the orchestra (Fig. 181) is occupied by sixty-seven arm-chairs, by ones, twos, or threes, hewn from blocks of Pentelic marble. These, as is proved by their inscriptions, were destined for the priests, archontes, and thesmothetai, the centre one, richly decorated with bas-reliefs, being reserved for the priest of Dionysos Eleuthereus. The wall of the proskenion, also decorated with bas-reliefs, was erected by the Archon Phaidros, perhaps in the third century after Christ, while the older wall and the oldest proskenion were placed, the former by six, the latter by eight, metres further back, owing to the orchestra required for the chorus of the old tragedy and comedy being much larger than that wanted for the mimic performances of late Roman times.

The orchestra, as we said before, was the scene of the choric dances in which the drama had its origin. Even in later theatres a large space was reserved for this purpose between the place for the spectators and the stage. This space was larger in the Greek than in the Roman theatres, in which latter no dances of this kind took place. Vitruvius describes the Greek orchestra as a circle into which a square had been designed, so that the four corners touched the periphery. The side of the square turned towards the stage terminates the orchestra, the space between this line and the tangent parallel to it being occupied by the stage. On the other side the orchestra is enclosed by the seats of the spectators. In the centre of it stands the thymele, the altar of Dionysos, which at the same time forms the central point of the choric dances. The soil was simply levelled; at meetings it was perhaps strewn with sand (hence κονίστρα); only in case dances were performed the thymele was surrounded with a floor of boards, resting most likely on several steps. In case of dramatic performances different arrangements became necessary. For the chorus had not only to sing and dance, but also to speak to the actors on the stage, and its place of action had to be raised accordingly. This was done by erecting a scaffolding over one half of the konistra as far as the thymele, and placing boards thereon. This raised part was called the orchestra proper, or the scenic orchestra, to distinguish it from the choreutic one. The latter, by some feet lower than the stage, was entered by the choreutai by the same passages (παρόδος), between the walls and the koilon, through which the spectators reached the konistra, and thence their seats. Steps led up to the orchestra, which again was connected with the stage by means of low movable stairs (κλίμακες) of three or four steps each (κλιμακτῆρες), as the course of the drama required frequently the ascending by the chorus of the stage, and its returning thence to the orchestra. Of these temporary arrangements naturally nothing remains, hence the various theories regarding them started by archæologists. Upon these, however, we cannot enter.

Of the stage-building we have fewer and less well-preserved remnants than of the place for the spectators. The stage was called ἡ σκήνη (tent), an expression dating most likely from the time when at the back of the orchestra a scaffolding was erected from which the actors entered as from a kind of tent. Afterwards the same expression was transferred to the stone theatre, its meaning being now either the whole stage-building, or, in a narrower sense, the back wall of the stage. Hence the expression found in Vitruvius of *scena tragica, comica,* and *satyrica,* from the different changes of scenery applied to it. Sometimes the small space in front of the back wall on which the actors performed was called σκήνη, instead of the more common προσκήνιον. Sometimes also the name λογεῖον was used for this place, or more particularly for the centre of it, from which the actors mostly delivered their speeches. This proskenion was considerably higher than the floor of the konistra, in order to raise, as it were, the actors into a strange sphere. Probably the whole space below the wooden floor of the proskenion was called ὑποσκήνιον ; its outer wall facing the orchestra was, according to Pollux, decorated with columns and sculptures. From it the " Charonic steps " (χαρώνειοι κλίμακες) led up to the proskenion, on which the ghosts of dead persons and river gods ascended the stage. The entrance was closed by a sliding slab of wood. Παρασκήνια were the two juttings of the stage-building enclosing the proskenion to right and left, ἐπισκήνια the different stories of the stage-wall.

Several stage-buildings have been preserved, particularly in

Asiatic cities, but in most of them Roman influences must be suspected, and they hardly can serve as specimens of purely Greek arrangements.   The theatre of Telmessos in Lykia is

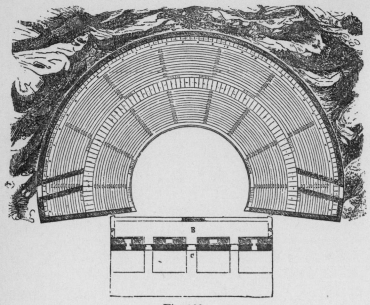

Fig. 182.

perhaps most adapted to this purpose, owing to its great simplicity (see Fig. 182).   The koilon is formed by a hill, the seats being closed in obtuse angles; one diazoma divides them into two

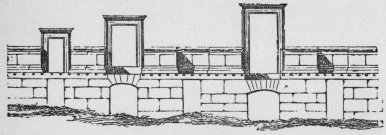

Fig. 183.

halves, another serves as an upper passage round them; eight stairs divide the place for the spectators into nine κερκίδες; the orchestra is very large, and agrees exactly with the statement of

Vitruvius; the proskenion rested on a wooden scaffolding. The
wall of the skene shows five doors, each of them originally
enclosed by two columns. Beneath these one still recognises the
hollows into which the beams of the floor of the proskenion
were placed (see Fig. 183); the doors underneath led into the
hyposkenion, the position of which we have described above.
Other specimens of preserved stage-buildings we shall mention in
speaking of the Roman theatre (§ 84); we conclude our description with a perspective view of a Greek theatre, designed by
Strack according to the statements of ancient writers and the
preserved remnants (Fig. 184).

Fig. 184.

31. In our description of the private dwellings of the Greeks,
we mentioned that more even than the public buildings they
have suffered from the influence of time. The same applies to
their interior fittings; only the utensils deposited in graves have
escaped the common destruction; in other cases pictures on vases
and sculptural representations must aid us in our description.
The different kinds of seats are specified by the following
expressions—δίφρος, κλισμός, κλιντήρ, κλισίη and θρόνος. Diphros
is a small, backless, easily movable stool, with four legs, either
crossed or perpendicular. The first-mentioned form of the
diphros, called also ὀκλαδίας δίφρος, ὀκλαδίας, or θρόνος πτυκτός,
δίφρος ταπεινός, could easily be folded, as the seat consisted only
of interwoven straps. It was therefore the custom amongst the
Athenians to have these folding-stools carried after them by

slaves. No less frequent were the diphroi with four perpendicular legs, which could naturally not be folded. Both forms of
the diphros are found on ancient monuments in many varieties.
Fig. 185, *a*, a diphros okladias, is taken from the marble
relief of a grave at Krissa. The two folding-stools, Fig. 185, *b*
and *c*, are from pictures on vases; the legs appear gracefully
bent and neatly carved. The second form of the diphros is
shown by Fig. 185, *d*, and Fig. 186, *c*. The first is taken from the
frieze of the Parthenon, where similar stools are carried on their
heads by the wives and daughters of the metoikoi who, at the
Panathenea, had to submit to the custom of stool-carrying
(διφροφορεῖν) : the second illustration is derived from a marble
relief at Athens; it is remarkable by its neatly bent legs and by
the turned knobs above the sitting-board, perhaps destined to
fasten the cushion placed thereon. If to this solid diphros we add

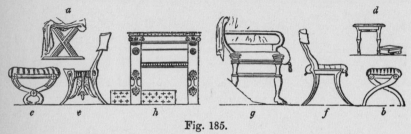

Fig. 185.

a back, we come to the second species of chairs, called κλισμός,
κλιντήρ, and κλισίη (see Fig. 185, *e*, *f*). They are like our
ordinary drawing-room chairs, but for the upper part of the
back, which is bent semicircularly, and therefore much more
comfortable than our straight-backed chairs. The legs bent
outward gracefully are in perfect harmony.

Under θρόνος we comprise all larger chairs with a straight
back and low arms; the former reaches either to the middle of
the back, or up to the head, of the sitting person. The thronoi in
the temples were the seats of the gods; in private houses they
were reserved as seats of honour for the master and his guests.
The thronoi in private houses were mostly made of heavy
wood; those in the temples, the ekklesiai, dikasteria, bouleu-
teria, the stadion, and hippodrome, reserved for the judges and
leaders of the people, were generally wrought in marble. The
thronoi were in different parts richly decorated with carved

garlands or figures; in sculptures they occur in various forms.
The low-backed thronos is shown in Figs. 185, *g*, and 186, *a*, the
former from the Harpy-monument at Xanthos, the latter from the
frieze of the Parthenon. The old wooden throne with a high
back appears in a marble relief of the best period (Fig. 186, *b*),
while several richly ornamented marble seats in the theatre of
Dionysos (Fig. 181), in the Akropolis of Athens (Stuart and
Revett, "Antiquities," iii., p. 19), illustrate the seats of honour of
the athlothetai in the market-places. The existence of thronoi
without backs is proved by the picture on a vase of a thronos
(Fig. 185, *h*) on which Aigisthos is being killed by Orestes. On
the seats of all these chairs woolly hides, blankets, or bolsters, used

Fig. 186.

to be put, as is mentioned by Homer (see Fig. 185, *b, c, e, f, g*).
To the throne belonged the footstool (θρῆνυς), either attached to
its front legs, and therefore immovable, or as a separate piece of
furniture. It was considered as indispensable both to rest the
feet and to mount the high throne. It was used, however, also
with low seats, resembling very much our modern footstool (Fig.
185, *d*, and Fig. 186, *c*). Something similar may have been the
massive wooden footstool (σφέλας) which, in the house of Odysseus,
Eurymachos applies as a missile. The width of the footstool
corresponds to that of the chair, those used for couches being
naturally longer (see Fig. 188).

32. The oldest specimen of a bedstead (κλίνη) is that
mentioned by Homer as joined together by Odysseus in his own
house. He had cut off the stem of an olive-tree a few feet from
the ground, and joined to it the boards of the bed, so that the trunk

supported the bed at the head. It therefore was immovable. The antique bed must be considered as the prolongation of the diphros. The cross-legged diphros prolonged became the folding bed; that with perpendicular legs, the couch. The former could easily be moved and replaced; they are perhaps identical with the δέμνια frequently mentioned in the "Odyssey," which were put into the outer hall for guests. One of them is shown as the notorious bed of Prokrustes in a picture on a vase (Fig. 187, *a*). The second diphros corresponds to the couch resting on four legs (Fig. 187, *b*), at first without head and foot-board, which were afterwards added at both ends (ἀνάκλιντρον or ἐπίκλιντρον). By the further addition of a back on one of the long sides, it became what we now call a *chaise longue* or sofa (Fig. 187, *c*, Figs. 188—190). This sleeping kline was no doubt essentially the same as that used at meals. The materials were, besides the ordinary woods, maple or box, either massive or veneered. The legs and backs, and other parts

a   c   b

Fig. 187.

not covered by the bedclothes, were carefully worked. Sometimes the legs are neatly carved or turned, sometimes the frames are inlaid with gold, silver, and ivory, as is testified in the " Odyssey " and elsewhere.

The bedding mentioned in Homer did not consist of sumptuous bolsters and cushions as in later times. It consisted, even amongst the richer classes, first of all of the ῥήγεα, *i.e.* blankets of a long-haired woollen material, or perhaps a kind of mattrass. Hides (κώεα), as spread by the poor on the hard floor, were sometimes put under the ῥήγεα and other additional blankets (τάπητες), so as to soften the couch. The whole was covered with linen sheets. The χλαῖναι served to cover the sleeper, who sometimes used his own dress for this purpose; sometimes they consisted of woollen blankets woven for the purpose. After Homer's time, when Asiatic luxury had been introduced into Greece, a mattrass (κνέφαλον, τυλεῖον or τύλη) was placed

immediately on the bed-straps (κειρία). It was stuffed with
plucked wool or feathers, and covered with some linen or woollen
material. On this mattrass blankets were placed, called by Pollux
περιστρώματα, ὑποστρώματα, ἐπιβλήματα, ἐφεστρίδες, χλαῖναι,
ἀμφιεστρίδες, ἐπιβόλαια, δάπιδες, ψιλοδάπιδες, ξυστίδες χρυσό-
παστοι, to which must be added the τάπητες and ἀμφιτάπητες
with the rough wool on either or both sides. Pillows, like the
mattrasses stuffed with wool or feathers, were added to complete
the bedding, at least in more luxurious times. Of a similar

Fig. 188.

Fig. 189.

kind were the klinai placed in the sitting-rooms, lying on which,
in a half-reclining position, people used to read, write, and take
their meals. They were covered with soft blankets of gorgeous
colours, while one or more cushions served to support the body in
its half-sitting position or to prop the left arm (Fig. 187, *c*).
Fig. 187, *a* shows the folding-bed, Fig. 187, *b*, the simple kline
covered with the ῥήγεα. Fig. 187, *c*
shows the kline with one upright end on
which two persons are reclining, one of
them resting the left arm on a cushion
covered with a many-coloured material,
the other leaning with her back against
two cushions. Much richer is the couch
in Fig. 188, which has a head and foot-

Fig. 190.

board and is covered with mattrasses and pillows; a long ornamented footstool has been added. Fig. 190, after a marble relief,
exactly resembles our sofa. Fig. 189 shows a peculiar kind of
kline, on which a sick person is lying, to whom Asklepios is giving
advice. Sometimes the drapery is evidently intended to hide the
roughly carved woodwork, as is shown by the picture of a symposion (Fig. 304), to which we shall have to return.

33. Tables were used by the ancients chiefly at meals, not for reading and writing. The antique tables, either square with four legs, or circular or oval with three connected legs, afterwards with one leg (τράπεζαι τετράποδες, τρίποδες, μονόποδες), resemble our modern ones but for their being lower. Mostly their slabs did not reach higher than the kline ; higher tables would have been inconvenient for the reclining person (see Fig. 187, *c*). In Homeric and even in later times, a small table stood before each thronos. The use of separate dishes for each guest is comparatively new. Originally the meat was brought in on large platters, divided by the steward, and each portion put on the bare table. In want of knives and forks the fingers were used. The pastry was put in baskets by the tables. Whether the Homeric tables were as low as the later ones, when lying instead of sitting had become the custom, we must leave undecided in want of sculptural evidence. The legs of the tables were carefully finished, particularly those of the tripods, which frequently imitated the legs of

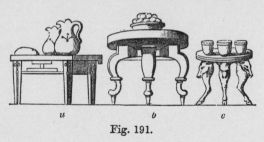

u   *b*   *c*

Fig. 191.

animals, or at least had claws at their ends (Fig. 191, *a, b, c*). The four-legged tables were more simple in design. The material was wood, particularly maple ; later on, bronze, precious metals, and ivory were introduced.

34. For the keeping of articles of dress, valuable utensils, ornaments, bottles of ointment, and documents, larger or smaller drawers and boxes were used. Chests of drawers and upright cupboards with doors seem to have been unknown in earlier times ; only in few monuments of later date (for instance, in the wall-painting of a shoemaker's workshop at Herculaneum) we see something resembling our wardrobe. The wardrobes mentioned by Homer (φωριαμός, χηλός) doubtlessly resemble our old-fashioned trunks (*Truhe*). The surfaces showed ornaments of

various kinds, either cut from the wood in relief or inlaid with
precious metals and ivory. Some smaller boxes with inlaid figures
or painted arabesques are shown in Fig. 192, *b, c, f, g, h*, all taken
from pictures on vases. The ornamentation with polished nails
seems to have been very much in favour (Fig. 192, *c, f, h*)—a
fashion reintroduced in modern times. The most celebrated
example of such ornamentation was the box of Kypselos, in
the opisthodomos of the temple of Hera at Olympia. It dates
probably from the time when the counting by Olympiads was
introduced, and served, according to Bötticher, for the keeping of
votive tapestry and the like. According to Pausanias, it was
made of cedar-wood, and elliptic in shape. It was adorned with
mythological representations, partly carved in wood, partly inlaid
with gold ivory, and encircling the whole box in five stripes, one
over the other. Boxes for articles of dress are seldom found in
old pictures on vases (Fig. 192, *a*) ; * very frequent are, on the

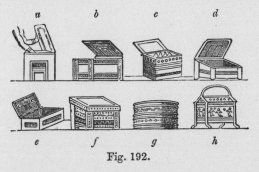

Fig. 192.

other hand, portable cases for ornaments, spices, &c. (Fig. 192, *b,
d, e, f, g, h*). Fig. 192, *c* contains evidently bottles of ointment.
Another box, standing before a reading ephebos, and showing the
inscription "**ΧΕΙΡΟΝΕΙΣ ΚΑΛΕ**," evidently contained documents (see Micali, " L'Italia avanti il dominio dei Romani," Tav.
CIII.). The cover was fastened to the box by a ribbon tied in a
knot. The custom of securing the ends of this ribbon by the impression of a signet-ring on wet sealing-earth or wax is of later date.
Locks, keys, and bolts, known at an early period for the closing of

* The inner surface of a drinking-goblet at the Royal Museum of Berlin
(Gerhard, " Trinkschalen und Gefässe," I. Taf. IX.) shows the large box in which
Hypsipyle, the princess of Lemnos, has hidden her father Thoas. See also our
Fig. 231.

doors, were later applied to boxes, as is sufficiently proved by the still-existing small keys fastened to finger-rings (see § 93), which, although all of Roman make, were most likely not unknown to the Greeks. For doors these would have been too small.

35. The furniture of Greek houses was simple, but full of artistic beauty. This was particularly displayed in vessels for the keeping of both dry and fluid stores, as were found in temples, dwellings, and even graves. Only the last mentioned have been preserved to us. Earthen vessels are the most numerous. The invention of the potter's wheel is of great antiquity, and was ascribed by the Greeks in different places to different mythical persons. The Corinthians named Hyperbion as its inventor. In the Kerameikos, the potters' quarter of Athens, Keramos, the son of Dionysos and Ariadne, was worshipped as such. The name of the locality itself was derived from this "heros eponymos." Next to Corinth and Athens (which latter became celebrated for earthen manufactures owing to the excellent clay of the promontory of Kolias), Ægina, Lakedæmon, Aulis, Tenedos, Samos, and Knidos were famous for their earthenware. In these places the manufacture of painted earthenware was concentrated; thence they were exported to the ports of the Mediterranean and the Black Sea for the markets of the adjoining countries. Owing to the beautiful custom of the ancients of leaving in the graves of the dead the utensils of their daily life, a great many beautiful vessels have been preserved which otherwise would have shared the destruction of the dwellings with other much less fragile implements. From the pictures on these vases we derive, moreover, valuable information as to the public and private habits of the Greeks. The greatest number of graves in their original condition, and filled with vessels, are found in Italy. The chief places where pottery has been and is still being found are—in Sicily, Gela and Girgenti (the old Akragas); in Southern Italy, the necropoles of the Apulian cities of Gnatia (Fasano), Lupatia (Altamura), Cælia (Ciglia), Barium (Bari), Rubi (Ruvo), Canusium (Canosa); in Lucania, the cities of Castelluccio, Anxia (Anzi), Pæstum, and Eboli; in the old Campania, the cities of Nola, Phlistia (Santa Agata de' Goti), Cumæ, and Capua; in Central Italy, the necropoles of the old Etruscan cities of Veii (Isola Farnese), Cære, Tarquinii, Vulci,

Clusium (Chiusi), Volterræ (Volterra), and Adria. In Greece
and Asia Minor things are different. The political conditions of
these countries have prevented their scientific investigation ; some
of the smaller vessels have been found only at Athens and
Ægina, some of the larger in Thera, Melos, and Rhodes. Besides
these we mention the discoveries in the grave-mounds of the old
Pantikapaion, the capital of the Bosphoric empire. They consist
of utensils worked in precious metals or bronze, and numerous
painted vessels belonging to the later period of pottery, which
must have been brought by merchants from Attika to this distant
outpost of antique culture. Of Athenian origin were also the
celebrated Panathenaïc prize-vases dating from the fourth century
B.C. which have been found amongst the ruins of the Kyrenaic Pen-
tapolis. They are amphoræ with two handles, and the picture of
Athene painted on them in an archaic style. In Greece, principally
in Attika, were un-
doubtedly the manu-
factures which sup-
plied the enormous
demands of both co-
lonies and barbaric
countries. In the style
of their paintings the

Fig. 193.   Fig. 194.

shrewd Attic men of business tried to hit the taste of their barbaric customers, not unlike our present manufacturers. The whole
trade was thus monopolised by Greece, a competition existing only
in those places where local manufacturers worked after Greek
patterns.

36. The *technique* of antique pottery may be learnt from two
gems. The first (Fig. 193) represents an ephebos clad in the
chiton, sitting in front of a handsome oven, from the top of which
he takes by means of two sticks a newly glazed two-handled
vessel. The second illustration also shows the interior of a
potter's workshop (Fig. 194). A nude potter gives the last
polish to a finished vessel (most likely with a piece of hard
leather) ; on a kind of baking oven, closed by a door, stand a
pitcher and a drinking-bowl for the purpose of drying. Two
pictures on vases, published by Jahn ("Berichte der kgl.
sächsischen Gesellschaft der Wissensch.," VI., 1854, hist. phil. Cl.,

p. 27 *et seq.*), show, one of them, a potter similarly occupied as ours (Fig. 194); the other, a little less finished in style, the whole interior of a potter's workshop with wheel and oven. Good (γῆ κεραμῖτις), particularly red, clay, was in demand for superior goods, and of this the promontory of Kolias, near Athens, furnished an unlimited supply. The potter's wheel (κεράμειος τροχός) was in use at a very early period. On it were formed both large and small vessels; with the difference, however, that of the former the foot, neck, and handles were formed separately, and afterwards attached, as was also the case in small vessels with widely curved handles. In order to intensify the red colour the vessel was frequently glazed and afterwards dried and burnt on the oven. The outlines of the figures to be painted on the vase were either cut into the red clay and filled up with a brilliant black varnish, or the surface itself was covered with the black varnish up to the contours, in which case these stood out in the natural red colour of the clay. The first mentioned process was the older of the two, and greater antiquity is therefore to be assigned to vessels with black figures on a red ground. In both kinds of paintings draperies or the muscles of nude figures were further indicated by the incision of additional lines of the colour of the surface into the figures. Other colours, like dark red, violet, or white, which on close investigation have been recognised as dissolvable, were put on after the second burning of the vessel.

37. About the historic development of pottery we know nothing beyond what may be guessed from the differences of style. As we said before, figures of a black or dark-brown colour painted on the natural pale red or yellowish colour of the clay indicate greater antiquity. The black figures were occasionally painted over in white or violet. These vessels are mostly small and somewhat compressed in form; they are surrounded with parallel stripes of pictures of animals, plants, fabulous beings, or arabesques (Fig. 195). The drawings show an antiquated stiff type, similar to those on the vessels recently discovered at Nineveh and Babylon, whence the influence of Oriental on Greek art may be inferred. This archaic style, like the strictly hieratic style in sculpture, was retained together with a freer treatment at a more advanced period. As a first step of development we notice the combination of animals and arabesques, at first with half-human,

half-animal figures, soon followed by compositions belonging
mostly to a certain limited circle of myths. The treatment
of figures shows rigidity in the calm, and violence in the active,
positions. The Doric forms of letters and words on many vases of
this style, whether found in Greece or Italy, no less than the
uniformity of their *technique*, indicate *one* place of manufacture,
most likely the Doric Corinth, celebrated for her potteries ; on the
other hand, the inscriptions in Ionian characters and written in
the Ionian dialect on vessels prove their origin in the manufactures of the Ionian Eubœa and her colonies.* The pictures on
these vases, also painted in stripes, extend the mythological
subject-matter beyond the Trojan cycle to the oldest epical myths,
each story being represented in its consecutive phases.

The latter vases form the transition to the second period.
The shapes now become more varied, graceful, and slender. The
figures are painted in black, and covered with a brilliant varnish ;
the *technique* of the painting, however, does not differ from that of

Fig. 195.

the first period. The outlines have been neatly incised and
covered up with black paint; the details also of draperies and
single parts of the body are done by incision, and sometimes
painted over in white or dark red. The principle seems to be that
of polychrome painting, also applied in sculpture. Single parts of
the armour, embroideries, and patterns of dresses, hair, and beards
of men, the manes of animals, &c., are indicated by means of dark
red lines. This variety of colour was required particularly for the
draperies, which are stiff and clumsily attached to the body. The
same stiffness is shown in the treatment of faces and other nude

* See the excellent preface of Jahn's description of vases in the Royal Pinakothek at Munich (p. cxlviii. *et seq.*), where the different periods of pottery have been
characterized. See also Jahn's essay, "Die griechischen bemalten Vasen," in his
"Populäre Aufsätze aus der Alterthumswissenschaft." Bonn, 1868 (p. 307 *et seq.*).

parts of the body, as also in the rendering of movements. The
faces are always in profile, the nose and chin pointed and
protruding, and the lips of the compressed mouth indicated only
by a line.   Shoulders, hips, thighs, and calves bulge out, the body
being singularly pinched (Fig. 196).   The grouping is equally
imperfect.   The single figures of compositions are loosely connected by the general idea of the story.   They have, as it were, a
narrative character; an attempt at truth to nature is, however,
undeniable.   The subjects are taken partly from the twelve-gods
cycle (like the frequently occurring birth of Athene, Dionysian
processions, &c.) or from Trojan and Theban myths; partly also
from daily life, such as chases, wrestlings, sacrifices, symposia,
and the like.   To this class belong most of those large Pana-

Fig. 196.

thenaïc prize-vases, which are of such importance for our knowledge of gymnastic competitions.

In our third class the figures appear in the
natural colour of the surface, which itself has
been painted black.   The character of the
figures in consequence appears gay and lively.
Both styles seem at one time to have existed
together, for we find them used severally on two
sides of one and the same vessel, till at last the
painting of black figures was disused entirely.   The drawings
now become more individual, and are freed from the fetters of
conventional tradition—a proof of the free development of both
political and artistic feelings, even amongst the lower classes of
artificers.   The specimens of the third class show the different
stages of this process of liberation.   At first the figures are still
somewhat hard, and the drapery, although following the lines of
the body more freely than previously, shows still traces of archaic
severity of treatment; the details, indicated by black lines, are
still carefully worked out.   For smaller folds and muscles, a
darker shade of the red colour is used; wreaths and flowers
appear dark; red white is used only in few cases—for instance,
for the hair of an old man.   The composition shows greater
concentration and symmetry in the grouping, according to the
conditions of the space at disposal.   The figures show a solemn
dignity, with signs, however, of an attempted freer treatment.

Kramer justly calls this period that of the "severe style," and compares it with the well-known "Æginetic" style in sculpture. The further development of the "severe style" is what Kramer calls the "beautiful style," in which grace and beauty of motion and drapery, verging on the soft, have taken the place of severe dignity. In high art this transition might be compared to that from Perugino's school to that of Raphael, or, if we may believe the ancient writers, from the school of Polygnotos to that of Zeuxis and Parrhasios.

Fig. 197.

The form of the vessels themselves next calls for our attention. The vases, two-handled amphorai and krateres, found most frequently during this period are slender and graceful. Together with them we meet with beautifully modelled drinking-horns (Fig. 201), and heads (Fig. 197, *d*) or whole figures, used to put vessels upon. The variety of forms, and the largeness of some vessels, overloaded as they were with figures, soon led to want of care in the composition. The moderation characteristic of the "beautiful style" was soon relinquished for exaggerated ornamentation, combined with a preference for representing sumptuous dresses and the immoderate use of white, yellow, and other colours. This led gradually to the decadence of pottery. Lucania and Apulia are the places where sumptuous vessels of the degenerating style are most frequently found (see Fig. 197, *a, b, c*). The handles of the splendid amphora (Fig. 197, *a*) are attached to the brim, adorned with an ovolo, the handles being in the form of volutes the centres of which contain heads of the Gorgon, their lower parts end in heads of swans. The neck of the vessel is adorned with three stripes of garlands, in the centre of which are female heads—a common feature of this style (see the vase, Fig. 197, *c*). The body of the vessel is occupied by pictures from the myth of Triptolemos, who himself is discovered in the centre on a chariot drawn by dragons. The pictures are in two rows, one above the other, a peculiarity frequently found in larger vases of this style. Above them we see a double ovolo; beneath them a "meandering" ornamentation. The arrangement of the figures in Fig. 197, *c*, is similar. In the centre of the picture is an open building (frequently met with on vases of this style), round which the figures are grouped in two rows, one over the other. The vessel itself is an amphora resembling a candelabrum, the excessively slender body of which, resting on a weak foot, shows its merely ornamental purpose (compare the picture on a vase in § 60, representing the burial of Archemoros). Fig. 197, *b*, shows Kadmos fighting with the dragon : the busts of gods being painted above the chief action, as if looking down upon it from heights, are also peculiar to this style.

The subject-matter of these pictures has undergone similar changes as the old mythical stories themselves, when looked at through the medium of poetry, both lyrical and dramatic. Attic myths were treated in preference. The infinitely varied treatment proves the popularity of those lyrical and dramatic versions. In the decaying style, not only battles of Amazons and Kentaurs, and scenes from the Hades, but also the subjects of tragedies, are depicted, the situations of the latter being evidently imitated from the stage, including even the variegated colours of the costumes. The whole impression becomes theatrical in consequence. Sometimes mythological scenes and characters have been caricatured as on the comic stage (see pictures of this kind in § 58).

The vases of Lucania and Apulia moreover show frequently representations of Greek burial-rites as modified by the South Italian populations. Jahn from this fact concludes the existence of local manufactures (*l. c.* p. ccxxxi.), which is confirmed by the inscriptions on the vessels. They belong to a post-Alexandrine period, those of the "beautiful style" dating from the time between Perikles and Alexander.

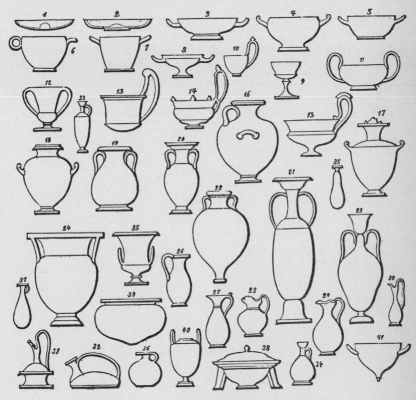

Fig. 198.

In some Etruscan cities earthenware was manufactured by local artists working after Greek patterns. The figures are distinguished from genuine Greek work by the contours being incised very deeply and filled up with red colour. The clay also is coarser. The compositions show an admixture of local myths and usages, not to mention Etruscan inscriptions.

38. Hitherto we have considered the various artistic styles of

vessels. Now we must try to distinguish their names and forms by the varieties of their uses. Ancient writers have transmitted to us a variety of names for them, which in some cases may be verified by inscriptions on individual vessels. The naming, however, of many of them is very difficult, and the attempts of Panofka in this direction have met with much contradiction amongst archæologists. Their nomenclature amongst the ancients seems to have been much more diversified than is the case at the present day. We have collected forty-one of the most striking forms (Fig. 198), by means of which the innumerable varieties in our museums may be to some extent classified.

Vessels may be divided, according to their uses, into those for storing, mixing, and drawing liquids. Amongst the vessels for keeping wine, oil, honey, water, &c., the pithos (πίθος) is the largest. It is made of strong clay, without a foot, either pointed or flattened at the bottom. If pointed, the pithos, in that case generally a small one, was dug into the earth to keep it upright ; if flat-bottomed, it was larger, and had a wide mouth. The cubic measure of the large pithos was equal, at least, to our large wine-vats, as is shown by the fact of those kept in the rocky cellars of Gallias at Agrigentum holding one hundred amphorai of wine each. During the Peloponnesian war, the poorer people seeking shelter in Athens lived in pithoi, also called πιθάκναι. Of mythological celebrity is the pithos of the Danaides in which Eurystheus hid himself ; the tub of Diogenes is generally known. Similar to the pithos, but smaller and more easily movable, must have been the στάμνος (Fig. 198, 18, called stamnos by both Panofka and Gerhard, and Fig. 198, 40, described by Panofka as a lekane, by Gerhard as an Apulian stamnos) and the βῖκος. Wine, oil, figs, and salt meat were preserved in them. About the forms of the wine-vessels called ὕρχη and πυτίνη we are quite uncertain. Equally uncertain is the form of the κάδος, a larger vessel, also for wine, unless we consider it as belonging to the class of amphorai. The form of the amphora (ἀμφορεύς), a two-handled vessel (ὁ ἑκατέρωθεν κατὰ τὰ ὦτα δυνάμενος φέρεσθαι) mentioned by Homer, is sufficiently known from many representations on vases, bas-reliefs, coins, and gems. They are more or less bulky vessels, with necks shorter or longer in proportion, but with mouths always of moderate

size compared to the bulk (Fig. 198, 20-23) ; frequently resting
on feet, but sometimes (Fig. 198, 22) ending in a flattened point,
in which case the amphora was either put against a wall or fitted
into a frame. The variety consists in the form of the handles,
essentially modified by the size of the vessel, and in the larger or
smaller opening of the mouth. Amongst the amphorai we count
the Panathenaïc prize-vases, in which the victor received the oil
from the sacred olive-tree, and which even during the period of the
" beautiful style " preserved the archaic manner of black figures
on a red background. Hydria (ὑδρία) and kalpis (κάλπις)
(Fig. 198, 16 and 17) seem to be different names of one and the
same kind of bulky, short-necked vessel, the use of which is
shown by its being carried on their heads, in the pictures on
vases, by maidens fetching water. Its characteristic is a third
handle in the centre of the vessel, which prevented its sinking
in the water, and, at the same time, made the lifting of the filled
pitcher on the head easier. The diminutive ὑδρίσκη signifies a
smaller vessel for the keeping of ointment, formed, most likely,
in imitation of the hydria. The krossos (κρωσσός, κρωσός,
κρωσσίον) was used for keeping water and oil, but also ashes.
It most likely resembled the hydria, but cannot with certainty
be recognised in any of the existing vessels. A smaller wine-
vessel, most likely bulky and long necked, was the λάγυνος.
Gerhard compares it to the modern Orvieto-bottle. The lagynos,
surrounded with wicker-work, called φλασκίον by Suidas, may
have been the model of our bottles or flasks. Travellers and
soldiers in the field used the κώθων, a bulky flask with a narrow
neck and a handle, which had the advantage of clearing the
water from muddy substances, most likely by means of a particular clay of which it was made. A similar drinking-flask was
the bombylios (βομβυλιός, βομβύλη), the narrow neck of
which emitted the fluid by single drops only, and in this way
produced a kind of gurgling sound, like the βησίον or βήσσα
used by the Alexandrines. Whether the little flask with
handles (Fig. 198, 37), .called bombylios by Gerhard and
Panofka, answers to the Greek term we will not venture to
decide. The λήκυθοι, mentioned by Homer, served for the
keeping of ointment; their form is sufficiently defined both
by pictures on vases and numerous still-existing specimens

(Fig. 198, 33). In these the oil was preserved for the rubbing of the limbs of wrestlers, or of bathers after their baths; out of them also was poured the sacred oil over the graves of the dead. All these vessels show very much the same type. The neck was narrow in order to let the oil pass only in single drops, by means of which the above-mentioned gurgling sound (λακεῖν, λακάζειν) was produced. The numerous vessels of this kind were chiefly manufactured in Attika; they were necessary both to men and women. About the form of the olpe (ὄλπη, ὄλπα, ὄλπις), also used for oil, and peculiar to the Doric tribe, we know nothing. According to Athenæus, olpe seems to have been an old name of the oinochoë; hence the notion of the vessels, Fig. 198, 26 and 27, being of the oinochoë kind. The former is called by Panofka, olpe, by Gerhard oinochoë; the latter Gerhard calls an olpe approaching the Egyptian style. About the form of the alabastron (ἀλάβαστρον, ἀλάβαστον) we are better informed. It is a small cylindrical vessel, narrowing a little in the neck so as to produce the gradual dripping of the perfumed ointment preserved in it. All the specimens preserved to us, although varying in size and form, agree in the essential points, but for the style of the pictures and the material of which the vessels are made. The use of the alabastron is shown in the wall-picture of the so-called Aldobrandini wedding (see Fig. 232).

The generic term for mixing-vessels used at meals and libations is krater (κρατήρ, κρητήρ, from κεράννυμι). Its form, greatly modified by different ages and tastes, is sufficiently known from pictures and existing specimens (Fig. 198, 25; compare Fig. 197, b). It had to hold larger quantities of wine and water (unless these were mixed afterwards in the drinking-glasses), and was accordingly bulky and broad necked. A handle on each side made the krater easily portable when empty. It rested on a foot divided into several parts, and on a broad base. Of the several divisions of the krater, as the Argolian, Lesbian, Korinthian, Lakonian, we have, no doubt, specimens in our collections, without, however, being able to distinguish them. Hypokreteria, i.e. large flat dishes, were placed under the krateres, to receive the overflowing liquid. Similar to the krater was the ψυκτήρ, a cooling-vessel for wine before it was mixed. Its dimensions varied greatly; in some cases topers emptied a whole ψυκτήρ of moderate dimensions. According to Pollux, this vessel was also called δῖνος, and rested on a base consisting of dice or knobs, instead of a foot. Its shape was somewhat like a pail, and resembled the kalathos, the working-basket of Greek women; this name was, indeed, also applied to it. We have in our collections several vases resembling this shape, to which, therefore, the names of ψυκτήρ and δῖνος may be applied.

Amongst vessels for drawing liquids we first mention those called ἀρύταινα, ἀρύστιχος, and ἀρύβαλλος, all derived from ἀρύω, to scoop. Of the aryballos Athenæus says, that it expanded towards the bottom, and that its neck narrowed like a purse with its string tightened, which latter was called by the same name. Specimens of it are numerous in our museums (Fig. 198, 34 and 36). It was also used for the keeping of ointment, and as such belonged, like the arytaina or arysane, to the bathing utensils. The οἰνοχόη, χοῦς, πρόχους, and ἐπίχυσις served, as their names indicate, for the drawing and pouring out of liquids, especially of wine. They had one handle, and resembled a jug. Their size varied considerably (Fig. 198, 26-31). Their use is sufficiently illustrated by pictures. Fig. 199 shows a picture on a vase in which the ephebos kneeling to the right is taking wine from the krater with the oinochoë, in order to fill the drinking-vessel of the other ephebos. The prochous seems to have been used chiefly as a water-jug. Accurate accounts of its different forms we do not possess. More-over, according to Athenæus, the terms had been changed. What originally was called pelike, afterwards received the name of choë. The pelike resembled the Panathenaïc vases;

Fig. 199.

and is said to have taken afterwards the form of the oinochoë, as used at those festivities. At the time of Athenæus the pelike was only a piece of ornament used at festive processions, the vessel in common use being called chous, and resembling the arytaina. The kotyle (κοτύλη, κότυλος) was used as a measure of both liquid and dry substances, but also for drinking purposes. The captive Athenians in the Syrakusian quarries, for instance, received one kotyle of water and two kotylai of food a day (see Fig. 198, 4 and 7; the former, called by Panofka, kotyle, by Gerhard, skyphos; the latter, by Panofka, kotylos, by Gerhard, kotyle). Its form was that of a deep, pot-like, two-handled dish, with a short foot. Several small kotylai with covers to them were sometimes combined and carried by one handle, similar to what we find amongst peasants in Central Germany at the present day. Athenæus calls this

combination a κέρνος (Fig. 200). Its elegant form makes its use at table as a kind of cruet-stand appear probable. The κύαθος was used both for drinking and drawing liquids. It resembles our drinking-cups but for the handle, which is con-siderably higher than the brim of the vessel (Fig. 198, 10, 13, 14), in order to prevent the dipping of the finger into the liquid on drawing it. It was used, as a measure at the symposia, before inebriation became the rule, when larger vessels were used.

Fig. 200.

Amongst drinking-vessels we mention the phiale, the kymbion, and the kylix. The φιάλη was a flat saucer without a foot (Fig. 198, 1 and 2), the centre of which was raised like the boss of a buckler, and called like it ὀμφαλός. Smaller phialai were used for drinking; larger ones served at libations and lustra-tions and as anathemata in the temples, particularly those wrought in precious metals. The kymbion (κυμβίον, κύμβη) is said to have been a deep, long dish like a boat, without a handle, used for drinking or libations; a specimen we do not possess, as far as we know. The κύλιξ is a drinking-cup with two handles, resting on an elegantly formed foot (Fig. 198, 8). We meet with it frequently in pictures and in museums. The kylix of Argos differed from that of Attika by having its brim bent inward a little. Whether the so-called Therikleic kylikes had their name from the animals painted on them, or from the potter Therikles, who was celebrated at Korinth at the time of Aristophanes, we must leave undecided. Athenæus describes these as deep goblets with two small handles, and adorned at the upper brim with ivy-branches. Fig. 199 shows an ephebos holding in his right hand the skyphos (σκύφος), while a kylix stands on his extended left. The former resembles a cup, sometimes with a flat bottom, at others resting on a small Doric base (Fig. 198, 6), at others,

again, ending in a point (Fig. 198, 41). It generally had two
small horizontal handles just underneath the brim. Originally
used by peasants (Eumaios, for instance, offers one to Odysseus),
it afterwards became part of the dinner-service. According to
different forms, peculiar to different localities, we distinguish
Bœotian, Rhodian, Syrakusian, and Attic skyphoi. The skyphos
was generally designated as the drinking-cup of Herakles. The
κάνθαρος was a goblet resting on a high foot, and having widely
curved thin handles : it was peculiar to Dionysos and to the
actors in the Dionysian thiasos (Fig. 198, 12, compare Fig. 199), and
appears frequently in their hands in pictures on vases and other
representations. The old kantharos was larger than that later in
use, as appears from a passage in Athenæus which says, that the
modern kantharoi are so small, as if they were meant to be
swallowed themselves, instead of having the wine drunk out of
them. As the oldest drinking-vessel the καρχήσιον is mentioned.
According to Athenæus, it was lengthy in form, with the centre
of the body slightly bent inward, and two handles reaching to
the bottom. Whether it had a foot or a flat base (Fig. 198, 11),
cannot be decided. Homer mentions a δέπας ἀμφικύπελλον, *i.e.*
double goblet, which, as appears from Aristotle ("Hist. Anim.,"
IX. 40), was also known at a later period. A specimen of it has not
been preserved, as far as
is known to us. Being
mostly wrought in precious
metals, they were pro-
bably, at a later period,
frequently remodelled into
more fashionable shapes.

To conclude we men-
tion the beautifully
modelled drinking-horns,
wrought partly in clay,
partly in metal, and used

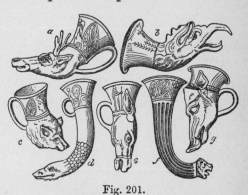

Fig. 201.

at feasts (κέρας and ῥυτόν) (see Fig. 201). The horn has been used
as a drinking-utensil since the oldest times, particularly amongst
barbarous nations. Both Æschylos and Xenophon quote examples
of this custom. In pictures on vases the Kentauroi and Dionysos
frequently appear with drinking-horns. The rhyton is an artistic

development of this primitive form. Its end has been modelled
into the head of an animal, according to the nature of which the
rhyton has received the surnames of γρύψ (Fig. 201, b), λύκος
(Fig. 201, c), ὄνος, ἡμίονος (Fig. 201, e), κάπρος (Fig. 201, g),
ἔλεφας, ἵππος, ταῦρος, &c. (compare the picture on a vase in § 56,
in which one of the topers pours the wine from a panther-rhyton
(πάρδαλις) into a goblet). The rhyton had to be emptied at one
draught, and was afterwards placed (probably to be filled again)
on a stand (ὑπόθημα, ὑποπυθμήν, περισκελίς). As appears from
the cited picture, the rhyton had an opening (which most likely
could be stopped) inside the mouth of the animal, from which the
wine was poured out, and had to be caught by the drinker in his
glass.

As another means of keeping wine and oil we now mention
the ἀσκός, the wine-skin, still in use in the East and in Southern
Europe, consisting of the hide of an animal sewed and tied
together. In pictures we often see it on the backs of fauns and
Sileni, and its form has even been imitated in clay in small vessels
for wine and oil. Our museums contain several vases of this kind
(see Levezow, "Gallerie der Vasen," &c., Table IX., No. 189).
Even that common form of handled vessels called by Gerhard
askos (Fig. 198, 32) may originally have been suggested by the
wine-skin.

Of Greek crockery nothing remains, with the exception of a
few dishes. It was destroyed with the dwelling-houses, and had
not the advantage of being deposited in the grave-chambers. On
the other hand, the kitchen utensils of the Romans are fully illustrated by the excavations at Pompeii; to these we refer the
reader. The χύτρα no doubt resembled our saucepans with one
or two handles. Porridge, meat, and vegetables were cooked in
it, and out of it the first portion was offered to the domestic gods
and to Zeus Herkaios at every meal, and at the consecration of
temples and altars. Sometimes the chytra had three feet (see
Fig. 198, 38), but usually, and particularly if it was oval in shape
and without feet, it was placed on a kind of tripod (χυτρόπους,
λάσανον). Homer already mentions large vessels (τρίποδες),
standing on tripods or having three feet, used particularly for
heating the bathing-water. Identical with the chytra was the
λέβης, mostly made of bronze. Both names occur frequently

amongst the enumerations of temple treasures. They were made
of bronze, silver, or gold. On a cameo (Panofka, "Bilder antiken
Lebens," Table XII., No. 5) we see a huge lebes, but without
the tripod, in which two boys are cooking a pig, while a third
one is poking the fire under the vessel. Besides these, we
possess some dishes in our museums the painting of which with
fish of various kinds indicates their being used for the preparing
of these; whence the name of ἰχθύαι applied to them.

As a domestic utensil we also mention the bath. In Homer
baths are mentioned, most likely made of polished stone (ἀσάμινθοι),
and large enough to hold one person. These
asaminthoi, however, were soon replaced by
large scale-like baths (λουτῆρες, λουτήρια,
Fig. 202) resting on one or several feet, and
filled by pipes in the walls, Fig. 202. They
appear in the pictures of bathing-scenes
in all kinds of varieties. Larger baths for
several persons, which were placed in the public or private bathing-chambers (βαλανεῖα),
were called κολυμβήθρα, πύελος, and μάκτρα.

Fig. 202.

They were either dug into the earth and surrounded with masonry,
or cut into the living rock. They may have also been built of
stone.

39. We now have to add a few remarks about vessels made of
metal, of stones more or less precious, and of glass. All these
were numerous, both as ornaments and for practical use. The
names mentioned for earthenware apply in general also to them.
Instead of paintings, however, we here find plastic ornamentations.
Amongst stones the fine white alabaster was most frequently used,
for those delicate little ointment-bottles called by the name of
alabastron (see p. 150), partly because of the softness of the
colour of the stone, partly because of its great coldness, which
tended to keep the ointment fresh. Its use for drinking-cups
was less frequent. Its sides were with great skill, by means
of turning, reduced to the thinness of note-paper, as can be
seen in an alabastron at the Museum of Berlin. For the same
purposes as the alabaster were also used the onyx and the agate.
Mithridates VI. Eupator had amongst his treasures two onyx
vases, which Lucullus brought to Rome as spoil. Only few of

these precious vessels are preserved at the present day. Amongst
these we mention the so-called "Mantuan goblet" in the possession of the late Duke Charles of Brunswick, formerly owned by
the Gonzaga family, an ointment-vase of onyx-agate in the
Münz- und Antiken-Cabinet at Vienna, an onyx vase in the Antiquarium of the Royal Museum at Berlin (all these decorated with
sculptures), and two onyx vases at the museums of Vienna and
Naples respectively. As the finest specimen of Oriental agate in
existence we mention a vase in the just-mentioned collection at
Vienna 28½ inches in diameter, including the handle. It was
brought to Western Europe after the conquest of Constantinople
by the Crusaders, and came afterwards into the possession of
Charles the Bold, Duke of Burgundy, whence it was transferred
to Vienna as part of the dowry of Maria of Burgundy, wife of the
Emperor Maximilian I. For larger vessels, like the krater or the
urn, white or coloured marble, porphyry, and also various metals,
were used, and we still possess numerous vases of this kind
adorned with beautiful reliefs. Particularly the krater is, according to its destination, frequently adorned with the Dionysian
attributes, such as Silenus-masks, goblets, musical instruments,
&c., beautifully grouped together with flower and fruit ornamentations; the handles and the finely developed foot are in
perfect harmony. Bronze vessels of this kind are frequently
mentioned by the ancients. Achilles offers a silver krater
wrought by Sidonian artists as a prize for runners at a race.
Crœsus made a votive offering to the Delphic oracle of one golden
and one silver krater, the latter holding 600 amphorai, being a
work of Theodoros, the Samian bronze-founder; a bronze krater.
resting on three colossal kneeling figures, was dedicated by the
Samians to Hera. Amongst the votive offerings at the Parthenon were numerous goblets of this kind, made both of gold
and silver. The most celebrated Greek toreutai, like Kalamis,
Akragas, Mys, Stratonikos, Antipater, Pytheas (who, however,
according to Pliny, worked only in silver and bronze), cultivated
this branch of their art, and the vessels from their *ateliers* were
sought after, up to the latest period, by the Romans. With the
exception of the smaller oil and drinking vessels, these vases
served only as ornaments in the houses of the rich, as votive
offerings in temples and graves, as decorations of the gables of

buildings, and as prizes at the games. The art of making vessels of glass seems to have been a later importation from the East, particularly from Egypt. At first vessels made of glass (λίθος χυτή) were appreciated as much as those of precious metals; afterwards glass bottles and drinking-glasses become more common. Still the Greek manufacture of this article never was equal to those of Rome and Egypt (compare § 91).

Amongst domestic utensils we also count articles made of basket-work, which frequently occur in antique pictures (see Fig. 203). The kalathos (κάλαθος, καλαθίς, καλαθίσκος), the basket for keeping wool (used for weaving and embroidering), and also flowers and fruit, is frequently met with in vase-paintings illustrating the life of Greek women (Fig. 203, a); perhaps Fig. 203, b, also went by the name of kalathos. As early as Homer's time baskets (κάνεον), probably round or oval, were used, at meals, to keep bread and pastry in. They had a low rim and handles (Fig. 203, c). The kaneon was also used at offerings, as is proved by Fig. 203, c, where it is filled with pomegranates, holy boughs, and ribbons. At the Panathenaia noble Athenian maidens carried such baskets, filled with holy cakes, incense, and knives, on their heads, whence the name κανηφόροι applied to them. These graceful figures were a favourite subject of antique sculpture. Both Polyklete and Skopas had done a celebrated kanephore—the former in bronze, the latter in marble. The σπυρίς, chiefly used for carrying fish, was also a flat basket, similar to that used at the present day by fishermen in the South. Other baskets used by peasants appear frequently in antique pictures, such as Fig. 203, d, in the original carried by a

Fig. 203.

peasant on a stick over his shoulder, together with another basket of the same pear-like shape; Fig. 203, f and e, are taken from a

bas-relief representing a vintage, in which the former appears
filled with grapes, while the latter is being filled with must
by a boy.   This proves, at the same time, the knowledge
amongst the Greeks of the art of making the basket-work dense
enough to hold fluids.   The same fact is shown by a passage in
Homer, in which Polyphemos lets the milk coagulate to cheese
in baskets (τάλαρος πλεκτός), which cheese was afterwards placed
on a hurdle (ταρσός), through which the whey trickled slowly.
Of plaited rushes, or twigs, consisted also a peculiar kind of
net (κύρτος), a specimen of which is seen on the reverse of a
medal coined under the Emperor Macrinus, as the emblem of the
maritime city of Byzantium (see Dumersan, " Descript. d.
Médailles ant. du Cabinet du feu M. Allier de Hauteroche,"
Pl. III., No. 8).   Baskets, roughly plaited, appear also in the
vase-painting of the " Weighing out of the Silphion " (Panofka,
" Bilder antiken Lebens," Taf. XVI., No. 3), where the silphion
is being carried in them.   According to Athenæus, basket-work
was imitated in precious metals.

40.   To light and heat the rooms, at Homer's time, fire-baskets,
or fire-basins (λαμπτῆρες), were used, standing on high poles,
and fed with dry logs of wood or splinters (δᾷδες).   The cinders
were, at intervals, removed by serving-maids, and the flames
replenished.   Such fire-baskets, on poles, are still used by night-
travellers in Southern Russia, and at nightly
ceremonies in India.   The use of pine-torches
(δαΐδων ὑπὸ λαμπομενάων) is of equal antiquity.
They consisted of long, thin sticks of pine-wood,
tied together with bark, rushes, or papyrus
(Fig. 204, c).   The bark of the vine was also
used for torches, called λοφίς.   The golden
statues on pedestals, in the hall of Alkinoos,
undoubtedly held such torches in their hands.

a   b   c
Fig. 204.

In vase-paintings we also see a different form of the torch,
carried chiefly by Demeter and Persephone, which consists of
two pieces of wood fastened crosswise to a staff (Fig. 204, *b*).
An imitation of this wooden torch was undoubtedly the torch-
case, made of clay or metal, in the shape of a salpinx.   Their
surface was either smooth or formed in imitation of the bundles
of sticks and the bark of the wooden torch, the inside being

filled with resinous substances. A different kind of torch was the phanos (φανός, φανή), which consisted of sticks tied together, and perforated with pitch, resin, or wax. They were put into a case of metal, which again was let into a kind of dish, turned either upwards or downwards (Fig. 204, *a*). This dish (χύτρα) served to receive the cinders or the dripping resin. The phanoi were either carried, or, when their case was prolonged to a long stem (καυλός), and had a foot (βάσις) added to it, might be put down (Fig. 205), and received, in that case, the names of λαμπτήρ or λυχνοῦχος. The further development of this form was the candelabrum, carrying either fire-basins or oil-lamps (see the Roman lighting-apparatus, § 92). The date of oil-lamps in Greece cannot be stated with accuracy : they were known at the time of Aristophanes. They were made of terra-cotta or metal, and their construction resembles those used by the Romans.

Fig. 205.

They are mostly closed semi-globes with two openings, one, in the centre, to pour the oil in, the other, in the nose-shaped prolongation (μυκτήρ), destined to receive the wick (θρυαλλίς, ἐλλύχνιον, φλομός). Amongst the small numbers of Greek lamps preserved to us, we have chosen two of the most graceful specimens, one of them showing the ordinary form of the lamp (Fig. 206), the other that of a kline, on which a boy is lying (Fig. 207). Both are made of clay, the latter being painted in various colours. The Athenians also used lanterns (λυχνοῦχος) made of transparent horn, and lit up with oil-lamps.

Fig. 206.

They were carried at night in the streets like the torches. Sparks, carefully preserved under the ashes, served both Greeks and Romans to light the fire. The ancients had, however, a lighting apparatus (πυρεία), consisting of two pieces of wood, of which the one was driven into the other

Fig. 207.

(στορεύς or ἐσχάρα), like a gimlet, the friction effecting a flame. According to Theophrast, the wood of nut or chestnut trees was generally used for the purpose.

41. We now come to the dress of the Greeks. We shall

have to consider those articles of dress used as a protection against the weather, and those prescribed by decency or fashion, also the coverings of the head and the feet, the arrangement of the hair, and the ornaments. Unfortunately, the terminology is, in many cases, uncertain. Many points, therefore, must remain undecided. Before entering upon details, we must remark that the dress of the Greek, compared with modern fashion, was extremely simple and natural. Owing to the warmth of the climate and the taste of the inhabitants, both superfluous and tight articles of dress were dispensed with. Moreover, the body was allowed to develop its natural beauty in vigorous exercise; and in this harmony and beauty of the limbs the Greeks prided themselves, which, of course, reacted favourably on the character of the dress.

The two chief divisions of garments are the ἐνδύματα, which are put on like a shirt, and the ἐπιβλήματα, or περιβλήματα, resembling a cloak, loosely thrown over the naked body, or the endymata. Weiss ("Kostümkunde," I., p. 703 *et seq.*) remarks rightly that the original character of Greek dress, consisting of the two parts just mentioned, remained essentially the same. The later changes apply only to the mode of using these, and to their material and ornamental qualities.

The χιτών, in its various forms, was used both by men and women as their endyma—*i.e.* the under-garment touching the naked body. A second under-garment like a shirt, worn under the chiton, seems not to have been in use. The expressions μονοχίτων and ἀχίτων only indicate that in the first case the chiton was worn without the himation; in the second, *vice versâ*. The chiton was an oblong piece of cloth arranged round the body so that the arm was put through a hole in the closed side, the two ends of the open side being fastened over the opposite shoulder by means of a button or clasp. On this latter side, therefore, the chiton was completely open, at least as far as the thigh, underneath of which the two ends might be either pinned or stitched together. Round the hips the chiton was fastened with a ribbon or girdle, and the lower part could be shortened as much as required by pulling it through this girdle. A chiton of this kind is worn by a soldier in Fig. 208, taken from a beautiful relief on an Attic urn representing the leave-taking

of an Athenian warrior from his wife and child. This sleeveless
chiton, made of wool, was worn chiefly by the Dorians. The
Athenians adopted it about the time of Perikles, after having
worn previously the longer chiton peculiar to the
Ionians of Asia Minor. Frequently sleeves, either
shorter and covering only the upper arm, or continued to the wrist, were added to the chiton,
which resembled, in consequence (at least, in the
former case), exactly the chemises worn by women
at the present day. The chiton, with sleeves
coming down to the wrist ($\chi\iota\tau\grave{\omega}\nu$ $\chi\epsilon\iota\rho\iota\delta\omega\tau\acute{o}s$), undoubtedly an invention of the luxurious Asiatic
Greeks, is worn, for instance, by Skiron (north-
west wind) and Boreas (north wind), amongst
the portraitures of the eight chief winds on the
octagonal tower of the winds at Athens (see

Fig. 158). The so-called pedagogue amongst

Fig. 208.

the group of the Niobides also wears this chiton ;
but the arms of this statue have been restored. The short-
sleeved chiton is frequently worn by women and children on
monuments. Of the sleeveless chiton, worn by men over both
shoulders, as in Fig. 208 ($\dot{\alpha}\mu\phi\iota\mu\acute{\alpha}\sigma\chi\alpha\lambda o\iota$), it is stated that it was
the sign of a free citizen. Slaves and artisans are said to have
worn a chiton with one hole for
the left arm, the right arm and
half of the chest remaining quite
uncovered. The $\dot{\epsilon}\xi\omega\mu\acute{\iota}s$ was another form of the chiton, worn
on monuments, chiefly by Hephaistos, Daidalos, and workmen,
$\kappa\alpha\tau$ $\dot{\epsilon}\xi o\chi\acute{\eta}\nu$, as also by fishermen
and sailors, whose occupations re-
quired the right arm to be quite

Fig. 209.

unencumbered. A bas-relief (Fig. 209) shows two ship-carpenters
dressed in the exomis, representing, perhaps, master Argos and
an assistant, working at the ship *Argo*, under the supervision of
Athene. Two charming statuettes of fisher-boys at the British
Museum and the Museo Borbonico of Naples (Clarac, "Musée,"
Nos. 881, 882), respectively, also illustrate this picturesque costume.

Identical with this in form is the chiton worn by Doric women. It was simple, short-skirted, and with a slit in the upper part at both sides. It was fastened with clasps over both shoulders, and shortened as far as the knees by means of pulling it through the girdle. In this form it is worn by two maidens in the Louvre, destined for the service of the Lakonian Artemis at Karyæ. They carry kinds of baskets (σαλία) on their heads, and are performing the festive dance in honour of the goddess (Fig. 210). The exomis, as described above, is worn by the female statue in the Vatican known as the "Springing Amazon"

Fig. 210.   Fig. 211.   Fig. 212.

(Müller's "Denkmäler," I. No. 138, *a*), and also by statues of Artemis, and representations of that goddess on gems and coins. The long chiton for women reaching down to the feet, and only a little pulled up at the girdle, we shall see in a vase-painting (§ 57, Fig. 310) representing dancing youths and maidens, the former wearing the short, the latter the long, chiton. A development of the long chiton is the double-chiton. It was a very large, oblong piece of woven cloth, left open on one side, like the Doric chiton for men. It was equal to about one and a half lengths of the body. The overhanging part of the cloth was folded round the chest and back, from the neck downwards, the upper

edge being arranged round the neck, and the two open corners
clasped together on one shoulder. On this open side, therefore,
the naked body was visible (Fig. 211). Over the other shoulder
the upper edge of the chiton was also fastened with a clasp, the
arm being put through the opening left between this clasp and
the corresponding corner of the cloth.

In the same way was arranged the half-open chiton, the open
side of which, from the girdle to the lower hem, was sewed up. A
bronze statuette (Fig. 212) illustrates this way of putting it on.
A young girl is about to join together on her left shoulder the
chiton, which is fastened over the right shoulder by means of an
agraffe. It appears clearly that the whole chiton consists of one
piece. Together with the open and half-open kinds of the chiton,
we also find the closed double-
chiton (χιτὼν ποδήρης) flowing
down to the feet. It was a piece
of cloth considerably longer than
the human body, and closed on both
sides, inside of which the person
putting it on stood as in a cylinder
As in the chiton of the second form,
the overhanging part of the cloth
was turned outward, and the folded
rim pulled up as far as the
shoulders, across which (first on
the right, and after it on the left
side) the front and back parts were
fastened together by means of clasps,
the arms being put through the two
openings effected in this manner.
Round the hips the chiton was
fastened by means of a girdle
(ζώνιον, στρόφιον), through which
the bottom part of the dress trailing

Fig. 213.

along the ground was pulled up just far enough to let the
toes be visible. Above the girdle the chiton was arranged in
shorter or longer picturesque folds (κόλπος). Most likely the
overhanging part of the chiton, which we shall meet with again
as an independent garment, was called by the Greeks διπλοΐς or

διπλοΐδιον. We have illustrated the chiton by two representations from the best period of Greek art. Fig. 213 shows a running female figure, the arms and feet of which have unfortunately been destroyed. The original is ten inches high. She seems to

implore the help of the gods against a ferocious animal, the claws of which have already caught her floating garment.* Chiton and diploïs are arranged most gracefully, and the violent motion of the body has been softened by a certain quiet treatment of the drapery. Fig. 214, on the other hand, shows one of the sublime female forms carrying the roof of the southern portico of the Erechtheion (compare Fig. 38). The attitude of the kanephore is quiet and dignified. Kolpos and diploïs are gracefully arranged in symmetrical folds. In spite of the calm attitude required by the architectural character of the figure, the artist has managed to convey the idea of motion by means of the left leg being slightly bent, and the straight folds of the chiton modified in consequence. The chief alterations of varying fashion applied to the arrangement of the diploïdion, which reached either to the part under the bosom or was prolonged as far as the hips; its front and back parts might either be clasped together across the shoulders, or the two rims might be pulled across the upper arm as far as the elbow, and fastened in several places by means of buttons or agraffes, so that the naked arm became visible in the intervals, by means of which the sleeveless chiton received the appearance of one

Fig. 214.

* On the back part of the garment the paw of a large animal is distinctly visible; for which reason we have adopted the above explanation in preference to that of her being a Bacchante, against which opinion moreover the modest dress and the absence of orgiastic emblems seem to speak.

with sleeves (Fig. 219). Where the diploïdion was detached
from the chiton, it formed a kind of handsome cape; which,
however, in its shape, strictly resembled the diploïdion proper.
This cape was most likely called by the
Greeks ἀμπεχόνιον. Its shape was considerably modified by fashion, taking sometimes
the form of a close-fitting jacket, at others
(when the sides remained open) that of a
kind of shawl, the ends of which sometimes
equalled in length the chiton itself (Fig. 215).
In the latter case, the ampechonion was
naturally at least three times as long as it
was wide. In antique pictures women
sometimes wear a second shorter chiton over
the χιτὼν ποδήρες. A great many varieties
of dress, more distinguishable in the vase-
paintings representing realistic scenes than
in the ideal costumes of sculptural types, we

Fig. 215.

must omit, particularly as, in most cases, they may be reduced to
the described general principles.

42. From the ἐνδύματα we now pass to the ἐπιβλήματα or
περιβλήματα, *i.c.* articles of dress of the nature of cloaks. They
also show throughout an oblong
form, differing in this essentially
from the Roman toga. The
ἱμάτιον, belonging to this class,
was arranged so that the one
corner was thrown over the left
shoulder in front, so as to be
attached to the body by means of
the left arm. On the back the
dress was pulled toward the right
side so as to cover it completely
up to the right shoulder, or, at least,

Fig. 216.   Fig. 217.

to the armpit, in which latter case the right shoulder remained
uncovered. Finally, the himation was again thrown over the left
shoulder, so that the ends fell over the back. Figs. 216 and 217,
taken from vase-paintings, show two male figures completely
enveloped in the himation according to the fashion of the time

($\dot{\epsilon}\nu\tau\dot{o}s$ $\tau\dot{\eta}\nu$ $\chi\epsilon\hat{\iota}\rho\alpha$ $\ddot{\epsilon}\chi\epsilon\iota\nu$). Both men and women wore the himation in a similar manner (see Fig. 218, taken from a terra-cotta at

Athens). The complete covering, even of the face, in this last figure indicates a chastely veiled Athenian lady walking in the street, or, according to Stackelberg, a bride.

A second way of arranging the himation, which left the right arm free, was more picturesque, and is therefore usually found in pictures (see, for instance, Fig. 219). The first-mentioned himation, however, was commonly given by the artist to figures meant to express noble dignity. The truth of these statements will be recognised in looking, for instance, at the statue of the bearded Dionysos in the Vatican enveloped in the himation according to strictest usage. In the beautiful statues of Asklepios at Florence and in the Louvre, the left side and the lower part of the body are covered by the himation, which is also the case in the figure of the enthroned Zeus in the Museo Pio Clementino, where one corner

Fig. 218.

of the garment rests on the left shoulder, and falls in beautiful

folds over the lap of the figure. The arrangement of the himation worn by women was equally graceful, as appears from the pictures, without, however, being subjected to a strict rule, as in the case of men. Perhaps the costume of the maidens carrying hydriai on the frieze of the Parthenon may be considered as the common type. The picturesque arrangement of the himation could undoubtedly be acquired only by long practice. In order to preserve the folds and prevent the dress from slipping from the shoulders, the Greeks used to sew small

Fig. 219.

weights into the corners.

Different from the himation was the much smaller and oblong

τρίβων, or τριβώνιον, worn amongst the Doric tribes by epheboi and grown-up men, while boys up to the twelfth year were restricted to the use of the chiton. At Athens also, the inclination towards the severe Doric customs made this garment common. Up to the time of the Peloponnesian war the dress of the Athenian boy consisted of the chiton only. On attaining the age of the ephebos he was dressed in the χλαμύς, introduced into Attika from Thessaly or Makedonia. The chlamys also was an oblong piece of cloth thrown over the left shoulder, the open ends being fastened across the right shoulder by means of a clasp; the corners hanging down were, as in the himation, kept straight by means of weights sewed into them. The chlamys was principally used by travellers and soldiers. Fig. 220, representing the statue of Phokion in the Museo Pio Clementino, illustrates this handsome garment. Hermes, Kastor, Polydeukes, the wandering Odysseus, soldiers, and horsemen (for instance, the epheboi on horseback on the frieze of the Parthenon) generally wear the chlamys.

Fig. 220.

Concerning the materials of the described garments, we have mentioned before that linen was used principally by the Ionians, wool by the Dorians; the latter material in the course of time became the rule for male garments all over Greece. The change of seasons naturally required a corresponding modification in the thickness of these woollen garments; accordingly we notice the difference between summer and winter dresses. For women's dresses, besides sheep's wool and linen, byssos, most likely a kind of cotton, was commonly used. Something like the byssos, but much finer, was the material of which the celebrated transparent dresses were woven in the isle of Amorgos. They were called ἀμόργινα, and consisted of the fibre of a fine sort of flax, undoubtedly resembling our muslins and cambrics. The introduction of silk into Greece is of later date, while in Asia it was known at a very early period. From the interior of Asia the silk was imported into Greece, partly in its raw state, partly worked into dresses. Ready-made dresses of this kind were

called σηρικά to distinguish them from the βομβύκινα, *i.e.* dresses
made in Greece of the imported raw silk (μέταξα, μάταξα). The
isle of Kos was the first seat of silk manufacture, where silk
dresses were produced rivalling in transparency the above-mentioned ἀμόργινα. These diaphanous dresses, clinging close to the
body, and allowing the colour of the skin and the veins to be
seen (εἵματα διαφανῆ), have been frequently imitated with astonishing skill by Greek sculptors and painters. We only remind the
reader of the beautifully modelled folds of the chiton covering
the upper part of the body of Niobe's youngest daughter, in a
kneeling position, who seeks shelter in the lap of her mother; in
painting, several wall-pictures of Pompeii may be cited.

The antiquated notion of white having been the universal
colour of Greek garments, a coloured dress being considered
immodest, has been refuted by Becker ("Charikles," III. p. 194).
It is, however, likely that, with the cloak-like epiblemata,
white was the usual colour, as is still the case amongst Oriental
nations much exposed to the sun. Brown cloaks are, however,
by no means unusual; neither were they amongst Greek men.
Party-coloured Oriental garments were also used, at least by
the wealthy Greek classes, both for male and female dresses,
while white still remained the favourite colour with modest Greek
women. This is proved, not to mention written evidence, by a
number of small painted statuettes of burnt clay, as also by
several pictures on lekythoi from Attic graves. The original colours
of the dresses, although (particularly the reds) slightly altered
by the burning process, may still be distinctly recognised. In
Fig. 320, from a vase-painting, the female form on the left wears
a chiton of saffron-yellow hue (κροκωτά), perhaps in imitation of
the colour of the byssos, and a violet peplos, the chiton of the
woman on the right being golden brown. Men also appear in
these pictures with the cherry-coloured chlamys and the red
himation; while Charon wears the dark exomis usual amongst
fishermen (see Stackelberg, "Gräber der Hellenen," Tafs. 43-45).
These dresses, both with regard to shape and colour, are undoubtedly taken from models of daily life.

The dresses were frequently adorned with inwoven patterns, or
attached borders and embroideries. From Babylon and Phrygia,
the ancient seats of the weaving and embroidering arts, these

crafts spread over the occidental world, the name "Phrygiones," used in Rome at a later period for artists of this kind, reminding of this origin. As we learn from the monuments, the simplest border, either woven or sewed to the dresses, consisted of one or more dark stripes, either parallel with the seams of the chiton, himation, and ampechonion (see Figs. 215-217, 219, 221), or running down to the hem of the chiton from the girdle at the sides or from the throat in front. The vertical ornaments called ῥάβδοι or παρυφαί correspond to the Roman *clavus.* Besides these ornaments in stripes, we also meet with others broader and more complicated; whether woven into, or sewed on, the dress seems doubtful. They cover the chiton from the hem upwards to the knee, and above the girdle up to the neck, as is seen in the chiton worn by the spring goddess Opora, in a vase-painting ("Collection des Vases gr. de M. Lamberg," Pl. 65). The whole chiton is sometimes covered with star or dice patterns, particularly on vases of the archaic style. The vase-painters of the decaying period chiefly represent Phrygian dresses with gold fringes and sumptuous embroideries of palmetto and "meandering" patterns, such as were worn by the luxurious South-Italian Greeks.

Fig. 221.

Such a sumptuous dress is worn by Medea (Fig. 221) in a picture of the death of Talos on an Apulian amphora in the Jatta collection at Ruvo. In the same picture the chitones of Kastor and Polydeukes, and those of the Argonautai, are covered with palmetto embroideries, the edges at the bottom showing mythological scenes on a dark ground. We also call to mind the rich peploi offered at high festivals to adorn the holy images, and also of the himation, fifteen yards long and richly ornamented, which was offered by the Sybarite Alkimenes to the Lakinian Hera in her temple near Kroton, and afterwards sold to the Carthaginians for 120 talents by the elder Dionysios. Plastic art in its noble simplicity has disdained to imitate these ornaments, which it introduces only in rare cases to adorn certain parts of the dress. The upper garment of a statue of Artemis in the Museo Borbonico, at Naples, shows a border imitating embroidery; and the archaic statue of Pallas in the museum of Dresden wears a peplos, imitated from the celebrated Panathenaïc peplos, covered with scenes from the gigantomachy (see Müller, "Denkmäler der alten Kunst," I. Taf. X., Nos. 36, 38).

43. In the cities Greeks walked mostly bareheaded, owing most likely to the more plentiful hair of southern nations, which, moreover, was cultivated by the Greeks with particular care. Travellers, hunters, and such artificers as were particularly exposed to the sun, used light coverings for their heads. The different forms of these may be classified as κυνῆ and πῖλος. The κυνῆ was a cap made of the skins of dogs, weasels, or cows; its further development was the helmet, to which we shall have to return. In Homer already we read of a peasant with a cap of goat's skin (κυνέη αἰγείη), most likely of the shape of a semi-globe, and fastened under the chin with straps. In a vase-painting in the Berlin Museum, representing the interior of a foundery, the workman poking the fire wears this cap as a protection against the heat (Fig. 222, a). The shape of the πῖλος was conical, either without a shade, like the κυνῆ (see Fig. 208), or with a small brim. It was made of felt. Sailors, merchants, and several gods and demigods may be recognised by it, particularly Charon, Odysseus and his companions, and Hephaistos the artificer; also Kadmos, the Dioskuroi (for instance, on Spartan coins), and the Amazons, in several vase-paintings. Tydeus also wears the pilos in a vase-painting (Fig. 222, b), and the cap worn by a shepherd blowing the double-pipe (Fig. 222, c) may lay claim to the same appellation (compare Fig. 208). It resembles in form the cap worn by South-Italian shepherds at the present day. Nearly related to the pilos is the well-known Phrygian cap, but for the top, which is turned over in front. The latter, now worn by Greek and Italian fishermen, was, in old times, used by the barbarous nations of Asia, which may be

recognised by it. Paris, Ganymede (Fig. 222, *d*), Anchises, Olympos, Atys, Mithras, and the Amazons are frequently represented with it, also barbarous warriors on Roman monuments of the imperial period. An interesting combination of head-coverings, with a flattened pilos amongst them, appears in a large vasepainting (Millin, " Galérie Mythologique," Pl. CXXXV.) representing a battle between Greeks and Amazons with their Scythian allies, perhaps an imitation of the battle of the Amazons represented by Phidias on the shield of Athene Parthenos. Similar to the Phrygian is another cap worn by Amazons and noble Asiatics. It consists of wool or leather, and resembles a helmet. The top is only a little turned down in front, the back part being prolonged by means of a flap (Fig. 222, *e*, compare Fig. 212).

Fig. 222.

It appears in paintings on the heads of Asiatic men and women, sometimes in the quaintest shapes (see Fig. 221). It is generally called μίτρα, although this word seems to imply the covering of the head with a scarf. Such a turban-like covering of the forehead, cheeks, and neck, with only the point of the Asiatic cap protruding from it, is worn, for instance, by the Persians in the Pompeian mosaic called the Battle of Alexander. The Oriental turban is undoubtedly a remnant of this costume. The third form of the hat is the πέτασος, originally worn in Makedonia and Thessaly, and introduced into Greece together with the chlamys worn by epheboi. It resembled our wideawakes, but for the very small headpiece, and was fastened to the head by means of straps, which, at the same time, prevented it from slipping when thrown over the back (Fig. 222, *f*), in the same way that the medieval biretta was worn occasionally. This petasos is worn by the epheboi on horseback on the frieze of the Parthenon (Fig. 222, *h*), and also by Kastor (Fig. 222, *g*) and Hermes in vase-paintings. The latter god may be recognised by a winged petasos peculiar to him (Fig. 222, *i*). What name must be assigned to a hat resembling a plate, which appears on coins of the Thessalian city of Krannon (Mus. Hunter., Tab. 21, No. XVII.), and of the Thrakian city of Ainos (Mus. de Hauteroche, Pl. III., No. 3), remains doubtful; it may be the καυσία worn by the Makedonians.

44. The hair is considered in Homer as one of the greatest signs of male beauty amongst the long-haired (καρηκομόωντες) Achaioi; no less were the well-arranged locks of maidens and women praised by the tragic poets. Amongst the Spartans it became a sacred custom, derived from the laws of Lykurgos, to let the hair of the boy grow as soon as he reached the age of the ephebos, while up to that time it was cut short. This custom prevailed amongst the Spartans up to their being overpowered by the Achaic federation. Altogether the Dorian character did not admit of much attention being paid to the arrangement of the hair. Only on solemn occasions, for instance on the eve of the battle of Thermopylæ, the Spartans arranged their hair with particular care. At Athens, about the time of the Persian wars, men used to wear their hair long, tied on the top of the head in a knot (κρώβυλος), which was fastened by a hair-pin in the form of a cicada. Of this custom, however, the monuments offer no example. Only in the pictures of two Pankratiastai, on a monument dating most likely from Roman times (" Mus. Pio Clement." vol. iv. p. 36), we discover an analogy to this old Attic custom. After the Persian war, when the dress and manners of the Ionians had undergone a change, it became the custom to cut off the long hair of the boys on their attaining the age of epheboi, and devote it as an offering to a god, for instance, to the Delphic Apollo or some local river-god. Attic citizens, however, by no means wore their hair cropped short, like their slaves, but used to let it grow according to their own taste or the common fashion. Only dandies, as, for instance, Alkibiades, let their hair fall down to their shoulders in long locks. Philosophers also

occasionally attempted to revive old customs by wearing their hair long.

The beard was carefully attended to by the Greeks. The barber's shop (κουρεῖον), with its talkative inmate, was not only frequented by those requiring the services of the barber (κουρεύς) in cutting the hair, shaving, cutting the nails and corns, and tearing out small hairs, but it was also, as Plutarch says, a symposion without wine, where political and local news were discussed. Alkiphron depicts a Greek barber in the following words (III. 66): "You see how the d——d barber in yon street has treated me; the talker, who puts up the Brundisian looking-glass, and makes his knives to clash harmoniously. I went to him to be shaved; he received me politely, put me in a high chair, enveloped me in a clean towel, and stroked the razor gently down my cheek, so as to remove the thick hair. But this was a malicious trick of his. He did it partly, not all over the chin; some places he left rough, others he made smooth without my noticing it." After the time of Alexander the Great, a barber's business became lucrative owing to the custom of wearing a full beard (πώγων βαθύς or δασύς) being abandoned, notwithstanding the remonstrances of several states.* In works of art, particularly in portrait statues, the beard is always treated as an individual characteristic. It is mostly arranged in graceful locks, and covers the chin, lips, and cheeks, without a separation being made between whiskers and moustache. Only in archaic renderings the wedge-like beard is combed in long wavy lines, and the whiskers are strictly parted from the moustache. As an example we quote the nobly formed head of Zeus crowned with the stephane in the Talleyrand collection. The usual colour of the hair being dark, fair hair was considered a great beauty. Homer gives yellow locks to Menelaos, Achilles, and Meleagros, and Euripides describes Menelaos and Dionysos as fair-haired (ξανθοῖσι βοστρύχοισιν εὔκοσμος κόμην).

45. The head-dress of women was in simple taste. Hats were not worn, as a rule, because, at least in Athens, the appearance of women in the public street was considered improper, and therefore

* According to tradition, many Makedonians were killed by the Persians taking hold of their long beards, and pulling them to the ground. Alexander, in consequence, had his troops shaved during the battle.

happened only on exceptional occasions. On journeys women wore a light broad-brimmed petasos (see p. 171) as a protection from the sun. With a Thessalian hat (Θεσσαλίς κυνῆ) of this kind Ismene appears in "Œdipus in Kolonos." The head-dress of Athenian ladies at home and in the street consisted, beyond

Fig. 223.

the customary veil, chiefly of different contrivances for holding together their plentiful hair. We mentioned before, that the himation was sometimes pulled over the back of the head like a veil. But at a very early period Greek women wore real shorter

or longer veils, called κρήδεμνον, καλύπτρα, or κάλυμμα, which
covered the face up to the eyes, and fell over the neck and back
in large folds, so as to cover, if necessary, the whole upper part
of the body. The care bestowed on the hair was naturally still
greater amongst women than amongst men. Fig. 223 shows a
number of terra-cotta heads of Athenian women published by
Stackelberg. These, and the numerous heads represented in
sculptures and gems, give an idea of the exquisite taste of these
head-dresses. At the same time, it must be confessed that most
modern fashions, even the ugly ones, have their models, if not in
Greek, at least in Roman antiquity. The combing of the hair
over the back in wavy lines was undoubtedly much in favour.
A simple ribbon tied round the head, in that case, connected the
front with the back hair. This arrangement we meet with in the
maidens of the Parthenon frieze and in a bust of Niobe (Müller,
" Denkmäler," I., Taf. XXXIV., *c*). On older monuments, for
instance, in the group of the Graces on the triangular altar in the
Louvre, the front hair is arranged in small ringlets, while the
back hair partly falls smoothly over the neck, and partly is made
into long curls hanging down to the shoulders. It was also not
unusual to comb back the front hair over the temples and ears,
and tie it, together with the back hair, into a graceful knot
(κόρυμβοι, Fig. 223, *e*, *c*). Here, also, the above-mentioned
ribbon was used. It consisted of a stripe of cloth or leather,
frequently adorned, where it rested on the forehead, with a plaque
of metal formed like a frontal, and called στεφάνη (Fig. 223,
a). This stephane appears on monuments mostly in the hair of
goddesses ; the ribbon belonging to it, in that case, takes the form
of a broad metal circle destined no more to hold together, but to
decorate the hair. This is the case in a bust of Here in the Villa
Ludovisi, in the statue of the same goddess in the Vatican, and
in a statue of Aphrodite found at Capua (Müller, "Denkmäler," II.
Taf. IV., Nos. 54, 56, 268). Besides this another ornamented
tie of cloth or leather was used by the Greeks, broad in the
centre and growing narrower towards both ends. It was called
σφενδόνη, owing to its similarity to the sling. It was either put
with its broader side on the front of the head, the ends, with
ribbons tied to them, being covered by the thick back hair, or *vice
versâ ;* in which latter case the ends were tied on the forehead in

an elaborate knot. The latter form was called ὀπισθοσφενδόνη. The στλεγγίς resembles the sphendone. The net, and after it the kerchief, were developed from the simple ribbon, in the same manner as straps on the feet gradually became boots. The different kinds of nets may collectively be called κεκρύφαλοι. The kekryphalos proper consists of a net-like combination of ribbon and gold thread, thrown over the back hair to prevent it from dropping. The large tetradrachmai of Syrakuse, bearing the signature of the engraver Kimon, show a beautiful head of Arethusa adorned with the kekryphalos. More frequent is the coif-like kekryphalos covering the whole hair, or only the back hair, and tied into a knot at the top (σάκκος) (see Fig. 223, b, i, Fig. 229, and the group of women to the right in Fig. 232). The modifications of the sakkos, and the way of its being tied, are chiefly illustrated by vase-paintings. Related to the sakkos is the μίτρα, at first only a ribbon, but gradually developed into the broad frontlet and the kerchief. The front of the head might, besides these coifs, be adorned with a stephane, as is shown by Fig. 223, i, and by the statue of Elpis in the Museo Pio Clementino (IV., Taf. 8), which shows the sphendone and stephane on the front and back parts of the head respectively. At the present day the Greek women of Thessaly and the isle of Chios wear a head-dress exactly resembling the antique sakkos (see v. Stackelberg, "Trachten und Gebräuche der Neugriechen," Part I., Tafs. XIII., XIX.). The acquaintance of the Greeks with the curling-iron and cosmetic mysteries, such as oil and pomatum, can be proved both by written evidence and pictures (see Fig. 223, b, d). It quite tallied with the æsthetical notions of the Greeks to shorten the forehead by dropping the hair over it, many examples of which, in pictures of both men and women, are preserved to us.

46. Gloves (χειρίδες), worn by the enervated Persians, were not usual amongst the Greeks. At home, nay even in the streets, Greeks often walked with naked feet, and, like modern Orientals, took off their shoes on entering their own or a stranger's house. Homer states how a man on leaving the house ties the splendid soles (πέδιλα) to his feet, which custom was continued for a long time. In a bas-relief representing the visit of Dionysos to Ikarios (Müller, "Denkmäler," II., Taf. L., No. 624), a Panisk bares

the feet of the god previous to his lying down to dinner. We
know a great many varieties of shoes from the monuments, and
we are, on the other hand, told of a number of terms by ancient
writers. But to apply the ones to the others will be in most
cases impossible. Three chief forms may, however, be recognised; which, according to our modern nomenclature, may be
denominated the sole, the shoe, and the boot. Our word sole,
whether fastened to the foot with one simple or with several straps
intertwined, may be rendered by ὑπόδημα. The simple sole
might be fastened by a strap (ζυγός) right across the instep, or
by two straps issuing from its two sides, and tied or buckled
together on the instep (see Fig. 224, 1, representing the foot of
the statue of Elpis, in the Vatican). Whether this arrangement

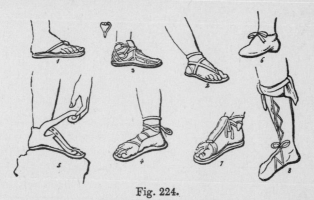

Fig. 224.

is identical with a kind of sandal called βλαύτη must remain
undecided. By the addition to the sole of several intertwined
straps the σάνδαλον is formed, worn originally by women, but
also by men, as is sufficiently proved by the monuments. In
the sandal a strap was sewed on the sole one to two inches from
the tip, and pulled through the big and first toes (sometimes
combined with a second strap between the third and little toes);
to it were added two or four other laces, fastened by twos to
the edges of the sole, and held together by a *fibula* in the form
of a heart on the centre-point of the foot, where the straps
crossed each other. The whole intertwined system of straps
terminated above the ankles. Fig. 224, 2, shows a female
foot with the simple, Fig. 224, 3, the foot of Apollo of Belvidere,

with the compound, sandal. Above the latter the *fibula*, in the form of a heart, is shown separately. Instructive is also the sandal worn by Dirke in the group called the "Farnesian Bull." The net-like entanglement of the straps, together with the leather laces of the compound sandal, gives it the appearance of a broken high shoe, as it appears, for instance, on the coins of the Thessalian city of Larissa, commemorating the one-shoed (μονοσάνδαλος) Jason. The sole itself, being mostly made of several layers of cow's hide, appears very thick in sculptures, making the otherwise graceful sandal look rather heavy.

By the addition of a closed heel, and of larger or smaller side-pieces sewed to the sole of the shoe, our second class was formed, perhaps identical with the ancients' κοῖλα ὑποδήματα. The sides of the shoe were tied with straps to the foot and ankle, leaving the toes and the upper part of the foot uncovered. The different forms of the shoe are illustrated by Fig. 224, 4, 5, 7—No. 5 being taken from the statue in the Vatican of a youth tying his shoe, formerly called Jason, at present Hermes. In No. 7, taken from the statue of Demosthenes in the Vatican, the juncture of the heel and side-pieces is covered by a dropping piece of the lace. The closed shoe, tied across the foot, we find in many statues of both men and women (Fig. 224, 6).

We now have to mention the boots (ἐνδρομίδες)—our third class. They were made of leather or felt, closely attaching to the foot, and reaching up to the calf. They were open in front and tied together with laces. To Diana a light hunting-boot is peculiar, resembling the mocassins of the Indians (Fig. 224, 8). The same kind of boots are worn by the so-called pedagogue amongst the group of the Niobides. A fringe of cloth generally surrounded the upper rim of the boot. We have purposely limited ourselves in our remarks almost entirely to monumental evidence, the explanation of many expressions in ancient writers, as, for instance, of ἐμβάς and κρηπίς, being throughout conjectural.

47. We conclude our remarks about dress with the description of some ornaments the specimens of which in Greek graves and in sculptural imitations are numerous. In Homer the wooers try to gain the favour of Penelope with golden breast-pins, agraffes, earrings, and chains. Hephaistos is, in the same

work, mentioned as the artificer of beautiful rings and hair-pins. The same ornaments we meet with again at a later period as important articles of female dress. Many preserved specimens show the great skill of Greek goldsmiths. Hair-pins, in our sense, and combs for parting and holding up the hair were unknown to the Greeks. The double or simple comb of Greek ladies (κτείς), made of box-wood, ivory, or metal, was used only for combing the hair. The back hair was prevented from dropping by means of long hair-pins, the heads of which frequently consisted of a graceful piece of sculpture (see Fig. 226, *a*, a gold pin found in a grave at Pantikapaion adorned with a hart's head). Well known are the hair-pins adorned with a golden cicada which, in Solon's time, were used by both Athenian men and women for the fastening of the krobylos.

It was the custom of the Greeks to adorn their heads on festive occasions with wreaths and garlands. Thus adorned the bridegroom led home the bride. Flowers full of symbolic meaning were offered on the altars of the gods, and the topers at carousals were crowned with wreaths of myrtle, roses, and violets, the latter being the favourite flower with the Athenians. The flower-market (αἱ μυρρίναι) of Athens was always supplied with garlands to twine round the head and the upper part of the body; for the latter also was adorned with garlands (ὑποθυμίδες, ὑποθυμιάδες). Crowns consisting of other flowers, and leaves of the ivy and silver-poplar, are frequently mentioned. Wreaths also found a place in the serious business of life. They were awarded to the victors in the games; the archon wore a myrtle-wreath as the sign of his dignity, as did also the orator while speaking to the people from the tribune. The crowning with flowers was a high honour to Athenian citizens—awarded, for instance, to Perikles, but refused to Miltiades. The head and bier of the dead were also crowned with fresh wreaths of myrtle and ivy (see Fig. 318—a vase-painting representing the adorning of the dead Archemoros). The luxury of later times changed the wreaths of flowers for golden ones, with regard to the dead of the richer classes. Wreaths made of thin gold have repeatedly been found in graves. The barrows of the old Pantikapaion have yielded several beautiful wreaths of ivy and ears of corn (Ouvaroff, " Antiquités du Bosphore Cimmérien," Pl. IV.) ; a gold imitation of a crown of myrtle has been found in a grave in Ithaka (Stackelberg, " Gräber der Griechen," Taf. 72). Other specimens from Greek and Roman graves are preserved in our museums. A golden crown of Greek workmanship, found at Armento, a village of the Basilicata (at present in Munich), is particularly remarkable (Fig. 225). A twig of oak forms the ground, from amongst the thin golden leaves of which spring forth asters with chalices of blue enamel, convolvulus, narcissus, ivy, roses, and myrtle, gracefully intertwined. On the upper bend of the crown

Fig. 225.

is the image of a winged goddess, from the head of which, amongst pieces of grass, rises the slender stalk of a rose. Four naked male genii and two draped female ones, floating over the flowers, point towards the goddess, who stands on a pedestal bearing this inscription:—

ΚΡΕΙΘΩΝΙΟΣ ΗΘΗΚΗ ΤΟΝ ΕΤΗΦΑΝΟΝ.

Earrings (ἐνώτια, ἐλλόβια, ἑλικτῆρες) were, in Greece, only worn by women; while amongst the Persians, Lydians, and

Babylonians they were common to both sexes. Their form varies
from simple rings to elaborate, tasteful pendants. Fig. 226, *b*,
shows a pendant, found in Ithaka, in the shape of a siren, holding
a double pipe in her hand. Fig. 226, *f*, shows an earring trimmed
with garnets, found in the same place, with the head of a lion
at one end, and that of a snake at the other. Fig. 226, *c*, is an

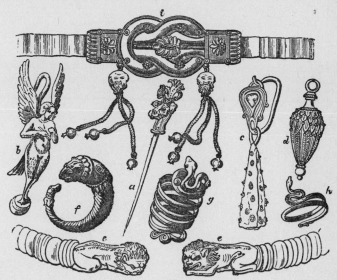

Fig. 226.

ornament, found near Pantikapaion, in the form of two clubs,
hanging on an earring of Syrian garnet. Fig. 226, *d*, shows a
pendant, found in the same neighbourhood, resembling those now
in use. Numerous other illustrations are supplied by vase-
paintings, coins, and gems; while works of sculpture reproduce
ornaments only in rare cases.

Necklaces (περιδέραια, ὅρμοι), bracelets for the upper and
under arm (ψέλια ὄφεις), and rings worn round the leg, above
the ankle (πάδαιχρυσαι περισκελίδες, περισφύρια), are frequently met
with on monuments.* Neck-ornaments either consisted of rings
joined into a chain, or of one single massive ring, spiral in form,
and made of bronze or precious metals, the latter being worn

* A statue of Aphrodite in the Glyptothek of Munich wears a broad ring round
the upper arm.

principally by barbarous nations.*   Fig. 226, *e*, shows a στρεπτὸς
περιαυχένιος of this kind, undoubtedly of Greek workmanship,
with figures of couching lions at each end.   It has been found
in a grave near Pantikapaion.   Armlets and anklets are mostly
of the form of snakes, whence their name ὄφεις.

It was an old custom, and the sign of a freeman, to wear rings
on the fingers, used both as signets and as mere ornaments.   With
the signet (σφραγίς) documents or property were marked.   Solon
made the forging of a seal a capital crime.   About the age of the
use of gems amongst the Greeks little is known : they most
likely belong to a period after Homer, instruments sufficiently
hard to cut them being wanting previously.   The beginnings of
the art of engraving amongst the Assyrians, Egyptians, and
Etruscans are of much earlier date.   The common use of the signet
soon caused the artistic treatment of the gem.   The setting
(σφενδόνη), on the contrary, was most simple, at least in most of
the rings preserved to us.   On the other hand, the *technique* of the
Greeks in cutting and polishing the stone has not been equalled
even by the great skill of the celebrated engravers of the Cinque-
cento and the eighteenth century.

The stones chosen were such as did not resist the drill too
much, and allowed of a smooth line of incision.   A further requisite
consisted in the stone being either of pure colour, or in its facili-
tating the varied representation of whole figures or parts of the
body and dress by means of patches, veins, or layers (*zonæ*) of
various colours.   The stones used most frequently were the
carnelian, sardonyx, chalcedony, agate, onyx, jasper, and
heliotrope, more rarely the nephrite, turquoise, and rock-crystal,
the silvery magnet-ironstone, the amethyst, green quartz, and
precious serpentine.   Of jewels proper only few were used, like
the ruby, genuine sapphire and emerald, the green beryl, the
felspath-opal, and the blueish genuine aquamarine.   Topaz,
hyacinth, Syrian and Indian garnets, and chrysophrase (the latter
being introduced into Greece after the time of Alexander) were
used equally.   The ancients also knew how to imitate jewels in
coloured glass, particularly the emerald in coloured crystal.
These paste copies were, according to Pliny, a most lucrative
article of counterfeiting industry.   They were the result of the

---

* A torque is seen, for instance, round the neck of the dying gladiator.

desire of the middle classes for rich ornaments, and are frequently
found in our museums. The accuracy and finish of the minutest
details justify us in supposing that the ancients knew all the
utensils of the trade, *e.g.* the wheel, the diamond point, diamond
dust, and even magnifying-glasses, which latter are generally
claimed as an invention of modern times. The figures were either
incised into the gem, which in that case was used as a signet,
or they were formed out of the different layers of certain stones
like onyx and sardonyx, in relief. In the former case they are
called gems (ἀνάγλυφα, *gemmæ sculptæ, exsculptæ, intaglio*), in
the latter cameos (ἔκτυπα, *gemmæ cælatæ*). The latter, only
used as ornaments, might, when small, be set in rings; when of
larger dimensions, they were used to adorn agraffes, girdles,
necklaces, and weapons, or they were let into the surfaces of vases
and precious goblets. The finest cameos and gems were made in
Alexander's time, who was not only painted by Apelles and
sculptured by Lysippos, but also had his portrait cut in a jewel
by Pyrgoteles. The passion for gems amongst all classes of both
Greeks and Romans is proved by the great number of them of
more or less good workmanship found in graves. Fig. 226, *g, h,*
shows two elastic gold rings trimmed with garnets, found in a grave
in Ithaka. Their form resembles the above-mentioned opheis.

Fig. 226, *i,* shows an ornamented girdle, also found in a grave
in Ithaka. It is made of gold, and is held together by means of
a gold clasp richly ornamented with hyacinthine stones. On it
hang two Silenus-masks, to each of which are attached three little
gold chains adorned with garnets (compare the girdle of the
marble statue of Euterpe in the Museo Bor-
bonico, XI., Taf. 59).

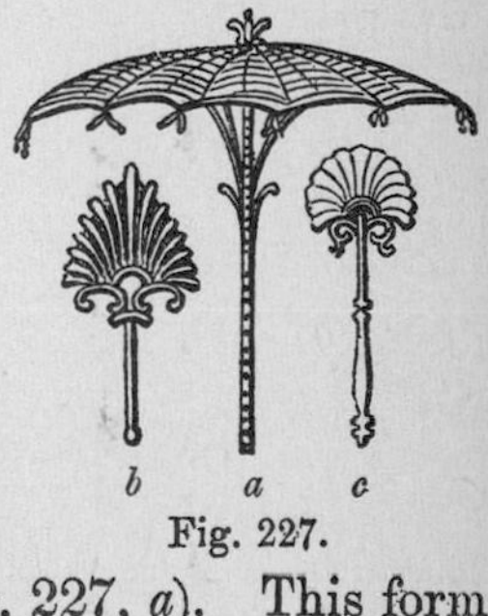

Greek, particularly Athenian, women
carried a sunshade (σκιάδειον), or employed
slaves to hold it over them. In the Panathenaïc
procession even the daughters of metoikoi
had to perform this service (σκιαδηφορεῖν).
Such sunshades, which, like our own, could
be shut by means of wires, we often see

b a c

Fig. 227.

depicted on vases and Etruscan mirrors (Fig. 227, *a*). This form
was undoubtedly the most common one. The cap-like sunshade
painted on a skyphos, which a Silenus, instead of a servant, holds

over a dignified lady walking in front of him, is undoubtedly intended as a parody, perhaps copied from the scene of a comedy (Gerhard, "Trinkschalen," II. 27). In vase-paintings we also see frequently the leaf-like painted fan (σκέπασμα) in the hand of women (Fig. 227, *b c*).

Of the secrets of Greek *toilette* we will only disclose the fact that ladies knew the use of paint. The white they used consisted of white-lead (ψιμύθιον) ; their reds were made either of red minium (μίλτος) or of the root of the ἄγχουσα. This unwholesome fashion of painting was even extended to the eyebrows, for which black colour was used, made either of pulverised antimony (στίμμι, στίμμις) or of fine soot (ἀσβόλη).

The mirrors (ἔνοπτρον, κάτοπτρον) of the Greeks consisted of circular pieces of polished bronze, either without a handle

or with one richly adorned.* Frequently a cover, for the reflecting surface, was added. The Etruscan custom (see § 97) of engraving figures on the back of the mirror or the cover seems to have been rare amongst the Greeks, to judge, at least, from the numerous specimens of mirrors found in Greek graves. Characteristic of these are, on the other hand, the tasteful handles, representing mostly Aphrodite, as in a manner the ideal of a beautifully adorned woman (see Fig. 228). These hand-mirrors frequently occur in vase-paintings, particularly in those containing bathing utensils (see Fig. 231).

Fig. 228.

The carrying of a stick (βακτηρία, or σκῆπτρον) seems to have been a common custom. It is mostly of great length, with a crutched handle ; young Athenian dandies may have used shorter walking-sticks (see Fig. 217). The first-mentioned sticks seem to have been used principally for leaning upon in standing still, as is indicated by frequent representations in pictures. Different from this stick was the σκῆπτρον proper, a staff adorned with a knob or a flower, which, as early as Homer, was the attribute of gods, and of rulers descended from the gods.

---

* Compare the collection of ornamented Etruscan mirror-handles in Gerhard's "Etruskische Spiegel," Pl. XXIV. *et seq.*

In regal families the sceptre was a valued heirloom. The sceptre serving as the emblem of judicial power (ῥάβδος) was a little shorter; it was also used by ambassadors, and a herald had to present it to the orator on his rising to address the council. In sculptures we frequently see the sceptre as the attribute of divinities, for instance, on the triangular altar in the Louvre. Our modern commander's staff is a modification of it.

48. The life of married women, maidens, children while in the care of women, and of female slaves, passed in the gynaikonitis, from which they issued only on rare occasions. The family life of Greek women widely differed from our Christian idea; neither did it resemble the life in an Oriental harem, to which it was far superior. The idea of the family was held up by both law and custom, and although concubinage and the intercourse with hetairai was suffered, nay favoured, by the State, still such impure elements never intruded on domestic relations. Our following remarks refer, of course, only to the better classes, the struggle for existence by the poor being nearly the same in all ages. In the seclusion of the gynaikonitis the maiden grew up in comparative ignorance. The care bestowed on domestic duties and on her dress was the only interest of her monotonous existence. Intellectual intercourse with the other sex was wanting entirely. Even where maidens appeared in public at religious ceremonies, they acted separately from the youths. An intercourse of this kind, at any rate, could not have a lasting influence on their culture. Even marriage did not change this state of things. The maiden only passed from the gynaikonitis of her father into that of her husband. In the latter, however, she was the absolute ruler, the οἰκοδέσποινα of her limited sphere. She did not share the intellectual life of her husband—one of the fundamental conditions of our family life. It is true that the husband watched over her honour with jealousy, assisted by the gynaikonomoi, sometimes even by means of lock and key. It is also true that common custom protected a well-behaved woman against offence; still her position was only that of the mother of the family. Indeed, her duties and achievements were hardly considered, by the husband, in a much higher light than those of a faithful domestic slave. In prehistoric times the position of women seems to have been, upon the whole, a more

dignified one. Still, even then, their duties were essentially limited to the house, as is proved, for instance, by the words in which Telemachos bids his mother mind her spindle and loom, instead of interfering with the debates of men. As the State became more developed, it took up the whole attention of the man, and still more separated him from his wife. Happy marriages, of course, were by no means impossible; still, as a rule, the opinion prevailed of the woman being by nature inferior to the man, and holding the position of a minor with regard to civic rights. This principle has, indeed, been repeatedly pronounced by ancient philosophers and lawgivers. Our remarks hitherto referred chiefly to the Ionic-Attic tribe, renowned for the modesty of its women and maidens. The Doric principle, expressed in the constitution of Sparta, gave, on the contrary, full liberty to maidens to show themselves in public, and to steel their strength by bodily exercise. This liberty, however, was not the result of a philosophic idea of the equality of the two sexes, but was founded on the desire of producing strong children by means of strengthening the body of the female.

The chief occupation of women, beyond the preparing of the meals, consisted in spinning and weaving. In Homer we see the wives of the nobles occupied in this way; and the custom of the women making the necessary articles of dress continued to prevail even when the luxury of later times, together with the degeneracy of the women themselves, had made the establishment of workshops and places of manufacture for this purpose necessary. Antique art has frequently treated these domestic occupations. The Attic divinities, Athene Ergane and Aphrodite Urania, as well as the Argive Here, Ilithyia the protecting goddess of child-bearing, Persephone, and Artemis, all these plastic art represents as goddesses of fate, weaving the thread of life, and, at the same time, protecting female endeavours; in which twofold quality they have the emblem of domestic activity, the distaff, as their attribute. Only few representations of spinning goddesses now remain; but many are the pictures of mortal spinning-maidens painted on vases, chiefly for female use. Fig. 229 is one of them. It shows a woman winding the raw wool from a kalathos round the distaff. For the spinning, a spindle was used, as is still the case in places where the northern spinning-wheel has not supplanted the antique custom. Homer describes noble ladies handling the distaff (ἠλακάτη, *colus*) with the spindle (ἄτρακ- τος, *fusus*) belonging to it. Helen received a present of a golden spindle, with a silver basket to keep the thread in. The distaff, with a bundle of wool or flax fastened to its point, was held under the left arm, while the thumb and first finger of the right hand, slightly wetted, spun the thread, at the end of which hung the spindle, made of metal. The web (κλωστήρ) was, from the spindle, wound round a reel, to be further pre- pared on the loom.

Fig. 229.

Akin to spinning are the arts of weaving (ὑφαντική) and embroidering (ποικιλτική). We frequently see in vase-paintings women with embroidering-frames in their laps. The skill of Greek ladies in embroidery is suffi- ciently proved by the tasteful embroidered patterns and borders on Greek dresses, both of men and women. The vase-paintings supply many examples. Fig. 230, after a vase-painting, shows a woman occupied with embroidering at a frame which she holds on her knees.

We know, from Homer, that next to spinning, weaving was one of the chief female

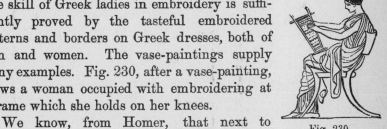

Fig. 230.

occupations. Even at that period the art must have been highly developed, as we conclude from the description of Penelope's work. In historic times the weaving of both male and female articles of dress was the business of women ; in some places we even hear of corporations of women being bound by law to weave the festive garments of certain holy images. The Attic maidens were obliged to weave a peplos for the statue of Athene Parthenos at the return (every four years) of the Panathenaïa. Into this were woven the portraits of men worthy of this high honour (ἄξιοι τοῦ πέπλου). These peploi, therefore, served, as it were, as an illustrated chronicle of Athens. Sixteen matrons were bound to weave a peplos for the statue of Here at Olympia. The same duty devolved on the noble maidens of Argos with regard to a statue of Artemis. Spartan ladies had to renew the chiton of the old statue of the Amiklaïc Apollo every year. Unfortunately, we have no pictures illustrating the weaving process itself. Our information, therefore, is but scanty. Originally weaving was done by means of a frame placed perpendicularly (ὄρθιος ἱστός), over which the long or chain threads (στήμιον, *stamen*) were pulled in parallel lines downwards, the bottom ends being made into bunches, and having weights (ἀγνῦθες) attached to them; the woof (κρόκη, ἐφυφή, *subtemen*) was drawn through them with a needle, in a horizontal direction. The improved horizontal loom, invented by the Egyptians, more resembled that at present in use (see Marquardt's "Handbuch der römischen Alterthümer," V., 2,

Fig. 231.

p. 130 *et seq.*). Ovid's description (Metam. VI., 53 *et seq.*) ought to be read in connection with it.

The pretty vase-painting, Fig. 231, refers to this branch of female occupation. Two maidens, in richly embroidered dresses, are occupied in folding a garment with a star-pattern embroidered on it, perhaps part of the dowry of a third maiden, standing to the right of them. Other garments are either hung up on the wall (together with the inevitable hand-mirror) or lie piled up on a chair between the two girls. The large press on the left most likely also contains garments. In case we wish to give mythologic significance to the picture, we may take it as an illustration of Nausikaa bidding two servants to prepare the garments that are to be taken to the washing-place (compare the picture of Nausikaa and two servants drying garments in Panofka's "Bilder antiken Lebens," Pl. XVIII., 5).

Our remarks about female duties in preparing the meal must be short. The heavy parts of the duty, like grinding the corn in hand-mills, were performed by servants. In the palace of Odysseus twelve female slaves were employed all day in grinding wheat and barley in an equal number of hand-mills, to supply the numerous guests. The hand-mill ($\mu\acute{\nu}\lambda\eta$, $\chi\epsilon\iota\rho o\mu\acute{\nu}\lambda\eta$) consisted (like those still used in some Greek islands) of two stones, each about two feet in diameter, the upper one of which was made to rotate by means of a crooked handle, so as to crush the corn poured through an opening in it (compare the Roman hand-mills found at Pompeii, § 101). Baking and roasting meat on the spit were amongst the duties of female slaves. In every house of even moderate wealth, several of these were kept as cooks, chambermaids, and companions of the ladies on their walks, it being deemed improper for them to leave the house unaccompanied by several slaves. How far ladies took immediate part in the preparing of dainty dishes we cannot say. In later times it became customary to buy or hire male slaves as cooks.

Antique representations of women bathing, adorning themselves, playing, and dancing are numerous. The Athenian maiden, unlike her Spartan sister, did not think it proper to publicly exhibit her bodily skill and beauty in a short chiton, but taking a bath seems to have been amongst her every-day habits, as is shown by the numerous bathing scenes on vases. In one of them, a slave pours the contents of a hydria over her nude mistress. Cowering on the floor in another we see an undressed woman catching in her hand the water-spout issuing from a mask of Pan in the wall into a bath. An alabastron and comb are lying on the floor (see Panofka "Bilder antiken Lebens," Pl. XVIII., 10, 11). A picture on an amphora in the museum of Berlin offers a most interesting view of the interior of a Greek bath-chamber. We see a bathing establishment built in the Doric style. By a row of columns the inner space is divided into two bath-chambers, each for two women. The water is most likely carried by pressure to the tops of the hollow columns, the communication amongst which is effected by means of pipes about six feet from the ground. The openings of the taps are

formed into neatly modelled heads of boars, lions, and panthers,
from the mouths of which a fine rain spray is thrown on the
bathers. Their hair has been tightly arranged into plaits. The
above-mentioned pipes were evidently used for hanging up the
towels; perhaps they were even filled with hot water to warm the
bathing linen. Whether our picture represents a public or
private bath seems doubtful. The dressing after the bath has
also been frequently depicted. We need not enter upon the
subject here, having mentioned the chief utensils, as the comb,
ointment-bottle, mirror, &c., on a former occasion. The scenes
thus depicted are undoubtedly borrowed from daily life, although
Aphrodite, with her attendance of Cupids and Graces, has taken
the place of mortal women. For music, games, and dances, we
refer to §§ 52 *et seq.* Here we mention only a game at ball, which
was played in a dancing measure, and therefore considered as a
practice of graceful movements. Homer mentions Nausikaa as a
skilled player of this game. It is remarkable that wherever
women playing at ball appear in pictures they are represented
in a sitting posture.

The swing (αἰώρα) was essentially a female amusement. In
commemoration of the fate of Erigone, daughter of Ikarios, a
festival had been ordained at Athens at which the maidens
indulged in the joys of the swing. Illustrations of this pastime
occur frequently on vases, free from any mythological symbolism,
even in cases where Eros is made to move the swing (see Panofka,
"Griechinnen und Griechen nach Antiken," p. 6, and the same
author's "Bilder antiken Lebens," Pl. XVIII., 2).

49. We now come to the point in the maiden's life when she
is to preside over her own household as the legitimate mate
of her husband (γαμετή, in Homer κουριδίη ἄλοχος). In
most cases a Greek marriage was a matter of convenience, a
man considering it his duty to provide for the legitimate continuation of his family (παιδοποιεῖσθαι γνησίως). The Doric tribe
does not attempt to disguise this principle in its plain-spoken
laws; the rest of Greece acknowledged it but in silence, owing
to a more refined conception of the moral significance of marriage.
The seclusion of female life, indeed, made the question of personal
charms appear of secondary importance. Equality of birth and
wealth were the chief considerations. The choice of the Athenian

citizen (ἀστός) was limited to Athenian maidens (ἀστή); only in that case were the children entitled to full birthright (γνήσιοι), the issue of a marriage of an Athenian man or maiden with a stranger (ξένη or ξένος) being considered illegitimate (νόθοι) by the law. Such a marriage was, indeed, nothing but a form of concubinage. The laws referring to this point were, however, frequently evaded. At the solemn betrothal (ἐγγύησις), always preceding the actual marriage, the dowry of the bride (προίξ, φερνή) was settled; her position as a married woman greatly depended upon its value. Frequently the daughter of poor, deserving citizens were presented with a dowry by the State or by a number of citizens. In Homer's time the bridegroom wooed the bride with rich gifts; Iphidamas, for instance, offers a hundred heifers and a thousand goats as a nuptial present. But afterwards this was entirely reversed, the father of the bride having to provide the dowry, consisting partly in cash, partly in clothes, jewellery, and slaves. In case of separation the dowry had, in most cases, to be returned to the wife's parents. The most appropriate age for contracting a marriage, Plato in his Republic fixes, for girls, at twenty, for men, at thirty. There was, however, no rule to this effect. Parents were naturally anxious to dispose of their daughters as early as possible, without taking objection to the advanced years of the wooer, as is tersely pointed out by Aristophanes (Lysist., 591 *et seq.*).

The actual marriage ceremony, or leading home, was preceded by offerings to Zeus Teleios, Hera Teleia, Artemis Eukleia, and other deities protecting marriage (θεοὶ γαμήλιοι). The bridal bath (λουτρὸν νυμφικόν) was the second ceremony, which both bride and bridegroom had to go through previous to their union. In Athens the water for this bath was, since the earliest times, taken from the well Kallirrhoë, called after its enclosure by Peisistratos, Enneakrunos. Whether a boy or a girl acted as water-carrier on this occasion (λουτροφόρος) is differently stated by ancient authors. The latter supposition is supported, amongst other things, by an archaic picture on a hydria (Gerhard, "Auserlesene griechische Vasenbilder," III., 306). To the left of the spectator lies, as the inscription indicates, the holy fountain Kallirrhoë, flowing from the head of a lion under a Doric super-structure. A girl, holding in her hand branches of laurel and myrtle, as used at lustrations, looks musingly down on the hydria which is filling with the bridal water. Five other maidens occupy the remaining space of the picture. Some of them, with empty pitchers on their heads, seem to wait for their turn ; others are about to go home with their filled pitchers. Gerhard's opinion of their forming a sacred procession is contradicted by the evidence of ancient writers. As most weddings took place in the month of marriage (γαμήλιον), the meeting of several bridal water-carriers was, in a populous city like Athens, anything but unlikely ; and a scene of this kind is evidently the subject of our picture.

On the wedding-day, towards dark, after the meal at her parental home (θοίνη γαμική) was over,* the bride left the festively adorned house, and was conducted by the bridegroom in a chariot (ἐφ' ἁμάξης) to his dwelling. She sat between the bridegroom and the best man (παράνυμφος, πάροχος) chosen from amongst his relatives or intimate friends. Accompanied by the sounds of the hymenæos, and the festive sounds of flutes and friendly acclamations from all passers-by, the procession moved slowly towards the bridegroom's house, also adorned with wreaths of foliage. The mother of the bride walked behind the chariot, with the wedding torches, kindled at the parental hearth, according to custom immemorial. At the door of the bridegroom his mother was awaiting the young couple with burning torches in her hand. In case no wedding meal had been served at the bride's house, the company now sat down to it. To prognosticate the desired fertility of the union, cakes of sesame (πέμματα) were distributed. The same symbolic meaning attached to the quince, which, according to Solon's law, the bride had to eat. After the meal the couple retired to the thalamos, where for the first time the bride unveiled herself to her husband. Before the door of the bridal chamber epithalamia were sung, a charming specimen of which we possess in the bridal hymn of Helena by Theokritos. On the two first days after the wedding (ἐπαύλια and ἀπαύλια) wedding-presents were received by the pair. Not till after these days did the bride appear without her veil.

Antique art has frequently illustrated the various customs of the marriage feast. A series of archaic vase-paintings (Gerhard,

* At this meal, contrary to the usual custom, women were present.

"Auserlesene griechische Vasenbilder," III. Pl. 310 *et seq.*) show *bigæ* and *quadrigæ* containing the bridegroom with the veiled bride, followed by the paranymphos, and surrounded by female relatives and friends, who carry the dowry in baskets on their heads. Hermes, the divine companion and herald, precedes the procession, looking back on it. Another vase-painting (Panofka, " Bilder antiken Lebens," Pl. XI. 3) shows the crowned bridegroom on foot leading the veiled bride to his house, at the entrance of which stands the nympheutria with burning torches waiting for the procession. A youth preceding the couple accompanies the hymenaios on a kithara ; the bride's mother, recognisable by her matron-like dress, with a torch in her hand, closes the procession. The most remarkable of all wedding scenes is the glorious wall - painting known as the " Aldobrandini Wedding " (Fig. 232). It is 4 feet high by $8\frac{1}{2}$ long. It represents three dif-

Fig. 232.

ferent scenes painted on one surface, without regard to perspective, as is frequently the case in antique bas-reliefs. The straight line of the wall in the background is broken by two pillars, by means of which the artist undoubtedly intended to open a view into two different parts of the gynaikonitis, while the third scene is meant to take place in front of the house. The picture illustrates three different scenes of the marriage ceremony such as might take place inside or in front of the bride's house before the starting of the bridal procession. From this point of view we must first consider the centre picture. In a chamber of the gynaikonitis we see the bride* chastely veiled and reclining on a beautiful couch. Peitho, the goddess of persuasion, sits by her side, as appears from the crown on her head, and from the many-folded peplos falling over her back. She pleads the bride-groom's cause, and seems to encourage the timorous maiden. A third female figure to the left of the group, leaning on a piece of column, seems to expect the girl's surrender, for she is pouring ointment from an alabastron into a vase made of shell, so as to have it ready for use after the bridal bath. Her peplos, only held by the shoulder-clasp, leaves the upper part of her body almost uncovered. Most likely she represents the second handmaiden of Aphrodite, Charis, who, according to the myth, bathed and anointed her mistress with ambrosial oil in the holy grove at Paphos. The pillar at the back of Charis indicates the partition-wall between this chamber and the one next to it on the left, to which we now must turn. We here see a large basin filled with water, standing on a columnar base. The water is perhaps that of the well Kallirrhoë, fetched by the young girl stand-ing close by for the λουτρὸν νυμφικόν. The girl seems to look inquiringly at a matronly figure approaching the basin on the other side, and putting her finger into the water as if to examine it. Her sublime form and priestly dress, together with the leaf-shaped instrument in her hand (probably the instrument used at lustrations), seem to betray her as Here Teleia, the pro-tecting goddess of marriage, in the act of examining and blessing the bridal bath. The meaning of the third figure in the background holding a large tablet is difficult to explain. Bötticher (" Die aldobrandinische Hochzeit," p. 106) believes that on the tablet is

* Compare the statuette, Fig. 218.

written the horoscope of the impending marriage. The third
scene, to the right of the spectator, is placed at the entrance of
the bride's house. The bridegroom, crowned with vine-branches,
is sitting on the threshold, as if listening impatiently for the close
of the ceremony inside the house. In front of him we see a group
of three girls, one of whom seems to be offering at a portable
altar, while the two others begin the hymenæos to the accompaniment of the kithara.

Very different from the social position of chaste women was
that of the hetairai. We are not speaking of the lowest class of
unfortunates, worshipping Aphrodite Pandemos, but of those
women who, owing to their beauty and grace of conversation,
exerted great influence even over superior men. We only remind
the reader of Aspasia. In the graces of society the hetairai were
naturally superior to respectable women, owing to their free
intercourse with men. For the hetairai did not shun the light of
day, and were not restrained by the law. Only the house of the
married man was closed to them.

50. Before passing from private to public life, we must cast
a glance at the early education of the child by the mother. We
begin with the earliest days of infancy. After the first bath the
new-born child was put into swaddling-clothes (σπάργανα), a
custom not permitted by the rougher habits of Sparta. On the
fifth or seventh day the infant had to go through the ceremony of
purification ; the midwife, holding him in her arms, walked several
times round the burning altar. The day was called in consequence δρομιάμφιον ἦμαρ, the ceremony itself, ἀμφιδρόμια (the run
round). A festive meal on this day was given to the family, the
doors being decorated with an olive-crown for a boy, with wool for
a girl. On the tenth day after its birth, when the child was
named, another feast (δεκάτη) took place. This ceremony implied
the acknowledgment, on the part of the father, of the child's
legitimacy. The name of the child was chosen by both parents,
generally after the name of either of the grandparents, sometimes,
also, after the name or attributes of a deity, under whose particular
protection the child was thus placed. A sacrifice, offered chiefly
to the goddess of child-bearing, Here Ilithyia, and a meal,
concluded the ceremony. At the latter, friends and relatives
presented the infant with toys of metal or clay, while the mother

received painted vases. The antique cradle consisted of a flat swing of basket-work (λίκνον), such as appears in a terra-cotta relief in the British Museum, of the infant Bacchus being carried by a satyr brandishing a thyrsus, and a torch-bearing bacchante. Another kind of cradle, in the form of a shoe, is shown (Fig. 238) containing the infant Hermes, recognisable by his petasos. It also is made of basket-work. The advantage of this cradle consists in its having handles, and, therefore, being easily portable.

It also might be suspended on ropes, and rocked without difficulty. Other cradles, similar to our modern ones, belong to a later period. The singing of lullabies (βαυκαλήματα, καταβαυκαλήσεις), and the rocking of children to sleep, were common amongst the ancients. Wet-nurses (τίτθη) were com-

Fig. 233.

monly employed amongst Ionian tribes; wealthy Athenians chose Spartan nurses in preference, as being generally strong and healthy. After the child had been weaned it was fed by the dry nurse (ἡ τροφός) and the mother with pap, made chiefly of honey.

The rattle (πλαταγή), said to be invented by Archytas, was the first toy of the infant. Other toys of various kinds were partly bought, partly made by the children themselves on growing older. We mention painted clay puppets (κόραι, κοροπλόθοι, κοροπλάσται), representing human beings or animals, such as tortoises, hares, ducks, and mother apes with their offspring. Small stones were put inside, so as to produce a rattling noise; which circumstance, together with the fact of small figures of this kind being frequently found on children's graves, proves their being toys. Small wooden carts (see Panofka, "Bilder antiken Lebens," Pl. I., 3), houses and ships made of leather, and many other toys, made by the children themselves, might be instanced. Up to their sixth year boys and girls were brought up together under their mother's care; from that point their education became separate. The education proper of the boy (παιδεια) became a more public one, while the girl was brought up by the mother at home, in a most simple way, according to our notions. From amongst the domestic slaves a trustworthy companion (παιδαγωγός) was chosen for the boy. He was, however, not a tutor in our sense, but rather a faithful servant, who had to take care of the boy in his walks, particularly on his way to and from school. He also had to instruct his pupil in certain rules of good behaviour (εὐκοσμία). The boy had, for instance, to walk in the street with his head bent, as a sign of modesty, and to make room for his elders meeting him. In the presence of the latter he had to preserve a respectful silence. Proper behaviour at table, a graceful way of wearing his garments, &c., might be mentioned as kindred subjects of education. Boys were accompanied by pedagogues up to their sixteenth year. The latter appear frequently in vase-paintings, and are easily recognisable by their dress, consisting of chiton and cloak, with high-laced boots; they also carry sticks with crooked handles, and their hair and beards give them a venerable aspect; while their pupils, according to Athenian custom, are clad more lightly and gracefully. The pedagogue of the group of the Niobides is well known.

Education was, at Athens, a matter of private enterprise. Schools were kept by private teachers, the government supervision extending only to the moral not to the scientific qualification of the schoolmaster. Grammar (γράμματα), music (μουσική), and gymnastics (γυμναστική), to which Aristotle adds drawing (γραφική), as a means of æsthetic cultivation, were the common subjects of education at schools and gymnasia. The expression γράμματα comprised reading, writing, and arithmetic. The method of teaching how to write consisted in the master's forming the letters, which the pupils had to imitate on their tablets, sometimes with the master's assistance. The writing materials were small tablets covered with wax (πίνακες, πινάκια, δέλτοι), into which the letters were scratched by means of a pencil (στύλος, γραφεῖον) made of metal or ivory. It was pointed at one end, and flattened or bent at the other (Fig. 234, *a*) so as to extinguish the writing, if required, and, at the same time, to smooth the surface again for other letters. The burnisher Fig. 234, *b*, the broad side of which is about equal in width to a tablet, most likely served to smooth the wax cover of a whole tablet at once. By means of joining several tablets together, in the manner of a book, the so-called πολύπτυχοι δέλτοι were formed (Fig. 234, *c*). Waxed tablets were used also for letters, note-books, and other requirements of daily life. A young girl in a charming Pompeian wall-painting ("Museo Borbonico," vol. vi., Pl. 35) has in her hand a double tablet (δέλτιον δίπτυχον), while with her other hand she holds a pencil to her chin, as if pondering over a letter. Her nurse looking over her shoulder tries to decipher the contents of the love-letter. Besides these tablets, Herodotos mentions the use of paper (βίβλος) made of the bark of the Egyptian papyrus-plant. The stalk (three or

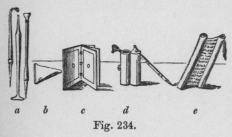

a   b   c   d   e

Fig. 234.

four feet in length) was cut longitudinally, after which the outer bark was first taken off; the remaining layers of bark, about twenty in number (*philuræ*), were carefully severed with a pin; and, afterwards, the single stripes plaited crosswise; by means of pressing and perforating the whole with lime-water, the necessary consistency of the material was obtained. The lower layers of bark yielded the best writing-paper, while the outer layers were made into packing-paper (*emporetica*); the uppermost bark was used for making ropes. Names of different kinds of paper, such as *charta Ægyptiaca, Niliaca, Saitica, Taneotica*, were derived from different manufacturing places in Egypt, which, down to late Roman times, remained the chief market for paper; other names, like *charta regia* (βασιλική), *Augusta, Liviana, Fanniana, Claudia, Cornelia*, were invented after emperors and empresses. Of at least equal antiquity with the use of papyrus was that of hides (διφθέραι) for writing materials. The Ionians used, according to Herodotos, the hides of goats and sheep for this purpose from time immemorial; but the more careful preparation of the material was invented not before the reign of Eumenes II. (197-159 B.C.) at Pergamum, whence the name περγαμήνη—anglicè, parchment. The leaves of the papyrus had writing only on one side, those of parchment on both. The latter were rolled on sticks (Fig. 234, *e*), kept in cylindrical cases, a small piece of parchment (σίλλυβος), with the title written on it, being fastened to the upper end of each roll (compare § 102) for convenience sake. A case of this kind full of parchment-rolls (κύλινδροι), with a cover to it, stands by the side of Klio in a wall-painting of Herculaneum (Fig. 235). In her left hand the muse holds a half-opened roll on which are inscribed the words ΚΛΕΙΩ ΙCΤΟΡΙΑΝ (Klio teaches history). The ink (τὸ μέλαν) was made of a black colouring-substance; it was kept in an inkstand made of metal, with a cover to it (μελανδόχον or πύξις). As is proved by Fig. 234, *d*, it could be fastened to the girdle by means of a ring. Double inkstands, frequently seen on monuments, were most likely destined for the keeping of black and red inks, the latter of which was frequently used. To write on paper or parchment, the ancients used the Memphic, Gnidic, or Anaitic reeds (κάλαμος, *calamus, harundo, fistula*, Fig. 234, *d*), pointed and split like our pens. As

Fig. 235.

we mentioned before, it was the custom of adults to write either reclining on the kline, with the leaf resting on the bent leg, or sitting in a low arm-chair, in which case the writing apparatus was supported by the knee of the writer. The latter posture is exemplified by a reading ephebos in a vase-painting (Panofka, "Bilder antiken Lebens," Pl. I. Fig. 11); it was, undoubtedly, also that of the boys sitting on the rising steps used as forms (βάθρα) at the schools. After his elementary education was completed, the boy was made acquainted with the works of national poetry, particularly with the poems of Homer, the learning by heart and reciting of which inspired him with patriotic pride.

51. Musical instruction formed the second part of general education (ἐγκύκλιος παιδεία). Technical virtuosity was a secondary consideration, the ethic influence of the art being the guiding principle. The playing of one instrument, generally a stringed one, was an important subject of education. At games and meals, or in the throng of battle, the exhilarating and inspiring influence of music was felt. Into the intricacies of Greek harmony, as developed amongst different tribes, we cannot enter here, no more than into the relations of music to the sister-arts of poetry and the dance; or into the monodic and choral divisions of vocal music (μέλος). We must restrict ourselves to instrumentation proper, collectively called κροῦσις, so far as it may be illustrated by the remaining specimens of antique instruments. It ought to be remembered that the music of stringed instruments only was called κιθαριστική, or ψιλή κιθάρισις,

κιθαρῳδική being the term for vocal music accompanied by strings. In the same way αὐλητική or ψιλὴ αὔλησις signified music of wind instruments ; αὐλῳδική the combination of these instruments with the human voice. We shall mention first the stringed instruments, after them the wind-instruments, and conclude with the clanging instruments, chiefly used for orgiastic music.

a. The Greeks used no bows in playing on stringed instruments. The strings were placed all at equal distance over the sounding-board ; a low, straight bridge (ὑκολύριον, μάγας, or μαγάδιον) only served to prevent the vibrating strings from touching the sounding-board. The strings were fastened at one end to the so-called "yoke" (ζυγόν or ζύγωμα) by means of pegs (κόλλοπες, or κόλλαβοι) ; at the other they were attached to the inside, or outside, of the sounding-box. The use of the bow was thus made impossible, by the want of a curved bridge (as it exists in our stringed instruments), by means of which the relative height of the position of the single strings is modified. The stringed instruments of the ancients were played with the fingers, or with the straight or curved plectrum (πλῆκτρον), made of wood, ivory, or metal. Sometimes also both fingers and plectrum were employed severally or simultaneously. Both the shape and the use of the plectrum are illustrated by Fig. 237, *c, e, g.* It was held in the right hand, and fastened to a long ribbon (Fig. 237, *g*). Large-stringed instruments, played with both hands, or with the plectrum and the fingers of the left hand simultaneously (see Fig. 237, *c, e*), were held in a convenient position by means of a strap slung over the shoulder ; other instruments, played only with the plectrum or the fingers of the right hand, might rest on the left arm, without being tied to it.* This strap, fastened by means of rings to either surface of the sounding-board, appears most distinctly on the statue of Apollo in the Museo Pio Clementino. The god wears the costume of a kithara-player, accompanying his own song on the instrument (see Müller, "Denkmäler," Part I., No. 141, *a ;* compare a statue of Apollo in the same collection, *ibid.*, Part II., No. 132). In vase-paintings these straps have been generally omitted ; but their necessity may be easily conjectured from the position of

* In this sense the words ἐπωλένιον κιθαρίζων in the hymn on Hermes verses 432 and 510) must be understood.

the instrument, which seems to float in the air. The numerous
specimens in pictures, and the varied terms in authors, make
it here again next to impossible to explain the *nuances* of
nomenclature, the more so as the statements of the authors
are frequently very brief, and the representations of the artists
(particularly with regard to the number of strings) inaccurate.
The last-mentioned feature can, for this same reason, be no
criterion in classifying the different instruments : the construction
of the sounding-board, as illustrated by the monuments, must
be our only principle of division. Most likely the artists
rendered essentially the forms of the real instruments, although
the whole conception of Greek art forbade a slavish imitation of
details. The rich ornamentation of some stringed instruments,
as proved by the vase-paintings, is quite in accordance with the
general taste of the Greeks.

Three fundamental types of stringed instruments must be
distinguished—viz. the lyre, the kithara, and the harp. They
are exemplified by an in-
teresting vase-painting in
the old Pinakothek of
Munich (No. 805), the
centre group of which consists of the three Muses,
Polymnia, Kalliope, and
Erato, playing respectively
on the three mentioned
instruments—the lyra, the
kithara, and the trigonon
(Fig. 236). The inven-
tion of the lyre (λύρα) is

Fig. 236.

ascribed, by the myth, to Hermes, who first drew strings
across the oval hollow of a tortoise-shell, which in this way
became the sounding-box of the instrument. This primitive
form is still in use amongst some of the South Sea populations; in Greece it was only known traditionally. The remaining
evidence, both literary and artistic, refers only to the developed
form of the lyre. In this not only the back-shell of the tortoise,
but also the part covering the animal's chest, was used, the whole
forming a closed sounding-box, the natural openings for the

front legs of which were used for the insertion of the roots of the curved horns of a goat. Near their points these were joined together by a transverse piece of wood, called the yoke. Across this frame the strings were drawn, being more than twice as long as those of the mythical lyre. On the chest part of the shell (for only this flat part could be used for the purpose) was placed a bridge, across which the strings were drawn, being at one end tied in knots and fastened to the sounding-board, at the other, either simply wound round the yoke, or fastened to pegs. Figs. 237, *a, b, c, d, e,* illustrate a number of lyres, of which *c* shows most distinctly the entire tortoiseshell. The arms (πήχεις) are, in *c, d, e,* made of goats' horns, which, as we shall see in speaking of weapons, were also used for bows; in *a* and *b* they consist of wood. In *e* the construction of the sounding-

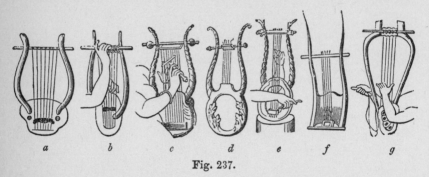

Fig. 237.

board is somewhat difficult to understand, showing as it does a large round opening in the centre. Equally difficult is the classification of the instrument in Fig. 237, *f.* Fig. 237, *g,* shows an instrument nearly related to the lyre. From the sounding-box, consisting of a small tortoiseshell, two wooden arms issue in divergent directions; towards their upper ends they approach each other, and are joined together by a yoke. In vase-painting this instrument appears generally in the hands of either Alkaios or Sappho, from which circumstance archæologists have (not without good reason) conjectured it to be the barbiton (βάρβιτον, βαρύμιτον), a low-toned instrument, which Terpander is said to have introduced from Lydia into Greece. The πηκτίς and μαγάδις, both of Lydian origin, may also have been of the nature of lyres. Both expressions are applied by Greek authors pro-

miscuously to one and the same, and to different instruments.
In Greece Sappho is said to have played on a pektis; in Sicily it
seems, at a later period, to have been used at mysteries. The
magadis is said to have been one of the most perfect instruments. It comprised two full octaves, the left hand playing the
same notes as the right, an octave lower. Still more perfect
was the ἐπιγόνειον, the name being derived from that of its
inventor, Epigonos. It had forty strings, most likely in double
rows—twice as many as the magadion. Neither of the two
instruments was played with a plectrum. They cannot be with
certainty recognised in the pictures; but the large lyre with
fifteen strings, standing before a sitting agonethis, in a marble-
relief on a grave at Krissa (see Stackelberg, "Gräber der
Griechen," Pl. II.), doubtlessly belongs to the same species.

The second class of stringed instruments, differing from the

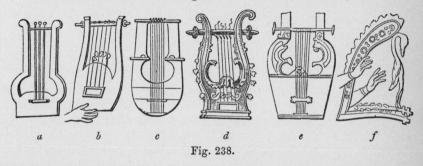

Fig. 238.

lyre both in shape and material, is called kithara (κιθάρα); it
was invented by Apollo, and therefore belonged to the kitharodes
κατ᾽ ἐξοχήν. The sounding-box here consists of thin plates
of wood, ivory, or metal; it is generally angular, in other cases
semi-oval in shape, and is continued, in order to increase its
resounding power, by two arms, also hollow, and at their base equal
in thickness to the sounding-box itself. The size of the latter,
as well as the length of the arms, and their distance from each
other, depended on the greater or smaller number of strings, also
on the desired stronger or weaker resonance, not to speak of
the individual taste of the maker (λυροποιός), which, moreover,
could show itself in the rich ornamentation of this particular
kind of instrument. The sounding-board may have been equal
in power to that of our guitars. Fig. 238, *a, b, c, d, e,* show a few

of the numerous variations of the kithara. Some of them (particularly *c*) resemble perfectly the guitar (*cither*) used in South Germany at the present day. Their forms are pleasing, that of *d* (most likely an imitation of the ornamental kithara, made of ivory or metal) magnificent. The distinction between lyre and kithara, founded on the different constructions of their sounding-boards, is not mentioned by ancient writers. The existence of *a* distinction between these two species, however, may be proved by written evidence, and is, moreover, confirmed by the vase-painting in Fig. 236, where the three muses represent the three chief classes of stringed instruments. The more complicated construction of the kithara, compared with the primitive tortoise and goat's horns of the lyre, seems to prove its later invention. The lyre was most likely of Thrakian origin ; Orpheus, Musaios, and Thamyris were there celebrated as masters on it, and thence it was most likely, together with the orgiastic worship of Dionysos, introduced into Greece. Its connection with that particular phase of religion is sufficiently proved by the monuments. In Greece the musical education of the youth began with the lyre ; together with the flute, it was the instrument most commonly used, for instance, at festive meals. The kithara, on the contrary, introduced from Asia into Greece by the Ionians, was used at musical competitions, sacrifices, and pageants, as is proved, for instance, by the Panathenaïc procession on the frieze of the Parthenon. The players always appeared on such occasions in the costume of the kitharodes, *i.e.* crowned and clad in long flowing robes. The phorminx seems not to have differed essentially from the kithara. Homer, at least, uses the expressions φόρμιγγι κιθαρίζειν and κίθαρις φορμίζειν as meaning the same thing. The explanation by Hesychius of phorminx, as a kithara carried on a ribbon over the shoulder (φόρμιγξ. ἡ τοῖς ὤμοις φερομένη κίθαρις), is most inappropriate, seeing that a difference, if it existed at all, must have appeared in the construction of the sounding-board, or the number of strings ; while, on the other hand, the strap is common to all the forms of the kithara.

As the third form of stringed instruments we mention an instrument resembling our harp, called by archæologists trigonon (τρίγωνον). It was of triangular shape, as indicated by the name, and of Syrian or Phrygian origin. We are therefore justified in applying to the harp-like instruments (Figs. 236 and 238, *f*), both taken from vase-paintings, the name of trigonon, or, perhaps, that of σαμβύκη, an instrument defined by Suidas as εἶδος κιθάρας τριγώνου. As in our harp, the sounding-board was on the side turned towards the player ; in the trigonon, however, the broader side is turned upwards, differing in this from the modern instrument. To the sounding-board the strings were fastened by means of studs ; the side of the instrument resting on the player's lap, took the place of the yoke. The strings, therefore, ran parallel to the third side or arm of the instrument. From Fig. 238, *f*, compared with similar representations, it would appear as if the yoke had been a double one, with double rows of strings drawn across it, as was the case in the above-mentioned epigoneion. The third side of the trigonon consisted either of a simple stick, connecting yoke and sounding-board, or it was shaped like an animal (Fig. 238, *f*). In Fig. 236 it is wanting entirely, and the trigonon, in consequence, resembles the harps, of different sizes, found frequently on Egyptian monuments.* An instrument with two wooden arms and ten strings, appearing in a wall-painting of Herculaneum ("Pitture d'Ercol." Tav. I., Pl. 171), belongs undoubtedly to the same class ; analogous forms of this instrument have also been found on Egyptian monuments (Wilkinson, " A Popular Account of the Ancient Egyptians," vol. i., p. 119), and, indeed, are still in use amongst certain tribes of the valley of the Upper Nile. The names of other instruments we must omit, as not sufficiently explained by monumental evidence. We only mention a four-stringed instrument, with a sounding-board in the form of a semi-globe, to which a long and narrow neck is attached just as in the modern guitar. It appears in a marble-relief of late Roman origin in the Louvre, held by a muse (Clarac, "Musée," II., Pl. 119). Instruments of this kind do not appear on Egyptian monuments.

b. The wind-instruments (αὐλοί) may be divided into pipes (σύριγγες), clarionets (αὐλοί proper), and trumpets (σάλπιγγες). The oldest and simplest form of wind-instrument is the reed-pipe (σύριγξ). The sound was produced by blowing either into the

---

* Amongst the "Swanes," a tribe of the Caucasus, a harp called *Tschungi*, resembling the trigonon, is still in use. See Radde, "Berichte über biolog.-geograph.," " Untersuchungen in den Kaukasusländern," I. (Tiflis, 1868), where a picture of the instrument may be seen.

orifice of a broken reed, or, as in the fife (*Querflöte*), into a hole made to the side of the reed. The sound of the wind in the reeds led most likely to the invention of the syrinx, which is ascribed to Pan. According to the myth, Syrinx, the daughter of the Arkadian river-god Ladon, pursued by Pan, was changed into a reed, which the god thereupon cut into several pieces, joining together seven of them, decreasing in size, by means of wax. The result received the name of syrinx, or Pan's pipe. The number of reeds varied from seven to nine, as is proved both by the statements of ancient

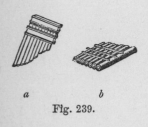

authors and by the monuments. Fig. 239, *b*, shows the simpler syrinx, taken from a wall-painting at Herculaneum; the pipes are seven in number, and seemingly of equal length. Fig. 239, *a*, taken from a candelabrum in the Louvre, shows nine pipes of different sizes. The syrinx, together with other

a   *b*

Fig. 239.

wind-instruments and the lyre, appears most frequently in the hands of Sileni and satyrs in scenes from the Bacchic myth —for instance, on a gem in the Florence gallery (Fig. 240), which shows two Sileni with a syrinx, an aulos, and a lyre. In practical music the syrinx seems to have been used little, although it appears occasionally, together with other instruments,

in pictures representing concerted music. An Etruscan bas-relief (Micali, "L'Italia avanti il dominio dei Rom.," Atlas, Tav. 107) shows three girls playing severally on a syrinx, a flute, and a kithara ; and in another Etruscan representation (Müller, "Denkmäler," Part II., No. 757) the sirens use it to allure Odysseus. Nearest akin to the syrinx is the πλαγίαυλος (fife), said to be invented by the Libyans. It was not a favourite instrument with the Greeks, and is rarely found on monuments. Fig. 241, *m*,

Fig. 240.

shows a youth playing on it, after a bas-relief in the Louvre (compare the statue of a young satyr in Müller's "Denkmäler," Part II., No. 460). Generally both the instruments in Fig. 241, *g* and *h*, are also called plagiauloi ; whether rightly or wrongly we will not venture to decide.

The αὐλός proper resembles our hautboy or clarinet, differing, however, from the latter in the fact of its lower notes being more important than the higher ones. The aulos consisted of two connected tubes and a mouthpiece, to the latter of which belonged two so-called tongues (γλῶσσαι), in order to increase the trembling motion of the air. The myth connected with the invention of the aulos illustrates, at the same time, the mutual position of wind and stringed instruments amongst the Greeks. Athene played for the first time on an aulos, made from the bone of a hart, at a feast of the gods. Here and Aphrodite rallied her on account of her blown-up cheeks, and the goddess, after having ascertained the truth of these objections by looking at her image, while playing, in the fountain on Mount Ida, threw down the instrument in disgust. It was found by Marsyas, the Phrygian Silenos, who, on the strength of it, dared to compete with Apollo, the inventor of the lyre, the Muses being appointed as umpires. The victory of the god symbolized that of stringed over wind instruments. It took a long while before the playing on the pipe was fully received in Greece; and although in Athens it formed part of the musical education, it never was there appreciated as much as in Bœotia, whose inhabitants were celebrated for this art. Perhaps the particularly fine reeds growing in the marshy plains of Orchomenos tend to explain this phenomenon.

The materials of the aulos were, besides reeds, the wood of box or laurel, the bones of the hart, and ivory; metals were chiefly used in it for ornamental purposes. At first the aulos had only three or four holes (τρήματα, τρυπήματα, παρατρυπήματα), but Diodoros of Thebes added to the number. The addition of side holes, with keys to them, completed the aulos. It was blown by means of a removable mouthpiece; which, if not used, was kept in a case (γλωσσοκομεῖον). The βόμβυξ (reed) itself was mostly straight; sometimes it was bent upwards near the opening, which was wider or narrower according to the strength of tone required. The simplest and oldest form of the aulos is seen Fig. 241, *b* and *n;* it resembles a short shepherd's pipe (*schalmei*), and the figures holding it in both cases are taken from the statues of shepherds. The form of the mouthpiece appears distinctly in Fig. 241, *a, d, e, f.* The clarinet (μόναυλος, μονοκάλαμος) with one tube only is seen also on the frieze of the

Parthenon; but still more common was the double clarinet, called by the Romans *tibiæ geminæ*. It consisted of two tubes blown simultaneously by means of one common or two separate mouthpieces (Fig. 241, *a, d, e, f, i, k, l*), and comprises as many notes as the syrinx. The tube held in the right hand, and blown with the right side of the mouth, had three holes, and was called by the Romans *tibia dextra*, by the Greeks the "male" clarinet (αὐλὸς ἀνδρήϊος); the left tube had four holes, and was called *tibia sinistra*, or "female" aulos (αὐλὸς γυναικήϊος). The former produced the lower, the latter the upper notes.* The tubes are

Fig. 241.

either both of the same length and shape (used to accompany revels and gymnastic exercises, Fig. 241, *a, d, f, k, l*), or of unequal length but equal shape (αὐλοὶ γαμήλιοι); or, finally, differing totally both in shape and length (Fig. 241, *e, i*). The pipes might be with (Fig. 241, *d*) or without keys (Fig. 241, *a, f, k, l*). The first-mentioned instrument (*d*) appears on a sarcophagus in the Vatican, in the hands of a genius displaying the

* Double shepherd's pipes, called "dutka," are still used by peasants in certain parts of Russia.

attributes of Euterpe. Sometimes the lower opening was shaped like a bell (κώδων) (Fig. 241, c d), as in our clarinets. The Phrygian double-pipe (ἔλυμοι αὐλοί), with one tube straight and the other bent downwards like a horn, shows the largest extension of the tube-opening. Fig. 241, i, shows a female figure playing the Phrygian double-pipe, taken from a sarcophagus in the Vatican ; the two Phrygian pipes, put crosswise (e), are taken from one side of a square altar in the Vatican, and appear in exactly the same form in a relief representing an Archigallus surrounded by the attributes of his dignity (Müller, "Denkmäler," Part II., No. 817). The difference in shape between the two mouthpieces is remarkable. Other varieties appear frequently (see, for instance, "Museo Borbon.," vol. ix., Tav. 37 ; and Fig. 247, b, representing a dancing bacchante, from a marble relief). Both Greek and Roman players occasionally tied a leather bandage round their lips and cheeks (φορβειά, στόμις, χειλώτηρ), through the hole of which, bound with metal, the mouthpieces of the double clarinet were put (Fig. 241, l). The purpose of this bandage was to soften the tone by preventing violent breathing. It was used particularly at theatrical representations, sacrifices, and pomps, to play long pieces on the large double clarinets ; while the female players in representations of symposia always appear without it. It was never used with single clarinets. The bagpipe is of antique invention. Fig. 242, taken from a bronze statuette, shows a bagpipe-player (ἀσκαύλης, *utricularius*). His instrument resembles those used by modern *pifferari*. Its squeaking notes naturally appealed only to the taste of the lower classes.

The σάλπιγξ (trumpet) consists of a tube considerably increasing in circumference towards the lower opening, and a mouthpiece in the shape of a drinking-vessel. The long trumpet, unknown to the Greeks in Homer's time, is said to have been introduced by the Pelasgic Tyrrhenians ; the Hellenic salpinx was undoubtedly identical with it. The far-sounding salpinx was a warlike instrument, no less than the pipe and kithara, used as such chiefly by the Spartans and Cretans ; it also accompanied religious ceremonies. By the sound of an Argive salpinx Agyrtes rouses the warlike spirit of Achilles, hidden amongst the women of Deïdameia in the isle of Skyros (Fig. 243, taken from a marble

relief'), while Diomedes and Odysseus display shining weapons to
the young hero. Of other trumpets and horn-like instruments
ascribed by Greek authors to Oriental nations, but not to the
Greeks themselves, we mention the Egyptian χνοῦς, used to call
the people to the sacrifice; it resembled the curved salpinx
(σάλπιγξ στρογγύλη), the *cornu* of the Romans (Fig. 245). We
further name the trumpet called the Galatian, bronze, or shrill
(ὀξύφωνος) salpinx, with a leaden mouthpiece and a kodon in the
shape of an animal's mouth; by the Galatian Celts it was called
κάρνυξ. The Paphlagonian trumpet was low-toned (βαρύφωνος),
and larger than the Greek salpinx; from its kodon, bearing the
shape of a bull's head, it was called βόϊνος. The Medes used
a hollow-sounding salpinx, made of a bulrush, with a wide kodon.

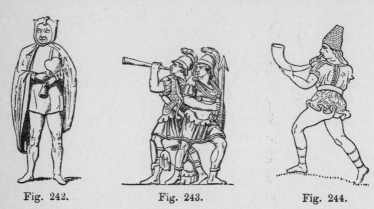

Fig. 242.   Fig. 243.   Fig. 244.

This Median trumpet seems to be depicted in two vase-paintings;
in one of them (Micali, "L'Italia avanti il dominio dei Romani,"
Atlas, Tav. 100) we see an Asiatic archer, in a Median or
Parthian dress, blowing on a very thin, long tube, with a
screwed-on mouthpiece, which he has fastened to his mouth by
means of a bandage in the manner of an aulos-player; the other
(Gerhard, "Griechische Vasenbilder," Part II., Pl. 103) shows the
same instrument in the hands of the Amazon Antiope clad in
Greek armour. It appears from the position of both these figures
that this instrument was turned towards the ground on being
played, differing in this from the Greek trumpet. We finally
mention the Tyrrhenian bronze trumpet, the kodon of which was
bent upwards (κώδων κεκλασμένος); it was also called the curved

or Etruscan lituus (λίτνον), and resembled, in its shape, the Phrygian pipe (compare Fig. 241, *i*); it was used as a signal-trumpet in battles, and at games and ceremonies. Horns (κέρατα), as warlike instruments, seem to have been unknown to the Greeks. Barbarian nations frequently used them for that purpose. Fig. 244 shows a player on the horn (κεραταύλης) whose *pileus* of black lamb's wool betrays him as an Armenian or Persian. In the vase-painting in which he occurs, he seems to encourage Asiatic warriors fighting with Greeks, while the latter are called to battle by the sounds of Hellenic trumpets.

To conclude, we mention the water-organ (ὕδραυλος, ὑδραυλίς, *organon hydraulicum*), invented by Ktesibios the mechanician, and described by his pupil, Hero of Alexandria. It was constructed on the syrinx principle, and contained seven pipes made partly of bronze, partly of reed. The sound was produced by waving the air-columns through the means of water. It was played, *organo modulari*, on a keyboard. Ktesibios' invention was afterwards considerably improved. Nero took a particular interest in it, and during his reign hydraulic organs of a new construction

Fig. 245.

were built (*organa hydraulica novi et ignoti generis*). Fig. 245 shows an organ taken from a Roman mosaic floor at Nennig. A man is playing on the horn to the sound of the organ.

c. We now come to the "clanging instruments" used chiefly at religious ceremonies connected with the worship of Dionysos and Kybele—castanets, the cymbal, and the tambourine. They were also used as a rhythmical accompaniment of social dances, played by the spectators, or the dancers themselves, as is still the custom amongst

Fig. 246.

peasants in the south of Europe. The castanets (κρόταλοι) said to be invented by the Sicilians, consisted, like our modern ones, of small pieces of reed, wood, or metal, or of shells, tied together with a ribbon. They were struck against each other by the fingers at rhythmical intervals. The three pairs of castanets seen in Fig. 246 appear in the hands of dancing-women in wall-paintings and on vases. Their manipulation requires no other explanation.

The cymbals (κύμβαλα) consisted, like those of our military bands, of two metal bowls in the form of semi-globes (Fig. 247, *a*).

a   *b*

Fig. 247.

They were held in the hollow of the hand or by means of straps (see "Museo Borbonico," vol. xv., Tav. 47). They were used at the above-mentioned religious ceremonies, and were also hung upon the branches of holy trees (compare Fig. 1). Still more noisy was the tambourine (τύμπανον), a broad ring of wood or metal with a covering of hide. Bells and pieces of brass were added to increase the noise (Fig. 248). In vase-paintings the tympanon appears with a sounding-bottom in the form of a semi-globe, which makes it resemble our kettle-drum. To conclude, we mention the *sistrum* (σεῖστρον, Fig. 249), not used by the Greeks, but introduced to the Romans as part of the secret worship of Isis.

Fig. 248.   Fig. 249.

It consisted of a sounding-box resembling that of the lyre, made of brass or precious metals, into which were inserted loosely small bars of metal, bent down at the end so as to prevent their sliding out. By means of a handle the instrument was shaken, whereat the vibrating motion of the bars produced a not inharmonious sound.

52. It was a distinguishing feature of the Greeks amongst ancient nations to consider corporeal exercise as a no less important factor of education than mental progress itself. The harmonious development of the body, and, indeed, of every single limb, was thought to be of the utmost importance for the attainment of self-conscious determination in the practical demands of life. This principle of acting, through means of the body, on the mind, was realised in the gymnastic and agonistic institutions of Greece.

Lucian, in his "Apology of Gymnastics," insists upon the ethic bearing of athletic exercise on the mind of young men in directing their ambition into the right channel, in preventing them from laziness and its accompanying vices, and in endowing them with that combination of good qualities which is collectively called καλοκαγαθία. The physical as well as the intellectual (for instance, musical) education varied greatly amongst the different tribes of Greece. Amongst the Doric tribes, chiefly in Sparta, it consisted principally in hardening the body of the young citizen-warrior against the influence of pain and exertion ; amongst Ionian tribes, and chiefly at Athens, the harmonious development of body and soul, *i.e.* grace and ease of bearing and demeanour (εὐρυθμία and εὐαρμοστία), were the objects chiefly aimed at.

The beginnings of gymnastic and agonistic exercises, although lacking at first the systematic development of later times, date back to prehistoric ages. Games were held at an early period in honour of gods and heroes ; and the laws of Solon and Lykurgos only served to regulate and further develop the skill thus acquired.

To our previous remarks (§ 25) we must add a few words as to the important question of the separation of the gymnasion from the palæstra. The separation of the two localities, destined as they were for different branches of athletic exercise, seems established beyond doubt, notwithstanding the utterances of ancient writers frequently contradicting each other. Herodotos, for instance, calls both the dromos and the palæstra γυμνάσια, while Vitruvius uses palæstra for gymnasion and palæstra collectively. At one time the palæstra was undoubtedly a building by itself, connected with, or detached from, the gymnasion. At the time of the emperors, but not before, this distinction seems to have disappeared ; hence the mixing up of the two terms by Vitruvius. At Athens the gymnasia were public institutions, supported by private or public means, at which epheboi and men spent a part of their day in athletic exercise and in instructive and social intercourse. There were the Lykeion, the Kynosarges, the Academy, the Ptolemaion, the splendid gymnasion of Hadrianus, and the small gymnasion of Hermes. The number of palæstrai at Athens was still greater. They were all private institutes kept by single pædotribai, and destined for the athletic education of boys only.

In smaller cities, the joint practice of youths and grown-up men
in the same locality was frequently inevitable. But it is erroneous
to suppose that the palæstra was exclusively the resort of
athletai. The separation of youths and men from boys was
desirable both for moral and educational reasons. For the
difficulties of the task increased in proportion to the age of the
aspirant. Classifications according to age and abilities are
contained in the expressions παῖδες νεώτεροι and πρεσβύτεροι, or
πρώτη and δευτέρα ἡλικία—the former applying to younger, the
latter to older boys. A more advanced stage was the τρίτη
ἡλικία, denoting the transition from the age of the boy to that of
the ephebos; another name for these youths was ἀγένειοι. Similar
distinctions existed undoubtedly amongst the epheboi of different
ages. These distinctions were especially marked in Sparta, where
each age had its particular amount of sufferings and exertions
to go through.

Before entering upon the single exercises we must try to
define the three general appellations, γυμναστική, ἀγωνιστική, and
ἀθλητική. The first term comprises all kinds of regulated
bodily exercise for the purpose of strengthening the body or
single limbs. The expressions ἀνταγωνιστής and ἀγών apply to
those games on which the emulation of several persons was brought
to bear. The ἀγωνιστική comprises the gymnastic exercises
tending to prepare the athletai for the wrestling-matches, which
formed an important feature of national festivities, particularly of
the games of Olympia, celebrated once every five years, at the time
of the first full moon after the summer solstice. Here assembled,
invited by the peace-messengers of Zeus, the delegates of empires
and cities; not to speak of crowds of enthusiastic spectators from
the most distant shores. The flower of Greek youth came to test
their skill in the noble competition for the crown of Zeus. Only
he whose unstained character and pure Hellenic descent had been
certified by the Hellanodikai was allowed to approach the silver
urn which contained the lots. A previous training of at least ten
months at a Greek gymnasion was further required for obtaining
the permission of taking part in the holy contest. Supreme were
the honours conferred on the victor. The umpires crowned him
with the fresh olive-wreath and the palm in the temple of Zeus;
poets like Pindar sang his praise; inscriptions and statues of brass
announced his fame to coming generations.

The ethic purpose of gymnastic art came to be more and more neglected when artificiality and affectation began to prevail. It was then that the noble art deteriorated into a mechanical profession ; the *ἀθλητική* is the later signification of that term.

To the fine arts the palæstra and gymnasion yielded an inexhaustible supply of beautiful models both for youthful grace and manly strength. The national pride of the Greeks further encouraged the artist in the choice of athletic subjects ; hence the innumerable plastic monuments in the native cities of the victors, and on the sites of their triumphs. Pausanias, who wrote after the wholesale spoliation and destruction of Olympia by the Roman conquerors, mentions no less than 230 bronze statues of Olympian victors adorning her streets and squares as the remnants of past glories. We possess only few specimens of this branch of Greek art, but their excellence and technical finish demonstrate the reciprocity between the feeling of the nation and its artistic expression. Scenes from the palæstra and gymnasion frequently occur in vase-paintings. There we see older or younger men clad in himatia, leaning on crooks, and looking down on the wrestlers, or directing their movements by means of peculiarly forked staffs (Gerhard, "Auserlesene griechische Vasenbilder," Taf. CCLXXI.), the destination of which, however, seems somewhat doubtful. These men are the gymnastai and pædotribai ; the former having to superintend the general development and deportment of the body, the latter directing the single exercises. These were the real teachers in gymnastics, and their place was amongst the wrestlers. Amongst other officials we mention the sophronistai, who were responsible for the good behaviour (*σωφροσύνη*) of the boys. Their number at Athens was ten, one being selected by each phyle. During the imperial times we meet with a kosmetes, with one anti-kosmetes and two hypo-kosmetai as assistants, who had to watch the epheboi at the gymnasia. The gymnasiarchos was the superintendent of the whole gymnasion, an honorary and, moreover, expensive post. He had to pay the expenses of the torch-races, and also for the oil used at the games, which afterwards was supplied by the State. He also had to arrange memorial processions in honour of great men.

It may be assumed that the simplest bodily exercises, viz. those that required no weapons or antagonists, were also the oldest. The most primitive of these was the foot-race (δρόμος), which always came first amongst the contests at the great Hellenic festivals. At the Olympic games, indeed, the foot-race continued for a long period the sole athletic exercise; and the Pythian, Nemean, and Isthmian games, which were modelled after them, always began with the foot-race whenever the pentathlon was enacted in its entirety. The foot-race consisted of the simple race (στάδιον or δρόμος), in which the racecourse had to be run over once from beginning to end. The race of the boys, however, comprised but half the racecourse, and those of the ageneioi of two-thirds. This race of the boys was incorporated with the Olympic games in the 37th Olympiad, and the names of the youthful victors are invariably first quoted in old inscriptions. But in those states in which the *physique* of the female sex was likewise trained and developed, the foot-race was regarded as the most suitable of gymnastic exercises for maidens, the length of their course being shorter by one-sixth than that reserved for men. In the second species of race, the diaulos (δίαυλος), the competitors had to run twice over the whole length of the racecourse. The goal had to be doubled in a curve (καμπή), whence the name κάμπειος δρόμος. But the greatest exertion of strength and endurance had to be displayed in the third species of races, the long-run (δόλιχος), in which, without stopping, the course had to be measured so often that the whole distance, according to various reports, consisted of 12, 20, or 24 stadia, that is, more than half a geographical mile, if we accept the highest computation.

We can understand, therefore, that the Spartan Ladas, when crowned conqueror in the foot-race, after having, for twelve successive times, run backwards and forwards over the course, should have dropped down dead on reaching the goal. Strength of limb and breath were, according to Lucian, the necessary requisites in running this race; while the greatest possible speed, on the other hand, was required by those who took part in the shorter course. The race in complete armour (ὁπλίτης δρόμος) also belonged to these exercises. At first this was executed by young men fully equipped with helmet, shield, and greaves; but at a later period their armour for this race was reduced to the simple shield. This armed race was undoubtedly of the greatest importance as a preparation for active service; and

Plato, with a view to this military object, demanded its being practised both in the long and short running-matches. For the Greeks, like the French, were wont to attack the ranks of the enemy at a running pace. This is said to have been the case at the battle of Marathon. At foot-races, as in all other exercises, the combatants used to appear quite naked, except in earlier times, when they girded their loins with a cloth. The runners who presented themselves at the agon as candidates were ranged in divisions (τάξεις) (each consisting, as may be seen from monuments, of four agonistai) and led to the starting-point, where it was decided by lot in which order the different divisions were to follow each other. Any kinds of tricks, bribery, or force, employed by racers to gain an advance upon the others, were strictly prohibited. After the various divisions had run their race, the victors of each had again to compete with each other; and only in the last race was it settled to whom the prize or garland should be awarded. Races of this description, run by four men or epheboi, are often represented on Panathenaïc vases. The runners here appear perfectly naked, and their lifted arms look as though they were to increase the swiftness of their legs.*

The torch-race (λαμπαδηδρομία) may also be regarded as belonging to this species of athletic sports. It was held at night in honour of various gods and goddesses in different parts of Greece. The principal object at these night races was to reach the goal with one's torch alight. Two epheboi, armed with round shields, and flourishing torches in their hands, are thus depicted on a vase (Gerhard, "Antike Vasenbilder," Cent. I. 4, Taf. 63). On two other vessels (Tischbein, "Vas. d'Hamilton," Taf. III., Pl. 48, and II. 25) Nike presents the crown, in sign of victory, to one of three youthful torch-bearers competing for the prize. Other races were connected with festivals of a religious character, such as the Oschophoria at Athens, where runners, clad in female garments, bore vines covered with grapes from the temple of Dionysos to that of Athene Skiras in the Demos Phaleros. These and others, however, do not properly come under the category of races.

Leaping (ἅλμα) ranked next in the series of gymnastic exercises. Homer already introduces practised leapers in his

* "Mus. Gregorianum," II., Tav. 42. "Monum. in edit. d. Inst. di Corrisp. archeol." I. Tav. 22. Gerhard, "Antike Bildwerke," Cent. I., Taf. 6, etc.

description of the games of the Phaiakai, and the same exercises
were afterwards introduced amongst the gymnic agones; they, as
well as the foot-race, formed a part of those sports to be presently
described as the pentathlon. The leaps upwards, forwards, and
downwards appear to have been practised at the palæstra and the
gymnasia, in a similar manner as in our modern gymnasiums.
But it is doubtful whether the Greeks were acquainted with the
long pole now habitually used in gymnastics; the poles depicted
on many vases held in the hands of leaping epheboi having rather
the appearance of spears than poles. But if we consider that the
Greeks regarded gymnastics as a preparation for military service,
and that the spear was often employed in war to leap over ditches,
we may safely assume that poles were also used for gymnastic
purposes. This surmise is further strengthened by the Amazon

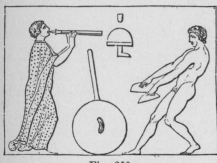

Fig. 250.

on a gem (Müller's " Denkmäler," I., Taf. XXXI., No.
138, *b*), who, grasping such
an instrument in her hands,
prepares for the leap. Written and monumental evidence
proves, on the other hand,
that the Greeks, in order to
secure accuracy of motion for
the distant leap, made use of
so-called ἁλτῆρες. The form
of this instrument, not unlike that of our own dumb-bells, though
rarely mentioned by ancient authors, appears in numerous pictorial
representations. On a vase where an ephebos is just preparing for
the leap, a pair of these instruments is depicted (Fig. 250). They
were either pieces of metal of semi-oval form, in the curved lines of
which orifices were left for the hands, or they consisted of short
iron bars having knobs at each end, thus resembling our dumb-bells
in shape; this latter kind was that in use at the pentathlon. The
mode of using these dumb-bells was probably as follows. The
person about to leap, whether first stepping back a few paces or not,
stretched his arms, laden with the dumb-bells, back in a straight
line; and then, in the very act of leaping, swung them forwards
again with a sudden motion (Fig. 250). But as this violent
motion of the arms necessarily imparted an oblique and receding

position to the body, in coming down the person would necessarily
have fallen on his back had not the equilibrium been restored by
a rapid backward motion of the arms. It has, in fact, recently been
proved by practical experiments that a person in the act of
leaping is capable of taking a much wider leap by the aid of
dumb-bells : still, even acknowledging the greater practice of the
Greeks, it remains inexplicable how Phayllos could, by aid of
these dumb-bells, have leaped to a distance of fifty-five feet,
considering that the most practised gymnasts of our time only
succeed in leaping one-third of that distance. As is the case in
our gymnasiums, the ancients marked, by a line dug in the
ground, or a board, the spot whence the leap had to be taken
(βατήρ). Such a board, of a very lofty height, whence a palæs-
trites takes the *salto mortale,* is depicted in a wall-painting in an
Etruscan burial-chamber (Micali, " L'Italia avanti il dominio dei
Romani," Atlas, Tav. 70), where, in fact, the most varied exercises
of the palæstra are most graphically represented. The goal which
had to be attained in leaping was marked either by a furrow dug
in the earth (σκάμμα), or the distance to which each of the
competitors leaped was marked by an incision in the ground.
This drawing of furrows is probably indicated by those agonistic
representations on vases, of men with hoes (Gerhard, "Auserlesene
griechische Vasenbilder," Taf. CCLXXI.). Others, again, depicted
in these paintings, carry long red ribbons in their hands, probably
pieces of tape, by which the length of the leaps as well as other
kinds of athletic exercises were determined. Although the use of
the dumb-bells as weights to be held in leaping has not been
introduced into modern gymnastics, its strengthening the muscles
of the arms, neck, and chest has, nevertheless, been as fully
recognised as it was by the ancients.

Wrestling (πάλη) was the third species of athletic exercise.
The custom of preparing for this exercise by anointing the body
(ἔλαιον) seems to have been introduced in post-Homeric times.
It contributed to the suppleness and elasticity of the limbs, and
was soon not only used in wrestling but in all other kinds of
athletic exercises. But in order to obviate the too great facility of
extricating the limbs from the embrace of an antagonist, the
wrestlers used to sprinkle their bodies with sand. Besides, as
Lucian says, this double covering of the skin prevents a too

copious perspiration by closing the pores, which, owing to the violent exercise, are open, and thus more exposed to the bad effects of draughts; it also strengthens the powers of endurance generally. The duty of anointing the limbs devolved on the ἀλείπτης. At the end of the combat the body, of course, was thoroughly cleansed; and the ancients for that purpose used an instrument of the nature of a scraper, which they called στλεγγίς (*strigilis*). Both sexes were also in the habit of employing the same scraper after every bath for the cleansing of their limbs. This instrument, hollowed out in the shape of a spoon, and consisting of metal, bone, or reed, was provided with a handle, and we naturally find an instrument so constantly used in daily life depicted in various paintings (Gerhard, " Auserlesene griechische Vasenbilder," Tafs. CCLXXVII.

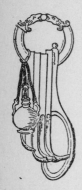

CCLXXXI. "Mus. Gregor.," vol. ii., Tav. 87), the subjects of which are taken from the palæstra or from domestic life. As a rule, it appears together with a vessel of a globular shape, in which the oil was kept. Fig. 251 may assist the reader in forming a correct idea of a complete apparatus of this sort, consisting of an oil-flask suspended by cords, of scrapers of various lengths, and of a flat dish; the original is at the Museo Borbonico. The manner of using this instrument is exemplified in a particularly vivid manner by the beautiful statue of an athlete scraping himself, in the Museo Chiaramonti, Fig. 252, generally known under the name of Ἀποξυόμενος. In no other kind of contest was a professional training as necessary as in the wrestling-matches. Not only rude strength was required, but also firmness of eye in finding out an antagonist's weak points. No less useful were certain dexterous thrusts learned at the wrestling-schools, and quickness in out-witting an antagonist by feigned turns and positions, all of which had, at the same time, to be executed in a pleasing and decorous manner. Certain rules were enforced at the wrestling-school which the combatants were not allowed to transgress. They do not, it is true, harmonize with our more humane ideas; for, although the beating of an opponent was then, as now, forbidden, not so were pushing (ὠθισμός), and spraining his fingers and toes,

Fig. 251.

nor grasping his throat with the hands. The combatants were
also allowed to knock their heads against each other (συναράττειν
τὰ μέτωπα), unless this is to be understood as a mere pressing
together of foreheads, a position which is also permitted in our
modern gymnasiums. This latter species of combat seems depicted
on a vase of the Blacas collection ("Musée Blacas," t. i., Pl. 2,
compare with it a similar representation in the "Museo Pio
Clementino," vol. v., Pl. 37), where two naked
wrestlers, with their heads pressed against each
other, endeavour to grasp each other's arms.
The Greeks had two species of wrestling. In
the first the wrestlers strove to throw each
other (πάλη ὀρθή, ὀρθία) while standing in an
upright position, and, if thrown, to rise again to
renewed contest. If the opponent was thrown
three times in the same contest he had to declare
himself beaten. The other species of wrestling
formed the continuation of the first; the custom in this being, that as soon as one of the
combatants had been thrown the other knelt
down upon him to prevent his rising, the contest
(ἀλίνδησις, κύλισις) being carried on in this
recumbent position. In both species of wrestling
certain tricks were used, by means of which the
wrestlers tried to deprive their opponents of
the free use of their arms and legs, by closely

Fig. 252.

embracing them. The opponents (Fig. 253) first approached
each other, at the beginning of the contest, with uplifted arms,
at the same time advancing the right leg, and taking a firm position with the upper body drawn back (ἐμβολαί).

The contest, then, was begun with arms and fists (Fig. 253),
each antagonist try-
ing to encircle the
other's arms and
shoulders (δράσσειν).
Another σχῆμα (the
technical name for

Fig. 253.

the different tricks of wrestling) was done with the legs; Odysseus,
in his contest with Aias, applies it by knocking his heel against the

bend of the knee of his antagonist, and flooring him by that means (ὑπέλυσε δὲ γυῖα). Another similar trick consisted in suddenly lifting up the antagonist's leg with one's hands, and throwing him down in that manner; this is frequently depicted in vase-paintings (" Monumenti dell' Istit.," vol. i. 22, No. 8, *b*).

Fig. 254.

The encircling of the antagonist's legs, continued even after the wrestlers had fallen to the ground, also belongs to this species of combats; it is illustrated by the celebrated marble group of "The Wrestlers," at Florence. The technical name for it was ὑποσκελίζειν, and it formed an important feature of the art. In the above-mentioned group (Fig. 254) the uppermost wrestler has laid his left leg tightly round that of his antagonist; the latter endeavours to lift himself up by means of his disengaged left arm and of his right knee. But his right arm has been firmly grasped by the victor, and is being pushed upwards. Many other schemata of wrestling mentioned by ancient authors we omit as not sufficiently explained.

The fourth kind of gymnastic exercise is the throwing of the diskos (δισκοβολία). Our illustration (Fig. 255) is taken from the statue of a Diskobolos found in 1781 at the Villa Palombara, belonging to Principe Massimi. It is undoubtedly a copy of the celebrated statue by the sculptor Myron. The upper part of the body is bent down towards the right, and rests on the left arm, the left hand itself resting on the knee of the right leg, which is slightly bent. The weight of the body, therefore, is thrown on the right foot; while the left one, with the toes bent slightly, only touches the ground to keep up the equilibrium. The heavy diskos lies on the lower part of the arm and the right hand. The right arm is bent backwards up to the height of the shoulder, so as to add force to the throw. The neck and head are turned towards the hand holding the diskos, so as to control the right direction of the throw. The same position is also mentioned by Philostratos ("Imag.," I., 24) in his description of a diskobolos, and was, undoubtedly, the regular one. It somewhat resembles that of our players at nine-pins, with the difference, however, that in our game the ball is thrown in a straight line, while the diskos was propelled in a curve. This game is connected with mythical gods and heroes; Homer mentions it as a favourite occupation of men.

The Homeric diskos (σόλος) consisted of a heavy piece of cast iron (αὐτοχόωνος) or of stone; as, for instance, amongst the Phaiakai. The historic diskos has the shape of a lens. It resembled a small round shield without a handle, and was, therefore, difficult to manage. The diskobolos bent his fingers over the side of the diskos which rested on his palm and on the lower part of the arm (Fig. 255). A diskos found at Ægina is 7· 7″ in diameter, and weighs 3 lbs. 29 oz. It is at present in the antiquarium of the Royal Museum of Berlin (Bronzen, No. 1273); on it are represented two epheboi, one of them throwing a spear, the other holding dumb-bells.* The diskobolos stood on a small earth-mound (βαλβίς), and the longest distance obtained decided the victory, whether or not a goal had previously been marked.

Fig. 255.

Still more than was the case with the diskobolia another exercise, viz. the throwing of spears (ἀκόντιον, ἀκοντισμός), was considered as a preparation for actual warfare. It was well known in Homer's time, and afterwards counted amongst the gymnastic and agonistic exercises. In Homer's time the game was performed in full armour and with sharp spears; later on, only pointless spears were used, as is confirmed by several vase-paintings, in which epheboi appear with one or two spears without points. In the pentathlon light, short spears, with long, thin points, were used either in throwing at aims or only for long distances. We shall return to the spears in treating of Greek weapons (§ 54).

The five exercises thus described, viz. running, leaping,

* See the picture of a diskos (original size) in Ed. Pinder, " Ueber den Fünfkampf der Hellenen." Berlin, 1867.

wrestling, throwing the diskos, and the spear, formed the so-called πένταθλον. At the four great national festivals all these had to be gone through on one and the same day, and the prize was awarded to him only who had been victorious in all of them. According to Böckh, the pentathlon began with leaping; after it followed running; after that, the throwing of the diskos and of the spear, the last game being the wrestling. Other philologists prefer a different order. It remains doubtful whether the whole pentathlon was gone through each time. According to Krause ("Gymnastik und Agonistik der Hellenen"), the τριαγμός (viz. leaping, and throwing of diskos and spears) was obligatory in all cases, the running and wrestling being omitted occasionally.

The most dangerous of all contests was the boxing-match (πυγμή, πύξ). In order to increase the force of the clenched fist each fighter (πύκτης) tied straps of bull's hide (ἱμάντες) round both his clenched fists, so as to leave only the fingers uncovered.

Fig. 256.

The ends of these straps were tied several times round the wrists, so as to protect the artery in that place. Such was the older custom mentioned by Homer. The name of this covering was μειλίχαι, perhaps, as Krause remarks, because it caused a softening of the blow dealt with it (see Fig. 256, *a*). In other cases, strips of hardened leather, or even nails and lead buckles, were attached to these coverings, inflicting wounds at each well-aimed blow. The name of this dreadful weapon was σφαῖραι (see Fig. 256, *b*, taken from the statue of a fighter in the Villa Pamfili). The fingers there are put through a ring of metal or leather, while round the arm are wound numerous straps, to which is added a piece of metal resembling a shield. A still more dangerous weapon is exemplified by the statue of a fighter in the Dresden Museum (Fig. 257); perhaps we there see what the ancients called μύρμηκες. The fighters entered the "ring" perfectly naked. After their straps had been adjusted by experienced men, they chose their places. After the signal had been given, they began the combat with the upper part of the body bent forward, but with the throat drawn back so as to remove it from the grasp of the antagonist. Fig. 257, and many other statues and vase-paintings, exemplify this position. All kinds of tricks were used by the fighter to tire out the antagonist and protect himself from blows. Both hands were used alternately to deal blows, the unemployed arm being used to ward off attacks from the head, the chest, or the belly. Quickness and agility in changing the position were no less required than strength of muscles. Illicit means of gaining the victory were severely punished, as was also the intentional killing of the antagonist. Blows were chiefly aimed at the chest, temples, ears, cheeks, nose, mouth, and chin. The teeth were frequently knocked in, and the ears squashed, as appears from several statues. Ear-cases of wool or leather (ἀμφωτίδες) were used in the gymnasia and palæstrai, but not at public fights. Fighters of about equal strength and dexterity

Fig. 257.

sometimes used to break their combat by short intervals of rest. Strongly contested fights, however, were generally continued without interruption till either of the combatants confessed himself beaten by lifting up his hand.

To conclude, we mention the παγκράτιον, a combination of wrestling and boxing. It was unknown in heroic times, and does not appear amongst public games previous to Olympiad 33. Straps were not used in it, as these would have impeded the motion of the hands in wrestling. According to rule in the pankration, the blow was not dealt with the clenched fist but only with the bent fingers. Otherwise all tricks and schemata of both wrestling and fighting were permitted, barring illicit means of weakening the adversary (κακομαχεῖν).

53. After having considered the gymnic agones (ἀγὼν γυμνικός), we now come to the ἱππικὸς ἀγών, *i.e.* racing in chariots and on horseback. Both these agones were considered as the highest and noblest kinds of public games. Horses and

chariots, of course, could be owned only by the richer classes, whence the fashionable character of these games. Firmness of hand and eye in directing the horses was the most important requisite of the art. The owners of horses, therefore, employed frequently substitutes at the chariot races (ἁρματηλασία). The architectural arrangements (aphesis, goal, &c.) of the racecourse have been described in § 28. We add a few remarks about the chariots themselves. The two-wheeled chariot used by Homeric heroes, both in the racecourse and on the field of battle, remained in use at races during the historic period. The charioteer alone occupied it. (Compare our remarks about the battle-chariot, § 54.) The number of chariots admitted at one race most likely varied according to the width of the hippodrome; in large hippodromes, like that of Olympia, the aphesis of which, on each side, was about 400 feet long, it was, no doubt, considerable. The number of horses attached to each chariot was originally four of full-grown size (δρόμος ἵππων τελείων), afterwards two (ἵππων τελείων συνωρίς). The first kind of race was introduced Ol. 25, the second, Ol. 93. The occurrence of three horses is proved by the frieze of the Parthenon. After Ol. 99, the custom of using colts (πῶλοι), either by fours or twos, was introduced. The use of mules in the hippodrome occurs only between Ol. 70—84. The places of the chariots were decided by drawing lots. At a given signal the horses started simultaneously, animated by the driver's shouts, and urged on to the utmost speed by his whip (μάστιξ) or goad (κέντρον); thick clouds of dust followed the wild race.* Just as in the foot-race, the course was either run through once, without returning round the goal (ἄκαμπτον), or the chariots had to run back, as in the diaulos of the foot-race. The equivalent of the dolichos would be the running twelve times through the whole course with grown-up horses (δωδέκατος δρόμος), as done at the Olympia, Pythia, and Isthmia. We also find, analogous to the ὁπλίτης δρόμος of the foot-race, a chariot-race at which both horses and drivers appeared in full armour. Usually, however, the charioteers were naked, while

---

* The mastix consisted of a short stick with a number of thongs attached to it (Fig. 259); the kentron was a long pointed staff similar to that used in southern Italy and Spain at the present day. Sometimes rattles were attached to the point of the kentron (see Müller, "Denkmäler," Part I. No. 91 b).

the horses were harnessed as lightly as possible. Great danger of upsetting, or even smashing, the chariot was incurred in going round the goal, not to speak of many other inconveniences connected with the imperfect levelling of the course. Nestor refers to the former danger in the instruction addressed to his son.

Chariot races have been frequently the subjects both of sculpture and painting. A wall-painting in an Etruscan grave-chamber (Fig. 258) illustrates the preparation for the race. On the left a charioteer drives his biga into the racecourse, while an expert seems to examine the horses of the next-following chariot before admitting it to the hippodrome. On the right, two horses are put to a chariot by two servants. Other monuments show the

Fig. 258.

chariots amidst the dangers of the race. In a vase-painting (Panofka, "Bilder antiken Lebens," Taf. III. 10) we see a running horse with the rein torn; a wall-painting (Micali, "L'Italia avanti il dominio dei Romani," Atlas, Tav. 70) shows a chariot smashed by the kicking horses, while the charioteer is thrown up into the air (see also the representation of Circensic games on a mosaic floor at Lyons, § 104).

We now have to consider the races on horseback (ἱπποδρομία). The art of riding, as applied to both warfare and racing, belongs essentially to historic times, when the Homeric chariot began to disappear from the field of battle. Only barbarous nations retained the chariot as an implement of war. In horse-racing we also meet with the distinction between grown-up horses (ἵππῳ κέλητι) and colts (κέλητι πώλῳ), the race with the former dating from Ol. 33, that with the latter from Ol. 131. The rules of horse-racing were most likely identical with those of chariot-racing. The turning round the goal in the former was much less dangerous than in the latter; but accidents, nevertheless, were not impossible, as appears from a vase-painting (Panofka, "Bilder antiken Lebens," Taf. III. 4), where a rider is dragged along the ground by his horse. The arrival at the goal is illustrated by a vase-painting (Fig. 259), in which the umpire receives the victor; he is one horse's length in advance of his competitors. The so-called κάλπη was a peculiar kind of race in which the rider, while racing round the course for the last time, jumped off his horse, and, holding it by the bridle, made for the goal. Something similar to the kalpe (which, however, was soon discontinued) occasionally took place at chariot races. Two persons, viz., the driver (ἡνίοχος) and the competitor, stood in the chariot. While the course was measured for the last time the latter jumped from the chariot and ran by the side of it, until very near the goal, when he jumped into it again, assisted

Fig. 259.

by the heniochos; hence his name ἀποβάτης or ἀναβάτης. At the Panathenaïa this kind of race was most commonly practised, and the frieze of the Parthenon undoubtedly contains examples of it. There we see chariots with three horses, driven by charioteers, while warriors, armed with helmet and shield, run by the side of them, or are seen jumping into them.

Amongst gymnastic exercises we also name the game at ball (σφαιριστική), greatly recommended by Greek physicians as strengthening the limbs, and, moreover, considered by the Greeks as a chief means of developing the grace and agility of the body. Boys and men, girls and women, practised it. It was played, like other gymnic exercises, according to certain rules which had to be learnt. At the gymnasia a separate place (σφαιριστήριον, σφαίριστρα) was reserved for it, where a teacher (σφαιριστικός) gave instruction in the art. The balls were of various colours, made of leather, and stuffed with feathers, wool, or fig-seeds. With regard to size the distinctions were—small, middle-sized, and very large, empty balls. The game with the small ball (μικρά) was again divided into three classes, according as the smallest (σφόδρα μικρά), the slightly larger (ὀλίγῳ τοῦδε μεῖζον), or the relatively largest ball (σφαιρίον μεῖζον τῶνδε) was used. The chief difference between games with the larger and smaller balls seems to have con-sisted in the position of the hands, which in the former were not allowed to be raised above the height of the shoulders; while in the latter they might be lifted above the head. The explanations of ancient authors are, however, not very perspicuous. Our monumental evidence consists chiefly of women, in a sitting position, playing with one or several balls. For want of a Greek representation, we have chosen a scene from a Roman sphairisterion (Fig. 260). It is taken from a wall-painting in the thermæ of Titus, in Rome.

Three epheboi, superintended by a bearded teacher, are practising with six small balls. The position of their arms accords with the rule just mentioned. The ἀπόρ-ραξις was another game with small balls. In it the ball was thrown on the ground in an oblique direction, and was caught by the other player after having rebounded several times owing to its elasticity.

Fig. 260.

These bounds used to be counted. The players altered their positions only when the ball, in rebounding, had changed its direction. Another game with the small ball was called οὐρανία, in which the little ball was thrown into the air as high as possible, and had to be caught on falling down again. In another game, of Spartan origin, called ἐπίσκυρος or ἐφηβική, the players were divided into two parties, separated by a line (σκῦρον). Behind each party was drawn another line which they were not allowed to cross in catching the ball. The ball was placed on the skyron and thrown by a member

of one party towards the other party, who had to catch it, and throw
it back. As soon as either party were driven back behind their
boundary-line the game was ended. About the games with large
and very large balls we are instructed less fully. They were
thrown with considerable force, and had to be caught and thrown
back by the antagonist with his arm or the palm of his hand. A
similar game, played by young men in Italy at the present day,
may be an antique reminiscence. Whether the game called
φαινίνδα was played with large or small balls is uncertain. In it the
player pretended to throw the ball towards one of his antagonists,
but changed its direction unexpectedly. We know that the balls
used in this game were hollow. We finally mention the game
with the korykos (κωρυκομαχία, κωρυκοβολία). From the ceiling
of a room was suspended, down to about the chest of the player, a
rope with a balloon attached to it, which latter was filled with
flour, sand, or fig-seeds. The task of the player consisted in
putting the balloon in a gradually increasing motion, and in
throwing it back with his hands or chest.

Bathing also may be counted amongst corporeal exercises.
The warm bath as a means of refreshment after the day's labour
is mentioned by Homer. In historic times, also, the beneficial
influence of a bath, particularly before meals, was generally
acknowledged by the Greeks, although they never cultivated
bathing as a fine art like the Romans. The too frequent use of
hot baths was rare amongst the Greeks. For warm baths, public
and private buildings (βαλανεία δημόσια and ἴδια) were erected;
certain rooms in the gymnasia were reserved for the same
purpose (see page 106). To judge by the vase-paintings—our
chief means of information with regard to the interior arrangements of baths—the ablution of the body was effected in bathing-
tubs, constantly supplied with fresh spring-water (compare
Gerhard's "Auserlesene griech. Vasenbilder," Taf. CCLXXVII.).
In taking a sudatory or steam bath (πυρίαι, πυριατηρίαι), the
bather was seated in a tub, either standing free or let into the
floor (πύελοι, ἀσάμινθοι, Homer). After the bath, cold water was
poured over him by the master of the bath (βαλανεύς) or his
assistants (παραχύται). To the bath an anointing - room
(ἀλειπτήριον) was always attached, where the body was scraped
and rubbed with delicate ointment. Here, also, the bather

dressed ; at least, in earlier times. Separate dressing-rooms (ἀποδυτήρια) were a later addition. The peculiar arrangement of a bath for women, shown in a vase-painting, has been mentioned before.

54. The games practised at the gymnasion were, to the Greek youth, a preparation for actual warfare ; this we shall now have to consider. Our chief attention will be directed towards the various weapons and pieces of armature. The different phases of Greek strategy we shall touch upon only in so far as they imply at the same time a change in the implements of war. The description of complicated war-machines, invented by the Greeks, we shall reserve for the Roman division of our work, seeing that the only illustrations of them appear on monuments belonging to the times of the emperors.

Our knowledge of Greek arms, both from written and monumental evidence, is considerable. The preserved specimens, on the other hand, are few in number, the weapons made of iron being almost entirely destroyed by rust, the effects of which only bronze has been able to withstand. The stone weapons of the aborigines, found in Greece, we shall omit for the present, being chiefly concerned with the classic period of Greek antiquity. Vase-paintings and sculptures, our chief means of knowledge, must be used with great caution, owing to the fantastic exaggerations of archaic painters, and to the ideal treatment of sculptors, both of whom were prone to sacrifice realistic truth to artistic purpose. Moreover, our written and monumental means of knowledge are not easily applicable to each other, unless we accept the specimens on the great monuments of Roman imperial times as equally illustrative of contemporary Greek armour.

To give the reader an idea of the full armour (πανοπλία) of a Greek warrior, we will introduce him to the workshop of Hephaistos (Fig. 261), taken from a bas-relief in the Louvre. The god, dressed in a tucked-up chiton, is employed in adding the handle to a large shield which one of his satyr-assistants is scarcely able to hold. By the side of the master, another workman is sitting on the floor, polishing a greave. On a stele near him are placed a sword and a cuirass, both in a finished condition. To the left of this group we see a furnace blazing with flames, and sitting near it a dwarfish figure, perhaps meant for Kedalion, the

faithful companion of the god. He somewhat resembles the
gnomes of northern mythology. In our picture he is looking

Fig. 261.

with the eye of a
connoisseur on a hel-
met with a crest of
a horse's mane. A
satyr standing be-
hind the furnace jest-
ingly extends his
hand towards the
pileus of the old man.
Supposing this to be
an illustration of the lines in the Iliad descriptive of Hephaistos
working at the armour of Achilles, we may consider ourselves as
perfectly informed with regard to the outfit of a Homeric hero.

As the chief weapons of defence we mention the helmet, the
coat of mail, the greaves, and the shield. The covering of the head
and the upper part of the body, to protect them from the weather
and the enemy's weapons, originally consisted of the hide of wild
animals. Thus the hunter's trophy became the warrior's armour.
Herakles, the extirpator of ferocious animals, always wears the
hide of the Nemæan lion as his attribute; other warriors appear
on the monuments with a similar head-dress. On an Etruscan
box of ashes, the relief-ornamentation of which shows the combat
between Eteokles and Polyneikes, one of the less important
figures wears a cap of lion's skin (Fig. 262, *a*). The same custom
prevailed amongst Germanic nations, and seems to have been
adopted by the Roman standard-bearers and trumpeters, as is
proved by the monuments of the imperial period. As a medium
between this primitive head-dress and the helmet of metal, we
mention the leather cap (κυνέη), made originally of the raw hide
of an animal. A cap of this kind is worn by Diomedes on his
nightly expedition with Odysseus. It was close fitting, without
crest or knob, and was made of bull's hide (κυνέη ταυρείη or
καταῖτυξ). Odysseus wore a similar head-covering on that
occasion. His cap was entirely made of leather, lined with felt,
and fastened with straps inside; on the outside it showed the
tusks of a boar, reminding one of the cap made of an animal's hide
which we mentioned before. Dolon wore a morion made of otter's

skin (κυνέη κτιδέη). According to Homer, a cap of leather was generally worn by younger warriors; Fig. 262, *b*, taken from a bronze statuette of Diomedes, may serve to illustrate its form. The casque of metal (κράνος, by Homer called κόρυς, or κυνέη πάγχαλκος) was a further development of this form. It was semi-globular in shape, and made of brass. Gradually front, back, and cheek pieces, visors and demi-visors, were added ; a crest served to protect the skull. On a hydria of Vulci, showing the taking leave of Amphiaraos and Eriphyle, the hero wears a semi-globular helmet of brass (Fig. 262, *c*).

Fig. 262, *d*, is taken from the group of the Æginetai at Munich. It represents the bowman, Teukros. His helmet protects the head to a much greater extent than that just mentioned. The semi-globular cap has been made to fit the

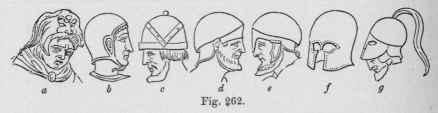

Fig. 262.

back of his head, and to it have been added a neck-piece, of about the width of a hand, and a narrow front-piece. Still more perfect is the helmet worn by Telamon in the same group (Fig. 262, *e*). The difference consists in a small piece of metal to cover the bridge of the nose being added to the front-piece. Besides this, short cheek-pieces (φάλαρα) have been attached to the sides by means of hinges, as appears from numerous vase-paintings ; these cheek-pieces could be turned upwards, which gave the helmet the appearance of a winged helmet. Still more protection is offered by the helmet in Fig. 262, *f*, found in the river Alpheios, near Olympia. Front, neck, and cheek pieces are made of one piece with the helmet, and completely cover the head down to the shoulders ; only mouth, chin, and eyes remain uncovered. The αὐλῶπις was another form of the helmet, lighter and more graceful than the one just described. The neck-piece is severed from the front-piece by an incision, and the latter has been developed into a complete visor, with small slits for the eyes (Fig. 262, *g*). In the battle it was pulled down so as to cover the skull with the cap, and the face with the visor ; otherwise it was worn pushed back over the neck, so that the visor rested on the top of the head (see Fig. 263, *b* : a head of Athene, from the Villa Albani). Frequently the elegant Greek helmet appears without any front-piece, and with a broad border bent upwards (στεφάνη), not unlike the open visor of a mediæval helmet (see the head of Athene, Fig. 263, *a*).

The leather cap, and frequently, also, the simple casque of metal, were without a crest (φάλος, see Fig. 262, *d, e, f*). Hence the name ἄφαλος applied to them. But Homer already mentions a heavy helmet of metal, with a crest proceeding from top to neck, and covering the seam which joins the two

a   *b*   *c*   *d*   *e*

Fig. 263.

sides of the helmet (Figs. 263, *a, c*, 264) : it served to protect the head from blows, and also to fasten the crest (λόφος). Vase-paintings of the archaic kind also show this crest. To increase its power of resistance, it was frequently made of four layers of metal. Hence the name τετράφαλος, τετραφάληρος.[*] Holes or notches were made into the upper side of the phalos for the insertion of bunches of horsehair (ἵππουρις) or feathers (Fig. 262, *g*). The κύμβαχος ἀκρότατος mentioned by Homer ("Iliad," XV. 536) is, perhaps, identical with the φάλος. When the phalos was wanting the crest seems to have been fastened to the casque by means of a small tube (Figs. 262, *g*, 263, *d*).

The helmets of the common soldiers were generally without ornaments, those of the officers only being decorated with figures or patterns ; the cap, visor, and stephane were frequently covered with these. The crest appears in many variations (Fig. 263, *b, c*), and sometimes was increased to overloading by the addition of feathers (Fig. 263, *d*). Decorated helmets of various kinds are generally worn by the statues of Athene, Ares, and

* According to Göbel's explanation ; see " Philologus," 1862, p. 213.

several heroes; we also see them on the head of Athene and various portrait-heads on coins and gems,—for instance, on cameos with the heads of Ptolemy I. and II., in the collections of St. Petersburg and Vienna. Fig. 263, *c*, shows the head of Athene from a silver coin of Herakleia; Fig. 263, *e*, the head of Neoptolemos, taken from a bas-relief, most likely of Roman origin, published by Orti di Manara.

The second defensive weapon is the cuirass (θώραξ). Pausanias describes its older form on speaking of the lesche painted by Polygnotos at Delphi. "On the altar," he says, "lies an iron cuirass of an unusual form, such as were formerly worn by the heroes. It consists of two iron plates, connected by means of buckles (περόναι), one of which covers the chest and stomach, the other the back. The former is called γύαλον, the latter προσῆγον. They seem sufficient to protect the body, even without a shield." Pausanias here speaks of the solid cuirass (θώραξ στάδιος or στατός) worn, in Homer, by the leaders, and, in conse-quence, frequently depicted in the older vase-paintings (Fig. 264). We also refer to the figure of Teukros in the Æginetan group at Munich. This cuirass was made of strong plates, and went down only as far as the hips, where it either was cut off or had a curved border added to it. Later on the plates were made thinner, and more in ac-cordance to the lines of the muscles (see Fig. 261). The chief difference between this and the older cuirass, besides its being lighter and more elegant, consists in the prolongation of the front plate over the navel. Altogether, it was more adapted to the altered warfare of later times. It was most likely worn only by officers. Round the waist was worn a belt

Fig. 264.

(ζωστήρ, ζώνη) over the cuirass, both to keep the parts of the harness together, and to protect that part of the body. It was fastened with buckles (in Homer, made of gold—ὀχῆες χρύσειοι). Odysseus wears a zoster of this kind over his jerkin, seemingly a leather one, on an Etruscan box of ashes (Fig. 265). Under the armour, but over the chiton, another broad belt, made of thin metal and lined inside (μίτρα), was usually worn. It is, of course, invisible in pictures, being covered by the armour; but one specimen of it (Fig. 266) has been preserved to us. It was purchased by Brönsted in Euboea, and described by him in his

pamphlet, "Die Bronzen von Siris." It consists of bronze, and is eleven inches long. On the inside fifteen larger and thirteen smaller indentures have been made which, on the outside, look like so many small semi-globes; the hooks at each end served to attach it to the lining of the real belt. This definition of zoster and mitra explains, at the same time, Homer's description ("Iliad," IV., 135 *et seq.*).

Fig. 265.

We mention, together with the iron cuirass, the linen jerkin (λινοθώρηξ) worn

Fig. 266.

by Aias, the son of Oïleus and Amphios, in Homer; and the iron chiton (χαλκοχίτων). Both were tight-fitting, made of leather or linen, and had pieces of iron attached to them to protect the heart and the shoulders (Figs. 265, 267). A belt was added, to protect the abdomen. The shoulder-pieces tied to the belt or to the jerkin itself (Fig. 267) were, as appears from numerous representations, richly ornamented. The

reliefs on two bronze shoulder-pieces, representing Aias fighting with an Amazon, are amongst the masterpieces of Greek art. Both are in the British Museum. The incorrect statement of their having been found on the banks of the Siris has given rise to the conjecture of their having been part of the splendid armour worn by Philip in the battle on the Siris. Notwithstanding the erroneousness of this supposition, their common name, the "Bronzes of Siris," will probably remain unaltered. Both these light jerkins (said to have been introduced amongst the Athenian army by Iphikrates) and the cuirasses

Fig. 267.

modelled after the lines of the body, had longer or shorter stripes of leather or felt attached to their bottom parts. These stripes consisted frequently of two layers, and were covered with plates of metal (πτέρυγες). They served to protect the abdomen, and were, like the shoulder-pieces, frequently ornamented. (Fig. 267; compare, as an example of the older armour, the statue of a warrior on the stele of Aristion, in Overbeck's "Geschichte der griechischen Plastik," Part I., p. 98). Such πτέρυγες of smaller size were also attached to the arm-holes of the cuirass, to protect the upper arm.

The coat of mail, consisting of a linen or leather shirt covered with iron scales, occurs at an early period. The large scales were imitated from those of a fish, the smaller ones from those of a snake; hence the names θώραξ λεπιδωτός or φολιδωτός, respectively applied to the two different kinds of armour.* Scale-chitons are worn, for instance, by Achilles and Patroklos on the vase known as the "Kylix of Sosias" in the Royal Antiquarium of Berlin. The Persian bowman amongst the Æginetai, generally called Paris, wears a tight-fitting armour of this kind. The cuirass of chain (θώραξ ἀλυσιδωτός) is of late Roman date, and, most likely, of Oriental invention.

The lower part of the leg was protected, even in Homer's time, by bronze greaves (κνημῖδες) covering the leg from the ankle to over the knee. They were made of flexible metal, and, in being put on, they were first bent back (Fig. 268) and afterwards placed round the leg, and their open sides bent together. They were tied across the ankle with beautifully wrought ribbons (ἐπισφύρια), as is proved by some fragments of legs belonging to the Æginetan group.† They do not, however, appear on other monuments. Besides this, the greaves were fastened round the calf with buckles or straps. The putting-on of greaves is frequently depicted on vases.

Fig. 268.

The principal weapon of defence was the circular or oval shield. The circular shield (ἀσπὶς παντὸς ἐΐση, εὔκυκλος)—also called the Argive, or more correctly the Doric, shield (Figs. 269, a, b; 270, b, c), owing to its being first substituted for the long shield by that tribe—was the smaller of the two, covering the

---

* The fragments of a coat of mail have been found amongst the ruins of the old Pantikapaion. See "Antiquités du Bosphore Cimmérien," Pl. xxvii.

† These ribbons have been preserved on the restored figures.

soldier from about the chin to the knee. As in battle it frequently had to be raised up to the helmet, an elastic cloth, made of leather or felt, was added at the bottom (λαισήϊα πτερόεντα ?),* sufficiently strong to ward off blows and thrusts (Fig. 269, b). This cloth was of Asiatic invention, but adopted by the Greeks at an early period. The oval shield (σάκος), about 4½ feet long by over 2 wide, covered the warrior almost from head to foot (ποδηνεκής, ἀμφίβροτος, Fig. 264). As mentioned before, the older long shield was soon changed for the round shield; but the oval shield, although considerably shortened, occurs up to

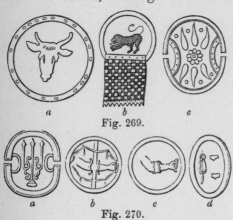

Fig. 269.

Fig. 270.

a very late period. Such oval shields as had semi-circular or oval incisions in the centre were called Bœotian (Figs. 264, 269, c, 270, a). The use of these incisions is not sufficiently explained; perhaps they served as peep-holes. This form of the shield appears in the scutcheon of most of the Bœotian cities (see Fig. 270, a, from a coin of the Bœotian city of Haliartos) and numerous archaic vase-paintings. The outer surface of the shields was more or less bent. The older way of carrying the shield, slung over head and neck by means of a strap (τελαμών) fastened to the inside of the shield, must have been very inconvenient. For the left hand there was a handle (πόρπαξ) inside the shield to direct its position. The Karians, according to Herodotos, improved this weapon considerably by introducing a band of leather or metal (ὄχανον), placed in the centre of the hollow for the upper part of the arm; to which was added another handle for the arm near the rim of the shield (Figs. 264, 265, 270, c). Whether the τελαμών was dropped entirely, or kept by—in order to carry the shield over the back on the march, as was the Roman fashion— seems uncertain. The straps fastened to a ring which occurs, together with the two handles, on the shield of Ares, in the Villa

* Compare Aristophanes, Achon, v. 1088 : τὰ στρώματ' ὦ παῖ δῆσον ἐκ τῆς ἀσπίδος.

Ludovisi (Fig. 270, *d*), is undoubtedly a telamon. In the older round shield we often see, instead of the two handles, a broad bar (κανών) reaching from one rim to the other. Through it the arm was put, the hand taking hold of the thong of leather or cloth fastened round the whole inner edge of the shield (Fig. 270, *b*). The numerous handles thus effected had the advantage of enabling the soldier to change the position of the shield in case one side of it was damaged. This mode of holding the shield belongs, most likely, to earlier times, being met with only on vase-paintings of the archaic period.

The shield was made of bull's hides, and frequently consisted of several, sometimes of no less than seven, layers, sewed one over the other, with a metal plate fastened on the top of them by means of nails. These nails protruded from the rim of the shield like buckles (ὀμφαλοί, Fig. 269, *a*); hence the epithet ὀμφαλόεσσαι applied to the shield by Homer. The centre boss, generally richly ornamented, and used to parry blows, was the omphalos κατ᾽ ἐξοχήν. The Greeks also had massive round shields of metal (πάγχαλκος ἀσπίς), which, owing to their weight, were soon disused. The beauty of some shield-decorations appears from the verses in the "Iliad" descriptive of the shield of Achilles made by Hephaistos, and from Hesiod's description of that of Herakles. The dreadful head of the Gorgon, lions (Fig. 269, *b*), panthers, boars, bulls (Fig. 269, *a*), scorpions, snakes, anchors, tripods, chariots, etc., appear frequently in vase-paintings as emblems (ἐπίσημα, σημεῖα) on shields, mostly with some reference to the character of the wearer. The shield of Idomeneus, for instance, showed a cock, in allusion to his descent from Helios, to whom that bird was devoted; Menelaos's scutcheon consisted of the image of the dragon which had appeared to him in Aulis as a divine message. A similar emblem, on the shield placed on Epaminondas's grave at Mantinea, indicated the descent of the hero from Kadmos; the shield of Alkibiades showed Eros throwing the lightnings. We also recall Æschylos's description of the shields of his seven heroes before Thebes. Besides these individual signs (οἰκεῖα σημεῖα), there existed, also, national emblems of the different Greek tribes. This custom dates from the Persian wars. The shields of the Sikyonians showed a brilliant Σ, those of the Lakedæmonians an archaic lambda Ʌ (whence their

name, lambda, or labda), those of the Mykenians a **M**, those of
the Athenians an owl, and those of the Thebans an owl or a
sphinx. Inscriptions also occur; on the shield of Kapaneus was
written, πρήσω πόλιν; on that of Demosthenes, ἀγαθῇ τύχῃ.
Only *one* Greek shield has been preserved; it is in the Museum of
Palermo.

The Persian wars caused an entire change of Greek strategy.
In the heroic age the valour of the individual showed itself in
single combats; in more modern times the hoplitai, *i.e.* the heavy-
armed foot-soldiers, decided the battle.
These warriors retained the Homeric oval
shield, while the heavy iron cuirass was
changed for leather or linen jerkins with
iron plates; helmet and greaves also were
made of lighter materials. After the
Persian wars we meet with light infantry
as distinguished from the hoplitai. After
the expedition of the Ten Thousand, the
light infantry became an essential feature
of Greek armies; they were divided into
γυμνῆτες, γυμνοί, soldiers without any
armour, and πελτασταί, πελτοφόροι, *i.e.*
soldiers wearing a pelta as defensive
weapon. They were destined to fight
at a distance; their weapons were,
according to their national predilec-
tions, the bow, the sling, or the javelin.
The peltastai also wore a shield in the

Fig. 271.

form of a crescent (πέλτα). It was two feet long, made
of wood or osiers,
and covered with
leather. It is said
to have been of
Thrakian origin. In
vase-paintings the
pelta is generally
worn by Amazons,

Fig. 272.

Fig. 273.

and a comprehensive knowledge of its more graceful forms might
be gathered from the numerous representations of battles of

Amazons. Fig. 271, from a beautiful marble statue of the
Dresden collection, may serve to illustrate not only the pelta
but the whole warlike costume of the Amazons in Greek art.
This Amazon appears in a noble Greek dress; more frequently,
however, we meet with an Oriental costume, as worn, for
instance, by an Amazon shooting with a bow (Fig. 272). Sometimes the Amazons also wear the vaulted oval shield of the
Greek soldiers; on the above-mentioned bronze armour from
Siris we see one with a small flat pelta in the shape of a disk
with only one handle. Fig. 273 shows a peltastes from a skyphos at Athens. The figure is of particular importance to us as
being illustrative of the new mode of attack for foot-soldiers
introduced by Chabrias. Cornelius Nepos, in his biography of
that commander, says: *Reliquam phalangem loco retuit cedere,
obnixoque genu scuto, projectaque hasta impetum excipere hostium
docuit.*

The aggressive weapons of the Greeks were the spear, sword,
club, battle-axe, bow, and sling. The spear
(ἔγχος, δόρυ) consisted of a smooth shaft (in
Homer's time generally made of ash-wood,
μείλινον) about 6 to 7 feet long, over the
pointed end (καυλός) of which an iron head
(αἰχμή, ἀκωκή) was drawn by means of a
socket (αὐλός), and fastened to it with an iron
ring (πόρκης). The shape of this spear-head
varies greatly; it frequently resembles a leaf
or a broad bulrush (Fig. 274, *b, c, e, f*), at other
times it has a barb (Fig. 274, *i*); sometimes, also,
it is exactly like the spear's head used by our
modern lancers. To the other end of the shaft
(especially in post-Homeric times) a "shoe"
(σαυρωτήρ, Figs. 273, 274, *f, g*) was added,
which either served to fasten the spear in the
earth when not used, or supplied the spear's
head in case this was broken. Smaller spears
were used for throwing, longer ones for thrusting;
of the former, the Homeric heroes generally have
two in their chariots. Warriors in vase-paintings also generally carry two javelins; it appears, however,

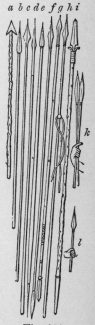

a b c d e f g h i

k

l

Fig. 274.

on comparing these two spears on numerous monuments, that they were of unequal length, whence it may be concluded that the longer was used for thrusting, the shorter for throwing (compare the lances worn by Achilles and Aias in Panofka, "Bilder ant. Lebens," Taf. X., 10, and by Peleus in Overbeck's "Gallerie heroischer Bildwerke," Taf. VIII., 6). Something analogous to this unequal length of the spears we observe in the fact of the Roman *hastati* and *principes* being armed with the *pilum* or *vericulum*.

Besides these spears, of an average length of 5 to 7 feet, we find in vase-paintings others only 2 to 3 feet long, in which latter the iron part is equal to one-third of the entire length (see Overbeck, ibid., Taf. XIII., 1, and Taf. XVIII., 3, in the latter of which the spear of Aias is still shorter, Fig. 274, *l*). The same custom of carrying several spears of unequal length was continued in historic times. The peltastai in Xenophon's army carried five shorter and one longer javelin, the latter having a strap (ἀγκύλη, *amentum*) attached to it, whence the name μεσάγκυλον, *hasta amentata* (Fig. 274, *h*). About the handling of these spears with straps opinions differed for a long time; both written and monumental proofs with regard to this point are, indeed, very scanty. Köchly was the first to treat the question comprehensively, illustrating it at the same time by means of practical trials (see "Verhandlungen der 26. Versammlung deutscher Philologen und Schulmänner," Leipzig, 1869, pp. 226-38). According to him, this weapon was adopted by

Fig. 275.

the peltastai from the gymnasion. It must be considered as a javelin, $2\frac{1}{3}$ to 3 Greek yards (*Ellen*) long by $\frac{3}{4}$ inch thick, to which, in its centre of gravity, a leather strap was tied. The two ends of the strap were tied round the shaft several times and arranged in a loop,

through which the fingers were put (διηγκυλωμένοι. Ovid, "Metamorph.," XII., 326: *inserit amento digitos*). At the moment of throwing the spear the loop was pulled violently, by means of which the strap, in being unwound, conveyed to the spear a rotating movement, similar to that of the missiles of our rifled guns. Fig. 275 is the only existing antique representation illustrative of the use of this weapon. From a passage in Plutarch's "Life of Philopoimen," it appears that the ankyle remained attached to the shaft. That commander is hit by a spear in both thighs, and, owing to the force of the throw, the strap also is pushed through one thigh, which makes the extraction of the weapon a difficult matter.

The longest of all spears, called σάρισσα, σάρισα, were used by the Makedonians. According to Greek authors they were at first 16, in later times 14 yards long, which, reckoning the Greek yard at $1\frac{1}{2}$ foot, would make 24 and 21 feet respectively. A spear of such length would have been unwieldy in the hands of the strongest soldier; we therefore agree with Rüstow and Köchly ("Geschichte des griechischen Kriegswesens," p. 238 *et seq.*) in changing the "yards" of antique measurements into feet. With this modification we will quote the description by Ælianus ("Theory of Tactics," c. xiv. *et seq.**) of the Makedonian phalanx ; our conjectural reductions of the measurements are added in brackets. "Every man under arms in the closed phalanx stood at a distance of 2 yards (2 feet, meaning the distance from the chest of the man in the first row to that of the man in the second row). The length of the sarissa was, according to the original pattern, 16 yards; in reality, however, only 14 yards (16 to 14 feet). From this the space between the two hands holding the spear = 4 yards (4 feet) must be deducted; the remaining 10 yards (10 feet) lie in front of the first row of hoplitai. The second row stands 2 yards (2 feet) behind the first, their sarissai, therefore, protrude by 8 yards (8 feet) from the front row, those of the third row by 6 yards (6 feet), of the fourth row by 4 yards (4 feet), of the fifth row by 2 yards (2 feet) ; those standing in the sixth row are unable to let their sarissai protrude from the first row. The five sarissai in front of every man of the first row naturally are of fearful aspect to the enemies, while, at the same time, they give fivefold strength to his attack."

Shorter than the sarissa, but still of considerable length, was the lance of the Makedonian cavalry. Representations of this

* Compare Ælianus, c. xiv., in "Griechische Kriegsschriftsteller," erklärt von Köchly und Rüstow.

weapon are scarce. A silver coin of the Thessalian city of
Pelina may serve to illustrate the arms used in northern Greece.

On one side of the coin (Fig. 276)
we see a horseman, covered with a
Thessalo-Makedonian felt hat, and
armed with sauroter and sword; the
reverse shows a light-armed foot-
soldier with the same kind of hat,
and armed with a Makedonian round
shield, a sword, and three short spears. The latter is perhaps
meant for one of the hypaspistai, introduced into the Makedonian
army during the reigns of Philip and Alexander; the horseman is
most likely a representative of the celebrated Thessalian cavalry,
who joined the Makedonians as allies.

The hunting-spear (ἀκόντιον) resembles, on monuments, that
used by soldiers; Fig. 274, *i*, shows one with a double barb.

The sword (ξίφος) was worn on the left side, about the height

Fig. 276.

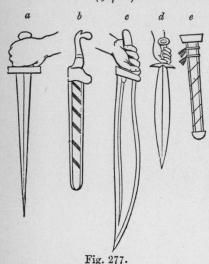

Fig. 277.

of the hip. It was fastened, by
means of a loop (ἀορτήρ), to
a belt (τελαμών) which was
thrown over the right shoulder.
The hilt (κώπη, λαβή), 4 to 5
inches long, had no guard; a
cross-hilt (Fig. 277, *a*) sometimes rounded (Fig. 277, *d*)
serving to protect the hand.
Hilt and blade were frequently
made of one piece; in more
ornamental swords the blade
was let into the hilt. The
blade, sharpened on both sides
(ἄμφηκες, ἀμφίγυον), was about
16 to 18 inches long by 2 to 2½
wide * (Fig. 277, *d*). A scabbard (κολεός, Fig. 277, *e* †), made

---

* A beautiful Greek sword, found near Pella in Makedonia, now in the Royal Antiquarium of Berlin, has a blade 17 inches long, and a handle measuring 4 inches.
The blade of another sword in the same collection is 19¼ inches in length, the hilt
being 4 inches long. The latter resembles perfectly our Fig. 277, *d*.

† Sword and scabbard (Fig. 277 *e*, *d*) belong to one and the same figure.

either of leather or metal, covered the blade up to the hilt.* The sword of heroic times was, like most weapons, modified by the changed mode of warfare of a later period. According to Cornelius Nepos, Iphikrates increased, according to Diodoros, he doubled, the length of the sword-blades of the infantry of the line ; the hoplitai, however, retained the shorter sword of earlier times. Besides this straight sword, ancient writers also mention another, the Lakedæmonian sword (μάχαιρα) ; its blade was slightly bent on one, the sharpened, side, while the other side was blunt like the backs of our knives ; the end was pointed obliquely towards the back (see Fig. 277, *c*, and Fig. 277, *b*, in the latter of which the form of the handle indicates a curved sword inside the scabbard). A third kind of sword, the blade of which is like that of a dagger, is repeatedly found on monuments (Fig. 277, *a*). Artistic ornamentation was chiefly applied to the hilt. The sword of the resting Ares in the Villa Ludovici has a hilt in the form of an animal's head (Müller, "Denkmäler," Part II., No. 250).

To conclude, we mention the sickle, the most primitive instrument for cutting grain, the form of which resembles that used at the present day. For pruning of vines and trees, the pruning-knife (ἅρπη) was used. Kronos first applied it in the fight with his father ; the harpe (Fig. 278, *a*) belongs to an image of that god. The knife used at sacrifices to cut off the animal's head resembles the sickle. It consists of a straight blade with a sickle or hook-like addition near its end (Fig. 278, *b*). In exactly the same form the harpe appears in renderings of the myth of Perseus, who with this instrument cuts off the head of the Gorgon (compare

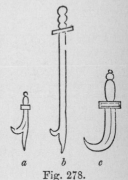

Fig. 278.

Fig. 278, *c*, another form of Perseus's weapon). Barbarous nations used swords shaped like sickles, as appears from the monuments of imperial Rome. Battle-chariots with sickles attached to the wheels and axle-trees (δρεπανηφόρον ἅρμα) were also used by barbarians, but never by Greeks ; in the battle of Gaugamela fifty sickle-chariots were placed in front of the centre of the Persian line

---

* The Royal Antiquarium of Berlin possesses a scabbard of chased silver, belonging to a dagger-like weapon.

A wooden and an iron club (ῥόπαλον, κορύνη), the former cut
by Hercules from the root of a tree, the latter made for that
hero by Hephaistos, are mentioned in the "Iliad." This weapon,
however, was never introduced into the Greek army. Herodotos
mentions amongst the weapons of the Assyrians in Xerxes' army
clubs covered with iron buckles (ῥόπαλα τετυλωμένα σιδήρῳ),
reminding one of the maces, clubs, and flails of the middle ages.

The battle-axe (βουπλήξ, ἀξίνη) appears chiefly in the hands
of Amazons; it is also carried by some of the heroes of the
"Iliad," for instance, by Peisandros in the hollow of his shield

a   b c d e
Fig. 279.

("Iliad," XIII. 611 *et seq.*). The later Greeks
never used this weapon. In the East it seems to
have been retained much longer; even in Alexander's time two thousand Barkanian horsemen
in the Persian army use battle-axes. Fig. 279,
c, shows the oldest form of the weapon as used
by the inhabitants of the isle of Tenedos, and
depicted by them on their coins. Fig. 279, *b* shows a bill, *d*
a double battle-axe, *a* and *e* fighting-hammers combined with
axes—all found in the hands of Amazons, and all resembling
mediæval weapons of the same kind.

We have to distinguish two forms of the antique bow (τόξον).
The one, simpler and more easy to bend, consisted of a curved
elastic piece of wood, the ends of which were turned slightly

Fig. 280.

upwards, for the purpose of fastening to them the string (νευρή).
This bow, called Skythian or Parthian, is frequently found on
monuments. Fig. 280 reproduces a vase-painting in which three

epheboi practise shooting with this bow. The aim is a cock placed on a column. Only in few Greek states archery was received amongst the gymnastic exercises, for which reason we have not mentioned it amongst the agones. Whether the just-mentioned bow, or that called the Greek bow proper, was the older of the two, is difficult to determine. The simpler con-struction of the former seems to indicate its greater antiquity, although the Greek bow was universally used as early as the heroic period. As to the construction and manipulation of the latter, we refer the reader to Homer's graphic description ("Iliad." IV., 105 *et seq.*).

Like the lyre, this bow was made of the horns (2½ feet long) of a kind of antelope (πῆχυς), the growing ends of which were joined together by a metal socket (κορώνη); on this the arrow rested; the other ends were tipped with iron, and to them the string, made of calf-gut, was tied. Including the socket, the Homeric bow must have been about 6 feet long, which allows 16 hands for each horn. To bend a bow of this kind required considerable strength. After being disused for some time it required greasing to recover its elasticity. At a later time these horns were imi-tated in wood, both because of the cheapness and the lightness of the material. The arrow (ὄϊστός, ἰός) consisted of a shaft (δόναξ) 2 feet in length, made of reed or light wood, and of a generally three-edged metal head 2 to 3 inches long, with or without a barb. The back end of the arrow was feathered. A notch (γλυφίς) was cut into the shaft where it lay on the string. The quiver (φαρέτρα, τοξοθήκη) was made of leather or basket-work. It usually held nineteen or twenty arrows (Fig. 281). It was carried on the left side by a strap slung across the shoulders (Figs. 272 and 280), and had a

Fig. 281. Fig. 282.

cover attached to it (Fig. 281, *b, c*). Sometimes both bow and arrows were kept in the quiver (Fig. 282), as is still the custom amongst Mongolians and Kirghis. Bending the bow the archer generally put one knee on the ground—a position taken, for instance by the archer of the Æginetan group (compare Figs. 272, 280). As early as Homer's time the Kretans were renowned as skilful archers. Kretan bowmen formed a peculiar feature of Greek armies up to the latest times, in the same way as Makedonian archers were a separate corps of the light infantry of Alexander the Great.   Amongst barbarians, the Skythians and Parthians were celebrated bowmen, both on foot and horseback.

The sling (σφενδόνη) consisted of a strap, broad in the centre and narrowing towards the two ends.   The stone or leaden bullet (μολυβδίς) was placed on the broader part of the strap; in throwing, the slinger held the two ends of the strap in one hand, and, after whirling the sling round his head several times, threw the bullet by letting go one end.   In the "Iliad" the sling is mentioned only once as used by a Trojan; it seems to have been

Fig. 283.

of Oriental origin.   Later on it seems to have been adopted by various Greek tribes, who had experienced its efficacy in the war with Xerxes. At first the Akarnarnians, afterwards the inhabitants of Ægium, Patræ, Dymæ, Rhodes, and Melos, were renowned as slingers.   According to Livy (XXXVIII. 29), the Greek sling consisted of three straps sewed together; the precision of which it was capable even surpassed that of the Balearic slingers.   The coins of the Pisidian city of Selge are the only Greek sculptures which represent slingers (Fig. 283); they frequently occur on Roman monuments.*

The use of battle-chariots belongs to the heroic period.   The warrior (παραβάτης), standing by the side of the charioteer (ἡνίοχος), was driven in front of the line to invite hostile warriors to single combat.   When the strategic skill of the commander superseded the demands on his personal valour, the chariot was transferred from the battle-field to the hippodrome, where alone its original form was preserved.   The description of the Homeric battle-chariot, therefore, to a great extent, also applies to the historic chariot of the racecourse.   Notwithstanding the plentiful monumental evidence, many important points, as, for instance, the harnessing of the horses, remain open to controversy.   The generic term for chariot was ἅρμα; its other name δίφρος is a *pars pro toto*, the denomination of the body of the chariot being applied to the whole.   The body of the chariot

---

* Compare § 107 as to the inscriptions on the missiles of slings.

rested on two wheels (τροχοί, κύκλα) connected by an axle-tree. The small diameter (30 inches) of the former must be explained from the desire of preventing the chariot from being upset by the impediments of the battle-field, such as *débris* or dead bodies. The axle-tree (ἄξων) was about 7 feet long, which, counting 1 foot for the nave of each wheel, leaves 5 feet for the chariot; a width sufficient not to impede the movements of the warrior. The nave (πλήμνη, χοινικίς) contained in its opening (σύριγξ) an inner ring (ἄταρνον, γάρνον, δέστρον), while two other metal rings, one before, the other behind, the spokes (πλημνόδετος, θῶραξ), surrounded it on the outside. The Homeric wheels had eight, those in vase-paintings generally four, spokes (κνῆμαι, hence ὀκτάκνημα). They were let into the four feliles (ἀψῖδες) forming the rim of the wheel (ἴτυς). In order to prevent the wheel from falling to pieces a tire of metal (ἐπίσσωτρον) was added. The body of the vehicle (ὑπερτερία, or δίφρος proper) rested on the axle. To the axle a wooden frame (τόνος, ἱμάντωσις τοῦ δίφρου) was fastened by means of nails and pegs, and on this frame the boards forming the bottom of the chariot (πτέρνα), elliptic in shape, were placed. Along the curved side of these boards rose the sides of the chariot (περίφραγμα, τάρριον), frequently made of osiers in the manner of trellis-work (hence Homer's expression δίφρος εὔπλεκτος), and reaching on the side of the horses up to the knee of the charioteer, while towards the back it became gradually lower (Fig. 258). The upper rim (ἄντυξ), made of wood or metal, was either prolonged towards the back in a large curvature (Fig. 258), or it was doubled all along the sides of the chariot (Fig. 284). Its form varies greatly in the vase-paintings.

Its destination was, most likely, twofold; the back part was grasped by the warrior on jumping on to the chariot, while the front part served for fastening the reins and the traces of the "wheel-horses"—an important point, hitherto unnoticed. The diphros was mounted from the back, which was open. The height of the sides in front was about 2 feet; in the

Fig. 284.

Roman triumphal chariot (an imitation of the Greek battle-chariot) it was increased up to about the chest of the charioteer. A cover of leather served to ward off missiles; where it was wanting the sides were composed of strong boards. Fig. 285, taken from a Roman relief, shows a chariot into which the corpse of Antilochos

Fig. 285.

is being lifted by his friends. About the construction of vehicles for every-day use we know little. As somewhat similar to the two-wheeled diphros, we mention the gig. The wheels resemble those of the chariot; a seat for two people, with a back and sides to it, rests on the axle (Fig. 286). In another vase-painting (Gerhard, "Auserlesene griech. Vasenbilder," Taf. CCXVII.) this seat resembles a chest; on it a female figure is seated; the driver sits at her feet close to the

Fig. 286.

pole with his legs hanging down at the side, a position similar to that of modern Neapolitan coachmen. On a coin of the city of Rhegium we see a one-horse vehicle on which the driver sits in a cowering position. We are ignorant of the names of these different forms of the gig. Ἀπήνη and ἅμαξα seem both to apply to four-wheeled vehicles of larger dimensions, used for carrying people and goods. The ἅμαξα, for instance, served as bridal chariot, on which the bride was seated between the bridegroom and parachos, a circumstance which proves the greater width of the vehicle. On journeys, or as a means of enjoyment, vehicles were used to a limited extent; walking, and riding on horseback, were deemed preferable.

The pole (ῥυμός) of the diphros was firmly inserted into the axle; its other end was bound with metal, frequently shaped like the head of an animal; the ends of the axle-tree were frequently adorned in like manner. To the point of the pole the yoke (ζυγόν, made of ash, maple, or beech-wood) was fastened by means of a very long strap (ζυγόδεσμον, *Archäol. Zeitung*, 1847, T. VI.).

The slipping off of the yoke was, moreover, prevented by

a long nail (ἔστωρ) being stuck through the pole, and a
ring (κρίκος) put over it. The yoke itself consisted of two
wooden half-rings joined together by a transverse bar, which
were put on the necks of the animals, the inner surfaces being
stuffed so as to prevent chafing. To prevent the horse from
shaking off the yoke, rings were attached to the curved parts
which, by means of straps, were connected with the girths and
the neck-straps (λέπαδνα). Only the two horses next to the pole
carried a yoke (whence their name ζύγιοι), the one or two
additional horses running by the side of them being called
σειραῖοι (σειραφόροι, παράσαιροι, παρήοροι), or trace-horses,
because they pulled by one trace only, fastened to the antyx of
the vehicle and to the neck-strap of the animal. The harnessing
of these trace-horses is illustrated by numerous vase-paintings
(Gerhard, "Auserlesene griech. Vasenbilder," Tafs. 107, 112,
122, 123, 125, 131, 136, and others). In one vase-painting
(Taf. 102, *ibidem*) this mode of fastening the traces to the antyx
has even been applied to the biga. Whether the yoke continued
to be used at a later period remains doubtful; Pollux, in his
description of the harnessing process, does not mention it. With
few exceptions (Fig. 258, compare Gerhard, " Ueber die Lichtgott-
heiten," in "Abhandlungen der Berliner Akademie der Wissenschaften," 1839, Tafs. III., 1, and IV., 2) the yoke is invisible
on the monuments, owing to the harness of the yoke-horses being
covered by the trace-horse nearest the spectator. The bridle
perfectly resembled that now in use. The Greeks had names
for the single parts of it, as, for instance, χαλινός for the bit, and
κορυφαία for the strap running from the bit upwards across the
head. The reins were fastened to both ends of the bit. As is
evident from vase-paintings, all the reins were drawn through a
ring just above the pole; they were held by the charioteer.

About the warlike equipment of the horses and horsemen of
historic times we know little; monumental evidence is almost
absent, seeing that the lancers occasionally met with on coins are
very imperfectly armed. The citizen-horsemen in the Panathenaïc procession on the frieze of the Parthenon are quite
unarmed. As appears from this monument and various representations of horse-races (Fig. 259), saddles were not used in
common life. Greek cavalry in battle used the saddle-cloth

(ἐφίππιον), fastened to the horse's back by means of a girth (ἔποχον). The horse of Alexander the Great in the Museo Borbonico (Müller, "Denkmäler der alten Kunst.," Part I., No. 170) wears a saddle-cloth. The ends of the cloth are there joined together over the chest of the horse by means of an elegant clasp; the bridle is adorned with rosettes. Stirrups and horse-shoes were unknown to the Greeks. The rider jumped on his horse, making use occasionally of stones lying by the road, or of his lance. The horse was protected by pieces of armour for the head (προμετωπίδιον), the chest (προστερνίδιον), and the sides (παραπλευρίδια). In a fragment of a vase-painting (" Micali, Monumenti inediti," 1844, Atlas, Pl. 45), a head-armour of this kind is depicted resembling a plate, which is fastened to the horse's head by means of iron bands.

Almost all the battle-scenes on Greek monuments represent mythical subjects. Historical battle-scenes, as frequently found on Roman coins and triumphal monuments, are very rare. Of historic representations we mention the battle between Greeks and Persians on the frieze of the temple of Nike Apteros, at Athens, the mosaic known by the name of "Battle of Alexander," and the assembly of the nobles of Darius Hystaspis, painted on a vase in the Museo Borbonico (Gerhard, "Denkmäler und Forschungen," 1857, Taf. CIII.).

To conclude, we mention the trophy (τρόπαιον) which, according to international custom, was erected from pieces of the booty, on the spot where the enemy had turned to flight (τρέπω, τροπή; τρόπαιον στῆσαι, στήσασθαι). Only in rare cases it was erected with a view to permanency; as, for instance, the trophy placed in the temple-grove Altis by the inhabitants of Elis, in commemoration of their victory over the Lakedæmonians. As a

Fig. 287.

rule, the trophy was temporary, and was frequently destroyed by the beaten party in case their defeat was not decisive enough to compel them to own it. The trunk of a tree, on which a complete armour has been hung, and at the foot of which pieces of booty have been heaped, appears as a tropaion on a coin struck by the Bœotians, most likely in commemoration of some victory (Fig. 287). The commemoration of victories and victorious generals at home by means of votive offerings, monuments, and inscriptions, was of a more lasting kind, although the Greeks never indulged in the self-glorifying exaggerations of the Roman emperors.

55. We add a few remarks about Greek war and merchant vessels. Many attempts at explaining the construction of antique ships have been made, but the mutual ignorance of seafaring men and philologists with regard to the technical terms of their respective branches of knowledge has, in many cases, led to bewildering confusion and wild conjectures. Moreover, antique representations of ships—partly from the total want of perspective, partly from the omission of the most important details—are of comparatively little assistance to us. Graser has attempted a new solution of this important problem, which is amongst the most difficult tasks of antique research.* Following the researches of Boeckh (in his celebrated work on the Attic navy) with regard to the construction and rigging of Greek ships, Graser has expounded an entirely new theory of the dimensions and rowing apparatus of Greek vessels. His intimate knowledge of modern ships has been of considerable assistance to him. We have essentially adopted the results of his investigations in preference to all previous conjectures.

We pass over the earliest attempts at navigation in hollow trees or on rafts. The invention of the art of ship-building, like that of most other arts, must be placed in pre-historic times; gods and heroes are mentioned as its originators. A bas-relief in the British Museum (Fig. 288) shows Athene supervising the building of the *Argo*, in which Jason and his companions are said to have ventured on the first long voyage. Homer's descriptions of the interior

Fig. 288.

arrangements of ships prove that at the time of the Trojan war the art of shipbuilding was considerably advanced. Rowers

* Graser, "De veterum re Navali." Berolini, 1864. "Philologus," supplementary volume iii. part ii.—"Das Modell einer athenischen Fünfreihenschiffs Penteres, aus der Zeit Alexanders des Grossen im kgl. Museum zu Berlin." Berlin, 1866.

(20 to 52 in number), sitting on benches (κληῖδες) along the sides of the ship, beat the waves simultaneously with their long oars (ἐρετμά) made of pine-wood. As in our sloops (*Schaluppen*), the oars of the Homeric vessel were made fast between pegs (σκαλμοί) by means of leather straps (ἠρτύναντο δ᾽ ἐρετμὰ τροποῖς ἐν δερματίνοισιν), so as to prevent their slipping. In case of a calm or of adverse winds the ship was propelled by the rowers ; the mast (ἱστός) was placed in a case, or rather on props (ἱστοδόκη), and kept in its position by means of ropes fastened to the prow and poop of the vessel. The sail (ἱστίον) was attached to a yard (ἐπίκριον). Wind and oars were thus conjointly made serviceable ; the helmsman (κυβερνήτης) directing the course of the vessel by means of the rudder (πηδάλια). The war-vessels sent against Ilion carried fifty to a hundred and twenty soldiers, who, undoubtedly, had also to act as rowers. Of the fifty men forming the crew of the smallest vessels, forty plied the twenty oars by turns, the others taking care of the rigging or acting as officers. The small draught of the vessels is proved by the fact of their being, without much difficulty, pulled ashore, where wooden or stone props (ἕρματα) served to keep them dry and protect them from the waves.

The development of ship-building was undoubtedly due to the Greeks. The numerous natural harbours of the Greek continent, combined with the growing demands of intercommunication with the islands, and the colonies of Asia Minor and southern Italy, favoured the rapid growth of navigation. The continual wars

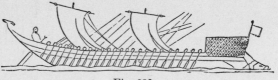

Fig. 289.

waged amongst the Greek tribes, and by them collectively against barbarians, necessitated the keeping up of large navies. The Homeric vessel, most likely only a transport, and unfit for battle, was soon supplanted by war-vessels of larger dimensions. Besides flat-bottomed vessels, called, according to the number of rowers sitting on both sides, εἰκόσοροι, τριακόντοροι, πεντηκόντοροι

(Fig. 289), and ἑκατόντοροι, we also hear of ships of greater draught in which the oarsmen sat in' two rows, one over the other. During the Persian and Peloponnesian wars the fleets consisted of τριήρεις exclusively. Vessels with more than three ranks of rowers, such as τετρήρεις and πεντήρεις, were first introduced by Dionysios I., tyrant of Syrakuse, after a Carthaginian pattern. Dionysios II. introduced ἑξήρεις. Even six rows were not always deemed sufficient. Ten and (with a modification of the system) more rows were placed one over the other, the result being a surprising velocity and handiness of the vessels thus constructed. In the battle of Actium we hear of ships with ten rows; Demetrios Poliorketes had even vessels of fifteen and sixteen rows, the seaworthiness of which is warranted by antique authors.

The construction of the war-vessel, as introduced shortly before the Persian wars, must now command our attention. The keel (τρόπις, *carina*) consisted of one horizontal beam, parallel to the longitudinal axis of the vessel; in older ships it rose from the centre to the ends in a wide curve. The large ships of a later period had keels composed of several straight beams joined together, into the ends of which stem (στεῖρα) and stern posts (ἀσάνδιον) were inserted almost in a right angle, being only slightly bent outwards. Under the keel another beam (χέλυσμα) was placed parallel to it, so as to add to its power of resistance; corresponding to this, a third beam (δρύοχον) lay on the top of the keel; into this, the ribs of the ship (ἐγκοίλια, *costæ*) were let. The upper ends of each pair of corresponding ribs, forming together one curvature, were joined together by means of a straight cross-beam (στρωτήρ), destined to carry the upper deck (κατάστρωμα, *constratum*). The bulwark, enclosing the two long sides of the latter, generally consisted of trellis-work. In larger vessels a second layer of boards (ζυγόν, *transtrum*), underneath the upper deck, was laid across the ribs of the vessel, destined to carry the second or lower deck (ἔςαφος, *pavimentum*). The two decks communicated with each other and the hull (κοῖλον) by means of steps, hatchways being cut in the boards for the purpose. The hull contained the ballast and the pump.

Both in the prow (πρώρα, *prora*) and poop (πρίμνα, *puppis*) of the vessel small half-decks (ἰκρίωμα), corresponding to our forecastle and quarter-deck, were placed considerably above the upper deck. They rested on the prolongation of the ribs nearest to stem and stern. The poop and prow were essentially identical in construction, differing in this from all modern vessels excepting our latest ironclads.

The planks of the vessel (σανίδες) were strengthened externally by a wooden ledge (νομεῖς) just above the water-line, corresponding to which a number of boards (ἁρμονίαι, δεσμοί) were placed along the ribs inside, so as to give firmness to the whole fabric. As a further means of increasing their compactness, war-vessels were provided with a band consisting of four stout ropes (ὑποζώματα) laid horizontally round the hull below the water-line; in case of a dangerous voyage, the number of these ropes might be increased. These hypozomata are distinctly recognisable on a small bronze in the Antiquarium of the Royal Museum, Berlin (No. 1329), representing the prow of a man-of-war (compare the small bronze statuette of Poseidon, No. 2469 of the same collection).

A little lower than the upper deck, just above the upper holes for the oars, a narrow gangway (πάροδος) runs along both sides of the vessel; in woodclad vessels (κατάφρακτοι, tectæ) this parodos is protected by strong massive boards (see Fig. 300, representing

a Roman bireme). Both stem and stern-post ended in a volute. The tent-like house (σκηνή) of the helmsman (Fig. 290) stood on the poop just underneath the volute. From this point he directed the two rudders (πηδάλιον, gubernaculum) to right and left of the stern, which are peculiar to all antique ships, by means of a rope (χαλινός) running straight across the vessel. The rudders were always kept parallel (Fig. 291). To the volute of the poop a leaf or feather ornament (ἄφλαστρον, aplustre) has

Fig. 290.

been added (Fig. 290). The prow frequently shows an ornament resembling the neck of a swan (χηνίσκος), which, perhaps, at the same time, served for fastening ropes. Between these two, the flagstaff (στηλίς), with the flag (σημεῖον) attached to it, was erected. In merchant vessels the flagstaff was frequently supplied by the image of the protecting deity. Athenian vessels, for instance, carried the image of Athene as ἀττικὸν σημεῖον. The prow, as we said before, exactly resembled the poop. Here, also, a strong wooden band encircled the vessel on a level with the parodos. The point where the outer ribs crossed each other was marked by a ram's head (προεμβόλιον) made of bronze, and serving either as an ornament or as a protection to the upper part of the vessel. Underneath this, on a level with the water-line, was the beak (ἔμβολον, *rostrum*), consisting of several rafters let into the

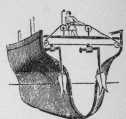

Fig. 291.

body of the vessel and ending in a point, which was made more formidable by the addition of a massive piece of iron divided into three blunt teeth of unequal length. Two beams (ἐπωτίδες), supported by props (ἀντηρίδες), protruded on both sides of the rostrum; on these the anchors were hung up. They also served to protect the vessel from the attacks of the enemy's beak. We finally mention an opening on each side of the prow, through which the cables were drawn; these holes were bound with iron, and somewhat resembled eyes, whence their name ὀφθαλμοί. The resemblance of a vessel thus constructed to a fish was not unnoticed by the ancients (see Fig. 289). Something similar we meet with in the imitation of dragons in the vessels of the Norsemen, and in the construction of Chinese junks.

The beam of merchant-vessels was usually equal to a quarter, that of men-of-war to one-eighth or one-tenth, of their length. Hence the name νῆες μακραί (*naves longæ*) applied to the latter. A trireme was 149 feet long by 14 wide (at the water-line) and 19½ deep. Her draught was 8½ feet, her tonnage 232. In the pentere the corresponding figures were 168 feet, 18 feet, and 26½ feet; the draught being 11½ feet, and the tonnage 534.

The main-mast (ἱστὸς μέγας) stood in the centre of the vessel. It was square-rigged (κεραῖοι, *antennæ*), and carried two sails (ἱστία μεγάλα), one above the other, answering to our course and top-sail. Above these was another square sail corresponding to our topgallant-sail (δόλων, *dolon*), and above that two triangular sails (σίπαροι, *suppara*). Besides the main-mast there were two

smaller masts (ἰστὸς ἀκάτειος), with two fore-and-aft lateen sails
each, one over the other, which were important in tacking.
Strong ropes supported the main-mast (stays, πρότονοι; back-
stays, ἐπίτονοι; and shrouds, κάλοι) and the two smaller masts;
thinner ropes served for lifting and bracing the yards, setting the
sails, etc.

Besides the ropes of the rigging, collectively called σκεύη
κρεμαστά, a war-vessel required various contrivances of a similar
nature to protect her both against high seas and the missiles
of the enemy. To this class belonged strips of tarpaulin
(ὑπόβλημα) hung round the hull to cover the apertures for the
oars, when these had to be pulled in owing to the roughness of
the sea; as also an awning (κατάβλημα) suspended over the
upper deck as a protection both from the sun and missiles; a
woven stuff was also pulled over the trellis of the bulwark
(παραβλήματα, παραρρύματα) to ward off darts and arrows.

To conclude, we mention the anchor, the ship's ladder, the
boat-hook, and the lead. The most primitive forms of the anchor
(ἀγκύρα, ancora) were blocks of stone, sand-bags, and baskets
filled with stones. Later, anchors in our sense, made of wood
and iron, and essentially like those at present in use, were
introduced. Their varieties are
illustrated by Fig. 292; *a*, *c*,
being taken from coins of the
city of Tuder; *b*, from one of
Luceria; *d*, of Germanicia Cæsa-
rea, and *e*, of Pæstum. The

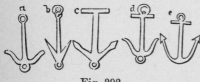

Fig. 292.

antique anchor, as appears from the pictures, has at the end of
the stem a ring, movable or immovable (*a*, *b*, *d*, *e*), to which
the cable is fastened; the cross-beam is underneath this ring
(*c*, *d*, *e*). The flukes of the anchor appear in many varieties on
the coins. Those on the coins of Pæstum (*e*) exactly resemble
our modern ones. At the point where the flukes met a loop or
staple (*a*, *b*, *c*, *d*) was attached to the anchor, to which a rope was
fastened for the purpose of lifting up the flukes so as to make
them catch. This could be done only where the water was not
very deep. The cable (σχοινία ἀγκύρεια, ancoralia, funes ancorales)
was wound round a capstan (στροφεῖον), by means of which the
anchor was weighed (see "Pitture d'Ercolano," t. ii., p. 14).

The cable ran through eye-like hawse-holes on both sides of the prow. Each ship had several boat-hooks (κοντοί) and ship's ladders (κλιμακίδες, *scalæ*). Fig. 293 and other monuments illustrate their use as bridges or gangways thrown from the side of the high vessel to the shore. As appears from a vase-painting (Micali, " L'Italia avanti il dom. dei Romani," Tav. 103), these ladders were secured to the rigging by means of ropes. Fig. 294, from a bas-relief in the British Museum, shows the lead (βολίς, καταπειρατήρ, *perpendiculum*) suspended on the volute of the prow.

Fig. 293.

Fig. 295 shows a design of a triere, by means of which the mutual position in the vessel of the parts hitherto mentioned may be recognised : *a* is the periphery of the vessel at the water-line ; *b*, θαλαμῖται; *c*, ζυγῖται; *d*, θρανῖται; *h*, πάροδος ; *i*, ἰκρία (forecastle and quarter-deck) ; *k*, κατάστρωμα; *l*, ἐπω-τίδες ; *m*, ἀντηρίδες ; *n*, ἔμβολον; *o*, point where the stern (στεῖρα) begins ; *p*, ἀσάνδιον ; *q*, ἱστὸς ἀκάτειος ; *r*, ἱστὸς μέγας ; *s*, χαλι-νός ; *t*, πηδάλιον ; *u*, διαφράγματα.

Fig. 294.

The interior arrangement of the antique ship, particularly with regard to the position and manipulation of the oars, is subject to many doubts. Here, also, Graser's investigation of the original sources, combined with practical experiments, has elucidated the question to a considerable extent. The rowing-apparatus (ἔγκωπον) was confined to the centre part of the hull. Poop and prow were unavailable, owing to their narrowness, and the former supposition of the uppermost rank of rowers having sat on deck has been completely abandoned, as has also the opinion that the space for the rowers was divided by horizontal partitions of any kind. The space for the rowers (ζύγωσις) was enclosed on the one hand by the long sides of the ship, on the other by two vertical partitions (διαφράγματα), with openings in them through which the rowers (ἐρέται, *nautæ*) filed off to their seats. The benches (ζυγά, *transtra*), reaching from the diaphragma to the side of the vessel, were arranged in rows of different heights.

Owing to the outward curvature of the hull, the rowers in the lower ranks naturally sat nearer to the side of the vessel than those in the higher. The width of seat necessary for each man may be counted at 8 square feet (Fig. 296). The benches were arranged so that the seats of the upper row were on a level with the heads of the lower. Fig. 297, *a*, shows the arrangement of the ranks which, in a manner, were dovetailed into each other (Fig. 297, *b*), in consequence of which the handles of the oars in one row required to be only two feet lower than those in the row above it. This arrangement, which left sufficient freedom to the movements of the rowers, explains why, in many-ranked vessels, the oars of the upper rows need not have been too long or too heavy to be plied by one man only. For Greek ships, unlike medieval galleys, had only one rower to each oar. In order to make this possible, the oar (κώπη, *remus*) was balanced as much as possible, the weight of the part inside the vessel being increased by the thickness of the handle and additional pieces of lead, so as to make it quite as heavy or even a little heavier than the outer part. Besides this, the aperture for the oar (τρῆμα, *columbarium*) was bound with metal, so as to reduce the friction to a minimum. The force of the beat of the different banks of oars on the water was made equal through the proportion of the inner to the outer part of the oar being in the same proportion in all oars (at first, 1 : 2 ; afterwards, 1 : 3).

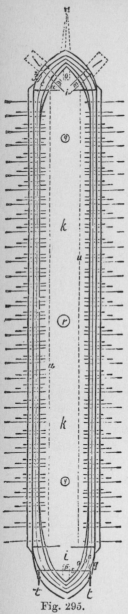

Fig. 295.

As we said before, the rowers of each bank sat horizontally behind each other, the ranks themselves lying perpendicularly over each other.

The number of these ranks determined the name of the vessel (τριήρης, *triremis;* τετρήρης, *quadriremis;* πεντήρης, *quinque-remis;* &c). In the triere the rowers of the bottom bank were called θαλαμῖται, those of the middle ζυγῖται, those of the top row θρανῖται; in the pentere the rowers of the fourth row were called τετρηρῖται, those of the fifth πεντηρῖται. The distance between the oars of the same row was exactly 4 feet; but they were always pushed 1 foot in front of the corre-sponding oars of the upper row (see Fig. 298, *b, c, d*). Reckoning the distance of the bottom row from the water-line, the thalamitai would have required oars of a length of 7½ feet. This length was increased by 3 feet in each ascending row, which determines the length of the oars of the zygitai at 10½ feet, of the thramitai (the topmost row of the triere) at 13½ feet, of the tetreritai at 16½ feet, of the penteritai (the top row of the pentere) at 19½ feet. The vertical distance of the handles of the oars was, as we said before, 2 feet (Fig. 298, *a, b*) ; but this distance was reduced to 1¾ feet by the curvature of the sides of the vessel (*c, d*) ; that between the apertures, seen from the outside, was, indeed, only 1¼ feet (*f, g*). The distance of the top row from the surface of the water in the pentere was only 8 feet, in the triere 5½ feet. For a ten-ranked ship this gives a distance of the apertures from the water of 14½ feet, the length of the oar being 34½ feet. Even in sixteen-ranked ships, such as were built by Demetrios Poliorketes, the length of the uppermost oars could be reduced to 27¾ feet, so as to make the vessel seaworthy. This was done by making the row-locks more slanting. This explains the possi-bility of the forty-ranked state-ship built by Ptolemaios Philopator ; which, however, could be used only in smooth water. The uppermost oars were, according to Athenæus, 57 feet long.*

Fig. 296.

Fig. 297 *a.*

Fig. 297 *b.*

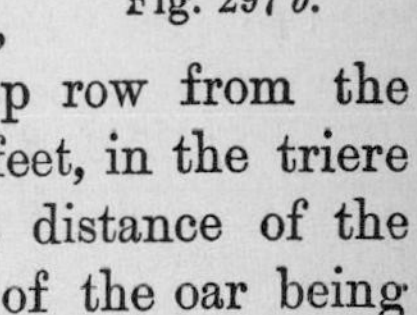

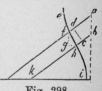

Fig. 298.

The celebrated state-ship of Hieron of Syrakuse was, however, not a vessel of war, but of burden.

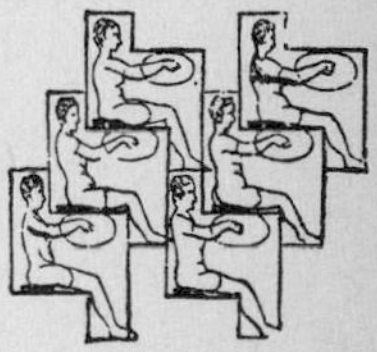

---

* See Graser, "De veterum re Navali," §§ 64—70, Tab. IV.

The number of rowers was increased by one in each ascending rank. The number of the thalamitai, counting both sides, was 54; of the zygitai, 58; of the thranitai, 62; of the tetreritai, 66; of the penteritai, 70. The triere, therefore, contained altogether 175 rowers; the pentere, 310. All these were under the command of the κελευστής (*hortator*) and his lieutenant, the ἐπόπτης. The rowing was accompanied by the rhythmical notes of a piper (τριηραύλης). The number of marines (ἐπιβάται) was comparatively very small. An Attic pentere contained only eighteen of them, besides twenty-four sailors (ναῦται, *nautæ*). The small number of marines is explained by the fact of a Greek sea-fight consisting chiefly in endeavours to knock a hole into the enemy's vessel by means of the above-mentioned rostrum, or, at least, to break her oars in passing close by her. Everything, therefore, depended upon skilful manœuvring.

The building and equipping of vessels was done in military harbours, of which that of Athens is in the best state of preservation. It was separated from the commercial harbour, commonly called Piraeus, and was divided into three basins, cut nearly circularly

Fig. 299.

into the Piraeus peninsula. The centre one, Munychia, could hold twice as many men-of-war (viz. 200) as each of the two others, Zea and Kantharos. The docks (νεώσοικος) lay round these basins close to the water, their openings being turned towards the centres or the outlets of the basin; in them the ships, when not in use, were protected from the weather. Further back were situated the arsenals (σκευοθήκη), containing the fittings of the ships not in use; the name for the whole dockyard was νεώρια. The docks, or ship-sheds, generally contained one vessel each; as, for instance, was the case in the celebrated harbours of Rhodes, Korinth, and Kyzikos, the latter of which could hold two hundred ships; in Syrakuse, however, and some other places, each dock contained two vessels. Graser's measurements of the Athenian harbours have fully confirmed his above-mentioned conjectures as to the construction of the vessels themselves. Further confirmation is derived from the bas-relief of an Attic τριήρης ἄφρακτος, but κατάστρωτος, in which, therefore, the uppermost bank of oars is visible (Fig. 299).

As the Roman vessel resembles the Greek in most points, we will here add a few remarks about the former. The Latin terms

Fig. 300.

have already been given. As long as Roman conquests were limited to Italy, their navy consisted only of long boats (*caudices, naves caudicariæ*) for river navigation, and of small sea-vessels as a means of intercommunication between the maritime provinces, not to mention the defence of the harbours. The Carthaginian wars necessitated the building of a powerful fleet. In a space of two months 130 penteres and trieres were constructed, after the pattern of a stranded Carthaginian pentere. The timbers were roughly cut, and the improvised sailors had to be trained on rowing-frames erected on shore; but the foundation was thus laid of a fleet of triremes, quadriremes, and quinqueremes, commonly called *naves longæ*. The Romans, differing in this from the Greeks, transferred the mode of close fighting to their sea-battles. Two or four towers (*navis turrita*) and catapults transformed the deck into a castle, from which the marines began the fight with missiles till the vessels approached within boarding distance. The marines, therefore, were much more numerous on board Roman than Greek vessels. The quinquereme contained 120. After the battle of Actium Roman ship-building underwent a thorough change. That battle had been won against the Greek-Egyptian fleet of Antony, built according to Greek rules, chiefly by means of the ships of the Liburnian pirates, which had only two banks of oars and a very light rigging. In consequence, the Roman fleet was reorganised according to the same principle (*navis Liburna*). Besides men-of-war, larger vessels of burden were required ; these *naves onerariæ* (φορταγωγὸς ναῦς or στρογγύλη) were about three or four times as long as they were broad. Many statements in ancient authors prove the quickness of voyage in those days. Balbilus went from Messina to Alexandria in six days (the French mail-steamers require 6½ days for the same distance). Valerius Maximus sailed from Puteoli to Alexandria *lenissimo flatu* in nine days, and the voyage from Gades to Ostia took only seven days, in case the wind was favourable ; that from Gades to Gallia Narbonensis (perhaps to Massilia), three days.

56. From the serious business of life we now follow the Greek citizen to scenes of merriment. We mentioned before (§ 33) that the chief difference between the customs at the meals of earlier and later periods consisted in the former being taken in a sitting, the latter in a reclining position (κατάκλισις). The Kylix of Sosias, in the Berlin Museum, where the gods appear at their meal sitting on thrones in couples, may serve to illustrate the older Homeric custom. Only the Kretans preserved this old custom up to a later period. Almost all the later representations show the men lying at their meals ; women and children, on the contrary, appear in an upright posture, the former sitting mostly on the further end of the kline at the feet of their husbands, or on separate chairs.* The sons were not allowed to recline till they came of age ; in Makedonia not till they had killed a boar. The women we occasionally see in pictures (mostly of later date) are probably hetairai

* Compare the specimens collected by Welcker, "Alte Denkmäler," vol. ii. p. 242 *et seq.*

(see Fig. 304). This, however, is different in Etruscan representations, where a man and a woman are seen reclining on one
and the same kline. Aristotle says expressly that men and their
wives used amongst the
Etruscans to lie down to
their meals under one and
the same coverlid. In
Greece, also, a kline was
generally occupied by no
more than two people. Fig.
301 shows two couches with

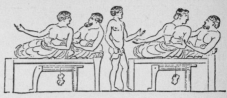

Fig. 301.

an older and a younger man reclining on each of them, talking to
each other in a lively manner. A cup-bearer is about to replenish
their emptied goblets. Where three or four persons are seen
on the same kline (see Fig. 304), we may suspect the introduction
of a Roman custom into Greece.

The gorgeous arrangement and more refined cookery of the
meals of latter days widely differed from the frugality of
Homeric times. Pieces of beef, mutton, goat meat, or pork,
roasted on the spit, were placed by the maid-servants on little
tables in front of the guests (see § 33); the bread was handed
round in baskets; and at the end of the meal wine was drunk,
which had been previously mixed with water in huge krateres.
The use of knives and forks remained unknown, whence the
custom of washing the hands (ἀπονίψασθαι) and drying them on
a towel (χειρόμακτρον) provided for the purpose. Tablecloths
and napkins were equally unknown. The latter were supplied by
a peculiar kind of dough, which served to clean the fingers from
grease. Sometimes temporary spoons were formed of the same
material, to eat the more fluid victuals. Such is still the custom
in the East. Greek cookery, even of a later period (not to
mention Spartan frugality), is described as simple, if not poor;
consisting chiefly of μᾶζα (flat round cakes of barley, still
eaten in Greece), various kinds of salad, garlic, onions, and
pulse, whence the derisive expressions μικροτράπεζοι or φυλλο-
τρῶγες applied to the Greeks. The more refined tastes of Grecia
Magna were only gradually introduced amongst the richer classes
of Greece itself. Various kinds of fish and shell-fish, and different
vegetables, gradually supplanted the huge joints of Homeric

times. The meals were prepared by cooks hired from the market, or by Sicilian "chefs," who, in Roman times, were amongst the slaves of every rich Greek family. The *menus* which might be composed from the statements of ancient authors seem little palatable according to our notions; but the rich and tasteful plate and other table-furniture described by us (§ 33 *et seq.*) give us a high idea of the elegant appearance of a Greek dinner-table.

Another characteristic of the meals of later times was the addition of the συμπόσιον to the meal proper (δεῖπνον). Deipnon was the name of the chief meal or dinner, about sunset; ἀκράτισμα that of the breakfast; ἄριστον that of the luncheon, about midday. In early times the meal was considered as finished as soon as the appetite was satisfied; later, the drinking-bout, animated by conversation, music, mimic representations, and games, became the most important part of the meal. Wit and humour were displayed to their fullest advantage, for the Greek, differing in this from the more indolent Roman, took an active part in the various amusements.

The removal of the dinner-table (αἴρειν, ἀπαίρειν, ἐπαίρειν, ἀφαιρεῖν, ἐκφέρειν, βαστάζειν τὰς τραπέζας), and the simultaneous cleaning of the floor from bones, peelings, and other remnants of the meal, gave the signal for rising. Sosus, the artist, imitated in mosaic a floor, covered with such remnants and other rubbish, for the dining-hall of the royal palace of Pergamon. At the end, as at the beginning of the meal, the hands were washed with scented soap (σμῆγμα or σμῆμα); the meal proper then was closed by a libation of unmixed wine, which was drunk by all round to the good spirit (ἀγαθοῦ δαίμονος), or to each other's health (ὑγιείας). A second libation (σπονδαί) introduced the symposion. Hymns and the solemn notes of a flute accompanied this libation, which, as it were, gave a sacred character to the beginning symposion.

The dessert, called, in opposition to the πρῶται τράπεζαι or δεῖπνον proper, δεύτεραι τράπεζαι or τραγήματα, later also ἐπιδόρπια, ἐπιδορπίσματα, ἐπιδόρπιοι τράπεζαι, ἐπίδειπνα, ἐπιδειπνίδες, ἐπιφορήματα, ἐπαίκλια, γωγαλεύματα, &c., consisted of about the same dainties as nowadays. Piquant dishes, stimulating the guests to drinking, were chosen in preference; amongst cheeses, those from Sicily and from the town of Tromileia in Achaia were particularly liked; cakes sprinkled with salt (ἐπίπαστα) were another important feature of the Greek dessert.

Dried figs from Attika and Rhodes, dates from Syria and Egypt, almonds, melons, &c., and salt mixed with spices, were seldom wanting. Many of these dainties, as various fruits and Attic cakes shaped like pyramids, may be recognised in pictures lying on little tables in front of the topers. The drinking began simultaneously with the appearance of the dessert; for during the meal no wine was served. Unmixed wine (ἄκρατον) was not as strictly forbidden to the Greeks as to the inhabitants of Lokri, in Southern Italy, where the law of Zeleukos made it a capital crime; still, the diluting of the wine with water was an old-established custom in Greece. This dietetic measure, made necessary by the universal custom even amongst the lower classes of drinking the fiery wine of the South, was so common in Greece, that the contrary was considered as a characteristic of barbarous nations. Habitual drunkenness was exceptional amongst the Greeks, although occasional inebriation at symposia was by no means uncommon; the severe Doric customs of Sparta and Krete for that reason forbade the post-prandial drinking-bout altogether. The wine was mixed with hot or cold water; in the latter case snow was frequently mixed with the wine, or the filled vessel itself was put into a wine-cooler filled with snow. The mixture always contained more water than wine; a mixture by halves (ἴσον ἴσῳ) was very uncommon. The proportion of water to wine was generally 3 : 1 (a mixture called by Athenæus in derision "frogs' wine"—βατράχοις οἰνοχοεῖν), or 2 : 1, more rarely 3 : 2. This proportion, however, was modified by the taste of the drinker and the quality of the wine. Large krateres of metal or burnt clay (see the vessels standing on the floor in Figs. 302 and 304) were used for mixing the wine. From this large vessel the wine was poured into the goblets (phiale, kylix, skyphos, kantharos, karchesion, keras, and rhyton) by means of the kyathos or oinochoë

Fig. 302.   Fig. 303.

(see the vase-painting, Fig. 302). Fig. 303 is taken from another vase-painting, in which the youthful cup-bearer there depicted approaches two girls on a kline with two kyathoi in his hands. As

soon as the goblets were filled a king of the feast (βασιλεύς, ἄρχων
τῆς πόσεως, συμποσίαρχος, ἐπίσταθμος) was chosen. His election
was generally decided by casting the dice, unless one of the
topers chose himself. This ruler had to decide the right mixture
of the wine, the number of goblets to be drunk by each guest,
and the general rules of the feast (τρόπος τῆς πόσεως), which
he occasionally had to enforce by penalties. The drinking
was begun with small goblets, soon followed by larger ones,

Fig. 304.

which had to be emptied by each guest at one draught (ἀπνευ-
στί or ἀμυστὶ πίνειν) to the health of his right-hand neigh-
bour. All this somewhat reminds one of the customs of German
students at their drinking-bouts. The southern vivacity and wit
of the Greeks gave a peculiar charm to these feasts, which,
however, frequently ended in sacrifices to Aphrodite Pandemos, as
is but too easily explainable from the presence of beautiful girls
as singers, players of flute and kithara and cup-bearers. Frequently these feasts were held at the houses of celebrated hetairai.*

* The presence of female slaves as cupbearers at these feats is proved by a bas-
relief (Micali, "L'It. av. il Dominio d. Rom." Atlas pl. 107), where a female slave
fills the goblets of two couples reclining on couches, while three girls are playing
on a flute, lyre, and syrinx, respectively.

Fig. 304 represents one of these scenes, which in later times were undoubtedly of frequent occurrence, and have often been the subjects of vase-paintings.

Jugglers of both sexes, either single or in gangs, were common all over Greece, putting up their booths, as Xenophon says, wherever money and silly people could be found. These frequently amused the guests at drinking-feasts with their tricks. The reputation of this class of people was anything but above suspicion, as is proved by the verse of Manetho ("Apotheles," IV., 276), in which they are described as the "birds of the country, the foulest brood of the city." Their tricks were innumerable, and outvied in boldness and ingenuity those of our conjurors, barring,

Fig. 305.

Fig. 306.

of course, such as are founded on the modern discoveries of natural science. Male and female jugglers jumped forwards and backwards over swords or tables; girls threw up and caught again a number of balls or hoops to the accompaniment of a musical instrument; others displayed an astounding skill with their feet and toes while standing on their hands. Rope-dancers performed the most dangerous dances and *salti-mortali*. In Rome even elephants were trained to mount the rope. Flying-machines of a construction unknown to us are also mentioned, on which bold aëronauts traversed the air. Alkiphron tells a story about a peasant who, on seeing a juggler pulling little bullets from the noses, ears, and heads of the spectators, exclaimed: "Let such a beast never enter my yard, or else everything would soon disappear." Descriptions of these tricks are frequent in ancient writers, particularly in the indignant invectives of the early fathers of the Church (compare § 100). Amongst the pictures of

female jugglers in all kinds of impossible postures we have
chosen three.   Fig. 305 shows a girl in short drawers and with a
cap on her head, performing the dangerous sword-dance (ἐς
μαχαίρας κυβιστᾶν) described by Plato ("Euthymed.," p. 294)
and Xenophon ("Symposion," § 11).   It consists in her turning
somersaults forwards and backwards across the points of three
swords stuck in the ground.   A similar picture we see on a vase
of the Berlin Museum.   Fig. 306 shows a female juggler dressed

Fig. 307.

in long drawers standing on her hands, and
filling with her feet a kantharos from a krater
placed in front of her.   She holds the handle
of the kantharos with the toes of her left
foot, while the toes of her other foot cling
round the stem of the kyathos used for drawing the liquor.   A woman sitting in front
of her performs a game with three balls, in
which the other artiste also seems to take

a part.   In Fig. 307 a girl, in a rather awkward position, is
shooting an arrow from a bow.

Of social games played by the topers we mention, besides the
complicated kottabos, the games played on a board or with dice.
Homer already mentions a game of the former class (πεττεία), and
names Palamedes as its inventor; of the exact nature of this
game we know little or nothing.   Neither are we informed of the
details of another kind of petteia played with five little stones
ψῆφοι, on a board divided by five lines.   The so-called "game
of cities" (πόλεις παίζειν) seems to have resembled our chess
or draughts.   The board was divided into five parts (πόλεις
or χῶραι).   Each player tried to checkmate the other by the
skilful use of his men.   Games of hazard with dice and astragaloi
were most likely greater favourites with the topers than the
intellectual ones hitherto described.   The number of dice (κύβοι,
κυβεία, κυβευτήρια, tesseræ) was at first three, afterwards two; the
figures on the parallel sides being 1 and 6, 2 and 5, 3 and 4.
In order to prevent cheating, they were cast from conical
beakers (πύργος, turricula), the interior of which was formed
into different steps.   Each cast had its name, sixty-four of which
have been transmitted to us by the grammarians.   The luckiest
cast, each of the dice showing the figure 6 (τρὶς ἕξ), was called

Aphrodite; the unluckiest, the three dice showing the figure 1, had the names of "dog" or "wine" applied to it (κύων, οἶνος, also τρεῖς κύβοι). Another game of a similar nature was played with the so-called astragaloi (ἀστράγαλοι, *tali*), dice of a lengthy shape made of the knuckles of animals. Two of the surfaces were flat, the third being raised, and the fourth indented slightly. The last-mentioned side was marked 1, and had, amongst many other names, that of "dog" (κύων, *canis*); the opposite surface, marked 6, was called κῶος. The Latin names of the two other sides marked 3 and 4 were *suppus* and *planus* respectively. The figures 2 and 5 were wanting on the astragaloi, the narrow end-surfaces not being counted. The number of astragaloi used was always four, being the same as in the game of dice. Here also the luckiest cast was called Aphrodite, with which at the same time the honour of king-of-the-feast was connected. Young girls liked to play at a game with five astragaloi, or little stones, which were thrown into the air and caught on the upper surface of the hand (πεντελιθίζειν, πενταλιθίζειν). This game is still in use in many countries. We possess many antique representations of these various games.* Two vase-paintings (Panofka, "Bilder antiken Lebens," Taf. X. Nos. 10, 11) show soldiers playing at draughts. Astragaloi and dice of different sizes, some with the figures as above described on them, others evidently counterfeited, are preserved in several museums. Of larger representations we mention the marble statue of a girl playing with astragaloi in the Berlin Museum, and a Pompeian wall-painting ("Museo Borbon.," vol. v., Tav. 23) in which the children of Jason play the same game, while Medea threatens their lives with a drawn sword. The celebrated masterpiece of Polykletes, representing two boys playing with astragaloi, formerly in the palace of Titus in Rome, has unfortunately been lost. Another wall-painting (Millin, "Mythologische Gallerie," Taf. CXXXVIII. No. 515) shows in the foreground Aglaia and Hileaira, daughters of Niobe, kneeling and playing the same game.

In connection with these social games we mention a few other

---

* Amongst the false dice of the R. Museum of Berlin one has the figure 4 twice over; another was evidently loaded with lead. Besides, there is a die in the shape of an octagonal prism; the surfaces show the following sequence of figures: 1, 7, 2, 6, 3, 5, 4, 8.

favourite amusements of the Greeks. The existence of cock-fights (ἀλεκτρυονομαχία) is proved by vase-paintings, gems, and written evidence. It was a favourite pastime with both old and young. Themistokles, after his victory over the Persians, is said to have founded an annual entertainment of cock-fights, which made both these and the fights of quails popular amongst the Greeks. The breeding of fighting-cocks was a matter of great importance, Rhodes, Chalkis, and Media being particularly cele-brated for their strong and large cocks. In order to increase their fury, the animals were fed with garlic previous to the fight. Sharp metal spurs were attached to their legs, after which they were placed on a table with a raised border. Very large sums were frequently staked on them by owners and spectators. Here again we see antique customs reproduced by various modern nations. The Italian game of *morra* (*il giuco alla morra* or *fare alla*

Fig. 308.

morra) was also known to the ancients. In it both players open their clenched right hands simultaneously with the speed of lightning, whereat each has to call out the number of fingers extended by the other. Fig. 308, from a vase-painting in the Pinakothek of Munich, shows Eros and Anteros playing this game. It was called by the Greeks δακτύλων ἐπάλλαξις, by the Romans *micare digitis.* (Compare similar representations in *Archæologische Zeitung*, 1871, Taf. 56.)

57. Mimetic dances were another favourite amusement at symposia. They mostly represented mythological scenes. A few words about Greek dancing ought to be added. Homer mentions dancing as one of the chief delights of the feast; he also praises the artistic dances of the Phaiakian youths. This proves the esteem in which this art was held even at that early period. In the dances of the Phaiakai, all the young men performed a circular movement round a singer standing in the centre, or else two skilled dancers executed a *pas de deux*. Homer's words seem to indicate that the rhythmical motion was not limited to the legs, as in our modern dances, but extended to the upper part of the body and the arms. Perhaps the germs of

mimetic art may be looked for in this dance. According to Lucian, the aim of the dance was to express sentiment, passion, and action by means of gestures. It soon developed into highest artistic beauty, combined with the rhythmic grace peculiar to the Greeks. Like the gymnastic and agonistic arts, the dance retained its original purity as long as public morality prevailed in Greece : its connection with religious worship preserved it from neglect. Gradually, however, here also mechanical virtuosity began to supplant true artistic principles.

The division of dances according to their warlike or religious character seems objectionable, because all of them were originally connected with religious worship. The distinction between warlike and peaceful dances, called by Plato $τὸ πολεμικὸν εἶδος$ and $τὸ εἰρηνικόν$, is more appropriate. Amongst the warlike dances particularly adapted to the Doric character, the $πυρρίχη$ was the oldest and that most in favour. It dates from mythical times. Pyrrhichos, either a Kretan or Spartan by birth, the Dioskuroi, also Pyrrhos the son of Achilles, are mentioned as its originators. The Pyrrhic dance, performed by several men in armour, imitated the movements of attack and defence. The various positions were defined by rule ; hands and arms played an important part in the mimetic action, hence the name $χειρονομία$ also applied to this dance. It formed the chief feature of the Doric gymnopaidia and of the greater and lesser Panathenaïa at Athens. The value attached to it in the latter city is proved by the fact of the Athenians making Phrynichos commander-in-chief owing to the skill dis-

Fig. 309.

played by him in the Pyrrhic dance. Later a Bacchic element was introduced into this dance, which henceforth illustrated the deeds of Dionysos. A fragment of a marble frieze (Fig. 309) shows a satyr with a thyrsos and laurel crown performing a wild Bacchic dance between two soldiers, also executing a dancing movement ; it most likely illustrates the Pyrrhic dance of a later epoch. Of other warlike dances we mention the $καρπεία$, which rendered the surprise of a warrior ploughing a field by robbers, and the scuffle between them. It was accompanied on the flute.

More numerous, although less complicated, were the peaceful choral dances performed at the feasts of different gods, according to their individualities. With the exception of the Bacchic dances, they consisted of measured movements round the altar. More lively in character were the gymnopaidic dances performed by men and boys. They were, like most Spartan choral dances, renowned for their graceful rhythms. They consisted of an imitation of gymnastic exercises, particularly of the wrestling-match and the Pankration ; in later times it was generally succeeded by the warlike Pyrrhic dance. Another dance, performed by noble Spartan maidens in honour of Artemis Karyatis, is depicted, Fig. 310. The chain-dance (ὅρμος) belongs to the same class. It was danced by a number of youths and maidens

Fig. 310.

placed alternately in a ring, and holding each other's hands ; they each performed the softer or more warlike movements suited to their sex, so that the whole, according to Lucian, resembled a chain of intertwined manly courage and female modesty (compare Fig. 310). We pass over the names of several dances, of which nothing is known to us beyond their connection with the worship of Dionysos. In this worship, more than in any other, the symbolic rendering of natural phenomena was felt by the people. The dying throbs of Nature in autumn, her rigid torpor in winter, and final revival in spring, were the fundamental ideas of the Bacchic myth. The joy and sorrow expressed by the Bacchic dances were in a manner inspired by these changes in nature. This dramatic element in the Bacchic dance was the germ of theatrical representations. The grave and joyful feelings excited

by the approach of winter or spring found their expressions both
in hymns and choric dances. In the intervals between two
hymns the choragos, disguised as a satyr, stepped forward, and
recited in an improvised oration the feats of Dionysos, celebrated
in the dithyrambos. His language was either serious or jocular,
according to the facts related. Thespis, by distinguishing the
actor from the chorus, and introducing a dialogue between him
and the choragoi, initiated the artistic drama. The choruses sung
at the Lenaia, the Bacchic winter celebrations, were descriptive of
the death of Nature, symbolized by the sufferings of Dionysos.
Tragedy owed its origin to them, while comedy was the development of the small rural Dionysia at the conclusion of the vintage.
In the latter the phallus, the symbol of Nature's creative power,
was carried in festive procession, surrounded by a crowd, adorned
with wreaths and masks. After the Phallic and Ithyphallic songs
had been sung, unbounded merriment, raillery, and satire became
the order of the day. Our remarks about the Greek theatre
will be limited to the decorative arrangement of the skene (as far
as it has not been considered in § 30), and the costumes of the
actors.

58. The assembled people in a crowded theatre must have
been an imposing spectacle, in which the gorgeous colours of the
dresses were blended with the azure of a southern sky. No
antique rendering of this subject remains. The spectators began
to assemble at early dawn, for each wished to secure a good seat,
after paying his entrance-fee ($\theta\epsilon\omega\rho\iota\kappa\acute{o}\nu$). This, not exceeding
two oboloi, was payable to the builder or manager of the theatre.
After the erection of stone theatres at Athens, this entrance-fee
was paid for the poorer classes by Government, and formed,
indeed, one of the heaviest items of the budget. For not only at
the Dionysian ceremonies, but on many other festive occasions,
the people clamoured for free admission, confirmed in their
demands by the demagogues. Frequently the money reserved
for the emergency of a war had to be spent for this purpose.
The seats in a theatre were, of course, not all equally good,
and their prices varied accordingly. The police of the theatre
($\dot{\rho}\alpha\beta\delta o\phi\acute{o}\rho o\iota$, $\dot{\rho}\alpha\beta\delta o\hat{\upsilon}\chi o\iota$) had to take care that everybody took his
seat in the row marked on his ticket. Most of the spectators
were men. In older times women were allowed only to attend at

tragedies, the coarse jokes of the comedy being deemed unfit for the ears of Athenian ladies. Only hetairai made an exception to this rule. It is almost certain that the seats of men and women were separate. Boys were allowed to witness both tragedies and comedies. Whether slaves were admitted amongst the spectators seems doubtful. As pedagogues were not allowed to enter the schoolroom, it seems likely that they had also to leave the theatre after having shown their young masters to their seats. Neither were the slaves carrying the cushions for their masters' seats admitted amongst the spectators. It is, however, possible that when the seats became to be for sale, certain classes of slaves were allowed to visit the theatre. Favourite poets and actors were rewarded with applause and flowers; while bad performers had to submit to whistling and, possibly, other worse signs of public indignation. Greek audiences resembled those of southern Europe at the present day in the vivacity of their demonstrations, which were even extended to public characters amongst the spectators on their entering the theatre.

The frontage of the skene consisted in the oldest times of only one story, to which, however, several others were added when the development of the drama by Aischylos demanded a greater perfection of the scenic apparatus. According to Vitruvius, the skene was developed architecturally, like the façades of large buildings, and, like these, adorned with columns, architraves, and friezes. His statement is confirmed by the well-preserved skene of the theatre at Aspendos, which, however, was built after a Roman pattern (see the view and description of it, § 84). According to Vitruvius, five doors were situated in the background, the centre one being called the gate of the royal palace (*valvæ regiæ*), most likely owing to the action of the antique tragedy generally taking place in front of a king's palace. The two gates to both sides of this led into buildings connected with the palace destined for the reception of guests, whence their name *hospitalia*. The two remaining doors, lying near the corners of the skene-wall and the wings of the stage, were called *aditus* and *itinera* respectively; the former indicating the road to the city, the latter that to foreign countries. In theatres where there were only three doors, the latter names were applied to the two doors to the right and left of the *valvæ regiæ*. The chorus entered the orchestra through the parodoi ; the actors coming from home or foreign parts could therefore conveniently enter and retire from the stage by means of the steps ascending from the orchestra to the logeion. Immediately before the skene-wall, perhaps only a few feet distant from it, was placed a wooden framework, across which the back scene was fastened. The doors in this piece of scenery corresponded to those in the stone wall. The back scene could undoubtedly be made to slide to right and left from the centre (*scena ductilis*), so as to produce a change of scenery, which, as we shall show, could be made complete by the turning of the periaktoi. Whether the back scene consisted of only two, or, as is more likely, of four or eight, movable pasteboard partitions we must leave undecided. Lohde * says that, in order to make the parts of the back scene, pushed behind the periaktoi, quite invisible to the public, "slight frames of woodwork, covered with painted paper-hangings, were placed at the further end and to both sides of the pulpitum, which were immediately connected with the side wings of the stage-building." By means of these pieces of scenery the excessive length of the stage was considerably shortened—the remaining space being still quite sufficient for the few actors of the Greek drama. In order to cover the stone wall of the skene, the artificial wall alluded to had to be of considerable height. To give it firmness, a second wooden erection was placed several feet behind it, running parallel to it ; both were connected by means of cross beams, and rested on firm foundations, the remains of which have been discovered in the theatres of Herculaneum, Pompeii, Orange, and Arles, belonging, it is true, all of them to Roman times.

Besides the back scene, two side scenes (περίακτοι, μηχαναί) existed in Greek theatres. They consisted of slight wooden frames in the form of three-sided prisms, covered with painted canvas. By means of pegs they could easily be revolved on their axis, so that always one of their painted surfaces was turned towards the spectators. Each of these three surfaces was painted in a different manner, and the changed position of the periaktoi indicated a total or partial change of locality on the stage. In case the periaktos to the left of the spectator was moved, the

---

* "Die Skene der Alten." Berlin, 1860. The chief points of which investigation we have adopted in our description.

direction of the foreign road was supposed to be changed. The revolving of both periaktoi implied a modification of the back scene, an entire change of locality being thus indicated. The periaktos to the right of the spectator could never be turned by itself, for it indicated the position of home, which, as long as the centre scene was unchanged, naturally remained the same. The few changes of scenery occurring in the antique drama could easily be effected. To complete the skene, a kind of ceiling of boards was necessary, traces of which can still be distinguished on the wall of the skene of the theatre at Aspendos. On these boards stood the crane on which was suspended the flying apparatus (called μηχανή in general, or more especially γέρανος, αἰώρημα, στροφεῖον, and ἡμιστρόφιον). By means of it gods and heroes and spectres entered and left the stage, or floated across it. A floating-machine of this kind was also the θεολογεῖον, on which, for instance, Zeus, with Eos and Thetis, appeared in Aischylos's *Psychotasia.* The upper conclusion of the stage was effected by means of a piece of painted canvas (κατάβλημα) hanging down, which covered the woodwork of the ceiling and the machinery placed there from the eyes of the spectators. The Charonic stair we have mentioned before. Quite recently* a hollow, of the shape of a coffin, has been discovered on the stage of the Greek theatre of Azanoi in Asia Minor, just in front of the *porta regia.* This was undoubtedly the opening of the Charonic staircase. Whether the old Attic stage had a curtain seems doubtful: later a curtain (αὐλαία, παραπέτασμα, originally called also προσκήνιον) is mentioned. Perhaps it used to be parted in the middle, and the two divisions pushed behind the sides of the proskenion.

An important part of the costume of the actors was the mask (πρόσωπον). Its origin must undoubtedly be looked for in the grotesque jocularities of the Dionysian worship. Disguises, the painting of the face with the lees of wine, afterwards with minium, or the wearing of masks made of leaves or bark, were customary from the earliest times. Thence the drama adopted its masks of painted canvas. It must be remembered that the antique actor was not so much the expounder of individual passion as the representative of the different phases and classes of society. The

---

* Sperling, "Ein Ausflug in die isaurischen Berge im Herbst 1862," in *Zeitschrift für allgemeine Erdkunde.* New Series, XV., 1863, p. 435.

expression of his face, therefore, was of much less importance than in the modern drama. K. O. Müller justly remarks that types like Aischylos's Orestes, Sophokles's Aias, or Euripides's Medea did not demand the *nuances* of facial expression that would be expected from Hamlet or Tasso. Moreover the masks could be changed so as to render the more general gradations of passion. Owing to the large size of the Greek theatre, acoustical and optical means had to be applied to convey the words and movements of the actors to the more distant rows of spectators. One of the latter was the apparent increase of the actor's size by means of κόθορνοι and high masks. The development of the mask into a covering, not only of the face, but of the whole head with side and front hair attached to it (ὄγκος), was ascribed to Aischylos. Openings were left for mouth and eyes, the latter not being larger than the pupil of the actor, and the former only just wide enough to afford egress to the voice. This was the case at least in tragedy : comic masks, on the other hand, showed distorted features, and a mouth widely opened, the lips serving as a kind of speaking-trumpet. Varieties

a   b   c   d   e

Fig. 311.

of modelling and painting, combined with the numerous changes of hair and beard, tended to greatly modify the character of the masks. The parts of young or old men and women and of slaves had their characteristic masks assigned to them, all of which are enumerated by Pollux. All this tended to some extent to remove the stiffness of the mask. Figs. 311 and 312 show a number of masks found on monuments. Fig. 311 *a*, *b*, *c*, *d* are tragic masks, *b*, *c* being remarkable by their high onkoi; *d* shows a female countenance with waving locks, *e* the ivy-crowned and nearly bald mask used in satyr-dramas. Fig. 312 illustrates the varieties of comic masks ; it would, however, be difficult to identify the masks described by Pollux on the monuments. The height of the onkos demanded a proportionate increase of the size of the body, which was effected by the actors walking on buskins (κόθορνος) (see Fig. 313, illustrative of a scene from a tragedy);

a   b   c   d   e

Fig. 312.

they also used to pad their limbs. The remainder of the actors' costumes was also to a great extent borrowed from the Dionysian

feast, both with regard to shape and colour. Tragic actors wore chitones and himatia of light colour richly embroidered, and embellished by brilliant gold ornaments. In comedy the dress of daily life was essentially reproduced, with the difference, however, that the old comedy caricatured this dress by attaching to it the frequently indecent emblems of Dionysian worship, while the

Fig. 313.

later comedy retained the caricatured mask, but discontinued the grotesque costume of older times. The monuments contain only

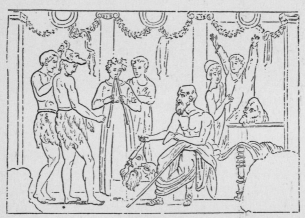

Fig. 314.

few representations of scenes from tragedies: scenes from the satyr-drama and the older comedy are, on the contrary, very frequent. Only in very few cases, however, are we able to trace these scenes back to the dramas preserved to us. Fig. 314 opens a view into the χορηγεῖον or διδασκαλεῖον of a poet or choragos before the performance of a satyr-drama. The aged poet seems to instruct some choreutai in their parts, and to call their attention to the masks lying before them ; a pipe-player is practising his music. In the background to the right an actor is putting on his costume with the aid of a servant; his mask is lying by his side. A similar rehearsal of a satyr-drama is illustrated by a large vase-painting, in the centre of which Dionysos and Ari-

Fig. 315. Fig. 316.

adne are reclining on a couch. A second female figure, perhaps the Muse, is sitting on the other end of the couch, by the side of which stand two actors (Fig. 315), one in the dress of Herakles, the other in that of Seilenos. The third actor, in the rich costume of an unknown hero, appears on the other side of the kline. The whole group is surrounded by eleven choreutai in a similar costume as those in Fig. 314. We also discover one kitharodos and one pipe-player, and the youthful master of the chorus. Fig. 316 depicts a scene from a comedy. Herakles, in a grotesque boorish dress, presents two Kerkopes, caught and imprisoned by him in market-baskets, to the ruler, whose mask resembles the head of an ape—quite in accordance with the ape-like form of the imps.

59. Agones, hymns, and choric dances were performed in honour of the gods ; sacrifices and prayers, on the other hand, established the immediate *rapport* between man and God. They were offered either to pray for a divine gift, as a successful chase,

harvest, etc., or they were intended to soften the wrath of the gods in impending or actual danger, such as illness and storms. A thank-offering eventually followed the grant of these prayers. A third sacrifice was that of expiation and atonement for a breach of the law, human or divine. The mode of prayers and sacrifices varied with their motives; but, before a man entered into intercourse with the deity, he had to undergo a symbolic process of external purification (καθαρμοί, ἱλασμοί, τελεταί). This was exacted not only from those who sacrificed, but from all who entered the precinct of a temple. Vessels with consecrated water stood at the entrances to such places, the sprinkling being done either by the person himself or by a priest. These lustrations were even performed in daily life, previous to acts in any way connected with religious ideas. The bridal bath described by us, the lustrations before feasts, the vessel with water placed at the door of a dead person for the use of the mourners on leaving the house—all these had the same significance. The contact with a dead body especially required a lustration, being considered as a taint which temporally prohibited the intercourse with the deity. Another kind of purification was that by fire and smoke. Odysseus performs a lustration with the steam of " curse-removing sulphur " (περιθείωσις) after the murder of the wooers; the fire burning on the altar, and the torches carried at religious ceremonies, had the same significance of moral purification. The carrying of the new-born infant round the flames of the domestic altar has been mentioned before. The lustration with fire and water even extended to the garments and to the utensils used at sacrifices. Herakles purified the goblet with water and sulphur before sacrificing to Zeus; Penelope took a bath, and dressed herself in clean garments, before sacrificing and praying for the safety of her son. To certain plants, such as myrtle, rosemary, and juniper, purifying qualities were ascribed. A twig of Apollinian laurel was supposed to free the murderer from his guilt. These purifications were also performed collectively by tribes and nations; in Homer, for instance, the Achaioi "purify themselves and throw their stain into the sea." In historic times collective lustrations of cities after epidemics or civil wars are mentioned repeatedly. Epimenides, for instance, purified Athens after the Kylonian massacre.

The act of purification was followed by the prayer. Plato says that it ought to precede every enterprise, great or little, and that for a virtuous man there is nothing better than keeping up the intercourse with the gods by means of offerings, prayers, and vows. Almost all important events or customs in the daily life, both of individuals and communities, were accompanied by prayers, consisting chiefly of old traditional formulas. Three gods—for instance, Zeus in conjunction with Athene and Apollo—were usually addressed together. In order not to offend the deity by omitting one of its names, certain formulas were usually added to the prayer, such as "whether you be a god or goddess;" or, "whoever you may be;" or, "whether this or another be your favourite name." The Olympian gods were prayed to in an upright position with raised hands; the marine gods, with hands held horizontally; the gods of Tartarus, with hands held down: the latter were also invoked by knocking or stamping the foot on the ground. Kneeling was not a custom of the Greeks: whenever it is mentioned amongst them, Oriental influence must be suspected. Only those craving protection used to embrace the statue of the god in a kneeling position, which is frequently represented on the monuments. Akin to the prayer was the curse against criminals: the Erinies were implored to execute it. Zeus Horkios, the revenger of oaths, punished the perjurer with his wrath. The solemn oath was taken on hallowed ground before the altar or statue of a god. The swearing person either touched these or immersed his hand in the blood of a sacrificed animal, calling, as in the prayer, usually on three gods as witnesses. This was the later custom: in Homer the heroes taking an oath raised their sceptre against the sky.

Prayers were always accompanied by gifts, to propitiate the gods. They were either gifts for the moment, to be deposited on the altar or consumed by fire; or they took the shape of votive offerings, which remained the property of the sanctuary. Gifts, as an old proverb says, determine the acts of gods and kings. Offerings of the former class consisted of the first-fruits of the field, such as onions, pumpkins, grapes, figs, and olives. Prepared eatables, such as cakes (πέμματα, πέλανοι) and other pastry, frequently in the shapes of animals, and in the place of real ones, were also offered to the gods. Roasted barley (οὐλαί, οὐλοχύται)

was another common gift; it was either thrown into the flames or
sprinkled on the necks of the animals brought for sacrifice. A bloodless offering is depicted in Fig. 317. The laurel-crowned priest
stands in front of the fire on the altar, throwing into it the barley
which is presented to him by an attendant in a basket adorned
with sacred twigs. On the other side another youthful attendant
is holding a long staff resembling a torch, to the upper end of
which is fastened some wool or oakum, serving most likely to
light a fire. By other archæologists this figure is explained as
a neokoros with a besom of laurel branches; a musician accom-

Fig. 317.

panies the ceremony on the pipe. Libations formed an essential
feature of sacrifices, just as they did at the meals of mortals. To
some gods unmixed wine was offered; others, for instance the
Erinies, Nymphs, Muses, and deities of Light, received honey,
milk, and oil. A libation of this kind is represented in the
frequently repeated choragic bas-reliefs, where Nike pours the
sacred beverage into a vase which is offered to her by the victorious Kitharoidos (Millin, "Galérie mythol.," Pl. XVII., No. 58).

The choice of the animals to be sacrificed depended on the
individual qualities of the various gods. The Olympian gods preferred white animals; those of the sea and the nether world, black
ones. To Demeter a pig was sacrificed, to Dionysos a he-goat,
because these animals destroyed the gifts granted to man by
these gods. Heifers, sheep, goats, and pigs were offered in larger
or smaller numbers, according to the wealth of the worshipper;

sometimes these different animals were promiscuously offered on one and the same occasion. In Homer sometimes twelve, at others ninety-nine, bulls are slaughtered together; in later times we repeatedly hear of hekatombs of a hundred and more bulls being killed. The original custom of burning the entire animal gradually disappeared; and, even in Homer's time, the gods received only the haunches and small pieces of flesh as their share, the remainder being eaten by those present. These sacrificial meals, shared, as it were, by gods and men, became an integral part of the sacrifice; only offerings for the dead, and the sacrifices on which lay a curse, were buried entire. The animals had to be strong and healthy, and their previous use for human purposes made them inadmissible; only in Sparta, where luxurious sacrifices were altogether unusual, owing to Doric frugality, this absolute purity of the animals was less strictly insisted upon.

For a graphic account of the sacrificial ceremonies, which remained essentially unaltered in later times, we refer the reader to two passages in Homer (Od., III. 436 *et seq.*, and Il., I. 458 *et seq.*).

The custom of gilding the horns mentioned by Homer was afterwards changed into adorning them with wreaths and tainiai. It was considered a favourable omen if the animal went to the sacrifice without opposition, or even nodded its head, as if consenting to its death. According to the sacrifice being for the Olympian or nether world, the head of the animal was bent upwards or downwards. Its throat was then pierced with a knife. Vase-paintings frequently show Nike in the act of sacrificing a bull. The animals, as well as the baskets and other sacrificial utensils, were adorned with twigs or wreaths; the latter, or instead of them a woollen tie, were worn by the Greeks at all religious acts. Criminals only were forbidden to wear them, and were by that means excluded from sacrificial cere-monies. Barring a few representations not easily to be explained (*e.g.* "Museo Borbon.," vol. v., Tav. 23), Greek monuments, as a rule, illustrate only simple sacrificial acts, as the adorning of divine images or the offerings of gifts of various kinds: we therefore refrain from entering into details. To the sacrifices for the dead we shall return hereafter.

The most brilliant exhibitions of religious worship were the festive processions. The Panathenaïa, in which the whole Athenian population took part, are rendered, on the cella frieze of the Parthenon, by the master-hand of Phidias. Theseus, who united the Attic komai into one city, was also named as the originator of this celebration of fraternity. At first only horse and chariot races took place, to which were added, in Peisistratos's time, gymnic agones, and, since Perikles, poetical and musical competitions. The performance of all these agones took place in the third year of every Olympiad, between the twenty-fifth and twenty-seventh days of the month of Hekatombaion. The climax of the feast—the procession—was held on the twenty-eighth day of that month. It moved through the streets of the city to the seat of the goddess, in the Akropolis. On the morning of that day the citizens of Athens, together with the peasants of the neighbouring country, assembled before the chief gate of the city, and formed themselves into a procession according to a fixed ceremonial. Kitharoidoi and auletai opened the procession; the reason of this distinction being that the musico-poetical agones were those last introduced at the Panathenaïa. After them followed, in good order, citizens on foot, armed with spear and shield, and others on horseback. Next came the victors in the horse and chariot races; the former riding on their horses, or leading them; the latter standing on their splendid quadrigæ. Priests, with their attendants, guarded the hekatombs to be sacrificed; old men, chosen for their dignified appearance, held olive-branches, from the holy tree of the Academy, in their hands (θαλλοφόροι); other distinguished persons carried the votive offerings destined for the goddess; a select band of citizens' daughters carried baskets containing the utensils of the sacrifice (κανηφόροι); while epheboi brought valuable plate, wrought by the most celebrated masters. After them followed the wives and daughters of the tribes protected by the Athenians; the matrons holding in their hands oak-branches, the emblem of Zeus Xenios, so as to mark them as guests; the maidens carrying the sunshades and chairs of the citizens' daughters (σκιαδηφόροι, διφροφόροι. The centre of the procession was formed by a ship resting on wheels, which carried, by way of a sail, the peplos of Athene, woven by Attic maidens, and richly embroidered, in which the old Xoanon of the goddess in the Akropolis was dressed. In this order the procession moved through the most splendid streets of the city, past the most celebrated sanctuaries where gifts were offered, round the rock of the Akropolis, entering, at last, through the celebrated Propylæa. Here the procession divided, to gather again on the east side of the Parthenon. All arms were taken off, and hymns were sung to the goddess by the assembled crowd, while burnt-offerings blazed on the altars, and votive-offerings were deposited in the sanctuary.

Although the frieze of the Parthenon-cella does not systematically render the procession, we can easily reconstruct it from the indications thus offered; indeed, all the important components of the festive crowd appear in the different groups. According to Bötticher,* however, the subject of the frieze is not the procession itself, but the preparations for it, such as the division, amongst the persons destined to carry them, of chairs, couches, and bolsters, which were kept in the Hekatompedon, and other preparatory arrangements. The various scenes represented are, according to him, divided both by space and time. Bötticher's conjecture was started in contradiction to all previous archæologists.

60. We now have to follow the Greek to his last place of rest, to see how the holy rites (τὰ δίκαια or τὰ νόμιμα) are duly performed for him. To watch over the rights of the dead, and to do him the last honour, so that his spirit might not wander restlessly on the banks of Acheron, excluded from the Elysian fields —this was the beautiful Greek custom sanctified by the precepts of religion. Hence the pious usage of adorning the dead for their last journey, of burying them with becoming ceremonies, and of considering their graves as holy places not to be profaned. With the same view the bodies of those who died in foreign countries were brought home, or, where this proved impossible, an empty tomb, a kenotaphion, was erected in their birthplace. It would have been disgraceful to deprive even enemies of the honour of a burial, and it was the custom, after a battle, to interrupt hostilities till both parties had buried their dead. Solon's laws discharged the son from all obligations towards his father in case the latter

---

* In "Königliche Museen. Erklärendes Verzeichniss der Abgüsse antiker Werke." Berlin, 1871, pp. 188—228.

had committed an immoral act against him, with the exception only of the duty " of," to use the words of Aischines, "burying his father according to prescribed custom in honour of the gods and the law. For he who receives the benefit is no more able to feel it." Only he who had betrayed his country or committed a capital crime was deprived of the honour of a burial. His corpse remained unburied, the prey of wild beasts, with no friend near to throw at least a handful of earth on it. On the other hand, an honourable burial (ὑπὸ τῶν ἑαυτοῦ ἐκγόνων καλῶς καὶ μεγαλοπρεπῶς ταφῆναι) was, as Plato says in Hippias Maj., the most beautiful conclusion of a life prolonged to old age, and surrounded by wealth, health, and the esteem of men.

We first turn to the burial rites of heroic times. The closing of lips and eyes of the dead was, as early as Homer's time, the first service of love (τὸ γὰρ γέρας ἐστὶ θανόντων) on the part of the surviving relatives or friends. After it the body was washed, anointed, and clothed in white thin garments; only the head remaining uncovered. Thus arranged, the body was placed on a kline, the foot end of which was turned towards the door of the house. Thereupon began the lament, for a specimen of which we refer the reader to the passage of the 'Iliad' in which the death of Patroklos is announced to Achilles. The ceremonies performed at the couch of the slain Hektor prove the existence of a regulated lament for the dead at that time. We there hear of singers intoning chants of complaint (θρῆνοι), interrupted by the loud lamentations of Andromache, Hekabe, and Helen. The corpse was exhibited for several days (*e.g.*, that of Achilles seventeen days, that of Hektor nine), during which time the lamentations were renewed incessantly; ultimately it was placed on the funeral pile to be given to the flames, numerous sheep and heifers being sacrificed simultaneously round the pyre. As soon as the funeral pile was consumed by the flames, the fire was extinguished with wine. The ashes, after having been sprinkled with oil and wine, were collected into urns or boxes of valuable materials. The urn itself was covered with gorgeous purple draperies, and deposited in the grave.* On this grave was heaped a high earth-mound, as

---

* Ross states that in the large graves of the Isle of Rhenæa ("Archæolog. Aufsätze," i. p. 62) two different kinds of vessels containing ashes (ὀστοθῆκαι) have been dis-covered. The first kind consists of semi-globular vases (κάλπις) of thin bronze, 10

examples of which custom we mention the grave-mounds raised in honour of Achilles and Patroklos by the Greek army. Agones and a festive meal concluded the ceremonies, as described by Homer.

In early times the Attic burial-rites are said to have been very simple. The grave was dug by the nearest relatives, and the corpse buried in it; whereupon the mound was sown with corn, by means of which the decaying body was supposed to be pacified. A meal, at which the *real* worth of the deceased was extolled by the survivors (*nam mentiri nefas habebatur*), concluded the ceremony. The more luxurious habits of a later period made the great funereal pomps originally reserved for heroes a common

Fig. 318.

custom amongst all classes. Solon had to prescribe distinct burial regulations, by which the protracted exhibition of the dead and other abuses were forbidden. Upon the whole, however, the ceremonies described by Homer remained essentially unaltered. An obolos, being the ferriage (ναῦλον, δανάκη) for Charon, was put into the mouth of the corpse; the body then was washed and anointed by the relatives (particularly the women), and clothed in a white shroud. It was crowned with flowers and wreaths, also provided by the relatives, and thus prepared for the customary lying-in-state (πρόθεσις, προτίθεσθαι). This adorning of the corpse is illustrated by an interesting Apulian vase-painting, representing the crowning of the body of Archemoros (Fig. 318).

to 12 inches in diameter, which, owing to their brittleness, have been fitted into marble cases with covers to them. Such marble shells, containing bronze vases covered with rust and partly destroyed, have been discovered in the graves of the Peiraieus. The second kind consists of square or round boxes of lead, also with covers to them.

On a kline covered with bolsters and cushions is lying the body of
Archemoros, who, when little more than a boy, had been killed by
a dragon. Hypsipyle, the careless nurse of the boy, stands by
the side of the bier about to put the myrtle-wreath on the curly
head of the dead; another, younger, female, standing at the head
of the kline, holds a sunshade over the bier, in allusion, as
Gerhard thinks, to the old notion that the light of Helios should
accompany the dead to his dark house, a night-burial being
considered dishonourable (compare Euripides, Troad., 446 : ἡ
κακὸς κακῶς ταφῇσῃ νυκτός, οὐκ ἐν ἡμέρᾳ). At the foot of the bed
we observe the pedagogue, recognisable by his dress and the
inscription over his head. In his left hand he is holding a lyre,
in order, perhaps, to add it to the gifts destined to adorn the
chamber of the dead. Under the kline stands a pitcher, the
contents of which had undoubtedly served as a libation. Next
to the pedagogue are standing two attendants, carrying on their
heads tables, on which various vessels adorned with tainiai are
placed. All these, as well as the splendid amphora standing on
the ground, and the krater carried by an ephebos on the left,
belong to the vessels which a pious custom deposited in the grave
or on the funeral pile. At the lying-in-view of the corpse, which
by Solon was considerably shortened, and of which Plato approved
only as a means to prevent burying alive, the relatives and friends
assembled to begin the lamentation. To avoid violent outbreaks
of grief, such as described by Homer,
Solon forbade a demonstrative behaviour, particularly on the part of women : the severe law of Charondas even
prohibited all kinds of complaints at
the bier of the dead. Frequently women were paid on such occasions for
singing woful songs accompanied by
the flute. Fig. 319, taken from a bas-relief on an Etruscan ash-
box, shows three women, most likely of this kind, at the kline
of a deceased person; a fourth seems to lacerate her face with
her hands; a smaller figure, standing near the bier, whose raised
arms indicate deep grief, seems to be the son of the deceased.

Fig. 319.

After the lying-in-view of the corpse, the burial proper
(ἐκφορά) took place early in the morning of the following day.

The *cortège* was opened by a hired chorus of men chanting mourning songs (θρηνῳδοί), or by a number of females playing on flutes (καρίναι), who were followed by the male mourners in grey or black garments and with their hair cut off. All these preceded the corpse, generally carried by relations or friends. The female mourners walked behind the bier: by Solon's law, however, women under sixty, unless the nearest relatives, were excluded. The old custom of burying those fallen for their country at the public expense is thus alluded to by Thukydides (II., 34):— "According to custom, the Athenians prepared a public funeral for those fallen in battle in this manner: three days previously they erected a tent, in which the remains of the killed lay in view; every one there might bring offerings for his deceased relatives. At the funeral, the coffins of cypress-wood are placed on carts, one being assigned to each phyle; in the coffin of each phyle the remains of those belonging to it are laid. An empty covered kline is carried for those missing, whose bodies have not been recovered. Citizens and friends follow the procession, the women attending at the funeral with lamentations. The remains are buried in a public grave lying in the most beautiful suburb of Athens. This place is always used for burying those fallen in battle, with the exception of those killed at Marathon, who were buried on the spot, their courage being deemed worthy of that distinction. After the bones have been covered with earth, a wise and respected man, chosen by the citizens, pronounces the eulogium of the slain, standing on a tribune erected for the purpose." Funeral orations of this kind at the grave were in classic times usual at public funerals only.

The choice of a place for the burial, and the ceremonies accompanying it varied according to the means of the deceased and the customs among different tribes. In the earliest times the burial-places seem to have been in the houses of the deceased themselves. This immediate contact with the dead, however, being considered unclean, burial-grounds were prepared outside the city walls both at Athens and Sikyon. Sparta and Tarentum had burial-grounds in the city in order (as the law of Lykurgos has it) to steel the minds of the youths against the fear of death. Such burial-grounds lie along the roads outside the gates of almost every city, and yield the most important specimens of the grave-monuments described in §§ 23 and 24. The Athenian law forbidding monuments of greater splendour than could be completed by ten men in three days must have been often infringed. Private persons were allowed to bury their dead in fields belonging to them instead of in the nekropolis. That the burning of the bodies—at least, of the Greek nobles—and the preserving of their ashes were customary in the heroic age, is sufficiently proved by Homer. According to Lucian, the same practice continued to be the most usual amongst the Greeks; recent investigations of numerous graves in the Attic plain, however, seem to prove that the burial of unburnt bodies in wooden or earthen coffins (λάρναξ, σορός), or in grave-chambers cut from the living rock, was at least equally frequent; according to Cicero (De Legg. 2, 22), the latter custom was even the older of the two. Most likely the wish of the

Fig. 320.   Fig. 321.

deceased or his relatives, and also the greater or less abundance of timber in a country, decided the matter. The rocky soil of Attika, bare of trees, necessitated the burial in grave-chambers for the majority of the inhabitants. The expression θάπτειν, applied to either kind of burial; καίειν signified cremation; κατορύττειν, interment in particular. Cremation became necessary particularly when the accumulation of bodies after a battle, or, for instance, after the plague of Athens, caused dangerous evaporations. The same process facilitated the transfer home of the remains of a person dying in a foreign country.

After the burial the *cortège* returned to the house of the deceased and sat down to a meal (περίδειπνον), they being considered, in a manner, as the guests of the dead person. The first (τρίτα), second (ἔνατα), and third (τριακάς) sacrifices at the grave took place on the third, tenth, and thirtieth days after the funeral. The last concluded the mourning period at Athens, that at Sparta being still shorter. The tomb adorned with flowers was a hallowed spot where on certain days of the year oblations and libations were offered in memory of the deceased (ἐνάγισμα, ἐναγίζειν, also χοαί used chiefly of libations).

Representations of this pious custom are common, particularly on the lekythoi, which, in a more or less preserved condition, are frequently found by the side of stelai, or amongst the remains of funeral piles. For it was the custom, particularly of the Athenians, to throw behind them the vessels used on such occasions, no utensil used at funerals being allowed to serve the wants of the living. Figs. 320 and 321 are pictures taken from Athenian lekythoi. The former represents a stele adorned at the top with a

"meandering" ornamentation and crowned by a capital of coloured acanthus-leaves. A blue tainia has been wound round the stele. On either side a woman is approaching. She to the right of the spectator carries a large flat dish, on which stands a lekythos, with a tainia laid round it. The figure on the left carries a similar dish in her left hand, while her right

Fig. 322.

hand holds a large flat basket, destined most likely for carrying flowers and cakes. The second picture, only partially reproduced here (Fig. 321), represents the adorning of the tombstone. A crown of ivy and a lekythos containing the sacred oil are seen on the steps of the simple stele, round which a woman is employed in tying red tainiai, with lekythoi attached to them. Fig. 322 shows Hermes Psychopompos gently leading a female shade to the boat of Charon, on her way to the thrones of Hades and Persephone, where stern judgment awaits her.

THE ROMANS.

THE ROMANS.

61. THE design of the Greek temple, in its highest perfection, was, as we have seen, a gradual development of the dwelling-house. This simple, necessary, and logical growth of artistic perfection would be looked for in vain in Roman sacred architecture. The numerous indigenous and foreign elements observable in the general development of that nation have produced a variety of forms in their sacred edifices which makes the methodical evolution of a purely artistic principle, like that of Greek architecture, impossible. It is true that all the forms of the Greek temple described by us also occur among the Romans ; at the same time essential differences occur, owing to the above-mentioned mixture of indigenous and Greek elements in the national life of the Romans. In speaking of the architecture of the Roman temple we therefore shall have to consider three points—viz., firstly, the requirements of the original Italian religion ; secondly, the introduction of Greek forms ; and, lastly, the reciprocal influence of Roman taste and culture on the forms borrowed from the Greeks, and the modification of the latter resulting therefrom.

Concerning the religious ideas of the old Italian tribes, we have to bear in mind that their notions of the Deity did not approach the human type as nearly as did those of the more artistic Greeks. The rational and reflecting Romans considered the gods as the rulers of human affairs and the prototypes of human virtues. Even the names of the old Italian deities were identical with those of the particular phases of moral and physical life protected by them ; hence the symbolism and want of individuality of type in Roman mythology. The notion of the god as an idealized man into which the Greeks had developed the original symbolism of their religion was absent from the Roman mind. Roman deities, therefore, were not in want of a protecting dwelling.

Nevertheless, statues of gods and houses for them occur amongst the Romans at a very early period, originating partly in the universal tendency of primitive nations in that direction, partly in the influence of Greek on Italian culture, which dates back to farthest antiquity. But whenever these houses are of purely Italian origin, their form differs essentially from that of the Greek temple. For to the desire of giving protection to the deity another purpose of no less, perhaps even greater, importance was added.

For, instead of humanising their gods, the Romans were intent upon pointing out, in the strongest ·manner, the divine influence on human affairs. Hence their anxiety to know the will of the god so as to regulate their actions accordingly. This knowledge, however, they did not derive from the utterance of a god-inspired person, as was the case in Greek oracles; the practical mind of the Romans was directed entirely upon obtaining from the gods a decisive Yes or No with regard to a particular action or resolution. Hence the development of augural science, which, by certain signs in the sky, as the flight of birds or the flashes of lightning, determined the positive or negative decision of the divine will. The observation and explanation of these signs most likely belonged originally to the head of the family, in whom centred the authority with regard to both religious and legal questions. As social and political relations grew more complicated, and the prediction of the future itself took the form of a science, the function of an augur seems to have devolved, first upon the king, afterwards on students of the science, who took the official name of augurs, and formed one of the most important priestly colleges amongst the Romans. Individuals were allowed, and representatives of the State compelled, to consult the augurs on all important occasions.

For the observations of these augurs a space in the temple had to be assigned, and protected against the intrusions of the profane. The Romans derived the origin of the science from the Etruscans, in whose theology, it is true, the limitation of the *templum* was determined in its minutest details ; it seems, however, certain that the science itself was common to all old Italian tribes. The observatory of the augurs was originally a square piece of ground, enclosed in the simplest and, at the same time, most appropriate manner. The generic term for such a space was *templum*, from an old Italian root related to the Greek word τέμνειν (to cut off, to border), whence τέμενος, the Greek analogue of *templum*. In order to enable the augurs to decide the favourable or unfavourable character of the auspices, the space alluded to, and, in accordance with it, the sky, was, by a line drawn from east to west (Fig. 323, *e, f*), divided into a day and night side; a second line drawn through it in a right angle to the first, from north to south (*g, h*), marked the sides of the increasing and decreasing day, or of morning and evening. The former line (*e, f*) was called

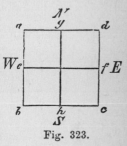

Fig. 323.

decumanus, the latter (*g, h*) *cardo*. The whole space was thus divided into four equal rectangular regions. The augur stood in the point of section (*decussis*) of these lines, the regions taking their different denominations according to the lines. The cardo divided the space into a right or western half (*a, g, h, b*), called *pars dextra*, or *exortiva*, and into an eastern one (*g, d, c, h*), called *pars sinistra*. The former comprised the third and fourth (0 to 180°), the latter the first and second (180° to 360°), chief regions; that is, the range of sight of the augur, when turned towards the south, comprised the south-east on the left and the south-west on the right. The decumanus, on the other hand, divided the space into a northern half (*a, e, f, d*), *pars postica*, lying at the back of the augur, and a southern half (*e, b, c, f*), *pars antica*, lying in front of him; that is, the augur looking towards the east had the north-east on his left and the south-east on his right. Signs appearing on the left were always considered as lucky, those on the right as the reverse. This division of the templum into four chief regions was the common one in the times of Cicero and Pliny, the older rule being observed no more. The older division of the temple into sixteen regions originated with the Etruscans; it implied a close observation of the constellations. This division is of the utmost importance for the investigation of Roman temples, which, according to Nissen's

clever researches, are by no means all built in the same direction.*
The axis of the temple was directed towards the point of the
horizon in which the sun rose on the day of the foundation-stone
being laid, which coincided with the native day or chief feast of
the god to whom the temple was dedicated.   This point changes
in Italy during the course of the year by 65°, in consequence of
which the Italian temples lie in almost all directions of the
compass.   The old Etruscan rule of building temples from north
to south seems to have been adhered to by the Romans only in
rare cases, as is proved by Nissen's investigations.   As the
Romans during their prayer always turned towards the east, the
image to which their prayer was directed had to look westwards.

The square form of the templum necessitated an almost
identical shape of the temple-enclosure.   In this respect the old-
Italian, or as it was called by the Romans Tuscan, temple differs
essentially from the Greek, the latter being an oblong with a
depth almost twice as long as its frontage ; in the Tuscan temple
the proportion of depth to frontage was 6 : 5.   No examples of

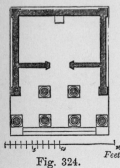

Fig. 324.

the Tuscan temple remain, it having been
supplanted by the forms of Greek architecture ; but with the assistance of Vitruvius's
description (iv. 7) we are able to gain a
tolerably clear notion of its appearance. Fig.
324 shows the plan of an Etruscan temple
according to Hirt's conjectures.   It strikes
us at once that inside the cellæ, which occupy
about one-half of the whole area, no columns
are to be seen. The pronaos has four columns
in front, the two corner ones of which cor-
respond with the *antæ*-pillars.   Two other columns are placed
between these pillars.   Peculiar to the Tuscan style is the slender
smooth column seven diameters in height and tapering by one
quarter.   It has a base divided into two parts, viz., a circular
plinth and a torus, of equal height, and a capital consisting of three
parts, of equal height.   This older form of the column occurs frequently in the decorative semi-columns of later Roman architecture.

62. The design of larger temples was much more varied.   The
style seems to have attained its climax in the temple of the

Capitoline deities, which, according to Roman tradition, Tarquinius Priscus intended for a national sanctuary of the Roman people. He chose for the purpose the highest summit of the Capitoline Hill, which, however, was found insufficient both with regard to size and level surface, and therefore had to be extended and propped by means of enormous substructures. In this manner an all but square area 800 feet in circumference was formed for the reception of the temple, either on the western (present site of the Chiesa Araceli) or eastern (present site of the Palazzo Caffarelli) summit of the hill. The undertaking however, both with regard to working power and expense, was so enormous that Tarquinius Priscus did not even begin the temple itself, which was brought nearer its completion only by Tarquinius Superbus, after (according to some writers) Servius Tullius had made efforts in the same direction. To the Republic was reserved the honour of completing the national sanctuary. M. Horatius Pulvillus, who was consul together with P. Valerius Poplicola in the third year of the Republic, is said to have inaugurated the temple. It stood in its original form for 413 years, when it was totally destroyed by fire.

It was rebuilt by Sulla, essentially unaltered with regard to the original measures and proportions, although modified as to architectural details, as appears from Tacitus's expression : *"iisdem rursus vestigiis situm est"* ("Hist.," iii. 72).* The description, therefore, of the later temple by Dionysios of Halikarnassos (iv., pp. 251, 260) applies to some extent to the original Tarquinian structure. Fig. 325 gives the

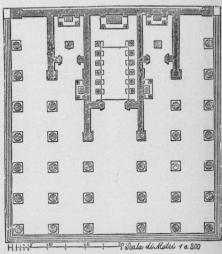

Fig. 325.

plan, Fig. 326 the view, of the temple according to L. Canina's

---

* It was again burnt down during the Vitellian riots, and rebuilt by Vespasian. After this new structure had also been destroyed by fire it was rebuilt, and inaugurated for the fourth time, by Domitian.

conjectural designs. In Fig. 325 we recognise the above-mentioned divisions of the temple into a front and a back half, the former of which, turned towards the south, is enclosed by columns without a wall, while the latter contains under a common roof the three cellæ of the Capitoline deities to whom the temple was dedicated. The centre cella belonged to Jupiter, the two smaller ones to left and right being assigned to Minerva and Juno respectively. By diminishing the dimensions of these two latter cellæ, Canina has succeeded in making his reconstruction to some extent tally with that part of Dionysios's description according to which the temple had three rows of columns in front and only two on each

Fig. 326.

of the long sides. Differing from Dionysios, and not quite free from objection, is Canina's conjecture of there being only six columns in the façade, to which he was led by the representation of the Capitoline temple on Roman coins, where it undoubtedly appears as a hexastylos. At any rate the illustrations offered by us will give the reader a correct general notion of this and other temples with three cellæ. For Fig. 326, old Roman and Etruscan monuments have been consulted to determine not only the columns and their proportions, but also the beams and their ornamentation with triglyphs and metopæ. The statues on the gable were, according to Etruscan custom, of burnt clay.

63. So much about the original Roman or Tuscan style of architecture which, as we said before, was founded on the requirements of old Italian worships. The detailed rules given by Vitruvius for the Tuscan order of columns remind one of Greek forms, and may serve to prove Greek influence on this as on other branches of earliest Italian development—an influence which will appear still more distinctly in our remarks about old Italian graves and wall-structures.

In following the further history of Roman civilisation one observes this influence becoming stronger and stronger. During the times of the kings, to which the development of Tuscan architecture belongs, the relations of the two nations were of the simplest kind; a conscious imitation of Greek customs cannot be thought of, least of all in Latium, the poverty and simplicity of whose inhabitants prevented a deeper-going influence in that direction. This, however, was different in Etruria, the political security and greater wealth of which made it more susceptible to the charms of Greek culture. Hence the notion common amongst the Romans, although considerably shaken by modern science, of the Etruscans having introduced Greek culture to them.

After the expulsion of the kings the influence of Greek on Italian manners begins to increase. The time when first the Roman people were enabled to model more fully their political and legal institutions coincided with the highest climax of Greek culture with regard to political, military, and artistic phases of development. No wonder, therefore, that over the whole Italian peninsula a new civilisation, akin to the Greek model, and fashioned after it, began to gain strength more and more. Etruria began to abound with Greek works of art, and even to rival those great models; Apulia had, from the first, followed Greek examples; in Lucania and Campania Greek language and Greek characters of writing prevailed to a great extent—the surest sign of mental affinity. Rome, which always must claim our chief attention, was, by its constitutional struggles and the warlike spirit of its inhabitants, prevented from receiving with a collected mind the germs of Greek civilisation. Nevertheless, the world-conquering power of this civilisation could not wholly be evaded, and we can look for no more striking proof of the civilizing mission of the Hellenes than in the fact of the Romans becoming more and more subjected to their genius, notwith-standing these unfavourable circumstances.

This influence is recognisable in political no less than in legal and commercial matters. After the conquest of Campania, in the fifth century of the city, the knowledge of Greek institutions, formerly limited to individual statesmen and lawgivers, became diffused amongst wider circles. But, besides this strong and ever-increasing intrusion of Greek uses and (but too frequently) abuses, we have to consider another point of affinity which, from the very beginning of this new epoch, became more and more important, particularly as far as sacred architecture is concerned.

We are alluding to the old religious connections between Greece and Rome, which remained unobliterated in the conscious-ness of the two nations—the signs, as it were, of a common origin, and which led to continued intercourse. The want of personality in the old Italian myths was thus supplied from the rich stores of Greek mythological lore, and the worships of certain gods were, by public authority, transferred from Greece to Rome. This enlargement of the religious horizon is not without political signi-ficance. At first the priestly office was entirely monopolized by the patricians; but, with the growing power of the plebeian element, the introduction of new objects of public worship became necessary. The kings already tried to mediate between plebeians and nobles by erecting a centre of national worship, and the frequent intro-duction, in the following centuries, of Greek deities by government was, in a manner, a continuation of this attempt at conciliating these classes.*

The adoption of Greek architectural forms was, therefore, due to religious causes, previous even to the entering of æsthetical considerations into the question. During the last century of the Republic the attachment to the old indigenous form of worship was more and more supplanted by the influence of modern Greek civilisation. This admixture of Greek mythology and, but too often, Greek scepticism soon tended to abolish the deep religious

---

* The temple of the Capitoline deities must be considered as this centre of *national* worship (Ambrosch, "Stud.," i. 196), independent of patrician exclusiveness. Similar transformations of the Roman religion seem to have been attempted by the earlier Tarquinians. Tarquinius Priscus is said to have erected the first images of gods, and, after him, Servius Tullius ordered the statue of the Aventine Diana to be fashioned after the model of the Artemis of Ephesos, known to the Romans through the Greeks of Massilia.

feeling characteristic of the old Romans. The religious indifference of the upper classes grew into a decided aversion to religion itself, and soon complaints began to be raised of the temples standing empty and being allowed to go to ruin. Augustus restored as many as eighty-two temples, most of them undoubtedly according to the principles of Greek taste, which at that time prevailed in all artistic and poetical creations of the Romans.

Such were the different phases of the influence of Greek on Roman sacred architecture, which gradually led to the entire transformation of the old Italian temple. Indeed, all the different forms of the Greek temple are met with amongst the sacred edifices of the Romans.

The simplest form of the *templum in antis* (see § 5) occurred, according to Vitruvius (III., 1), in a temple of the Three Fortunes, outside the Porta Collina : the prostylos (see § 7) was very frequent. To this we shall have to return (§ 65). Even of the amphiprostylos (see § 8), which was rare amongst the Greeks themselves, and of which Vitruvius mentions no example either in Greece or Rome, we have at least one specimen in the temple on the Forum of Velleja (compare § 82). Of the peripteros (see § 9) Vitruvius mentions two examples, viz., the temple of Jupiter in the Hall of Metellus, and that of Virtus and Honos, also in Rome, which the architect Mutius had built for Marius. The form of the pseudo-dipteros, of which only one specimen exists in Greece (see § 10), was frequently used by Roman architects, as we shall see hereafter. Vitruvius mentions one specimen of the dipteros (see § 12), viz. the temple of Quirinus, erected by Augustus on the Quirinal. It had double colonnades of seventy-six columns, and was counted amongst the most splendid edifices of Rome. Of this temple no traces remain. We, therefore, shall specify the influence of Greek on Augustan architecture by some remains of a Greco-Roman temple at Athens. We are speaking of the beautiful columns standing south-east of the Akropolis, 60 feet in height, and partly still showing their architraves. They belonged to the temple of the Olympian Zeus, the building of which was begun by Pisistratos, but not continued till the reign of Antiochus Epiphanes. On the latter occasion we hear of a Roman knight, Cossutius, acting as architect. The temple was finished by the art-loving Emperor Adrian. Vitruvius, in the preface of his seventh book, says that Cossutius built the walls and the double colonnade, and also covered the beams. The additions of Adrian must therefore have consisted either of the ultimate completion of the last-mentioned parts, or of the decorative arrangements of the interior. Fig. 327 shows the plan of the

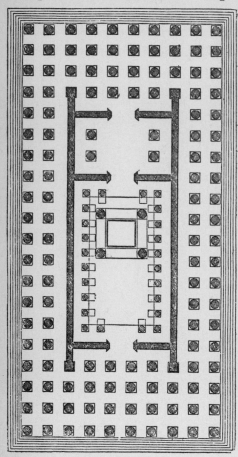

temple. It was a dipteros 173 feet broad by 359 long. Livy (XLI., 20) justly designates it as unique. It had ten columns on the narrow and twenty on the long sides; on the narrow sides it had three rows of columns instead of the two usually found in the dipteros, as may still be seen from the remains. Of the two other orders of the temple, the pseudo-dipteros (§ 13) and the hypæthros (§ 11), there were, according to Vitruvius, no specimens in Rome. The temple of Venus and Roma, however, to which we shall have to return (§ 66), undoubtedly showed the essential characteristics of the pseudo-dipteros; and Vitruvius's own description (III., 2) proves that the just-mentioned temple

Fig. 327.

of Jupiter Olympius was, like the Parthenon in its vicinity, a hypæthros.

64. The forms of Greek architecture thus adopted by the Romans were considerably modified by them. These modifications were of a twofold kind. They either originated in the reaction of the Italian on the Greek temple, in which case the

design and local division of the building were affected; or they
were caused by entirely new modes of construction being applied
either to the purely Greek or Greco-Roman temple. In that case
the whole character of the edifice was altered.

Before, however, entering into these more important modifications, we must mention a few minor changes, chiefly with
regard to the order of columns. All the Greek orders of columns
described by us were also used by Roman architects. As examples
of the Doric order, we name the temples of Quirinus at Rome
and of Hercules at Cori: not to mention several other specimens
of the Doric style col-
lected by Canina, " Arch-
itettura Romana," Tav.
67. The graceful forms
of Greek architecture
have, however, been fre-
quently misunderstood;
and have, in consequence,
lost their original purity
and harmonious propor-
tions. The Tuscan order,
frequently used by the
Romans, is itself nearly
related to the Doric style.
It must be explained from
the adoption and partial
modification of the Greek
original by the Etruscans,
from whom it again was
borrowed by the Romans,
the latter developing the
forms thus received into
a system of their own.
The statements of Vitru-
vius, together with some
archaic specimens found
on Etruscan graves (for

Fig. 328.

instance, the fragments of columns of the Cucumella of Vulci), and
other examples of this style in later Roman buildings, enable us

to form a distinct notion of this old-Etruscan order of columns. It must suffice to refer the reader to the façade of the Capitoline temple (Fig. 326), which displays the Tuscan order with the modifications alluded to.

The Ionic order of columns, likewise, is found in Roman edifices; for instance, in a small temple of Tivoli (see Fig. 330), and in the still standing temple of Fortuna Virilis in Rome ; also in that of Saturn in the Roman Forum. The second stories of both the Coliseum (§ 85) and the theatre of Marcellus are adorned with Ionic semi-columns; a few specimens of this style have been found at Pompeii. Almost all these specimens show more or less important deviations from the pure Greek form. Particularly, the graceful sweep of the curvatures and the spiral lines of the volutes have been lost—an observation which also applies to the large Ionic temples of Asia Minor (see Figs. 9 and 10). A characteristic example of the Roman form of the Ionic capital occurs in Desgodetz's description of the temple of Fortuna Virilis in Rome (Pl. III.).

While the Ionic and Doric orders were thus deteriorated by Roman architects, the Korinthian column, and especially the Korinthian capital, received a richer and more splendid development at their hands. The peculiarities of this style seem to have been congenial to the Roman mind ; it is, indeed, particularly adapted to an architecture which derives its effects more from the grandeur of massive structure than from the harmonious proportions of architectural lines. The capitals are formed by two or three rows of delicate acanthus-leaves, from between which appear volutes, flowers, or the forms of men and animals, the richer development of the beams being in harmony with this splendid style of ornamentation. This order has been most frequently applied by the Romans, the greater number of whose edifices are, indeed, built in the Korinthian style. We have met with it already in the temple of the Olympian Zeus at Athens, and shall find it again in almost all the monuments we shall have to mention. One of the finest specimens of the style is the Pantheon (see Figs. 342 to 344), a column of which, with the beam resting on it, is shown in Fig. 328. In later times, the style became overloaded, and by the addition of Ionic volutes the so-called "composite capital" was arrived at, of which Desgodetz

(V., 17) and Cameron ("Baths of the Romans," Pl. 30) show examples (compare, also, the triumphal arch of Titus, Fig. 448).

65. The requirements of the old Italian religion led naturally to the adoption of that more or less modified form of the Greek temple which was most suited to its peculiar rites; this form was the prostylos. The Tuscan temple, the frontage of which consisted only of colonnades, so as not to obstruct the view of the sky, was itself a prostylos. At the same time the prostylos could, by means of a simple enlargement, be easily adapted to the demands of Italian worship. This enlargement was effected by adding one or more rows of columns to the one which in the Greek temple formed the portico of the building. In this manner the front part, surrounded only by columns (*pars antica*, § 61), became of almost equal size with the back part (*postica*), occupied by the cella. The door of the cella, therefore, where the augur used to stand, was exactly, or at least

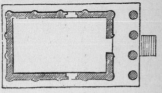

Fig. 329.

very nearly, in the centre of the temple. This form of the prostylos with a far-protruding portico occurs so frequently that it may be called that of *the* Roman temple *par excellence*. As such, it is distinguished from both the Tuscan and purely Greek temples, the elements of which it amalgamates to artistic unity.

The simple form of the prostylos, protruding in front by one column only, is also frequently found amongst Roman edifices, more frequently, indeed, than in Greece, where it was used very rarely. Vitruvius, for instance, mentions no specimen of it in Greece, but two in Rome, viz., the temple of Faunus and that of Jupiter in the Island of the Tiber. Figs. 329 and 330 show the design and view of a small half-ruined prostylos at Tivoli, near the well-known round temple (see Fig. 340 *et seq.*). It is preserved up to the height of the capitals; the wall of the cella is adorned with Ionic half-columns, and therefore appears in the form of

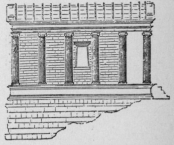

Fig. 330.

a pseudo-dipteros (§ 10), frequently applied by the Romans. On each of the long sides, between the two pairs of centre columns, (counting those of the portico) we see a small window growing narrower towards the top, and adorned with an elegant cornice. According to Canina, from whom our woodcuts are taken, the temple was built towards the end of the republican era, and dedicated most likely to the Sibylla Tiburtina or Albunea.

The first and most natural enlargement was effected by the addition of another column to the projecting one which carried the portico. This form also occurs frequently. Besides the above-mentioned temple of Fortuna Virilis (at present S. Maria

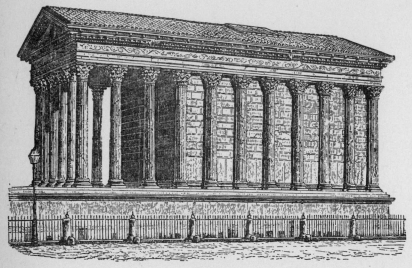

Fig. 331.

Egiziaca) in Rome, the temple of Isis at Pompeii shows this enlarged form of the portico. The all but square size of this temple reminds one of Vitruvius's rules for the Tuscan temple. A small oblong temple at Palmyra, most likely from the time of Aurelianus, shows the same form of the enlarged prostylos. Like that of Isis at Pompeii, it has four columns in the façade, which, together with the two on each side, form the pronaos, almost equal in size to the cella.

The design is more interesting where the portico projects by three columns. This arrangement is shown in the beautiful temple of Antoninus and Faustina, the portico of which is carried by six columns in front and three on each side, each of the columns consisting of one piece of green-veined marble. The walls of the cella, also preserved, consist of the stone called commonly travertine.

Fig. 331 shows an unusually well preserved temple of the same order at Nismes (the old Nemausus), in southern France. It belongs to the best period of Roman architecture, and was erected, according to an inscription on it, by Augustus, in honour of the sons of the faithful Agrippa, Caius and Lucius, adopted by the emperor. The temple, known as *Maison quarrée*, consists of a cella (pseudo - dipteros) adorned with Korinthian half-columns, and a portico formed by six columns in front and three on each side. The beams, in perfect preservation, resting on the wall and the columns, show a frieze with beautiful bas-relief ornaments. The old pediments with their beautiful cornices are also preserved. The interior of the temple is at present used as a museum, in which the numerous antiquities found in and near Nismes are kept.

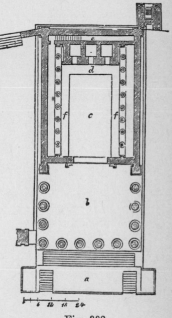

Fig. 332.

A further development of the same principle of Roman architecture appears in the large temple of Jupiter at Pompeii, which at the same time may be considered as one of the finest examples of this style. Fig. 332 (scale 24 Par. feet) shows the plan, Fig. 333 a restored section, of the building. The protrusion of the portico is increased by a further column, six columns standing in front and four on each side. In front of the portico (*b*) lies a platform, with steps leading up to it (*a*), by means of which the whole front part was made equal in length to the back part, in accordance with Vitruvius's rules for the Tuscan temple. The position of the temple from north to south also accords with these rules. Through the door which lay exactly in the centre of the building one entered the cella, on both sides of which there were galleries of eight Ionic columns each (*f f*). In front of the back wall of the cella lay a kind of substructure containing three small cellæ (*d*). The Ionic columns (as appears from Fig. 333) seem to have carried a gallery of Korinthian columns, up to which led a staircase in the back wall of the cella (Fig. 332, *e*). The substructure (*d*) may have supported a statue, the head of which, in the character of Jupiter, has been discovered there. The three cellæ most likely served to keep documents and treasures, as was frequently the case in temples. The walls of the cella were richly

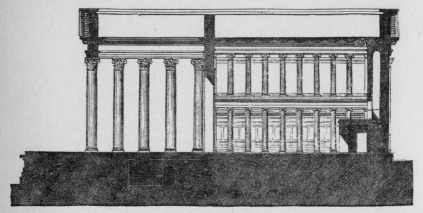

Fig. 333.

painted, as were also the columns of the portico, consisting of lava. The floor of the temple was adorned with mosaic. The temple itself lay in the most beautiful part of the Forum. A tasteful and clever reconstruction of both it and the Forum is found in Gandy's "Pompeiana" (Pl. 51).

In connection with these specimens of the Roman prostylos we mention the temple of Concordia in Rome, differing in design from all other similar buildings. It was built in consequence of a vow made by Camillus after he had spoken in the senate in favour of the claims of the plebeians to the consular dignity. It was intended as a symbol of the restored concord between patricians and plebeians. It lay at the northern end of the Forum

Romanum, close to the enormous foundations of the Tabularium (see § 81). The remains found on the spot do, however, not belong to the older temple of Concordia, but to the splendid temple built by Tiberius on its site. Only the large substructure of the temple, to which led a flight of steps from the Forum, may be recognised by some remnants of masonry, which, together with the Capitoline plan of the city, enable us to define the original situation of the building. The entire building (see plan, Fig. 334) formed an all but regular square stretching from north to south, one half of which (*postica*) was occupied by the transverse cella, while the other half (*antica*) consisted of the substructure and the portico, projecting by six columns. The cella was used at the same time

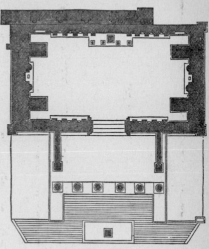

Fig. 334.

as the meeting-hall of the senate, and therefore was known at first by the name of *senaculum*, in later imperial times by that of *curia*. (The same was the case with the cella of the above-mentioned temple of Jupiter at Pompeii.) To judge by the few preserved pieces of the architrave, with the cornice, and by the slabs of painted marble which formed the floor, the beauty and purity of the style of this temple must have been unsurpassed in Rome. According to ancient writers, the interior, most likely the senate-hall, contained twelve statues of gods by the hands of the greatest masters.

66. The third modification of the Roman temple above referred to was caused by the introduction of a mode of construction seldom used by the Greeks, and never on a large scale. It enabled Roman architects to cover the cellæ of the temples in an imposing monumental manner. We are speaking of the vault, by the bold and consistent development of which Roman architecture differs essentially from the art of the Greeks. We cannot here discuss whether and when the art of vaulting became known to the

Greeks, or whether it was invented by the Italians. Suffice it to say, that vaulted buildings occur at a very early period amongst the Etruscans and other Italian tribes; but that it was left to the Romans to carry this important principle to its technical and æsthetical perfection. We shall have frequently to speak of the vault, as applied to canals, bridges, aqueducts, gates, and triumphal arches. By its means the Romans were enabled to get over architectural difficulties in a manner differing from, and much grander than, any known to the Greeks. At present, we must consider the vault in its influence on the development of the temple. The exterior of the temple never displays vaults or arches in any noticeable manner; the interior, on the other hand, was considerably transformed by the new principle, even the

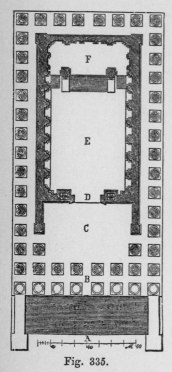

Fig. 335.

largest cellæ now being spanned by bold and richly decorated vaults, instead of the flat *lacunaria*-ceiling formerly in use. As an example of this style we mention the smaller of the two temples at Heliopolis, in Syria, to the larger of which, the so-called Temple of the Sun, we shall return (§ 68). Fig. 335 shows the plan (scale 80 feet English measure), Fig. 336 the view, of a prostylos of the above-described kind, which, in addition, has been surrounded by a colonnade. Excepting the front row of columns of the façade, it has been perfectly preserved. A flight of steps (A) leads to the colonnade (B), through which one enters into the pronaos (C), the ceiling of which consists of a transverse barrel-vault. A splendid door (D), on each side of which a staircase has been let into the wall, opens into the inner cella. It is divided into two parts; the first of which, lying on a level with the pronaos, is spanned by a bold barrel-vault richly adorned with *laquearia*. The side walls are adorned with beautiful Korinthian half-columns enclosing niches. Opposite the entrance lies a raised space (F), up to which seem to have led steps. It was separated from the space in front of it by two columns, and most likely

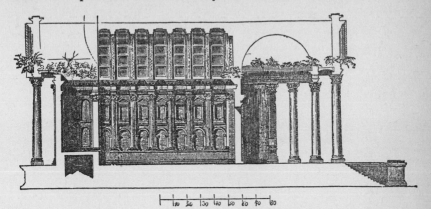

Fig. 336.

contained the statue of the temple. In the inside of the raised platform is a space evidently destined for the reception of sacred implements and other valuable objects. The style of the archi-

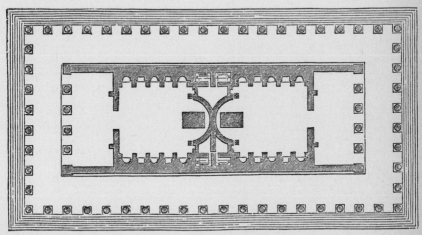

Fig. 337.

tecture is splendid, as was usual under the Emperor Caracalla, who seems to have finished the building begun most likely by his father Severus.

Fig. 338.

The temple of Venus and Roma in Rome shows the same principle of vaulting, although belonging to an earlier period. It is, at the same time, one of the few specimens of a double temple in Roman architecture. It stood between the Forum Romanum and the Coliseum, rising on a strong substructure. It was begun by Adrian, a lover of art, and himself an amateur architect, and most likely finished by Antoninus Pius. It belonged to the most splendid monuments of Rome, and its ruins are still of imposing aspect. These remains at the same time enable us to distinguish the position of the two separate cellæ belonging to the above-named goddesses.

In the centre of the temple were two semicircular niches touching each other, adorned with beautiful semicupolas, and containing the statues of Venus and Roma. One of them was turned towards the west, the other towards the east. Fig. 337

shows the plan of the temple. It must be described as a pseudo-dipteros dekastylos, having ten columns in the façades. The distance of the colonnade from the wall was sufficient to leave space for another omitted row of columns (compare § 13). Each of the long sides had twenty columns. The entrances to the two divisions of the cella lay towards east and west respectively; the entrance to them was through pronaoi, formed by the prolongations of the cella-walls, and by four columns placed between the *antæ* of these walls. The two cellæ were covered by richly adorned barrel-vaults (see Fig. 338), which were in beautiful harmony with the semi-cupolas over the two niches. The side walls contained niches with half-columns enclosing them, additional splendour being produced by coloured tablets of marble. The outside consisted entirely of Prokonnesian marble. Steps led from the Forum to the terrace (500 feet long by 309 wide) on which the temple stood. Some remains of these steps are still in existence. The two long sides had no steps. Fragments of shafts of columns made of grey granite have been found near the edges of the substructure. They tend to prove the existence of a colonnade round the building. The temple itself lay on a separate platform inside the colonnade, by six or seven steps above the level of the substructure

67. In the examples of vaulted temples hitherto cited a so-called barrel-vault was joined immediately to the quadrangular shape of the cella or the pronaos. Another no less important kind of the vault is the cupola applied to circular buildings. The Romans used it frequently, sometimes with great effect.* We have mentioned the round temple in Greek architecture (§ 14), without, however, being able to cite examples of this style, barring, perhaps, the monument of Lysikrates at Athens (Fig. 152) and the conjectural design of the Philippeum of Olympia (Fig. 36). In Rome these buildings were both more frequent and more developed than amongst the Greeks; they indeed form a considerable fraction of Roman edifices. According to Servius (see

---

* Adler ("Das Pantheon zu Rom," 31. "Programm zum Winckelmannsfest der archæolog. Ges. zu Berlin, 1871, p. 16 *et seq.*), contends that the cupola was an old Oriental, not a Roman, invention. In Alexander's time it attained its climax in Western Asia and Lower Egypt, whence it came to the Romans, who brought it to its highest perfection in the cupola of the Pantheon.

"Æn.," IX., 408), they were dedicated chiefly to the goddesses Vesta and Diana, also to Hercules and Mercury. Vitruvius (IV., 7) mentions two kinds of this temple, one of which he calls monopteros, the other peripteros. The monopteros consists of a number of columns, arranged in a circular form, standing on a base with steps (*stylobat*), and carrying the beams, also circular in shape, and, by means of them, the vaulted cupola, made either of stone or wood. These temples, in the centre of which the statue of the deity was placed, had therefore no separate cella; which want was perhaps supplied by railings between the single columns, as appears from a bas-relief. No specimens of this style are preserved. To judge by a coin of Augustus, the temple of Mars Ultor (not to be mistaken for the splendid temple of later origin) in the Capitol, built by that emperor, was a monopteros,

Fig. 339.

which form also appears on another coin representing an open temple containing the statue of Vesta (Fig. 339). On the top of the cupola is a flower-like ornament quite in accordance with Vitruvius's statement, who (IV., 7) prescribes a certain measure for this flower (*flos*). The inaccuracy of such representations, however, prevents us from deciding with certainty whether our illustration is not perhaps intended to represent the Roman temple of Vesta still in existence, although that belongs to the second form of round temples.

The temples of the second kind also rest on a circular base;

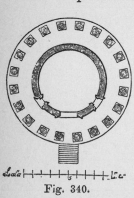

Fig. 340.

but here the separate columns encircle a round cella, which is covered by a cupola resting on the colonnade. This arrangement is specified by the above-mentioned temple of Vesta, more commonly called the temple of Hercules Victor. It has been transformed into a Christian church (S. Maria in Cosmedin), to which circumstance it owes its preservation. The celebrated temple of Vesta, which now has entirely disappeared, lay at the foot of the Palatine, near the church S. Maria Liberatrice, a little way from the Via Sacra.

The ruins of another temple, ascribed to Vesta with more certainty, are found at Tivoli. Its original appearance can distinctly be recognised. It is one of the finest specimens of the class of round temples called by Vitruvius peripteroi. Fig. 340 shows the design, Fig. 341 the view, both after Valladier's drawings of the remains, to which Canina has added the missing parts. The cella is formed by a circular chamber (see Fig. 340), whose wall contains a handsome door and two elegant windows.

Fig. 341.

The cella is surrounded by twenty Korinthian columns, carrying richly ornamented beams (see Fig. 341). The upper part of the cella-wall, surrounded by a graceful cornice, rises above these beams, the conclusion being made by the cupola, crowned by an ornament. The whole structure stands on a base, also surrounded by a slight cornice, up to which base leads a narrow flight of steps in accordance with Vitruvius's rule. The building must be considered as one of the finest specimens of late republican architecture.*

* Weiss in his "Costümkunde" (Part I., p. 1169) suggests that the round temple may have been a reminiscence of the circular huts of the old-Italian populations.

Hirt has called attention to the remarkable circumstance of Vitruvius limiting his description to these two kinds of the round temple without mentioning a third class, in which the circular body of the building (in that case generally of larger dimensions) is not enclosed by columns at all, but only shows a projecting portico like the other Roman temples (prostyloi). This omission on the part of Vitruvius is all the more remarkable, as in his time already Roman architecture had achieved its highest success in that particular style.

We are speaking of the Pantheon, the splendid building erected by M. Agrippa, the friend of Augustus, in immediate connection with the Thermæ, built and dedicated to Jupiter Ultor by him. This building, which embodied, as it were, the highest aspirations of Roman national pride and power, was completed, according to the original inscription preserved on it, B.C. 25, in which year Agrippa was consul for the third time. According to the statement of Pliny (" Hist. Nat.," 36, 24, 1), which, however, has been disputed, it was originally dedicated to Jupiter Ultor, whose statue, therefore, undoubtedly stood in the chief niche opposite the entrance. The other six niches contained the statues of as many gods ; those of the chief deities of the Julian family, Mars and Venus, and of the greatest son of that family, the divine Cæsar, being the only ones amongst the number of which we have certain knowledge. Was it that the statues of Mars and Venus showed the attributes of the other principal gods, or that the statues of the latter stood in the small chapels (*ædiculæ*) between the niches, or that the unequalled enormous cupola was supposed to represent heaven, that is, the house of all the gods ? Certain it is that, together with the old appellation, the new name of the Pantheon, *i.e.*, temple of all the gods, was soon applied to the building. This latter name has been unanimously adopted by posterity, and has even originated the Christian destination of the edifice as church of all the martyrs (S. Maria ad Martyres). Without entering into the consecutive changes the building has undergone in the course of time, we will now attempt a description of its principal features. The temple consists of two parts, the round edifice and the portico (see plan, Fig. 342). The former was 132 feet in diameter, exclusive of the thickness of the wall, which amounts to 19 feet. The wall is perfectly circular, and

contains eight apertures, one of which serves as entrance, while
the others form, in a certain order, either semicircular or quadrangular niches; the former are covered by semi-cupolas, the
latter by barrel-vaults. Only the niche opposite the entrance is,
at the present time, uninterrupted, and open up to its full height,
thus corresponding with the formation of the entrance (compare
section, Fig. 344); in front of each of the others, two columns
have been erected, the beams of which close the opening of the
semicircular vault. To this chief portion of the building is
attached the splendid portico which, in the manner of the above-

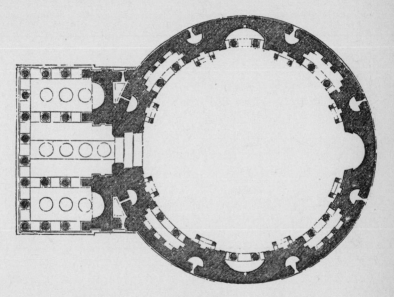

Fig. 342.

mentioned temples, projects by three columns, besides a massive
wall-structure. The frontage shows eight columns. As a rule,
the whole space of the pronaos was without columns; contrary to
this rule we here see it divided into three naves by means of two
pairs of columns. The centre nave, which was also the widest
led to the entrance-door, each of the two others being terminated
by an enormous niche. Not to mention æsthetical considerations,
these columns were required as props of the roof covering this
vast space (the portico is about 100 feet long).

The columns of the portico (one of the capitals is shown, Fig.

328) carried beams, on the frieze of which the following inscription in large letters has been placed : M·AGRIPPA·L·F·COS· TERTIUM·FECIT.   Another inscription below this one, in smaller characters, states the building to have been restored by Septimius Severus and Caracalla.   The beams carry a large pediment, originally adorned with groups of statues representing Jupiter's victories over the Gigantes.   Behind and above this gable rises a second one of the same proportions, serving as an ornament of the projecting wall which connects the round building with the portico (see also plan, Fig. 344).   The roof of the portico was supported by beams made of brass.   According to

Fig. 343.

the drawing of Serlio, these beams were not massive, but consisted of brass plates riveted together into square pipes—a principle frequently applied by modern engineers on a larger scale in building bridges, &c.   Unfortunately, the material of the roof, barring some of the large rivets, has been used by Pope Urban VIII. for guns and various ornaments of doubtful taste in St. Peter's Cathedral.   The large columns carrying the ugly tabernacle on the grave of St. Peter are one of the results of this barbarous spoliation.   The old door, also made of brass, which leads from the portico into the interior has, on the contrary, been preserved.   The outer appearance of the round building is simple and dignified.   It most likely was originally covered with stucco and terra-cotta ornaments, of which, however, little remains at present; but the simple bricks, particularly in the upper stripes, where the insertion of the vault becomes visible, look, perhaps, quite as beautiful as the original coating.   The whole cylinder of masonry is divided into three stripes by means of cornices, which break the heaviness of the outline, the divisions of the inner space corresponding to those of the outer surface (see Figs. 343 and 344).   The first of these stripes is about 40 feet high, and rests on a base of Travertine freestone.   It consists of simple horizontal slabs of stone, broken only by doors which lead to chambers built in the thickness of the wall between the niches (see plan, Fig. 342).   It corresponds to the columns forming the first story of the interior, the two cornices, in and outside, being on a level. The second stripe, about 30 feet in height, answers to the second story of the interior, where the semicircular arches of the niches are situated.   The horizontal stone layers outside are accordingly broken by large double arches, destined to balance the vaults in the interior.   They alternate with smaller arches, thus forming a decoration of the exterior at once dignified and in harmony with the general design of the building.   The two cornices in and outside are again on a level.   The third stripe corresponds to the cupola, the tension of which is equal to 140 feet.   The outer masonry reaches up to about a third of its height, from which point the cupola proper begins to rise in seven mighty steps.

The height of the dome is equal to the diameter of the cylindrical building, which adds to the sober and harmonious impression of the whole building.   The lower of the above-mentioned interior stories is adorned with columns and pilasters, the latter of which enclosed the niches.   Eight of these columns, over thirty-two feet in height, are monoliths of *giallo antico*—a yellow kind of marble beautifully veined, and belonging to the most valuable materials used by ancient architects.   Six other columns are made of a kind of marble known as *pavonazzetto;* by an ingenious mode of colouring these columns are made to harmonize with those consisting of the rarer material.   Above the first lies a second lower story, the architectural arrangements of which may be recognised from Adler's ingenious attempt at reconstruction (see Fig. 344).   Its original decoration consisted of tablets of coloured marble, the effect being similar to that of a sequence of narrow pilasters. This original decoration has later been changed for another. Above the chief cornice which crowns this story, and at the same time terminates the circular walls, rises the cupola, divided into five stripes, each of which contains twenty-five "caskets" beautifully worked and in excellent perspective. In the centre at the top is an opening, forty feet in diameter, through which the light enters the building. Near this opening a fragment has been preserved of the bronze ornamentation which once seems to have covered the whole cupola. Even without these

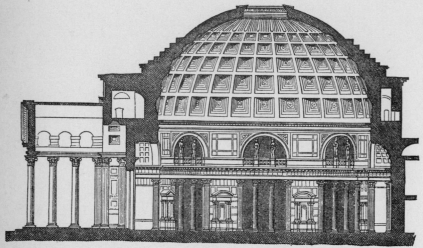

Fig. 344.

elegant decorations the building still excites the spectator's admiration as one of the masterpieces of Roman genius.

68. The temple-enclosures of the Romans were, as a rule, still more splendid than the periboloi of the Greeks. Although few in number, the remaining specimens of these surrounding courts are sufficient to give us a distinct idea of the whole arrangement. The original purpose of these courts was to seclude the sanctuary from the profane bustle of the world, for which purpose the enclosure of the space immediately in front of the temple was sufficient. Several enclosures of this kind have been preserved at Pompeii. In front of a prostylos with a colonnade projecting by two columns, commonly designated as the temple of Æsculapius,

is situated a simple court enclosed on two sides by a bare wall, only the third side fronting the temple being adorned with a portico of two columns. Another still smaller sanctuary, without columns, at Pompeii, formerly described as the temple of Mercury, at present as that of Quirinus, shows an entrance-court the walls of which on two sides are adorned with pilasters, the third consisting of a portico of four columns. Through the latter one enters the court of the temple, in the background of which, on a broad base, rises the cella containing the statue of the god; in the centre of the court stands an altar remarkable for its relief-ornamentation

In other cases the courts were richly decorated and of larger dimensions, surrounding the temple on all sides. This seems to

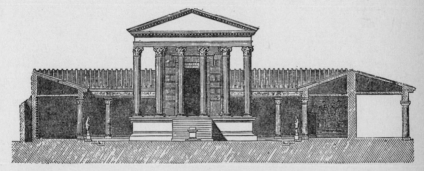

Fig. 345.

have been the case in almost all the larger and in most of the smaller temples wherever the locality would permit it. In Pompeii we again refer to the above-mentioned temple of Isis, which is built in a regular space surrounded by walls. The court is surrounded by a colonnade; in the centre of it lies the cella with the pronaos. A similar arrangement, on a larger scale, we see in the so-called temple of Venus, occupying the western side of the Forum of Pompeii. It is a peripteros surrounded by twenty-eight splendid Korinthian columns, with a portico of considerable projection in front. The temple is enclosed by a covered court adorned with columns; the colonnades on the narrower sides consisting of nine, those on the broader sides of seventeen, detached Korinthian columns. The wall on the right is joined on the outside by a

similar colonnade (Fig. 345 *a*) of Doric columns, which belongs to
the surroundings of the forum. The remnants of both the temple
and the court are in a state of tolerable preservation. Mazois has
attempted a trustworthy conjectural design of the original building (see Fig. 345). The temple rises in beautiful proportions
over the surrounding colonnades. Both with regard to elegance
of proportions and splendour of decorations it ranks amongst the
finest buildings of Pompeii. In front of the steps leading to the
base stands the small altar, occupying the centre of the foreground.
The surface of the inner walls of the cella is divided into several
parts separated by pilasters of stucco. They are of a light-yellow
colour, while those of the peribolos are richly adorned in the
manner of perspective room-decorations—only rarely met with in
temples. The back wall of the peribolos is joined by a number
of small chambers destined, perhaps, for the priests. Their walls
are decorated with beautiful figure-pictures.

In Rome no temple-enclosures of this kind have been preserved, but their existence in ancient times is proved by the
temple of Venus and Roma described by us (Figs. 336 and 337).
Of a very early structure of a similar kind, we have knowledge
from the plan of the city of Rome, which, made of marble, was
placed in the temple of Romulus, and the fragments of which are
now let into the walls of the staircase of the Capitoline Museum.
In this fragment we see two temples standing near each other, and
enclosed at a moderate distance by a single oblong colonnade.*
This colonnade was built most likely of common material by Q.
Cæcilius Metellus ; Augustus reconstructed it on a larger scale in
marble in the name of his sister Octavia. In front of the two
temples stood, as appears from the Capitoline fragment, groups of
twenty-five horsemen, the work of Lysippus, which had been
brought as spoil from Macedon by Metellus. In the reign of
Titus (A.D. 70) both temples were burnt down in a fire which
destroyed a great part of Rome. They were rebuilt, according to
an inscription found on them, by the emperor L. Septimius Severus
(A.D. 203). Both temples were dedicated to Jupiter and Juno.
Remains of the portico leading to the court are found in the

---

* See F. Reber, " Die Ruinen Roms und der Campagna."   Leipsic, 1863, p. 210
et seq.   P. 211 contains a view of the portico of Octavia ; p. 213, the fragment of the
Capitoline plan referring to it.

Piazza di Pescaria ; some columns of the temple of Juno belong to a private house in the Via di S. Angelo di Pescaria.

The largest temple-enclosure amongst the monuments known to us belonged to the temple of the Sun at Palmyra, the mighty city of the desert, situated on the frontier of the Roman and Parthian empires. In it the most gorgeous specimens of almost all classes of Roman architecture are found. The open colonnade, for instance, more than 4,000 feet long, consisting of four rows of Korinthian columns, had not its equal in Rome, no more than the just-mentioned temple-enclosure. The latter occupies a square nearly 3,000 feet in circumference. The outer wall, of considerable height, is broken on three sides by windows cut into it at regular intervals between the pilasters, which adorn the wall both in front and at the back. The fourth side has no windows, but instead of them a high entrance-portal in the centre, which may be considered as one of the most splendid specimens of Roman architecture under the Emperor Aurelianus. The court which one enters through this portal is of proportionate size and splendour. Each of the sides (over 100 feet in length) is adorned with colonnades ; those on three sides being double (*i.e.* formed by two rows of columns), that on the side of the entrance single. The whole area of the court is covered with slabs of marble, and it contains, on both sides of the entrance, two large regular hollows, most likely used as ponds. Opposite the entrance, facing it with its long side, lies the temple, a dipteros about 110 feet wide by 200 long; the entrance to it lies on the long side of the cella, opposite the portal of the enclosure-wall. This is a deviation from the ordinary design of temples; another irregularity consisting in the windows which are broken into the walls of the cella. The inner sides of each of the two narrow walls of the cella contain a quadrangular niche destined to receive the statue of a god. This fact accords with the statement of Aurelian having placed here the statues of Helios and Belus. The same emperor restored the older temple in a manner the splendour of which is frequently praised by ancient writers, and still is apparent from the remains.

Less in size, but not in splendour or individual peculiarities, were the courts of the temple of the Sun in Heliopolis, the modern Balbek. One of the chief temples of that city we have mentioned in § 66 (see Figs. 335 and 336). The other one, larger than the first, and most likely devoted to Jupiter, as god of the sun, was a peripteros with ten columns in front, and nineteen on each of the long sides. Its width was 160 feet; its length, exclusive of the steps, about 300 feet. The cella of the temple has been destroyed beyond restoration; only the beautiful Korinthian columns of the colonnade (about 7 feet in bottom diameter) may still be recognised. The courts in front of the temple, and the entrance-portal belonging to them, are comparatively well preserved. The latter (see plan, Fig. 346; scale 200 feet) consists of a portico of twelve columns, up to which led a broad flight of steps, the entrance into the first court being formed by three magnificent gates. The court itself shows the unusual shape of a hexagon. Op-

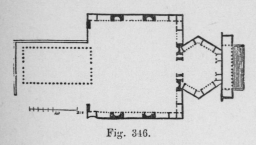

Fig. 346.

posite the entrance lies the chief portal, leading to the second court. The four remaining sides show halls, opening towards the court through colonnades; the niches in the walls of these halls, with their beautifully vaulted ceilings, may still be recognised from the ruins. The second court, square in shape, was designed in a similar manner, each of three of its sides (400 feet in length) containing open halls (*exedræ*) alternating with semicircular niches. The walls of the halls are adorned with niches, most likely containing statues. On the fourth side, opposite the splendid portal with three gates above mentioned, rises the façade of the temple, concerning the arrangement of which we have spoken before.

So much about the enclosures and courts of temples. Frequently these temples were also erected in public squares, to which arrangement we shall have to return in speaking of the Fora of Rome and Pompeii (see § 82). The grand impression of a temple is frequently increased by the artificial base on which it stands. We have spoken of such a base in reference to the Capitoline sanctuary (§ 62). The foundations of the court of the temple of Venus and Roma were, as we have seen, on the largest scale. Similar preparatory works were necessary for the base of the just-mentioned temple of Heliopolis. Large walls of freestone had been erected for the purpose on three sides, consisting of stones of thirty or even of sixty feet in length. In a temple erected on rising ground, the base itself could be architecturally developed; terraces, frequently of imposing proportions, often led up to the temple. As an instance, we add the temple of Fortuna of Præneste, at Palestrina, conjecturally re-designed by Canina (Fig. 347). According to this design, the mountain, on the slope of which the old town of Præneste lay, was converted into terraces up to half its height, which were propped by mighty basements of different kinds and ages. The midmost terraces, for instance, show front walls of Cyclopic-Pelasgic workmanship (see § 17),

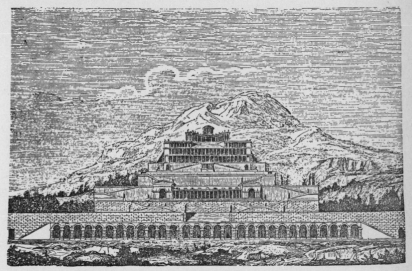

Fig. 347.

and are therefore dated by Canina back to the time in which the similarly constructed walls of Præneste itself were built. This structure was afterwards enlarged towards both top and bottom, these later parts accordingly showing regular freestone architecture. Other parts again show the so-called *opus incertum* (see § 69), and, also, the regular brick-architecture of imperial times. The modern town of Palestrina has been built amongst these ruins, which latter have been an object of continued research ever since the sixteenth century (we mention only the important works on the subject by Pirro Ligorio and Pietro da Cortona). In com-

paring the remains with the statements of ancient writers, we
find that the temple of moderate dimensions lay about half way
up the mountain resting on the above-mentioned terraces, which
again were architecturally adorned in various ways. The bottom
story, if we may use that expression, was formed by a grand
archway carried by pillars; it extended to a considerable length,
running parallel with the highway which passes the mountains
on that side. On both sides of it two large covered cisterns have
been discovered. From here, stairs led up to a terrace of large
size, on which two other large tanks were situated—an arrangement met with also in the court of the temple of the Sun at
Palmyra. From here stairs led up to a second terrace, in the
centre of which remains of a gorgeous building have been
discovered. It consisted of two large halls connected by means
of a colonnade; in one of the halls a celebrated mosaic floor has
been discovered. Pietro da Cortona transferred it to the palace
of the Barberini family, built on the ruins of this structure,
where it still remains. Double flights of steps led up to a third
and a fourth terrace; on the fifth terrace stood an archway
running along the front edge; on the sixth we see a large square
court surrounded by colonnades (peristylos), joined by another
similar court of semicircular shape. From this a flight of steps,
semicircular in design, led up to the temple of Fortuna itself, of
which, however, nothing now remains.

69. We now have to consider the wall—the most primitive
form of protective architecture. A great similarity exists between
the first attempts of this kind in Greece and Italy, which
proves the relationship and analogous development of the two
nations. The oldest Italian town-walls known to us consist of
large stones, in the cutting and placing on each other of which
we notice the same different modes of proceeding as in the
Pelasgic walls (compare Figs. 53 to 56). We therefore need not
repeat our previous remarks, and only add, that not only towns,
but also other places, were enclosed with walls for purposes of
safety or religious worship. Wall-enclosures of this kind are frequently found on heights in various parts of Italy; it is indeed
probable that one of the chief centres of Rome, the Capitoline
hill, was enclosed originally for the purpose of defence rather than
of habitation. In this manner it became, like the akropolis of

a Greek city, the centre point round which the first dwelling-houses of the city were grouped.

When a town was to be founded systematically, as frequently was the case with a colonising nation like the Romans, certain religious ceremonies had to be observed. A bull and a cow were harnessed to a plough in order to encircle the place destined for the city with a furrow. For the gates, the number of which was also determined by holy traditions, a space was left by lifting up the plough. The ploughed-up earth had to lie towards the town, the furrow itself towards the country, this arrangement being in a manner suggestive of the wall and moat of Italian and Roman cities. Where the locality permitted it, the space for the town was designed as a square, an instance of which was the old *Roma quadrata* on the Palatine Hill: this arrangement recalls the form of the templum (see § 61 *et seq.*), the centre of the town being, like that of the temple, considered as holy, and marked as such by the deposition of gifts and offerings.

The walls of the Romans were generally made of bricks. Recently, however, some remains of the oldest fortifications of Rome have been dis-covered which are built of freestone in the Greek manner. On the Aventine Hill, for instance, may be traced for a considerable distance the line of a free-stone wall, which undoubt-edly belongs to the so-called fortifications of Ser-

Fig. 348.

vius. It lies on the top of a large earth-wall (*agger*), which is expressly mentioned amongst those fortifications, and it contains, like the walls of the Greeks, projections for the purpose of defence ; the arches placed at intervals for the sake of increasing the firmness of the layers of stones are thoroughly Italian in cha-racter. Of a similar kind are the substruction-walls which have been recently found on the Palatine Hill, forming, most likely, the original fortification of that hill (see Fig. 348).

In later times, as we mentioned before, brick was used in fortifications. Vitruvius states, that first of all masses of earth

were heaped up, and the erection thus gained was enclosed on
both sides with strong brick walls.   In these walls, as well as in

those made of massive stone,
different modes of structure were
in use, by means of which the
appearance of the walls was considerably modified.   Either the
whole wall consisted of a mixture
of mortar and unbaked bricks
(called *opus incertum* by Vitruvius), or the outer surface of
the wall was faced with regular
bricks of equal size.   In this
case, also, two modes of construc-

Fig. 349.

tion became possible, the stones being either triangular in shape
and arranged in horizontal layers (Fig. 349), or being cut into

quadrangular prisms
which were pressed into
the soft mortar, so that
the joints crossed each
other in a net-like man-
ner (*opus reticulatum*).
Fig. 350 illustrates the
latter mode of structure,
which also appears, for
instance, in the walls of
a conduit of the Alsie-

Fig. 350.

tine aqueduct.   The inside of these walls consists of irregular
bricks joined together by mortar (*opus incertum*), while the outer
surface consists of reticulated brickwork coated over with
stucco.   Sometimes the reticular and horizontal principles appear
combined, in which case the reticular surfaces are interrupted by
narrower pieces of horizontal layers.   This is the case, for instance,
in several parts of the Roman town walls.

We quote two instances of town walls, in illustration of the
principles hitherto insisted upon, viz., the walls of Pompeii and
the so-called Aurelian fortification of Rome.   In the former the
wall consists, according to Vitruvius's rule, of an irregularly
heaped mass of stones, faced both in front and at the back with

flag stones (scarp and counterscarp), to which additional firmness
is added by means of buttresses. The upper surface of the wall
is, towards the outside, protected by battlements four feet in
height, into which, at intervals of nine feet, embrasures have
been cut; they project towards the inside by three feet, thus
yielding a safe position to the besieged.
Towards the town side the wall is considerably raised, reaching a height of
forty-two feet from the level of the
ground. Broad but rather steep steps
lead from the town up to the wall.
Square towers communicated with the
top of the wall by means of (generally
round-arched) gates.

In our second example (Fig. 352),
the Aurelian fortification of Rome,
the wall towards the inside is propped by strong buttresses connected

Fig. 351.

with each other by means of round arches. The top of the
wall here, also, is protected by battlements. A sort of gallery
is formed by these arches, in the single divisions of which
semicircular niches are cut into the thickness of the wall

Fig. 352.

which communicate with the outside by means of narrow shot-
holes, thus yielding a strong position both for attack and defence
(another arrangement of the wall is illustrated by Fig. 359).
Here also turrets are placed at certain intervals, such as we have

met with before at Pompeii (Fig. 341) and in Greece (compare § 19, Figs. 70—77). Upon the whole, Roman towers differ little from the Greek but for the vault, which adds to their strength. Fig. 353 (scale, 18 feet) shows a section of a turret at Pompeii, rising in three stories to a height of about forty feet. The ceiling between

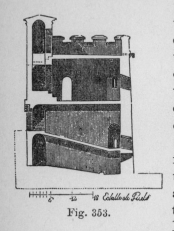

Fig. 353.

the two lower stories inclines slightly towards the outside, which is also the case with the openings above referred to. The steps necessary for communication lie in the back part of the turret, which is slightly raised. The topmost chamber communicates with the circuit of the wall by means of a vaulted gate (compare Fig. 351). The upper platform also inclines outward so as to let the rain run off, stone eaves being added for the same purpose, as is also the case with the circuits of the wall. Battlements protect the platform.

A few words ought to be added about fortified camps, so important in Roman warfare. They were erected at considerable distances from each other, to protect the frontier from the barbarians, sometimes connected with each other by long lines of wall with intervening smaller fortifications. They, of course, required large garrisons. The remains of a large fortified camp are still visible in the Taunus Mountains, about an hour's walk from Homburg vor der Höhe, and 250 paces from the large Roman line of defence commonly called the *Pfahlgraben.* The present name of the camp is *Saalburg;* it is most likely identical with the Arctaunon (Arxtauni) mentioned by Ptolemæus. It was built by Drusus in the year 11 (B.C.), and re-erected by his son Germanicus after its partial destruction by the Germans (A.D. 9). Continued, but not yet finished, excavations have made it possible to discern the whole plan of the camp (see Fig. 354, after the designs of Archivrath Habel). The shape of the fortification was quadrangular, being 700 feet long by 450 wide. The outer wall, consisting of irregular blocks of stone, had a thickness of 5 feet, slightly increased on the north side, which was most exposed to the attacks of the enemy. The four angles are rounded. The original height of the wall cannot be determined with certainty ; in some parts the remaining portions rise to six feet from the ground. Outside of this wall lies a double moat ; inside of it we see a second higher line of wall, about 7 feet wide, which, in our plan, is marked by a double line of dots. Behind this wall lies a road 30 feet wide, the *via angularis* (E) (marked by a single dotted line in our plan), destined for the reception of larger bodies of troops. The other arrangements of the camp perfectly tally with the descriptions of ancient writers. On the front side, between two towers projecting inside, lies the chief gate, *porta prætoria* (A), with which corresponds, on the opposite side, the *porta decumana* (D). On the two long sides we have the *porta principalis dextra*, also protected by towers (B), and the *porta principalis sinistra* (C). In the centre of the camp, where the connecting lines between the opposite gates meet, stands the dwelling of the commander, the *prætorium* (F).

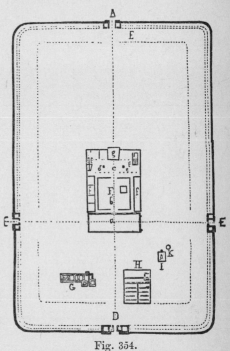

Fig. 354.

Erected without much care and in a hurry, it still shows several compartments, partly for the private use of the general, partly for military purposes. There is no entrance on the side of the *porta prætoria*, in the place of which we see a square tower (*g*) ; on the opposite side the building terminates in an oblong room (*a*), the three outlying sides of which contain three doors exactly opposite the three gates in the corresponding walls of the camp. Near G and H remains of buildings have been discovered, most likely those of dwelling-houses. The narrow intervals between the cross walls of H seem to indicate the existence of a heating apparatus. I marks a small sanctuary, K a well. The prætorium was reserved for the staff and the *corps d'élite;* the rest of the army lived, according to the rules of *castrametatio,* in the open spaces between the prætorium and the wall of the camp. Light huts, made of earth or wood, were most likely constructed for the purpose, the German climate being too cold to permit living in tents for long. Stone foundations of the soldiers' dwellings have not been discovered.

Another camp, at Gamzigrad in Servia, carefully investigated for the first time by F. Kanitz, is much larger and in a better state of preservation than the one just described. It dates, undoubtedly, from late Roman times. It was erected to protect the Timon valley, and is of enormous dimensions. It formed an

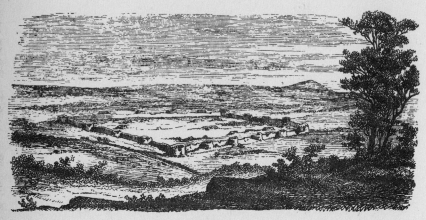

Fig. 355.

irregular square (Fig. 355), the narrow sides having a length of 1,461 and 1,351 feet respectively, while the two long sides show the enormous measures of 1,908 and 1,896 feet. Round towers, 180 feet in diameter, and with walls 24 feet thick, stand at the four corners, a number of smaller round towers projecting almost circularly from the wall at irregular intervals. At a distance of about 108 feet from this wall the remains of a second row of towers have been discovered also, most likely connected with each other by walls. The substructure of a square building of 84 by 132 feet occupies the centre of the fortification. Unfortunately no excavations have taken place, by means of which the name of this camp might, perhaps, be discovered.

70. The Roman gates differ from the Greek ones more than is the case with towers or walls. It is true that their position in the wall remained essentially unaltered ; that is, they were inserted mostly in the parts most protected by nature, and further strengthened by projections of the wall, built in such a manner as to afford a point of attack on the left side of the besieging enemy. As we have seen before, the gates were flanked by towers (compare also our description of the castle of Salona, § 76, Fig. 392).

All these points the Roman gates have in common with the Greek. The chief difference consists in the principle of vaulting applied to the Roman structures. By means of this principle, applied also to subterraneous canals, the Romans were able to cover wide spaces without difficulty. We quote a few examples of Roman gates, classed according to the number of their openings.

The simplest form naturally consists of one arch, either flanked by projections and cut into the thickness of the wall, or else repeated on the opposite sides of a tower. A beautiful specimen of the first kind is the gate of Perusia, where a second decorative arch is added above the actual opening. An example of the second kind we see in the gate of Volterra, which shows all the simplicity of the old Italian arch. The gate of Pompeii, leading to Nola, is of later date ; its simple arch does not lie in the wall but at the end of a small passage, which touches the wall at an obtuse angle, thus compelling the besiegers to

Fig. 356.

expose themselves to the attack of those standing on the side walls of this passage. Later still, and evidently erected with a view to decoration as well as to safety, is one of the gates of the above-mentioned villa of Diocletianus, at Salona, called *porta aurea*, most likely owing to its splendid ornamentation (see § 78). Like the other gates of this building, it is flanked by towers, and contains one opening only. The latter shows a round arch, closed at the bottom by a straight ledge of stone (see Fig. 356). The surface of the wall is decorated in the late Roman style, with small columns on bases, enclosing niches. A cornice, partly destroyed, adds to the beauty of the gate even in its present condition.

Fig. 357.

Gates with two openings are of rarer occurrence. As an example we quote one of the oldest and most beautiful gates of Rome, at present called Porta Maggiore, the original aspect of which is shown Fig. 357.* The design is very complicated, owing to various considerations; but it shows, at the same time, the artistic skill of the Romans in getting over architectural difficulties. Two high arched portals afford an opening to two Roman highways, the Via Labicana and Via Prænestina, which here met at a pointed angle. These portals are enclosed by two mighty piers, the upper parts of which are broken by smaller arches and decorated with two semi-columns each, on the latter of which rest beams and pediments. The centre pier

---

* Compare the gate of Messene (Fig. 67), the opening of which seems to have been divided into two halves by a pillar.

shows, below the just-mentioned opening, another small round-
arched gate. The arches served at the same time to carry two
aqueducts. Just above them lies an "attic," which, however,
does not contain water; but above this we see two other "attics:"
the lower one forms the conduit of the Aqua Claudia, the upper
one that of the Anio Nova. Three large inscriptions cover the
three attics. The first states that the Emperor Claudius built the
aqueduct called Aqua Claudia, by which the waters of the two
wells called Cæruleus and Curtius, lying near the forty-fifth

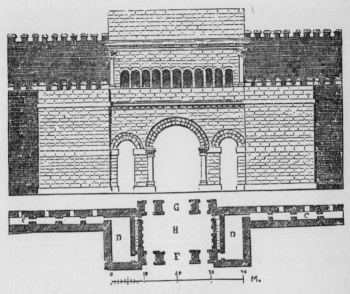

Fig. 358 and 359.

milestone, were conducted into Rome. The second inscription says
that the same emperor conducted the Anio Nova to Rome from a
distance of sixty-two Roman miles. The third inscription
mentions Vespasian and Titus as the restorers of the gigantic
building of Claudius.

More frequent than two, are three gate-openings, of which the
centre one is usually wider and higher than the two others: the
former being destined for horses and carriages, the latter for foot-
passengers. The two purposes of defence and traffic are beautifully combined in a gate belonging to the fortifications of Aosta.

built by Augustus (see view, Fig. 358, and plan, Fig. 359). The wall to which the gate belongs differs essentially from those of Pompeii, the interval between the lower and outer (Fig. 359, *a*), and the higher and inner, wall-facings (B) being not filled up with earth, but left empty. The connection between the two wall-facings is effected by means of arches. This interval is thus transformed into a number of small vaulted chambers (C) which

Fig. 360.

open towards the town, and thus somewhat resemble the inner divisions of the Aurelian walls. Two towers (D D), enclosing the outer gate (F), project from this double wall. The gate shows the just-mentioned division into three openings, all of which could be closed by strong portcullis. After this gate follows an open space (H), called by Vegetius *propugnaculum*, because here the besiegers that might have advanced so far could be attacked from the platforms of the low towers. On the opposite side of this space lies the inner gate (G), the three openings of which were closed by doors studded with iron. The architecture is dignified and even severe in style, and this work of Augustus may be counted amongst the finest of its class.

A similar though less fortified structure we see in one of the gates of Pompeii, called, from the direction of the road passing through it, the Herculanean gate (see the outer view of it, Fig. 360, from the conjectural designs of Mazois). On the left it is protected by a projection of the wall; it has one centre and two side entrances, the latter for foot-passengers. The inward side of the gate shows the same arrangement. The narrow space lying between the two chief portals was uncovered, thus forming a kind of *propugnaculum*, similar to that of the gate of Aosta. The side entrances are vaulted in their full length; they were each connected with the uncovered space in the centre by means of two arches, through which the necessary light is conveyed into the long and narrow passages. The large portals could, at one time, be closed by portcullis which, however, at the time of the destruction, seem to have been no more in use. The side entrances contained doors, as indicated by the still-preserved hinges. The whole structure consists of pieces of tufa and mortar, coated with stucco. The remains show how carefully the surface was smoothed. The whole gate was 16·80 metres deep by 14 wide. The width of the centre passage is 4·70 metres, that of each side passage 1·30.

71. The structures of utility, to which we have now to turn, differ from those of the Greeks by their greater variety of purpose, and of the means used to accomplish this purpose. It is here that the practical sense of the Romans shows to greatest advantage.

The Romans soon discovered the political importance of roads, and showed great energy and consistency in carrying out their ideas, differing in this from the Greeks. With the latter, religious purposes formed an important consideration in the building of roads; the Romans only considered the necessities of the State. Artistic road-building commenced as soon as the Roman dominion began to extend beyond its original limits. Conquered provinces had to be connected with the heart of the State, *i.e.* the city of Rome. The roads thus became a means of political, commercial, and intellectual interchange between Rome and the provinces.

The chief and first purpose, however, was of a military kind; large masses of troops had to be conveyed with ease to distant provinces. In this way originated the first artistic road, the Via Appia, and its continuation to Arminum, the Via Flaminia : the subjection of the Boii, on the Po, led to the construction of the Via Æmilia ; while that of the Gallic and Germanic nations caused the grand system of roads in the Alps and the countries on the Rhine and Danube. The gradual extension of the Roman territory may be followed in the history of road-building. These large political considerations, of course, were out of the question amongst the numerous and, to a great extent, isolated states of Greece. This difference of purpose between the two nations also influenced their modes of constructing roads. The Greeks built their roads according to the nature of the locality, or even to old traditional routes of travellers, heedless of occasional detours. The Romans, on the contrary, true to the indomitable energy of their character, follow the *one* plan of building as nearly as possible in a straight line. The nature of the ground is almost totally disregarded ; where mountains intervene they are broken

Fig. 361.

through ; hollows are made level by means of dams ; deep valleys or rapid streams are spanned by bridges, the bold design of which still excite the admiration of modern engineers, far superior though they are to the Romans in technical, scientific, and mechanical resources.

Of tunnels through mountains we mention the so-called " Grotto of the Posilippo," near Naples, which is still daily passed through by thousands (Fig. 361). It is cut through a promontory between Naples and Baiæ, being in length 2,654 Neap. palms by 24 wide. The height inside varies from 26 to 74 palms. At the two ends there are arches of 94 and 98 palms respectively, tending to increase the firmness of the structure. The tunnel is bored through the solid rock.

Other difficulties had to be overcome in marshy places. The soil here had to be made firm and its level raised by means of a dam. The Via Appia, for instance, was thus conducted through the Pontine marshes. In other places, again, the road had to be carried on along precipices on walled substructures or viaducts.

This is the case in that part of the Via Appia which descends from Albano to the valley of Ariccia; just below the village of Ariccia it runs for a considerable distance on an embankment faced with freestone. Fig. 362

Fig. 362.

shows this part of the road with massive balustrades and seats on both sides of it. Vaulted openings in the basement evidently served as outlets for the mountain streams.

As to the technical arrangements of the roads, such as pavement, gutters, &c., full information is derived from Hirt's work, " Die Lehre von den Gebäuden bei den Griechen und Römern," which we have followed in many points. The roads were either strewn with sand and gravel (*glarea viam sternere*) or paved with

Fig. 363.   Fig. 364.   Fig. 365.

solid stones. In the latter case generally polygonal blocks of some hard stone, generally basalt, are chosen for the roadway, the surface being made as smooth as possible (*silice sternere viam*) as is shown by the part of the Via Appia in Fig. 363. In case there were raised pavements for foot-passengers, they were generally made of the softer common tufa (*lapide sternere*). The middle of the road was generally raised a little, so as to make the rain-water flow off; small outlets for the water, such as we mentioned in speaking of the wall (see Fig. 353), also occur on roads. Figs. 364 and 365 illustrate the draining-apparatus of the Via Appia, where an arched passage under the road serves as an outlet for the water, perhaps also as a means of communication. Fig. 364 shows the front view; Fig. 365 the sections. The roadway itself is about 18 feet wide; it has a massive stone balustrade on each side.

The streets of Pompeii were of similar construction, drains being frequently found below them; the pavements for foot-passengers to both sides are generally raised a little, posts, connected by kerb-stones, being placed at certain intervals to prevent the intrusion of horses or vehicles. At intervals of 1,000 paces, milestones (*milliaria*) were placed on the highways, with the distances from the larger towns written on them. Frequently seats for exhausted travellers were placed near these milestones.

72. In their construction of bridges the Romans differ widely from the Greeks, owing to the use of the arch in Roman architecture. The viaducts and bridges of the Romans are amongst the

Fig. 366.

most remarkable monuments of antiquity. At the ninth milestone from Rome, on the road to Gabii, is a viaduct across a broad valley, which only during the rainy season of the year is partly flooded. Nevertheless, the viaduct is built on as many as seven arches. It is 285 feet long, and consists of blocks of "peperin" and red tufa. Owing to the softness of the material the pillars are very stout, and the intervals spanned by the arches small. From the simple and solid structure of the work (which is now called Ponte di Nona, and still in use), Hirt believes it to belong to the time of Caius Gracchus, who, while a tribune (124—121 B.C.), constructed a great many roads, and of whom Plutarch distinctly remarks (C. Gracchus, c. III.) that he considered not only usefulness but also beauty and elegance (χάριν καὶ κάλλος).

Where a stream had to be crossed, the arch naturally became

of still greater importance. Bridges, moreover, seem to have been regarded almost like religious monuments. In the early history of the city of Rome, so closely connected with the Tiber, the bridges across that river were of such religious import that the care of them was assigned to a fraternity of priests (*pontifices, i.e.* bridge-makers), of which the highest college of priests in Rome was a further development. The name *Pontifex Maximus* remained attached to the office of high priest, and is at present that of the pope.

Although of great importance, the arch was not indispensable in Roman bridge-architecture. Not to speak of temporary bridges of boats, we mention permanent wooden bridges, such as the Pons Sublicius, the oldest bridge in Rome, and the bridge that Cæsar threw across the Rhine. In other bridges woodwork and masonry occur combined, as, for instance, in the splendid bridge built across the Danube by Trajan. It rested on twenty strong stone pillars, standing at distances of 170 feet, and connected with each other by wooden arches instead of stone vaultings. A representation of this bridge is seen on the column of Trajan.

Arched structures made of stone marked the highest perfection of the art, combining, as they did, firmness of structure with the capability of spanning wide spaces without impeding (owing to the height of the arches) the navigation on the river. Without entering into details we will, in the following pages, quote a few examples of bridges, classing them according to the number of their principal arches. The bridge near Volci, across the river Fiora

Fig. 367.

(Fig. 367), shows one chief arch, with two smaller ones on the banks of the river. This bridge also serves to carry an aqueduct across the river (compare § 74).

Fig. 368 shows a still-existing Roman bridge with two principal arches, generally known as the Ponte de' Quattro Capi, owing to the two heads of *Janus Quadrifrons* on stelai placed on the balustrade above the *têtes-du-pont*. According to the inscriptions it was built in 62 B.C. by L. Fabricius, at that time *curator viarum*. Its condition was, in 21 B.C., examined and testified as safe by the consuls Q. Lepidus and M. Lollius. It connects the city with the island of the Tiber, and consists of two arches extending in graceful lines from a strong pillar in the centre of the river to its two banks. On the base of the pillar, between the

Fig. 368.

two chief arches, the masonry is interrupted by a third arch, which gives an appearance of grace to the whole structure. The side of the pillar turned towards the current of the stream is made into a sharp edge. Two other smaller arches, nearer the banks, add to the firmness of the structure, being filled up with earth.

One of the first Roman bridges is the Pons Ælius, built across

Fig. 369.

the Tiber by the Emperor Hadrian. It opened the access to the tomb erected by him on the right bank of the river (compare § 78). The bed of the river was crossed by three semicircular arches, joined to right and left by four smaller vaultings. It is in a state of excellent preservation, and well known by the name of Ponte S. Angelo. On its restoration at a later date one of the arches has been filled up, and is hidden by the extended embank-

ment. Fig. 369 shows the original design of the bridge ; Fig.
370 its present aspect at low water, which shows the massive
structure of the foundations and piers.

73. Of still greater magnificence and boldness of construction
than the bridges were the harbours, canals, and similar structures.
Hirt ("Lehre von den Gebäuden," p. 367) justly remarks, "that
even the splendour of Nero's golden house dwindles into nothing
compared with the harbour of Ostia, the drainage works of the
Fucinine Lake, and the two large aqueducts, Aqua Claudia and
Anio Nova, all built by Claudius. In their waterworks the
ancients seem to have surpassed themselves." Of the harbours
of the Greeks, partly of considerable dimensions, we have spoken

Fig. 370.

before (§ 20) : in comparing them with those of the Romans we
find the same difference as between the roads of the two nations;
that is, the Greeks adapt their structures to the conditions of the
soil, while the Romans, without neglecting local advantages, as a
rule, force Nature to their powerful will. In Greece, harbours
generally consisted of natural bays enlarged and fortified by dams
and similar structures : the Romans built their harbours where no
such natural opportunities offered themselves. It is true that
their coasts, compared with Greece, were wanting in bays and
promontories. Instead of these, therefore, the Romans built

dams and walls far into the sea, to obtain safe anchorage for their ships; nay, entire artificial islands were produced in the sea so as to protect equally artificial harbours from the waves. This was the case, for instance, in the harbour of Centumcellæ (the modern Civita Vecchia), built by Trajan. Of the gradual progress of this structure we are told by the younger Pliny (§ 31): two enormous

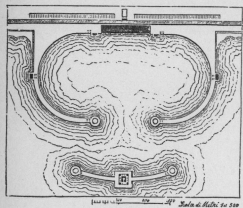

Fig. 371.

piers were being built, of which that to the left was finished first; at the same time an artificial island in front of them was in progress of construction. Enormous loads of blocks of stone were brought in flat vessels, and thrown into the sea in proper places. In this manner a powerful stone wall was formed under the water, which, at the time when Pliny wrote, already protruded from the surface of the sea.   (See the plan of the harbour, Fig. 371, according to Canina's design.)

Similar structures, although on a different plan, had been attempted at a much earlier period. When the harbour of Ostia (built at the mouth of the Tiber by Ancus Martius, and already covered with sand about the end of the Republic) was being restored, we hear of an artificial island of this kind. It formed a breakwater in front of the large piers of the harbour, and carried a lighthouse almost equal in size to the celebrated Pharus in the harbour of Alexandria. Instead of rough stones, the Emperor Claudius, who took a particular pride in buildings of this kind, used chalk, mortar, and Puzzuolan clay. Of these materials three enormous pillars were built and sunk into the sea together with the colossal ship on which they stood.* The clay received an indestructible firmness by the accession of the salt water, and in this manner the foundation of the island was formed. As to

---

* This was the same vessel in which, under Caligula, the obelisk of the Vatican had been brought to Italy. By the Romans it was believed to be the largest vessel that ever sailed on the ocean.

the rest, this harbour resembled that at Centumcellæ. Like the
latter, it consisted of an outer harbour built into the sea by
Claudius, and of a large basin afterwards dug into the shore
by command of the Emperor Trajan. The basin was enclosed by
freestone walls, and communicated with the outer harbour by
artificial canals, as also with the open sea by means of the Tiber,
the stream of which was well regulated and embanked. Fig. 372
(scale 1,000 metres) shows Canina's design, made according to the
existing remnants of the harbour. The ruins of the harbour of

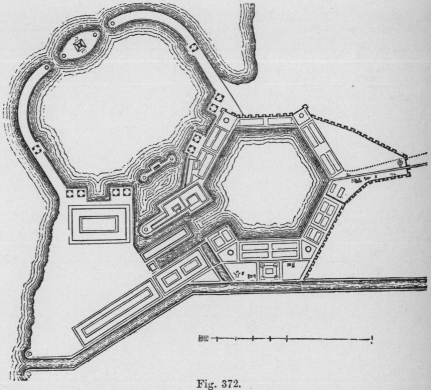

Fig. 372.

Claudius now lie one miglia inland, owing to the deposits of the sea.
Our design also indicates the storehouses for grains and other
merchandise by which the inner hexagonal basin was surrounded. A coin struck during the fifth consulate of Trajan
(A.D. 103) gives a distinct view of this harbour and the buildings
surrounding it. As to the arrangements of such storehouses we

may perhaps derive some knowledge from the remains of a building discovered by Piranesi near the Emporium in Rome, on the left bank of the Tiber (see Fig. 374). It rose from the river to the city in terraces in accordance with the natural conditions of the ground. The ceilings of the store-rooms were vaulted; graceful arches in the enclosing walls effected an easy communication with the street.

Fig. 373.

Fig. 374 shows the view of a harbour from a Pompeian wall-painting. Walls crowned by towers serve as a means of protection. Storehouses surround the basin, connected with the shore by means of a bridge. On an island connected with one of the jetties we see a temple and a dwelling-house adorned with columns, both standing on artificial

Fig. 374.

Fig. 375.

terraces, to which lead steps. Groups of trees add to the picturesqueness of the whole. The most remarkable feature is the jetty, to the right of the harbour, projecting far into the sea, and containing a number of arcades destined for the keeping out of mud or for the reception of smaller vessels.

74. We now have to consider the drainage works of the Romans—less imposing, but no less useful, than their harbours. We mention particularly the drainings of the Pontine marshes, the meadows of the Po, &c., where, by means of canals, ditches, and drains of various kinds, damp, boggy stretches of country have been transformed into arable land. A still more remarkable example of a complicated system of drainage is the city of Rome itself. Lying on several hills, with a river flowing through it, the lower parts of the city naturally were liable to the formation of unhealthy swamps. To remove this nuisance, a system of subterraneous canals was built, whose grand and skilful design still excites our admiration; they serve their purpose, after about 2,500 years, in the most perfect manner. The fundamental idea was to collect the water by means of a system of smaller canals into one large sewer, which conducted it, together with the refuse of the city, to the river. This chief canal, known as Cloaca Maxima, is still preserved for a distance of nearly 1,000 feet. It served, and still serves, to conduct the waters from the Capitoline and Palatine hills, collecting in the Velabrum, into the Tiber (see its open-ing towards the river, Fig. 376). A barrel-vault of tufa, with arches of travertine inserted into it at intervals of 10 feet, covers the canal, which is about 20 feet wide. Its ori-ginal height was 12 feet, now reduced to 6-7 feet

Fig. 376.

by the mud and dust which have collected in its bed, in spite of frequent clearings out. The commencement of cloaca-buildings in general, and that of the Cloaca Maxima in particular, is generally ascribed to the three last kings; several additions to the latter were necessitated by the increasing size of the city. Frequent clearings out of the canal were required, owing to the gathering of mud;

some of them, carried on at great expense, are mentioned by contemporary writers. One of the late extensions is ascribed to M. Agrippa, the friend of Augustus. He seems to have constructed a new system of canals underneath the Campus Martius, one of which still passes under the floor of the Pantheon.

Of no less importance were the structures serving as outlets of lakes, either to prevent inundations or to regain arable land from the water. Such outlets, *emissaria*, also are mentioned at a very early period. They were either open or covered, and served to conduct the superfluous water from the lake to lower ground. The greatest difficulty naturally consisted in cutting the canals through solid mountains, or in conducting them in subterraneous tunnels. This was, for instance, the case with the drainage of the Albanian Lake, which Livy (V. 15 *et seq.*) connects with the story of the conquest of Veii by M. Furius Camillus (396 B.C.). The waterworks are still in use at the present day. From the high level of the lake, which lay in the crater of the old Albanian volcano, the water was let off by means of a shaft cut through the mountain for a distance of several thousand feet. According to the precept of the Delphic oracle, it was not led into the sea, but divided over the neighbouring fields, which thus were made fertile, the periodical inundations being at the same time prevented.

In a similar manner, but by an open canal, the drainage of the Veline Lake, in the country of the Sabii, was effected, after the conquest of those parts by Curius Dentatus (290 B.C.). By this means the country round Reate was converted into one of the most fertile regions of Italy. These works also are still in use.

The largest structure of this kind were the drainage works of the Lacus Fucinas, in the country of the Marsi, which had been desired for a long time by the inhabitants, owing to the dangerous inundations, and were planned by Cæsar, but not executed till the reign of Claudius. Here the whole basin of the lake was to be laid dry, and thus gained for agricultural purposes. This was effected by means of a shaft cut through the living rock from the lake down to the river Liris (at present called Garigliano), which discharged the water into the Mediterranean, near Minturnæ. According to ancient authors, the shaft was

3,000 *passus* long by 14 high and 9 wide. Fig. 377, *a c*, gives
the section of the shaft in its full length, the line *a b* marking the

Fig. 377.

horizon so as to show the strong incline of the shaft. The vertical
and oblique lines indicate shafts and galleries leading from the
surface to the canal ; the former destined for carrying off the
rubbish, the latter for the descent of the workmen, thirty thousand
of whom were occupied for eleven years in constructing the canal.

From the emissaria we turn to the *aquæductus*, destined to
conduct the water necessary for human use from distant places.
The care and skill bestowed on their construction and preservation
was equal, if not superior, to that required by the first-mentioned
canals.

The first thing required after the discovery of a spring in a
high place was to collect the water in a sheltered spot. This led
to the erection of fountain-houses, specimens of which, in Greece,
we have before described (see Figs. 90 and 91). In Italy also
some archaic buildings of this kind are extant, as, for instance,
the fountain-house discovered at Tusculum, and made known in
his description of Tusculum by Canina. It consists of an oblong
chamber divided into several compartments, the ceiling being
constructed by the overlaying of stones on the old Greek system,
afterwards supplied amongst the Romans by the vault. The
manner of conducting the water to the cities was, of course,
modified by the nature of the soil, as well as by the material
at hand. One way was to conduct it underground in pipes (*tubi,
fistulæ*) or subterraneous canals. The pipes were generally made
of lead or clay ; in some towns some of these have been preserved
with the municipal stamp on them. The canals were, like the
emissaria, either cut into the rock or, where the soil was soft,
dug into the earth and walled in. In either case shafts or other
openings placed at certain intervals served as communications
of the water with the fresh air. Such openings were also

contrived where the canal, owing to the nature of the soil, was sunk below its ordinary level. A hollow extension of this kind was called *venter*, and above it a perpendicular shaft was laid as far as, or beyond, the surface of the earth, from which in the latter case it protruded like a chimney. In this shaft the water rose again to its ordinary level, by means of which it not only communicated with the open air, but also received additional pressure. The expenses of these aqueducts, so far as they were used for public purposes, were borne by the municipal governments; the private use of the water for houses, land, or the carrying on of a trade was subjected to a tax.

Where the aqueducts lay aboveground, it was usual to place them on the tops of walls (see Fig. 378). In that case the

water-channels usually were made of freestone or brick, and covered, in the former case, with slabs of stone, in the latter with vaults. In either case the interior of their walls received a watertight coating, consisting of chalk and fragments of bricks, instead of the more common sand. The same coating was used in canals cut through the rock.

Fig. 378.

An uninterrupted wall would have been a great obstacle to the traffic, for which reason here also the all-important vaulting principle was applied. By means of intervening arches the wall of the aqueduct was divided into pillars at intervals, sufficiently large to leave space for the passage of roads, or even of rivers, without endangering the firmness of the structure. As an example we cite the arches of different dimensions across the Fiora Valley, near Volci, which carry both a road and an aqueduct (see p. 345, Fig. 367).

The Porta Maggiore in Rome (see p. 338, Fig. 357) ought also to be mentioned again as being part of two of the most celebrated Roman aqueducts. We have stated above how across the arches of this gate the waters of the Aqua Claudia and of the Anio Nova were conducted into the city in two different channels. Both aqueducts were begun by Caligula (A.D. 38), and finished fourteen years later by Claudius. The former, comparable by the excellency of its water to the celebrated Aqua Marcia,* began

* Called since its restoration by Pius IX., 21st June, 1870, Aqua Pia.

near the thirty-fifth milestone of the Via Sublacensis, in the Sabine Mountains, and was fed by two plentiful springs, besides receiving part of the Aqua Marcia. Owing to some turns necessitated by local conditions the length of the aqueduct was extended to forty-five miles, thirty-five of which were taken up by subterraneous canals, the remaining ten by open-air structures. The Anio Nova was fed, as its name indicates, by the river Anio, the word *nova* being added to distinguish it from an older aqueduct, Anio Vetus. It commenced at the sixty-second milestone of the same road, and received its water not immediately from the river, but from a basin into which it was led for the purpose of purification; near the thirty-eighth milestone a spring of still purer water, the Rivus Herculaneus, joined the aqueduct. Its whole length amounts to sixty-two Roman miles, partly above, partly under ground. About six miles from the city the two aqueducts join, and are carried on to the end by a common structure of arches, in some places 109 feet high; the channel of the Anio Nova, lying above that of the Aqua Claudia, was considered to be the highest aqueduct in Rome.

Some provincial aqueducts reach a still greater height. One of them is found near Nemausus (Nismes), in southern Gaul, whose beautiful temple we have mentioned before. The magnificent aqueduct, which crosses a valley, is in a good state of preservation. Its highest portion, known as *Pont du Gard*, rises in two stories to a height of nearly 150 feet. A row of smaller arcades is added on the top of the chief structure. The arcades are wide-arched, and convey the impression of a bold, graceful construction. Of a similar kind were the aqueducts of Segovia and Tarragona in Spain. The former is 2,400 feet long, and consists of a row of vaulted arcades: where the valley is deepest, the arcades rise in two stories up to a height of 100 Castilian feet, combining grace with firmness of structure. Owing to its excellent construction the aqueduct is still in good preservation.* The aqueduct of Tarragona is 876 feet long by 83 high.

So much about the aqueducts themselves. Many other contrivances were, however, required to make and keep the water fit for human use, as also to distribute it regularly. For the

---

* See Andres Gomez de Sommorostro, "El Acueducto y otras Antiguedades de Segovia." Madrid, 1820.

former purpose we mention, besides the shafts described above, the so-called *castella*, or reservoirs for collecting and purifying the water. At the beginning of the Anio Nova, for instance, lay a large mud-reservoir (*piscina limaria*), destined for filtering the water from the river. At the Aqua Virgo the waters of several springs had to be collected in separate reservoirs before being led into the common aqueduct.

The above-mentioned castella also served different purposes (see Fig. 379, representing a castellum of the Aqua Claudia).

Fig. 379.

According to Vitruvius, they had to be repeated at intervals of 24,000 feet, particularly in high aqueducts, their purpose being chiefly to give opportunities for distributing the water amongst the inhabitants of the surrounding countries; in case of stoppages, they also considerably facilitated the finding of the damaged places. Particular care was required for the castella at the ends of the aqueducts, from which the distribution of the water for the different purposes of the town took place. According to Vitruvius, the water seems to have been divided into three portions—one for the public fountains, the other for the thermæ, and the third for private use. For these three purposes three reservoirs served, each fed by a separate pipe; by means of other pipes the water was further distributed from these reservoirs. As, moreover, the water had to be divided over several quarters of the town, a number of smaller castella, and indeed a whole system of canals and reservoirs (247 of such are counted), became necessary, the excellent management of which, by a numerous staff, is a brilliant proof of the practical capacities of the Romans. Besides the usefulness of this quantity of water, it also served to embellish Rome. Numerous fountains adorned the city; M. Agrippa alone is said to have placed 105 jets. Rome still has the reputation of possessing a greater number of fountains than any other city in the world.

The above-mentioned *piscinæ* could also be constructed on a larger scale, in which case they became real reservoirs. In order to keep the water pure and cool a vault was constructed over the basin. As an example of these magnificent structures, we

quote the piscina at Fermo (see section, Fig. 380), which contains
in two stories six wide oblong compartments covered with so
called barrel-vaults, and connected
with each other by means of smaller
openings. Fig. 381 shows the large
reservoir still preserved near Baiæ,
which is known as *Piscina Mirabile.*
It is 270 palms long by 108 wide, and
is covered with a vault broken by ven-
tilation holes, and carried by forty-eight
detached slender pillars. Two stairs of
forty steps each lead to the bottom
of the reservoir, in the centre of which
is a considerable cavity for the reception
of the settling mud. Walls and pillars
are coated with a peculiar kind of very
hard stucco, impenetrable, it is said, even
to iron.

Fig. 380.

Fig. 381.

75. In the private buildings of the
Romans we discover the same mixture
of old Italian and Greek elements as in
their temples.

In order to understand the peculiarities of the Roman
dwelling-house as distinguished from the Greek (see § 22) we
have to consider the three most important parts of the former,
as they can be plainly recognised from existing specimens. As
is generally known, the three towns of Pompeii, Stabiæ, and
Herculaneum were buried by an eruption of Vesuvius in 79 A.D.
While the two latter towns were more or less destroyed by
streams of lava, Pompeii was only covered with ashes; after,
therefore, the ashes and the arable land on the top of them
have been removed the buried buildings reappear in their
original condition, unless they have been damaged by fire. In
this way we gain a perfect idea of a provincial town, which,
although Oscio-Samnitic by origin and Greek by development,[*]
still, by its long connection with the Roman empire, may,
in its present condition, be considered as essentially Roman.

* Some of the oldest buildings, as, for instance, the so-called temple of Hercules,
show the old Doric style.

The dwelling-houses there preserved may therefore be fairly quoted as proofs, and indeed the only remaining proofs, of the Greek influence on private architecture.

The historic Roman house must be divided into a front space partly covered (*atrium*), a centre space wholly covered (*tablinum*), and adjoining it an open court surrounded by columns (*peristylium*). These three parts are found in the same order in almost every house, other smaller rooms being grouped round them in various ways. The atrium seems to be of exclusively Italian origin, as is proved by its mode of design entirely differing from Greek architecture, as also by its name. It consists of a square space covered by a roof which projects from the four walls, only a square opening being left in the centre. In this simplest form, of which several examples are known to us, the atrium is called *Tuscanicum*, for, like most other old Italian institutions, it was believed to owe its origin to the Etruscans (compare § 61 *et seq.*). Varro and other Roman antiquarians adhering to this notion have derived the name from the Etruscan town of Hatria; others derive the word from the Greek αἴθριον, or from the Latin *ater* (black). According to the former etymology, atrium would mean a room open to the sky (ὑπ᾽ αἰθρίῳ); according to the latter, which is now generally accepted, a room blackened by the smoke of the hearth placed here. The latter explanation implies that the atrium was the chief room of the Italian house, owing to its containing the hearth, or, which is the same in other words, that, with the rooms immediately adjoining, it originally was the Italian house itself.

In sacred parlance, which retains the oldest ideas and expressions longer than any other, the house of King Numa is called *atrium regium*, which perhaps is identical with the *atrium Vestæ*, for this house lay close to the temple of Vesta, *i.e.* the common hearth of the Roman State. An old legal custom also proves the high age of the atrium. The opening in the centre of the roof was, as we said before, an essential feature of the atrium. Through it the smoke ascended, but also the rain entered, for which latter reason it was called, in conjunction with the slight excavation of the floor just underneath it, the *impluvium* and *compluvium*. The old law alluded to prescribed that if a man in fetters entered the house of the

Flamen dialis, these fetters were to be taken from him and thrown through the impluvium into the street, which proves sufficiently that at the time the law was made the atrium was an essential part of the house.

The simplicity of early times easily leads to the conclusion of the atrium having been the old Italian house itself; it was, like the court surrounded by columns in the Greek house, at once the starting-point and the remaining essential feature of later developments. Marini (see his "Vitruvius," c. III., Fig. 2) has attempted to reconstruct the old Italian house on this basis. As an important, though indirect, proof of our opinion we also mention an old Etruscan box of ashes discovered at Poggio Gajello (see Fig. 382). It is evidently intended for the imitation of a house, as is not unfrequently the case with similar boxes. We can distinguish the protruding roof (mentioned by Vitruvius as a feature of the old Etruscan temple), the doors, and the impluvium, which is indicated by a cavity in the raised centre portion of the house, which accordingly consisted only of the atrium, surrounded perhaps by some smaller rooms.

Fig. 382.

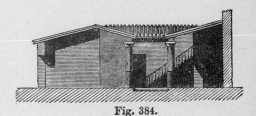

Fig. 384.

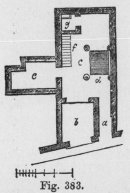

Fig. 383.

Amongst the numerous houses of Pompeii are moreover several which show this simple structure, and are evidently reminiscences of the original form. Fig. 383 shows the design, Fig. 384 (scale, 18 feet) the section, of one of these; besides a shop (*b*) lying towards the street, and a small passage (*a*), it consists exclusively of the atrium. The roof, protruding on three sides (on the fourth there is a simple wall), is supported by two columns (*c*), to which correspond two semi-columns in the wall; *d* indicates the impluvium. Within the atrium, and under the same roof with it, we see a small separate compartment (*g*), to the upper story of which (most likely the bedroom of the slaves) leads a staircase (*f*); a larger room (*e*) adjoining the atrium is evidently the sitting and bed room of the owner (*cubiculum*), the small compartment observable in it being most likely a sort of alcove for his bed.

Another house, the design of which is shown, Fig. 385 (scale, 18 feet), is of no less importance. Here again we see nothing but an atrium (*c*), enclosed on two sides by the walls of the house, while the two other sides open into various rooms. We first observe the entrance-hall (*a*) and a small chamber (*h*), to the upper story of which leads a staircase (*b*); the other rooms (*f, f, g*) communicate with the atrium by means of narrow doors. The atrium itself, like the above-mentioned Tuscan one, is without columns; the roof protrudes equally from the four walls without further props; the impluvium (*d*) is comparatively small. A particularly important feature of this house is another room (*e*) not hitherto met with, which adjoins one long side of the atrium, into which it opens completely, and not by means of doors, as in other cases. On comparing the design of the older Greek house (Fig. 92) we shall find that this room (*e*) lies in a similar position to the atrium as the prostas (Fig. 92, C) does to the court (B), with the only difference that in our present case, for want of space, the room could not, like the prostas, be placed opposite the entrance. This room (*e*) therefore becomes the chief apartment of the whole house, and we recognise in it the simplest form of the tablinum, to which we shall return presently.

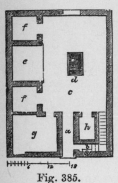

Fig. 385.

The modifications of this original type of the dwelling-house were, as in the temple, caused by the intrusion of Greek elements. Here also they consist, first of all, of an enlargement of the house. As we remarked before, the greater number of existing Roman dwelling-houses contain, besides the atrium, a second important part, viz. the court surrounded by a colonnade.

The mode of extending the house for natural reasons resembled that explained by us with regard to the Greek dwelling (compare Fig. 93 *et seq.*). We there recognised the court and the prostas as the oldest parts, to which afterwards a second back court was added. This court we also observe in most Roman houses. Between it and the atrium lies an open hall, called *tablinum*, which thus forms the centre of the house. It lies in the same place and served the same purpose as the prostas in the Greek dwelling. It was reserved to the master of the house, who from it could overlook the two other divisions; here he kept his money and documents, here he transacted his business. Zumpt calls it the office, or writing-room, of the owner, and derives its name from *tabellæ* (writing-tablets); another derivation is that from *tabulæ, tabellæ, i.e.* family-pictures, which are said to have hung in the tablinum.* Notwithstanding its being open and lying between the atrium and peristylium, the tablinum was not used as a passage between the two; slaves and other domestics rarely entered it; some remaining traces seem to indicate that it could be closed by means of sliding doors or curtains. The communication between the atrium and peristylium was effected by means of narrow corridors (*fauces*) running mostly alongside the tablinum.

The peristylium † is the court added to the Roman house at a later period, after Greek architecture had become prevalent. According to Greek patterns, it was surrounded by columns; its name also is Greek; while tablinum and atrium are derived from Latin roots. It is natural, and moreover confirmed by Vitruvius's statement and the remaining specimens, that in the houses of the less wealthy classes the peristylium, if found at all, was of secondary importance compared with the atrium; in many cases it certainly was very unlike the regular court surrounded by colonnades on its four sides prescribed by Vitruvius. Some houses in Pompeii have a court without any columns, instead of the peristylium. The Casa della Toeletta del Ermafrodito, or di Adone ferito (called so from the pictures found in it), at

---

* According to other accounts, these family pictures were kept in separate rooms, called *alæ*, the position of which seems uncertain but for the undisputed fact of their being part of the atrium.

† The expression, *cavum ædium*, which occurs frequently, and has been explained in various ways, seems to be applicable to the peristylium.

Pompeii shows a regular and spacious atrium ; while the peristylium (the open part of which is not longer than the atrium) shows columns only on two sides, the two others being occupied by the walls, which enclose the house towards two streets crossing each other. A similar design we find in the peristylium of the Casa della Caccia, or di Dedalo e Pasifae, but for its being still more irregular, owing to the want of a rectangular termination ; the atrium of this house also is spacious, and perfectly regular. The latter is the case also in the house of Sallustius, the peristylium of which, is surrounded by columns on three sides.

We must omit other more or less irregular designs, and turn to a house at Pompeii which is remarkable both for the regularity of the *corps de logis* of the owner, and also for the manner in which other parts of the premises have been made useful for mercantile purposes, or let out to other persons. We are speaking of the house of Pansa, so called after the inscription on the façade, which, however, does not indicate the owner. The house, including the

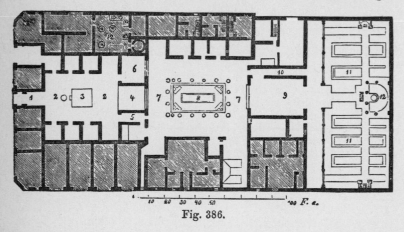

Fig. 386.

above-mentioned smaller habitations, is a complete oblong, surrounded by streets on all four sides (in front by that of Delle Terme), and therefore forming a so-called insula. The dwelling of the owner is surrounded on three sides by smaller houses (see Fig. 386), which appear hatched in our Plan. Part of the façade and the right side of the premises are occupied by various buildings, used partly as shops, partly let to so-called minor lodgers. The chief part of the opposite side is taken

up by a bakery, with the mill (12) belonging to it, and by
three shops (*tabernæ*) with small apartments attached to them. The
entrance to the dwelling-house lies between two shops, let separately. A narrow hall (*vestibulum*, 1),* the inner threshold of
which shows a "Salve" in mosaic, leads to the spacious atrium
(2 2), the impluvium of which is marked 3 in our plan. Six side-
chambers (*cubicula*) communicate with the atrium by means of
doors; two other rooms being entirely open towards it may
be considered as the side-wings of the atrium, whence their
name *alæ* (compare the Greek house, Fig. 92, 4, 5, and Fig. 93).
Opposite the entrance lies the tablinum (4), which, both by
its position and the beautiful mosaic on its floor, is marked as
the chief room of the house. Although open towards both sides
of the house, it did not serve as a passage, the communication
being effected by narrow corridors (*fauces*, 5) to the right of the
tablinum. On its left, towards the atrium, lies a good-sized room
(6), which shows a mosaic floor similar to that of the tablinum.
Remains of written documents have been found in it, whence
it is believed to have been the archive or library of the owner.
On the opposite side, separated from the tablinum by the fauces,
lies a smaller apartment, the entrance of which lies towards the
peristylium. Overbeck believes this to be a winter *triclinium*,
frequently met with in a similar situation. We now come to the
beautiful symmetrical peristylium (7) (20·15 × 13·10 metres),
the open centre space (8) of which is surrounded by sixteen
graceful columns of the Ionic-Korinthian order; its floor is
occupied by a fountain (*piscina*), the sides of which, two metres in
height, are painted with fish and water-plants. A narrow passage
between two of the out-houses led from the peristylium into
the side street. Several rooms open into the colonnade of the
peristylium, those to the left of the entrance being bedrooms
(*cubicula*); while a larger room on the right was the triclinium,†
or dining-room, the adjoining room serving as pantry, or as assem-

* Some authors (in accordance with Vitruvius, vi. 8) call vestibulum an open space
in front of the house. In Pompeii there is no example of such, unless we call the
small space immediately before the door (*ostium, janua*) by that name, in which case
the word *iter* (used by Vitruvius) would apply to the entrance-hall. Vestibulum
seems to have been used by the ancients in different senses.

† About the arrangement of the triclinium we shall speak at greater length (§ 88),
but we omit the description of the banqueting-halls (*œci*).

bling-room for the jugglers and dancers appearing towards the close of the meal. Behind the peristylium lies a garden, the connection between which and the peristylium is formed by a second kind of tablinum, the *œcus* (9) or state-room of the house. A corridor (10) by the side of the œcus, and communicating with it by means of a door, proves that the œcus itself was not used as a passage. To the left of the last-mentioned corridor lay the kitchen, and another room in which the dishes were dressed. The back façade, adorned with a portico, is joined by a garden (11), the regularly shaped beds (where most likely vegetables were grown), as also the lead pipes for watering the garden, are still visible; in the background, opposite the entrance to the œcus, seems to have been a sort of open hall (12).

One of the shops adjoining the dwelling-house was connected with the atrium by means of a back room (the blank compartment of our plan, the second to the left of the entrance). Perhaps the owner here sold the produce of his garden or estate. The largest and best preserved of the offices is the bakery (*pistrinum*), lying in the left division of the façade, next to the last-mentioned shop. Here we see the well-preserved oven, the mills, baking-table, water-reservoir, &c. Other shops were used for the sale of different goods, as, for instance, the colours used for wall-paintings. The owners lived in the dark rooms behind their shops, or in the rooms on the upper flats, to which led stairs from the shops. There are indisputable indications of the existence of a second story in this house, even parts of the floors of the upper rooms have been preserved. Mazois, to whom we owe a masterly publication of Pompeian buildings, remarks that here objects of female toilette have been discovered, which makes it appear probable that the sitting and bed rooms of the women lay on the second floor. According to Mazois's trustworthy design the rooms of this upper story were lower than those of the ground-floor ; they were grouped round the two large open rooms of the house, so however that their walls did not take away air and light from the atrium and peristylium. Their windows, as far, at least, as the chief dwelling-house is concerned, looked towards the interior. The staircases in the outhouses here also prove the existence of a second floor, the windows of which, of course, lay towards the street (see Fig. 388).

Rome, of course, differed in many respects from provincial towns. Originally built without a plan and on uneven ground, its narrow angular streets were inhabited, about the time of the Antonines, by nearly a million and a half of people. Only the wealthy could have houses of their own, the middle and poorer classes living in hired lodgings. Speculators erected houses of many stories, of light woodwork or bad material, repairs were neglected, and enormous rents had to make up for the losses of the owners caused by their houses breaking down or being consumed by fire—daily occurrences in Rome. As early as the Republic houses of three or four flats were common in Rome. By a law of Augustus the street-frontage of no private house was allowed to exceed 70 feet (Roman measure), which limit was, after the fire of Nero, further reduced to 60 feet.

Fig. 387.

To conclude we add (Fig. 387) the section of a regular and tasteful middle-class house, the so-called Casa di Championnet, at Pompeii: *a* indicates the passage leading from the street to the atrium; *b* the atrium, the ceiling of which is carried by four slender columns: here lies the altar-like mouth (*puteal*) of a cistern, also met with in the peristylium of the house of Pansa; *c* is the tablinum, the walls of which are still adorned with paintings; *d* the peristylium, the open space of which is occupied by a cavity used as a conservatory; underneath this is a vaulted cellar (*hypogæum*) for the keeping of stores.

76. We add a few further remarks about the outward appearance of the houses, as also about certain modifications of their ordinary design. About the façades we know but little, seeing that in Pompeii all the upper stories of houses have

been destroyed. Most likely they were generally in very simple taste ; for antique private architecture was chiefly intent upon the decoration of the inner apartments. The frontages of houses may, however, have been adorned in a simple way. We must distinguish between houses with or without shops in front. Of such shops we have already seen some examples (Figs. 385 and 386). They seem to have been open towards the street in their full width. The want of architectural beauty was supplied by a tasteful arrangement of the goods, in which the Italians of the present day, particularly with regard to fruit and other eatables, are still unsurpassed.

Of a house without a shop, opening towards the street only by a door, Mazois has attempted the reconstruction (Fig. 388), The façade shows a door in the centre between two Korinthian pilasters; the walls to the right and left are coated with stucco imitating freestone, the lower part representing large slabs, the upper

Fig. 388.

regular layers of small stones. A simple ledge finishes the lower story, over which a second story has been erected, with three small windows in it. The second story protruded from the surface in the manner of a bow-window, as is proved by several houses in the lane del Balcone Pensile at Pompeii. As to the manner of closing the window-holes we are uncertain in most cases. Sometimes movable wooden shutters have been used, as is proved by the wooden frames found beside the windows of the house of the "tragic poet" at Pompeii ; in other cases thin broken tablets of clay served the purpose, of which also several specimens have been preserved at Pompeii ; we further hear of a transparent stone (*lapis specularis*) being used for the same purpose; window-panes of artificial glass have also been found at Pompeii.

Several specimens of doors (see Fig. 389) have been preserved to us : about the construction of their leaves and the manner of closing them we shall speak hereafter (§ 93). Fig. 389 shows a very simple door found at Pompeii. We there see the small window-like opening in the pilasters, through which the

porter (*ostiarius*) could look at the callers after they had knocked
with the knocker, also visible in our illustration. The most
striking point on entering the house is the painting of the walls.
The thorough artistic taste of all classes is
proved by the fact of the walls of even
poorer houses being always either decorated
pictorially or at least painted. The careful plastering of the walls, much superior to our present method, is equalled by
the execution of the paintings themselves,
which, although sometimes technically imperfect and mechanical in design, still give
us some notion of the proportionately higher
finish of real antique art. The large mytho-
logical figure-pictures painted on, or let into, the centre-pieces of
walls at Pompeii and Herculaneum show the prevailing in-

Fig. 389.

Fig. 390.

fluence of Greek art, while the landscapes, still lives, and architectural decorations are more specifically Roman in taste.

To these wall-paintings also we shall have to return (see § 93).
We add a few illustrations of single parts of houses, designed

in accordance with the remaining specimens. Fig. 390 shows
the open court of the house of Sallustius (also called the house of
Actæon) turned into a garden. One side of it is occupied by the
wall of the house, while the other shows a colonnade with a low
wall (*pluteus*) in the columnar interstices; on the third side, near
a fountain, the remains of which still exist, stands a sort of
verandah or bower, decorated by Mazois in the well-known
manner of a triclinium.

Fig. 391 shows the interior of the house of Pansa, from the
reconstructive design of Gell. We first see the atrium, containing statues and other objects; several alæ and cubicula open

Fig. 391.

into it (compare Fig. 386); we further see the triclinium, to the
left of which lies a cabinet; while to the right we discover the
corridors or fauces leading to the large peristylium, which itself
is visible in the distance with its lofty colonnades. Everything
gives the idea of a secluded comfortable home.

Where the wealth of the owner or the situation of the house
in the country gave additional space to the architect, he was
naturally tempted to develop new and enlarged modes of design.
This led, in the former case, to the palace; in the latter, to the
villa. This distinction, however, cannot always be preserved;
for, on the one hand, the town-palaces of later times sometimes
comprised pleasure-grounds, &c., belonging properly to a country

residence; while, on the other hand, the villa of a rich, luxurious Roman took the form of a monumental palace.

During the last century of the Republic the splendid mansions of private persons begin to be mentioned more and more frequently. We only remind the reader of the house built on the Palatine by M. Æmilius Scaurus, the stepson of the dictator, L. Cornelius Sulla, a man celebrated for his wealth. He first bought one of the most celebrated houses of the time, that of Cn. Octavius, with adjacent pieces of ground, to erect his own mansion on the site. As a specimen of great luxury Pliny mentions the marble columns, thirty-eight feet in height, which adorned the fore-court. They most likely had formerly belonged to the theatre built by Scaurus (see § 84), and their size certainly implies a locality of more than ordinary dimensions, even if compared with the larger dwelling-houses at Pompeii. Mazois has attempted a conjectural design of the palace of Scaurus, which gives an idea of the splendour and variety of its single parts. But all this was far surpassed by the buildings of imperial times, of which we will only mention the " golden house " of Nero, the product of an exaggerated love of splendid architecture which did not shrink from incendiarism to satisfy its craving on the ruins of Rome. The palace was built on the Palatine, and extended from there, by means of intermediate structures (*domus transitoria*), to the Esquiline, containing all the luxuries and conveniences imaginable. A fore-court surrounded by a triple colonnade (a Roman mile, or 1,478·50 metres, long) contained the statue of the emperor, 37 metres in height; ponds of the size of lakes, with rows of houses on their banks, gardens, vineyards, meadows, and woods inhabited by tame and ferocious animals, occupied the various courts; the walls of the rooms were covered with gold, jewels, and pearls; the ivory with which the ceiling of the dining-halls was inlaid was made to slide back, so as to admit a rain of roses or fragrant waters on the heads of the carousers. Under Otho this gigantic building was continued at an expense of about £525,000, but only to be pulled down for the greater part by Vespasian. On the site of the above-mentioned ponds stood the large amphitheatre finished by Titus (see § 85), and on the foundations of Nero's buildings on the Esquiline the thermæ of the same emperor were erected. The Palatine proper remained the chief residence of the later emperors, who greatly altered the original arrangements. The excavations ordered by Napoleon III. and Pius IX., and conducted by the architect Rosa, have yielded the most important contributions to the history of the Palatine edifices, from the oldest times of the Roma Quadrata down to the Flavii.

A work of later date must serve to give us a more distinct idea of Roman palatial architecture. We are speaking of the palace erected by the Emperor Diocletian on the coast of Dalmatia, near his birthplace, Salona, where he spent the last years of his life after his abdication. On the few occasions when this large and splendid building is mentioned by ancient authors it is simply called a villa. It might more properly be described as a castle fortified in the manner of a camp (see § 70), for the whole area occupied by the palace and other houses adjoining it is enclosed on three sides by a solid wall, protected by square or octagonal towers. The whole space thus enclosed is about 500 feet wide by 600 long. Amongst the ruins of the house now lies a great part of the town of Spalatro. Between the

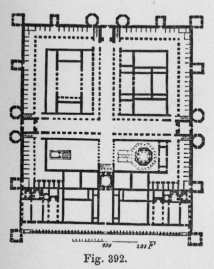

Fig. 392.

centre pair of the above-mentioned towers on each of the three sides lies a gate (compare Fig. 356), those on the two long sides being connected by means of a street, just as we found it in the Saalburg, near Homburg (compare Fig. 354). Another street, crossing the first in the centre, starts from the gate on the third, narrower side, without, however, being continued to the opposite side. This street, after passing between two temples, ends in what may be considered as the vestibule or entrance-hall of the imperial palace proper. This palace occupied the fourth side towards the sea. Instead of the solid walls we here see an open passage with arcades, into which open the numerous different apartments of the imperial dwelling. The view of the sea and surrounding country is beautiful. The space of the whole area not occupied by the palace itself (see plan, Fig. 392) is divided into four quarters by means of the above-mentioned streets, the two outer ones being taken up by the houses for the body-guard and other attendants of the emperor, while the two remaining quarters form open spaces, with a temple standing in the centre of each. One of these temples, to the left of the palace-entrance is a simple prostylos of moderate dimensions; the other is a fine specimen of the vaulted round temple, for, although octagonal in its outer shape, it is circular in the interior. The wall is adorned with two rows of columns, one above the other, and by an elegant cupola.

There is no room within the enclosing wall for gardens and fields, and it is moreover mentioned expressly that these lay outside. The character of the architecture is rich and splendid, but shows a decline if compared with the purity of the end of the Republic and the beginning of the Empire.

Villas proper, *i.e.* country residences, were greatly in favour with wealthy Romans, and we in consequence possess numerous descriptions of them of various dates, on the authority of which architects and scholars since Pirro Ligorio have attempted various reconstructive designs. The old *villa rustica*, of which Cato and after him Varro speak, comprises a combination of the dwelling-houses and of the various buildings required for farming purposes. Varro already complains of the latter consideration being thrown into the background by the desire of transforming large agricultural districts into beautiful landscapes, the villas themselves being at the same time reconstructed on the luxurious system of town architecture (*villa urbana*). Vitruvius, whose statements about the villa rustica tally with those of Varro, says that the villa urbana was constructed like a town house, with the distinction of its being more regular in design, and that of its site being chosen better than the narrow space between the adjoining houses of a street would permit. The increasing scale of luxury and comfort may be marked by comparing the simplicity of the older Scipio's Linternum in Campania, or the family-seat of Cicero at Arpinum, with the more comfortable villa of the latter at Tusculum or his Formianum, and finally with the splendid country residences of Métellus and Lucullus. We possess the description and partly the remains of some of the villas of imperial times, which give us a high idea of the variety and splendour of their architectural arrangements. The younger Pliny has described in two letters his Tuscum (Ep. V., 6; compare § 94) and his villa at Laurentum (II., 17). He there mentions a great number of apartments, halls, courts, baths, and other conveniences for the enjoyment of life in different weathers and seasons; he at the same time notices the absence of fish-ponds, museums, libraries, &c., such as were considered indispensable at other villas. These statements refer to the time of Trajan. Of the time of Hadrian we know the villa constructed for himself by that art-loving emperor at Tibur, the former splendour of which is still visible in the numerous remains of it found near the modern Tivoli; a short description of the same villa by Spartianus (v. Hadriani, 26) assists us further in realising its grand design. The ground belonging to it had a circumference of seven Roman miglie. We are still able to distinguish two larger theatres, and an odeum, smaller in size, and destined, most likely, for musical performances; a great number of chambers, still recognisable, seem to have been destined for the pilgrims visiting a temple and oracle here situated; other rooms in a still better state of preservation (" le Cento Camarelle ") may have belonged to the emperor's body-guard. Near them lie the ruins of what is supposed to have been the emperor's dwelling. Other structures were called by the names of celebrated buildings in different provinces of the empire. The Canopus (an imitation of the temple of Serapis at Canopus) mentioned by Spartianus has been recognised in the ruin of a round temple lying in a valley, enclosed architecturally. It was adorned with numerous statues in the Egyptian style, the remains of which are in the Capitoline Museum. Other ruins containing the remains of baths are said to have been the Lyceum and Academy; a large square surrounded by columns was the Poikile, adjoining which lie a basilica and a round building, most likely the Prytaneum mentioned by Spartianus. Even the valley of Tempe had been imitated, while Hades is recognised by some in a still-preserved labyrinth of subterraneous chambers. The architecture was technically perfect, as is shown by the remaining brick walls and vaults: some

of the ruins seem to prove that the walls were adorned with slabs
of marble, and that the vaulted ceilings were coated with stucco.
Numerous fragments of columns, beams, valuable pavements, and
sculptures have been (during the last three centuries) and are still
being recovered from the ruins.

To illustrate the simpler villas of the higher middle class we
have inserted the plan of the so-called *villa suburbana* of M. Arrius
Diomedes at Pompeii (Fig. 393; scale, 100 feet). It lies near the
city in the street of graves, which passes the building in an
oblique direction. The ground in this place slopes downwards

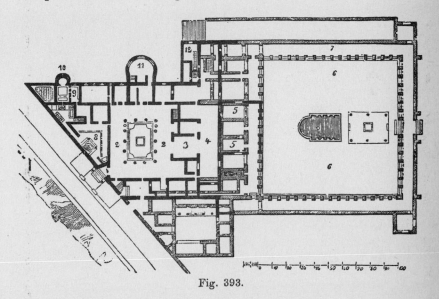

Fig. 393.

from the street; and as the house has to follow this declivity,
the front parts (marked in our plan by black lines) lie higher
than the back ones (marked by hatched lines), rising above them
in the form of terraces. Near the entrance the pavement of the
street is raised, and from it seven further steps ascend to the door
(1) through which one enters the peristylium (2), quite in
accordance with Vitruvius's (VI., 8) rules for such villas, called by
him *pseudourbanæ;* in the position of the peristylium they therefore differ essentially from town-houses. Fourteen Doric columns
(the lower third of which is not fluted, but painted red, while the
two upper thirds are white and fluted) form the peristylium, and

surround a compluvium, the water of which communicated with two fountains (*puteal*) between the columns. On the side opposite the door of the peristylium lies the tablinum (3), the other sides being adjoined by smaller chambers, some of which were bedrooms, as appears from the beds worked into the walls. The tablinum opens into a sort of gallery (4), connected on one side with the peristylium by means of fauces, and opening on the other into a large hall (5), the œcus. This again opens into a second large court with colonnades by means of a window reaching almost to the ground. The enclosing walls of the space hitherto

Fig. 394.

described are marked black in our plan, the hatched lines between them being meant for the walls of smaller chambers on the ground floor underneath it. The just-mentioned court (6), measuring 33 square metres, was surrounded by a vaulted passage (7), supported by pillars (*cryptoporticus*), two sides of which are in perfect preservation; to judge by some of the remains it must have had a second story. In the centre of the court lies a large piscina adorned with a jet, and behind it an open structure resembling a temple, which most likely served as triclinium in the summer. The six columns formerly supporting it are partly

preserved. To the left of the street-door we notice a triangular
court (8) enclosed on two sides by a covered passage, the third
longer side being occupied by a cold plunging-bath. We also
find a tepidarium (9) and calidarium (10) for tepid and hot baths,
in the latter of which the tub for the hot water, the niche for the
labrum, and the heating apparatus are preserved (compare § 80).
Remarkable is also a beautiful bedroom (11), the semicircular
projection of which contains three large windows, to let in the
sun in the morning, afternoon, and evening; the view from these
windows is beautiful. The back wall of this room contains the
alcove for the bed, that could be closed by means of a curtain,
as is proved by the rings still in existence ; 12 marks a small
chamber, through which, by means of a staircase, one passed
into the lower story and the rooms lying near the large court.
To conclude we add (Fig. 394) the view of a villa by the sea,
from a Pompeian wall-painting.

77. From the houses of the living we pass to graves and
grave-monuments. Amongst the numerous and variegated
Roman graves we must limit our remarks to a few specimens.
Almost all the different kinds of Roman tombs have their analogies in Greek architecture. We cannot discuss the question
whether, as seems likely, the old Latin or Italian custom consisted
in simply covering the corpse with earth; neither will we try
to determine when this custom was superseded by the construction of grave-chambers or detached monuments for the reception
of the ashes of burnt bodies. Certain it is that at the time when
this was done models for all the varieties of tombs as developed
by the Greeks (see §§ 23 and 24) were to be found amongst
the neighbouring Etruscans. Amongst the Etruscan tombs we
distinguish the subterraneous grave-chamber, the tomb cut into
the rock with a more or less elaborate façade, and finally the
detached grave-mounds. Of the first kind the old graves of
Cære and the burial-places of Vulci and Corneto offer numerous
examples.

Amongst the former we have chosen the grave known as
Tomba delle Sedie (see plan, Fig. 395, and section, Fig. 396).
The plan shows an inclined passage leading (partly by means
of steps) down to a vestibule, into which open three doors; the
two at the sides lead each into a chamber all but square in shape

(*d*) ; the third between these two is the entrance to the chief burial-chamber (*a*). It is an oblong, and shows on the wall opposite the entrance two stone chairs (see Fig. 396), whence the name

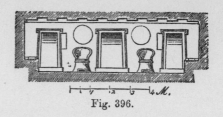

Fig. 396.

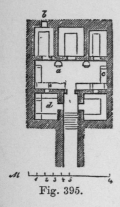

Fig. 395.

of the grave is derived ; along the other three walls run benches (*c*). After this chief apartment follow three smaller chambers, of which that on the right contains a niche in the wall (*b*).

Of graves cut into the rock we find several examples in the narrow valleys of Norchia and Castell d'Asso, the steep slopes of which contain the entrances to the graves; steps lead up to them. Some of the façades are adorned with columns (compare Lenoir, "Tombeaux de Norchia." Ann. dell' Instit., IV. 289 ; "Mon. Ined.," I., tav. XLVIII. 4), while others (see Fig. 397)

Fig. 397.

show no artificial work beyond the doors and the steps leading up to them.

Of the third or detached grave we find numerous specimens in the burial-places of Vulci and other towns. Most of these resemble the above-mentioned grave-mound in the isle of Syme (see Fig. 98) ; our illustration (Fig. 398), the so-called Cucumella, differs from it only by its larger diameter (200 feet) and by the careful stone-border surrounding its whole circumference. On the slope of the mound we also discover ruins of old Etruscan structures which indicate a more elaborate architectural decoration of this grave.

Fig. 398.

We now come to the subterraneous Roman graves built after the Etruscan pattern. Like the Greek tombs they varied in design according to the conditions of the soil, being either cut into the hard rock, or dug into the earth and enclosed with walls where the softness of the soil required it; in the construction of the ceiling the vault became an important element. Of graves in rocks we possess a very primitive example in the tombs of the Scipiones—a kind of labyrinth of irregular subterraneous passages, previously used as a quarry. Originally

Fig. 399.

they lay outside the city in the Via Appia, but on the enlargement of Rome they came within the circle enclosed by the Aurelian wall. Of the monuments found there we quote (Fig. 399) the sarcophagus containing the remains of L. Cornelius Scipio Barbatus (Consul, 298 B.C.). It is made of common stone, and may be considered as one of the most important proofs of the early influence of Greek on Roman art, showing an ornamental border resembling the frieze of Doric art, and a cornice of dentils, which, like the volutes of the top decoration, remind one of Ionic patterns.

More regular is the tomb of the Nasones, in the Via Flaminia. It consists of a subterraneous chamber, with semicircular niches for the coffins. The grave of the Gens Furia, near Frascati, consists of a semicircular chamber surrounded by a narrow passage, the entrance to which, on the slope of the mountain, is adorned with a façade.

We finally mention the subterraneous grave-chambers common to a tribe or to the slaves and freedmen of the imperial or other

noble families. The urns (*olla*), with simple covers to them, stand
in niches somewhat resembling pigeon-holes, whence the name of
columbarium (dovecot) applied to these graves; a small marble tablet

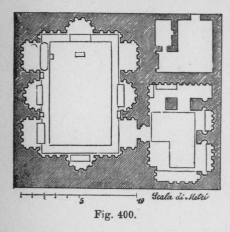

above each niche records the
name of the deceased. Several of these columbaria have
been found in and near Rome.
Figs. 400 and 401 give the
plan and view of the columbarium in which the freedmen of Livia, the wife of
Augustus, were buried. It
lies in the Via Appia, and
consists of several apartments,
of which the one nearest the
entrance is very simple, while
the larger ones, reached by

Fig. 400.

descending a staircase, are decorated more richly. Large niches,

Fig. 401.

square or circular in shape, were destined for the reception of sarcophagi; while seven ascending rows of smaller

openings in the walls contained the cinerary urns. Another
columbarium in the Vigna Codini contains 425 niches in nine rows.

The interior arrangements of
detached graves are of a
similar kind (compare § 78).
Fig. 402 illustrates the interior of a detached tomb,
the exterior of which we
shall consider hereafter (see
Fig. 412). The simple room
covered with a barrel-vault
receives its light from a
single window in the ceiling. Niches in the walls

Fig. 402.

and in the benches contain the urns, others of which are standing
on these benches.

78. The simplest forms of detached graves aboveground are
nearly related to Etruscan structures of the same kind. We pass
from the simple earth-mounds (*tumuli*) to those tombs which show
a distinct architectural design. Fig. 403 shows Hirt's reconstructive design of a partly destroyed, but still recognisable, grave

Fig. 403.

Fig. 404.

near Naples, generally called the tomb of Virgil. It consists
of a square base made of bricks, the frontage of which contains
a round-arched door leading into the grave. On this base stands
a flattened cone, also made of bricks, except the bottom layers,
which consist of hewn stones.

A similar, though more artistic, design appears in the so-called
tomb of the Horatii and Curiatii, standing on the road from Rome

to Albano, near the last-mentioned place (see view and design,
Figs. 404 and 405). It seemingly belongs to the time of the
Republic. Its material is a stone found in the quarries of
Albano, generally called "Peperin." The substructure is nineteen metres in circumference, and shows a base and a cornice
carefully worked out. On it stands a conical structure, similar to that of the grave of Virgil. Here,
however, several smaller cones are grouped round
the centre one, the former occupying the four
corners of the substructure. The centre cone is
both thicker and higher than the others. Perhaps
an individual Etruscan model has here been imitated; the descriptions, at least, of the tomb of the Etruscan King Porsenna indicates a similar arrangement of four conical turrets.

Fig. 405.

Akin to these conical erections is the round tower on a square
base, such as found in the grave in the Via Appia belonging,
according to its inscription, to Cæcilia Metella, daughter of
Q. Creticus, and wife of the triumvir C. Crassus, celebrated for

Fig. 406.

his riches (Fig. 406). The base is made of quarry-stone, the
round tower being carefully faced with freestone, and adorned
with frieze and cornice. The decoration of the frieze is composed
of alternating flowers and skulls of animals, whence the popular
name of the monument "Capo di Bove." A small door leads
into the circular grave-chamber. What the original roof of the

building has been can no more be ascertained; the battlement
seen in our illustration dates from the Middle Ages, when the
Cætani turned the tomb into a tower of defence, connecting it
with other fortifications still preserved.

Another monument built in imitation of the Egyptian pyramids belongs to the age of Augustus (Fig. 407). The pyramid
is of rather steep ascent, its base being 30 metres in circumference, its height 37 metres. It is built of a very firm composition of mortar and small stones faced with tablets of white
marble. The grave-chamber is comparatively small, and still

Fig. 407.

shows traces of beautiful wall-paintings. The original entrance
was effected by means of an inclined shaft about half-way
up the northern side of the pyramid. This shaft, covered
outside with a stone, led straight to the centre of the vault,
covering the grave-chamber. Columns and statues adorned the
exterior. Several inscriptions record the dignities of the deceased
inmate, amongst which we count those of prætor and tribune of
the people. His name was C. Cestius. The monument was
erected to him by his heirs, one of whom was M. Agrippa. In

accordance with the last will of the deceased it had been completed in 330 days.

Other forms of the grave resemble the design of a temple,
as does, for instance, a monument discovered near the northern
corner of the Capitol (Fig. 408). It

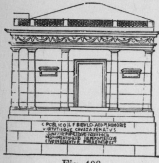

is built of freestone, and shows on
its base an inscription, according to
which it was dedicated by the people
and senate to the memory of the ædile
Caius Poblicius Bibulus. The upper
part contains on the side shown in
our illustration a door between two
Doric or Tuscan pilasters, which at
the same time carry the beams, with
a sort of balustrade on the top of

Fig. 408.

them. The frieze shows a decoration of flowers and skulls of
bulls, similar to that of the tomb of Cæcilia Metella. Another
tomb at Palmyra shows a still closer resemblance to the temple;

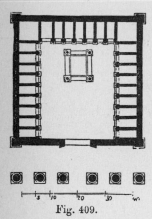

it may, indeed, be described as a prostylos hexastylos (see Fig. 409; scale,
40 feet). It forms an all but perfect
square, with a portico of six detached
columns added to it. The arrangement
of the interior proves its destination as
a family-grave: on three sides we see
rows of narrow cellæ or grave-chambers, while almost in the centre of the
building stands a structure of four
columns (*tetrastylos*), most likely destined for the reception of the chief

Fig. 409.

sarcophagus. Another grave in the
form of a tower is also found at Palmyra (Fig. 410; scale, 24 feet),
the front side of which shows the statue of the deceased in a
lying position; while the interior contains, in different stories, a
number of niches for the reception of cinerary urns.

All the monuments hitherto mentioned are, if not small, at
least of moderate dimensions; the increasing luxury of later
times, however, also extended to grave monuments. This was
particularly the case where the dignity of the State itself was

represented by the deceased person. The monument erected by
Augustus to himself and his descendants shows colossal dimensions.
On a square base rose an enormous round building (similar to
that of the tomb of Cæcilia Metella), on which
was heaped an additional tumulus, while underneath it lay the imperial grave-chambers. The
enclosing walls are preserved sufficiently to give
an idea of the original grandeur of the structure.

When, in the course of a century, it had been
filled with the remains of emperors, Hadrian
determined upon erecting a similar structure for
himself and his successors.

The site chosen lay on the other side of the
Tiber, opposite the tomb of Augustus, connected
with the city by means of the above-mentioned
Pons Ælius (Figs. 369 and 370), at present
called Ponte S. Angelo. This tomb also con-

Fig. 410.

sists of a square basis (90 metres), and, standing on it, a colossal
round tower (67 metres in diameter by 22 high), originally faced

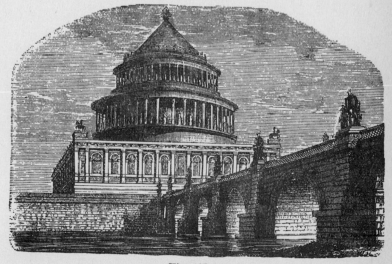

Fig. 411.

with Parian marble, and decorated more richly than the mausoleum
of Augustus. According to a tradition, the twenty-four Korinthian

columns in the centre nave of St. Paul's Basilica originally
belonged to this Moles Hadriani, which indicates its having been
surrounded by colonnades in the manner of a round peripteros.
This conjecture becomes still more probable from the fact of
plastic works of art being mentioned in connection with the
mausoleum, which statues most likely stood in these colonnades :
excellent works of art have indeed been found in the neighbourhood.   The chief part of the edifice has been preserved in the
round tower of the Castello S. Angelo, which makes a careful
investigation of the interior a matter of some difficulty.   Several

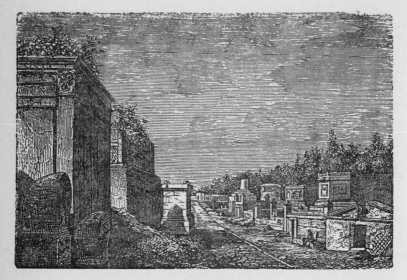

Fig. 412.

designs of the original form of the building have been attempted.
Fig. 411 shows that of Canina, who, in opposition to Hirt,
assumes the existence of two external colonnades.   Canina
crowns the building with a pyramidal roof, the top ornament
being a large pineapple of bronze, found in the neighbourhood,
and at present in the garden of the Vatican.

Of other smaller grave-monuments, partly containing the
grave-chambers, partly built above them, we possess a variety
of forms.   They either resembled small round or square altars
(*cippi*), or they consisted of simple pillars (*hermæ*), the tops of

which were rounded on one side, so as to almost resemble a human head cut in half. Of all these forms we see specimens in the street of graves at Pompeii (Fig. 412). On both sides of the street (our view is taken from a point near the villa of Diomedes, Fig. 393) we see numerous graves, generally with the names of individuals or families inscribed on them. Where space permitted the monument was, like the temple, surrounded by a small court, separated from the street and other graves by a wall. These enclosures, besides indicating the hallowed character of the place, were, in some cases, used for the solemn burning of the body and the collecting of the remains according to prescribed rites (*ossilegium*). In case the enclosure served this purpose it was denominated *ustrina* (from *urere*, to burn). In some places, however, the burning of the body near the grave was forbidden, besides which the poorer classes could not afford separate enclosures; for these reasons public ustrina had to be provided, one of which, in the form of a square space enclosed by a wall, has been discovered at Pompeii. Another large public ustrinum, in the Via Appia, about five miglie from the Porta S. Sebastiano, has been discovered by Piranesi, and described by him in his "Antichità di Roma" (III., 4). It is a vast square, surrounded on all sides by walls of large blocks of Peperin stone. On the wall is a path with a low parapet, evidently intended to enable the mourners to witness the burning of the body in the square, after which the collecting of the ashes took place.

Amongst the tombs of the Pompeian street of graves (Fig. 412) we discover on the left, first a small monument like a temple, with two columns; it lies just opposite the villa of Diomedes, and was, according to its inscription, the common grave of the family of M. Arrius Diomedes; to it belong the two cippi which lie on a common base with the chief monument, and are inscribed to two members of the same family. The second larger monument on the same side is devoted to the memory of L. Ceius Labeo; his and his wife's busts, which formerly stood on the grave, are now in the Museo Borbonico. On the right side of our illustration we see a wall covered by a gable; a low door in this wall leads into an uncovered square court adjoining one corner of the villa of Diomedes, in which court the arrangements for the funereal repast, the last ceremony of the burial, have been found. In this court we recognise a *triclinium funebre* resembling the dining-rooms of private houses, with their gently inclining couches; its walls were covered with paintings, now in an all but destroyed condition. Next to this triclinium stands, on a rich base, an altar-like monument, which is amongst the finest and best preserved tombs of Pompeii. It lies in a court, the wall of which is adorned with small turrets; a door in this wall opens into the street. The grave-chamber lies inside the base (see the view of the interior, Fig. 402); the cippus, resembling an altar, which rises above the base on several steps to a height exceeding

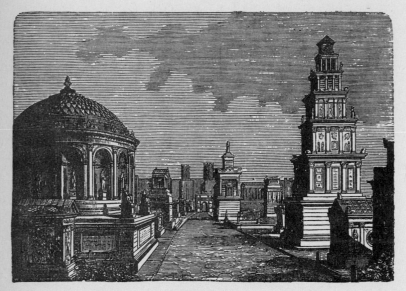

Fig. 413.

that of the enclosing wall, is richly adorned with bas-reliefs. The inscription on its front side says that Nævoleia Tyche, the freedwoman of Luccius Nævoleius, has erected the monument during her lifetime to herself, to L. Munatius Faustus, and to their liberated slaves of both sexes. Amongst the monuments following on the same side, and still visible in our illustration, we mention the cenotaphium of C. Calventius Quietus, in the form of an altar. After it follows a family-grave without inscription, consisting of a round flat tower surrounded by a wall, crowned by turrets, with decorations in relief. We further mention the tomb of

Scaurus, interesting by its bas-reliefs representing gladiators (compare Figs. 505, 507, 508).

To conclude we add an illustration of a portion of the Via Appia, near Rome. This important highway was peculiarly adapted to be adorned with tombs and other monuments, the traces of which have been discovered for a distance of several miles from Rome. After carefully examining the remains and comparing them with other monuments, the architect Canina has tried to illustrate parts of the Via in their original appearance. Fig. 413 is a reproduction of one of these attempts.

79. We now come to those monuments which, instead of being the receptacles of dead persons, served to prolong the memory of their deeds and merits. Some monuments served both as tombs and memorial structures (compare our remarks about the kenotaphion of the Greeks, § 24, c). The most striking illustration of the combination of these two different purposes is the column of the Emperor Trajan, to which we shall have to return. Fig.

Fig. 414.

414 shows a monument, which in a manner forms the connecting link between the two species of edifices alluded to. It
lies near the village of Igel, in the vicinity of Treves; our
illustration shows the north side. It is built of freestone, and
rises in several divisions to a height of 64 feet, according to the
lowest of the different measurements. The sides towards north
and south are 15, those towards east and west 12 feet wide. The
steep roof, resembling a pyramid with curved outlines, is adorned
with decorations not unlike scales. It is crowned by a sort of
capital, adorned with human figures in the four corners, on which
rests a globe supported by four small sphinxes. Some fragments
on the top of this globe seem to indicate that here was placed
originally an eagle carrying a human figure to heaven—an
apotheosis of the persons to whom the monument was dedicated.
Besides these greatly injured sculptures we observe a profusion of
figures in relief on all sides and in all divisions of the structure.
Like the chief representation on the south side they refer partly to
the individuals to be honoured by the monument, partly to mythological objects (the centre bas-relief visible in our illustration, for
instance, shows the god of the sun in his chariot), partly also they
illustrate scenes of actual life in reference to the persons alluded to.
Of this more anon. The style of the sculptures and architecture
belongs to late imperial times. An inscription, although partly
destroyed, and explained in many different ways, seems to prove
beyond doubt that the monument was erected by L. Secundinius
Aventinus and Secundinius Securus in honour of their parents
and their other blood-relations. It was the common monument
of the Secundinii, several members of which family are mentioned in inscriptions found near Treves as holding offices of
various kinds. Similar monuments of Roman origin have been
found by Barth in the south of the Tripolitan country (the
Syrtica Tripolitana of the Romans), in the Wadi Tagidje, and
near the fountain of Taborieh (see H. Barth, " Reisen und
Entdeckungen in Nord- und Central-Afrika," I., pp. 125
and 132).

In turning to the monuments of honour proper we must
premise that amongst such may be counted all structures, be they
temples, halls, theatres, columns, pillars, or gates, erected in
honour of a person or in celebration of an event. To Cæsar and

several emperors temples have been erected; small buildings resembling chapels, built in honour of individuals, occur at Palmyra; halls and colonnades in Rome served, as they did amongst the Greeks, to perpetuate the memory of great men; even a theatre in Rome was built in honour of a favourite of the Emperor Augustus. We must refrain from describing these and similar structures. We mention only two forms of the monument of honour, one of which has been invented, the other applied in preference, by the Romans. To the latter class belong the columns; to the former the triumphal arches. Columns were frequently erected by the Greeks for the same purpose, and in that case bore the statue of the person to be honoured (as, for instance, that of the orator Isokrates), or some object referring to the deeds or merits of this person. A second column erected to the same Isokrates showed the image of a syren as a symbol of eloquence; other columns, partly still preserved, carried tripods, such as were awarded to the victors of the agones.* Sometimes the columns showed only inscriptions without sculptural decorations. Columns of all three kinds may have occurred amongst the Romans, who at an early date adopted this mode of honouring meritorious citizens from the Greeks. Originally they were awarded only by the senate, afterwards also by the people, the expenses being either raised by private collections or paid by the State. Having frequently described the architectural characteristics of the column, we shall here refer to such columnar monuments only as greatly deviate from the common type. We first mention the oldest of all such columns, viz. the Columna Rostrata, built in the Forum, and adorned with the prows of ships, to celebrate the naval victory of C. Duilius over the Carthaginians (B.C. 261). A modern imitation of it with the antique inscription is preserved in the Capitoline museum. This venerable monument became the model of other *columnæ rostratæ* found on various coins of imperial origin, struck in celebration of naval victories. Whether these columns (as, for instance, those on silver coins of Augustus and Titus, with the statues of these emperors on the top of the columns) were actually erected remains uncertain. Other columns

---

* On the south side of the Akropolis, near the castle-wall, above the theatre of Dionysos, are still standing several columns of this kind, the Korinthian capitals of which have been made triangular, so as to fit the tripods to be placed on them.

show the deeds of their heroes in relief representations, winding generally in a spiral line round the shaft of the column from base to capital. A column of this kind was the chief ornament of the Forum built by Trajan, to which we shall later have to return (see § 82). The column stands on a square base covered with the inscription and with numerous warlike trophies of various kinds. The pedestal is 17 feet high; the column itself, including base and capital, 92 feet. Above the capital rises a pedestal, on which the bronze statue of the emperor stood: it has been lost and replaced by that of St. Peter. The column itself, consisting of twenty-three drums of marble, is in surprisingly good preservation. The bas-reliefs surrounding it, in twenty-two spiral curves, form a consecutive number of scenes from Trajan's wars with the Dacians. The inscription on the base gives the date and purpose of its erection.* According to a doubtful tradition the ashes of the emperor were enclosed in a globe held by the statue; while, according to another more trustworthy account, Hadrian deposited the remains of his predecessor in a golden urn underneath the column. A winding staircase of 185 steps inside the column (the entrance to which lies in the pedestal) leads to the top of the capital.

Resembling the column of Trajan, although not equal to it in workmanship and beauty, is the column erected by senate and people to the memory of the noble Marcus Aurelius Antoninus. It seems to have been connected with a temple devoted to the same emperor. Like the column of Trajan, it is well preserved, and, like it, it has lost the original statue of the emperor, the present one of St. Paul having been placed on it by the same pope, Sixtus V., who put the statue of St. Peter on the column of Trajan, on the occasion of both these monuments being cleaned and restored. Fig. 415 shows a design of Canina of the column with its original surroundings. Like the first-mentioned column, it consists of large cylindrical blocks of marble worked, on the inside, into a winding staircase of at present 190 steps. According to an inscription found near it, its height is 100 old Roman feet.

---

* SENATUS POPULUSQUE ROMANUS IMP CAESARI DIVI NERVAE F NERVAE TRAIANO AUG GERM DACICO PONTIF MAXIMO TRIB POT XVII IMP VI COS VI P P AD DECLARANDUM QUANTAE ALTITUDINIS MONS ET LOCUS TANTIS OPERIBUS SIT EGESTUS.

The shaft is like that of the column of Trajan, but the pedestal is considerably higher in this case; part of it is now hidden by the earth. The bas-reliefs winding round the column in twenty spiral curves refer to the wars of the emperor with the Marcomans and other tribes to the north of the Lower Danube (compare § 107).

Triumphal arches were frequently erected by the Romans, in

Fig. 415.

this case without the aid of numerous models in Greek architecture. Both by their character and destination these structures are essentially Roman. The custom of arranging festive pageants in celebration of happy events soon led to the erection of triumphal gates for the procession to pass through. Besides decorating the gates of the city for the occasion, the Romans used to erect detached gates of a monumental character. Such triumphal arches might be the reward of all kinds of civic merit. An arch erected to Augustus at Araminium (Rimini) celebrated his construction of the Flaminian road from that town to Rome; an arch, still standing, on the jetty of Ancona records Trajan's restoration of that harbour; another arch at Beneventum was dedicated to the same emperor for his restoration of the Via Appia; an arch still preserved, near the Olympicum, commemorates the building of a new splendid quarter of Athens by Hadrian. The so-called arch of the Sergii at Pola records the merits of a family; a small but richly decorated triumphal gate in the Forum Boarium in Rome was erected to Septimius Severus by the goldsmiths and cattle-dealers.

In most cases, however, these arches were designed for the triumphal entrance of a commander at the head of his army after a victorious war. These triumphal entrances (compare § 109) are essentially representative of the national spirit of the Romans, quite as much as the public games were of that of the Greeks. The sculptural decorations of the arches generally represent the processions that were to pass through them: on the arch of Titus we even see a sculptural reproduction of this monument itself. As the arch itself is a product of Roman national spirit, so its design is pre-eminently representative of that specifically Roman element in architecture — the vaulting or arching principle. Nowhere is this principle displayed more simply and more effectively, nowhere does the mixture of Greek columnar architecture with Roman elements appear in a more striking manner, than in these detached triumphal gates, the arcades of which are in a manner framed with columns or semi-columns appearing to support the flat coverings of the arches and the second lower stories on the top of them. Into the architectural varieties of the triumphal arch we cannot enter here; we only shall quote two examples, representative of the two principal divisions of these monuments. Like the city gate, the triumphal arch can have either one (compare Fig. 356) or three openings (358—360), the possibility of two openings occurring in some Roman gates (Fig. 357) being naturally excluded.

A beautiful example of the first species is the arch of Titus in Rome, built of Pentelic marble (see design, with the statue of the emperor in a quadriga added to it, Fig. 416). Its height is 15·40 metres, its width 13·50, its depth 4·75 metres. The arched opening is 5·36 metres wide by 8·30 high. In the Middle Ages a tower of fortification had been built on it ; but it was restored to its present form in 1822. Its construction is very simple : two strong piers have been connected by means of an arch for the triumphal procession to pass through. To right and left of

Fig. 416.

the arch the piers show two fluted semicolumns of the " composite" order, being the earliest specimens of that order (the two outside ones in travertine and without flutes are a modern addition) ; they stand on a common base, and enclose on each side of the arch a so-called false window. The beams, which are supported by the columns, and which at the same time cover the arch, are richly decorated ; the frieze shows a small bas-relief representation of a sacrificial pageant. Above the beams rises the attic, divided, like the lower story, into three parts, the centre one of which shows the inscription. The sculptural decorations of the arch itself are beautiful; the triangular surfaces between the arch and the columns are occupied by winged Victories with warlike attributes. Inside the opening the walls to right and left are adorned with bas-reliefs, one of which represents the emperor in his triumphal chariot, the other groups of soldiers with the booty of the Jewish war, amongst which we discover the seven-branched candlestick of the temple of Jerusalem (compare § 109). The barrel-vault of the archway is adorned with laquearia, a bas-relief in the centre showing the apotheosis of the emperor, who is carried to heaven by an eagle. According to the inscription, the monument has been erected to the memory of Titus by senate and people in the reign of his successor Domitian. It lies in a beautiful position, between the temple of Venus and Roma and the Coliseum above the Via Sacra, and is one of the most remarkable architectural monuments of Rome.

Still more important for the history of art, although of later date, is the triumphal arch of the Emperor Constantine. In it the traces of two very different periods are distinguishable. For it marks the closing period of the old empire and the rise of Christianity, being erected in celebration of the victory of Constantine over his rival Maxentius, by means of which Christianity was established as the official religion of the Roman State. On the other hand, it takes us back to one of the most glorious epochs of Roman history, viz. the time of Trajan's victories over the Dacians. For when, after the vic-

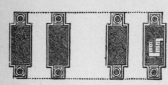

Fig. 417.

tory at the Pons Milvius (A.D. 312), people and senate decided upon erecting an arch for the victor, the shortness of time or the want of artistic means at their disposal compelled them to make use of the plastic and architectural decorations of an older monument for their new structure.* This latter (see plan, Fig. 417) has three openings, the centre one of which is both higher and wider than the two others, being destined for the triumphal chariot of the emperor. The three entrances were enclosed by detached columns, instead of

* Height, 21 metres; width, 25·70; depth, 7·40. Height of centre arch, 11·50, of side arches 7·40.

the usual semi-columns (see Fig. 418), four of which, made of yellow
Numidian marble (*giallo antico*), stood on each side of the structure.
According to Hirt, their workmanship denotes the purer style of
the reign of Hadrian. The greater part of the sculptures, on
both sides of the structure and inside the centre arch, are
taken from the triumphal gate (according to Hirt, two different
gates) erected to Trajan for his victories over the Dacians and
Parthians. The arrangement of these sculptures is very tasteful.
They begin at the bases of the columns, which are adorned with

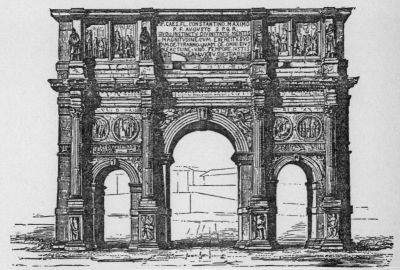

Fig. 418.

large relief-figures in standing postures; on each side of the
richly decorated arch-enclosures we see two seated Victories.
After them follows, in the manner of a frieze, over the smaller
entrances, a series of smaller bas-reliefs; above each of these
lower bas-reliefs are two circular bas-reliefs ("medallions," eight in
all), representing scenes from the private life of Trajan, to which
correspond eight square bas-reliefs with larger figures in the so-
called Attic. The scenes represented by the last-mentioned
sculptures begin, according to Braun's description, on the side
turned towards the Aventine. "They commence," he says,*
"with an illustration of the triumphal entrance of Trajan after

* In his work on the Ruins and Museums of Rome, p. 8.

the first Dacian war, and then turn to his merits in conducting the Via Appia through the Pontine marshes, and in founding an orphanage. They also refer to his relations to Parthamasires, King of Armenia, and to Parthamaspates, to whom he gives the Parthian crown ; also, finally, to Decebalus, king of the Dacians, whose hired assassins are brought before the emperor. The remaining groups show the emperor addressing the soldiers, also the usual sacrifices of pigs, sheep, and oxen." About the "medallions" representing the private life of the emperor, " in simple and graceful compositions," Braun makes the following remarks:—"They begin with the setting out for the chase. The second group represents a sacrifice to Sylvanus, the protecting god of the forest. The third shows the emperor on horseback hunting a boar ; the fourth, the thank-offering to the goddess of the chase. The groups on the side of the Coliseum show a boar-hunt, a sacrifice to Apollo, the inspection of a killed lion, and, lastly, an unexplained oracular scene, most likely referring to the miraculous escape of Trajan from an earthquake at Antiochia."

The above-mentioned frieze continued over the central opening represents consecutively the battle, the flight, and chase of the enemy, and the crowning of the emperor by the Goddess of Victory. It is dedicated to Constantine as the "founder of peace," and the " liberator of the city ; " which inscriptions refer to Constantine's victory over Maxentius, and his occupation of Rome. Only the latter sculptures—the seated Victories, and the standing figures on the pedestals of the columns—date from Constantine's time. By their bad execution and clumsy composition they denote the decline of Roman art ; while the bas-reliefs from the time of Trajan, together with the figures of captive barbarians over the columns, are perfect in both these respects (compare §§ 107 to 109).

80. We have described (§ 25) the development of the Greek gymnasia from private institutions for the requirements of individuals to centres of public intercourse and recreation. A similar position in Roman life was held by the public baths. They also grew from private into public institutions of great magnificence indispensable to the Romans, and, therefore, found in all important towns.

These baths, from the greater importance of the warm baths

ROMAN BATHS. 397

contained in them, generally called *thermæ*, are, in many respects, comparable to the Greek gymnasia, which name was, indeed, occasionally applied to them in later times; in other points, however, the two differ entirely. Although the gymnastic exercises, together with their Greek names, were adopted by the Romans, they never gained national importance amongst them : war, and warlike evolutions in the field, remained the chief means of their corporeal education. In their bathing-establishments the thermæ or baths had, therefore, the largest space assigned to them, smaller localities being reserved for agonistic games ; the Greek notions about the relative importance of these two purposes were thus exactly reversed. Common to both Greek and Roman institutions were the localities serving as walks and places of meeting and conversation to all visitors. The luxury of imperial times added to the thermæ means of intellectual enjoyment, such as libraries and museums.

In older times, before bathing had become a necessity of daily existence, the *lavatrina*, or washhouse, lying next to the kitchen, and connected with it by a heating-apparatus, served also as bath-room. But this simple arrangement soon became insufficient. Hot, sudatory, tepid, and cold baths, shower-baths, rubbing and oiling of the body—all these required separate apartments, to which, at the thermæ, were added dressing and undressing rooms and other apartments for conversation and various kinds of amusement. From numerous remains of baths discovered in various points of the Roman empire we have a distinct idea of their original arrangements ; these remains, moreover, tally in a remarkable degree with Vitruvius's rules. We ought to add, that the picture of the interior of a bath supposed to have been found in the thermæ of Titus, and reproduced in most compendiums of Roman antiquities for a century and a half, has been proved by Marquardt* to be an invention of the architect Giov. Ant. Rusconi (1553).

All the bath-rooms lay over a substructure (*suspensuræ*) about two feet high, the ceiling of which rested on rows of pillars standing at distances of one and a half foot. The furnace (*hypocausis*), with the firing-room (*propnigeum, præfurnium*) lying

---

* In "Handbuch der römischen Alterthümer, etc., begonnen von W. A. Becker, fortgesetzt von J. Marquardt," Part v. Division i., p. 283 *et seq.* Leipsic, 1864.

in front of it, occupied the centre of the establishment. From here the heat was diffused through the basement, and ascended in earthen or leaden pipes (*tubi*) in the walls to the bath-rooms. The cold, tepid, or hot water required for the baths came from three tanks lying above the furnace, and connected with each other by means of pipes. The bath-rooms, over the basement, grouped round the furnace at greater or less distances, were divided, by the different degrees of heat attained in them, into *tepidaria* (sudatory air-baths), *caldaria* (hot baths), and *frigidaria* (cold baths). Tanks (*piscina*), or tubs (*solium, alveus*), occupied the centre of the caldaria and frigidaria; benches and chairs were ranged along the walls, or stood in niches; a flat tub (*labrum*, see Fig. 202), placed in a niche on the narrow side of the oblong calidarium, was filled with cold water for a plunge after the hot bath. In larger, particularly public, baths separate rooms served for dressing and undressing (*apodyterium*), rubbing (*destrictarium*) and oiling the body (*unctorium*). In smaller baths, the latter process was occasionally gone through in the tepidarium. After the end of the Republic, larger establishments used to have a separate steam-bath (*laconicum*) in imitation of the Greek πυριατήριον. Next to the tepidarium, but separated from it by a wall, lay, according to Vitruvius, a small circular building covered by a cupola, which received its light through an aperture in the centre of the dome. By means of a separate heating apparatus its temperature could be increased to an enormous degree. A brass plate (*clypeus*) was suspended on chains from the dome; by lowering it, or pulling it up, the hot air in the apartment became more or less condensed.

So much about the general arrangements of the bath. We now must turn our attention to some of the remains of baths preserved to us. A house at Pompeii shows very simple arrangements. A small dressing-room (*apodyterium*), with a chamber for a tepid air-bath (*tepidarium*) and a hot bath (*caldarium*), may still be recognised. A similar arrangement we see in the above-mentioned *villa suburbana*, where to the tepid and hot baths (Fig. 393, 9 and 10) is added a court for a cold bath (8). The reservoir of the latter, as well as the apparatus for heating the water of the hot bath, is still recognisable.

The same arrangements, although increased in number and

varied in form, we meet with in the thermæ proper, or public
baths; as the simplest specimen of such we quote the thermæ
of Veleia. Veleia, or Velleia, was built in the first century of
the Christian era by the Veleiates, a Ligurian tribe dwelling
previously in villages in the country traversed by the Via Æmilia,
not far from the modern Piacenza. Under one of the successors of
Constantine the town was buried by the fall of a mountain, and
all knowledge of it was lost till 1747, when the discovery of the
largest existing bronze inscription, the so-called *tabula alimentaria*
of Trajan, near the village of Macinisso, indicated the existence
of a Roman settlement. In 1760, by command of Don Philip
of Parma, systematic excavations were begun, which, after five
years, resulted in the discovery of a moderate provincial town of
the first centuries of the Empire. Fig. 419 shows the plan of the

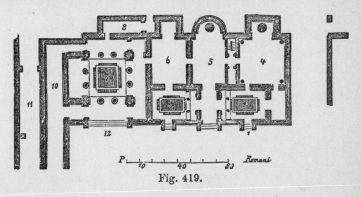

Fig. 419.

partly destroyed thermæ of Veleia according to the design of the
architect Antolini. The façade (1 to 12) contains several
entrances. That lying on the extreme right (1) leads into the baths
for women, consisting of a sort of entrance-hall (2) and of a larger
apartment for hot baths (4). The smaller room lying between the
two may have contained the heating apparatus (*hypocaustum*).
On the other side of the vestibule common to both divisions lies
the entrance-hall of the men's baths (3). After it follows the
bath-room for men (5), separated from that for women by a space
containing a staircase. The room adjoining it (6) was intended
for social intercourse, after it follows the swimming-bath (*natatio*)
of the men (7), surrounded by a colonnade. Into this peristylium
open a narrow apartment (8), in which a mosaic floor has been

discovered, and a covered passage (*crypta*, 10). The street (11)
runs parallel with the latter : on the opposite side of the building
was also a street, while in front of it seems to have been an open
square.

More complicated in design and larger in size are the thermæ
excavated at Pompeii in 1824 (see plan, Fig. 420). Like the
house of Pansa (Fig. 386), they are surrounded by a number of
shops and lodging-houses, which, however, are unconnected with
the bathing-establishment. The whole block of houses (*insula*)
forms an irregular square bordered on all sides by streets. Here,

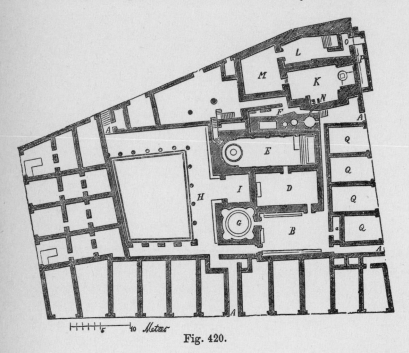

Fig. 420.

also, the baths of women and men are separate, and have different
entrances. The former comprise the rooms *K L M N O P*, the
entrance being near *O* ; the latter, the rooms *B D E G H I*.
Four entrances lead into them from the street on three different
sides (*A A A*). The heating-apparatus (*F*) is common to both
divisions, and lies between them. The remainder of the area
(marked in our plan *Q*, or left blank) is occupied by shops and
private lodgings belonging to them. *O*, as we mentioned before,

marks the entrance to the women's bath in a projection of the wall. To the left of it lies a small apartment furnished with benches, undoubtedly a sort of waiting-room. The larger room *L* is generally believed to be an apodyterium; it also is fitted up with stone benches. In the small alcove-like part of it nearest the entrance we recognise the frigidarium, with the piscina belonging to it, to which latter descend steps (see Plan). From the apodyterium one enters the tepidarium (*M*), under the floor of which, as well as under that of the caldarium (*K*) adjoining it, the suspensuræ for the diffusion of the hot air are still recognisable. In a sort of niche in the latter room we discover the labrum, intended for cold ablutions. Near *N* is the opening of the canal through which the hot air and hot water were conducted from the firing-room (*F*) to the caldarium. Here we see the heating-apparatus enclosed in thick walls : it consists of a circular furnace, about 8 to 9 feet in diameter, from which the hot air was conveyed to the two caldaria for women (*K*) and men (*E*) by means of canals of brickwork which pass underneath the raised floors. We also mention two cauldrons in which the bathing-water was heated ; they were filled with cold water from a quadrangular reservoir lying behind them. The fuel was kept in a court, perhaps covered, and connected with *F* by means of narrow passages.

The rooms for the baths of the men were also grouped round this central heating-apparatus, those requiring the greatest heat lying nearest to it. The caldarium of the men (*E*), lying close to the furnace, consists of an oblong apartment, covered with a barrel-vault, containing openings to admit the light and let out the steam. The slightly raised floor of the centre part lies above the suspensuræ. On the sides narrow openings were left between the stones of the wall and its outer surface to let the hot air pass through. On the narrow eastern side of the room lies a large tub for hot baths (*lavatio calda*) ; several steps led up to this tub or tank, which is connected with the wall itself. The opposite western side, ending in a semicircular niche, contains a detached round labrum, for cold ablutions, about eight inches deep and raised above the ground by one metre ; a bronze pipe at the bottom of it admitted the water. An inscription in bronze letters on the border of the tub says, that it had been purchased by decree of the *decuriones* for the sum of 5,250 *sestertii* (about £38).

A door connects the caldarium with the tepidarium (*D*), smaller in size, but more richly decorated with sculptures and paintings: a bronze hearth and three benches of the same material have been discovered in this elegant and comfortable apartment (Fig. 421). Inscriptions on the seats of the benches name M. Nigidius Vaccula as the donor. Parallel with the tepidarium, and connected with it by means of a door, we see another slightly larger room (*B*). It also has a barrel-vault, but

Fig. 421.

is decorated less richly than the tepidarium. It served as apody-terium, and was surrounded by stone benches with a low step in front of them. On one of the narrow sides of this room lies a small chamber (*A*) belonging to the keeper of the bathers' clothes (*capsarius,* from *capsa, i.e.* cupboard where valuables are kept). On the opposite side the apodyterium is adjoined by a round room (*rotatio, G*), covered with a cupola, in which room a round marble basin served for cold baths, and which may therefore be described as frigidarium. A small aperture in the conical ceiling admitted the light, while the tepidarium was lighted by means of a window closed with *one* pane of ground glass. In accordance with its destination, the tepidarium was connected with the street (*A*) by means of a narrow corridor. In the wall opposite the opening of this corridor, by the side of the entrance to the frigidarium, lies the door of another narrow corridor leading to an open court (*H*). This court, accessible from the street by two other entrances (*A A*), resembles a peristylium, two of its sides being occupied by covered Doric colonnades, while on a third lies a vaulted hall, *crypto-porticus*, receiving its light from several large windows. One of the colonnades is adjoined by a hall (*I, exedra*), serving for purposes of conversation and amusement. The court itself was used for gymnastic exercise and walks, whence its name *ambulatio*. It was particularly adapted to advertising purposes, whence the numerous inscriptions on the walls, most of which, however, are no longer legible. Here has been found a box, in which, most likely, the entrance fees were collected by the janitor.

Much larger than those just described are the so-called "new thermæ" at Pompeii, the excavation of which was finished in 1860. Here all the walls are covered with rich paintings; the upper rooms, moreover, are larger in size, and several new accommodations have been added. Amongst these, we principally count an uncovered marble swimming-bath (*natatio* ; compare Fig. 419, 7), 16·5 by 8 metres in size, opening with its full width towards the palæstra.

The thermæ of Pompeii were naturally surpassed by those of Rome ; nevertheless, they are to us of almost greater importance than the latter, owing to their better state of preservation. The dimensions and splendour of the Roman thermæ may, for instance, be seen from the fact that the Pantheon itself, one of the grandest monuments of Roman architecture, formed only a small portion of the thermæ built by M. Agrippa. In later imperial times, even this splendour was surpassed : Seneca already mentions the coating of the walls with the most valuable kinds of marble, the introduction of silver mouthpieces for the water-pipes, and the placing of numbers of columns and statues in the public baths— a statement which is confirmed by the fragments of beautiful statues found amongst the ruins of thermæ ; an ancient author justly compares their extensive grounds to whole provinces.

Fig. 422 shows the plan of the thermæ of Caracalla, designed

by Cameron. His design, however, only represents the chief
building: an enormous court with which the emperor Decius
afterwards surrounded it has been omitted; but, even without
this addition, the thermæ finished by Caracalla in the fourth year
of his reign (A.D. 217) must be considered as the most magnificent Roman structure of the kind. The walls and part of the
vaults are well preserved; the latter are made of porous tufa,
lighter than the common one, which adds to the boldness of
their design. This applies particularly to the magnificent
entrance-hall, a rotunda (A) with eight niches, similar in design
to the Pantheon, which it almost equals in size, its diameter being

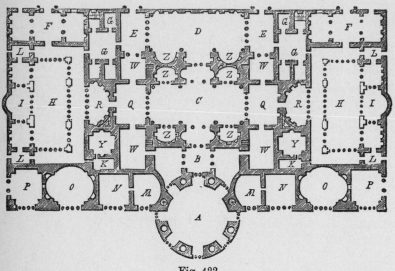

Fig. 422.

111 feet. The vault is not, as in the Pantheon, spherical,
but surprisingly flat in design, and has, for that reason, been
compared by the ancients with a sole, whence the name of the
structure *cella solearis*. The architects of the time of Constantine
explained the possibility of this kind of vaulting by presuming
that metal sticks were placed in the interior to support the
ceiling; Hirt, however, thinks that the lightness of the material
is sufficient to account for the difficulty. After having passed
through the cella solearis one entered the apodyterium (B), behind
which lay the chief hall—the ephebeum (C) (compare the

gymnasium of Ephesos, Fig. 154, *C*), by Roman authors also called *xystus.* Eight colossal granite columns, one of which now stands in the square S. Trinità in Florence, carried the intersecting vaults of the ceiling (see view of the interior, Fig. 423): the length of the whole room was 179 feet. Adjoining the two narrow sides of the ephebeum, and separated from it by columns only, lay smaller rooms (*Q Q*) destined for spectators or wrestlers; *exedræ* resembling niches (*Z Z Z Z*) lay on the longer sides of the hall. We next come to another hall (*D*) of equal length, in which lay the swimming-bath (*piscina*); this room also was

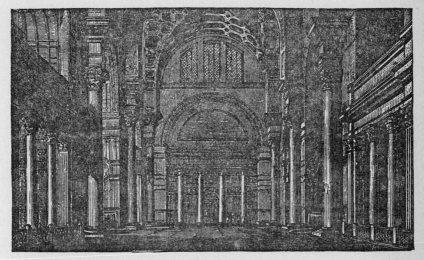

Fig. 423.

adjoined by niches (*Z Z*) and other apartments for the spectators (*E E*). The rooms hitherto mentioned formed the chief part of the building, distinguished from the other divisions by its greater height. The destination of these latter lying to both sides of the centre structure cannot always be determined with certainty. According to Cameron, *F* marks vestibules or libraries; *G*, the dressing-rooms for the wrestlers, near which the remains of stair-cases to the upper stories have been found. He further mentions peristylia with swimming-baths (*H*), rooms for practising (*I*), elæothesia (*K*), with konisteria (*Y*) adjoining them; also vesti-bules (*L*), above which rooms with mosaic pavements have been

discovered.   *M, N, O, P*, respectively mark the laconicum,
caldarium, tepidarium, and frigidarium; *R* indicates larger rooms
(*exedræ*) for conversation.   Fig. 423 shows the interior of the
chief hall (*C*) in its original condition, for the reconstructive
design of which the analogous hall of the thermæ of Diocletian,
preserved in the church S. Maria degli Angeli, has been of considerable assistance.   Other reconstructive designs of the whole
building may be found in the comprehensive work, " Les Thermes
de Caracalla," by the French architect, Abel Blouet.

81. The enormous development of their political power
naturally reacted on the architecture of the Romans ; its tasks
were greater and more varied than those of Greek architecture.
With the extension of the empire, the number of officials in the
central seat of government increased proportionately, for whose
accommodation large public buildings were required.   Other
buildings served to supply the demands of the more extensive
and varied judicial and commercial developments of the people,
while further structures were required to satisfy the craving of
the populace for pageantry and theatrical splendour.   Hence the
number of basilicas (both for judicial and commercial purposes),
of colonnades (for social intercourse), of forums and theatres ;
hence, also, the enormous extension of the circus to accom-
modate the cruel populace of the metropolis : the amphitheatre of
Vespasian may, in a manner, be considered as the embodiment of
the power and splendour of the empire.   The same phenomena,
though on a smaller scale, we see repeated in the provincial towns
in proportion to their growing wealth and independence.

The remains of political buildings of the time of the
republic are scarce ; republican Rome soon became transformed
into imperial Rome, the different phases of which latter are
illustrated by numerous monuments.   Our knowledge of the
official buildings of republican magistrates is, to a great extent,
conjectural ; sometimes their meetings may have taken place in
certain parts of the Forum or in temples.   About the meeting-
place of the senate, generically called *curia*, we know little,—
neither as regards the *curia Hostilia* belonging to the times of the
kings, nor the *curia Julia* instituted by Cæsar, nor, indeed, those
other curiæ called by the names of Marcellus, Pompey, &c.
Most likely they were roomy oblong halls of some kind, which

view is supported by the fact that the cellæ of the temples, where the sittings of the senate frequently took place, show the same form. Of particular importance, in this respect, are the remains of the temple of Concordia in the Forum Romanum, already described by us (see Fig. 334) : it was here that Cicero delivered his fourth oration against Catilina and several of his Philippics ; here also the condemnation to death of Ælius Seianus, the notorious favourite of Tiberius, was pronounced by the senate.

The meeting-place of the quæstors also was a temple, viz. that of Saturn, of which eight columns on a high base are still preserved in the Forum. Here the treasure of the State (*ærarium*), with the documents belonging to it, as also the standards of the army, were kept. The tablets of the law and other political documents (*tabulæ*) were kept in the so-called Tabularium or archive. This building, lately investigated, rests on a large sub-structure, seventy-one metres in length, which seemingly adds to the firmness of the Capitoline Hill on the side of the Forum. It lies immediately above the just-mentioned temple of Concordia (compare Fig. 428, *E F G H*). One wall of the Tabularium, and a row of arcades erected on it, are still in existence (see Fig. 334, *a*). The arcades rest on strong separate pillars of freestone, adorned, towards the Forum, with Doric semi-columns. Above them rises the "Palazzo del Senatore," built in the sixteenth century, and supposed to occupy the site of the Tabularium, which, therefore, must have been of considerable dimensions. Ac-cording to an inscription, both the substructure and the Tabularium itself were built by Q. Lutatius Catulus (B.C. 78). Under Nero the Capitol and the archives were destroyed by fire. Vespasian undertook the new building. According to Suetonius (Vespas. 8), " the emperor restored 3,000 bronze tablets melted by the fire after having searched for copies of their contents, the finest and oldest collection of documents (*instrumentum*) of the empire, in which, since the foundation of the city, all the decrees of the senate, and the plebiscites with regard to the right of confede-ration, and the privileges granted to each community, were kept."

The censors had their office in the so-called *atrium libertatis*—to judge by its name, a building of some religious character (com-pare what has been said about the atrium in § 74). The prætors performed their judicial function at first in "tribunals" (*i.e.*

square raised substructures standing in the Forum), afterwards in
basilicas.   Before describing the latter most developed form of
Roman architecture we must mention a few smaller buildings as
examples of simple meeting-places of municipal officials and
boards.

We are alluding to three buildings in the immediate vicinity
of the forum of Pompeii (see their plans, Fig. 424). They
consist of three halls (9 to 10 metres broad by 16 to 18 long)
of simplest design.   The entrances lie on the narrow side
towards the forum, separated from the latter by a double
colonnade.   On the side opposite the entrances there are niches,
destined evidently to receive the seats of the functionaries.   In *a*
this niche (*tribunal*) is semicircular in form; in *b* it is smaller,

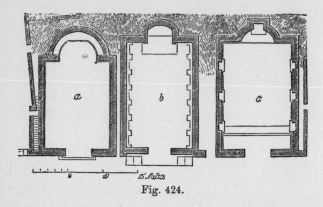

Fig. 424.

and appears terminated by two parallel walls to which a flattened
segment has been affixed; in *c* we see a further square indenture
in the centre of the wall of the otherwise semicircular niche.
Everything indicates that these buildings were used for the
meetings of some board, and not as temples or treasure-houses
as has been conjectured.

The destination of another building in the forum of Pompeii
as the meeting-house or *senaculum* of the decurions can be determined with more certainty.   It consists of a large square hall
(20 by 18 metres), to the back of which is added a semicircular apse
11 metres wide (at the opening) by 6·50 deep.   In the background
of this apse is situated a broad daïs for the seats of the presiding
magistrates.   These and similar buildings may be safely classed as

curiæ, a name which was generically applied to council-houses of magistrates: a building, for instance, devoted to Mars, where the priestly college of the Salii held their meetings, was called a curia.

Still more often occurs the name of *basilica*, a kind of structure frequently described by antique authors, and, moreover, sufficiently illustrated by the remaining specimens. The name was derived from the kingly hall (στοὰ βασίλειος) at Athens where the archon basileus sat in judgment. This derivation is confirmed by the fact that the first basilica was erected at a period when the influence of Greek on Roman architecture had already become powerful. When, during the consulate of Q. Fabius Maximus and M. Marcellus (B.C. 214), a fire destroyed part of the Forum, no basilica was in existence: a fact which Livy (XXVI.— 27) thinks it necessary to tell his contemporaries, to whom the ideas of forum and basilica had become inseparable. About thirty years after this event, M. Porcius Cato, while censor (B.C. 184), erected the first basilica at public expense, after having purchased two plots of ground in the Latomia, besides four shops, for the site of the building. The latter lay beside the curia in the Forum, of which it was in a manner a continuation, being destined for commercial and judicial purposes. For which of these two purposes Cato intended the building, called by himself Basilica Porcia, is difficult to decide, seeing that written testimony is wanting, and that the building itself has been totally destroyed during the riots of Clodius. Vitruvius (Arch., V. 1) seems to think only of commercial convenience. "Basilicas," he says, "ought to be built in the warmest quarters of the market-places, in order that, in winter, the merchants assembling there may not be inconvenienced by bad weather." In his description, on the other hand, of the basilica built by himself at Fanestrum (the modern Fano), he mentions the "tribunal," which he calls "hemicyclium;" but says that the curve was not a complete semicircle, its depth being 15 feet by 46 wide, "in order," he adds, "that those who stand near the magistrates may not be disturbed by those doing business in the basilica."* The twofold use of the basilica appears suffi-

---

* The first passage (edition of Rose and Müller-Strübing) reads, *Ut per hiemem sine molestia tempestatium se conferre in eas negotiatores possint;* the second, *Uti qui apud magistratus starent negotiantes in basilica ne impedirent:* according to this version, here also the commercial interest is put in the foreground.

ciently from these two passages. With regard to the construction
of such buildings Vitruvius adds the following rules. "Their
width must not be less than one-third, and not more than one-
half, of their length, providing the nature of the locality does not
necessitate different proportions. If the site is of considerable
length, *chalcidica* ought to be added at both ends of the building."
The latter seem to have been halls added to the narrow sides of the
basilica, in order to make use of the whole space at disposal. The
basilica is divided lengthwise into three parts, the two at the sides
being called *porticus;* their width is to be equal to one-third of
that of the centre space ; the height of the columns is to be equal
to this width ; above the first porticus lies a second, with columns
lower by one-quarter than the bottom ones; between these lies a
high parapet. From the further description of the basilica of
Fanestrum, it appears that all the rooms were covered. All these
rules, however, must be taken in a general sense only ; individual

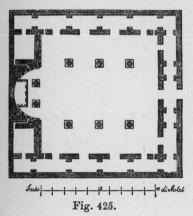

Fig. 425.

buildings frequently deviate from
them. One class of exceptions
are, for instance, the basilicas with
one instead of three naves; other
basilicas occurring at an early
period had as many as five
naves. Of such with one nave, and
therefore without porticus, we
mention the remains of a basilica at
Aquino (the old Aquinum in
Latium), where the walls of the
tribunal built of freestone are
still recognisable ; also that at
Palestrina (the old Præneste), where the "hemicyclical"
tribunal, with a "chalcidicum," has been preserved. The design
of the three tribunals in the forum of Pompeii is, in a more
or less modified way, repeated in most of these buildings ; this
is, for instance, the case in a basilica at Palmyra, consisting of
an oblong hall, to one of the narrow sides of which a perfectly
semicircular niche has been added, while the opposite side shows
an entrance-portico of four columns. To the other sides of the
building wings have been added, which, however, are enclosed
by detached columns instead of walls. Each of these wings

contains twenty columns arranged in five rows of four columns each; they were covered with roofs, and thus formed convenient places of meeting for the merchants whose disputes were decided in the interior of the building.

We also possess several specimens of basilicas with three naves; one of them has been discovered near the modern Otricoli, in 1775. It has been recognised as the basilica of the old Roman *municipium* of Ocriculum, one of the larger towns of Umbria, situated on the Via Flaminia (Fig. 425). The shape of the basilica considerably differs from Vitruvius's rule, forming an all but perfect square. It is divided by two rows of columns (three in number) into three naves, the centre one of which is the widest. To this has been added a semicircular tribunal, up to which lead

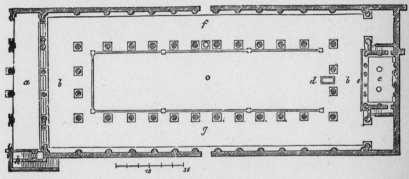

Fig. 426.

steps. On the floor of the first a second daïs seems to have been raised. On both sides of the hemicyclium lie two small quadrangular chambers, accessible also from the two side naves, besides being connected with the niche of the tribunal. A narrow passage (*cryptoporticus*) surrounds the space on three sides. Of other basilicas with three naves, we mention the church of Alba on the Fucine Lake, and a basilica at Treves (233 by 88 feet); as also the so-called " Temple of Peace " in Rome, lying between the Coliseum and the temple of Venus and Roma. It was begun by Maxentius, and finished by Constantine; its ruins are amongst the most splendid of Rome. Four enormous piers divided the inner space into a wide centre and two narrower side naves, the former being covered with an intersected vault, the two latter with barrel-vaults. Two apses were reserved for the seats of the judges. The form of the principal hall in the thermæ of Caracalla (Fig. 423) is exactly like that of the present building, but for the absence of a tribunal in the former.

Fig. 426 (scale 36 feet) illustrates the basilica with three naves at Pompeii, from which we are able to derive a distinct idea of the arrangement of such buildings. With its narrow side it touched the forum, the colonnade of which hid the front of the basilica. *a* in our plan marks a small fore-hall, most likely a chalcidicum. On four steps of the same width as the building we ascend the basilica proper—an oblong edifice with five doors, surrounded on all four sides by a colonnade (*porticus, b b, f g*), by means of which the whole is divided lengthwise into three naves. These columns were of the Ionic order. Thinner pilasters, of Korintho-Roman order, were let into the walls, which latter most likely contained windows, seeing that in all probability the centre space (*c*) also had a roof to it. The quadrangular tribunal (*e*) is raised several feet above the ground, and is adorned in front with a row of smaller Korinthian columns. From two chambers stairs led up to this seat of the judges; another staircase led into the vaulted chamber under the tribunal, which received its light from an opening in the floor of the tribunal, not to mention several small side openings. This chamber was most likely a temporary prison. The ruins show traces of rich mural decorations all over the building; the pavement consisted of marble. Near *d* a pedestal has been discovered, which, to judge by some sculptural fragments, carried an equestrian statue. According to Mazois, the three naves were of nearly equal height, the centre one only being raised a little. The entire length of the basilica was 67 metres, by a width of 27·35 metres. The staircase (*h*) in our plan is not connected with the basilica; it leads up to the roof of the colonnade surrounding the forum.

Of basilicas with five naves we mention the Basilica Julia, built by Cæsar for the centumviral courts of justice in the Forum, between the temple of the Dioscuri and that of Saturn. According to the latest excavations, it was a large building surrounded by a double porticus, and divided by four rows of strong travertine stone pillars into five naves. The pavement consists of grey, reddish, and yellow slabs of marble, which are in an excellent state of preservation. The building (some arches of which were still in existence in 1849) was so large that four judges could sit in its different parts simultaneously. Fig. 427 shows the plan of the Basilica Ulpia, built by Trajan as part of the splendid decoration of his forum. A fragment of the antique plan of Rome,* frequently mentioned by us, distinctly shows the five naves, and even the large niche of the tribunal. The covering of the building with beams of bronze is mentioned with admiration by ancient writers.

82. About the places where public meetings were held in republican times we know but little. In most cases open spaces

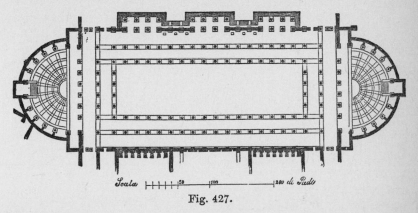

Scala |++++|⁵⁰ |¹⁰⁰ |²⁰⁰ di Piedi

Fig. 427.

without much monumental decoration served the purpose. Only the *curiæ, i.e.* the divisions of the people according to old tribal traditions, form an exception to this rule. The buildings where they met, originally situated in the old parts of the town, were for the greater part afterwards transferred to the more modern quarters, whence the distinction between *curiæ veteres* and *curiæ novæ.* The importance of the curia as a tribal community, although to a great extent divested of its political character, remained unaltered. Their original places of meeting were undoubtedly of the simplest construction, the curiæ of later date, mentioned in § 81, being most likely fashioned after their model.

* This plan engraved on slabs of marble, represents Rome under Septimius Severus and Caracalla. Fragments of it were found, under Pope Pius IV., behind the church of SS. Cosmo e Damiano, and deposited by Benedict XIV. in the Capitoline Museum founded by him. According to Canina, the scale of the plan barring some inaccuracies, was 1 : 250.

They were connected with sanctuaries (*sacella*) of Juno Quiritis, the protecting goddess of the old tribal unions. They were destined for deliberations and sacrificial acts under the presidency of the *curio*, as also for common meals of the members (*curiales*). The *comitia*, on the other hand, were the places of meeting of the whole sovereign people : the name was applied both to the assemblies themselves and to the place in the upper part of the Forum Romanum where they were held (see Fig. 428, R). The meetings were held in the open air till 208 B.C. (546 of the city), in which year, on the occasion of a census (which fixed the number of citizens at 137,108), the comitium was for the first time (see Livy, XXVII. 36) covered,—most likely with canvas, in the manner of the theatres and amphitheatres.

The *comitia tributa* and *comitia centuriata* were frequently held in the Campus Martius, where for that purpose certain places called sheep-pens (*ovile*) were fenced in ; later they were called *septa*, or lists. They were made of wood till Julius Cæsar erected splendid marble ones (*septa marmorea, septa Julia*). About their form nothing is known, beyond what appears from the old plan of Rome, and various coins relating to them : the space in the interior must have been very large, seeing that at a later date fights of gladiators and naval battles took place in it. They were completed by Agrippa, destroyed by fire under Titus, and afterwards restored by Hadrian. In the same Campus Martius, most likely connected with the septa, lay the *diribitorium*, a splendid building, used for counting, perhaps also for giving, votes ; of its original roof, a beam 100 feet long used to be shown in the septa as a curiosity.

We have to add a few remarks about the market-places (*fora*), in which many of the public buildings mentioned by us were situated. Their importance for political life was still greater amongst the Romans than amongst the Greeks (compare § 26). Particularly the Forum Romanum appears like the heart of the body politic. In the course of centuries it was adorned with numerous structures of both historic and artistic importance. Fig. 428 shows the plan of the Forum Romanum in accordance with the latest investigations by Reber and Detlefsen : we shall, in the following remarks, attempt to convey to the reader an idea of what the Forum was during the first centuries of the empire. Upon a discussion of controverted minor points we cannot enter.

The Forum (A) occupies the valley to the north-west of the ridge of mountains connecting the two Capitoline hills (S S) ; to the south-east it extends as far as the Velia, a part of the Palatine (T). Its shape is an irregular oblong, the south-western long side of which is determined by the recently discovered antique pavement of the Via Sacra and several buildings touching it. The north-eastern side is still covered by a mass of rubbish (30 feet deep), on which later structures have been erected. The antique buildings formerly situated there are for that reason indicated in our plan by dotted lines, with the exception only of the Mamertine prison and the temple of Faustina. Of the two narrow sides, that lying towards the slope of the Capitoline hills has been determined by the discovery of the substructures of several temples, identifiable both by their inscriptions and by the testimony of ancient authors ; the opposite side (at a distance of 570 feet) can be distinguished from the vicinity of the Rostra Julia (W) ; the arch of the Fabii, formerly standing there, has, on the other hand, entirely disappeared. We first enumerate the buildings bounding the south-western side of the Forum, also called *sub veteribus sc. tabernis.* According to antique authors, the Atrium of Vesta (Q) lay at the foot of the Palatine (T) ; its exact situation can no more be determined. By the side of it rose the temple of Castor and Pollux, of which three Korinthian columns, connected by a richly ornamented architrave, are still standing erect. It was devoted to the memory of the victory near the Regillus Lake (B.C. 485), but was most likely burnt down together with the Basilica Julia in its vicinity. Tiberius rebuilt it A.D. 6. The excavations, begun in October, 1871, have already laid open three sides of the building, the pavement of which lies 10 metres below the surface of the modern street. The above-mentioned Basilica Julia (C) was separated from this building only by a street ; its substructure has been laid open in its full length. After it follows the temple of Saturn, the *œrarium* or public treasury (D), eight granite columns of which (six belonging to the frontage, the two others to the two long sides), with the architrave resting on them, are still in existence. The first erection of this temple dates back to early republican times ; it

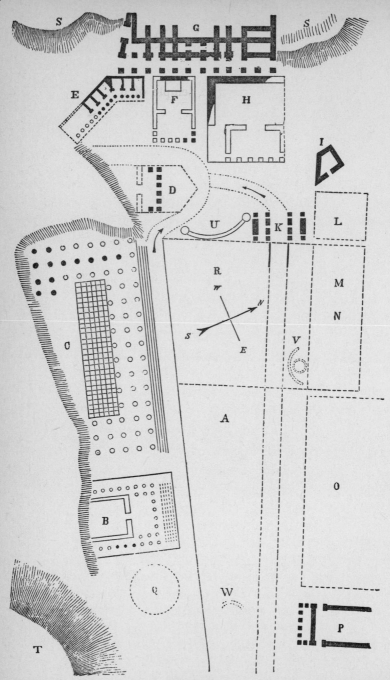

Fig. 428.

was, however, restored repeatedly, for the last time in bad style, under one of the later emperors.

The north-western side of the Forum was bounded by four buildings, viz. the porticus of the Dii Consentes (E), the temple of Vespasian (F, formerly called temple of Jupiter Tonans), the temple of Concordia (H, see also Fig. 334), and, towering above them all, the Tabularium (G) already mentioned. The porticus of the advice-giving gods (Dii Consentes), or twelve chief Roman deities, has been partly restored in modern times with the aid of excavated fragments of antique columns and architraves. The statues of the gods stood, most likely, in front of, or between, the columns. Of the temple built by Vespasian in honour of Domitian (a prostylos hexastylos), three Korinthian columns with their beams are still standing.

Our knowledge of the buildings on the north-east side of the Forum is to a great extent conjectural. Only the two corners are distinctly marked by the ruins of the Mamertine prison (I) and those of the temple of Antoninus and Faustina (P). The foundations of the intervening buildings, viz. the Curia Hostilia (M; the senate-house till B.C. 55, when it was destroyed by fire), the Curia Julia built by Augustus (N), and the Basilica Æmilia et Paulli (O), have been built over at a later date. The Mamertine prison lies underneath the church S. Guiseppe de' Falegnami and the chapel S. Pietro in Carcere, from which a modern staircase leads down to the uppermost of the two subterraneous chambers (according to tradition the prison of the Apostles Peter and Paul). From here another staircase descends to the lower chamber, under which lies the so-called Tullianum (from the old Latin word *tullii*, which, according to Festus, means "fountain-vault"), in which Jugurtha, Sejanus, and others found their death. No trace remains of the notorious staircase leading from the prison to the Forum, on which the corpses of the executed were exhibited, and on which the Emperor Vitellius was killed. In comparatively the best state of preservation is the temple of Antoninus and Faustina (P), a prostylos hexastylos, inside of which the church S. Lorenzo in Miranda has been erected.

The upper part of the space surrounded by these buildings was, in republican times, occupied by the comitium (R); the

lower part formed the Forum proper. The two divisions were of
about equal size : on the north-east side stood the old tribune
for the orators, the *rostra vetera* (V), protected from the populace
thronging the Forum by a semicircular balustrade ; behind it lay
the above-mentioned Curia Hostilia and the older Græcostasis, an
uncovered terrace (*locus substructus*) surrounded by a balustrade,
where foreign ambassadors waited for the decision of the curia.
After Cæsar's time the rostra was transferred to the lower Forum,
where it existed during the two first centuries of the empire under
the name of Rostra Julia (W).   After the downfall of the
Republic, the comitium and the whole republican arrangements of
the Forum lost their political significance ; new buildings were
erected, the old ones remodelled. Septimius Severus at last
(203 A.D.) built a triumphal arch (K), of Pentelic marble, on the
north-west side of the Forum, and at the same time transferred
the Via Sacra (which previously ran along the older booths—*sub
veteribus*—on the south-west side of the Forum) to the opposite
side, directing it straight towards the triumphal arch ; behind the
latter the road most likely turned westward in a curve (marked
by a bent arrow), joining the old Via Sacra at the foot of the
Clivus Capitolinus.   Near the arch of Severus lies, at present, a
terrace (U), slightly curved towards the Forum, and showing the
remains of a marble balustrade ; a brick base in the corner
nearest the arch of Severus is believed to be a remnant of the
milliarium aureum, built by Augustus, *i.e.* the central milestone,
and at once the centre (*umbilicus*) of the Roman empire. The
terrace itself is, by some modern archæologists, believed to be the
Rostra Capitolina of imperial times ; others call it Græcostasis.

Vitruvius (V. 1), in his rules for the building of regularly
planned fora, says that their shape ought to be oblong, instead of
showing the square form of the older Greek agora ; the reason for
this modification being the public games (combats of gladiators)
which, according to old Italian custom, were held in them.   For
this purpose the oblong form seems to have been the more convenient one.   In order not to obstruct the view of the spectators
the columns of the surrounding colonnades ought to stand at
considerable distances from each other.   Inside these colonnades
shops (*tabernæ argentariæ, i.e.* money-changers' offices) ought to
be built, with a second story above them.   The width of the

forum ought to be equal to two-thirds of its length. The latter
rule is strictly followed in the forum of the Ligurian town of
Veleia, formerly mentioned by us (see Fig. 429, from Antolini's
design). The open space (1) is 150 Roman palms long by 100
wide ; it is surrounded on three sides by colonnades (14), the
single Doric columns of which are ranged at considerable distances
from each other. In the open space several pieces of solid
masonry (2), most likely the remains of decorative monuments,
have been discovered. A still-existing canal surrounded the
whole area, in order to drain off the water ; a stripe of marble
(marked in our Plan by thinner lines), with a bronze inscription

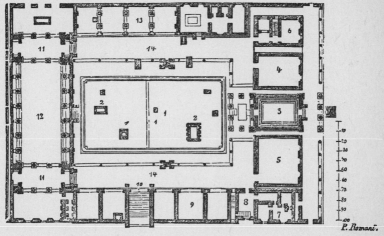

Fig. 429.

on it, lay right across the Forum : according to the inscription,
L. Lucilius Priscus had the Forum paved with stone slabs (*laminis
stravit*) at his expense. A temple (3) occupies the centre of the side
on which one enters the square, the entrance being through small
passages leading past the temple, not unlike the fauces of private
houses.* To right and left of the temple lie two good-sized
rooms, one of them (4, 6) believed to be the dwelling of the priest,
the other (5) a meeting-hall (*comitium*) reserved for the deliberations of religious communities. On entering the forum through
the temple or the fauces, one sees to the left a row of shops (9),

* The temple itself has been mentioned by us (§ 63) as one of the rare examples
of an amphiprostylos.

opening into the surrounding colonnades; 10, on the same side, marks another entrance, through which one ascends the forum by means of steps; 7 and 8 have been explained as prisons. Opposite the temple lies a large building, generally called a basilica (12), with chalcidica (11) on both sides; it bounds the area in its full width. 13 is supposed to be another larger and detached chalcidicum: an inscription found there says that Bæbia Basilla presented a chalcidicum to her fellow-citizens. The space between this chalcidicum and the supposed dwelling of the priest is generally considered as the site of the ærarium. In this Forum was undoubtedly kept the large inscription, the finding of which led to the rediscovery of Veleia itself: it is written on a plate of bronze 8 feet 8 inches long by 4 feet 4 inches high, and is believed to be the largest inscription on metal in existence; it is known by the name of *tabula alimentaria*, because it contains the regulations of Trajan for the keeping of the orphans and other poor children of the town, the number provided for being 246 boys (*pueri alimentarii*) and 35 girls (*puellæ alimentariæ*). Besides a separate fund for 19 other children, a sum of 1,044,000 sestertii (about £11,344) was mortgaged on houses and land in Veleia, the interest of which at 5 per cent. was divided amongst the children.

Much more splendid than the Forum of Veleia was that of Pompeii: the remains of the buildings surrounding it seem to indicate a uniform architectural design. Including the colonnades in front of the curiæ its length is 160 metres, its medium width from north to south 42 metres. An uninterrupted colonnade surrounds the forum on the western long side, the southern narrow side, and part of the eastern long side. On the remaining sides the colonnade is interrupted in several points. The continued colonnades carried (in accordance with Vitruvius's precept) a second story, the former existence of which is proved by the preserved staircase leading up to it. On the north side stands the temple of Jupiter, already described (see Figs. 332 and 338); to both sides of it lie two gates, that on the right being, to judge by its remnants, a triumphal gate. It was, at the same time, the chief entrance to the Forum. On the eastern long side, to the left of the triumphal arch, lie the so-called Pantheon, with the money-changers' shops (*tabernæ argentariæ*) in front of it, the curia of the decuriones, the small so-called temple of Mercury or Quirinus, the chalcidicum of Eumachia, and, separated from these by a street, another edifice, perhaps a public school. On the south side (adorned with a double colonnade), opposite the temple of Jupiter, lie the council-houses (shown in Fig. 424) ; on the west side the basilica (see Fig. 426) and the so-called temple of Venus, the long side of which latter, with its splendid colonnade, is turned towards the Forum, but is accessible from it only by a gate, the chief entrance to the temple lying in a street leading to the Forum. By the side of the last-mentioned gate, in a niche, stands an interesting monument, viz. the gauging-stone, consisting of two tables, one on the top of the other, into the slabs of which the normal measures have been inserted. The original is at present in the museum of Naples, being supplied at Pompeii by a rough imitation. On the same side of the forum and opening on to it lies also a large hall (10 metres deep by 34 wide), considered by some as a picture-gallery (*stoa pœkile*); by Overbeck, with better reason, as a public room for conversation.

Hitherto we have considered only the fora reserved for civic intercourse (*fora civilia*), from which mercantile pursuits (barring the shops of the money-changers) were excluded. Market-places for the latter purposes (*fora venalia*) also occur in Rome and other towns, as, for instance, markets for vegetables (*forum olitorium*), oxen (*f. boarium*), pigs (*f. suarium*), fish (*f. piscarium*), meat and vegetables conjointly (*f. macellum*), &c. In Rome itself there were, besides the Forum Romanum, several other fora civilia, originated by the increasing number of citizens and by the desire on the part of the emperors to gain popularity by the erection of splendid structures for common use. Whole blocks of houses had frequently to be bought and levelled for the purpose. The Forum of Julius Cæsar, surrounded by double colonnades and adorned with the splendid temple of Venus Genitrix, has almost entirely disappeared. We mention besides the fora of Augustus, Vespasian, Nerva (also called *Forum Transitorium* or *Palladium*), and of Trajan, the last of which surpassed all the others in size and splendour. All these fora lay grouped together on the north side of the Forum Romanum, of which they were in a manner a splendid continuation.

83. Our remarks about the buildings for public games and

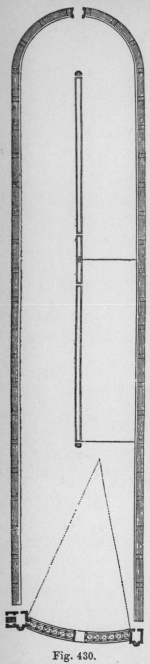

Fig. 430.

similar enjoyments, so important for Roman life, and so fully illustrated by the remaining specimens, can be couched in few words. What we have said about the Greek hippodrome (§ 28), stadion (§ 29), and theatre (§ 30) applies to a prevailing extent also to the Roman circus and theatre. Peculiar to the latter nation is only the amphitheatre; but here also the architectural principles of the Greek theatre in conjunction with those of the stadion and hippodrome may be recognised. About the games of the circus (*ludi circenses*), the theatrical representations, and the fights of the gladiators, we shall have to speak at greater length hereafter.

Fig. 430 shows the plan of a *circus* or racecourse discovered, in 1823, amongst the ruins of the old Bovillæ, a small town in Latium lying on the Via Appia, at the foot of the Albanian mountains. It is comparatively small, much smaller, for instance, than the racecourses in Rome. The foundations are of simple construction, and show a very moderate use of the vault, generally one of the grandest and most characteristic features of similar structures. On the other hand, it is more than usually well preserved, particularly that part of it where the race began; it resembles the hippaphesis of the hippodrome of Olympia, and is one of the most essential features of the whole arrangement. We are speaking of the compartments for the single chariots (*carceres*), being placed in a line at once curved and oblique, in order to produce equal distance from the point where the real race began (see Plan, Fig.

430). The number of these carceres, in the middle of which lay the entrance-portal, was twelve : on the two sides are tower-like buildings (*oppida*), occurring also in other racecourses. In one of these towers we discover steps leading to the seats on the roofs of the carceres. In the middle of the course lies the *spina* (a raised line), with the *metæ* (goals) at both ends ; round these the chariots had to race a certain number of times. In the centre of the semicircular curve of the course, opposite the carceres, lies the triumphal gate (*porta triumphalis*) through which the victor left the circus.

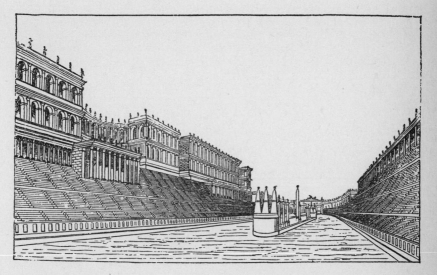

Fig. 431.

The same arrangements, on a large scale, we find repeated in the numerous racecourses of Rome itself. We mention only the Circus Maximus, lying in the broad valley between the Palatine and Aventine hills. This circus (afterwards, in comparison to other smaller ones, called "the largest") is said to have been built by King Tarquinius Priscus, who also arranged the seats of the people, according to their division, into thirty curiæ. In Tarquinius Superbus's time already the circus was enlarged and the seats re-arranged, which process of enlargement and embellishment was, in the course of a thousand years, repeated frequently, the last restorer being Constantine or his son Constantius. The additions consisted of massive buildings in several stories, by means of which the number of seats was gradually increased from 150,000 to 260,000, according to a later account even to 383,000.* The circus has entirely disappeared, the regulated formation of the sides of the valley being the only trace of its existence. Fig. 431 shows its original aspect; we there see the raised substructure (*podium*) and the different stories of the spectators' seats (*mæniana*), overlooked on the left by the imperial palaces, also the spina with its manifold decorations (the goals, several sanctuaries, an obelisk, &c.) and the porta triumphalis.

The stadia, of which there was a considerable number in Rome, exactly resemble those of the Greeks.

84. "After the market-place has been designed," Vitruvius continues (V., 3 *et seq.*), "a very healthy spot must be chosen for the theatre, where the people can witness the dramas on the feast-days of the immortal gods." Unless a natural rising of the ground had been made use of, as was mostly the case in Greece, foundations and substructures had to be built. "On this basement marble or stone steps (*gradationes*) must be raised." The latter remark refers to the place for the spectators, which, in analogy to the κοῖλον (see § 30), was called *cavea* (hollow). Part of it was the orchestra, which was not, as in Greek theatres, used for the performance, but contained seats for the spectators. The seats were, as in the Greek theatre, interrupted by parallel passages (*præcinctiones*—διαζώματα), the name of the several divisions being *mæniana*.

"The number of the præcinctiones," Vitruvius continues, "must be in proportion to the height of the theatre. They ought not to be higher than they are broad; for if they were higher they would throw the voices back towards the top, and thus prevent those occupying the uppermost seats above the præcinctiones from hearing the words distinctly. A line drawn from the highest sitting-step (*gradus*) ought to touch all the corners or edges of the steps, so as nowhere to impede the voice." After having treated in the following chapters (IV. and V.) of several acoustic calculations and contrivances, Vitruvius (chapters V. and VII.) adds some prescriptions as to the size and proportions

* According to the latest calculations, the circus, in late imperial times, must have had contained 480,000 seats. It is about 21,000 feet long by 400 wide.

of the stage and of the place for the spectators. The orchestra, like the sitting-steps rising round it, ought to be semicircular in shape. Between the orchestra, where the arm-chairs of the senators are placed, and the back wall (*frons scenæ*) lies the stage (*pulpitum*), which ought to be twice as long as the diameter of the orchestra, and wider than the Greek stage, because in the Roman theatre "all the actors act on the stage." "The height of the pulpitum must be above five feet, so as to enable those sitting in the orchestra to see the gestures of the actors."

The sitting-steps of the spectators are to be divided not only horizontally by the præcinctiones, but also into wedge-like parts (*cunei*) by means of stairs. In the same manner, radiating from the centre of the orchestra, are to be designed the entrances, lying between the walls of the substructure (also designed as radii).

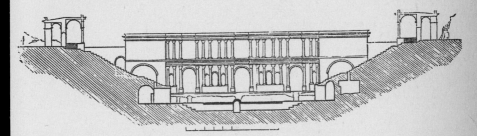

Fig. 432.

Care must be taken not to let the entrance-passages to the upper seats cross those to the lower, so that on leaving their seats the people may not press on each other (chap. III.).

Having considered Vitruvius's precepts, we now must turn to some of the remaining specimens of theatres. Fig. 432 (scale, 100 Sicilian palms) shows the cross-section of the theatre of Syracuse, being, as we mentioned before (§ 30), a Greek structure with Roman additions. The cavea lying on the slope is of Greek origin. The seats are made of the rock itself. The remaining parts of the stage-wall indicate Roman origin : with the aid of these remnants a reconstructive design of the two stories of the skene has been attempted. The colonnade of the spectators' place also is a Roman addition.

Of Roman theatres we mention that built by Pompeius, B.C. 55.

All previous theatres, although splendidly decorated,* had been
built of wood, to be pulled down after the festive performances
were over.   Of the theatre of Pompeius little remains ; but a
fragment of, the old plan of Rome enables us to distinguish its
general design, and even the arrangement of the single parts
(see Fig. 433).   The cavea (*a*) contained, it is said, 40,000 seats ;
it shows the above-mentioned radiating direction of the walls,
between which the entrance-passages of the spectators lay, and

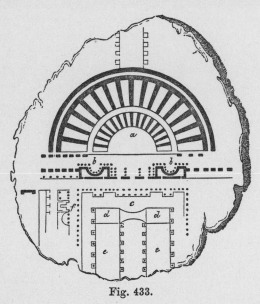

Fig. 433.

on which the sitting-steps rested.   The stage (*b b*) shows a skene-
wall richly decorated with columns and semicircular niches.
" Behind the stage lies a portico (*c*), in order," as Vitruvius adds
(chapter IX.), " that, in case the play is interrupted by a shower of
rain, the people may find refuge there ; also in order to give the
choragi room for arranging the chorus."   The design of this
portico indicates various embellishments : the ancients indeed boast

* The theatre of Scaurus already mentioned, built 52 B.C., had 80,000 seats. The
stage-wall was three stories high and adorned with 360 marble columns partly of
colossal size. The wall of the first story was coated with marble, that of the
second with glass (most likely coloured glass mosaic), that of the third with plates
of gilt metal. Between the columns bronze statues, to the almost incredible number
of 3,000, were placed, not to mention various other decorations.

of its statues and valuable tapestry, also of the groves, fountains, wild animals, &c., found in it.

Another theatre, in a better state of preservation, is that built by Augustus (after a plan of Cæsar), and called by him after the name of his nephew Marcellus. It was opened B.C. 13, the same year in which the theatre of Cornelius Balbus was completed. These three were the only theatres in Rome. The theatre of Marcellus stood near the hall called after his mother Octavia : during the Middle Ages the Savelli family used the remains of the theatre for the erection of their palace, at present owned by the Orsinis. The passages between the foundation-walls of the theatre are at present used as offices, and part of the old wall of the cavea may still be recognised in the enclosing wall of the palace. The cavea was semicircular in shape, and rose in three stories, the two lower of which were adorned with arcades and Doric and Ionic semicolumns, while the upper one consisted of a massive wall adorned with

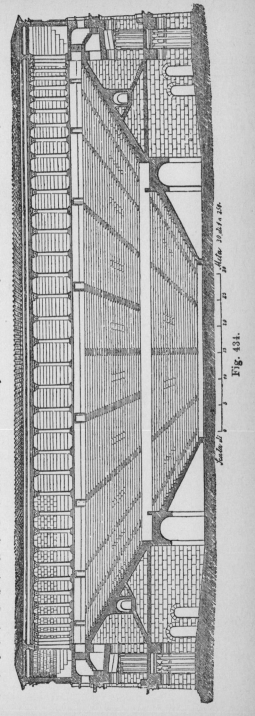

Fig. 434.

Korinthian pilasters—an arrangement which (but for the additional fourth story, here wanting) resembled that found in the Coliseum (compare Fig. 439). Fig. 434, after Canina's design, shows the cross-section of the interior, containing 30,000 seats. We there see the form of the substructure with the stairs and passages, also the corridors, already described in the theatre of Pompeius, which surround the cavea and open into the arcades, also mentioned in the above. The rows of seats of the cavea rise in beautiful proportions from the orchestra and the low podium ; they are divided into two parts by a præcinctio, tallying in this respect, and also as regards the cunei, with the precepts

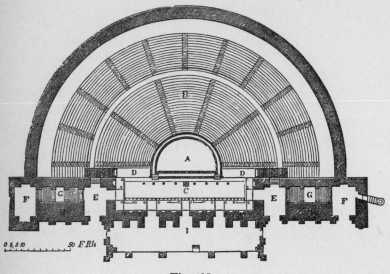

Fig. 435.

of Vitruvius. The upper end is finished off by a colonnade, which also contains places for the spectators, and which is mentioned by Vitruvius amongst the necessary requirements of a Roman theatre. "The roof of the arcade," he says (chap. VII.), "ought to correspond with the height of the skene, because in that case the voice spreads simultaneously to the upper ranks and the roof; while if the two differ in height the voice is broken by the first lower point it encounters." On the roof of the arcade the ropes were fastened, by means of which a canvas could be stretched over the cavea, so as to protect the spectators from the sun (see § 85).

About the stage itself little was known till the discovery of the theatre of Aspendos in Pamphylia; the closer investigation of the Roman theatre at Orange, in the south of France, has also yielded interesting results as to this important portion of the antique theatre (see Lohde's work, "Die Skene der Alten"). Besides these two buildings we mention the theatre of Herod at Athens, the stage of which seems to show a similar arrangement. The latter theatre, counting amongst the best-preserved antique buildings of Athens, lies on the western side of the southern slope of the Akropolis, the seats being worked into the rock. Skene and paraskenia have been well preserved, rising partly up to three stories, interrupted by arcades. The end wall of the hyposkenion, which carried the logeion, and the stairs leading up to the stage have been partly recovered by recent excavations. These arrangements have been imitated from Greek architecture, while the magnificent stage-building itself shows the Roman method. The cavea (Fig. 435, B) lying towards the rock of the Akropolis is divided into two ranks of sitting-steps by means of a præcinctio 4 feet wide: the lower division contained twenty, the upper most likely thirteen steps; the latter are completely destroyed. The height of each step is $1\frac{1}{4}$ foot: the lower section of steps is again divided by six, the upper one by twelve, staircases. The orchestra (A) is semi-elliptical in shape, its diameter being 60 feet long; it is paved with square slabs of white Pentelic marble and of Cipollino from Karystos, the latter with green, yellow, or grey veins. As in Greek theatres, the lowest row of steps does not immediately touch the stage, but is divided from it by the parodoi (D D). The stage, 24 feet deep, lies $4\frac{1}{2}$ feet above the floor of the orchestra. The skene-wall contains three doors, through one of which one enters a room (I), the remains of which, like those of the rooms marked E E and F F, show the traces of a vaulted ceiling. The theatre was built between 160 and 170 A.D. by Herodes Atticus of Marathon, celebrated for his wealth and his oratorical talents: to him Athens also owes the Panathenaïc stadion on the Ilissos. When Pausanias visited Athens this theatre had not yet been erected; in another passage he speaks of it as an odeum, and counts it amongst the most splendid buildings in Greece. Philostrates calls it the theatre of Annia Regilla, the deceased wife of Herod, in whose honour her husband erected it. According to the same author its roof consisted of cedar-wood, a remarkable feature in a building of such dimensions.

Fig. 436 gives a perspective view of the repeatedly mentioned theatre of Orange, the stage of which is in perfect preservation. The cavea lies on the slope of a hill. Behind the richly decorated skene-wall lies a narrow building of three stories, the façade of which, adorned with arcades, is seen in our illustration. Between the wall of the skene and the outer wall are several staircases. The stage-building is 103·15 metres long by 36·821 high; the length of the proskenion, from paraskenion to paraskenion, is

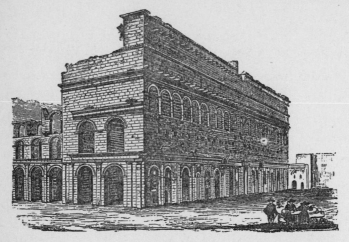

Fig. 436.

61·20 metres; the distance between its facing wall and the centre door of the skene-wall is 13·20, that from the two side doors 18 metres: an oblique roof of timber covered this whole space (see Lohde, "Die Skene der Alten," p. 5 *et seq.*).

Of a similar kind was the arrangement of the theatre of Aspendos (see Fig. 437, where the position of the oblique roof of the stage may be distinguished). The spectators' seats lie on the slope of the hill on which the town of Aspendos is situated. The rows of seats rise from the semicircular orchestra, which first is surrounded by a podium of considerable height. A diazoma divides the rows of seats into two stories, the upper one of which is surrounded by arcades, with a barrel-vaulted niche attached to each of them. The cavea is more than usually well preserved. The top of the arcades is on a level with that of the skene-wall, in accordance with Vitruvius's precept. The wall of the skene rises in three stories, richly adorned with columns, which have disappeared; the projecting beams carried by them are, however, still visible, as are also the gables. All these projecting parts, and the window-sills of the first stories, are made of marble; the wall itself consists of large blocks of a kind of *breccia*, joined together without mortar; the whole back wall of the skene was once adorned in an encaustic manner. Above the third series

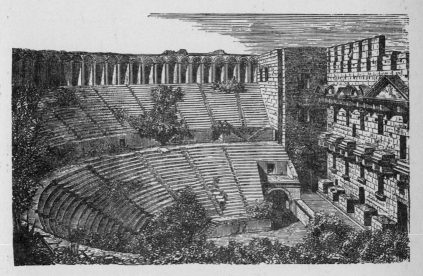

Fig. 437.

of columns lay the oblique roof covering the whole stage: traces of its insertion into the wall of the proskenion may be discovered in our illustration. Besides the usual three doors, two apertures in the wall of the paraskenion opened on to the stage, similar to those in the theatres of Herod and at Orange. Above each of these two doors the walls of the proskenion contain two other openings, leading, most likely, to small balconies or boxes for distinguished spectators. The building behind the wall of the skene is narrow, as at Orange. It had three stories, the middle one of which communicated by a door with the space which lay between the wall of the skene and the back scene, put in front of it during the performance.

85. We now have to mention a building unique as regards mechanical appliances, and important for us in so far as it undoubtedly was the intermediate step to another class of edifices for public amusement. We are speaking of the building erected by C. Curio during his tribunate (B.C. 50) for an enormous sum of money, given to him by Cæsar for the furthering of party-

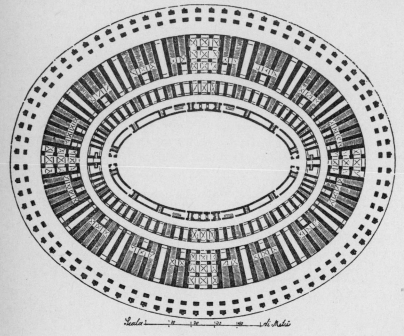

Fig. 438.

purposes. Both the stone theatre of Pompey (55 B.C.) and the wooden one of Scaurus were already in existence. A new contrivance of astonishing boldness had to be invented, so as to excite the admiration of the multitude. Pliny (Hist. Nat., XXXVI., 24, 8) gives the following description of the astonishing structure. "He (Curio) built two wooden theatres by the side of each other, each of them kept its balance by means of movable pegs. In the forenoon comedies were performed on them, and the two theatres were turned away from each other, so that the noises

on the two stages should not interfere with each other. All
of a sudden they were whirled round, so as to stand opposite each
other; in the evening the wooden partitions of the stages were
removed, the ends of the sitting-steps (*cornua*) touched each
other, and an amphitheatre was thus created, in which Curio,
after having endangered the lives of the people themselves,
arranged battles of gladiators." Pliny strongly reproves both
tribune and people for trusting their lives to a fragile wooden
machinery.

Whether this was the first attempt at constructing an amphitheatre we cannot tell; certain it is that four years later Cæsar
built an edifice for the battles of gladiators and the fights of
animals, which resembled the bold attempt of Curio, and to which
the name of *amphitheatrum* was technically applied.* It was
built of wood, but richly decorated. The first stone amphitheatre
in Rome was built during the reign of Augustus by Statilius
Taurus, the friend of that emperor ; it was destroyed by fire
under Nero. The amphitheatres, to which the gladiatorial
battles formerly fought in the forum or circus were transferred, became so popular in consequence, that even provincial
towns went to enormous expenses in erecting them. Fig. 438
shows the plan of the amphitheatre of Capua, consisting of an oval
arena surrounded by rows of seats. It was built at the expense of
the town, after the model of the Flavian amphitheatre in Rome,
from which the substructure, and the arrangement of the sitting-
steps and of the stairs leading up to them, are imitated almost
exactly. It nearly equalled the size of its model, being the
second largest of all the amphitheatres known to us. An inscription says that the Emperor Hadrian added the columns and their
roof, meaning the colonnade surrounding the highest row of steps,
as in a theatre (compare Fig. 434). Underneath the arena were
vaulted chambers (also found in the Flavian amphitheatre), destined

* Amphitheatrum means literally a building with a θεάτρον, spectators' place or
cavea, on two sides. The buildings for the so-called naumachia (naval battles) also
had the form of amphitheatres. Hirt (*loc. cit.*, III., 159) points out that the
elliptical shape was chosen in preference to the circular as it held more spectators
on an equal space; the greater length of the arena, moreover, left more freedom to
the movements of men and animals than a circle would have done. Acoustic
considerations were out of the question, as there was nothing to be heard, but only
something to be seen.

for the keeping of the wild animals, also for making the necessary preparations for the performances.

The Flavian amphitheatre, better known as the Coliseum, was begun by Vespasian, and completed by his successor Titus, on the site of a large pond (*stagna Neronis*) in the "Golden House" of Nero. Augustus is said to have planned an amphitheatre to be erected on the same spot. It is said to have contained 87,000 seats (*loca*), and was, owing to its central situation, one of the most favourite places of amusement of the Roman people. Its plan is shown in Fig. 438. The arena, underneath which vaulted

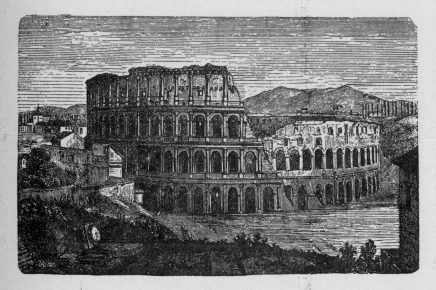

Fig. 439.

chambers have been discovered, has the form of an ellipse, the larger diameter measuring 264, the smaller 156 feet. The surrounding edifice has a uniform depth of 155 feet, which gives a total diameter of 574 feet, or of 466 feet for the enclosing outer wall. The latter was interrupted by eighty arcades, forming the openings of the numerous systematically arranged corridors and staircases of the interior. The lowest row of these arcades (*vomitoria*) is adorned with Doric, the second story with Ionic, and the third with Korinthian semi-columns. The fourth story consists of a wall adorned with Korinthian pilasters, and inter-

rupted by windows. The total height is 156 feet. Figs. 439 and
441 show views of the exterior and interior of the Coliseum in
its present state. In the upper story 240 small projections are
conspicuous, to which answer as many openings in the chief
cornice. These were destined to carry masts, to which ropes were
fastened, to support an awning (*velarium*) stretched across the
enormous space. The section (Fig. 440, from a design by Fontana,
modified by Hirt) serves to illustrate the interior arrangements
(compare also Fig. 434). The Coliseum consists almost entirely of
travertine freestone, carefully hewn ; the interior, partly built of

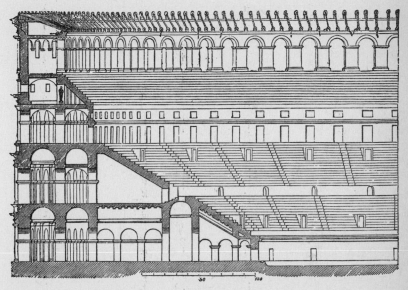

Fig. 440.

bricks, has considerably suffered during the Middle Ages. At
one time it served as the castle of the Frangipani family ; at
another it was systematically ransacked for building materials
(the Palazzo della Cancelleria, Palazzo Farnese, and Palazzo di
S. Marco have been built of such) ; but its grand forms have
withstood all these attempts at destruction. In the substructure
of the rows of seats, the corridors (*itinera*), passages, and stairs
leading up to them are still recognisable. The lowest part of the
spectators' place, viz. the *podium*, has been built higher than was the
custom in theatres : as a further means of protection against the

wild animals in the arena other contrivances were added. Near
the podium were the seats of the imperial family, of the highest
magistrates, and of the Vestals; at the back of them followed the
ordinary rows of seats in three stories (*mœniana*, corresponding to
those of the exterior arcades), the lower of which, containing about
twenty steps (*gradus*, no more in existence), was reserved for magistrates and knights, the next following one (of about sixteen steps)
for Roman citizens. The præcinction-wall, between the second and
third stories, is higher than usual, and the upper rows themselves
show a steeper ascent than the lower ones, in order to enable the
spectators seated there to overlook the arena. This high præcinc-

Fig. 441.

tion-wall, called *balteus*, was richly decorated (according to Hirt,
with glass mosaic) in the same manner as that of the theatre of
Scaurus. The fourth story, the steps of which were considerably
higher than those of the lower rows, was surrounded with an open
portico, also richly decorated. Here were the seats for the
women, and, perhaps at both ends of the longer diameter, those
for the common people. The differences of rank and station
co-existing with the legal equality of the Roman people appear
thus distinctly marked in the Coliseo, which, in a manner, becomes
the symbol of the grandeur and variegated development of the
nation itself.

86. We now turn to the consideration of the implements of domestic use; our knowledge of these is much more accurate than of those of Greek origin, owing, to a great extent, to the preservation of the dwelling-house itself, to which these utensils belong. We have mentioned before how, during the eruption of Vesuvius (79 A.D.), Herculaneum and Stabiæ were more or less destroyed by a stream of lava, while Pompeii was first covered with a shower of glowing *rapilli*, on which lava afterwards collected. Only in 1748 Pompeii was rediscovered by an accident. At Herculaneum the hardened lava could only partially be removed; at Pompeii, on the other hand, the layers of loose ashes, to a depth of seven to eight metres, offered comparatively little difficulty to attempts at excavation. At first these excavations were made without plan or system; the recovered objects were left for a long time at the mercy of the weather, not to speak of the spoliation of uncultivated or unprincipled persons. Arditi, in 1812, was the first to bring system into the work; and, after the expulsion of the Bourbons, Fiorelli has continued his predecessor's efforts, introducing at the same time a new method, viz. that of horizontal instead of vertical digging; in this manner the former danger of the houses breaking down as soon as their props were taken away, has been removed. A little less than one-half of Pompeii has thus been discovered. The wall, about 10,000 feet long, surrounding the whole town in the shape of an irregular oval, shows Pompeii to have been of moderate dimensions; but the numerous public buildings and the comfort of many of the private houses proves the wealth of the citizens. Pompeii, and (in a lesser degree) many other seats of Roman culture, have yielded from amongst their ruins a rich harvest of utensils and implements of daily life and

intercourse, such as vessels (of metal, glass, and earthenware), lamps, armour, jewellery, coins, &c. Most of these have passed into private and public collections; numerous valuable objects have been purloined and destroyed by the finders.

In looking at these utensils, and comparing them with similar objects of Greek origin, we have to consider the question whether they were really of Roman make,—that is, worked by Roman artificers. In trying to answer this question we must briefly touch upon the political history of Rome. To south and north of the Roman territory, the country was inhabited by nations superior to the Romans in both material and intellectual respects. We are speaking of the Greek colonies in the southern, and of the Etruscan cities in the more northern, parts of Italy. The splendour of both nations, however, was waning when they came into contact with their less-civilised neighbours : first the Etruscans, and after them the Greeks, had to submit to the superior military tactics of the Romans. The military spirit of the conquerors prevented them at first from adopting the higher culture of the vanquished. At the same time it must be remembered that at an early period Etruscan artists adorned the public edifices of Rome with the works of their handicraft; moreover, the statues of gods and other works of art, brought to Rome as booty from the conquered and devastated Etruscan cities, formed an intellectual and religious link between conquerors and conquered. Political motives thus co-operated with growing artistic culture. The statue of the Juno Regina was brought from Veii by Camillus, that of Jupiter Imperator from Præneste by Cincinnatus, with a view to amalgamating the nations.

Of still greater importance was the treasure of masterworks of art and culture found by the Romans in the cities of Magna Græcia and Sicily, such as Capua, Tarentum, and Syracuse, further augmented by the spoils of the Greek peninsula, Macedon, and the Asiatic empires. The art-treasures paraded in the three days' triumph by Quinctius Flaminius and Paullus Æmilius, the conquerors of Philip and Perseus of Macedon, were of enormous value. Roman prætors used to ransack their Greek provinces for valuable objects of art : Scaurus, for instance, adorned his theatre with Greek statues and pictures acquired in this manner; and when his villa at Tusculum was burnt by his enraged slaves, Greek works of art to the value of about £600,000 are said to have perished in the flames. Omitting many other instances of spoliation, we remind the reader only of that of Nero, by which Delphi and Olympia were deprived of the statues still remaining there. Thus Italy was flooded with the creations of Greek genius, and the craving for foreign art diffused amongst all classes of the Romans could not but throw into the background the productions of native artists. Many Greek artificers, moreover, came to Rome as the best market for their wares : even amongst the Greek slaves artistic talent was of no rare occurrence. In this way Greek patterns became prevalent, not only in high art but also in mechanical handicrafts. Even at a later period, when Greek art itself had declined, and Roman customs and ideas had, to a great extent, absorbed the national peculiarities of the conquered races, the artistic creations of what is generally called the national Roman style are, for the greater part, only reminiscences of originally Greek ideas. At Pompeii also, much of what we now call Roman is undoubtedly of Greek origin; the compositions of the best wall-paintings and mosaics breathe Greek spirit, as might be expected in a town which, although Romanised to a great extent, still retained traces of its Greek origin. Nevertheless, most of these wall-paintings, mosaics, and other objects of art and industry, although perhaps composed by Greek artists, or after Greek patterns, are justly denominated Roman, as they undoubtedly belong to the period of municipal power and independence, which fostered the growth of the Roman national element.

87. Seats and couches are sufficiently illustrated by wall-paintings at Pompeii and Herculaneum, and by the remaining specimens. The simple folding-stool with crossed legs, the backless chair with four perpendicular legs, the chair with a low or high back, and the state-throne (see § 31),—all these were made after Greek patterns. The word *sella* is the generic term for the different classes of chairs comprised in the Greek diphroi and klismoi ; only the chair with a back to it is distinguished as *cathedra*. The form of the cathedra resembles that of our ordinary drawing-room chairs but for the wider, frequently semicircular, curve of the

back, which greatly adds to the comfort of the seated person.
Soft cushions, placed both against the back and on the seat, mark
the cathedra as a piece of furniture belonging essentially to the
women's apartments; the more effeminate men of a later period,
however, used these *fauteuils* in preference.   The marble statues

of the younger Faustina (Fig. 469)
and of Agrippina the wife of Germanicus, both in the gallery of Florence (Clarac, "Musée," Pls. 955, 930),
are seated on cathedræ.   The legs of
the chairs were frequently shaped in
some graceful fashion, and adorned
with valuable ornaments of metal and
ivory; tasteful turnery was also often
applied to them: all this is sufficiently proved by the wall-paintings
(compare Fig. 471).   Different from
these chairs is the *solium*, the dignified
form of which designates it as the seat
of honour for the master of the house,

Fig. 442.

or as the throne of rulers of the State and gods; it answers,
therefore, to the *thronos* of the Greeks.   The richly decorated
back rises perpendicularly sometimes up to the height of
the shoulders, at others, above the head, of the seated person;
two elbows, mostly of massive workmanship, are attached to
the back.   The throne stands on a strong base or on high legs;
it was generally made of solid, heavy materials.   Of the wooden
solium, seated on which the patron gave advice to his clients,
naturally no specimen remains; but we possess several marble
thrones, most likely the seats of emperors, and others placed,
according to Greek custom, near the divine images in the temples.
A marble throne of the first-mentioned class, richly decorated with
sculptures, is in the Royal Collection of Antiques at Berlin.   Fig.
442 shows a throne from a temple—one of the two of the kind
preserved in the Louvre.   The symbolical sculptures on the inner
surface of the back, both above and below the seat, consisting of a
pair of winged snakes, the mystical basket, and the sickle, also
the two torches serving in a manner as props of the back, seem

to indicate its connection with the worship of Ceres. The seat is supported by two sphinxes, the wings of which form the elbows of the chair. The companion chair in the Louvre shows the Bacchic attributes arranged in a similar manner. Similar thrones of gods occur frequently in Pompeian wall-paintings and on Roman coins; we also mention in connection with the subject a wall-painting at Herculaneum ("Pitture antiche d'Ercolano," vol. i. p. 155). These thrones generally show light, graceful forms of legs, and broad seats covered with soft cushions; the back and elbows are frequently enveloped in rich folds of drapery. Of the two thrones in the Herculaneum wall-painting referred to, one has a helmet, the other a dove, on its seat—the respective emblems of Mars and Venus. The solium used by the magistrates of the republic was without back or elbows.

Peculiar to the Romans was the *sella curulis*, a folding-stool with curved legs placed crosswise; at first it was made of ivory, afterwards of metal: it most likely dates from the times of the kings. At that period it was in reality a seat on wheels, from which the kings exercised their legal functions: afterwards the sella curulis, although deprived of its wheels, remained the attribute of certain magistrates; it was placed on the tribunal, from the height of which the judge pronounced his sentence. The use of the sella curulis was permitted to the consuls, prætors, proprætors, and the curulian ædiles; also to the dictator, the magister equitum, the decemviri, and, at a later period, the quæstor. Amongst priests, only the Flamen Dialis enjoyed the same privilege, together with a seat in the senate. On some of the *denarii* of Roman families, such as the Gens Cæcilia, Cestia, Cornelia, Furia, Julia, Livineia, Plætoria, Pompeia, Valeria, we frequently see the sella curulis connected with the names of those members of the gens who held one of the curulian offices. Fasces, lituus, crowns, and branches frequently are arranged round the chair to indicate the particular function of the magistrate.

Fig. 443.

Fig. 443 shows the reverse of a coin of the Gens Furia, with a sella curulis depicted on it. On the chair are inscribed the words P. FOVRIVS; underneath it we read, CRASSIPES: the other side of the coin shows the crowned head of Cybele

with the inscription, AED. CVR. The emperors also claimed
the privilege of the sella curulis. The marble statue of the
Emperor Claudius in the Villa Albani (Clarac, "Musée," Pl.
936, *B*) is, for instance, seated on a sella curulis, or rather *sella
imperatoria.* Several bronze legs of chairs, in the Museo Borbonico,
worked like necks of animals and placed crosswise, most likely belonged to chairs of this kind. The *subsellium,* a low bench with

Fig. 444.

room for several persons, was
destined for the magistrates of the
people, *i.e.* for the tribuni and ædiles
plebis. Silver coins of the Gens
Calpurnia, Critonia, Fannia, and
Statilia show this bench always
occupied by two ædiles (see
Riccio, "Le Monete delle antiche
Famiglie di Roma," Tavs. X.,
XVII., XX., XLV.). Another seat of honour was the *bisellium,*
a very broad chair, or rather double chair, without a back,
destined for the decuriones and augustales. Two bronze bisellia
have been found at Pompeii, one of which is shown, Fig. 444.

88. The couches and beds show the same elegance and comfort
as the chairs. We need only add a few remarks to what we
have already said about Greek couches (§ 32). The body of
the bed, made either of wood inlaid with ivory and tortoiseshell,
or of valuable metal (*lecti eborati, testudinei, inargentati, inaurati*),
rested on gracefully formed legs. Sometimes the whole bed-
frame was made of bronze, and in a few cases (*e.g.* the bed of
Elagabalus) of solid silver. A bronze bed-frame somewhat
resembling our iron truckle-beds may be seen on an Etruscan
tomb (see "Museum Gregorianum," vol. i., Tav. 16). A bronze
trellis-work here carries the mattrass, instead of the more usual
webbing (*fasciæ, institæ, tenta cubilia*). The mattrass (*torus*), originally filled with straw, was afterwards stuffed with sheep's wool
(*tomentum*) or the down of (particularly German) geese and swans;
Elagabalus chose the soft plumage under the wings of the partridge
for his mattrasses. Bolsters and cushions (*culcita*) were stuffed
with the same material (see, for instance, Zahn's "Schönste
Ornamente," Series III., Taf. 41). Blankets and sheets (*vestes*

stragulæ), according to the owner's wealth, made either of simple material or dyed and adorned with embroidered or woven patterns and borders, were spread over the cushions and bolsters. One or several pillows (*pulvinus*) served to prop the head (whence their name *cervicalia*) or the left elbow of the sleeping or reclining persons (compare the couches in Fig. 232 and those in Figs. 187—190, the latter of which, although taken from Greek vase-paintings, are equally illustrative of Roman forms). Footstools (*subsellia, scabella, scamna*), used for mounting high thrones and beds, or with cathedræ for resting the feet, were as general amongst the Romans as amongst the Greeks. Wooden bed-frames, like all other wooden utensils, have been destroyed at Pompeii; but we see many couches (on the average 2·50 metres long by 1 wide) let into the walls of the niches of bedrooms; these niches, as, for instance, that in the villa of Diomedes, could be closed by means of curtains or pasteboard partitions ("Spanish walls").*
As we said before, the couch was used, not only for sleeping, but also for meditating, reading, and writing in a reclining position, the left arm leaning on the cushions. This custom was undoubtedly adopted from the Greek. The two names, derived from the different purposes, *lectus cubicularius* and *lectus lucubratorius,* most likely apply to one and the same kind of couch; perhaps in the latter there was attached to the back of the couch (*pluteus*) nearest the head a contrivance like our reading-desks, to put books and writing materials on; a similar contrivance is mentioned in connection with the cathedra.

In later times, when the simpler custom of sitting at their meals was abandoned by the Romans, men used to lie down to their meals on couches. The wife sat on the foot end of the lectus, the children on separate chairs, and the servants on benches (*subsellium*). This custom, as illustrated by numerous bas-reliefs, was limited to the family circle. In the dining-rooms (*triclinium*), where guests were received, a particular arrangement of the couches became necessary. A square table stood in the centre of the triclinium (several of which are perfectly preserved at Pompeii) surrounded on three sides by so many low couches

---

* See a picture of the remains of such a partition found at Pompeii in Overbeck's "Pompeji," 2nd ed., ii. p. 48.

(*lectus triclinaris*), while the fourth side remained open to the access of the attending slaves. Fig. 445 shows the arrangement of a triclinium. M indicates the table surrounded by the three couches. The latter, as is proved by several couches made of masonry

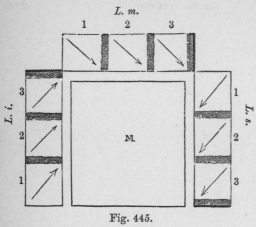

Fig. 445.

at Pompeii (Mazois, "Ruines de Pompei," t. i., Pl. 20), had the edge nearest the table slightly raised (compare the summer triclinium in the background of Fig. 390). The couch was ascended by the guests (*accubare*) on the lower side, the space between the edge of the table and the couch being too narrow for a person to pass. Each couch had room for three persons reclining in the direction of the arrow in our plan; the left arm rested on the cushions, while the disengaged right hand was used for eating. *L. i.* mark the lowest (*lectus imus*), *L. m.* the middle (*lectus medius*), and *L. s.* the highest (*lectus summus*) couch. In the same manner the single seats on each couch were distinguished as *locus imus, medius,* and *summus.* On the lectus imus 1 marks the lowest, 3 the highest, and 2 the middle places. On the lectus medius 3 marks the highest, 1 the lowest, and 2 the middle. The last-mentioned place was the place of honour; 1 was called the *locus consularis*, because if a consul was present this place was occupied by him, in order that he might be able to receive important communications during dinner. The place on the lectus imus (3) touching his was occupied by the host. On the lectus summus the places followed in the reverse order of that on the lectus imus. The stronger lines on the edges of the loci summi mark the low backs against which the cushions belonging to these seats were placed; the cushions belonging to the other places lay in the middle of the couch, and, therefore, did not require a prop. In later times three or more triclinia were frequently placed in one dining-room, which must have been of considerable size, taking into account the additional space required for the servants, dancers, musicians, &c.

About the end of the Republic the use of round tables (*orbes*) instead of square ones became more frequent; the three couches standing at right angles were accordingly transformed into one, the shape of which, following the curve of the table, became semicircular, resembling the form of a Greek C, whence its name *sigma* or *stibadium*. The two corner seats (*cornua*) now became the places of honour, that on the right (*in dextro cornu*) being considered superior to that on the left (*in cornu sinistro*). On a sigma of this kind are reclining several Cupids, round a table covered with drinking-cups (see the graceful Pompeian wall-painting, "Museo Borbon.," vol. xv., Tav. 46). One large bolster on the edge of the couch nearest the table serves as prop for the left arms of the topers; a light awning protects them from the sun. A different arrangement we see in the wall-painting found near the tomb of the Scipiones in the Via Appia (Campana, "Di due Sepolcri Romani del Secolo di Augusto, &c." Roma, 1840. Tav. XIV.). Here the table has the form of a crescent (*mensa lunata*); along its outer edge is placed the sigma, on which eleven persons are reclining, partaking of the funereal repast (compare the description of a similar scene in "Bullettino arch. Napoletano," 1845, p. 82). We refrain from describing the rich ornamentation of these couches, with their bolsters and valuable carpets, harmonizing with the wall-decorations and the mosaic pavement of the dining-room itself.

To conclude, we mention the benches of bronze found in the tepidarium of the thermæ at Pompeii (Fig. 421), as also the *hemicyclia*, semicircular stone-benches, holding a greater number of persons, such as were placed in gardens and by the side of public roads. Two marble hemicyclia may be seen by the side of the street of graves, near the Herculanean gate at Pompeii; a third bench occupies the background of a small portico opening into the street (see "Mus. Borb.," vol. xv., Tav. 25, 26).

89. We have already made mention of square, round, and crescent-shaped tables. The brick leg of a table, the wooden slab of which has disappeared, may be seen in the *triclinium funebre* at

Pompeii; it is surrounded by three well-preserved couches. The above-mentioned mensa lunata in a wall-painting is, on the other hand, supported by three legs shaped like animals. Besides these larger tables, others of smaller size, and more easily movable, were in frequent use. They might be either round or square, and were placed by the side of the couches : like the dining-tables, they were not higher than the couches. For their various forms we refer the reader to the Greek tables shown in Fig. 191. The way of ornamenting the tables was far more splendid and expensive amongst the Romans than amongst the Greeks. Not only were the legs beautifully worked in wood, metal, or stone (the graceful forms of the numerous marble and bronze legs found at Pompeii have become the models of modern wood-carvers), but the slabs also consisted of metal and rare kinds of stone or wood wrought in elegant and graceful shapes. Particularly the slabs of one-legged tables (*monopodia, orbes*) used to be made of the rarest woods; the wood of the *Thyia cypressiodes,* a tree growing on the slopes of the Atlas, the stem of which, near the root, is frequently several feet thick, was chosen in preference ; the Roman name of this tree was *citrus*, not to be mistaken for the citron-tree. The value of large slabs of citrus-wood was enormous. According to Pliny, Cicero (by no means a wealthy man according to Roman notions) spent 500,000 H S. (about £5,400), Asinius Pollio £10,800, King Juba £13,050, and the family of the Cethegi £15,150, for a single slab of this

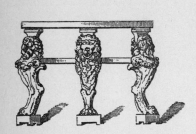

material. The value of this wood consisted chiefly in the beautiful lines of the veins and fibres (*maculæ*), shown to still greater advantage by the polish. The Romans classified the slabs by their designs into tiger, panther, wavy, and peacock feather, &c., patterns. The

Fig. 446.

enormous price of the massive slabs naturally led to the custom of veneering other wood with citrus. Valuable tables of this kind were taken out of their covers only on festive occasions. The plate and nicknacks, always found in elegant Roman houses, were displayed on small one or three legged tables (*trapezophoron*), the slabs of which

(*abacus*, a word which, like trapezophoron, is sometimes used for
the whole table) had raised edges round them : several richly
ornamented specimens of such tables have been found at Pompeii.
Fig. 446 shows a small abacus resting on three marble legs, which
has been found in the house of the "Little Mosaic-Fountain" at
Pompeii. Another table ("Museo Borb.," vol. xv., Tav. 6),
with a slab of *rosso antico* resting on four graceful bronze
legs, deserves attention on account of an ingenious contrivance
between the legs, by means of which it could be lowered or
heightened at will : a similar contrivance occurs in several
tripods.

A table of a different kind was the tripod (*delphica sc. mensa*),
imitated from the Greek τρίπους,
and used chiefly at meals to put
vessels and dishes on : several
elegant specimens of the tripod
have been discovered at Pompeii.
The ends of the three legs
were generally shaped like the
paws of animals; the legs, connected by means of metal bars
and generally ornamented with
figures or foliage, carry a metal
basin, either flat-bottomed or of
semi-globular shape (Fig. 447).
Whether the tripods found in
the rooms of houses were used
for sacred or profane purposes
cannot always be decided with
certainty. The skulls and garlands surrounding the top of our
tripod (Fig. 447) seem to indicate

Fig. 447.

its sacred character : other tripods are without any decoration. The
top of the sacred tripods generally consisted of deep caldron-
like basins : specimens of them have been found in Etruscan
graves ; they also occur in various forms on coins and vases.

90. The numerous vases found in the graves of Italy (see
§ 38 *et seq.*) are, as we have seen, of Greek origin, although
frequently manufactured on Roman territory. The pictures

on them illustrate myths, or scenes from the daily life of Greeks or Etruscans; we therefore have refrained from referring to them in speaking of Roman customs and artistic achievements. As to the degree of skill with which native Roman artificers worked after Greek patterns we are unable to judge, seeing that most of the specimens of Roman native pottery preserved to us belong to a low class of art. Local potteries were found in almost all places of any importance; and the former existence of manufactures is betrayed by the heaps of potsherds found in such places,—as, for instance, in the valley of the Neckar. Whole vessels are, however, found very rarely. More numerous are the specimens of clay vessels found in Roman graves: their style and material are far inferior to those of Greek make. About the forms of the smaller drinking and drawing vessels and ointment-bottles (to which classes they chiefly belong), we have spoken before (compare Fig. 198): new to us only are the kitchen utensils of clay, numerous interesting specimens of which have been dug up. The destinations of most of these can be determined from their similarity to vessels now in use. Besides these earthen-

a   b   c   d

Fig. 448.

ware vessels a great many others made of bronze have been found at Pompeii and other Roman settlements; their elegant and, at the same time, useful forms excite our highest admiration. In most cases the names occurring in ancient authors cannot, unfortunately, be applied with certainty to the remaining specimens. Figs. 448 and 449 show a variety of vessels, all found at Pompeii, Fig. 448, *c*, shows a kettle, semi-oval in shape and with a comparatively narrow opening, to the rim of which the handle is fastened; it rests on a tripod (*tripes*). Similar kettles, with covers (*testum, testu*) fastened to their necks by means of little chains,

have been found in several places ("Mus. Borbon.," vol. v., Tav.
58). A pot (*olla, cacabus*), similar to those now in use, the handle
of which is made in the shape of a dolphin, is represented,
Fig. 448, *d*. Porridge, meat, and vegetables were cooked in it.

Of pails we possess a considerable number (Fig. 448, *a, b*).
Their rims are adorned with graceful patterns, and the rings to
which the handles are fastened often show palmet to ornaments.
The pail, Fig. 448, *b*, shows small pegs on both sides of the rings
to prevent the heavy handle from falling on the graceful rim of
the vessel ; the double handle (Fig. 448, *a*) served to steady the
vessel while being carried ; thus usefulness and elegance of
form were combined.

Fig. 449, *f*, resembles our saucepan. Two vessels of this kind,
the ends of whose horizontal handles are shaped like heads of

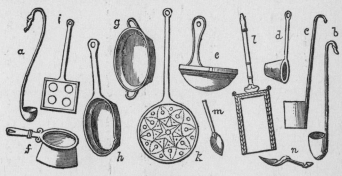

Fig. 449.

swans, have recently been found, the one at Teplitzin Bohemia,
the other at Hagenow in Mecklenburg ; both show, on the upper
surface of the handle, the stamp of the same manufacturer—
TIBERIVS ROBILIVS SITALCES. The vessel found in
Bohemia shows underneath this inscription another name,
GAIVS ATILIVS HANNO, which Mommsen (*Archäologischer
Anzeiger*, 1858, Nos. 115—117) takes to be that of the modeller.
The flat pan (*sartago*, Fig. 449, *h*) was used to heat the oil—an
important ingredient of Southern cookery. Fig. 449, *i*, shows a
pan with four indentures, used most likely for poaching eggs ;
Fig. 449, *l*, a sort of shovel with a handle and an elegant border-
pattern ; and Fig. 449, *g*, a two-handled vessel, also for kitchen
use. In Fig. 449, *m* and *n*, we see two forms of the spoon

(*cochlear, ligula*) ; they were used not only for eating soup and porridge, but also for the opening of eggs, oysters, and snails, whence their pointed ends. Fig. 449, *e* and *d*, show ladles for drawing water ; Fig. 449, *a, b, c,* specimens of the long-handled *trua* or *trulla* (the Greek kyathos, compare Fig. 303), to draw the wine from deep butts, &c. Of sieves (*colum,* Fig. 449, *k*), funnels (*infundibulum*), and similar kitchen utensils, most of the larger museums contain specimens; we refer the reader to the numerous works illustrative of the kitchen utensils found at Pompeii.

Meat and fish were put on small or large flat dishes (*patina*) with raised edges, mostly made of clay. Those of rich people were made of precious metals beautifully chiselled (*argentum cœlatum*). But even those made of clay frequently were bought at enormous prices. Pliny relates that the tragic actor, Clodius Æsopus, possessed a dish worth 100,000 sestertii. Vitellius had an earthenware dish made for himself at the price of one million sestertii ; an oven had to be erected in the fields for the purpose. Amongst dishes resembling plates we mention the *lanx.* According to Pliny, there were in Rome, after Sulla's wars, more than 150 *lances* of silver, weighing each 100 Roman pounds. Drusilianus Rotundus, the slave of the Emperor Claudius, owned a dish of 500 Roman pounds weight, while his fellow-slaves possessed eight, weighing each 250 Roman pounds. The *patella, catinum, catillum,* and *paropsis* resembled our plates ; the latter was chiefly for dessert (*opsonium*).

91. The names of Roman drinking-vessels, *calix, patera, scyphus, cyathus,* sufficiently indicate their Greek origin; their shapes show the same variety as those of their Greek models (see § 38). Their names cannot always be identified, but the existence of a few measuring-vessels with the gauge marked on them enables us to speak with certainty about the cubic contents of some of their forms.* Here, however, we must limit ourselves to the outer appearance of the vessels, and the material of which they are made. All vessels made of precious metals were either *pura, i.e.* without any relief-work, and therefore of smooth surface, or they were *cœlata,* that is, adorned with bas-reliefs, either wrought of the material itself or soldered to its surface. Many

---

* Compare Hultsch, "Griechische und römische Metrologie," p. 87 *et seq.*, and Becker's "Gallus," herausgegeben von Rein, Third Edition, Part III. p. 280 *et seq.*

Greek and Oriental vessels of great value were brought to Rome, and kept in Roman families as precious heirlooms; others made of precious metals were melted and recast according to Roman taste. The custom of adorning drinking-vessels with precious stones, known to the Greeks, was exaggerated by the luxurious Romans of imperial times to an unprecedented degree (Pliny, "Hist. Natur.," XXXIII. 2). Such vases (*gemmata potaria*) were sent by foreign kings to the Roman people, and with them the emperors rewarded the services of their generals or of the chieftains of Germanic tribes (Tacitus, "Germania," V.). We possess numerous vessels of earthenware, adorned with garlands of leaves and flowers, and inscribed with gay devices; such as, COPO IMPLE; BIBE AMICE EX ME; SITIO; MISCE; REPLETE, &c. Vessels of precious metal are of rarer occurrence.

We have mentioned before the luxurious custom, common amongst the Romans after the conquest of Greece and Asia, of having their utensils of the table, and even of the kitchen, made of solid silver. Valuable plate (*argentum escarium* and *potorium*) was of common occurrence in the houses of the rich. According to Pliny, common soldiers had the handles of their swords and their belts studded with silver; the baths of women were covered with the same valuable material, which was even used for the common implements of kitchen and scullery. Large manufactories of silver utensils were started in which each part of the work was assigned to a special artificer; here the orders of the silver-merchants (*negotiatores argentarii vascularii*) were executed. Amongst the special workmen of these manufactories were the *figuratores* (modellers), *flatuarii* or *fusores* (founders), *tritores* (turners or polishers), *cœlatores* (chisellers), *crustarii* (the workmen who attached the bas-reliefs to the surface of the vessel), and the *inauratores* or *deauratores* (gilders). Many valuable vessels have been recovered in the present century; others (for instance, several hundred silver vessels found near the old Falerii) have tracelessly disappeared. Amongst the discoveries which happily have escaped the hands of the melter we mention the treasure of more than one hundred silver vessels, weighing together about 50 lbs., found by Bernay in Normandy (1830). According to their inscriptions, these vessels belonged to the treasury of a temple of Mercury; they are at present in the late imperial library at

Paris.   In the south of Russia the excavations carried on in 1831,
1862, and 1863, amongst the graves of the kings of the Bosphoric
empire, have yielded an astonishing number of gold and silver

Fig. 450.

vessels and ornaments belonging to the third century of our era.
At Pompeii fourteen silver vases were discovered in 1835; at

Fig. 451.

Cære (1836) a number of silver vases (now in the Museo Grego-
riano) were found in a grave.   One of the most interesting discoveries was made near Hildesheim, 7th October, 1868, consisting of

seventy-four eating and drinking vessels, mostly well preserved ; not to speak of numerous fragments which seem to prove that only part of the original treasure has been recovered; the weight of all the vessels (now in the Antiquarium of the Royal Museum, Berlin) amounts to 107·144 lbs. of silver. The style and technical finish of the vases prove them to have been manufactured in Rome ; the form of the letters of the inscriptions found on twenty-four vessels indicates the first half of the first century after Christ. The surfaces of many of them are covered with alto-relievos of beaten silver—a circumstance which traces back their origin to imperial times, distinguishing them, at the same time, from the bas-relief ornamentations of the acme of Greek art. The gilding of the draperies and weapons, and the silver colour of the naked parts, in imitation, as it were, of the gold-and-ivory statues of Greek art, also indicate Roman workmanship. Figs. 450 and 451 show some of the finest pieces of this treasure. The composition of the figures on the surface of the vase in Fig. 450 shows true artistic genius : naked children are balancing themselves on water-plants growing in winding curves from a pair of griffins ; some of the children attack crabs and eels with harpoons, while others drag the killed animals from the water. The graceful groups on the drinking-vessels in Fig. 451 are mostly taken from the Bacchic cycle of myths.

Besides vessels of precious metals and stones, those of glass were in favourite use amongst the Romans. The manufactory of glass, originating in Sidon, had reached its climax of perfection, both with regard to colour and form, in Alexandria about the time of the Ptolemies. Many of these Alexandrine glasses have been preserved to us, and their beauty fully explains their superiority in the opinion of the ancients to those manufactured in Italy. Here also, after the discovery of excellent sand at Cumæ and Linternum, glass works had been established. Most of our museums possess some specimens of antique glass manufacture, in the shape of balsam or medicine bottles of white or coloured glass. We also possess goblets and drinking-bottles of various shapes and sizes, made of white or common green glass ; they generally taper towards the bottom, and frequently show grooves or raised points on their outer surfaces, so as to prevent the glass from slipping from the hand ; urns, oinochoai, and dishes of various

sizes made of glass are of frequent occurrence (Fig. 452). Some
of these are dark blue or green, others party-coloured with stripes
winding round them in zigzag or in spiral lines, reminding one of
mosaic patterns. Pieces of glittering glass, being most likely fragments of so-called *allassontes versicolores* (not to be mistaken for
originally white glass which has been discoloured by exposure to
the weather), are not unfrequently found. We propose to name
in the following pages a few of the more important specimens of
antique glass-fabrication. One of the finest amongst these is the
vessel known as the Barberini or Portland Vase, which was found
in the sixteenth century in the sarcophagus of the so-called tomb
of Severus Alexander and of his mother Julia Mammæa. It was
kept in the Barberini palace for several centuries, till it was purchased by the Duke of Portland, after whose death it was placed

Fig. 452.

in the British Museum. After having been broken by the hand of
a barbarian it has fortunately been restored satisfactorily. Many
reproductions of this vase in china and terra-cotta have made it
known in wide circles. The mythological bas-reliefs have not as
yet been sufficiently explained. Similar glass vases with bas-
relief ornamentation occur occasionally either whole or in fragments. The present writer saw in the collection of the late Mr.
Hertz in London a small tablet of transparent green emerald
resembling a shield, in the centre of which appears an expressive
head of a warrior in gilt opaque glass similar to the bas-reliefs of
the Portland vase; this tablet is said to have been found at
Pompeii. According to a story told by several writers in the time
of Tiberius, a composition of glass had been invented which could
be bent and worked with a hammer.

We further mention a small number of very interesting goblets, which, to judge by their style, evidently belong to the same place of manufactory as the Portland vase. They perhaps belong to the class of goblets known as *vasa diatreta*, some specimens of which were sent by Hadrian from Egypt to his friends in Rome. The goblet, Fig. 453, found near Novara may serve as specimen. Winckelmann, in his "History of Art," gives a description of it. He speaks of a reticulated outer shell at some distance from the glass itself, and connected with it by means of thin threads of glass. The inscription: BIBE VIVAS MVLTIS ANNIS, is in projecting green letters, the colour of the net being sky-blue, and the colour of the glass itself that of the opal, *i.e.* a mixture of red, white, yellow, and sky-blue, such as appears in glasses that have been covered with earth for a long time. Three vases of a similar kind have been found at Strasburg and Cologne (see "Jahrbücher des Vereins von Alterthumsfreunden im Rheinlande," Year v., p. 337, Tafs. XI., XII.);
all these distinctly show that they have been made of solid glass by means of a wheel, together with the net and letters. The highest prices were paid for the so-called Murrhine vases (*vasa Murrhina*) brought to Rome from the East. Pompey, after his victory over Mithridates, was the first to bring one of them to

Fig. 453.

Rome, which he placed in the temple of the Capitoline Jupiter. Augustus, as is well known, kept a Murrhine goblet from Cleopatra's treasure for himself, while all her gold plate was melted. The Consularis T. Petronius, who owned one of the largest collections of rare vases, bought a basin from Murrha for 300,000 sestertii; before his death he destroyed this matchless piece of his collection, so as to prevent Nero from laying hold of it. Nero himself paid for a handled drinking-goblet from Murrha a million sestertii. Crystal vases also fetched enormous prices. There is some doubt about the material of these Murrhine vases, which is the more difficult to solve, as the only vase in existence which perhaps may lay claim to that name is too thin and fragile to allow of closer investigation. It was found in the Tyrol in 1837 (see *Neue Zeitschrift des Ferdinandeums*, vol. v., 1839). Pliny describes the colour of the Murrhine vases as a mixture of white and purple; according to some ancient writers, they even improved the taste of the wine drunk out of them.

Fig. 454 shows two bronze jugs, at present in the Museo Bor-

Fig. 454.

bonico, for the drawing or pouring out of liquor (compare the corresponding Greek forms, Fig. 198). The metal admitted of a more artistic treatment than the clay used by the Greeks. The more or less bent handles are adorned at their ends with figures, masks, or palmetto ornaments; the gracefully curved mouths of the vessels frequently show borders of leaves and branches; the body of the vessel is either smooth or decorated by toreutic art. These vessels served for domestic uses, such as pouring water over the hands of the guests after dinner, or keeping the wine in. One particular kind of them, similar in form to the wine-vessels found on Christian altars, was reserved for libations (compare § 103).

We finally mention two graceful vessels, one of which, made of

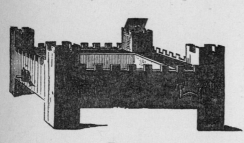

Fig. 455.

bronze (Fig. 455), represents a Roman fortified camp; the walls, as well as the towers flanking them, are hollow; into these boiling water was poured, in order to keep warm the dishes placed on the parapet of the walls, or fitted into the centre hollow,

which was also filled with water. The tower in the right corner of our illustration shows a lid; the water ran off through a tap on the left. The handles visible in Figs. 455 and 456 tend to show that both vessels were meant to be lifted on to the table. The construc-

tion of the latter heating apparatus is of a complicated kind.
A square box on four graceful legs supports a high barrel-like
vase with a lid to it; the mask just underneath serves as a
safety-valve for the steam inside the vases; a similar contrivance
appears on a semicircular water-box connected with the former.
Three birds on the upper brim of the latter served as stands for
a kettle. Whether the open box contained hot water or burning
coals seems uncertain.

The Greek custom mentioned in § 39 of decorating buildings
with ornamental vases was further developed by the Romans, who

Fig. 456.

loved to place krateres, amphoræ, urns, and pateræ in their rooms
or on the outsides of their houses; open halls and gardens were
adorned in the same manner. Marble, porphyry, bronze, and
precious metals were used for these ornamental vases, several
specimens of which, in stone and bronze, have been preserved to
us. The Museo Borbonico in Naples possesses a pitcher or kettle
with a richly ornamented border, resting on three fabulous
animals; also a bronze krater of great beauty. Fig. 457 shows a
bronze mixing-vessel of Etruscan workmanship, of noble simplicity
in form and decoration. Another vase of marble (Fig. 458) belongs

both by its graceful shape and by the execution of its ornamental details to the finest specimens of antique art.   It most likely came

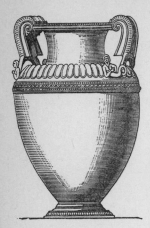

from a Greek workshop (some say from that of Lysippus), and has been found amongst the ruins of Hadrian's villa at Tivoli; at present it is in Warwick Castle, whence the name of Warwick Vase by which it is generally known. It has been frequently reproduced on a smaller scale; a copy, in the original size, adorns the staircase of the Royal Museum, Berlin.

Amongst the earthen vessels used for keeping wine and other liquors we mention the *dolia*, and the *amphoræ* and *cadi*, specimens of which are to be found in all our larger museums.   They are

Fig. 457.

of rude workmanship, showing either two small handles or none at all.   The former resembles a pumpkin; the bodies of the latter are slender, ending in a point (see Fig. 459); they were

dug into the earth about half-way, or put against the wall in an oblique position in order to prevent them from falling.   In the latter position a number of these vessels have been found in the house of Diomedes at Pompeii.

We subjoin a few remarks about the Roman way of making wine.   After the grapes

Fig. 458.

for eating had been sepaated, the remainder was put into coops and stamped on with the feet.   After this the grapes were once more operated upon with a wine-press.   The juice thus produced was poured into *dolia* or large tubs, and taken to the wine-cellars (*cella vinaria*), which, in order to make them cool, were always built facing the north.   In these open tubs the wine was left to ferment for a year: after that it was either drunk or (in case its quality was to be improved by longer keeping) poured from the dolia into the amphoræ and cadi (*diffundere*). The amphoræ, after having been pitched (hence *vinum picatum*) and cleaned with sea or salt water, were further rubbed with ashes of vines and smoked with burnt myrrh, after which they were closed with clay stoppers, and sealed up with pitch, chalk, or cement (*oblinere, gypsare*). A small tablet (*tesseræ, notæ, pittiacia*) attached to the body of the vessel indicated the size of the vessel and the name of the wine, also the consul under whom it had been stowed away. One amphora, for instance, bears the following inscription—RVBR. VET. V̄. P. CII. (*rubrum vetus vinum picatum CII.*), *i.e.* old pitched red wine, contents 102 lagenæ. The amphoræ were put in the upper story of the house, in order that the ascending smoke should give the wine a mild flavour (compare Horace, Od. III., 8, 9). Owing to the copious sediment produced by this method, the wine had to be strained each time before it was drunk. Several strainers (*colum*) made of metal have indeed been found at Pompeii. Sometimes a basin filled with snow (*colum nivarium*) was put on the top of a larger vessel. The wine was poured on the snow, through which it dripped into the amphora both cooled and filtered. Wooden barrels were not used in Rome in Pliny's time; they seem to have been introduced from the Alpine countries at a later period.

Innumerable different kinds of wine were grown in Italy, not to mention the Greek islands. The Romans became acquainted with the vine through the South Italian Greeks, who brought it from the mother-country. Italian soil and climate were favourable to its growth, and Italian growers were moreover encouraged by laws prohibiting the planting of new vineyards in the provinces. According to Pliny ("Nat. Hist.," XXXIII., 20), the Surrentum (*sc. vinum*) was the favourite wine of earlier times, afterwards supplanted by the Falernum or Albanum. These and other celebrated wines were frequently imitated. Of great celebrity were also the Cæcubum (afterwards supplanted by the Setinum), the Massicum, Albanum, Calenum, Capuanum, Mamertinum, Tarentinum, and others. Altogether eighty places are mentioned as famous for their wines, two-thirds of which were in Italy. Besides these we count about fifty kinds of liqueurs made of odoriferous herbs and flowers, such as roses, violets, aniseed, thyme, myrtle, &c., also several beverages extracted from various fruits.

We possess several representations of vintages and of the process of pressing the grapes. In the centre of a bas-relief in the Villa Albani (Panofka, "Bilder antiken Lebens," Taf. XIV., 9) we see a large tub, in which three boys are stamping with their feet on grapes brought to them in baskets. The must runs from the large tub into a smaller one, whence another boy pours it into a vessel made of osiers secured with pitch; to the right another boy pours the contents of a vessel of the same kind into a dolium. A wine-press is seen in the background. In another picture (Zahn, "Die schönsten Ornamente," &c., 3rd Series, Taf. 13) we see three Sileni occupied in the same manner as the three boys.

We mentioned before (§ 38) that the custom, still obtaining

Fig. 459.

in the South, of keeping the wine in hides of animals is of antique origin. The hairy part, rubbed with a resinous substance, was turned inside. Both Roman and Greek peasants brought their cheap wines to market in such skins (*uter*). In case larger quantities had to be transported, several skins were sewed together, and the whole put on a cart. Fig. 459 shows a wine-cart from a wall-painting, with which the interior of a tavern at Pompeii is appropriately decorated. The picture, which requires no further explanation, gives a vivid idea of a Roman market-scene.

92. Amongst all domestic utensils dug up, the lamps, par-

ticularly those made of bronze, claim our foremost attention,
both by their number and by the variety of their forms. Lamps,
like other earthenware utensils, were made in the most outlying
settlements, or were (in case their designs were of a more elaborate
kind) imported there from larger towns. The older Greek custom
of burning wax and tallow candles (*candelæ cereæ, sebaceæ*), or
pine-torches (see § 40) was soon superseded by the invention of
the oil-lamp (*lucerna*); these candles, moreover, were always of
a primitive kind, consisting of a wick of oakum (*stuppa*) or the
pith of a bulrush (*scirpus*) dipped into the liquid wax or tallow,
and dried afterwards. Even the lighting of the rooms by lamps

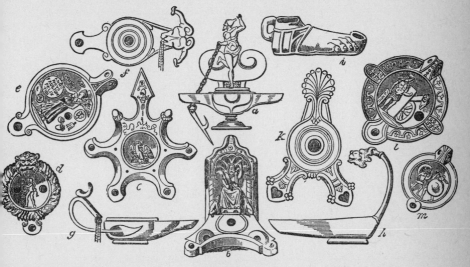

Fig. 460.

(notwithstanding the elegant forms of the latter) was not on a
par with other comforts and luxuries of Roman life. Glass
chimneys were unknown, and the soot of the oil-lamps settling on
furniture and wall-paintings had to be carefully sponged off by
the slaves every morning.

The lamp consisted of the oil-reservoir (*discus, infundibulum*),
either circular or elliptic in form, the nose (*nasus*), through which
the wick was pulled, and the handle (*ansa*). The material
commonly used was terra-cotta, yellow, brownish red, or scarlet
in colour, frequently glazed over with silicate. The simplest

forms of the lamp are specified in Fig. 460, *d, e, l, m*. All these lamps have only *one* opening for the wick (*monomyxos, monolychnis*), others (*b, c, k*) have two such openings (*dimyxi, trimyxi, polymyxi*). Birch ("History of Ancient Pottery," vol. ii., pp. 274 and 275) gives earthenware lamps with seven, and even twelve, *nasi* from originals in the British Museum. The Royal Antiquarium in Berlin also possesses two earthenware lamps with twelve nasi. The disks and handles of many of these lamps are adorned with graceful bas-reliefs, representing mythological events, animals, domestic life, or battles, fights of gladiators, flowers, garlands, &c., frequently original in composition. Fig. 460, *d*, shows Apollo, *l* a Roman warrior standing by a battering-ram, *m* two soldiers fighting.

b　　　　　　　　a　　　　　　　　c

Fig. 461.

Of particular interest is Fig. 460, *e*, representing an earthenware lamp, which, according to its inscription, was intended for a New Year's present (*strenæ*).* The device on the shield of the Goddess of Victory reads: ANNO NOVO FAVSTVM FELIX TIBI.

A number of lamps show on their bases inscriptions, either incised or in relief, indicative of the name of the potter, the owner, or the reigning emperor, &c.; sometimes we also meet with trade marks affixed to the lamps.

* Several lamps, intended as new year's gifts, such as were habitually exchanged by friends amongst the Romans, are in the R. Antiquarium of Berlin.

The forms of the lamps in Fig. 460, *b, i,* are of an unusual kind. The former shows a sacellum with the enthroned figure of Pluto; the latter has the semblance of a sandalled foot. Greater elegance and variety are displayed in the bronze lamps frequently found in our museums (Fig. 460, *a, f, g, h, k*). Herculaneum and Pompeii have yielded a number of beautiful specimens, counting amongst the most graceful utensils of antique times. To snuff the wick (*putres fungi*) and to pull it out small pincers were used, numbers of which have been found at Pompeii; another instrument serving the same purpose appears in Fig. 460, *a,* where the figure standing on the lamp holds it by a chain.

In order to light up larger rooms these lamps were either put on stands or they were suspended by chains from lamp-holders or from the ceiling. These stands or lamp-holders (*candelabrum*) were, amongst the poorer classes, made of wood or common metal; the rich, on the other hand, had them executed in the most graceful and elegant forms. The thin stem, sometimes fluted, some-times formed like the stem of a tree, rises to a height of 3 to 5 feet, on a base generally formed by three paws of animals; on this stem rests either a diminutive capital or a human figure, destined to carry the plate (*discus*) on which the lamp stands. The shaft is frequently adorned with figures of all kinds of animals. Sometimes we see a marten or a cat crawling up the shaft of the candelabrum, intent upon catching the pigeons carelessly sitting on the disk— a favourite subject, which occurs, with many variations, in the candelabra found in Etruscan grave-chambers. Besides these massive candelabra, there were others with hollow

Fig. 462.

stems, into which a second stem was inserted, which could be
pulled out and fastened by means of bolts; in this manner
the candelabrum could be shortened or lengthened at will.
Fig. 461, *a*, shows a candelabrum in the shape of a tree, the
branches of which carry two disks for lamps. At the foot of the
tree a Silenus is seated on a rock—an appropriate ornament,
seeing that the lamp was destined to give light to merry
topers.

Different from the candelabrum is the *lampadarium*. Here

the stem resembles a column or pillar, and is
often architecturally developed; from the capital
at the top issue several thin branches gracefully
bent, from which the lamps are suspended by
chains. Fig. 461, *b* and *c*, represents two elegant
specimens of lampadaria; in the latter the base
takes the shape of a platform, on the front part
of which we see an altar with the fire burning on
it, and on the opposite side Bacchus riding on a
panther. Each of the four lamps is made after
a different pattern, which is also the case with
the lamps in Fig. 461, *b*.

All the candelabra and lampadaria hitherto
mentioned could be placed and replaced as convenience required; others were too heavy to be
moved. We are speaking of the long marble
candelabra, specimens of which are shown in
Figs. 462 and 463; they were placed as anathemata in temples, or in the halls of the rich, and on
festive days blazing fires were lit on them.

Fig. 463.

The sacred character of the candelabrum (Fig.
462) is proved by the altar-like base resting
on three sphinxes, and by the rams' heads at the corners.
Cicero, in his impeachment of Verres, mentions a candelabrum
adorned with jewels destined by the sons of Antiochus for
the temple of the Capitoline Jupiter, but appropriated by
Verres before it had reached its place of destination. The
candelabrum (Fig. 463), the stem of which is supported by
kneeling Atlantes, most likely belonged to a private mansion.

Lanterns also (*laterna*) have been found at Pompeii; they

consist of cylindrical cases protected by a cover, and attached to a chain. Transparent materials, such as horn, oiled canvas, and bladder, were used instead of glass, which was introduced at a later period.

To conclude we mention some Greek lamps, mostly found in Roman catacombs, which, by the Christian subjects of their bas-reliefs and by the sign of the cross and the monogram of Christ frequently found on them, can be distinguished from other contemporary lamps, from which, however, they do not differ in form.

93. To complete our description of domestic utensils, we must once more pass through the different rooms of the Roman house with the assistance of our Plan (Fig. 386). Entering the ostium from the street we first observe the folding-doors (*fores, bifores*), made of wood, frequently inlaid with ivory or tortoiseshell; in public buildings, particularly in temples, these always open outwards, in private houses inwards. They, however, did not, like the doors of our rooms, move on hinges, but on pivots (*cardines*) let into the lintel (*limen superum*) and the stone sill (*limen inferum*). Holes for this purpose have been found in the thresholds of houses at Pompeii. Like the threshold, the doorpost (*postes*) in good houses consisted of marble or of elegant woodwork. Knockers, fastened in the centre of the panel, may be seen in wall-paintings; a few specimens of these have been preserved. The janitor or porter (whose office was held in every good house by a particular slave, and whose box, *cella ostiarii*, was near the door) opened the door by pushing back the bolt (*pessuli*) or bar (*sera*, whence the expression *reserare*, to unbolt). Doors opening outward, particularly those of cupboards, &c., were not bolted, but closed with lock and key. Most of our larger museums possess specimens of iron or bronze keys (Fig. 464). They are of all sizes, from the small ring-

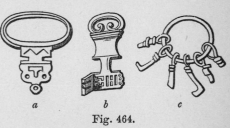

a   *b*   *c*

Fig. 464.

key (Fig. 464, *a*) attached to the finger-ring, or the small skeleton-key (Fig. 464, *c*), to the large latch-key. Frequently they are of a peculiar shape (Fig. 464, *b*), and the locks to which they were fitted must have been contrived with great mechanical ingenuity. A few locks have been preserved; but most of them, like, for instance, those found at Neuwied, are in an almost decayed condition.

There were no separate doors to the single rooms, which were closed only by curtains (*vela*), so as not to shut out the fresh air from the generally small bedrooms and sitting-rooms. Poles and rings for these curtains have been found at Pompeii.

We now enter the interior of the house, undeterred by the rod (*virga*) or threatening fist, which the porter (*ostiarius*) was wont to oppose to unwelcome visitors. A "SALVE" on the threshold bids us welcome. We first come to the atrium, the centre of house and family, where stood the hearth with its Lares and Penates and the venerable marital couch (*lectus genialis*). Here, in ancient times, the matron, surrounded by her children and hand-maidens, used to sit and weave. These old customs, however, soon disappeared. It is true that even at a later period the altar was reflected in the waves of the fountain; but no fire was lit on it; it remained in its place only as a tradition of former ages. Another memorial of ancient times are the family-portraits (*imagines maiorum*) looking down upon us from the opened wall-presses (*armaria*) surrounding the room. In the atria of old family houses were found masks of wax (*ceræ*), taken from the features of the dead persons, with tablets (*titulus, elogium*) telling of their names, dignities, and deeds attached to them. "The lines of the pedigree" (Pliny, "Nat. Hist.," XXXV. 2) "were drawn to the pictures, and the family archives filled with written and monumental evidence of their deeds. By the doors were seen representations of their valour, and near these were hung the weapons captured from the enemy, which even subsequent owners of the house were not allowed to remove." This custom was abandoned when upstarts bought the old mansions, and placed the marble or bronze busts of fictitious ancestors in their niches. Needy scholars were not wanting to trace back pedigrees to Æneas himself. The craving for portrait-statues is ridiculed by Pliny, who says that the libraries frequently contain sculptural reproductions of features invented for the purpose, as, for instance those of Homer.

The wall-paintings found at Pompeii and Herculaneum, although belonging to provincial towns, afford us sufficient

Fig. 465.

insight to judge approximately of the art of painting as practised
amongst the Greeks ; for this art also the Romans had adopted
from them.   How far the Greeks used this art for wall-decoration
of their private houses is difficult to decide, seeing that all such
houses have disappeared and that Greek authors only mention the
large paintings found in public buildings.   Perhaps private wall-
painting, although certainly not unknown to the Greeks, was practised amongst the Romans more extensively than amongst their
instructors.   Most of the better wall-paintings were undoubtedly
executed by Greek artists living in Italy.   In most cities there
were guilds of painters, presided over by a master, perhaps of
Greek birth, who himself made the designs of the better pictures,
leaving the mechanical part of the work to his assistant.   Many
of the imperfect designs, however, found at Pompeii are evidently
the work of inexperienced mechanics ; but even in these a certain
grace of workmanship betrays the influence of Greek schools.
The same influence is displayed still more distinctly in those
fantastic arabesques, which Vitruvius (" Arch.," VII. 3) considers
as the excrescences of a degenerated taste.   With this censure we
are unable to agree fully ; for these compositions, although
frequently bizarre, surprise us by the boldness and accuracy
of their designs, which, at any rate, betray a thorough artistic
training.

Whether the remaining wall-paintings are originals or copies
is in most cases impossible to decide : four monochromes at Herculaneum have the name of the artist, Alexandros of Athens,
added to them.   The fact, however, that amongst the numerous
paintings found in two neighbouring towns, and frequently
treating the same subjects, not two compositions exactly like each
other have been discovered, seems to prove that the copying of
pictures, barring a few celebrated masterpieces, was not customary ;
single features of compositions are, however, frequently repeated,
which, like the uniform treatment of colour and design, and the
almost unvaried repetition of certain figures, tends to prove the
existence of schools of decorative painters.

All the different classes of wall-paintings specified by Vitruvius—viz. architectural design, landscapes, still lives, scenes from
daily life, tragic and satirical representations, and renderings
of mythical subjects—are specified by one or more examples

amongst the wall-pictures of Pompeii and Herculaneum. Imitations of architectural materials, particularly of marble, occur frequently, as do also fanciful architectural designs, used mostly as frames of large surfaces adorned with pictures (Fig. 465); lofty buildings resting on thin columns, with winding staircases, windows, doors, and roofs of fantastic, almost Chinese, shape, throughout adorned with statuettes, garlands, and small animal pictures, are drawn in white or light yellow contours on a dark background. Small views of the sea, with ships on it, of harbours, temples, villas (see Figs. 375, 394), halls, forests, and rocks, with figures in the foreground, painted generally on friezes and bases of columns, give us an idea of Greek landscape-painting. The painter Tadius, in the reign of Augustus, was, according to Pliny, the inventor of this style of painting. Still life is represented by numerous culinary subjects, such as game, fish and other marine creatures, fruits, and pastry (see Fig. 479). Amongst *genre* pictures we count numerous scenes from daily life, such as interiors of workshops

Fig. 466.

with genii as carpenters and cobblers, a fullonica with (Figs. 472, 473) workmen, vintners carting home their grapes (Fig. 459), symposia, sales of Cupids, &c.; also representations connected with the theatre, both on the stage and behind the scenes, dancing-girls and floating figures, the latter particularly being amongst the highest achievements of antique painting. We, moreover, refer to the above-described charming picture of a young lady with a pencil and writing-tablet in her hands, as also to that of a female painter (Fig. 466). The artist dips her brush into a colour-box standing on a piece of column; in her left she holds her palette; her eye rests on the herme of a bearded Bacchus, which she has been copying; a boy kneeling by the base of the herme holds the canvas, with the picture of the god nearly finished. We mention in connection with this picture the name of Iaia of Kyzikos, who, according to Pliny, lived in Rome when Marcus Varro was a young man: she painted with the brush and also engraved on ivory, chiefly female portraits; in Naples she painted on a large tablet the portrait of an old woman, and also. her own likeness from a looking-glass.

Of mythological subjects we see specimens in all the more important houses at Pompeii, as, for instance, in the Casa delle Pareti Nere, Casa delle Baccanti, Casa degli Scienziati, Casa delle Sonatrici (with life-size figures), Casa di Adone, di Meleagro, del Poeta Tragico : consisting of larger compositions or of single figures, these pictures occupy the centre spaces of the walls, either in square or round frames. Amongst single figures, we frequently meet with those of Jupiter and Ceres. Of subjects we mention the finding of Ariadne by Bacchus, Adonis bleeding himself to death in the arms of Venus, Mars and Venus, Luna and Endymion, not to mention numerous other amorous adventures of the gods, with which the lascivious taste of the time was wont to adorn bedrooms and triclinia. The same preference for erotic and sentimental subjects appears in many pictures representing the mythical adventures of heroes ; others are treated in a purely artistic spirit without sensuous admixture. Amongst the latter we refer to the graceful picture of Leda, holding in her hand the nest containing Helen and the Dioscuri ; also to the pictures of the sacrifice of Iphigenia, Chiron giving a music-lesson to the youthful Achilles, the discovery of the same hero amongst the daughters of Lykomedes, and the abduction of Briseis from Achilles's tent. The backgrounds of these pictures are black, reddish brown, deep yellow, or dark blue ; particularly on black and dark blue backgrounds the figures appear with a distinctness rivalling plastic art. This contrast of colours, no less than the effects of light and shade, and the grace and truth of many of the compositions, more than fully make up for occasional inaccuracies of drawing.

In order to preserve the pictures, the most important ones amongst them have been sawed from out of the walls and removed to the Museum of Naples, where, after many of them have been partly destroyed by unskilful treatment, the remainder are now placed in a favourable position. Many of those not removed have partly or entirely been destroyed by the influences of daylight and weather; only in cases where the pictures had been protected in time by roofs has the process of decay been, at least, retarded. Two Germans, Zahn and Ternite,* deserve our gratitude for having copied and published a number of the chief pictures at a time when they were still in a good state of preservation. The accurate reproduction of designs and colours leaves nothing to be desired, which is more than can be said of the much more numerous copies which have appeared in the " Museo Borbonico." † The latter reproductions are without colours. In judging of the effects of colour in these pictures it ought to be remembered that they were intended to be seen by the subdued light of the atria and peristylia, or of the adjoining chambers, which had no windows of their own.

A few words ought to be added about the mechanical method of painting amongst the ancients. Many authors speak about the gradual development of the art from the first silhouettes (*linearis pictura*) attempted at Korinth and Sikyon, to the painting of the outlines in monochrome. Darker lines were added to express the various parts of the body and drapery ; and this led ultimately to a perspective, life-like conception of the human figure, in exactly the same gradual manner which we observed in vase-painting. About the time of Polygnotos the use of four colours, viz. white earth of Melos, red earth of Sinope, yellow-ochre of Attika, and black, began to supersede painting in monochrome. The use of these four colours and their mixtures implied the fundamental notions of light and shade, the first introduction of which has been severally ascribed to Apollodoros of Athens, Zeuxis, and Parrhasios, the founder of the Ionic school. The highest degree of artistic skill was attained by the school of Sikyon, founded by Eupompos, and brought to its climax of perfection by Apelles. Unfortunately no pictures of the great

* W. Zahn, "Die schönsten Ornamente und merkwürdigsten Gemälde aus Pompeji, Herculanum und Stabiae." Series 1—3. Berlin, 1827—1859. Ternite, " Wandgemälde aus Pompeji und Herculanum." 11 parts. Berlin, 1839.

† "Real Museo Borbonico," vols. i.—xvi. Napoli, 1824—1857.

Greek artists have come to us. The canvases of the great Greek masters were either brought to Rome as spoil or they were imported by the dealers. Even wall-pictures were sawed from out of the walls, in order to be framed and taken to Italy by the conquerors; this was done, for instance, in several buildings of Sparta. All these paintings have been lost in the course of centuries. Only the burial-places of Etruria, the houses of Pompeii and Herculaneum, some parts of the imperial thermæ in Rome, and a few remnants of wall-paintings found in various other places, bear witness of the great perfection of Greek *technique* preserved in Italy even after the decay of Greek art itself. It has been proved by careful and still-continued investigations that the substances used for the colour were almost exclusively minerals: of animal substances we only know the slimy matter of the purple snail mixed with chalk; the only vegetable substance used was the black of charcoal. As unmixed colours were used the white of chalk and the yellow of ochre, the admixture of chalk and minium to the latter producing light yellow and orange; for blue, was used oxidised copper; for red, red chalk or minium; and for brown, burnt ochre. Green was only produced by mixture. Previously to applying the colour (see Vitruvius, VII. 3, 8) one layer of plaster was laid on the wall, on the top of which one or more thin layers of fine mortar were added; over these several layers of mortar mixed with powdered marble or chalk were laid, the upper one being added before the lower had quite dried, by means of which the whole surface received a firmness and consistency almost equalling marble. The upper layers were finally beaten down and smoothed by means of a wooden instrument called *baculus* (stick), the impressions of which are, according to Mazois, still recognisable on several walls at Pompeii. The painting was done either *al fresco* or *a tempera*. In the former case the colours, moistened with water, were put on the damp wall; by means of a chemical amalgamation the picture was thus indelibly affixed to the hardening surface. In *a tempera* painting the colours, after having received an admixture of size in order to make them adhesive, were put on the dry surface. Both methods have been used at Pompeii (see Overbeck, "Pompeji," 2nd edition, vol. ii. p. 182 *et seq.*). The backgrounds were always painted *al fresco*, as were also generally the architectural ornaments, imitations of coloured stones; and, in a few cases, the subject pictures in the centre. As a rule, the latter, however, were painted *a tempera* on the *al fresco* background or immediately on the wall, a space being in that case left free for them; the latter pictures may be removed from the wall in thin layers, while a removal of the *al fresco* paintings implies the destruction of the surface underneath.

Encaustic colours were never applied in wall-decorations, although frequently in pictures painted on tablets or canvas. Colours prepared with a resinous substance have been found in the shop of a colourman belonging to the Casa del Arciduca, at Pompeii. In order to preserve them from the influence of the open air the pictures were frequently coated over with varnish made of wax or resinous matter.

94. The floors of the rooms consisted originally of clay, stamped or beaten to make it smooth, and mixed with potsherds to add to its firmness (*pavimentum testaceum*). Soon, however, this primitive method was superseded by a pavement consisting of slabs of white or party-coloured marble, placed together in geo-metrical figures of three, four, or six angles (*pavimentum sectile*); sometimes also square tablets were composed into checkered patterns (*pavimentum tessellatum*). The latter kind of pavement was common in Italy even before the Cimbrian war; it was applied, for the first time on a large scale, in the temple of the Capitoline Jupiter, after the beginning of the third Carthaginian war (see Pliny, " Nat. Hist.," XXXVI. 25, 61). From this kind of pavement (which remained in use down to late Roman times) the mosaic proper was developed, the larger tablets being changed for small parti-coloured pieces of marble, valuable stones (such as onyx or agate), and glass, placed together in various patterns. The art of working in mosaic had been practised in the East from a very early period. The method of surrounding the centre pictures with decorative designs was adopted for these pavements from wall-painting. The dark stripes of the geometrical figures thus form, in a manner, the frames of the pictures themselves. Sometimes the whole floor of a room was occupied by one design, at other times by several smaller medallion-like pictures. Work of this kind received the name of mosaic (*pavimentum musivum*). Before the mosaic was placed, the ground underneath was

firmly stamped down, or received a foundation of slabs of stone;
to this foundation a layer of plaster, slow in drying and very
adhesive, was added, into which the above-mentioned small pieces
were inserted after a certain pattern; the whole formed a compact
mass, impenetrable to dust and rain.

The mosaic floors found in almost every Roman house have
mostly been well preserved under the rubbish of centuries. In
the various Roman temples, baths, and dwelling-houses we see
numerous specimens of mosaic, varying from rude attempts to the
highest perfection of workmanship. Remains of Greek mosaic
preserved in Greece have not as yet been discovered, barring a
rather rude composition of coloured stones in the pronaos and
peristylos of the temple of Zeus at Olympia.

The compositions of the mosaic pictures are of the most varied
kind, not to speak of the numerous decorative patterns of generally
black lines on a white ground. Masks and scenic representations
(mosaic of Palestrina), races in the circus (mosaic found at Lyons,
see § 104), mythological representations (fight of Theseus with
Minotauros, found amongst the ruins of Iuvavia, the modern
Salzburg), historical battles (battle of Alexander in the Casa
del Fauno, at Pompeii), musical instruments (mosaic pavement in
the villa at Nennig, Fig. 245),—such are the subjects chosen, and
executed with admirable neatness, by antique artists. Amongst
the most celebrated mosaics no more in existence we mention the
pavement of the dining-hall of the royal palace of Pergamum,
executed by Sosus. It imitated a floor with the remains of a
dinner lying on it; the name applied to this hall was "the
unswept" (οἶκος ἀσάρωτος), afterwards transferred to all mosaic-
work of a similar kind (opus asarotum). Pliny also mentions
another mosaic in the same palace representing a dove sitting on
the rim of a fountain, with the shadow of its head thrown on to
the water. Perhaps the two mosaics seen in the villa of Hadrian
and at Naples were imitations of those of Pergamum. Amongst
mosaics still preserved, we mention particularly the large battle-
scene found, in 1831, in the Casa del Fauno, at present to be seen
in the Royal Museum, Naples. With regard to both size and
beauty of composition it ranks amongst the finest works of
antique art. It represents, most likely, the final victory of
Alexander over Darius at Issos: both kings appear in the *mêlée*,

the former piercing with his spear a noble Persian, the latter standing on his chariot surrounded by a few faithful followers; a horse is kept ready for his flight. From the left the Greek cavalry are making an irresistible attack on the wavering lines of the Persians. Helen, the daughter of Timon the Egyptian, is said to have painted a picture of this battle, which Vespasian brought to Rome; perhaps our mosaic is a copy of it. The accuracy of the details

Fig. 467.

may be concluded from the fact that each square inch is composed of one hundred and fifty pieces of glass or marble. Fig. 467 represents a mosaic found in the house of the Poeta Tragico at Pompeii.

Before leaving the house, we must cast a passing glance at the *viridarium*. Homer already mentions a large garden belonging to the palace of Alkinoos, king of the Phaiakai. Enclosed by a quadrangular wall, it contained the choicest kinds of pears, figs, pomegranates, olives, apples, and grapes, not to speak of beautiful beds of flowers. The water supply was plentiful. Horticulture, however, limited itself to the indigenous productions of the soil: the importation of tropical plants was unknown both to Greeks and Romans. We quote a letter of the younger Pliny to give some idea of Roman horticultural art; it somewhat reminds us of the style of the time of Louis XIV., as displayed in the gardens of Versailles. "In front of the portico of the house," Pliny says, speaking of his Tuscan villa, "lies a terrace cut into all kinds of shapes, and edged with box; it is adjoined by a sloping lawn, at the side of which the box is cut into the forms of various animals looking at each other. In the plain stands a cluster of delicate acanthus-plants, round which there is a walk, the latter being inclosed by a hedge of evergreen cut into different shapes and always kept under the shears. By the side of it an avenue resembling a race-course winds round clusters of box cut into various shapes, and trees not allowed to grow high. The whole is inclosed by a wall hidden from sight by box planted in a terrace-like manner. Behind the wall follows a meadow, pleasing by its natural beauties no less than the garden by its artificial charms. Fields and many other meadows and groves lie around." After this follows a glowing description of the villa itself, and the summer-house with its beautiful view of garden, fields, and woods. " In front of this building," he continues, " lies a roomy *manége*, open in the centre and surrounded by maple-trees; ivy encircles their stems and branches, winding from one tree to another. Here you see a small meadow, there clusters of box cut into a thousand shapes, sometimes in the form of letters indicating the name of the owner or that of the gardener. You next come to a grove with a bench of white marble, overshadowed by a grape-vine propped by four small columns of Carystian marble. A small waterspout issues from the bench, as if caused by the pressure of those sitting on it ; the water falls into a hollowed stone, from whence it flows unnoticeably into another marble basin. In case people want to dine here, the heavy dishes are put on the rim of the basin, while the lighter ones, shaped like birds or fish, are set afloat on the water." Pliny, of course, is describing one of those large gardens belonging to the country-residences of the rich. In large cities, particularly in Rome, where every square foot of ground was of great value, gardens even of very moderate dimensions could be indulged in only at great expense. Such *viridaria*, deprived of the charms of living trees and flowers, but still showing the remains of verandahs, statuettes, and fountains (compare "Pitture antiche d'Ercolano," vol. ii., Tav. 21), ponds, and borders of flower-beds, have been discovered amongst the ruins of Pompeii ; for instance, in connection with the houses of Diomedes, of Sallustius (see Fig. 390), of Meleager, of the Small Fountain, and of the Centaur. The existence of glass houses to protect tender plants from the cold of the winter is proved by the verses of Martial (VIII. 14).

95. The art of arranging in a picturesque manner the few pieces of clothing required by the southern climate of Italy, or by their feeling of propriety, the Romans had adopted at an early period from their Greek neighbours, aided in this respect by their own sense of the picturesque. The old republican type of the Roman dress, although to some extent modified with regard to shape and colour by the luxurious habits of later times, still remained essentially unaltered.

The Greek distinction between epiblemata and endymata reappears in the *amictus* and *indutus* of the Romans ; the former class being chiefly represented by the *toga*, the latter by the *tunica*.

The toga, the specifically national dress of the Romans, was originally put on the naked body, fitting much more tightly than the rich folds of the togas of later times. About the shape of this toga, which is described as a semicircular cloak (περιβόλαιον ἡμικύκλιον), many different opinions prevail. Some scholars consider it to have been an oblong piece of woven cloth like the Greek epiblemata described by us (§ 42) ; others construct it of one or even two pieces cut into segments of a circle. Here again we shall adopt in the main the results arrived at through practical trials by Weiss (" Costümkunde," p. 956 *et seq.*). The Roman toga therefore was not, like the Greek epiblemata, a quadrangular oblong, but "had the shape of an oblong edged off into the form of an oval, the middle length being equal to about three times the height of a grown-up man (exclusive of the head), and its middle breadth equal to twice the same length. In putting it on, the toga was at first folded lengthwise, and the double dress thus originated was laid in folds on the straight edge and thrown over the left shoulder in the simple manner of the Greek or Tuscan cloak ; the toga, however, covered the whole left side and even dragged on the ground to a considerable extent. The cloak was then pulled across the back and through the right arm, the ends being again thrown over the left shoulder backwards. The part of the drapery covering the back was once more pulled towards the right shoulder, so as to add to the richness of the folds." Counting the whole length of the toga at three lengths of a full-grown man, the first third of the toga would go to the front part of the drapery up to the height of the left shoulder, the second third to the part pulled across the back and under the right arm, the remaining third being occupied by the part pulled across the chest and again thrown over the left arm. If the toga is folded so that the two half-ovals are not congruent to each other, and that therefore the lower edges of the cloak do not fall together, the result will be that in putting on the toga two layers of clothing will appear, the longer one reaching down to the calves (*media crura*), the shorter one only to the knee (see Fig. 468). The former part of the cloak touches the body, the latter one lying outside.

The simpler, that is narrower, toga of earlier times naturally clung more tightly to the body ; a wide bend of the part reaching from the right arm across the chest to the left shoulder was therefore impossible. This rich fold in the later toga is compared by an author to the belt of a sword (*qui sub humero dextro ad sinistrum oblique ducitur, velut balteus.* Quinctil., XI. 3, 137). The same author adds, that the old Roman toga had no such fold (*sinus*), which in the later toga was large enough to hide objects

Fig. 468.

in. The part of the toga touching the ground was pulled across the sinus and arranged in large folds, as appears, for instance, from the statue of the emperor Lucius Severus (Fig. 468). Whether the part thus arranged was called *umbo* we will not venture to decide. Although the older toga impeded comparatively little the motions of the body, soldiers thought it necessary to tie the end thrown over the left shoulder round their waists, so as to keep their arms free. This sort of belt (*cinctus Gabinus*) remained the military costume till the *sagum* was introduced : even after that time the belted toga used to be worn at certain religious rites, such as the founding of cities or the opening of the temple of Janus ; also by the consul when performing certain religious ceremonies previously to setting out on a campaign. The Romans had undoubtedly adopted this costume from the inhabitants of the neighbouring Gabii, who on their part received it from the Etruscans. The later toga, with its rich folds covering the whole body, prevented each rapid motion which might have disturbed their careful arrangement. In order to produce, and give a certain consistency to, these folds, they were arranged by slaves on the preceding evening; sometimes small pieces of wood were put between the single folds, so as to form them more distinctly. Pins or clasps to fasten the toga seem not to have been used. Small pieces of lead sewed into the ends, hidden by tassels, served to preserve the drapery : a similar practice we noticed amongst the Greeks.

The toga as the Roman national dress was allowed to be worn by free citizens only. A stranger not in full possession of the rights of a Roman citizen could not venture to appear in it. Even banished Romans were in imperial times precluded from wearing it. The appearance in public in a foreign dress was considered as contempt of the majesty of the Roman people. Even boys appeared in the toga, called, owing to the purple edge attached to it (a custom adopted from the Etruscans), *toga prætexta*. On completing his sixteenth, afterwards his fifteenth, year (*tirocinium fori*) the boy exchanged the toga prætexta for the *toga virilis, pura,* or *libera*—a white cloak without the purple edge. Roman ladies (for these also wore the toga) abandoned the purple edge on being married. The toga prætexta was the official dress of all magistrates who had a right to the curulean chair and the fasces; the censors, although not entitled to the latter, also wore the toga prætexta. Amongst priests, the Flamen Dialis, the pontifices, augures, septemviri, quindecimviri, and arvales wore the prætexta, while acting in their official capacity; tribunes and ædiles of the people, quæstors and other lower magistrates were prohibited from wearing it. The *toga picta* and the *toga palmata* (the latter called so from the palm branches embroidered on it) were worn by victorious commanders at their triumphs; also (in imperial times) by consuls on entering on their office, by the prætors at the *pompa circensis*, and by tribunes of the people at the Augustalia. Being originally the festal dress of the Capitoline Jupiter, this toga was also called *Capitolina;* it was presented by the senate to foreign potentates. Masinissa, for instance, received a golden crown, the *sella curulis*, an ivory sceptre, the *toga picta*, and the *tunica palmata.*

Besides the somewhat unwieldly toga, there were other kinds of cloaks both warmer and more comfortable. In imperial times the toga was indispensable only in the law courts, the theatre, the circus, and at court ; under the Republic it was considered improper to appear in public without it. Amongst other cover-ings we mention the *pænula*, a cloak reaching down to the knees, adopted most likely from the Celts. It was without sleeves and fastened together at the back (*vestimentum clausum*), a round opening being left to put the head through. It was open at both sides, and had a seam in front at least two-thirds of its length from the neck downwards. It consisted of thick wool or leather, and was worn by both men and women, over the toga or tunica, during journeys or in bad weather. At first it used to be made of a sort of foreign linen (*gausapa*), the outer side being rough, the inner smooth ; the woollen cloak (*pænula gausapina*) was an introduction of later date. The pænula was, most likely, worn by soldiers sent to a rough climate. Another kind of cloak, also worn over the toga or tunica, was the *lacerna*. Its cut resembles that of the Greek chlamys, being an oblong open piece of cloth, fastened on the shoulder by means of a fibula. Although introduced much later than the pænula, it had become the common costume of imperial times, in which Romans appeared even on festive occasions. Being made of thinner material than the pænula, the lacerna gave more opportunity for the artistic arrangment of the folds. Large sums were spent on well-made and particularly well-dyed lacernæ. As a further protection from wind and weather a hood (*cucullus*) was affixed to both pænula and lacerna ; to this we shall have to return.

Similar in cut to the lacerna was the warrior's cloak, called originally *trabea*, later *paludamentum* and *sagum* ; it is essentially identical with the Greek chlamys. The *paludamentum*, always red in colour, was in republican times the exclusive privilege of the general-in-chief, who, on leaving for the war, was invested with it in the Capitol, and on his return changed it for the toga (*togam paludamento mutare*). In imperial times, when the military commandership was concentrated in the person of the emperor, the paludamentum became the sign of imperial dignity. It was laid round the body in rich, picturesque folds. The *sagum* or *sagulum* was a shorter military cloak, also fastened across the shoulder like a chlamys ; it was worn by both officers and private soldiers in time of war. The sagum of imperial times was longer than that of the Republic. In the representations of "Allocutions," frequently occurring on monuments (for instance, on the arch of Septimius Severus and the Columna Antoniniana, Fig. 530), both officers and privates appear in richly draped saga, reaching down to the knees. The name sagulum most likely applies to the short mantle reaching hardly lower than the hips which is worn by the barbarian soldiers in the bas-relief of the arch of Severus.

About the form of an article of dress called by the Greek name of *synthesis* we are entirely uncertain; we do not even know whether to class it as *amictus* or *indumentum*. Out of doors it was only worn by the highest classes of society at the Saturnalia; indoors it was usually worn at dinner (*vestes cenatoriæ*). Nevertheless the synthesis never appears in the numerous representations of festive meals. An epigram of Martial, in which Zoilus is made fun of for changing his synthesis eleven times, owing to its being saturated with perspiration, seems to indicate that it must have been a close-fitting dress like the tunica.

The *tunica* was put on in the same way as the Greek chiton. Its cut was the same for men and women, and its simple original type was never essentially modified by the additions of later fashion. It was light and comfortable, and was worn especially at home; out of doors the toga was arranged over it. Like the chiton, it could be worn with or without sleeves, and reached down to the calves; underneath the chest it was fastened round the body with a girdle (*cinctura*), across which it was pulled and arranged in folds in the Greek fashion. The persons carrying the temple-treasure of Jerusalem on the arch of Titus (see Figs. 536 and 537) wear the simple tunica arranged in this manner. In statues clad with the toga, the dress covering the upper part of the body to the neck must be designated as tunica (Fig. 468, compare the statues of Julius Cæsar, Augustus, Tiberius, and Claudius in Clarac, "Musée de Sculpture," Nos. 916, 924, 912 *A*, 936 *B*). The soldiers on the monuments of imperial times wear the tunica underneath their armour or sagum. About the time of Commodus sleeves were added to both male and female tunics (*tunica manicata*), covering the arm almost to the wrist; in a late Roman bas-relief we even see a prolongation of the sleeve resembling a cuff; this kind of tunica is also called *dalmatica*. At a later

date two or three tunics were put on in cold weather: Augustus
is said to have worn four in the winter. The tunic nearest to the
body was called *subucula;* the one over this, *intusium* or *supparus.*
A tunic with a purple edge was the privilege of senators and
knights, the sign of the *ordo senatorius* being one broad stripe,
that of the *ordo equester* two narrower ones; the former ornament
was called *clavus latus,* the latter *clavus angustus,* whence the
distinction between *tunica laticlavia* and *tunica angusticlavia.*

Fig. 469.

Women also used to wear a double tunica, the one nearest to
the body (*tunica interior*) being a close-fitting sleeveless chemise
reaching down over the knee. No girdle was required for it;
a thin band (*mammillare, strophium*) served to support the bosom.
Above the lower tunica the long *stola* fell in many folds: as to its
cut and the way of putting it on we refer the reader to our
remarks about the simple Doric chiton of Greek women. Like

this, the stola was an oblong chemise, cut open on the two upper sides, the open ends being fastened on both shoulders by means of clasps (compare the statue of Livia in "Mus. Borbon.," vol. iii. Tav. 37). Underneath the bosom the stola was fastened to the body by means of a girdle, through which it was pulled, so that its lower edge just touched the ground.

In case the tunica had sleeves, the stola worn over it had none, and *vice versâ.* The sleeves of the tunica or stola were cut open, and the ends fastened together by means of buttons or clasps, in the same manner as described by us in speaking of Greek dress (see the celebrated marble statue of the younger Faustina, Fig. 469; also Fig. 471). An essential part of the stola is the furbelow (*instita*) or ornamental border attached to the bottom of the dress (see Fig. 471).

Out of doors women wore a cloak (*palla*), appearing frequently on statues. Its cut resembled either that of the toga or that of the Greek *himation*, arranged in graceful folds according to the taste of the wearer, unrestricted by the laws of fashion, which exactly prescribed the folds of the male toga. A third kind of palla seems to have consisted of two pieces of cloth fastened over the shoulders with fibulæ, and either falling down in loose folds or fastened round the body by means of a girdle. These three kinds of the palla occur on monuments, the first-mentioned being seen most frequently on the statues of matrons of the

Fig. 470.

imperial family, or other portrait-statues of imperial times. Sometimes the back part of the palla is drawn over the back of the head in the manner of a veil (see the statue of the younger Agrippina, Fig. 470). Other graceful arrangements of the palla appear in Fig. 469, and on a seated statue of Agrippina, the wife of Germanicus,

in the museum of Florence. Before the introduction of the palla
Roman ladies used to wear a shorter and tighter square cloak,
called *ricinium*, which afterwards seems to have been worn only
at certain religious ceremonies. Similar articles of dress were
the *rica* and *suffibulum*, the former worn by the Flaminica, the latter
by the Vestals in the manner of a veil. Fig. 471 reproduces a

Fig. 471.

graceful picture found in a room at Herculaneum (1761), with
several others, leaning against the wall. It is generally
designated as the "Toilette of the Bride." On a throne is
seated the still youthful mother of the bride, dressed in the stola,
tied round the body with the strophium. The lower part of the
body is covered by the folds of the palla; down her back floats a

long veil fastened to the back of her head. Her right arm tenderly embraces the neck of her daughter; both are gazing at the bride standing in the middle of the room. The stola of this, her second, daughter shows the broad instita already mentioned; its open sleeves, or those of the tunica underneath, are fastened to the upper arm by means of buttons. She wears a palla of the toga kind over her other garments. A maid-servant, standing behind her, is clad in a stola (with sleeves reaching down to the wrists) and a palla.

Up to the end of the Republic the only materials used for these dresses were wool (*lanea*) and linen (*lintea*). The togæ were made of various kinds of wool, those of Apulia and Tarentum being considered the best amongst Italian, and those of Attica, Laconica, Miletus, Laodicea, and Bætica, the finest of foreign materials. Women's underclothing was made of linen, the materials of Spain, Syria, and Egypt being preferred to those of Italian origin. Both materials were worked into lighter dresses for the summer, and warmer ones for the winter. Silk dresses (*holoserica*) and half-silk dresses (*subserica*) began to be worn by ladies about the end of the Republic; under the Empire they were even adopted by men, notwithstanding the prohibitory law of Titus. About the importation of raw silk from Asia into Greece, and thence into Italy, we have spoken before. We only add that the transparent sea-green veils, made principally in the isle of Kos, occur repeatedly in wall-pictures (see "Mus. Borbon.," vol. viii., Tav. 5, III. 36, VII. 20). Goat's-hair was used only for coarse cloaks, blankets, and shoes.

The usual colour of the dress was originally white (for the toga this was prescribed by law): only poor people, slaves, and freedmen wore dresses of the natural brown or black colour of the wool, most likely for economical reasons. Only the mourning dresses of the upper classes showed dark colours (*toga pulla*, *sordida*). In imperial times, however, even men adopted dresses of scarlet, violet, or purple, colours formerly worn only by women. Fig. 471 may serve to illustrate the different colours of the dresses. The veil of the mother is blue, her stola of a transparent white, through which one sees the flesh-colour of the bosom; her palla is reddish white, with a bluish-white border. The stola of the daughter nearest the mother is also reddish white, her palla being yellow, with a bluish-white border. Yellow was, according to Pliny, a favourite colour with women, particularly for brides' veils. The bride wears a reddish-violet stola, adorned with an embroidered *instita* of darker hue; her palla is light blue. The servant wears a blue upper dress with white underclothing. Frequently the inside of dresses appears in the pictures of another colour than the outside. In a picture, for instance, representing Perseus and Andromeda (Zahn, "Die schön. Orn.," Series 3, Taf. 24), the outside of Perseus's dress is reddish brown, the inside white; while Andromeda's dress is yellow outside and blue inside. Perhaps these dresses were lined with material of a different colour.

Particularly interesting are the purple-coloured silk or woollen dresses of the Romans; the raw materials were subjected to the dyeing process. Two kinds of snails, the trumpet-snail (*buccinum, murex*) and the purple snail proper (*purpura, pelagia*), yielded the colour; the exudations of the latter were, in reality, of a yellowish-white colour, but by the combined influence of the sun and of dampness they turned into a rich violet colour. The scarlet juice of the buccinum was generally mixed with purple colour in order to prevent its fading. The purple colour proper had two shades, a black and a red one; it was applied either pure or mixed with other substances. By means of these mixtures, and by dipping the cloth into the colour more than once, the ancients contrived to produce no less than thirteen different shades and *nuances* of colour. By mixing blackish purple with the buccinum juice the favourite amethyst-violet and hyacinth-purple colours were produced (*ianthinum, violaceum*). In order to gain brightness and intensity of colour the dress was dyed twice (*bis tinctus, δίβαφος*), being dipped first into the purple juice and afterwards into that of the buccinum. Looked at straight, the blood-red dress thus prepared had a blackish tint, looked at from underneath it showed a bright red colour. The double-dyed purple dresses, particularly those of Tyrian and Laconic origin, fetched the highest prices, a pound of double-dyed Tyrian wool being sold at 1,000 denarii (about £43), while a pound of the above-mentioned violet-amethyst-purple wool cost only £15.

At first only the broad or narrow hems of togas and tunicas (worn by senators, magistrates, and knights) were coloured with

genuine purple (*blatta*); those of private persons being dyed with
an imitation purple. The white toga, with a hem of genuine
purple, remained the official dress of certain magistrates; but as
early as the last years of the Republic it became the fashion
amongst men to wear entire purple togas. The first to wear one
of these as the sign of highest dignity was Julius Cæsar, who,
like several successive emperors, tried to stem the luxurious habit
by restrictive laws; which, however, became soon disregarded.
The wearing of genuine purple, however, remained the exclusive
privilege of the emperors. Even women were punished for
infringing this law, as were also merchants for trafficking in the
genuine article.

After being woven the materials of the dresses were further
prepared with needle and scissors, as is sufficiently proved by the
cut of most of the underdresses, particularly of the pænula and
tunica. Most of the Greek dresses were worn unsewed. In
Rome each wealthy household counted amongst its slaves several
tailors (*vestiarii, pænularii*). The existence of guilds of professional
tailors is established beyond doubt. The guilds of fullers and
dyers carried on two important trades connected with clothing.
The old Greek custom for kings' daughters to superintend
personally the cleaning of clothes was, if ever imitated by the
Roman ladies of noble families, soon abandoned by them. The
cleaning, moreover, of the white woollen materials chiefly worn
amongst the Romans required arti-
ficial means. For this purpose the
guild of the fullers (*fullones*) was
established at an early period; like
that of the cloth-weavers (*collegium
textorum panni*), it did a large and
profitable business. The shop and
the work of a fuller are illustrated
by the remains of a fullery (*fullonica*) found at Pompeii, and also
by several paintings on its walls

Fig. 472.

(see Figs. 472 and 473). Near the back wall are four large tanks
consisting of masonry, and connected with each other, but on a
different level, in order to let the water run from the highest to
the lowest. A raised platform runs along these tanks, which one

ascends on several steps.   To the right of it lie six small compartments destined, most likely, to receive the washing-tubs. To the right of the peristylium there is, moreover, a vaulted chamber containing a large tub and a stone table to beat the clothes on.   Large quantities of soap have been found in this apartment, which was the washing-room proper.   On one of the corner pillars of the peristylium four wall-paintings have been

Fig. 473.

discovered illustrative of the work of a fuller.   In the first (Fig. 472) we see, standing in niches, several tubs filled with water, in the centre one of which a fuller is treading on the clothes, for the purpose of cleaning them; in the tubs on both sides (we only reproduce part of the picture) two other men are occupied in pulling the clothes out of the water, and in rubbing off such stains as may remain on them.   After this the clothes were once more rinsed with pure water, to remove the nitre or urine frequently used in fulling.   The other picture (Fig. 473) introduces us to a different part of the fullery.   In the background a workman is brushing a white dress with a purple hem which hangs over a pole; on the right another workman approaches with a frame resembling a hen-coop, across which the clothes were drawn for the purpose of sulphuration; the vessel carried by the man most likely contains the necessary sulphur.   On the top of the frame the bird of Athene Ergane, the goddess of industry, has appropriately been placed.   In the foreground is the seated figure of a richly dressed woman, who seems to examine a piece of cloth given to her by a young work-girl.   The third picture, not here reproduced, shows the drying-chamber, with pieces of cloth hung on poles for drying.   A fourth picture shows a press with two screws, for the final preparation of the cloth.

96. With regard to Roman head-coverings of men we have

little to add to our remarks about Greek hats (see § 43, Fig. 222). Most of the forms there shown also occur amongst the Romans. The Roman, like the Greek, generally wore his head uncovered, the toga pulled over the back part of the head being sufficient shelter in case of need. The pileus and petasus, however, were worn by the poorer working-classes continually exposed to the weather, and by rich people on journeys or at public games as a protection from the sun. The pileus was occasionally replaced by the hood (*cucullus, cucullio*), introduced into Rome from northern countries, most likely from Gaul, North Italy, and Dalmatia. The cucullus was either fastened to the pænula or lacerna like the cowl of a monk, or it was worn as a separate article of dress. A cucullus of the latter kind, covering head and body down to the knees, is

Fig. 474.

worn in a bas-relief by a traveller who is just settling his bill with the hostess of his inn ("Bullet. Napoletano," VI. 1); the smaller cucullus is worn in a wall-painting by several persons at a rural feast (Fig. 474).

The custom of leaving the head uncovered naturally led to a careful treatment of the hair. According to Varro, Romans used to wear long hair and long floating beards covering chin and cheeks till the year 454 of the city. At that time the first barbers (*tonsores*) came to Rome from Sicily ; Scipio Africanus is said to have been the first Roman who had himself shaved (*radere*) with a razor (*novacula*) every day. The fashion of wearing the hair cropped short seems to have made slow progress, and only amongst the higher classes. The hair was either worn in wavy locks, or it was arranged in short curls (*cincinni*) by means of a curling-iron resembling a reed, and for that reason called *calamistrum ;* the slaves charged with this manipulation were called *ciniflones.* The different ways of wearing the hair become apparent from a comparison of the numerous male portrait-heads occurring on coins and statues. " Swells " of the period of moral decline managed to twist their hair into all kinds of unnatural shapes. A common fashion was, for example, to wear curls arranged in several steps (*coma in gradus formata*), such as found on the head of M. Antonius at Venice. Of the Emperor

Gallienus it is told that he had his hair powdered with gold-dust. About the beginning of the Empire it was a common custom, both amongst men and women, to wear false hair (*capillamentum*), either to hide bald places or to give a fuller appearance to the natural hair. Sometimes also hair was painted on the bald head, so as to produce the semblance of short hair, at least at a distance (compare Martial's Epigram, VI. 57). The close-cropped hair seems to have been the fashion from the time of the Emperor Macrinus to that of Constantine.

Full beards became again the fashion about the time of Hadrian. Up to the time of Constantine an uninterrupted series of portrait-heads of emperors on coins yields excellent information with regard to these matters ; afterwards the type of the coins degenerates. Between the reigns of the two above-mentioned emperors the heads appear with full beards, with only a few exceptions, as, for instance, the heads of Elagabalus, Balbinus, Philippus the younger, and Hostilianus, which are always represented with smooth chins. Barber-shops (*tonstrina*) were naturally of frequent occurrence amongst the Romans. They were the gathering-places of all idlers and the centres of town-gossip in Italy, as well as in Greece. They were well furnished with razors (*novacula*), tongs (*volsella*) to pull out the hairs of the beard, scissors (*axisia*), several pomatums to destroy the hair in certain places, combs (*pecten*), curling-irons (*calamistrum*), mirrors (*speculum*), towels, &c. The small so-called barber's shop in the street of Mercury at Pompeii, next to the fullonica, can, it is true, not have accommodated many persons at a time; but, most likely, the establishments in the capital were on a larger and more splendid scale.

Women do not seem to have worn hats; they generally pulled their palla over the back of their heads (see Fig. 470). Still more picturesque was the veil fastened to the top of the head (Fig. 471), and dropping over neck and back in graceful folds. The *mitra* was a cloth wound round the head in the manner of a cap ; it resembled the Greek sakkos, and served to keep the hair in its position (see the servant, Fig. 471 ; and Fig. 232, where the woman sacrificing in front of the bridal chamber wears the sakkos). This cap frequently consisted of the bladder of an animal; it never reached higher than the top of the head;

the front hair was always arranged in graceful wavy lines. A more handsome head-covering was the net made of gold thread (*reticulum*), also worn by Greek and indeed by our modern ladies (see Fig. 473, where the seated female wears it).

More variegated were the ways of dressing the hair as illustrated by the numerous female statues of imperial times. Ovid remarks "that the different ways of dressing the hair in Rome were equal in number to the acorns of a many-branched oak, to the bees of the Hybla, to the game on the Alps, every new day adding to the number." Compared with this variety even the numerous hair-dresses appearing on coins, representing empresses, ladies of the imperial court, or private persons, seem few in number. At the same time they are representative of the leading fashions. In the first centuries of the Republic the hair was arranged in a simple graceful manner, in accordance with the general character of the dress. The long hair, either parted or unparted, was combed back in wavy lines, and plaited or tied in a knot (*crines in nodum vincti, crines ligati*), sometimes arranged round the top of the head like a crown, at others fastened low down the neck by means of ribbons or clasps (see the daughter standing by the mother's side, Fig. 471). Another fashion was to arrange the hair round the head in long curls, or to arrange the front hair in thick plaits, connecting it with the back hair, &c. The form of the face and the taste of the lady naturally were decisive in this matter (compare Ovid, "Ars Amat.," III. 137 *et seq.*). Married ladies were, at least in earlier times, excluded from this licence; they always used to arrange their hair in a high *toupé*, called *tutulus*, fastened on the top of the head by means of ribbons. This, at least, seems to us the right explanation of the description of the tutulus by Varro (VII. 44): "*Tutulus appellatur ab eo quod matres familias crines convolutos ad verticem capitis quos habent vitta velatos, dicebantur tutuli, sive ab eo quod id tuendi causa capilli fiebat, sive ab eo quod altissimum in urbe quod est, arx, tutissimum vocatur.*" Perhaps the arrangement of the mother's hair in Fig. 471 ought to be described as a tutulus fastened with gold rings instead of ribbons. The original simple and beautiful arrangement of the hair was soon superseded by fantastic structures of natural and artificial hair, justly described by Juvenal (VI. 502) as "towers of many stories." Hairdressing became a science, and occupied a considerable part of a fashionable lady's time. Special maid-servants were employed for the purpose, whose naked arms frequently had to suffer the pricks of the needle of the fastidious beauty, who perhaps all the while seemed to listen to the speeches of philosophers and rhetoricians. Amongst the numerous heads illustrating the hair-fashions of imperial times we have chosen the portraits of three empresses (Fig. 475), viz., those of Sabina, wife of Hadrian (*a*), of Annia Galeria Faustina, wife of Antoninus Pius (*b*), and of

a   *b*   *c*

Fig. 475.

Julia Domna, wife of Septimius Severus (*c*). The natural hair was frequently insufficient for the tower-like *coiffures*, and the want had to be supplied either by false plaits or by complete wigs. Even plastic art imitated this custom by adding to the head a removable marble hair-dress, which could be replaced by a new one according to fashion. In the Royal Collection of Antiques, Berlin, there is a bust with movable hair, ascribed to Lucilla. The custom of dyeing their hair became common amongst Roman ladies at an early period. As early as Cato's time the Greek custom of dyeing the hair a reddish-yellow colour had been introduced in Rome; caustic soap (*spuma caustica*, also called *spuma Batava*), made of tallow and ashes, was imported from Gaul for the purpose. The long wars of the Romans with the Germans engendered amongst Roman ladies a predilection for the blond hair of German women (*flavæ comæ*); this hair became, in consequence, a valuable merchandise: Roman ladies used to hide their own hair under fair wigs of German growth.

We have already mentioned the numerous pomatums and balsams used for dressing and scenting the hair, by both men and women. Cicero speaks of the demoralised companions of Catilina as shining with ointments. Kriton, the body-physician of the Empress Plotina, gives in his work on "Cosmetics" the receipts of twenty-five different pomatums and scents.

Ribbons and pins served at once to fasten and adorn the
hair. These ribbons (worn, for instance, by the daughter
standing by the mother's side, Fig. 471) were adorned with
pearls and jewels; frequently they were replaced by a ring of
thin gold or gold thread (see the hair of the mother and the
bride, Fig. 471). Strings of pearls also were tied up with the
hair (see the hair-dress of the Empress Sabina, Fig. 475, *a*),
with the addition of a stephane studded with jewels (Fig. 475, *a, b*).
Not the least graceful adornment of the hair were the wreaths,
consisting either of leaves of flowers joined together (*coronæ
sutiles*) or of branches with leaves and blossoms (*coronæ plexiles*).
In a wall-painting of Pompeii ("Mus. Borb.," vol. iv., Tav. 47)
we see four Cupids sitting round a table, occupied in arranging
wreaths and garlands.

Hair-pins, made of metal or ivory, have been found in great
numbers and varieties. We reproduce (Fig. 476, *a, b, c, h, i, k*)
some of the more grace-
ful ones worked in
ivory, one of which (*c*)
shows Venus rising
from the sea and strok-
ing back her wet hair,
a common subject of
antique sculpture. Fig.
476, *e*, shows a poma-
tum-box with a reclin-
ing Cupid in bas-relief

Fig. 476.

represented on it; *f*, a bronze comb (*pecten*), which was used (as by
the Greeks) only to comb, never to fasten, the hair. A very elegant
bronze comb adorned with coloured stones was found some time
ago near Aigle, and is at present in the museum of Lausanne.
Combs made of box or ivory are preserved in many of our museums.

We have given (§ 46) a comprehensive account of the sandals,
the boots, and the shoes used amongst the Greeks. The same
remarks apply essentially also to Roman foot-coverings; little
remains to be added. The equivalent of the Greek sandal is the
Roman *solea* (worn by the mother, Fig. 471). They were worn
by men and women at home, and on all occasions where the
official toga did not require a corresponding foot-dress. At table

the soles were taken off, for which reason the two expressions, *demere soleas* and *poscere soleas*, are synonymous with lying down to, and getting up from, table. It is, however, unlikely that even in older times the Romans ever appeared in public with naked feet, as is told of the Greeks. The solea, like the tunica and lacernæ, belonged to private life; the official toga required the corresponding *calceus*, a closed high shoe resembling our ladies' boots. Calcei are frequently worn by male and female statues. Official distinctions were, however, made. The calceus fastened to the ankle and calf with four strings (*corrigiæ*), and, moreover, adorned with a crescent-shaped piece of ivory (*lunula*) on the top of the foot, was most likely worn by senators, being, in that case, identical with the black *calceus senatorius*, as distinguished from the *calceus patricius* or *mulleus*. The mulleus, made of red leather, and with a high sole like a cothurnus, was originally worn by the kings of Alba, but afterwards adopted by the patricians : it reached up to the calf; little hooks (*malleoli*) were attached to its back leather for the purpose of fastening the laces. The calceus was cleaned with a sponge, as is proved by the bronze statuette (in the late Hertz collection) of an Ethiopian slave occupied in that manner.[*]

Besides the calceus, we find on statues numerous varieties of the sandal, and also a sort of stocking tied with laces from the instep to the calf; the name of the latter is entirely unknown to us ; it appears frequently on the warlike statues of emperors, the upper borders, made of cloth or leather, being adorned with the heads of lions and other animals, worked most likely in metal (see, for instance, the statues of Cæsar, Tiberius, Caligula, Vitellius, Hadrian, and others, in Clarac, "Musée," pl. 891 *et seq.*). The just-mentioned combination of toga and calceus has, however, not always been preserved by the artists : the statues, for instance, of Cicero in the museum of Venice, of Sulla at Florence, and of M. Claudius Marcellus in the Museo Chiaramonti, wear sandals ; while, on the other hand, the statue of Balbus in the Museo Borbonico, and many other portrait-statues, correctly wear calcei with the toga.

The *caliga* was a sort of military boot of imperial times.

---

[*] "Catalogue of the Collection of Assyrian, &c., Antiquities formed by Hertz." Revised by W. Koner. London, 1851. Tab. III.

Caius Cæsar received his nickname Caligula from this boot.
The caliga was most likely a boot with a short top, turned over
at the upper edge, resembling the Spanish boots of the middle
ages (compare Fig. 523).

Sandals and shoes were fastened to the foot by means of straps
tied round the foot and the leg, from the ankle upwards. These
straps mostly covered about half of the calf (*fasciæ crurales*,
tibiales), extending, however, sometimes up to the thigh (*fasciæ
feminales*) ; the latter mode of wearing them was considered to be
effeminate. On historic monuments of imperial times we see
Roman legionaries clad in socks reaching up to the middle of
the calf, and fastened with straps covering the heel, foot (with
the exception of the toes), and the leg, up to some inches above
the ankle ; they were, most likely, part of the military dress, and
very convenient for marching.

Breeches (*braccæ*) were originally worn by barbarous nations,
but adopted by Roman soldiers exposed to northern climes. The
trumpeters opening the procession, and the soldiers carrying
Victories (Figs. 532, 533), are clad in trunk-hose, similar to those
worn by the barbarians following the triumphal chariot (Fig. 538,
compare Fig. 526). The Persian warriors in the Pompeian
mosaic of the "Battle of Alexander" wear close-fitting breeches
similar to the tights in which Amazons are generally depicted (see
Fig. 272).

97. We add a few remarks with regard to the numerous
ornaments made of precious metals, ivory, jewels, and pearls,
some of them of artistic value, which have been found at Pompeii
and other places, particularly in graves. Hair-pins, earrings,
necklaces, bracelets, girdles, and agraffes compose what was
collectively called *ornamenta muliebria.** Most of these objects
have already been mentioned as worn by Greek ladies (compare
§ 47, Figs. 225 and 226) ; the specimens found in Italy distinctly
betray Greek workmanship.

---

* A complete set of a lady's ornaments, consisting of bracelets, necklaces, rings,
earrings, brooches, and pins, has been found near Lyons in 1841 (see Comarmond,
"Description de l'Ecrin d'une dame Romaine trouvé à Lyon en 1841," Paris et Lyon,
1844). Of particular value are the seven necklaces, consisting of emeralds, garnets,
sapphires, amethysts, and corals. Pliny, "N. H.," ix. 117, relates that Lollia
Paulina, the wife of Caligula, used on ordinary occasions to wear ornaments to the
value of 40 millions sestertii (about £450,000).

About hair-pins (*crinales*) we have spoken above (see Fig. 476). Simpler specimens, about seven-eighths of an inch long, with round or angular heads, or with eyes for the fastening of the strings of pearls, are found in most collections. The bride (Fig. 471) has her hair fastened with elastic gold *bandeaux*, open in front.

The neck and bosom were adorned with necklaces (*monilia*) or chains (*catellæ*, see mother and daughter, Fig. 471) of gold, studded with jewels and pearls. A necklace of beautiful workmanship, consisting of elastic gold threads twisted together, has been found at Pompeii ("Mus. Borbon.," vol. ii. Tav. 14); attached to it is a lock adorned with frogs. A gold chain for the neck, 5 feet 6 inches in length, and equal in weight to

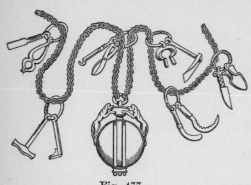

203 ducats, has been found near the Magura mountain in Siebenbürgen (Austria), and is at present in the Münz- und Antiken - Cabinet, Vienna: fifty different instruments, *en miniature*, such as scissors, keys, anchors, saws, tongs, hammers, &c., are attached to it by means of

Fig. 477.

thirty rings (Fig. 477; compare the description of the necklace found at Lyons in Marquardt, "Römische Privatalterthümer," 2nd Series, 1867, p. 294). Other chains, wound several times round the neck, and falling down to the bosom, had frequently a little case (*bulla*) attached to them. It contained a charm against sickness and the evil eye, and was worn by boys of noble families, afterwards also by the legitimate sons of freedmen, up to the time of their relinquishing the toga prætexta. The custom was of Etruscan origin. At a later period grown-up persons, particularly victorious generals at triumphs, used to wear a protective bulla (*inclusis intra eam remediis, quæ crederent adversus invidiam valentissima*). It appears on several statues of Roman youths, as also on the statue of a young man clad with the toga in the Dresden gallery (Clarac, "Musée," pl. 906). A bulla fastened to an elastic gold thread, found at Pompeii, was evidently meant to be worn by a woman (compare the bulla, Fig. 477).

Bracelets (*armillæ, bracchialia*) in the form of snakes (compare the Greek ὄφεις) or simple ribbons, also of rings or plaited gold thread, adorned the lower and upper parts of women's arms. Bracelets frequently appear on statues ; others, made of bronze or precious metals, have been found in Roman graves. They were used as male ornaments by the Etruscan and other Italian nations, as is proved by the story of Tarpeia's treason, as also by the male figures on Etruscan cinerary boxes. In imperial times massive arm-rings were given to Roman men as the reward of prowess (see the centurion, Fig. 531).

Pendants (*inaures, pendentes*) were worn by Roman as well as by Greek ladies, as is proved by several specimens found at Pompeii ; the form of the segment of a globe was, in the first century of the Empire, used frequently for them. We also hear of pearls and jewels fastened to the ear by means of hooks of gold thread (see Fig. 471). "Two pearls beside each other," Seneca complains, "with a third on the top, now go to a single pendant. The extravagant fools probably think their husbands are not sufficiently plagued without their having two or three heritages hanging down from their ears." Another fashion was to wear a single large pearl (*unio*) as a pendant. White pearls, resembling the colour of alum, fetched the highest prices, their value being proportionate to their size, smoothness, and roundness. Cæsar presented to the mother of Marcus Brutus a pearl which had cost him six million sestertii ; the pearl which Cleopatra drank dissolved in vinegar was worth ten million sestertii.

Enormous sums also were spent on rings adorned with jewels and cameos. According to the simpler custom of old times, adopted from the Etruscans, an iron signet-ring was worn on the right hand : even after the introduction of gold rings old families continued wearing the primitive iron signet-ring. Originally only ambassadors sent to foreign nations were allowed to wear gold rings, and were supplied with such at the public expense as a sign of their dignity ; later, senators and other magistrates of equal rank, and soon afterwards knights, received the *jus annuli aurei*. After the civil war, when many *equites* had to drop their knighthood owing to the loss of the census, the privilege was frequently encroached upon. The first emperors tried to re-enforce the old law, but as many of their freedmen had become entitled to wear gold rings the distinction lost its value. After Hadrian the gold ring ceased to be the sign of rank; Justinian granted it to all citizens, free-born or liberated. This *annulus aureus* most likely was a plain and heavy ring, like our wedding-rings. To distinguish it from other rings adorned with stones, &c., the wearing of which was free to men or women of all classes, the gold ring retained its original shape unimpaired by fashion. The passion for rings adorned with jewels and cameos (compare our remarks about Greek rings, p. 182) seems to have been common to all classes. Almost every excavation adds new specimens to our collections of cameos, the number and variety of which enable us to follow the history of the art of engraving from its rise in the time of Alexander the Great to its deepest decline. It is true, however, that a strictly historic basis cannot be established, seeing that the names of artists occasionally found on their works can be fixed historically only in the fewest cases; while, on the other hand, the portrait-heads occurring on cameos give but an approximate indication of the time of their origin. Moreover, the work of incompetent beginners occurs but too frequently contemporaneously with the highest achievements of the art, the general passion for cameos making cheapness appear an almost more important consideration than perfection of workmanship. In this art, also, the Romans were seldom creative, as appears from the Greek names of most of the artists found in the inscriptions, or mentioned by ancient authors. Roman men and women used to cover their fingers with rings of this kind, used partly for sealing, partly as ornaments; small boxes of a peculiar kind (*dactyliothecæ*) served to keep the rings. "At first," Pliny says, "it was the custom to wear rings on the fourth finger only; later, the little and second fingers also were covered with them, the middle finger only remaining free. Some people put all the rings on their smallest finger; others put on it only one ring, to distinguish that which they use for sealing." Rich people had several sets of rings; lighter ones for the summer, heavier ones for the winter. Large public and private dactyliothecæ existed in Rome, where the cameos brought home from foreign wars were exhibited. The well-known Scaurus, for instance, owned a collection of cameos amongst his Greek art-treasures ; Pompey placed a rich collection of cameos, taken from Mithridates, in the Capitol as a votive offering ; Cæsar gave six collections of the same kind to the temple of Venus Genetrix.

To conclude, we mention the buckles and brooches (*fibulæ*) destined to fasten the palla of women, and the ends of the toga and paludamentum of men, on the right shoulder ; they stood the ancients in the stead of our buttons, hooks, and pins, and are frequently found on the sites of habitations or on battle-fields. At first they consisted of bronze, afterwards of silver and gold, frequently studded with jewels and cameos, *fibulæ gemmatæ.* Aurelian permitted the wearing of gold instead of silver buckles, even to common soldiers. The most common forms of the buckle are shown, Fig. 478.

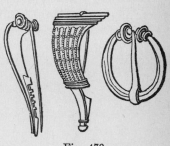

Fig. 478.

Mirrors of glass were unknown to the Romans : their mirrors were made of polished metal, either square or round in form. The handle attached to it served to hold the mirror in the hand, or to suspend it by, if not used (Fig. 476, *g*, compare Fig. 228). Mirrors hanging on the wall appear in numerous vase-paintings ; valuable specimens were kept in cases. Other mirrors could be placed upright (Fig. 476, *d*). The handle and the back and border of the mirror afforded opportunities for engraved or bas-relief ornamentation. At first mirrors were made of a composition of tin and copper ; Pasiteles, a contemporary of Pompey, is said to have introduced silver mirrors. In Pliny's time the back of the mirror used to be gilt, which was thought to add to the power of the reflecting surface. Seneca (" Quæst. Nat.," I. 17) complains that for one of the large upright gold or silver mirrors, equal in size to a grown-up person (*specula totis corporibus paria*), larger sums were expended than were given by the State as dowry to the daughters of poor generals. The poorer classes had to be satisfied with a composition of copper and lead, imitating, or plated with, silver. Numerous specimens of a peculiar kind of mirror have been found amongst the ruins of the old Præneste,

and in several burial-places of Etruria. Their form and ornamentation distinguishes them from other mirrors. They are
known by the name of Etruscan metal mirrors, and have been
described by Gerhard in his work, "Die etruskischen Spiegel"
(4 vols., Berlin, 1838—1869). They are either perfectly round or
have the shape of a pear ; their backs show engravings of mythological or realistic scenes, for the greater part slovenly imitations
of Greek originals ; the treatment of the figures is repulsively soft
and sensuous ; only few of them have artistic value. Many of
these mirrors, particularly those found at Præneste, have been
discovered together with other toilette articles in cylindrical boxes
with curved lids, made of wood covered with leather and studded
with metal, or consisting entirely of metal. These boxes, owing
to their resemblance to the holy snake-baskets, frequently occurring on monuments, have been called mystic boxes (*cista mystica*).
Owing to the engravings on the back of the mirrors (resembling
those on the *cista*), and to the slightly bent borders of the
reflecting surface, these mirrors have been for a long time
mistaken for pateræ, which they somewhat resemble in form.
Gerhard's opinion, however, of their being nothing but mirrors
of early Etruscan make has, at present, been generally adopted.

About the mysteries of the toilette of Roman ladies, merci-
lessly laid bare by the authors of imperial times, we shall say
little. Great care was particularly bestowed on the complexion,
and on the artificial reproduction of other charms, lost too soon in
the exciting atmosphere of imperial court-life. During the night
a mask (*tectorium*) of dough and ass's milk was laid on the face,
to preserve the complexion ; this mask was an invention of
Poppæa, the wife of Nero, hence its name *Poppæana*. Another
mask, composed of rice and bean-flour, served to remove the
wrinkles from the face. It was washed off in the morning with
tepid ass's milk (Juvenal, VI. 467), and the face afterwards
bathed in fresh ass's milk several times in the course of the day.
Poppæa was, for the purpose, always accompanied in her travels
by herds of she-asses (Pliny, "Nat. Hist.," XXVIII. 12). The
two chief paints used for the face were a white (*creta, cerussa*) and
a red substance (*fucus minium, purpurissum*), moistened with
spittle. Brows and eyelashes were dyed black, or painted over ;
even the veins on the temples were marked with lines of a tender

blue colour. Many different pastes and powders were used to
preserve and clean the teeth. Artificial teeth made of ivory and
fastened with gold thread were known to the Romans at the time
when the laws of the twelve tablets were made, one of which laws
prohibits the deposition of gold in the graves of the dead,
excepting the material required for the fastening of false teeth.

98. In order somewhat to illustrate our remarks on the Roman
cuisine, we reproduce (Fig. 479) one of the numerous wall-paintings at Pompeii and Herculaneum, illustrative of the various
dainties of the table, such as grapes, apples, pears, quinces, figs,
mushrooms, sometimes kept in transparent glass vessels; also
game, fish, and shell-fish; the composition of these groups

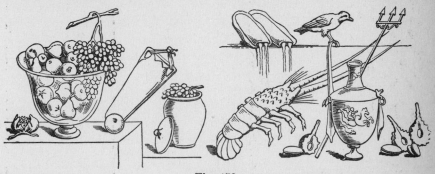

Fig. 479.

reminds us somewhat of the still-lives of the older Dutch
school.*

The breakfast (*ientaculum, iantaculum*) of the Romans, taken
earlier or later according to the hour of rising, consisted of bread,
dipped in wine or flavoured with salt, grapes, olives, cheese, milk,
and eggs. Luncheon (*prandium*), consisting of more solid dishes,
both hot and cold, was taken about the middle of the day, or at
the sixth hour, according to Roman nomenclature. The chief
meal, or dinner (*cena*), was taken about the ninth hour, between
noon and sunset. The poorer classes at all periods chiefly fed on
porridge (*puls*) made of a farinaceous substance (*far, ador*), which
served them as bread, besides vegetables, such as cabbage

* Compare "Mus. Borb.," VIII., Tavs. 20, 57. "Pitture antiche d'Ercolano,"
vol. ii. Tavs. 56 *et seq.*; iii. Tav. 55.

(*brassica*), turnips and radishes (*napus, beta, pastinaca*), leak (*porrum*), garlic (*allium*), onions (*cepa*), pulse (*legumina*), cucumber (*cucumis*), pumpkins (*cucurbita*), melons (*melo*), &c. Meat was eaten only on festive occasions. In early times the arrangements of the kitchen were in harmony with the simplicity of the dishes prepared there; slaves and masters partook, according to Pliny, of the same fare. On particular occasions professional cooks were hired, who offered their services in the *macellum* or market. After the Roman conquests in Greece and Asia the diet of the richer classes, with regard to both the number and quality of the dishes, became essentially altered. Simple vegetables sufficed no longer; various kinds of meat and fish, delicately flavoured, salads, and rare fruits were found in their stead. A numerous staff of domestic cooks and scullions was required to prepare even the ordinary meals. A particular slave was retained for baking the pastry—an office formerly held by the women of the household. Experienced cooks and pastrycooks received high wages. Upon the whole, however, over-refinement of taste was less the fault of the Romans than disgusting gluttony—a vice which reached its climax between the battle of Actium and the reign of Vespasian, during which period prohibitive laws against luxury, repeated eight different times, were vainly put in force to put a stop to it.

The smaller kind of fish, such as *lacertus, mœna*, and *mullus* (mullet), were eaten chiefly by the poorer and middle classes; the larger mullus, on the contrary, was one of the most expensive dainties. Its price increased with its size, one of 4 lbs. being paid with 1,000 sestertii, one of 6 lbs. with 6,000 sestertii, and so forth in increasing proportion. Other fish much appreciated were the *murœna* (a sort of salt-water eel, caught particularly in the Straits of Sicily and Tartessus), the *rhombus* (flounder, generally imported from Ravenna), the *aurata*, the *lupus* (pike, kept in ponds), also the various kinds of salt and preserved fish (collectively called τάριχος), which were imported from the Pontine, Sardinian, and Spanish coasts. Various sauces (*garum, muria alec*) served to flavour the fish. Amongst shell-fish or mussels we mention the eatable purple snail (*murex*), the *echinus*, different slugs (*cochlea*), and, most important of all, the oyster (*ostrea*), called by Pliny ("Nat. Hist.," XXXII. 6, 21) *palma mensarum divitum.* In order to have the fish always ready at hand the Romans constructed fish-ponds (Lucinius Muræna is said to have set the example), filled with salt or fresh water (*dulces* or *salsæ*), according to the nature of the fish kept in them. These *piscinæ*, or *vivaria piscium*, were connected with canals, to renew the water, the openings of which were closed with iron grates. Lucullus had a canal dug through a ridge of mountains by the sea in order to supply his piscinæ with salt water. Other celebrated piscinæ were those of the orator Hortensius at Bauli, near Baiæ; according to Pliny (IX., 55, 81), he shed tears at the death of one of his murænæ. Antonina, the wife of Drusus, is said to have adorned a favourite fish of the same kind with ear-rings. The breeding and taming of fish was a favourite occupation with fashionable idlers. The invention of oyster-banks (*vivaria ostrearum*) is ascribed to the gourmand, Sergius Orata (his second name was given him from his preference for the fish called *orata*). Snail-preserves were first kept by Fulvius Lupinus, in the neighbourhood of Tarquinii. The different kinds of snails (Illyrian, African, &c.) were carefully kept apart, and fed on flour mixed with thickened must. The Romans also had preserves of birds (*vivaria avium*, or *aviaria*), as, for instance, of ordinary poultry, fig-thrushes, guinea-fowls, pheasants, peacocks, and of the favourite fieldfare. As the inventor of the aviaries M. Lænius Strato, of Brundusium, is mentioned. Hortensius was the first to treat his guests to roast peacock, having imported the bird from Samos. Peacocks, like pheasants (introduced from Asia) and fieldfare, were kept in great numbers in the aviaries; the two latter birds, and the eggs of the former, being considered great delicacies. For many of the wealthy Romans their ponds and aviaries were, moreover, a considerable source of income, derived from the sale of fish and birds.

Hares and rabbits were favourite dainties, the former being kept in so-called *leporaria*. In the Balearic Islands the rabbits repeatedly destroyed the harvest, and the inhabitants had to apply to Augustus for military assistance, in order to diminish their number. We also mention kids (of which the finest were imported from Ambracia), pigs, and boars. Pliny ("Nat. Hist.," VIII. 51, 77) remarks that, while other animals are only partly eatable, the pig furnishes no less than fifty different dainties.

The parts eaten in preference were the udder (*sumen*), the womb (*vulva*), and the liver, the latter being artificially enlarged by a diet invented by the *chef* Marcus Apicius. Pork ham (*perna*) and sausages (*botulus, tomaculum*) also were much liked, the latter being carried about the streets in portable ovens, and cried out by the sausage-vendors (*botularii*).

Amongst plants used for the excellent salads of the Romans we mention rue (*ruta*), lettuce (*lactuca*), cress (*lepidium*), mallows, (*malva*), and sorrel (*lapathum*). To these indigenous plants others, brought from the kitchen-gardens of the provinces, were added.

Italy was particularly rich in fruit-trees, both indigenous and acclimatised. Varro calls the Peninsula one large orchard. Apples, particularly honey-apples (*melimela*), pears, plums, cherries. quinces, peaches, pomegranates, figs, nuts, chestnuts, grapes, olives, &c., were found on all good tables. Other fruits and cereals, however, now commonly found in Italy and most parts of Southern Europe, were unknown to the Romans. Melons, oranges, lemons, citrons, and bitter oranges (*Pomeranzen*) were not grown in Italy in Pliny's time. Melons and citrons began to be cultivated in the first century after Christ. Lemons and bitter oranges came to Europe in the time of the Crusades; while the orange was imported from China by the Portuguese as late as the sixteenth century. Of corn the Romans only knew wheat and barley; oats, rye, maize, and rice were unknown to them.

Of particular importance from a culinary point of view was naturally the *cena*. In older times it consisted of two—later of three—courses, the entrées (*gustus, gustatio*) being composed of such dishes as were supposed to excite the appetite, for instance, mussels, light kinds of fish, soft eggs, salad, cabbage, &c. With these was drunk a mixture of honey and wine or must (the proportions being four-fifths wine to one-fifth honey, or ten-eleventh must to one-eleventh honey), so as to prepare the stomach for the richer wines. This mixture was called *mulsum*, whence this part of the meal also received the name *promulsis*. After these entrées the cena proper was put on the table. It con-sisted of three courses (*ferculum*), called respectively *prima, altera*, and *tertia cena*. The dishes of each of these courses were brought in simultaneously on a tray (*repositorium*). The dessert (*mensæ*

secundæ) consisted of confectionery, preserves, and dried and fresh
fruits. We subjoin the *menu* of a *cena pontificalis* given by
Lentulus about the middle of the last century of the Republic,
in celebration of his entering on his priestly office. We give the
original words of Macrobius, leaving it to the reader to find
or imagine approximate modern equivalents for the dainties specified : " *Cœna*," Macrobius says ("Saturn.," III. 13), " *hæc fuit :*
Ante cœnam *echinos, ostreas crudas, quantum vellent, peloridas,
sphondylos, turdum asparagos subtus, gallinam altilem, patinam
ostrearum peloridum, balanos nigros, balanos albos: iterum sphondylos,
glycomaridas urticas ficedulas, lumbos capraginos, aprugnos, altilia,
ex farina involuta, ficedulas murices et purpuras.* In cœna *sumina,
sinciput aprugnum, patinam piscium, patinam suminis, anates,
querquedulas elixas, lepores, altilia assa, amulum, panes Picentes.*"
We also refer the reader to the amusing description of Trimalchio's
feast in Petronius.

Of drinks we have already mentioned the *mulsum* and the
various kinds of wine. Like the Greeks, the Romans used to
mix the wine with water ; as to the strength of the mixture
we are not informed accurately. To drink unmixed wine (*merum
bibere*) was considered a sign of intemperance ; even the adding
of but little water (*meracius bibere*) did not escape reproof; a
rather weak mixture was considered proper for a sober man
(*homo frugi*). The strength of the mixture, however, was left
to the decision of every individual; youthful slaves (*pueri ad
cyathos, ministri vini, pocillatores*) prepared the mixture, adding
either hot water or snow, according to taste and season. The
hot beverage was called *calda*, and we still possess a beautiful
chiselled bronze vessel destined for its preparation. It has two
handles, and rests on three lions' claws ; the cover, fastened to it
with a hinge, is of conical shape (see the picture of the vessel in
Overbeck's "Pompeii," p. 312). In the middle of the vessel
is a cylindrical case for the hot coal, with a receptacle for the
ashes at the bottom. A separate cover closes the space round this
cylinder, containing the calda. A tap, about the middle of the
vessel, served to emit the fluid, which was poured in by means of
a pipe let into the upper rim on the opposite side. During the
cena the drinking was moderate ; but after, it not seldom followed
a drinking-bout (*comissatio*), at which the customs and jokes of

the Greek symposion were frequently imitated *(Græco more bibere)*. With their heads and lower limbs crowned with flowers, the topers reclined round the table after the dishes had been removed. A master or king of the feast *(magister,* or *rex convivii, arbiter bibendi)* was chosen by a cast of the dice, the cast of Venus being decisive, as in the case of the βασιλεύς. The healths were drunk of present persons (who had then to drain the goblet), with the words, *bene tibi, vivas,* or of absent friends ; in later times, particularly of the emperor and the army. In case a lady was the object of the toast, the number of cyathi (wine-glasses of moderate size) to be drained consecutively was equal in number to the letters of her name *(nomen bibere;* compare Martial, I. 72). Cicero compares the end of a convivium given by Verres (Verr., V. 11) to the end of the battle of Cannæ, where some were carried away disabled, while others remained in an unconscious state on the field of battle.

Besides witty conversation, many games of hazard and bets tended to enliven and excite the guests. Particularly games of dice *(alea),* although prohibited by the law, were often secretly indulged in (compare our description of this game, p. 270). Prohibitive laws, and the legal determination that complaints of cheating or misconduct at gambling-places were not admissible in courts of justice, were unable to check the passion for gambling, which was carried on on an enormous scale in private houses and *popinæ.* Games at dice were permitted only when no money was staked, as were also the various more intellectual games played on a board, such as the *ludus latrunculorum,* resembling our chess, played on a *tabula latrunculoria* divided in squares ; the purpose was, by means of clever drawing *(ciere),* to take away or block up *(ligare, alligare, obligare)* the men of the adversary, so as to checkmate him *(ad incitas redigitur).* The men *(latrones)* consisted of pieces *(calculi)* of glass, ivory, or metal, coloured in different ways, and used in a different manner ; the *mandræ,* for instance, were a particular kind of men in one game. Another game of this class was the *ludus duodecim scriptorum,* played on a board divided into twenty-four parts by means of twelve parallel lines and one transverse line. Each move *(dare calculum)* of the fifteen men, black and white in colour, was determined by a previous cast of the dice. Augustus diverted his guests by a lottery with valuable prizes, such as pictures of Greek masters, turned with their backs to those partaking in the game. Culti-vated people used to amuse their guests with reading or vocal and instrumental music, to which, however, objection was occasionally taken (compare Martial, IX. 77). Less innocent were the dances and scenic representations performed at these feasts by actors and dancers of both sexes since the time of Sulla; even fights of gladiators are said to have taken place at meals on a few occasions.

99. Public bathing-establishments have already been men-tioned (§ 80). Originally bathing was with the Roman a matter of health and cleanliness only, in consequence of which the older bathing-establishments were undoubtedly of a very simple kind. Of these older buildings no traces remain; all the splendid buildings described by us (compare Figs. 419—423) belong to a later and more refined period. The chief additions made to the simple cold and tepid baths of older times were the sudatory bath, and the numerous accommodations for walks, conversation, and gymnastic exercises found in all later establishments.

The usual time of taking a bath was the eighth or ninth hour, or indeed any time shortly before the hour of the cena, which greatly varied according to the occupation or convenience of individuals. For that reason the public baths were open during the greater part of the day till sunset. In imperial times they continued open during part of the night, as is proved by numerous lamps found in thermæ, and by the marks of lamp-soot on the walls of the baths of Pompeii. The opening and closing of the establishment was announced by the sound of a bell. Each visitor had first to pay an entrance-fee, which differed according to the accommodation offered, but amounted on the average to a *quadrans* for men. The janitor threw the money into a box (as has been concluded from a box of this kind found in the portico of the thermæ of Pompeii), and returned to the bather a ticket to be delivered to the bathing-master. Some-times this entrance-fee was remitted to the people by the ædiles desirous to gain popularity. The ædile Agrippa, while in office, built one hundred and seventy bathing-chambers, to which every-body was admitted gratis for the space of one year; on his death, he left his magnificent private thermæ to the people. In the apodyteria of the Pompeian thermæ we still see the holes in the walls into which the pegs for suspending the clothes were inserted. The bather next entered the tepidarium (sudatory bath), where the dry rubbing (*destringere*) also took place, whence he proceeded to the *caldarium* to take a hot bath originally in a tub (*alveus*), in later times in a large reservoir; in a niche of this room stood the flat *labrum* with cold water. A cold plunge in the *cisterna* or *piscina* of the *frigidarium* terminated the bath proper. Afterwards the bather went into the *unctorium* to be rubbed, or rub himself, with oil; sometimes this took place in the tepidarium. Even before, and in the intervals of, the bath the bather was frequently anointed, a slave carrying the oil-bottles (*ampulla olearia*), the scraper (*strigilis*), to remove oil and perspi-

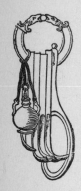

ration from the skin, and the linen towels (*lintea*) after his master to the bath (compare the bathing-apparatus Fig. 480). Soap became known only in imperial times; in its stead were previously used by the poorer classes a sort of paste made of the fruit of the lupine (*lomentum*), by wealthy people different ointments. After the bath the hair and skin were again rubbed with odoriferous ointment; even the clothes were scented. For these scented ointments were used native flowers, and shrubs like the rose, crocus, myrtle, cypress, or Oriental ingre-

Fig. 480.

dients, which, if genuine, were bought at enormous prices. Amongst the most valuable of these Oriental ointments was the *nardium oleum*, made of Indian or Arabian nard. It was kept in bottles of precious metals or stone, such as the alabastron mentioned by us on a former occasion. Scented powders (*diapasmata*) were strewn over the body; the water was mixed with saffron and other scents, in addition to which the limbs after the bath were stretched, and the whole body rubbed with swan's-down or purple sponges. The laconicum above described was the place for sudatory cures frequently repaired to by the gourmands of imperial times.

The increasing luxury of Roman manners became particularly visible in the interior arrangements of the baths. Seneca speaks of the decorations of private bath-chambers with the most valuable kinds of marble or with glass; even the taps of the

water-pipes had to be made of silver. The elder Pliny says,
that many Roman ladies would not think of entering a bath
without silver fittings. This luxury of private baths was far
surpassed by the enormous public thermæ of imperial times,
where fashionable Romans passed a great part of their day in
luxurious idleness or animating conversation. The large thermæ
of Agrippa, in the Campus Martius, have already been mentioned ; near them lay (between the modern Piazza Navona and
the Pantheon) the thermæ Neronianæ, called, after their enlargement by Alexander Severus, thermæ Alexandrinæ. After these
follow in chronological order the thermæ of Titus, Trajan, Commodus, the thermæ Antoninianæ built by Caracalla, the thermæ
of Decius, Diocletian, and of Constantine. The ruins of other
thermæ, although smaller in size than those of the metropolis,
are found in provincial towns, almost every year adding a new
discovery of substructures, which, by their hypocausta, can be
recognised as Roman baths. Besides these common baths, the
Romans knew and used the medicinal powers of mineral springs.
From the waters of the Rhenish country, such as the *aquæ Mat-
tiacæ* (Wiesbaden) or *aquæ Aureliæ* (Baden-Baden), to the numerous springs on the slope of the Atlas, the *aquæ Tibilitanæ,* and
other *aquæ calidæ*—from the "Baths of Hercules," near Mehadia,
in Siebenbürgen, to the waters of Bagnères in the Pyrenees—few
medicinal wells had escaped the notice of the Romans ; many
votive inscriptions tell of successful cures in these places, which
frequently also show the remains of old bathing-houses. The
watering-places of the Romans, like those of modern times, were
frequented by both sick and healthy ; some, indeed, Baiæ
foremost amongst them, became centres of fashionable life and
amusement. The beautiful air and scenery, and the vicinity of
Naples, Puteoli, Cumæ, and Misenum, the chief station of the navy,
not to speak of the hot sulphur wells, the steam of which led by
means of pipes into the sudatoria was considered a remedy of
various illnesses,—all this tended to make Baiæ a fashionable
watering-place. The dance, the chase, gambling and other vices,
were the order of the day, and indulged in with even greater
freedom than in Rome. Seneca calls Baiæ the seat of vice
("diversorium vitiorum "), a term which, in a modified sense, may
have applied to many of the smaller watering-places.

Of the accommodations for games, walks, and conversation connected with the thermæ we have spoken before. *H* in the plan of the Pompeian thermæ (Fig. 420) signifies a court surrounded on two sides by colonnades, while a third is occupied by a vaulted hall receiving its light through large windows. This court was the *ambulatio* (walk), the hall (Fig. 420, *I*) being destined for conversation. For gymnastic exercise previous to the bath no separate space is assigned ; in the thermæ of Cara- calla (Fig. 422) we find, on the contrary, ephebea, conisteria, and places for the spectators at wrestling competitions. Together with the youths, men of riper years took part in these exercises, the abstaining from which was a matter of reproof except in cases where bodily infirmities or a learned occupation (as in Cicero's case) were considered as sufficient excuse. These gym- nastic exercises, however, never attained amongst the Romans the high development of Greek agonistic games. In Rome these exercises were chiefly considered as a preparatory school for actual warfare : the principal ones amongst them were the throwing of the disc, the use of dumb-bells, fencing with a wooden sword against a pole (*palus*, *stipes*, frequently practised by grown-up people before their bath), wrestling, and running. Although the Greek scheme was thus essentially adopted by the Romans, their public games took an entirely different character from those of the Greeks : instead of the καλοκαγαθία, the chief aim of the Romans was enjoyment. They merely assembled to witness the agonistic prowess and skill of professional athletes, notwithstanding the attempts made in imperial times at intro- ducing the Greek agones in their full significance. The same was the case in the thermæ : members of the guilds of professional wrestlers showed their skill, the wealthy Roman looking on and preferring for himself some easier means of exercise. For this purpose a sphæristerium was added to most larger private houses, consisting, like those of the thermæ, of open or covered halls, in which young and old previously to taking a bath practised some easy kind of gymnastic exercise, as, particularly, the game at ball.

We have described at some length (p. 228) this game as played by the Greeks : we therefore add only a few remarks with regard to Roman peculiarities. Three kinds of balls were used, viz. the *follis* (a large ball filled with air), *pila*, and *paganica*. The ball was thrown up, and caught, and thrown back again by the different players—a game described in the words *datatim ludere*. Another kind of game at ball is described by the words *expulsim ludere :* as to its nature we know nothing ; it is, perhaps, identical with an exciting game played by modern Italians, in which the ball before touching the ground has to be caught, and thrown back with a wooden ring round the under part of the right arm. The *paganica* was a ball stuffed with feathers, as to the use of which we have no means of information. The game at ball could be played by two or more persons ; the name *trigon* or *pila trigonalis* indicates three players, who, if skilful, threw and caught the ball with the left hand. The *harpastum*, according to Athenæus originally called φαινίνϛα, admitted of any number of players ; it was a rough exciting game : one or more balls were thrown up into the air by one person, whereat the players standing next tried to catch them. The interior of a sphæristerium or tennis-court is shown in Fig. 260, taken from a wall-painting in the thermæ of Titus. Boys, however, used to improvise sphæristeria in the streets and squares of Rome, particularly in front of the butchers' booths in the Forum Romanum.

100. Trades and handicrafts were, according to the aristocratic notions of the Romans, somewhat beneath the dignity of a free citizen ; even commerce, particularly retail traffic, was little esteemed. Landed property on a large scale was the only source of income not unworthy of a free Roman of good position in society. Cicero in his " De Officiis " expounds this view at some length ; he, however, makes a distinction between the trades according to their usefulness and to the intellectual faculties required by them. Commerce, if carried on honestly and on a large scale, is to some extent approved of, particularly if its proceeds are invested in landed property, the only source of income quite worthy of the Roman gentleman.

Slaves and freedmen were the chief tradesmen and mechanics, the former supplying the various requirements of the household, the latter working for payment and selling their wares in shops. The list of slaves attached to a wealthy Roman household comprises handicraftsmen of almost every kind. For the present we omit the slaves employed in agriculture and horticulture : we mention a complete staff of architects, &c. (*architecti, fabri, tectores, pictores*), tailors and hairdressers (*vestiarii, pænularii, cosmetæ, tonsores*), cooks, pastrycooks, &c. (*pistores, coqui, dulciarii, fartores, placentarii*), together with slaves employed in the triclinium (*triclinarii*, with the triclinarchus at their head, *structores, scissores*) ; also musicians and troops of mimics and jugglers. Physicians and surgeons were mostly slaves or freedmen; the important post of private secretary of the master of the house also was occupied by a slave.

The numerous class of the slaves was recruited by the children of slaves, captives taken on the field of battle or in conquered cities, and sold at once by the quæstor accompanying the army,[*] and by slaves continually imported from other slave-holding countries. Slave-traders (*mangones, venalicii*) always followed the armies, or bought their human wares in the chief markets of Rome and Delos, &c. Ordinary slaves were exhibited on a scaffolding (*catasta*) erected for the purpose : a tablet (*titulus*) fastened to the neck of the captive indicated his country, age, corporal and intellectual achievements or debilities, as also his guiltlessness of crime. Accomplished slaves, particularly of Greek origin, were kept in separate rooms of taverns, and shown only to wealthy customers. To distinguish them from free-born captives, the children of slave parents or of a slave mother were called *vernæ* or home-slaves, in reference to the masters to whom they belonged by birth.

All the slaves belonging to a master were collectively called *familia*. In older times their number was small, the work of the simple town household or of the farm (the latter, for the greater part, performed by the owner himself) not requiring many hands. As town and country houses grew larger and more splendid, the number of slaves had to be increased accordingly. For almost every one of the many services required by the luxurious owner and his family a separate slave was kept, this perfect division of labour being considered characteristic of a grand house. The slaves employed in the town house were called *familia urbana*, those attached to the villa *familia rustica*, a distinction which, however, was not always strictly kept, the same slaves often serving both

---

[*] Such captives where crowned with a wreath to show their being for sale whence the expression—*sub corona venire.*

purposes, at least amongst the less wealthy classes. Some of the slaves even of rich people occasionally followed their master from the *villa urbana* to the *villa rustica*.

The *latifundia* taking the place of the old farms naturally required a much larger staff of labourers. Besides the agricultural slaves proper, employed in ploughing, sowing, reaping, or attending to olive-trees and vines, gardeners for orchard, kitchen, and flower gardens were required ; not to speak of those who had to take care of the poultry-yard, the fish-pond, the beehive, and the game cover. Sometimes several thousands of slaves were required for these various purposes.

Another class of slaves were those employed in the household, or waiting upon the master and his family. Amongst the lower domestic slaves (*vulgares*) we mention first the *ostiarius* or *janitor*, who, from his box (*ostiaria*), had to watch the entrance of the house, and the *cubicularii*, who had to keep bedrooms and sitting-rooms in order, and also to announce visitors. In the houses of rich people a particular *nomenclator* was appointed for the latter purpose, whose office it was to call out the names of clients who came to say their matutinal *Ave* (*salutatio*) to their patronus, and of numerous other visitors thronging the vestibule in the early hours of the day. The same nomenclator had often to accompany his master in his walks, to recall to his memory the names and circumstances of persons met in the street whose vote or assistance were required for a particular purpose.

The wealthy Roman was always accompanied by one or more slaves (*pedisequus*), who had to carry any object that might be required at the bath or a party, and also to act as torch-bearers on returning at night. Another class of slaves were the *lectiarii*, or carriers of sedan-chairs, which, about the end of the Republic, had become the usual means of conveyance in travelling. In town only senators and ladies were allowed to be carried in them, a law which, most likely, was often infringed. We have to distinguish the litter (*lectica*), a frame with straps to support a mattrass and pillow, and the sedan-chair (*lectica operta*) with a canopy (*arcus*), and curtains (*vela, plagæ, plagulæ*) that could be pulled up or down. The latter means of conveyance was always used by modest women ; it resembled the modern Oriental palankeen, and is said to have been introduced from the East, together with numerous other Oriental customs, after the defeat of Antiochus by the Romans. Strong slaves, in rich red liveries, carried the litter on their shoulders by means of poles (*asseres*) passed under its bottom.* Syrians, Germans, Celts, Liburnians, and Mœsians, in later times particularly Cappadocians, were employed as carriers, their number varying with the size of the litter. A portable chair (*sella gestatoria* or *portatoria*) was introduced by Claudius, and used chiefly by emperors and consulares; it was covered at the top, and could be closed with curtains. One or several litters, with slaves to carry them, were found in every good Roman household; there were, however, in Rome litters on hire, the stand (*castra lecticariorum*) of which was in the "XIV. regio trans Tiberim."

Besides litters, carriages were employed on travels; their use in Rome, and most likely also in the colonies and municipia, was restricted by law. Under the Republic respectable women were allowed to drive in town, a privilege taken away from them in imperial times. Vestals, Flamines, and the Rex sacrorum in certain sacred processions, as also the triumphing general, and the magistrates in the procession preceding the festive *ludi circenses*, were allowed to drive in carriages. Even carts with merchandise, &c., were forbidden to appear in the streets of Rome during the ten hours from sunrise to sunset (by the *lex Julia*, passed 45 B.C.), with the exception of those destined to transport the materials of the large buildings. With the beginning of the third century carriages became more frequent in the cities, although their use remained the privilege of the highest imperial officials. We possess many representations of carts and carriages, the classification of which according to the expressions found in the authors is not always possible. The body of the carriage is generally clumsy, while the wheels, with spokes (*rota radiata*), are almost always of a graceful shape. On the monument of Igel (Fig. 414) we see a small open carriage on two wheels drawn by mules, in which two persons are seated; perhaps we may recognise in it a *cisium* or *essedum*. Another richly decorated carriage (*carpentum*), also on two wheels, but with an awning to it, appears on the coins of Julia, daughter of Titus, and on those of Agrippina,

---

* A small terra-cotta, not yet reproduced, in the Museo Borbonico at Naples shows two men carrying a litter in the manner described.

daughter of Germanicus. Fig. 481 shows a two-wheeled travelling carriage (*covinus?*) with an awning. *Reda* and *curruca*, mentioned by the authors as large travelling-carriages for several persons, do not appear on the monuments; where, on the other hand, we frequently meet with carts and waggons loaded with rural produce, merchandise, armour, &c.; the generic term for these is *plaustrum*, the expressions *sarracum*, *carrus*, and *arcera* marking subdivisions no longer definable by us. Fig. 450 shows a four-wheeled market-cart with a wineskin on it; Fig. 482 (from a mosaic found at Orbe, in Switzerland), a cart, drawn by two oxen,

Fig. 481.

the load of which is secured against rain by a blanket; even the step to mount the cart has not been omitted. On the arch of Severus (compare Fig. 535) and the column of Antoninus we see a number of baggage-carts, some of them on two wheels with spokes, others on massive round discs of wood (*tympanum*), all laden with pieces of armour and provisions in sacks and barrels. Bronze rings attached to the collars of horses, bits, and other parts of the harness, as well as the ends of poles shaped like animals' heads, exist in numerous specimens.*

Numerous slaves followed the travelling-carriage or litter of the wealthy Roman, the scnty accommodation of the inns making a complete travelling apparatus a matter of necessity. The members of the imperial family and other wealthy Romans took a pride in their travelling equipment, and the precious plate and carpets carried after them by a numerous train of pack-horses. Numidian horsemen, forerunners, negroes, &c., saddle-

Fig. 482.

* See Lindenschmit, "Die Alterthümer unserer heidnischen Vorzeit," vol. i. Part II. 5, and vol. ii. Part X. 3, 5.

horses, grooms, domestic and body slaves, preceded the caravan
or brought up the rear.

Amongst the slaves (*vulgares*) we further mention the tailors of
the master and his family, also valets and chambermaids, besides
which lower slaves the Romans used to keep a number of other
menials to amuse them and their guests, particularly at table, such
as bands of musicians (*pueri symphoniaci*), mimics, dancers of both
sexes, gladiators (who frequently accompanied the master in his
walks), jugglers, and rope-dancers (compare our description of the
Greek symposion, p. 269, Figs. 305—

Fig. 483.

307). About the arts of these acrobats
and rope-dancers (*funambuli, schœnobatœ*)
we hear astonishing accounts from the
ancient authors. Even elephants were
trained to mount the rope (Pliny, VIII.
2, 3). Fig. 483 shows the reverse of a
coin of Cyzicus (a city celebrated for its
acrobatic feats) illustrating the mounting
of a rope. We also hear of *petauristœ*
amongst the domestic slaves, *i.e.* flying
men, who rose into the air by means of the *petauron* or flying-
machine, the construction of which, in the absence of monumental
evidence, cannot be sufficiently understood from the meagre
accounts of the authors.

Amongst domestic slaves we also mention the unfortunate
beings whose bodily or intellectual frailties were the laughing-stock
of their master (*moriones, fatui,* and *fatuœ*). Dwarfs of both sexes
(*nani, nanœ*), who were taught to fight and dance, were particular
favourites with ladies. A pet dwarf of Julia, the granddaughter
of Augustus, was only two feet one palm high; his name was
Canopas. Two bronze statuettes found at Pompeii represent two
crippled, misshapen forms with large heads, one of them dancing
and beating the castanets, the other clad in a toga, with a
bulla fastened to a chain round his neck, and holding a writing-
tablet in his hand (compare also " Pitture d'Ercol.," vol. ii.,
Tavs. 91, 92).

Several overseers were employed in keeping the numerous
slaves in order; the higher officials of this kind had also to
superintend the management of the house, the stores, &c. The

procurator, the first person amongst the *familia* of slaves, managed the income and domestic expense of his master. The agent of the landed property was called *actor*, to whom, in case he had no agricultural knowledge, a practical farmer (*vilicus*) was given as assistant. At the villa urbana the *atriensis*, or steward, kept the accounts, at least in older times; afterwards this became the business of a separate official, *dispensator*, the atriensis being limited to the superintendence of domestic arrangements. The *cellarius* or *promus* had the keys to store-room and wine-cellar. The higher slaves of the last-mentioned kind were collectively called *ordinarii*.

An important position was held by the *lectores* or *anagnostæ*, slaves who had to read out to their master while at table or in the bath, and to write from dictation, copy documents, or take care of the library.

We finally mention the physicians and surgeons, who, at least in republican times, belonged for the greater part to the classes of slaves and freedmen.

The position of the slave amongst the Romans was widely different from that of his fellow-sufferer in Greece. In the latter country the mutual positions of master and slave were legally defined, the right of punishing or even killing a slave being considerably limited by the law. Different in Rome: here the slave was the absolute property of the master, unprotected by the law against his cruelty. The harshness of this relation was, of course, in individual cases, modified by the humanity of the master or the usefulness of the slave; but as many of his numerous slaves were hardly known to the master, they were, particularly in the country, at the mercy of overseers. This, of course, was not to be feared in earlier times, when the slaves sat down to their meals on lower benches (*subsellia*) at the foot of their master's couch, or when the latter shared the labour of the field with his servants. But the attachment thus engendered disappeared with the increasing luxury of later times, which banished most of the slaves from any familiar intercourse with their owners. They now had their rations (*demensum*) dealt out to them by the day or month, and with the savings out of these (*peculium*), to which the master had no right, the slaves frequently bought their liberty; unless they tried the shorter way of theft and defraudation, undaunted by the cruel punishment to which their slightest misdemeanours were liable. The pride of a freeman made captive on the field of battle could ill brook such treatment, whence the furious determination with which the death-struggle of the revolted slaves was carried on. Refractory slaves had their legs fettered with *compedes,* so as to make their escape impossible, or, loaded with iron collars (*collare*) and manacles (*manica*), they were imprisoned in dungeons (*ergastulum, pistrinum*) built on most farms for the purpose, or condemned to hard labour in the quarries. Flagellation with a stick, rod, or whip was a common punishment (*fustis, virga, mastix*), as was also the carrying of the *furca,* a fork-like instrument laid round the neck, the arms being tied to the protruding front part of the furca. Runaway slaves, or those found guilty of theft, had the initial letters of the crime branded on their foreheads with a hot iron (*stigma,* whence their name *stigmosi* or *literati*). Their capital punishment was crucifixion (*in crucem ager, figere*), or being thrown into the *vivaria,* or opposed to wild animals in the amphitheatre.

Slaves were, of course, forbidden to wear the toga. Their costume was the tunica, of coarse dark materials, worn in the manner of the Greek exomis, to which workman's costume a pænula or lacerna might be added in bad weather. Other slaves, who had to wait personally on the master and his family, most likely wore a finer tunic of lighter colours.

After his liberation (*manumissio*) had been granted, the slave stood to his patron in the relation of a *libertus.* This manumissio was effected by the patron presenting himself with his slave before the highest magistrate of the city: after having proved his right of possession (*iusta servitus*), he pronounced the words, "Hunc hominem ego volo liberum esse," whereat the *assertor* (without whom the slave could not appear in a legal transaction, not having yet received his liberty) touched the slave with a rod on the top of his head, or, according to a later custom, boxed his ear. After this the patron took his former slave by the hand, turned him round, and ended the ceremony by once more repeating the just-mentioned formula. Besides this liberation, called *manumissio vindicta,* there existed the so-called *manumissio censu,* consisting in the name of *libertus* being entered in the census lists; and the *manumissio testamento, i.e.* the liberation of the slave by the owner's last will. After his liberation the former slave put on the pileus, donned the toga, wore a ring, and shaved his beard—the signs of a freeman.

101. The mechanical or intellectual occupations of the slaves were continued by them as freedmen, in consequence of which the trades were shared by the *plebs* with the *liberti*. The contempt against trades expressed by Cicero is further illustrated by the fact of tradesmen being, with few exceptions, debarred from serving in the legions. Roman tradesmen and mechanics, therefore, were a low, cowardly, and at the same time unruly class of people—*fæx urbana*, as Cicero calls them. Livy mentions particularly that when, in the year 426 of the city, the Gauls threatened Rome, the Consul L. Æmilius Mamercinus was compelled to recruit his legions from the just-mentioned classes, "*minime militiæ idoneum genus.*" The same Livy reproaches the Consul Terentius Varro, known by the battle of Cannæ, with his descent from a butcher's family. Epigrammatists loved to ridicule tradesmen grown wealthy, who, like true *parvenus*, made a show of their riches.

Mechanics' guilds (*collegia opificum*) existed at an early period, their origin being traced back to King Numa: they were nine in number, viz. pipers, carpenters, goldsmiths, dyers, leather-workers, tanners, smiths, and potters, and another guild combining, at first, all the remaining handicrafts, which afterwards developed into new separate societies. Amongst these later guilds, frequently mentioned in inscriptions, we name the goldsmiths, bakers, purple dyers, pig-dealers, sailors, ferrymen, physicians, &c. They had their separate inns (*curia, schola*), their statutes and rules of reception and expulsion of members, their collective and individual privileges, their laws of mutual protection, and their widows' fund, not unlike the medieval guilds. There was, however, no compulsion to join a guild. In consequence, there was much competition from freedmen—foreign, particularly Greek, workmen who settled in Rome, as also from the domestic slaves who supplied the wants of the large families—reasons enough to prevent the trades from acquiring much importance. They had, however, their time-honoured customs, consisting of sacrifices and festive gatherings at their inns ; on which occasions their banners (*vexilla*) and emblems were carried about the streets in procession.

A wall-painting at Pompeii (*Archäol. Zeitg.*, T. XVII., 1850, p. 177 *et seq.*) is most likely intended as an illustration of a carpenters' procession. A large wooden tray (*ferculum*), surmounted by a decorated baldachin, is being carried on the shoulders of young workmen. On the tray stands a carpenter's bench in miniature, with two men at their work, the figure of Dædalus being seen in the foreground.

The shops in which the mechanics worked and exhibited their wares were collectively called *tabernæ*, a name derived from the old booths (*quod ex tabulis olim fiebant*), such as stood in the Forum Romanum in old times. Under Domitian these wooden structures were banished from the streets and Forum of Rome, only the money-changers being allowed to retain their old places. Martial (VII. 61) highly approves of this measure. The shops lay in the ground floors of houses opening towards the street. The shops of a provincial town, as, for instance, of Pompeii, consisted of one large compartment with one or two smaller back rooms, the latter sometimes connected by means of stairs with bedrooms in the upper story (compare the house of Pansa, Fig. 386). The shops are open towards the street (in corner houses even on both sides), so as not to impede the view of the wares. Facing the street stood a stone counter, a narrow passage being left for those who wished to enter the shop; bottles containing the liquids for sale were let into this counter, cases in the back wall of the shop being filled with glasses, bottles, and stores. Shop-signs, mostly hewn in stone, indicated the nature of the objects for sale : the shop of a milkman at Pompeii shows the sign of a goat; that of a wine-merchant exhibits two men carrying an amphora on a stick over their shoulders; that of a baker, a mill put in motion by a donkey.

Private bakeries, as attached to every large household, have been found in several Pompeian houses, as, for instance, in those of Pansa and Sallustius; in an oven belonging to the Casa di Marte e Venere numerous loaves of bread have been found, completely burnt, but still distinctly recognisable. Close to the house of Sallustius lies a large bakery containing four mills made of coarse porous tufa. Fig. 484 serves to illustrate their construction, one half showing the exterior aspect, the other the cross-section of a mill. The stone base, in the form of a disc, is marked *a;* its upper surface shows a rill or groove (*b*), going all round it. On this base stands a massive conical stone (*c, meta,* μύλη), being worked of one piece, with the base or otherwise let into it. This stone is surmounted by a hollow double cone or funnel (*d d, catillus,* ὄνος), the corn being poured into its upper half, whence it dropped through another groove (*e*) into the narrow space between the lower half of the double funnel and the outer surface of the cone (*c*). On the double funnel (*d d*) being whirled round the corn was crushed, the flour dropping into the groove (*b*). The groove (*e*) could be closed by means of an iron plate with five holes, the centre one of which was connected with the top of the cone by means of a strong iron peg, so as to facilitate the action of the double funnel, the four other holes serving to admit the grain. Two bars (*ff*), fastened in the middle of the double funnel, served to work the mill, which was done either by men (*mola versatilis*) or animals (*mola jumentaria, asinaria*). Windmills were unknown to the Romans; not so water-mills

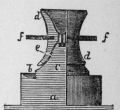

Fig. 484.

(*mola aquaria, hydraleta*), one of which is described by Vitruvius; its principle of action resembled that just explained: water-mills were introduced in Rome about the fourth or fifth century A.D. A Pompeian wall-painting ("Mus. Borbon.," vol. vi., Tav. 51) depicts the *Vestalia,* or millers' feast, celebrated on the 9th of June, genii taking the place of men, as is often the case in these pictures. The day was celebrated by the millers and bakers by a simple family dinner, consisting of bread, salt, vegetables, and fish, served in earthenware. The donkeys had a resting-day, animals and mill being adorned with flowers, and garlands composed of loaves strung together. In the just-mentioned bakery of Pompeii we see also an oven cleverly constructed, and furnished with a contrivance to retain the heat. The act of baking itself is illustrated on a small grave monument in Rome, just outside the Porta Maggiore, where the Via Labicana and Via Prænestina meet at a pointed angle. According to the inscription: EST HOC MONIMENTVM MARCEI VERGILEI EVRYSACIS PISTORIS REDEMPTORIS APPARET, it has been erected by M. Vergilius Eurysaces, baker and bread-dealer,

for himself and his wife, Atistia. The name of the monument is
panarium (bread-basket), and it is adorned with the emblems of
the trade, amongst which we distinguish heaps of corn, two mills
moved by donkeys, two flour-strainers, and two miller's knives ;
also a machine for kneading dough moved by horses. A similar
machine appears in a relief on a sarcophagus of the Lateran
(Gerhard, " Denkm. u. Forsch.," 1861, No. 148). Scales to weigh
large and heavy quantities (a pair of which also appears on the

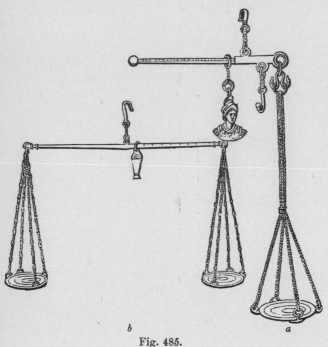

Fig. 485.

monument of Eurysaces) are frequently met with on Roman and
Greek monuments ; they resemble those at present in use.

Smaller quantities of dry or liquid substances, such as meat,
fish, oil, or chemicals, were weighed in the *libra* (Fig. 485), two
specimens of which have been found at Pompeii. The object to
be weighed is suspended from the smaller of the two unequal ends
of the beam (*jugum*), while to the longer end is attached a weight
(*æquipondium*), by means of a movable ring. By pushing this
equipoise to and from the point of revolution the weight of the

object could be determined exactly, this part of the beam being divided by means of incised points. Fig. 485, *a*, shows another balance, from the shorter end of whose beam are suspended a hook and a scale (*lanx*), the former for the fastening of bottles or pots with fluids, the latter for the reception of dry objects to be weighed. The longer end of the beam is here divided by a double system of points, the one to determine the weights of solid, the other that of fluid substances. In other balances the beam is divided into two equal parts (Fig. 486, *b*), a scale being suspended from each end. One of these ends, moreover, is marked in the manner described, the equipoise here showing the form of an acorn, while in the former case it was a head of Minerva; the heads or forms of animals occur often. Numerous other weights to be put in one of the scales have been found. They are made of bronze, lead, or stone; some of them have their value marked on them.

After the bakeries we mention cook-shops, low inns (*popinæ*), and wine-shops (*cauponæ*). They were frequented by the poorest classes, and were often the scenes of vice; it was considered disreputable for a gentleman to visit such places. There were, however, taverns, &c., for *roués* of the better classes, where debauchery and games of hazard were the order of the day; the trade of inn-keeper (*caupo*) was, for these reasons, considered disreputable. The interior arrangement of such places most likely resembled that of the modern *osterie*. Signboards (*insignia*), hung out at the door, proclaimed the name of the house : at Pompeii there was an Elephant inn; in Rome, near the Forum, a Cock; at Lyons, a Mercury and Apollo, &c. A wall-painting at Herculaneum ("Pitture d'Ercol.," vol. iii. p. 227) gives a vivid idea of an antique *taberna*. In the foreground of a square, which a colonnade shows to be a forum, mine host is helping a guest to some beverage brewing in a kettle on the fire; in the background a woman is selling pears and vegetables.

With the work of a potter we have already become acquainted (see § 90 and Figs. 193 and 194). In Pompeii a potter's oven has been found to the left of the street of graves. The fireplace has a flat top full of holes, through which the heat enters the baking-oven. A similar arrangement is shown in the tilers' and potters' ovens found near Rheinzabern (in 1858, thirty-six of the former

and seventy-seven of the latter kind had been discovered), as also
in those found near Waiblingen (Würtemberg) ; at the excavation of the latter, in 1840, the author was present.

The surface of a kylix in the Royal Museum, Berlin (Gerhard,
" Trinkschalen des Kgl. Museums," Tafs. XII., XIII.), represents
the workshop of a metal-founder; although taken from Greek
life, the picture will serve our present purpose. We there see the
large furnace with the cauldron standing on it; one workman is
poking the fire, while another, leaning on his sledge-hammer,
seems to wait for the melting of the metal. In another part of
the shop the bronze statue of a praying youth lies on the floor.
The head has not yet been soldered on to the body; a man is

Fig. 486.

working with a hammer at
one arm of the figure. On
the opposite side is seen,
under a scaffolding, the finished colossal statue of a
youthful warrior ; two workmen are polishing the legs
with a scraper, while two
men in long cloaks, most
likely the artist and the owner
of the foundry, are looking on.
Hammers, saws, modelled
arms, legs, and heads, and
sketches on tablets, cover the
walls. Vulcan's smithy has
been shown, Fig. 261: cyclops

at their work are frequently met with in bas-reliefs (Millin,
" Gallérie Mythol.," No. 383). A cutler's shop and workshop are
illustrated by two bas-reliefs on a cippus in the Vatican, the
former of which (Fig. 486) shows a rich choice of sickles, pruning-
knives, and long carving-knives. The owner of the business seems
to be selling a knife to a customer.

Fig. 487, from a bas-relief found at Capua, has, according to its
inscription, been let into the proscenium wall of a stage by
Lucceius Peculiaris, a builder, in consequence of a dream he had.
Near the figure of Athene Ergane we see a sculptor working at a
Korinthian capital, while two men are lifting the drums of a

column by means of a tread-wheel. Chisels, gravers, files, drills, and half-finished statues have been discovered in a sculptor's studio at Pompeii; pairs of compasses used by stone-masons and carpenters, leads, and folding foot-rules have also been found at Pompeii, the latter divided into twelve *unciæ* (by points on the side surface) and sixteen *digiti* (marked on the edge); * similar instruments appear as emblems on tombstones.

A blacksmith's workshop, recognisable by the axles of carts, fellies, and tools found there, has been discovered at Pompeii outside the Herculaneum gate. A carpenter's workshop appears in a wall-painting at Herculaneum, where two Cupids are sawing a board with a saw exactly resembling those at present in use.

Fig. 487.

The bottom of a glass vessel found in the catacombs of Rome represents the manipulations of a cabinet-maker and cutter of wood in six pictures painted on a gold ground ("Pitture d'Ercol.," vol. i. Tav. XXXIV., and Perret, "Catacombes de Rome," T. IV. 22, 14; see also Jahn, *loc. cit.*, Taf. XI. 1).

Tanneries are represented (Figs. 472 and 473) in Pompeian wall-paintings: the interior of a cobbler's shop appears in a wall-painting at Herculaneum ("Pitture d'Ercol.," vol. i. T. XXXV.), where one of two Cupids sitting by a table seems to beat the leather on a last, while the other is sewing at a shoe; rows of finished shoes stand in an open cupboard and on boards on the wall, which proves that the shop was used both for working and

* See "Mus. Borb.," T. VI., Tav. XV.

selling. In the street leading towards the Odeum at Pompeii there is the shop of an oil-merchant, with eight earthen vessels let into the counter, in which olives and clotted oil have been found; we also mention a perfumer's shop, the signboards of which, now illegible, announced the sale of pomatum, incense, and the ingredients for embalming the dead: in a colourman's shop in the Casa del Arciduca di Toscana, colours, partly in a raw state, partly prepared with resin, have been found. A series of market-scenes appear in a picture at Herculaneum (" Pitture d'Ercol.," vol. iii. Tav. XLII. *et seq.*) representing the colonnade of a forum, where clothes, bronze vessels, ironware, and cakes are sold, while shoemakers take the measure of people sitting on benches.

102. Three classes amongst the slaves and freedmen held a distinguished position by their intellectual accomplishments, viz., the *medici, chirurgi,* and *literari.* About physicians, their first appearance amongst the Romans and their social position, we gather interesting information from Pliny's remarks at the beginning of the twenty-ninth book of his " Natural History." In the first centuries of the Republic slaves and freedmen used to treat their patients according to certain old prescriptions and nostrums. In the year 575 of the city (219 B.C.) a Greek surgeon of the name of Archagathus settled in Rome, whose art was acknowledged by the erection, at the public expense, of a booth for him on the Acilian cross-road. To his passion for burning and cutting he owed the nickname of butcher: altogether he brought discredit on Greek doctors; they were called charlatans, filling their purses and endangering their patients' lives by their ignorance, there being no law to restrict or punish them. Nevertheless, the appearance of Archagathus and other Greek medical men gave rise to the establishment of a medical profession in Rome. Numerous physicians became known, one rejecting the remedies of the other, and seeking renown by the introduction of new methods. "Hence," says Pliny, " those disgraceful squabbles at sick-beds, when all the physicians disagree only in order to avoid the appearance of consent; hence the dreadful inscription on tombs— ' The number of his doctors has killed him.' Medical art is changed every day by new additions; we are sailing before a Greek wind, and the decision of life and death lies with him who has got most to say for himself, &c." The large income of a

physician (for want of chemists, they also sold their drugs, frequently composed of expensive ingredients) may be guessed from the fact that Quintus Stertinius, body-physician to the emperor, considered it highly meritorious on his part to be satisfied with 500,000 sestertii, as his private practice had brought him 600,000 sestertii (£6,450 according to the value of money in Augustus's time). Krinas, a contemporary of Pliny, left at his death ten million sestertii, after having spent almost as much on the building of fortifications at Massilia (his native town) and other cities. Under Nero the medical profession became organized, an upper class of physicians, the *archiatri,* being created, amongst which the body-physicians of the emperors (*archiatri palatini*) and the *archiatri populares* held again distinguished ranks. The former were amongst the most important court-officials,

Fig. 488.

their title being *spectabiles.* After the time of Antoninus Pius a certain number of the archiatri populares were appointed to reside in each town; they were elected by the citizens and examined by the college of *archiatri;* they received a salary from the city, besides being exempted from all *munera,* for which in return they had to attend the poor. Medical men were divided into physicians (*medici*), surgeons (*medici vulnerum, vulnerarii, chirurgi*), and oculists (*ocularii* or *medici ab oculis*); besides these, we hear of dentists, specialists for diseases of the ear, lady-physicians for the diseases of their own sex, midwives, and assistants (*intraliptæ*), whose chief business was to rub patients with medicinal ointment; we also mention the numerous sellers of Oriental salves, &c., who added their share to the grand system of quackery obtaining in Rome. Surgical instruments and medicine-boxes made of bronze with silver inlaid covers have been discovered; little weights, to exactly determine the quantity of the medicine used were also kept in these boxes. Fig. 488 represents a box found in the Rhenish country, at present in the Royal Museum, Berlin. On its sliding cover it shows the inlaid image of Æsculapius placed in a small temple. In Pompeii two chemists' shops have been found, the signboards of which show the snake of the same God, with a pineapple in its mouth; solid medical substances, liquids dried up in glasses, and a surgical apparatus of bronze (now in the Museum of Naples) have been discovered there. Fig. 489 represents a number of surgical instruments found in the house of a surgeon in the Strada Consolare at Pompeii: *a* is a bronze box containing probes (*specillum*), such as appear separately in *n, o, p*. Pincers (*forceps*) are seen *e, g, i; f* is a scalpel (*scalpellum*); *l*, a *spatula*; *m*, a sound; *q*, a straight pin; *k*, pincers to remove splinters of bones; *h*, a *speculum magnum matricis*; *d*, a chopper of unknown use.

Frequent diseases of the eyes occurring from about the end of the Republic, as the results of vice or exaggerated hot bathing, necessitated a separate class of oculists. The names of the oculists of the Empress Livia are found in her columbarium.

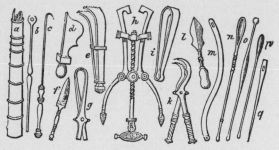

Fig. 489.

Many small vases, previously taken for children's toys, have turned out to be receptacles of drops and salves for diseases of the eye: one of them shows the inscription "*Lycium Iasonis,*" *i.e.* the prescription of the Greek oculist Iason. Particularly in the occidental provinces of the empire small tablets of slate are found in great numbers, indicating the names of oculists, their prescriptions, and the way of applying them: these were advertisements of Roman oculists. The quackeries of medical men were favourite subjects with both Athenian and Roman playwrights. A Greek vase-painting (Panofka, "Bild. antik. Leb.," Taf. VII. 5) represents a travelling quack practising his art in a booth standing in a market-place; he is feeling the head of a patient, whom, with the assistance of his servant, he is pulling up the stairs of his booth.

Numerous *tabernæ* were, by the advertisements on the door-posts or porticoes of the houses, marked as booksellers' shops. Such shops were found in Rome, in the Forum near the Curia, in the Vicus Sandalarius, and in many other much-frequented quarters. Several names of celebrated publishing firms are known to us. Inside the shops lay in pigeon-holes (*armaria, nidi*), carefully arranged, the book-rolls, in more or less costly bindings. The shops, at the same time, were meeting-places of literary men and persons interested in literature. In reading of the numerous private libraries, and the enormous quantities of books required by the reading public of the Empire, we naturally ask how this demand could be supplied without the printing-press. We answer this question in the words of Schmidt (" Geschichte der Denk- und Glaubensfreiheit im ersten Jahrhundert der Kaiser-herrschaft," p. 119) : " the place of the press in our literature was taken by the slaves." We have already mentioned the *literati*, cultivated slaves, generally of Greek origin, who had to copy books or write from dictation. By these slaves manuscripts were copied with astounding celerity, with the aid of abbreviations called, from their inventor, Tiro, a freedman of Cicero, Tironian notes. These copies, sometimes full of mistakes, went to the shops of the booksellers (*bibliopola*), unless these kept copyists in their own shops. Numerous copies were thus produced in little time. The satirical writings of Ovidius, Propertius, and Martialis were in everybody's hands, as were also the works of Homer and Virgil, the odes of Horace, and the speeches of Cicero ; grammars, anthologies, &c., for schools, were reproduced in the same manner ; indeed, the antique book-trade was carried on on a scale hardly surpassed by modern times. Augustus confiscated, for instance, in Rome alone, 2,000 copies of the pseudo-Sibylline books—by no means a recent work. Pomponius Atticus, the friend and publisher of Cicero, possessed a large number of slaves for the manufacturing of writing materials and the copying and correcting of manuscripts ; besides which he carried on a lucrative publishing business (see Cicero's speech "Pro Ligario"). More-over, authors used (according to a custom introduced by Asinius Polio in Augustus's time) to read their unpublished productions either to their friends or (after due advertisement) to public audiences in the Forum, at theatres, baths, &c. Hardly a day passed without an exhibition of this kind ; the younger Pliny, in one of his letters (I., 13) graphically describes the difficulties of attracting, and still more of retaining, the *blasé* audiences of the metropolis.

About the writing materials of the Greeks we have spoken before. The Romans also used wax tablets (Fig. 490, *c, d*), called *tabellæ, pugillares*, or simply *ceræ*, for writing letters, notes, first drafts, or school exercises. Only the inner side was written on, a raised wooden border serving to protect the writing when two or more tablets were joined together or made into a book (*duplices*, δίπτυχα, *triplices*, τρίπτυχα, *multiplices*, πολύπτυχα). The outer surface or cover was generally adorned with ivory carvings, jewels, or precious metals. Several of these diptycha, which, in imperial times, the new-appointed consuls and prætors used to present to each other, have been preserved. Several wax tablets, most of them with Roman, and a few with Greek, documents written on them, have been discovered at various times since 1786 in the old Roman mines near the towns of Abrudbanya (Gross Schlatte) and Vöröspatak, in Siebenbürgen ; most of them are at present in the Hungarian National Museum, Pesth, a few others in private collections.*

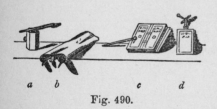

a   b   c   d

Fig. 490.

The pencil (*stilus, graphium*), used for incising or erasing the letters (*stilum vertere*), we have mentioned before. Fig. 490 shows a pencil lying on an open book (*c*). The tablets were also used for writing letters, separate slaves or freedmen being occasionally employed as *librarii ab epistulis*. On sending the letter the *tabellæ* were fastened together with a thread tied into a knot, on which the wax seal was pressed. The outside of the letter bore the address. Another kind of writing was done with ink (*atramentum librarium*), made of a solution of soot and gum, on papyrus or parchment (see Fig. 490, the inkstand, *a*, with the *calamus* lying on it, and the half-opened writing-scroll, *b*). Of the materials and manufactory of the papyrus

---

* The chronological enumeration of these discoveries from 1786 to 1856 is found in Erdy, "De Tabulis ceratis in Transsilvania repertis." Pesth, 1856. See Massmann, "Libellus aurarius sive Tabulæ ceratæ," Leipsic, 1840 ; and Detlefsen's Contributions to the Sitzungsberichte of the Wiener Akademie der Wissenschaften, Hist. Cl. vols. xxiii. and xxvii.

we have already spoken. The height of the scroll varied, according to the quality of the paper, from 6 to 13 inches; as to its length, no rule can be given. A papyrus found in 1821, containing a fragment of the twenty-fourth book of the Iliad, is 8 feet long by 10 inches high. One end of the papyrus was fitted into the hollow part of a cane, and rolled round the cane, the ends of which, slightly protruding, were adorned with buttons of ivory or metal (*cornua, umbilici*). To secure it against moths and dust the papyrus was put in a purple or yellow case (*membrana*) : to it, or (as appears from several wall-paintings) to the umbilici, the title of the book was tied. Several scrolls together were put into a cylindrical case (*scrinium*, compare Fig. 235) with a cover to it ; books or documents could thus be conveniently carried. Several statues, clad in the toga ("Augusteum," Tafs. 117, 119), have a scrinium standing at their feet ; and in a bas-relief (Micali, " Monumenti per servire alla Storia degli ant. Popoli Italiani," Atlas, Tav. 112), a scrinium, together with the sella curulis and several books, is carried by the attendants (*apparitores*) in front of a procession of magistrates. Most houses had a library, which, according to Vitruvius, ought to face the east in order to admit the light of the morning, and to prevent the books from becoming mouldy. At Herculaneum a library with book-cases containing 1,700 scrolls has been discovered. The grammarian Epaphroditus possessed a library of 30,000, and Sammanicus Serenus, the tutor of the younger Gordian, one of 62,000 books. Seneca ridicules the fashionable folly of illiterate men who adorned their walls with thousands of books, the titles of which were the delight of the yawning owner. According to Publius Victor, Rome possessed twenty-nine public libraries, the first of which was opened by Asinius Polio in the forecourt of the Temple of Peace; two others were founded during the reign of Augustus, viz. the Octavian and the Palatine libraries. Tiberius, Vespasian, Domitian, and Trajan added to their number ; the Ulpian library, founded by the last-mentioned emperor, being the most important of all.

Of agricultural implements we first mention the plough (*aratrum*). Originally the land was turned up by means of a long hoe, which soon was developed into the wooden plough, consisting of a strong wooden hook pointed at the bottom like a ploughshare,

or cased with iron, the back part forming the plough handle. This
plough, of Etruscan origin, but adopted by the Romans, is shown,
Fig. 491, from an Etruscan bronze group; it naturally could
only dig into the earth, without turning up the furrows. The
later Roman plough consisted of a share-beam (*dentale*), with the
ploughshare (*vomer*) at one end, and the *stiva* (plough-handle)
with a cross-bar (*manicula*) at the other; beam and handle might
be made of one piece, or the latter inserted into the former; the
manicula served to direct the plough by being either raised or
pressed down by the ploughman. About the middle of the
share-beam was fastened the *buris* or *bura* (plough-tail), about
eight feet long and slightly bent; in the Roman plough it served
at the same time as pole (*temo*), to the further end of which the
oxen were yoked (see Fig. 491, where the yoke itself is also

shown separately, above the
animals). To even the furrows
two mould-boards (*aures*) were
fastened behind the ploughshare. A particular kind of
plough was the *plaustraratrum*,
used in Gallic Rhetia and in
the north of Italy. In it the
plough-tail rested on two low

Fig. 491.

plough-tail rested on two low
wheels, into the axle-tree of which the pole was inserted.
The plough was drawn by two or more oxen, according to the
nature of the soil. We next mention the harrow (*occa, crater*)
and the *irpex*, an instrument consisting of iron hooks. It was
drawn by oxen, and served to tear up roots and weeds. We
further name the *bidens*, an instrument with two prongs, the rake
(*rastrum*), the *ligo* (a hoe used in gardens and vineyards), and the
spade (*pala, rutrum*). The *falx vinitoria* and *falx arboraria* were
used for pruning vines and trees. The former had a curved
blade and a spike, the latter a bent blade. Sickles were used
to cut grass or corn, not too near the root; the ears were gathered
in baskets and trodden out by oxen on an open piece of ground,
which had previously been made firm by being stamped upon;
a custom still obtaining in southern countries. Another way of
thrashing the corn was by means of the *tribulum*—according to
Varro, a board, portions of which were raised by means of inserted

stones or pieces of iron. It was pulled across the ears by oxen, the ploughman standing on it. The remaining husks were left to be blown away by the wind, or else removed. The corn was kept in subterraneous caves (*horreum subterraneum*), still in use in southern countries, or in dry, airy granaries resting on columns (*horreum pensile*). In times of famine these granaries were filled at public expense, according to the example set by C. Sempronius Gracchus. The ruins of the large *horrea populi Romani* were still visible in the sixteenth century, between the Aventine hill and the Monte Testaceo; at present they have entirely disappeared, as have also the granaries called by the names of their founders, *horrea Aniceti, Vargunteii, Seiani, Augusti Domitiani.*

The culture of the olive-tree in Italy dates from the times of the kings. Venafrum, Casinum, and the Sabine country were celebrated for their oils. The culture of the vine is of later date. It became of importance only when the growing of grain began to cease. The shoots were planted in furrows or holes, and the vines were trailed (*maritare*) on trees, chiefly elms, planted at distances of twenty feet; their distance apart was doubled in case the ground lying between was used for the growing of grain, as is still the case in modern Italy. The custom of trailing the vine on poles or trellis-work was equally known to the Romans. Hedges of briars, fences made of osiers, or walls protected the vineyards against the cattle. Numerous sculptural groups of reapers and herds of cattle illustrate the agricultural pursuits of the Roman people.

103. We propose in the following pages to give a short sketch of the priestly colleges, the sacrificial rites, and the festive games connected with them, always availing ourselves of monumental evidence. All religious acts performed in holy places (*locus sacer*) were called *sacra :* in case they were performed by individuals or by the head of a family in honour of the domestic gods, the Lares, Penates, &c., or by a priest in the name of a community (*gens*), they were called *sacra privata ; sacra publica*, on the other hand, were performed at the public expense by public priests (*sacerdotes populi Romani*) for the people (*pro populo*), or by certain societies (*sodalitates*) which were charged by the State with the veneration of certain deities, as, for instance, the Gens

Nautia with that of Minerva, the Gens Julia with that of Apollo, and the Gens Aurelia with that of Sol. The public priests (*sacerdotes*) were divided into three classes : the first class, that of the *sacerdotes publici populi Romani*, formed the great *collegia* of the *pontifices*, comprising the subdivisions of the *VII viri epulones*, the *XV viri sacris faciundis*, the *augures, Salii* and *Fetiales;* the second class comprised the *sodalitates*, which had to perform the *sacra popularia;* the third, those officiating at the *sacra gentilitia.*

The priests of the first class enjoyed many privileges ; they were allowed to wear the toga prætexta, they were exempt from military or civil service, and had seats of honour at feasts and games. They were also in possession of public land (*ager publicus*), the rental of which covered the expenses of the sacra ; moreover, the State kept for them a number of subaltern officials, partly slaves (*servi publici*), partly freemen. Amongst these we mention the *lictores*, mostly freedmen, who preceded priests and priestesses (just like the lictores of civil magistrates), in order to make room for them through a crowd; also the *pullarii* (keepers of the fowls), the *victimarii* (sacrificial butchers), the *tibicines* and *fidicines* (musicians), the *calatores* (messengers to announce meetings), and the *camilli* and *camillæ*, boys and girls partly officiating at the sacrifices, partly aspirants for the priestly dignity. For the last-mentioned class originally free-born children alone were eligible with parents still alive (*pueri patrimi et matrimi* and *puellæ patrimæ et matrimæ*).

The pontifices formed, in the time of the kings, a college of four priests, with the king himself as high priest at their head. When (300 B.C.) the tribunes of the people Q. and Cn. Ogulnius carried a plebiscite granting the plebeians admittance to the priestly offices, previously held by patricians only, four plebeians were added to the original four pontifices, the high priest (*pontifex maximus*) being chosen from amongst them. Sulla, the reformer of many priestly colleges, increased the pontifices to fifteen. In imperial times the dignity of pontifex maximus was, by the senate, conferred on, or on his own authority assumed by, the emperor. We possess, for instance, a statue of Hadrian in pontificals, with a sacrificial vase in his hand (Clarac, "Musée," Tom. II. pl. 945). Saturnus, Ops, and Vesta were the chief gods whose worship was committed to the pontifices. The high priest had his dwelling in the Regia, near the temple of Vesta in the Forum. The atrium of Vesta was the hearth of the State household, where the priests, as heads of the Roman family, and the Vestals, like the maidens in private families, performed sacrificial rites. The college of pontifices, therefore, formed the centre of Roman public worship, and to them was confided the keeping of the religious State-archive, where the religious annals (*annales maximi*), written by the high priest himself, the *leges regiæ* (the oldest customary laws referring to sacred matters), the *libri pontificii*, and the minutes and decisions of the meetings of pontifices (*commentarii pontificum*), were deposited. By this college was pronounced every year the *sollemnis votorum nuncupatio* (the vows of the State), and its advice was asked by the magistrates with regard to religious ceremonies, the pontifices alone being supposed to know the sacrifices agreeable to the gods. Previous to devoting a place or object (statue, vase, &c.) to the gods, men had to solicit the approbation of the pontifices, who also performed the *consecratio* preceding the act of devotion itself. They were consulted about the mode of *expiatio*, when faults had been committed against the sacred precepts, or at burials (where the *manes* had to be pacified), &c.

Amongst other offices connected with this college we mention that of "sacrificial king" (*rex sacrorum* or *rex sacrificulus*), a dignity held at first by the Roman kings, and, after their expulsion, by a priest, who had to perform certain acts of worship, particularly the *sacra* of Janus. Although his functions were of comparatively little importance, the sacrificial king occupied nominally a higher rank than the pontifices themselves, at whose festive meals the place of honour was granted to him. His wife, the *regina sacrorum*, shared the honour of his priesthood.

The pontifices, like several other priestly brotherhoods (*e.g.* the *fratres Arvales* and *sodales Augustales*), had sacrificial priests (*flamines*) attached to them, whose name was derived from *flare* (to blow the fire). The number of flamines attached to the pontifices was fifteen, the three highest of whom (*flamines maiores*), viz. the *flamen Dialis, Martialis,* and *Quirinalis,* were always chosen from old patrician families; the remaining twelve were called *flamines minores.* Free from all civil duties, the Flamen Dialis, with his wife and children, exclusively devoted himself to the service of the deity. His house (*domus flaminia*) lay on the Palatine hill. His marriage was dissoluble by death only; he was not allowed to take an oath, mount a horse, or look at an army. He was forbidden to remain a night away from his house, and his hand touched nothing unclean, for which reason he never approached a corpse or a burial-place. He always appeared in his official dress, consisting of a toga prætexta, woven by his wife of thick wool (*læna*), which was not allowed to be tied in a knot, but had to be fastened by means of fibulæ, the sight of fetters being forbidden to him. For the same reason the ring he wore on his finger had to be a broken one; neither was he allowed to approach

Fig. 492.

a trailed vine or touch ivy : a prisoner on entering his house was freed from his fetters, which were thrown through the impluvium into the street. His head-dress was the *albogalerus*, a sort of pileus, to the top (*apex*) of which was tied an olive branch with a white woollen thread (*filum*). This head-dress appears on several coins, of which we mention one of Julius Cæsar, bearing the inscriptions PONT. MAX. and AVGVR. The albogalerus, Fig. 492, *k*, resembles that seen in a bas-relief of the temple of Vespasian in Rome,* but for its apex, which is a little lower. The adornment of the albogalerus with a flash of lightning shows its being destined for a Flamen Dialis. In the daytime the Flamen Dialis was not allowed to take off his head-dress, and he was obliged to resign his office in case it fell off by

---

* Reber, "Die Ruinen Roms." 1863, p. 82.

accident. In his belt he carried the sacrificial knife (*secespita*), and in his hand he held a rod (*commetacula*), in order to keep off the people on his way to the sacrifice. For the same purpose he was preceded by a lictor, who compelled everybody on the way to lay down his work, the flamen not being allowed to see the business of daily life. The wife of the flamen (*flaminica*) had to submit to an equally strict etiquette ; she also appeared always in long woollen robes, her hair was tied in a tutulus with a woollen ribbon of purple colour, over which a kerchief (*rica*) was fastened with the bough of a lucky tree (*arbor felix*) attached to it. She wore a purple veil (*flammeum*), and her shoes had to be made of the leather of sacrificed animals. She also carried the sacrificial knife. Fig. 492 shows a bas-relief illustrative of all the utensils used at sacrificial acts by the upper priests, such as the sacrificial vase (*culullus*, *e*), the vessels for drawing liquids (*simpulum*, *f*), the sacrificial knife (*secespita*) in a case (*g*), and the albogalerus (*k*).*

Besides the flamines, the Vestals (*virgines Vestales, virgines Vestæ*) were closely connected with the college of pontifices. They are said to have come from Alba soon after the foundation of Rome : at first there were two Vestals for each of the two tribes Ramnes and Tities ; afterwards two others were added for the Luceres, and the number of six was exceeded at no period. The vestal, on being chosen, was not allowed to be younger than six or older than ten years ; she was to be *patrima et matrima*, and free from bodily defects. After having been examined she was clad in white garments and devoted to the service of Vesta for thirty years ; during the first ten years she was a novice, during the second ten an active priestess, and for the remaining period a teacher of novices. After this period she was at liberty either to remain in the service of the goddess (which was generally done) or to return to her family and get married. Her dress was always white ; round her forehead she wore a broad band like a diadem (*infula*), with ribbons (*vittæ*) attached to it. During the sacrifice, or at processions, she was covered with a white veil (*suffibulum*), fastened under her chin with a fibula (see Gerhard, "Antike Bildwerke," Taf. XXIV., and the Vestal Claudia Quinta, Fig. 493,

---

* Sacrificial utensils appear frequently on cameos and coins ; for instance, on the denarii of the families, Antestia, Antonia, Cassia, Cornelia, Domitia, Iulia, Hirtia, Sulpicia, &c.

from a bas-relief). She was carefully guarded against insult or temptation; an offence offered to her was punished with death: no man was allowed to enter her dwelling or approach the temple by night; in public every one, even the consul, made way to the lictor preceding the maiden. At public games and pontifical banquets she had the seat of honour; and a convicted criminal accidentally meeting her was released. Amongst her priestly functions was the keeping of the eternal fire in the temple of Vesta, each Vestal taking her turn at watching; in case the fire went out the negligent maiden was liable to corporal punishment at the hands of the Pontifex Maximus. The temple of Vesta had, moreover, to be sprinkled every day with the water of the fountain of Egeria; on the 1st of March of every year it was decorated anew with purifying laurel (see the laurel-branch lying on a censer, Fig. 492, *a*). The sprinkling with water was done with an *aspergillum*, sometimes in the form of a horse's leg with a horse's tail attached to it (see Fig. 492, *h*), sometimes with a spiral handle. In accordance with the simple offerings at the domestic hearth, the gift of the vestals consisted of different preparations of salt (*muries* and *mola salsa*), offered in earthen vessels. The sacrifice was accompanied by prayers for the people. Breach of chastity on the part of the Vestal was punished with death; the culprit was carried on a bier to the *campus sceleratus*, outside the Porta Collina, beaten with rods, and afterwards immured alive, the violent killing of a Vestal being considered *nefas*; only miraculous intercession of the goddess could save the culprit. We know of twelve cases of Vestals being punished in this manner.

We now come to the colleges independent of the pontifices, mentioning first the *VII viri epulones*. Their origin dates from the year 196 B.C., when, owing to the pontifices being overworked, a separate college of seven members was founded, chiefly in order to perform the rites of the sacrificial meal (*epulum Jovis*), taken in the temple of the Capitoline Jupiter, in the presence of the whole senate; the *ludi plebeii* always followed on the next day. In later times such meals were arranged on many public occasions, the *viri epulones* always presiding.

The colleges hitherto mentioned had the care of the worship of the old Roman gods (*dii patrii*); the *XV viri sacris faciundis*, on the other hand, presided over the religious rites of strange gods (*dii peregrini*) introduced in Rome. The number of these priests was, under Tarquinius Superbus, two; since the year 367 B.C. the college consisted of five patrician and five plebeian members, to whom five further priests were added, most likely by Sulla. They had to keep and expound the Sibylline books, and to choose the new decisions of oracles to be recorded in them. As is well known, nine books of oracular sayings were offered to Tarquinius Superbus by the sibyl of Cumæ, three of which the king bought, while the others were thrown into the flames by the sibyl. These three books were kept in the temple of the Capitoline Jupiter, together with which they were destroyed by fire (83 B.C.). A new collection of oracles was made in Asia Minor (the most fertile soil for such sayings) and other countries, which again was deposited in the rebuilt Capitol. The *XV viri* were charged by Augustus with the critical selection of these oracular sayings, many corrections and additions being made under subsequent emperors. Stilicho is said to have burnt these books. In times of plagues, earthquakes, and the like, these books were consulted by the priests, and the proper mode of expiation expounded from them. One of the expiatory acts was the introduction of new gods. The worship of Apollo, Artemis, Ceres, Dis pater, Venus, Salus, Mercury, Æsculapius, and Magna Mater (Cybele) were thus transferred to Rome on the authority of the Sibylline books, public games being at the same time introduced in honour of many of these gods, as, for instance, the Apollinaria and Secular games in honour of Apollo, the *ludi Cereris,* in honour of Ceres and the *Megalenses* to celebrate the Magna Mater. Fig. 493 refers to the worship of the latter goddess. The figure of the vestal drawing with her girdle the vessel on whose deck Cybele is seated, is Claudia Quinta. A late Roman bas-relief on a sarcophagus

Fig. 493.

represents a scene from the grand procession preceding the ludi circenses during the festive days of the Megalenses (see Gerhard, "Ant. Denkm.," Taf. CXX. 1). The image of Cybele in her chariot drawn by lions is carried on the shoulders of seventeen persons. The two figures clad with the toga, opening the procession, are most likely two of the *XV viri*.

The *augures* also were fifteen in number. Their institution coincided with the foundation of the city, Romulus himself being mentioned as the first augur. No public act or ceremony in peace or war, no inauguration or exauguration could be performed without the augurs' assistance, who, according to certain rules, derived the will of the gods from the appearance, non-appearance, or manner of appearance of the sign. Only the magistrate had a right to consult the augurs about the auspices with reference to public affairs (*spectio*); his questions only were answered by the augur (*nuntiatio*). The important political position of these priests is sufficiently explained by these facts. Standing in the centre of the temple, or temple-enclosure, under a tent (*tabernaculum*) the augur (after having divided the holy precinct into regions with a smooth stick slightly bent at the top, *lituus*, see Fig. 494) turned towards the south, and, offering prayers, expected the divine message. Lightning (*servare de cœlo*) and the flight of birds were the

principal signs. The lightnings coming from the left (*fulmina sinistra*) were considered favourable, those from the right unfavourable. The Etruscans had no less than eleven categories of lightnings, according to their direction, colour, &c. : the Roman theory was less elaborate,

Fig. 494.

the lightnings being classified only according to their occurring in the night or daytime ; in imperial times, however, the Etruscan theories were more generally adopted, which

had previously been the case only in a few instances, such as the purification of places struck 'by the lightning. For, like the body of the dead, the lightning had to be buried, which was done by building a shaft with walls of masonry, which protruded from the ground like the rim

Fig. 495.

of a fountain (whence the name *puteal*); this tomb of the lightning was inscribed, *Fulgus conditum ;* another name, *bidental,* was derived from the circumstance of an animal two years old being sacrificed on the spot. A puteal consisting of a round structure resting on eight Doric columns has been found at Pompeii. Fig. 493 represents a puteal from a denarius of L. Scribonius Libo, with the inscription, PVTEAL

SCRIBON.* We observe laurel-wreaths, lyres, and a pair of pincers on the puteal, which has the form of an altar. Scribonius had been commissioned by the Senate to find the spot struck by lightning, and had, in consequence, erected a puteal in the temple of Minerva.

The birds of omen (*signa ex avibus*) were divided by the augur into such whose cry (*oscines*) and into such whose flight (*alites*) signified the divine will. To the former class belonged the raven, the crow, the owl, the woodpecker, and the cock ; to the latter, the eagle (*Jovis ales*), hawk, and vulture. These auspices were in later times (particularly during campaigns, or on other occasions when no augur was present) supplied by the signs derived from the manner of eating observed in the sacred hens (*auspicia pullaria* or *auspicia ex tripudiis*). Hens were kept in a cage for the purpose ; in case the animals devoured their dump-lings (*offa pultis*) as soon as the hen-keeper (*pullarius*) opened the hen-coop, the omen was favourable, particularly if they dropped little pieces while eating (*tripudium sollistimum*) ; in case they refused to eat or to leave the cage, evil might be anticipated. Sometimes the pullarii or augurs used undoubtedly artificial means in bringing about the desired omen. Fig. 496 shows a hen-coop with two chickens eating, from a cameo (several cameos with similar representa-tions are in the Berlin Museum ; compare Toelken, "Verzeich-niss der antik vertieft geschnittenen Steine der kgl. Preuss. Gemmensammlung," p. 77, No. 175, and p. 250, No. 1484 *et seq.*). We finally mention the two less important auguria *ex quadrupedibus* and *ex diris*. To meet certain animals, such as a wolf, a fox, a snake, &c., was considered an evil augury.

Fig. 496.

The *haruspices*, nearly related to the augures, were of Etruscan origin : under the Republic they were consulted only in a few individual cases ; under the emperors they gained more import-ance, remaining, however, inferior to the other priestly colleges.

---

* On the puteal depicted on a gold coin of Æmilia Scribonia we see a hammer in-stead of these pincers; see Cohen, "Descr. gén. des Monnaies de la Républ. Rom.," pl. I.

They also expounded and procured lightnings and "prodigies," and moreover examined the intestines of sacrificed animals ; their more developed Etruscan method competing successfully with that of their Roman colleagues. Besides drawing down the lightning by their art, &c., the haruspices had made a speciality of the inspection of the intestines of animals. Heart, liver, and lungs were carefully examined, every anomaly being explained in a favourable or unfavourable sense. Although on solemn occasions the haruspices were officially invited to Rome for consultation, their art was never much esteemed by the more enlightened classes. Cato's saying, that no haruspex could look at his fellow without laughing, is significant in this respect.

The fifth college of priests, that of the *Salii*, was traced back to Numa. In his time a shield of peculiar form (*ancile*) is said to have dropped from the sky. To prevent it from being stolen the king ordered eleven other shields exactly like it to be made by the artist Mamurius. In order to keep these shields a college of twelve priests, the Salii, was instituted on the Palatine. Unfortunately for the story, however, there was another college of Salii, of Sabine origin, on the Quirinal hill, the former being devoted to the worship of Mars, the latter to that of Quirinus ; both were undoubtedly representatives of the oldest worship of Mars, whose name is also connected with the above-mentioned tradition of the shield. In the month of March, devoted to that god, the feast in his honour was celebrated. Clad in the toga picta and in full armour, the toga prætexta, worn above them, being tied in a Gabine knot, the head covered with the helmet (resembling the above-mentioned apex), armed with sword and lance, and carrying (on the left arm or fastened round the neck) the ancile, the Salii walked through the streets in solemn procession, dancing a warlike dance (whence their name) before every sanctuary, and beating their shields with their lances or staffs to the measure of an old song, the words of which (*axamenta, assamenta, carmina saliaria*) had, at a later period, become incomprehensible to the priests themselves. These songs celebrated Janus, Jupiter, Juno, Minerva, and Mars, the names of departed citizens being added to these as a mark of highest distinction. During the greater part of March these processions were repeated daily, and returned every evening to the quarters (*mansiones*) of the Salii, several of which existed in Rome.

The ancilia were carried into the house by servants on poles
(they were not allowed to touch them), a festive meal, celebrated
for its sumptuousness, ending the proceedings.
Fig. 497, from a cameo in the Florentine collection, shows several of these ancilia being
carried by servants in the manner described.
A silver coin of the Gens Licinia (Cohen,
"Desc. gén. des Monnaies de la Républ.
Rom.," pl. XXIV.) shows two ancilia and an
apex with the inscription, PVBL. STOLO III VIR.

Fig. 497.

The next college of priests, that of the *Fetiales*, also dates back
from the time of the first kings. They had to perform the sacred
rites accompanying declarations of war and treaties of peace or
alliance. Usually four Fetiales, with a speaker (*pater patratus*),
were sent by the king, and afterwards by the senate, to foreign
nations to demand satisfaction for injuries received. They were
clad in priestly robes, and in front of them were carried holy
herbs (*sagmina*), which the consul or prætor delivered to them in
the Capitol, after having touched with them the forehead of the
pater patratus. Thus equipped they demanded satisfaction from
the foreign nation, calling down the wrath of the gods upon their
own heads in case their requests were unjust. On this demand
being refused they returned to Rome, and after an interval of
from ten to thirty days the pater patratus declared war by
throwing a bloody spear across the frontier into the enemy's
country in the presence of three witnesses. When the Roman
territory began to extend more and more this ceremony was
performed in Rome itself, a piece of ground near the temple of
Bellona being considered as the enemy's country (*terra hostilis*),
on which a *columna bellica* was erected at a later period. At least
two Fetiales had to be present at the conclusion of treaties of
alliance, viz. the pater patratus and the herald carrying the holy
herbs (*verbenarius*). After the words of the treaty had been read,
a pig was killed with a pebble (*silex*) kept in the temple of
Jupiter Feretrius, whence the expression *fœdus ferire*. This
ceremony is represented on a silver coin of the Gens Antistia, and
on a number of coins of the cities of Capua and Atella.

The only remaining priestly college, that of the *Curiones* and
the religious sodalities of the *Luperci, Titii,* and *Fratres Arvales,*

we refrain from noticing for want of monumental evidence. The head-dress of the last-mentioned sodality consisted of a crown of wheat-ears.

The dress of those going to pray or sacrifice was usually white, a symbol of guiltlessness and chastity. The sacrificial utensils and the offering itself had to be free from stain; profane interruption by word or deed was considered a bad omen, whence the exclamation *favete linguis*, pronounced at the beginning of the sacrifice. A flute-player accompanied the holy act on his instrument, as appears from the representation of a sacrifice on an earthen lamp (Passerius, "Lucernæ Fict.," I. 35). To the right of the altar stands the priest, and an assistant carrying a box of incense; to the left we see the butcher with his axe; in the foreground several fettered bulls lie on the ground, and behind the altar a tibicen is playing on the double-flute.

Prayers to the celestial gods were offered standing and with hands held up to the eastern sky (see the bas-relief of a praying woman, Zoega, "Bassiril," vol. i. Tav. 18). The gods of the nether world were propitiated by touching the earth with the hands, and the *supplicationes* were offered kneeling; at the supplications for the averting of threatening evil, women appeared with loosened hair. Unlike the Greek, the Roman sacrificed with the toga pulled over the back of his head in the manner of a veil; only the sacrifices imported from Greece were performed (*Græco ritu*) bareheaded.

In the oldest time the offerings were bloodless: first fruits, *mola salsa*, milk, honey, wine, and cakes were offered. The animals (which began to be sacrificed under the last kings) were divided by the Romans into *victimæ* and *hostiæ*, *i.e.* heifers and smaller animals, offered to different gods according to holy custom. After having been examined, and found without blemish, the animal was led by the attendant (*popa*) to the flower-crowned altar, the resistance, and still more the flight, of the animal being looked upon as a bad omen. The horns of oxen and wethers were frequently gilt, and the animals always adorned with ribbons and ties (*vittæ, infulæ*), partly wound round the horns, partly spread over the back (compare Figs. 498, 539, and 492, *b*, *l*). The question "*agone?*" of the sacrificial butcher (*victimarius*) was answered by the officiating priest with "*hoc age*," after which the priest strewed mola salsa and incense on the head of the animal, and burnt a bunch of hair cut from between its horns; he also drew with a knife a line on the back of the animal from the forehead to the tail. The victim thus prepared (*macta est*) was killed by the victimarius with an axe (*securis, bipennis,* Fig. 492, *e*) or mallet (*malleus,* Fig. 492, *f*), provided it was a large animal: pigs, sheep, and birds had their throats pierced with a knife by the *cultrarius,* who caught the blood in a vase (Fig. 492, *e*); it was then poured over and round the altar. After this the body was opened with the *secespita* (Fig. 492, *g*), and the intestines taken out with smaller knives (*cultri,* Fig. 492, *d*), and examined by the haruspices. In case of an unfavourable omen the sacrifice had to be renewed; otherwise the intestines were sprinkled with wine and burnt on the altar amidst prayers. A libation of wine and incense, the former poured from an amphora (*præfericulum,* Fig. 492, *c*), the latter taken from a box (*acerra, turibulum,* Fig. 492, *i*), concluded the sacrifice, after which the priest dismissed those present with the word "*Ilicet.*" A meal followed; prepared by the priests in case the sacrifice

Fig. 498.

had been public, by the family in case it had been private.

To conclude we mention the expiatory sacrifice performed at the end of a lustrum and after the triumph; in the latter case by the triumphator in honour of the Capitoline Jupiter: the technical name was *suovetaurilia, i.e.* sacrifices of pigs, sheep, and oxen. The first-mentioned sacrifice is illustrated by a bas-relief (Clarac, "Musée," pl. 221, No. 751) composed of twenty-one figures. On the left we see the censor inserting the names of citizens and soldiers in the census lists; two musicians play on the cithara and flute respectively. To the right three crowned animals are brought forward by the servants, while another attendant carries a box of incense on his shoulders. The priest

is pouring the libation into a vase presented to him by a *camillus*.
Fig. 498, taken from the arch of Constantine, represents the
sacrifice of the emperor, surrounded by his army, in honour of
Jupiter after his triumph. The emperor pours a libation on the
burning altar. Suovetaurilia are led forward by crowned servants.
A camillus offers a box of incense to the emperor, while the tibicen
plays on his instrument.

104. Public games were, from the earliest times, connected
with religious acts, the Roman custom tallying in this respect
with the Greek. Such games were promised to the gods to gain
their favour, and afterwards carried out as a sign of gratitude for
their assistance. Such vows (*vota pro salute rei publicæ*) were
made on the 1st of January of every year by the new-elected
consuls, according to a formula first pronounced by the Pontifex
Maximus; after Cæsar's time special *vota pro salute principis* were
added to these. The expenses of the games thus promised
(whether the vow was made in Rome by the highest magistrate
or in the field by the general) were at once guaranteed, either
from the public treasury or from the booty. These *ludi votivi* were
either performed only once, or repeated annually (*ludi annui,
solemnes, stati, ordinarii*) on a certain day appointed for the
purpose. During the first years of the Republic the consuls had
to arrange the games; but after the creation of ædiles (494 B.C.)
this duty devolved upon them, the higher magistrates only
superintending. The expense was, at least for the greater part,
covered by the State; in later times, however, the public money
by no means sufficed for the splendid preparations required, and
the ædiles, and later on the imperial officials appointed for the
arrangement of the ludi circensis, had frequently to waste their
private property in the service of the multitude. The admission
to the games arranged by the State was gratis; private persons
who arranged games at their own expense (*editor ludi*) were
allowed to raise entrance-fees. In imperial times the number of
annual games increased enormously, the birthday of the emperor,
the anniversary of his accession, the delivery of the empress, the
memorial days of the dead members of the family, becoming
occasions for the ruler to gain the favour of the multitude by the
institution of splendid games. Augustus charged the prætors
with the arrangement of public games, but on the onerous offer

proving too much for them alone, the consuls and quæstors were conjointly made responsible; the arrangement of the most expensive games, however, the emperor reserved to himself, a court official (*curator ludorum*) being appointed for the purpose.

As early as the times of the kings horse and chariot races are said to have taken place in the circus; in 364 B.C. scenic representations introduced from Etruria were added to them. Both were performed either separately or on one and the same occasion, in which latter case the beginning was always made with the scenic representations. Fights of gladiators, at first arranged only by private individuals, soon became an equally important feature of the public games. The agon of gymnastic and musical arts, so highly developed amongst the Greeks, never became popular amongst the Romans. Augustus initiated one of these in memory of the battle of Actium. Nero instituted an agon consisting of horse-races and gymnastic and musical competitions, in the latter of which he took part himself; his agon was a *certamen quinquennale*. The agones were renewed for the last time by Gordianus III.

The nature of the games necessitated different local arrangements. Horse and chariot races took place in the circus, fights of gladiators and wild animals in the amphitheatre, and scenic representations in the theatre (compare §§ 83-85). The two earliest amongst the ludi circenses were the *consualia* and *equiria*, said to have been founded by Romulus; both were celebrated twice a year, the former on the 21st of August and the 15th of December, the latter on February 27th and March 14th; they consisted of chariot-races in the Campus Martius. The *ludi Romani*, also dating from the time of the kings, were celebrated in honour of the three Capitoline deities; they lasted at first only a few days: Augustus extended their duration from September 4th to 19th. The *ludi plebei* were instituted in memory of the confirmation of popular power after the secession on the Aventine; their duration was afterwards extended to a fortnight (November 4th to 17th), the final days being in this, as in the just-mentioned games, reserved for the ludi circenses. The *Cereales* were celebrated from April 12th to April 19th; their institution seems connected with the building, by the dictator Postumius, of a temple for Ceres, Liber, and Libera; at first they were *ludi votivi*, having to be decreed each time by the senate, afterwards they became annual : Cæsar appointed separate *ædiles Cereales.* The *ludi Apollinares* were instituted in consequence of an oracle contained in the *carmina Marciana* to the effect that the expulsion of the Carthaginians would be impossible till games in honour of Apollo were instituted. Ludi circenses took place on the final day, being preceded by dramatic representations. They dated from 212 B.C., being at first *ludi votivi,* afterwards *ludi stati,* celebrated on the 5th July; still later, from the 5th or 6th till the 13th of July. The prætor urbanus was charged with the arrangements. The *ludi Megalenses* (also comprising ludi circenses) were instituted to celebrate the arrival in Rome of the Magna Mater, on April 12th, 204 B.C. In order not to interfere with the Cerealia (April 12th to 19th), these games were celebrated from April 4th to 10th, it being always the custom to add new days not after, but before the day first appointed. We finally mention the *Floralia* (April 28th to May 3rd), the last day of which was occupied with the hunting of tame deer in the Circus Maximus; also the temporary games in honour of Cæsar Augustus (*ludi victoriæ Cæsaris, Augustalia*), &c., always ending in ludi circenses.

About the Circus Maximus we have spoken before (see Fig. 431). A second circus, that of Flaminius, was built 220 B.C. by the censor C. Flaminius in the meadows called after his name. Other buildings of the same kind, partly still recognisable by their ruins, were the results of later times ; we mention the circus built by Caligula in the gardens of Agrippina, commonly called the Circus of Nero, also the circus near the grave of Cæcilia Metella (erroneously called Circo di Caracalla), built by Romulus, son of Maxentius, not to speak of numerous racecourses in provincial towns (compare Fig. 430). From circumstantial evidence (such as the plan of the circus of Bovillæ, Fig. 430, sculptural representations, and descriptions by the authors) we are able to give an accurate account of the arrangements of the Circus Maximus, which itself has disappeared almost entirely.

On entering through the festive entrance-gate (to both sides of which lay the cages, *carceres,* for the racing-chariots) one observed, in the centre of the course, the spina, with three conical columns (*metæ, i.e.* goals) at each end. The spina itself was adorned with columns, small sanctuaries, statues of gods, and a tall mast, instead of which Augustus erected the obelisk now in

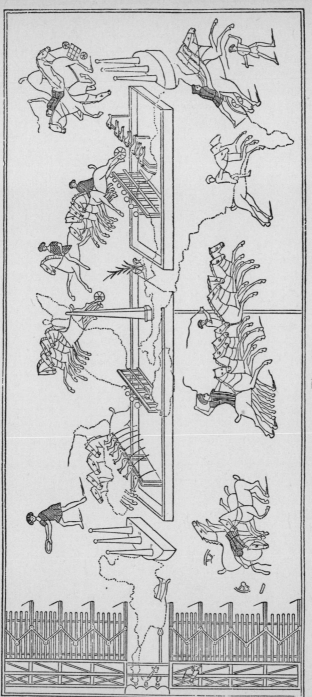

Fig. 499.

the Piazza del Popolo. Constantine added a second higher obelisk, now standing in front of the Lateran. M. Agrippa adorned the spina with seven water-spouts in the shape of dolphins, in allusion, most likely, to Neptunus Equester, to whom races were dedicated. Here also stood an altar (see Gerhard, "Antike Bildw.," Taf. CXX., 2) with seven egg-shaped objects (*ova*) lying on it, in remembrance of the origin of Castor and Pollux, horse-breakers *par excellence*. Each time the course had been run through, one of these eggs was removed as a sign to the spectators. Most of these arrangements may be observed in the mosaic, 15 feet 6 inches by 9 feet 6 inches, found in the circus of Lyons, Fig. 499. On both sides of the chief entrance we see four carceres; we further observe three conical metæ standing on semircircular bases at both ends of the spina, which is here formed by two water-reservoirs with brick facings, each of them filled by seven water-spouts in the shape of dolphins. Between the two ponds rises an obelisk, while the ova lie on two rows of poles standing in the water. A different arrangement appears in a bas-relief on a late Roman sarcophagus (Gerhard, "Antike Bildwerke," Taf. CXX., 2), the lower half of which most likely represents a chariot race in the circus, in the presence of the Emperor Maximus. The spina there is adorned with an obelisk, two Korinthian columns, and a Korinthian base, on which the dolphins are placed. The ova lie on a small altar at a little distance.

We have shown, Fig. 258, the light two-wheeled chariot used at races. The Roman charioteers (*auriga*, *agitator*), unlike the Greek who appeared naked, wore a short tunic strapped tightly round the upper part of the body; they used to have a curved knife in their belt, in order to cut the traces on the horses running away; the thighs had straps tied round them (see the statue of an auriga in the Museo Pio Clementino), or else the arms and legs were dressed in reticulated tights (see Gerhard, "Antike Bild-werke," Taf. CXX., 2). Their head-dress consisted of a leathern cap resembling a helmet. Bigæ and quadrigæ, and more rarely trigæ, were used for racing; an inscription mentions the victor of a race won with seven horses running in a row. In the biga the two horses were yoked together, in the quadriga only the two wheel-horses carried the yoke. Favourite charioteers and horses were received by the public with loud applause. Sicily, Spain, Africa, Cappadocia, &c., were celebrated for their race-horses, whose pedigree, age, and name were recorded with the utmost accuracy. The left wheel horse was watched with particular anxiety, because it had the most difficult task in doubling the meta; its running against, or being frightened at, the meta exposed chariot and charioteer to the danger of destruction. In inscriptions the name of the victorious horse is frequently mentioned together with that of the charioteer.

The umpire, sitting on a balcony above the chief entrance-portal, gave the sign for beginning the race by throwing a white cloth (*mappa*) into the arena (compare Fig. 499). On the towers or *oppida* mentioned by us stood musicians, who played in the intervals between the races. The chariots began the race from the right hand side of the entrance-portal, keeping on the right side of the spina, and returning on the left after doubling the meta; in this way the course was measured seven times without stopping. After the last time they left the circus through the carceres on the left side of the chief entrance. The whole race of seven courses was called *missus*, a single course being denominated *curriculum* or *spatium*. Usually four chariots ran at a time; the first arrival after the missus at a line marked with chalk in front of the carceres on the left being decisive as to the victory. In republican times about ten or twelve races were run in a day; after Caligula the usual number seems to have been twenty-four, an amount sufficient to fill up the whole day. Counting the length of the Circus Maximus, which had to be measured fourteen times, at three stadia, the whole distance run in each missus amounts to 25,176 feet, Rhenish measure. Making allowance for preparations, removing of impediments, and smaller intervals after the completion of six races, &c., and counting the day at twelve hours in which the twenty-four races were run, the time for each race may be roughly calculated at twenty-five minutes.

Sometimes the ordinary number of four chariots must have been increased to six, as appears from the temporary existence of six "factions" of the circus (of which more anon), and from the fact that the circus of Maxentius had twelve carceres.

In republican times already, two parties of the circus

(*factiones*) had been formed, each of which furnished two of the racing-chariots, the charioteers wearing either red or white tunics, according to the party they belonged to. The names of these parties were *factio albata* and *factio russata*. The increased *insania et furor circi* of imperial times called two new parties into life, the *factio prasina* (green) and the *factio veneta* (blue) ; under Domitian two other parties, the *aurea* and *purpurea*, were temporarily added to these. About the end of the third century A.D., the four original factions were combined into two, white joining green, and red blue, the *prasina* and *veneta* taking the lead, followed by the two other colours, whose separate existence, however, did not entirely cease. These four colours appear in the tunics of the mosaic of Lyons (Fig. 499) : in our illustration the oblique lines signify green, the horizontal ones blue, and the vertical ones red ; while the white tunics are left blank. In Constantinople these parties (δῆμοι) of the circus received a political character, and frequently made the circus the scene of their internecine warfare. In 501 A.D., under Anastasius, 3,000 citizens were thus killed in the hippodrome : during the so-called Nika revolt, A.D. 532, under Justinian, no less than 30,000 people were killed in three days, the throne being saved only by means of the German soldiers under Belisarius.

In older times the charioteers were free citizens ; afterwards this occupation, although never dishonourable, like that of the gladiators, was considered unworthy of a free Roman, and therefore mostly left to slaves and freedmen, who, previous to appearing in public, were trained at schools. Such schools, comprising a complete staff of chariot-makers, tailors, shoemakers, surgeons, teachers, &c., were kept by one or several *domini factionum*, who let out both chariots and charioteers to the highest bidding of the parties of the circus. Victorious charioteers received silver crowns, valuable garments, and money ; the successful ones amongst them frequently made large fortunes, and became *domini factionum* on their own account.

Horse-races were not run in the Roman circus : occasionally a horseman appeared with two horses (*desultores*), who jumped from one on the other while they were running at full speed, a trick learned from the Numidian cavalry (see Bartoli, "Lucerne Antiche," p. 24). The destination of the horsemen seen riding by the side of the chariots (see, for instance, Fig. 499, and Gerhard, *loc. cit.*, Taf. CXX. 2) seems uncertain.

Like the charioteers, the wrestlers and athletes appearing in the circus were, at least in later times, always professional men. Only exceptionally, and by express command of the emperor, Roman noblemen appeared in this capacity. Different in the military games and evolutions, *ludi sevirales* and *ludus Troiæ*; the former, instituted by Augustus in honour of Mars, were performed in the circus by six *turmæ* of Roman knights with three *seviri* at their head, and commanded by the *princeps iuventutis*, a title borne by the imperial princes, and, after Caracalla, claimed by the emperors themselves; the imperial coins with the inscription PRINC. IVV. showing a galloping horseman, refer to the *ludi sevirales*. The *ludus Troiæ* was a military exercise performed by boys of noble families on horseback.

Whether all ludi circenses were opened with a *pompa* seems uncertain; the fact is proved, however, of the *ludi Romani, Megalenses*, and the *ludi votivi*; it may be assumed with tolerable certainty of the *ludi Cereris*. The procession was opened by a band of musicians, followed by the officiating magistrate in a triumphal chariot, clad in the costume of a *triumphator*, and holding in his hand an ivory sceptre adorned with an eagle. A *servus publicus* held a golden crown studded with jewels over his head. His chariot was surrounded by white-robed clients (see Fig. 540), and followed by the images of the gods, with the priestly sodalities and colleges belonging to them, also by the statues of the reigning family, and of those of the deceased members of that family to whom the games were devoted. This splendid procession, starting from the Capitol, traversed the Forum, the Vicus Tuscus, the Velabrum, and Forum Boarium, entering the Circus Maximus through the chief entrance. Accompanied by the applause of the spectators, who rose to their feet, it once walked round the nearest meta, and repaired to the seats reserved for the purpose, whereat the sign for the beginning of the race was given in the manner described.

105. The fights of gladiators and the baiting of wild animals took place in the amphitheatre (see § 85). The former became known in Rome in the third century B.C., and were thence introduced into Athens, where at first they were little relished by

the refined inhabitants. Only after the conquered Greeks had become demoralised they accepted this, with other Roman customs. The origin of the gladiatorial games must, most likely, be looked for in Etruria, where they formed part of the funereal ceremonies, replacing the still older custom of human sacrifices; they seem to have been connected with the worship of Saturn—an opinion confirmed by the fact that in Rome duels of this kind originally formed part of the Saturnalia—a limitation soon swept away by the growing passion for such exhibitions. It was natural to the warlike spirit of the republican Romans to wish for the continuation of the scenes of war on a smaller scale at home; but the gloating over the sight of the *vilis sanguis* of the slaves, indulged in to an ever-increasing degree, was more apt to breed cruel tyrants than high-minded patriots.

The first *munus gladiatorium* was, according to Valerius Maximus, arranged by the brothers Marcus and Decimus Brutus in the Forum Boarium (264 B.C.) on the occasion of their father's burial. Rome did not possess an amphitheatre at that time. Several other gladiatorial fights are mentioned in connection with funerals. In the year 200 B.C. the sons of Marcus Valerius Lævinus arranged a fight of twenty-five pairs of gladiators at his funeral. In 174 B.C. T. Flaminius arranged a fight lasting three days in honour of his deceased father, seventy-four gladiators being hired for the occasion. The development of gladiatorial games as an established institution belongs to the last years of the Republic. Schools of gladiators (*ludi gladiatorii*), comprising the *familiæ gladiatorum*, owned by the State or private individuals (*lanistæ*), were formed in Rome and many other cities of the empire. They became the rallying-points of many of the most depraved elements of Roman society, and the revolts of the slaves and gladiators more than once endangered the State. Most of the fighters appearing at the public fights came from these schools. Soon these fights became an essential feature of the public games; the ædiles and other magistrates, and ultimately the emperors themselves, trying to gain popularity by means of them (*ad plebem placandam et mulcendam*). The lex Tullia against gladiatorial extravagance, moved by Cicero less from humane considerations than in order to stay the party intrigues furthered by such exhibitions, was but too soon forgotten. Augustus (22 B.C.) ordered that fights of gladiators should take place only twice a year after the consent of the senate had been obtained, the number of the gladiators being limited to 120 ; but this restriction was cancelled by Caracalla, who arranged battles of gladiators fighting not only in couples but *catervatim*. He even compelled twenty-six knights who had ruined themselves to appear in this dishonourable combat. Many characteristic incidents of the gladiatorial fights arranged by Claudius, Nero, and Domitian are recorded by the authors ; even Trajan, after his return from the victorious campaign on the Danube, arranged festive gladiatorial games lasting 123 days, 10,000 fighters being engaged for the occasion. Commodus, of whom Lampridius relates, " *et nomina gladiatorum recepit eo gaudio, quasi acciperet triumphalia*," and who designated himself as *primus palus secutorum*, brought the passion for exhibitions of this kind to its climax, the income of the State being squandered for this ignoble purpose. Even the Christian emperors were obliged to buy the favour of the populace, and divert its attention from political passions by inhumane spectacles of this kind. Private schools of gladiators, and gangs of them amongst the *familiæ* of rich Romans, were of common occurrence during the last years of the Republic. The emperors often used to establish imperial institutions of the same kind. Domitian built in Rome four large gladiatorial schools, viz., the *ludus Gallicus, Dacius, magnus*, and *matutinus*. Several towns, as Præneste, Ravenna, and Alexandria, were recommended for the same purpose, owing to their healthy situation. Capua was, from the first, celebrated for its gladiatorial schools. In Pompeii, barracks of gladiators have been recognised as such by Garrucci by the fittings, by inscriptions, and pictures of gladiators, &c., scribbled on walls and columns, and by the numerous gladiatorial weapons found there. The structure consists of an open court (55 by 40·10 metres) surrounded by colonnades, and adjoined by buildings of two stories, containing sixty-six separate rooms. Counting two gladiators to each room, the number of the inmates must have been 132. Captive Germans, Dacians, Gauls, Æthiopians, &c., as also slaves and criminals condemned to death, were received as members of the *familia gladiatorum ;* even free-born Romans, after having wasted their property, frequently sold themselves to the *lanistæ*, receiving sums of money (*auctoramentum gladiatorium*) as the price of their infamy (*auctorati*). Guided by the fencing-master (*doctores* or *magistri*), and fed on a peculiar diet (*sagina*, chosen with a view to strengthen the muscles), the apprenticed gladiator (*tiro*) practised the technical manipulations of his art at first with light wooden, and afterwards with exceedingly heavy, weapons against a post or a straw puppet. After having got successfully through his public *début*, he received an oblong tablet of ivory (*tessera gladiatoria*) as a reward, and sign of his proficiency, on which were written his name, that of his master, and the day of his first fight and

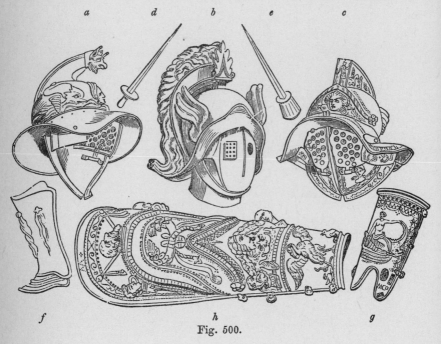

Fig. 500.

victory. The tiro was thus admitted to the rank of the *spectati* (distinguished persons) : a certain number of these decorations most likely entitled the gladiator to be received amongst the *veterani*. About sixty genuine *tesseræ* marked SP, in rare cases SPECT or SPECTAT (*spectatus*), have been discovered (compare Fr. Ritschl, "Die Tesseræ gladiatoriæ der Römer." München, 1864).

A number of weapons of gladiators have been found; by means of these, and of numerous specimens seen in pictures and plastic representations, we are enabled to give an accurate account of their form, which essentially differs from that of the weapons used by legionaries. Several gladiatorial helmets are kept in the Museo Borbonico : the one shown Fig. 500, *c*, has a massive crest adorned with sculptures ; a broad brim serves to protect neck and forehead. The visor consists of four plates, the two lower ones being massive, the two upper ones pierced with holes like a sieve for the gladiator to look through. The visor in Fig. 500, *b*, consists of two plates, with an opening for the eye in each ; the opening on the left being round, while that on the right resembles a sieve. Fig. 500, *a*, shows a helmet of a similar kind also kept in the Museo Borbonico. Many different kinds of the gladiatorial helmet appear on the monuments.

The shield of the gladiator was the square, oval, or circular *parma* (compare Fig. 505), differing from that used in the army by its lighter weight and more graceful form, &c. An oblong shield of a very different form, with rounded edges and a curve at the upper end to ease the movements of the shoulder and upper arm, is kept in the Museo Borbonico. The right hand and arm were protected by straps of leather (compare Fig. 505) or by iron splints (Fig. 500, *g*). The way of protecting the legs seems to have differed amongst the various classes of gladiators. Some appear with straps round their thighs, while their shins are protected by greaves (Fig. 505). Others wear greaves or leather gaiters (resembling the κάλτζα of the modern Greeks) on the right or the left leg only (Fig. 500, *f*, compare Fig. 505) ; others, again, wear the foot-coverings of the legionaries, or appear with naked feet (Fig. 501). Fig. 500, *g*, *h*, shows two richly ornamented, not to say overloaded, coverings for arm and thigh, from originals in the Museo Borbonico.

The aggressive weapons of the gladiators were the lance, the dagger, straight or curved, and the Roman sword, or, in its stead, the rapier (Fig. 500, *d*, *e*, compare Fig. 504). The gladiator's chest was uncovered ; his body was dressed in a loose garment fastened with a belt, and hanging down to the knees in front, but pulled up on the hips (Figs. 502, 503).

The different classes of gladiators were distinguished by their weapons and by their mode of fighting. The *Samnites* derived their name from their peculiar equipment, imitated from that

nation.* It consisted of a large oblong shield (*scutum*), a helmet
with visor, crest, and plume, a greave on the left leg, and a sleeve
of leather or metal for the right arm, to which a shoulder-piece
(*galerus*) reaching above the shoulder was attached (compare

Fig. 501 *a.*

"Bullet. Napol." New Series, I., Tav. 7). Their sword was short.
It is difficult to distinguish the Samnites amongst the numerous
statues of gladiators ; neither does it appear from the authors what
class of gladiators was usually opposed to them, for the gladiators

Fig. 501 *b.*

fighting with each other never belonged to the same class. A
second class of gladiators, much liked in imperial times, were the
secutores, whose antagonists were the *retiarii.* The latter wore a
short tunic or apron (*subligaculum*), fastened round the body with

* It is said that after the defeat of the Samnites by the Dictator Papirius Cursor
in the year 444 of the city, their national armour was adopted for the gladiators as
a sign of contempt.

a belt, and generally a sleeve on the left arm. Their head was
uncovered. Their weapons of attack were the trident (*fuscina,
tridens*) and the dagger; besides which they
carried a large net (*iaculum*), in which they
tried to entangle the *secutores*, the latter
being armed with helmet, shield, and sword.
Suetonius, in his life of Caligula (cap. 30), tells
of a fight between five gladiators of each class,
in which the retiarii were beaten without
offering resistance; but when by command of
the emperor they were to be killed, one of
them suddenly took a *fuscina* and killed all
the *secutores*. A mosaic (Fig. 501, *a*, *b*)
illustrates their mode of fighting. In Fig.

Fig. 502.

501, *a*, the secutor, entangled in the net, attacks
the retiarius lying on the ground, while the latter, having dropped
his trident, defends himself with a dagger. In Fig. 501, *b*, the
retiarius attacks his entangled
antagonist with the fuscina,
seemingly with success. According to Isidorus, the secutores
carried a stick with lead bullets
attached to it, with which they
tried to keep off the net.*

The *laquearii* also were light-
armed gladiators. They carried
a sort of lasso, which they threw
over their antagonist in order
to pull him down. They were
of late imperial origin. The
myrmillo and the *Gallus* were
frequently opposed to the retiarius. Their armour was that
of the Gauls, the name *myrmillo*

Fig. 503.

being derived from a fish (μορμύλος) adorning the crest of their
helmet. Fig. 502, taken from a tomb, most likely represents a

---

* " *Gestabat enim cuspidem et massam plumbeam, quæ adversarii iaculum impediret, ut
antequam feriret rete, iste superaret ;* " compare *Revue Archéol.*, IX., p. 80.

myrmillo. A fight between a myrmillo and a retiarius is represented in the mosaic pavement of the Roman villa at Nennig (see
v. Wilmowsky, " Die röm. Villa zu Nennig "). The *torques* round
the neck of the gladiator in our illustration (Fig. 502) indicates the
Gallus, while the crest of the helmet hung on the pole distinctly shows
the fish, characteristic of the myrmillo. Another class of gladiators,
frequently mentioned in imperial times, were the *Thraces.* They
were armed with a small round shield (*parma*), greaves, and a
dagger, either curved like a scythe (*sica,* frequently seen on
imperial monuments in the hands of barbarian warriors) or bent
in a straight-lined angle. The *hoplomachi* were completely armed
with helmet, cuirass, and greaves. Gladiators also fought in chariots
or on horseback. A large bas-relief at Pompeii (Fig. 505) contains
two *equites,* wearing helmets with closed visors; their arms, like

Fig. 504.

those of the scutores, were protected by straps; their offensive
and defensive weapons were the *spiculum* and *parma* respectively.
The gladiators fighting in chariots were called *essedarii.* This
mode of fighting seems to have been introduced by Cæsar, in
imitation of the skilful manœuvres of the chariot-fighters of
Brittany described by him (" De Bello Gall.," IV. 33). We
finally mention the *andabatæ,* who wore helmets with closed visors,
containing no opening for the eyes; and the *dimachœri,* who
fought with two swords, a mode of fighting belonging exclusively
to a later age. Fig. 503 perhaps represents a gladiator of this
kind—a supposition which, however, has been greatly doubted of
late.

The announcement of gladiatorial fights was made by *libelli*

sent to the people in the neighbourhood or by advertisements on
the walls (*programmata*). An inscription
on the Basilica of Pompeii announces the
appearance of the "family" of the lanista,
N. Festus Ampliatus, in these words : " *N.
Festi Ampliati familia gladiatoria pugnabit
iterum, pugnabit XVI kal. Iunias, venatio,
vela.*" In these advertisements the number
and names of the gladiators and the mode
of their fighting were announced. On the
day of the performance a solemn procession of gladiators, walking in couples,
went through the streets to the arena ;
there the weapons were examined, and a
sort of introductory fight (*prolusio*) with
blunt weapons (*arma lusoria*) opened the
proceedings. The sound of a bugle announced the commencement of the real
fight. The words of command were
shouted : " *Ponite iam gladios hebetes, pug-
natur iam acutis,*" whereat the lanista or
editor muneris gladiatorii determined the position of the antagonists, and drew the limits
within which the battle was to be fought.
Fig. 504, from a Pompeian wall-painting,
illustrates these preparations. In the
centre stands the lanista marking the lines
in the sand with a stick. One of the
gladiators stands ready for the fight, while
an assistant presents his sword to him ;
his antagonist is blowing the signal-horn,
while two attendants cowering in the
background hold his helmet and shield in
readiness. On one of the gladiators being
disabled, the words " *Hoc habet* " were
shouted. The wounded man dropped his
weapons (*arma submittit*) and, holding up
his forefinger, begged his life from the
people, or from the lanista or editor muneris in case he was their

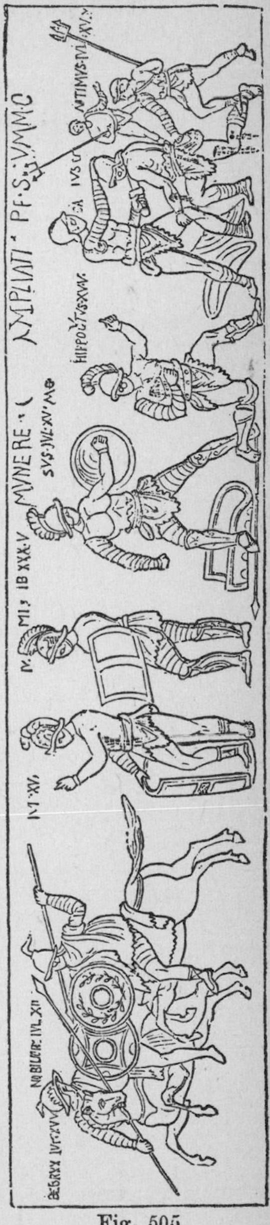

Fig. 505.

private property. In imperial times the emperor, of course, had the decision of life and death. In case the spectators lifted their clenched fists (*verso pollice*) the fight had to be continued; the waving of handkerchiefs was the sign of mercy granted. A gladiator who had behaved in a cowardly manner had no claim to mercy; he had to take up his weapon (*ferrum recipere*), and was, if necessary, compelled by whipping or burning with a hot iron to resume the fight. In case the fight was *sine remissione* (*i.e.* without quarter asked or given) no appeal to the people could take place. The victor was rewarded with a palm-branch, crowns, and, in imperial times, money. The blunt rapier (*rudis*) given to a gladiator signified his release; he then again became a slave till the granting of the pileus made him a freedman.

Fig. 505 shows a large bas-relief adorning the wall of the erroneously so-called tomb of Scaurus at Pompeii. The two equites in the left corner (armed both alike) we have mentioned before. The curved spike of their helmets is remarkable. The two next following gladiators are also armed alike, but for the coverings of their legs. One of them, bleeding from a wound in his chest, is leaning on his shield, and implores mercy with lifted forefinger, his unwounded antagonist seeming to wait for the permission to continue the fight. In the next group one of the gladiators, wounded in his chest, and sunk on his knee, implores mercy in the manner just described; he has dropped shield and lance, and turns his head towards his threatening antagonist. Here we notice a difference of greaves and shields in the two gladiators. The third group shows the final execution of a conquered gladiator by his victor. A figure holding a trident, most likely an assistant destined to carry off the killed gladiator through the *porta libitinensis* to the death-chamber (*spoliarium*), lays hold of the dying man. Another official of the same kind is seen in the background. If on arriving in the death-chamber there remained signs of life in the vanquished gladiator, it was the duty of these people to kill him.

Another spectacle, no less sanguinary, of which, in imperial times, the amphitheatre, and in some cases the circus, were the scene, is the *venatio* of wild animals, the introduction of which dates back to the year 186 B.C. Like the gladiators, the fighters with animals (*bestiarii, venatores*) were trained at schools (*familiæ venatoriæ).* Sometimes they were hirelings, sometimes captives or criminals, compelled to fight the ferocious animals in the arena. In the latter case the spectacle of untrained men imperfectly armed or quite without defence exposed to the fury of the animals must have been horrible. At other times these animals, made furious by hunger or fire, were let loose at each other. The rarest animals from the most distant regions

were brought to Rome for the purpose. Pompeius arranged a fight of 500 or 600 lions, 18 elephants, and 410 other ferocious animals brought from Africa. In a chase arranged by Augustus (A.D. 5), 36 crocodiles were killed in the Flaminian circus, flooded for the purpose. Caligula arranged a

Fig. 506.

fight between 400 bears and an equal number of African wild beasts. The authors are full of horrid descriptions of animal-fights under the later emperors, at which frequently numbers of captives lost their lives. Amongst the numerous plastic representations of such scenes we have chosen (Fig. 506) a bas-relief rendering a fight of armed bestiarii with animals near the theatre of Marcellus,

Fig. 507.

which is seen in the background. The animals (a bear, panther, and lion) wear the leathern girths with rings attached to them, by means of which they were fettered in their cages underneath the arena. Figs. 507 and 508 render subjects of a similar nature; they are taken from the above-mentioned gladiatorial bas-relief on a tomb at Pompeii. The former shows the fight between a bestiarius and a panther or tiger leashed to a bull, which latter is made to advance by the pricks of the lance of another bestiarius. This is one of the less dangerous tricks of professional bestiarii. Fig. 508 shows a bestiarius with arm and leg protected by straps, and holding in his hand a cloth to be thrown over the head of the attacking bear.

Fig. 508.

A third spectacle produced at some of the amphitheatres was the *naumachia,* or naval combat. The arena was flooded by means of a system of canals, pipes, and locks; in other cases large ponds were dug for the purpose. Cæsar built the first naumachia in the Campus Martius (46 B.C.), large enough for the manœuvres of two fleets manned by 1,000 soldiers and 2,000 rowers. Augustus (2 B.C.) built a naumachia of stone in the vicinity of the *horti Cæsaris,* near the Tiber, in which a naval battle between Athenians and Persians was fought by thirty vessels. Titus and Domitian used the Coliseum for the same purpose. Of existing amphitheatres that of Capua shows the flooding apparatus in the best state of preservation. The largest of all naval fights was that arranged by Domitian on the Fucine Lake (52 A.D.). One hundred men-of-war, manned by 19,000 soldiers and rowers, attacked each other at the signal of a trumpet blown by a Triton, who suddenly emerged from the water in the centre of the lake. The number of killed tends to prove that the battle was by no means a feigned one.

Sometimes mythological scenes were performed in the arena with cruel accuracy. Condemned criminals had to mount the pyre like Hercules, or to give their hand to the flames like Mucius Scævola, or to be crucified like Laureolus the robber; others were torn by bears, in imitation of the fate of Orpheus. Mythological scenes of a frivolous kind also were enacted : dwarfs and women performed sham-fights, &c. Seneca sternly reproves these levities.

106. The first scenic performances are said to have taken place in Rome in 364 B.C., when, during a plague, Etruscan actors performed mimic dances to appease the divine wrath. The mimic dances thus introduced were soon afterwards accompanied by the recital of comic verses in changing metres, the result being

the satirical drama (*satura*). The creator of the drama proper was Livius Andronicus, who first added to the pantomime, accompanied by flute-playing and singing, the dialogue (*diverbium*) founded on a story or plot (*fabula*). His successors were Nævius, Ennius, Plautus, Terentius, Pacuvius, Atticus, and others who, under the influence of Greek models, further developed the Roman drama. The close relation of Roman to the later Greek comedy explains the absence of the chorus, which, in its turn, accounts for the want of the orchestra in Roman theatres, the space assigned for it in Greek theatres being used for seats of spectators. The action, therefore, was limited to the stage itself, which was both wider and deeper than that of the Greeks, to give space to the numerous actors of the Roman drama,* and to the gorgeous pageants frequently introduced in imperial times. At first a temporary wooden stage was erected for the *ludi scenici,* mostly on the slope of a hill. There were no seats for the public, neither was a space reserved for the upper classes. The first distinction of this kind was made in 194 B.C., when the front part of the cavea was separated from the rest by a barrier, and reserved for senators. During the next forty years it became the custom of the rich to have chairs carried after them to the theatre by slaves ; but the original form of the cavea was retained till after the subjection of Greece, when the first theatre, with semicircular rows of seats rising in the manner of terraces, was erected; the seats of the senators were placed immediately in front of the stage, not without the indignant murmurs of the populace. Further distinctions soon were made. The fourteen rows behind the seats of the senators were assigned to the knights, the priestly colleges received seats of honour ; the women were placed higher up, separated from the men, only the highest steps of the cavea remaining to the populace. All the theatres built in the seventh century of the city consisted of wood, and were pulled down after being used. The first stone theatre was built by Pompeius in the year 699 of the city (55 B.C.), the second by Cornelius Balbus, 13 B.C., the third by Augustus in honour of Marcellus. All the other theatres mentioned in imperial times

---

* In the Greek drama the various parts were divided amongst three actors: not so in Rome, where each part was performed by a separate actor.

consisted of wood, and were pulled down after having been used once.

About the scenery and mechanical appliances of the Roman theatre nothing certain is known; most likely they resembled those of the Greek stage. The curtain (*aulæum*), after the performance, did not drop, but was raised. Besides this chief curtain there was a second (*siparium*) one, closed between the acts; it parted in the middle.

The professional actors were mostly slaves or freedmen, united in troupes (*greges, catervæ*), and kept by a manager (*dominus gregis*), frequently by an old principal actor (*actor primarum*). This manager treated with the magistrate, who had the *cura ludorum*, and who paid the salary of the actors. Not inconsiderable sums were paid to favourite actors, at least in later times, when the theatre had gained vast popularity: besides this, the actor who had gained the loudest applause was rewarded by the *curator ludorum* with the palm or crown of victory and honour, in imperial times also with costly robes and money.

Since the time of Terentius actors used to wear masks; up to that time a fair, black, or reddish head-dress (*galerus*), resembling most likely the onkos of the Greeks, served to mark the actor's age. The costume varied in accordance with the different kinds of masks required for tragedy and comedy (compare Figs. 311 and 312): in the former long floating garments (*syrmata*) and the high cothurnus were worn, while comedians appeared in an every-day dress of the loudest possible colours and in low shoes (*soccus*).

Amongst dramatic representations we also mention the *atellanæ,* the *mimus,* and the *pantomimus.* The *atellanæ fabulæ,* called after the Oscian city of Atella, were a thoroughly national and thoroughly Italian burlesque, played by young citizens in typical masks. Amongst these types still recognisable in those of the modern *commedia dell' arte* we mention *maccus* (arlechino); *pappus* or *casnar,* the grave old father of the piece (pantaleone); *bucco,* the glutton (brighella); and *dossennus,* the humpbacked charlatan, and soothsayer (dottore). At first these plays, partly improvised, contained only rough parodies of tradesman and peasant life; after the war with Carthage they were developed more regularly by special playwrights, and given on the regular stage as *postludes* (*exodium*) of the drama. At the same time the

parts were given over to professional actors, the citizens naturally
shrinking from an occupation which, even in later times, was at
least legally infamous.

The mimus, also, was a sort of burlesque, serving, like the
atellanæ, as interlude to the serious drama. The dialogue was
witty, frequently coarse, the whole being destined to parody real
life in a grotesque, not seldom indecent, manner. The chief actor
(*archimimus*) was dressed in the parti-coloured costume of an
harlequin (*centunculus*), over which a short cloak (*ricinium*) was
worn; he acted before a curtain which divided the front part from
the back of the stage. The other characters (amongst which we
mention particularly the bald-headed *parasitus* or *stupidus*) played
minor parts, mainly seconding, by occasional retorts or gesticulations, the chief actor. Actors of both sexes appeared in the
mimus, the grossest obscenities frequently adding to the attract-
iveness of the play,—at least, at a later period.

The pantomimus was an outgrowth of the *canticum* of the
comedy, in which the actor indicated by a dramatic dance or by
gesticulations the subject of the song. Already, in republican
times, this dance became to be a separate branch of art, brought to
its climax of perfection in imperial times by Pylades of Cilicia and
Bathyllos of Alexandria. The subjects of the pantomime were
taken from the myths of gods and heroes, the actor having
to represent male and female characters by turns, while a choir,
accompanied by flute-players, sang the corresponding canticum.
Sometimes several male and female dancers appeared in the
pantomime, which in that case became a sort of dramatic ballet
called *pyrrhicha* (not to be mistaken for the Pyrrhic dance of the
Dacians).

107. Notwithstanding many descriptions of the Roman army,
not to speak of the numerous remaining specimens of weapons, our
account of the equipment of the Roman soldier must be in many
cases imperfect and conjectural. We shall limit ourselves, in
accordance with the aim of our book, to a description of Roman
armour as far as it can be illustrated by the remaining monuments.
The comparatively small amount of weapons found on the numerous battle-fields is explained by the fact, that a century before
our era bronze weapons began to be replaced by iron ones, which
latter metal is more liable to destruction by rust.

We first turn to the weapons of defence. The Roman helmet (*cassis*, *galea*) differs from the Greek by the absence of a visor. The simplest form, specified by two helmets found in Etruscan graves (Fig. 509, *c*, *d*), resembles the pileus, and at the same time reminds one of the steel cap worn by common soldiers in the Middle Ages. A more developed form of the helmet is shown, Fig. 509, *f*, from an original in the Museo Borbonico. To the low semi-globular cap a stripe of metal has been added, surrounding the head on all sides, and considerably enlarged at the back so as to protect the neck. It covers the forehead to about the eyes. Cheekpieces (*bucculæ*) are added. The top of the common soldier's helmet consists of a simple button (see Fig. 509, *e*, from the arch of Severus) ; sometimes it is adorned with a short plume : a helmet of the latter kind is worn by almost all the soldiers on the arch of

a　　　　*b*　　*c*　　*d*　　*e*　　　*f*

Fig. 509.

Constantine. The helmet of centurions and higher officers are adorned with three feathers, or with a crest of horsehair (*crista*, *iuba*), which was taken off on the march, but put on again in the battle, so as to distinguish the leaders in the fight (see the two helmets, Fig. 509, *a*, *b*, from the arch of Constantine, where they are worn by foot-soldiers and horsemen). The upper part of the body was protected by an iron cuirass, fashioned according to the lines of the muscles both in front and at the back, like the old Greek θώραξ στάδιος. Servius Tullius re-organized the Roman army of citizens after the pattern of the Greek phalanx, and adopted the iron helmet, the oval shield, and the cuirass of the hoplitai for the two first ranks of the phalanx. At the later re-organization of the army the cuirass was dropped by the common soldiers, and perhaps retained only by the leaders in exceptional cases. The Latin name of the cuirass is unknown to us. The *lorica ferrea*,

which Tacitus (Hist. II. 11) mentions as worn by the Emperor
Otho, was most likely an iron cuirass. Several specimens of the
bronze cuirass are still in existence (Fig. 510, *a*). It was,
perhaps by Camillus, the great reformer of tactics and armour,
exchanged for the *lorica* proper, made of stripes of metal. It was
commonly worn by the legionaries of the empire. From five to
seven stripes of beaten iron or bronze (Fig. 510 *b*), each equal in
width to about three fingers, attached to leather straps, were
fastened round the body with hooks from the
waist up to the armpit, thus forming the breast-
armour (*pectorale*, Fig. 511) proper, while similar
stripes were laid across the shoulders (*humeralia*),
and fastened by means of hooks to the upper
stripes of the pectorale. Several stripes, hanging
down in front, protected the lower part of the
body. Quite as common as the lorica is the tight-
fitting leather jerkin, reaching down a little
lower than the thighs, and worn over the tunic
by the common soldiers on imperial monuments
(see the soldier to the right, Fig. 530). Occasionally (for instance, by a number of soldiers on
the arch of Severus) the lorica, or a portion of
it, is worn over this jerkin. Scale and chain-

Fig. 510.

armour (*lorica squamata* and *hamata*) was (owing
to its high price) worn in older times only by the hastati and
principes; at a later period, also, it remained the exclusive dress
of officers and of certain corps of the army (Fig. 512). The Antiquarium of the Royal Museum, Berlin (bronzes, No. 1025), possesses a fragment of a chain-and-scale armour, found near Rome,
in which the scales are put on the meshes of the fine iron mail.

Generals, and the emperor himself, wore undoubtedly the
more costly Greek chalkochiton, which, perhaps in an idealised
form, appears on monuments frequently adorned with inlaid or
chiselled ornaments (see, for instance, the military statue of
Caligula, Fig. 510, *c*). The marble statuette of Augustus, found
in 1863 in the villa of the Cæsars, nine miglie from the Porta del
Popolo, is most remarkable, both by the chiselled decoration of the
armour and by the perfect colours in which the marble is painted.

Greaves (*ocrea*) of bronze are found in many of our museums.

They were worn in the time of the Republic by the hastati, principes, and triarii, on the right leg, unprotected by the shield; the cavalry in Polybius's time wore greaves made of leather. In imperial times metal greaves were, at least by the

Fig. 511.   Fig. 512.

legionaries, altogether abandoned for leather or woollen stockings extending over the calf. The foot, to above the ankle, was covered with straps by the whole army (see Figs. 511 and 512).

According to Diodorus, the Romans, previously to becoming acquainted with the Etruscans, used square shields; from the Etruscans they adopted the common Argive *aspis* (see page 237), or the circular iron shield *clypeus*.* Besides this shield, the Romans are said to have adopted from the Samnites the four-cornered *scutum* (4 feet long by $2\frac{1}{2}$ feet wide), a wooden shield covered with leather, showing the form of a cylinder cut in half (compare our remark about the shield of the gladiators called Samnites, p. 557). The upper and lower edges of the shield were, by

Fig. 513.

* The Royal Museum, Berlin (bronzes, No. 1008), possesses an Etruscan shield (found in a grave near Corneto) of gilt bronze, richly ornamented. The thinness of the metal in this and other shields found in the graves of Cære and Tarquinii seems to show their purely ornamental character (see Friederichs, "Berlins ant. Bildwerke," II., 1871, p. 218 *et seq.*)

Camillus's order, lined with iron. In the old Roman phalanx the first class of legionaries carried the clypeus, the second, third, and fourth classes the scutum; after the Servian re-organization of the army the latter was worn by hastati, principes, and triarii, while the heavy iron clypeus disappeared entirely, the light circular *parma* made of leather being given in its stead to the light-armed soldier (*velites*). Of the time when the oval and hexagonal shields were introduced in the army we have no certain knowledge. Rectangular, hexagonal, and oval shields are worn by the Roman soldiers on the bas-reliefs of one and the same triumphal gate or column; for instance, on the arch of Septimius Severus. It therefore may be assumed with certainty, that the different parts of the army were distinguished not only by the form, but also by the painting on their shields (see Figs. 521, 523, 525, 526) of various signs, such as appear on the shields of larger or smaller divisions on the monuments of imperial times. We there see winged thunderbolts, lightnings surrounded by wreaths, single and double eagles ("Col. Traian.," 26, 91, 110; "Col. Anton.," 31, 45, 46, 58), rhombic figures, crescents, and crowns of lilies ("Col. Anton.," 21), laurel crowns round the umbo of the shield ("Col. Traian.," 71, 72), and other designs composed of rhomboids, crescents and rays. While marching, the foot-soldiers frequently hung their shields over their backs on straps ("Col. Anton."); horsemen fastened them under the saddle-cloth at the horse's side ("Col. Traian.," 66).

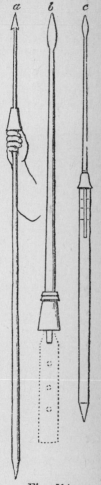

Fig. 514.

The spears used by the different divisions of the Roman army greatly varied in form; their shape also changed considerably in the course of centuries (see the different spear-heads, Fig. 513). The long Etruscan *hasta* (resembling the old Greek lance) is said to have been introduced by Servius Tullius; Camillus retained it for the triarii, while to the hastati and principes he gave an

additional javelin (*pilum*), used for throwing. Several heads
of *pila* have been found in the Rhinelands and Switzerland.
Lindenschmit and Köchly * have made careful researches both
with regard to the history and the varieties of the pilum. The
oldest pilum used by the triarii, chiefly for the defence of walls
against a storming enemy, was a long heavy weapon (*pilum
murale*) ; in later times it was used only on rare occasions. The
consecutive modifications of the pilum by Marius (Plutarch,
25) and Cæsar belong to the special history of Roman arms. The
entire length of the Cæsarian pilum was six feet, the iron head
and the shaft being each three feet long. Fig. 514, *a*, shows a
pilum from the tombstone of Q. Petilius Secundus, a private
of the 15th Legion, in the Museum of Bonn. Another tombstone
in the same museum, and two spear-heads (most likely of pila)
found near Mayence, and now in the museum of that city (see one
of them, Fig. 514, *b*), further illustrate the form of the pilum.
The two spear-heads consist of four-edged pieces of iron (two feet
long) with four-edged pyramidal points to them, and with a flat piece
attached to the bottom end, which was let into a split of
the shaft. A four-edged ring was pulled over the
spear-head up the shaft, besides which the iron was
made fast by means of cross nails (see the restored pilum,
Fig. 514, *c*).

Vegetius describes the *spiculum*, a kind of pilum used
in late imperial times. It was 5½ feet long, the size
of the three-edged spear-head being 9 inches to 1 foot.
The soldiers of later imperial times who objected to the
older heavy pilum, frequently used the *vericulum* (called

Fig. 515. in Vegetius's time *verutum*), 3½ feet long, with an iron
point 5 inches long. About the same time we hear of javelins
with a leathern strap (*amentum*) attached to them, so as to increase
their effect on being thrown (compare our remarks about the ἀγκύλη,
p. 242, as also Clarac, "Musée," II., pl. 148, No. 319). Some
of the troops of late imperial times were armed with arrows to be
thrown (*martiobarbuli, plumbatæ* sc. *sagittæ*), of which every soldier

---

* "Verhandlungen der 21. Versammlung deutscher Philologen und Schulmänner
in Augsburg." Leipsic, 1863, p. 139 *et seq.* Compare Lindenschmit, "Die vater-
ländischen Alterthümer der F. Hohenzoller'schen Sammlungen zu Sigmaringen."
Mainz, 1860, p. 17 *et seq.*

carried five fastened inside the shield. Their heads were made heavy with lead, and had a barb. Fig. 515 shows an arrow-head of this kind (8 inches long), found near Mayence, at present in the Museum of Wiesbaden.

Of swords (*gladius*) used by Roman soldiers we have to distinguish the older Gallic and the later Spanish swords. The Gallic sword was rather long and heavy; it had no point, and its blade was sharpened on one side only. After the battle of Cannæ, in which the Romans experienced the superiority of the lighter two-edged Spanish sword used by the Carthaginians, the latter weapon was adopted by them. The older sword does not appear on monuments. The two swords shown, Fig. 516, *a* and *b*, are such as were used by common soldiers; of these, numerous specimens are still in existence. Officers undoubtedly used superior weapons, distinguished by the graceful form of the handle (Fig. 516, *c*) or by the valuable material and ornamentation of the scabbard. Fig. 516, *d*, shows a scabbard adorned with gold and silver ornaments; it was found, in 1848, near Mayence, and is, perhaps, a sword of honour presented by Tiberius (whose portrait, *en médaillon*, appears on it) to one of his generals. The Spanish sword was carried in a shoulder-belt (*balteus*, Figs. 511 and 512) or waist-belt (Fig. 523); in the latter way it was worn chiefly by superior officers, and always on the right

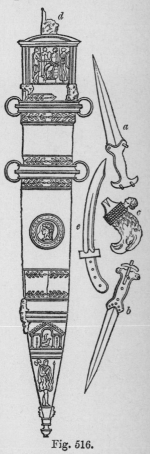

Fig. 516.

side, while the old Gallic sword was worn on the left. In close fights the soldiers used to advance the right leg, while in throwing the javelin the left leg was put forward. Besides the sword the soldiers on the imperial monuments frequently have a long narrow dagger on the right side (see the *signifer* in Lersch, "Centralmuseum," II., and the centurio, Clarac, "Musée," II., pl

148, No. 319), which considerably differs from the broad, short dagger, frequently found in the graves of barbarian nations. Longer swords (*spatha*) reappear after the time of Hadrian, used only by certain divisions of the army. Fig. 516, *e*, represents a sabre worn (on arches and columns) only by barbarian soldiers.

Bow (*arcus*) and arrows (*sagitta*) seem to have been first adopted in the time of Marius from the foreign allies, and their

Fig. 517.   Fig. 518.

use always remained limited to these. On imperial monuments we, therefore, see this weapon always in the hands of barbarians or of such soldiers of the Roman army who, by their dress, are marked as auxiliaries (see Figs. 517 and 518). After the wars with Carthage the bow gained greater importance, and troops of Cretan and Balearic bowmen ever since that time formed regular divisions of the Roman infantry. The Asiatic allies sent chiefly bowmen on horseback, covered from head to foot in scale armour (*cataphracti, loricati equites*, Fig. 518). They were renowned for their skill. The bow and arrows used by all these troops exactly resembled those of the Greeks (see two arrow-heads, Fig. 519). Three-edged arrow-heads are frequently found amongst Roman ruins; they were fastened to the shaft with a nail. The crossbow marked amongst the ancients the transition from light to heavy artillery. It was called *arcuballista* (γαστραφέτης), and to bend it the small three-spiked instruments found in our museums were most likely used.

Fig. 519.

Slingers (*fundibalatores*) we find, under the name of *accensi velati*, as a corps of the older Roman army attached to the *rorarii*. Like the bow, the sling gained its real importance after the Carthaginian wars, owing to the skill of the Balearic allies. Dressed in the tunic and sagum, in the folds of which latter thrown over the left arm the ammunition was kept (see Fig. 520), the slinger held his weapon (*funda*, compare p. 248) in the right. The slingers of the Columna Traiana are, moreover, armed with a short sword and a small one-handled shield, while a slinger on the Columna Antonina is without either. The missiles thrown by the slingers were either stones (*lapides missiles*) or pieces of lead in the form of acorns (*glans*); many such, found chiefly at Enna, in Sicily, and at

Fig. 520.

Asculum, are seen in our museums, some with defying inscriptions in Latin or Greek, such as, *pete culum Octaviani, fugitivi peristis, feri Pomp(ejum)*, δέξαι, &c. (see the missiles kept in the Royal Museum, Berlin, Bronzes, No. 1128-42).

Elephants appear in the Roman army for the first time during the war with Philip, after they had been used for many centuries by Asiatic nations, from whom they were adopted by the Greeks. The elephant was conducted by a *rector* riding on the neck of the animal, and pricking it with an instrument called *cuspis*, resembling a *harpe* (Fig. 278, *b*). A bronze coin of the city of Nicæa, with the head of Caracalla, shows on its reverse a *rector* riding on an elephant with the *cuspis* in his hand.

Soldiers on the march had to carry a rather heavy baggage besides their arms. Only a change of arms and the heavy baggage were carried by pack-horses and mules (*iumenta sarcinaria*). In imperial times carts on two or four wheels were used for the purpose, as appears from the baggage-trains on the column of Antoninus and the

Fig. 521.

arch of Severus. Amongst the heavy baggage were the tents (*tentorium, tabernaculum*), made of leather or canvas, and the poles and pegs belonging to them. The base of the tent was

about 10 square feet; it had a roof-like cover (see "Col. Anton.,"
Nos. 10 and 26), accommodating about ten men (*contubernium*).
Each *centurio* had, moreover, a separate tent, and each *tribunus*
two for himself and his attendants. The camp of a legion, therefore, consisted of about 500 tents. Poles to mark out the camp,
standards, and tools, and, on large expeditions, stores and hand-
mills, were carried after the army. The legionaries themselves
had, moreover, at least in older times, to carry saws, spades, axes,
hoes, sickles, linen, a cooking apparatus, a change of clothes, and,
on longer expeditions, stores for twelve days, to which list we
have to add, in ante-Cæsarean times, the gabions. The baggage
of the foot-soldier, including arms, weighed about sixty pounds,
or about as much as that of a soldier of the Prussian infantry in
former years. The soldier's knapsack was unknown to the Romans.
Marius greatly eased the burden of the soldiers by the so-called

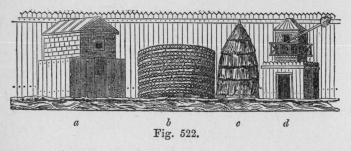

Fig. 522.

Marian mule (*muli Mariani*), that is, a pole with forked ends,
across which a piece of wood was laid; the victuals and dress, being
made into a bundle (*sarcina*) and fastened to the crosspole, were
thus conveniently shouldered, and taken off at the beginning of
the fight. This arrangement seems to have remained unaltered
in imperial times, as appears from a group of marching soldiers on
the column of Trajan (Fig. 521).

To supply the men and horses with food in barren countries
magazines containing corn (*horrea*) and hay (*fœnilia, palearia*) were
instituted on the line of march, places with good communications
by road and water being chosen in preference. Stores of fuel
and wood for gabions, bridges, and besieging engines also were
collected. Such magazines, fortified by palisades, are shown in
the first of the series of bas-reliefs on the columns of both Trajan

and Antoninus (Fig. 522, *a*, *b*, *c*). Fig. 522, *d*, shows one of the fortified sentry-boxes, which were placed at moderate distances from each other. The sentry who had to watch the enemy's movements stood on the gallery surrounding the building, and gave the signal of alarm by lighting a torch.

Fig. 523 shows two *prætoriani* from a bas-relief in the Louvre, restored, it is true, in rather an arbitrary manner.

Augustus instituted an imperial body-guard of nine cohortes (*cohortes prætoriæ* or *prætoriani milites*), stationed in Rome and the neighbouring towns; by Vitellius this guard was increased to sixteen cohortes or 16,000 men, after-wards reduced again to ten cohortes. Their pay was better and their time of service shorter than that of ordinary legionaries, from whom they were also distinguished by their dress. They had barracks (*castra*) assigned to them in Rome by Tiberius; they frequently exercised the most detrimental influence on political affairs, and on the decisions of the emperor himself. Our

Fig. 523.

group distinctly shows the proud, overbearing demeanour of these soldiers.

The standard had the same importance for Roman soldiers as for those of the Middle Ages and of modern times. By it the soldier was sworn; it formed the rallying-point in the battle; its preservation was a point of honour, and its loss brought contempt on the standard-bearer and the legion. In several cases officers threw the colours into the ranks of the enemy or across his fortifications, so as to excite the valour of the troops in its recovery. In the battle on the Trasimenus, the dying standard-bearer buried the eagle (*signum*) with his sword; and at the defeat of Varus the standard-bearer tore the eagle from its pole to hide himself with it in a bog.

The original form of the standard was that of a bunch of hay* fastened to the point of a lance. This hay was changed for

---

* The bunches of leaves tied together with ribbons frequently seen on the

a cloth (*vexillum*, Fig. 524, *a*) fastened to a transverse piece of wood; this standard belonged to smaller divisions of infantry or, more frequently, of cavalry (see "Col. Traian.," Nos. 6, 16, 66; "Col. Antonin.," Nos. 26, 51, 52). Different from the *vexillum* is the *signum*, consisting of an animal's form (*insigne*) fastened to a pole; the animals usually chosen were a she-wolf, horse, elephant, boar, and capricorn: we also meet with an open hand (Fig. 524, *c*, *d*, *h*, *i*), usually in the standard of a *maniplus*, while that of the *cohors* shows the above-mentioned animals. The common signum of the whole legion was, since Marius, a silver or golden eagle (*aquila*), always with extended wings, and frequently holding a thunderbolt in its fangs. Many signa found

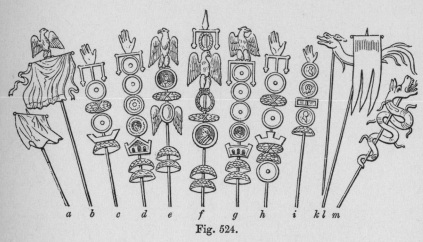

Fig. 524.

on coins or bas-reliefs cannot be classified for want of written evidence. The poles generally showed, besides animals, the images of generals or emperors (Fig. 524, *d*, *f*, *i*), disks (Fig. 524, *c*, *d*, *g*, *h*), walls with gates and battlements (Fig. 524, *d*, *g*, *h*), most likely memorials of conquered cities, *rostra*, and tablets with the number of the cohors written on them. The eagle-standards, however, are without these additional decorations (Fig. 541), showing only occasionally a *vexillum* (Fig. 524, *b*). The chief banner of the Christian emperors was the so-called *labarum*. Eusebius describes it as a long lance with a cross-piece; to the latter a square silk flag

standards of later times are perhaps a reminiscence of those primitive ones, Fig. 524, *a*, *c*, *e*, *f*, *h*.

was attached, into which the images of the reigning emperor and his children were woven. To the point of the lance was fastened a golden crown enclosing the monogram of Christ and the sign of the cross. A banner answering this description, save that the monogram of Christ is inscribed on the flag, is seen on the coins of Constantine the Great, Constantius II., Valens, and others; it was considered as the palladium of the army, and always protected by a guard of fifty picked men.

The standards of barbarian nations greatly differ from those of the Romans. Sometimes they resemble mediæval banners (Fig. 524, *l*), but most frequently they appear in the form of dragons with open mouths, showing rows of sharp teeth (Fig. 524, *k*, *m*); they frequently are seen amongst the trophies on Roman monuments. According to Suidas, these dragons were made of silk; they were inflated with wind through their mouths, emitting it again with a hissing sound through small openings in the tail.

Trumpeters (*tubicines*) and buglers (*cornicines*) formed the military bands. The former had to blow the signals of attack and retreat on their *tuba* or straight trumpet, as also to intone the fanfare at the sacrifice celebrated by the emperor in the presence of the army (see Fig. 498). The signal for the starting of the army was given on the horn (*cornu*), a marching-tune being perhaps played on the same instruments. Buglers, at least, walk in front of the marching army on the column of Antoninus and the arch of Constantine (Fig. 532). The signal of relieving the sentries at night was given on a smaller spiral brass instrument (*bucina*), while the cavalry used a brass instrument (*lituus*) curved like the shaft of an auger (compare Fig. 241, *i*). After the wars with the Germans it seems to have become the custom of the Romans to dress their standard-bearers and buglers in skins of animals (*Wildschur*), after the German fashion (compare Figs. 529, 530).

We now come to the heavy artillery and to the engines destined to protect the storming columns. In case fortifications were attacked without protecting engines, the second rank and those following used to hold their shields horizontally over their heads, while the first rank and the two end men of each rank held theirs vertically in front of them. In this manner a protecting roof resembling the shell of a tortoise (*testudo*) was formed (Fig. 525).

A regular siege of fortified places of course required many preparations. First of all, the besieged city was surrounded by a wall with bastions (*circumvallatio*), so as to cut off supplies. From this circumvallation the further operations were conducted. Sheds (*musculi*) were erected, under cover of which the miners worked and the storming party mounted the breach. Similar engines of protection for bowmen, slingers, and diggers were the *crates* (hurdle), *plutei* (sheds), *vineæ* (literally bowers of vine

Fig. 525.

branches), &c. The besieging wall (*agger*) and the walking towers (*turres ambulatoriæ* or *mobiles*) had to be erected, and the heavy besieging engines (*tormenta*) placed in favourable positions. Of the latter we have descriptions; while, on the other hand, the specimens seen on the columns of Trajan and Antoninus render us but little assistance in forming an idea of their aspect. Accurate descriptions, founded on technical knowledge and scholarly research, we owe to the joint efforts of Rüstow and Köchly.*

* Rüstow and Köchly, "Geschichte des griechischen Kriegswesens," p. 196 *et seq.*, 307 *et seq.*, 378 *et seq.* Rüstow, "Heerwesen and Kriegführung C. Julius Cæsar's," pp. 137—154. "Griechische Kriegsschriftsteller, griechisch und deutsch, mit kritischen und erklärenden Anmerkungen von Köchly und Rüstow."

We mention a few engines occurring on the monuments of the imperial epoch.

After the wall of the beleaguered city had been approached sufficiently, a strong beam, the end of which, cased in iron, had the shape of a ram's head (whence the name *aries, κριός*), was brought into action. The smaller and older battering-ram was knocked against the walls at regular intervals by a number of strong men (see the attack by barbarian soldiers on a Roman fortification on the column of Trajan, Fig. 526). Amongst the smaller battering-rams we also count the *aries subrotatus*, resting on wheels, which were used up to a late period (see Fig. 460, *l*, from a bas-relief on an earthen lamp). The Greeks greatly perfected the battering-ram by introducing, instead of

Fig. 526.

the short beam, a mast composed of several pieces, the whole from 60 to 100 feet long (that invented by Hegetor, of Byzantium, measured 180 feet), which was suspended from a horizontal beam, and put in motion by means of ropes fastened to the beams. Another large battering-ram stood on a sort of bank, and could be pushed backwards and forwards by means of rollers.

To protect the battering-ram, and the soldiers working it, against the enemy's missiles, another engine, the so-called *testudo arietaria* (χελώνη κριοφόρος), was erected—a wooden frame or house (Fig. 527) with a slanting roof, to which frequently a smaller structure of the same kind, with a ram's head protruding from its gable, was appended.

Fig. 527.

Wall-sickles (*falx muralis*) to tear the stones out of the wall, and the wall-drill (*terebra, τρύπανον*), consisting of a battering-ram with a sharp point, were protected by similar roofs. The besieged threw pots of fire, torches of pitch, melted lead, burning arrows, and stones on the storming columns (Fig. 525). They interrupted the work of the besiegers in various manners, tried to set fire to their engines or to crush them. Large stones, suspended by ropes, slings, and

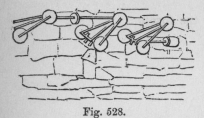

large pincers, were used to catch hold of and divert the ram; sand-bags or mats of reed were let down from the battlements to neutralise its force. An engine of defence difficult to explain appears on the Columna Traiana (Fig. 528). We have already mentioned the *musculus* (χελώνη διορυκτίς), a wooden structure covered with a roof, which, with its straight long side was pushed against the wall, to protect the sappers employed in undermining the foundation of the wall; an engine of this kind, resting on wheels (perhaps a *musculus*), appears on the Columna Antoniniana, pulled and pushed along by horses and soldiers on their march.

It is difficult to give a distinct idea of the working and moving of the large walking towers (*turris ambulatoria, mobilis*, πύργος), although their construction is sufficiently described by ancient authors. According to Diades, a Greek military authority, the smallest tower of this kind had a height of at least 90 feet by a base of 25½ square, and contained ten different stories, connected with each other by steps (*tabulata* or *tecta*, whence *turris contabulata*, στέγη). The beams protruding from the outer surface by several yards supported galleries with wooden battlements, surrounding the whole tower. The highest story, or, in other terms, the upper platform, covered with a roof, was the place for the light artillery, while the water and various contrivances for extinguishing flames were kept in the bottom story. On a level with the wall of the beleaguered city a drawbridge (*pons*, ἐπιβάθρα, σαμβύκη) was constructed to open the way to the top of the enemy's fortifications. About the way of moving the towers nothing appears in ancient writers.

To cross unfordable rivers light boats were used, consisting of wooden frames, timbered on the spot, the sides consisting of hides and osiers. In imperial times each legion carried ready-made pontoons with it. The bridges made of these boats were constructed by first placing the pontoons in their right position, which was done by means of light skiffs. They were anchored by means of pyramidally shaped baskets filled with stones. Beams with boards laid across them connected the boats with each other; wooden rails added to the firmness of the structure, and prevented accidents through falling over the edge of the bridge. Sometimes walking-towers were placed on one end of the bridge to protect it against the enemy. Fig. 529 illustrates the crossing of the Danube by the Roman army on a bridge constructed by the Emperor Trajan.

Fig. 529.

We add a representation of an *allocutio*, or speech of the general to his army (Fig. 530), a subject frequently treated on coins, and occurring on the columns of Trajan and Antoninus. Surrounded by his officers, standard-bearers, &c., the emperor used to address the army from a raised standpoint, praising, blaming, or encouraging to new deeds of valour, according to circumstances; from here he pronounced the punishment of cowardice, which was at once executed by his lictors*; from here

---

* We add a few remarks about the *fasces*, seen in the hands of the lictors, Fig. 530 (compare Fig. 540). The fasces were bundles of rods (*virgæ*) of elm or birch-wood, tied together round the handle of an axe (*securis*) with (most likely red) straps. The iron of the axe, which was the executioner's tool, protruded from the sticks. The fasces were carried on their left shoulders by the lictors, who walked in front of certain magistrates, making room for them, and compelling all people to move out of the way (*summovere*), barring Vestals and Roman matrons. To about

he divided the prizes awarded by him, or the army itself, to the bravest among them.

108. Military decorations and rewards of valour (*dona, præmia militaria*) occur in many forms amongst the Romans. We pass over such *dona* as a share of the booty, advancement, or the honourable mentioning of a soldier's name before the assembled

Fig. 580.

legion. The highest military decoration was the crown of grass (*corona graminea*), awarded, according to Pliny ("Hist. Nat.," XXII. 3, 4), only after a desperate deed of valour, and by common consent of the whole army. "All other rewards were given by the general to the soldiers, but this the soldiers gave to their leader. It was also called crown of siege (*corona obsidionalis*)

the end of the Republic, when a special executioner was appointed, the lictors inflicted capital punishment. The king was entitled to twelve fasces, the same number being granted to the consuls (after the passing of P. Valerius Publicola's law "de provocatione ad populum," only one of the two consuls within the walls of Rome was allowed to have the axe carried in front of him), or the officials endowed with *consularis potestas*, also to *decemviri*, war-tribunes, and proconsuls outside Rome. The dictator was entitled to twenty-four lictors, the magister equitum appointed by him to six, the Roman prætor to two, the provincial prætor to six, an equal number being allowed to proprætors. Since 42 B.C., the Flamen Dialis and the Vestals also were entitled to one lictor each. In case a higher official met his inferior in the street, he was saluted by the lictors of the latter withdrawing the axe and lowering the fasces (*fasces submittere*).

in case a whole camp had been delivered from a siege or dishonourable terms. It was composed of green herbs picked on the spot where the besieged had been delivered." This honour was conferred only in very rare cases.

The *corona triumphalis*, a laurel crown, was given to generals returning in triumph from a victorious campaign. Originally it was made of real leaves, afterwards imitated in gold; after Cæsar's dictatorship it became the diadem of the emperors, worn by them in the theatre and circus. The radiated crown (*corona radiata*), at first a decoration of the images of the dead, occurs after Nero's time on senatorial coins, but did not become the imperial crown till the third century. The myrtle crown (*corona myrtea*), worn by the generals at the so-called *ovatio* (small triumph, whence its other name *ovalis*), resembles the triumphal crown. The rescue of a citizen from the throng of battle was rewarded with the *corona civica*, made of oak-leaves. The heads of Augustus and Galba are crowned with it on several coins; still more frequently we see it on the reverses of imperial coins, with the surrounding motto: OB CIVES SERVATOS. He who first mounted the walls of a besieged city or camp received the golden *corona muralis*, also called *castrensis* or *vallaris*. The *corona rostrata, navalis*, or *classica* was the reward of him who first boarded the enemy's vessel. It was awarded on rare occasions, and only to commanders. Agrippa received it after the double victory of Actium. We see it, on a gold coin, adorning the head of Agrippa, a mural crown being placed on the top of the *corona navalis;* the latter, in the form of a laurel-wreath studded with rostra, also appears on a bronze coin of the city of Nikopolis, founded by Augustus after the battle of Actium.

Another class of decorations adorned the chest of the brave soldier. We first mention the chain of honour (*torques*), originally worn by barbarian leaders (we remind the reader of the single combat of T. Manlius with a Gallic warrior, to which he owed his surname Torquatus), but afterwards adopted by the Romans, who distinguished a heavy kind (*torques* proper) and a lighter kind (*catellæ*), wound several times round the neck and hanging down over the chest. To these we add the decorations in our modern sense, *i.e.* small round silver tablets (*phaleræ*) adorned with bas-reliefs, resembling the tablets found on the standard of the cohortes.

Since Caracalla they consisted of large gold medals, frequently adorned with jewels, and fastened by means of straps across the cuirass, as is proved by the *phaleræ* found on the Lauersfort estate, near Crefeld. We finally name amongst signs of honour, armrings (*armillæ*), the *hasta pura* (a lance of precious metal with a button instead of a point), and the different kinds of

vexilla, named according to their colours *pura, argentea, cærulea,* or *bicolora.* The tombstones of the centurio Q. Sertorius, at Verona, of the standard-bearer, Cn. Musius, at Mayence, and of the *legatus* Manius Cælius, killed in the battle lost by Varus (Fig. 531), show the profusion with which emperors and generals rewarded military merit.

Fig. 531.

Cælius is adorned with one or even two civic crowns, his neck is encircled with a massive torques; two heavy rings, held by a ribbon laid across the shoulders, hang down on his chest, which is adorned besides with five medals attached to straps; he also wears bracelets round his knuckles. L. Siccius Denatus, the tribune of the people, was rewarded for his valour, proved in one hundred and twenty battles, with 22 *hastæ puræ*, 25 *phaleræ*, 83 *torques*, 160 *armillæ*, and 26 *coronæ*, viz. 14 *civicæ*, 8 *aureæ*, 3 *murales*, and one *obsidionalis.*

109. The highest reward of the commander was the triumphal entrance. At first it was awarded by senate and people to real merit in the field, and its arrangement was simple and dignified; but soon it became an opportunity of displaying the results of insatiable Roman rapacity and love of conquest. Only the dictators, consuls, prætors, and, in late republican times, occasionally legates, were permitted by the senate to enter Rome in triumph, the permission to the legate being granted only in case he had commanded independently (*suis auspiciis*), and conducted the army to Rome from a victorious campaign *in sua provincia.* As in later times it was impossible to conduct the whole army from distant provinces to Rome, the last-mentioned condition was dispensed with, the claim of the commander to a triumph being

acknowledged in case in one of the battles gained by him 5,000 enemies had been killed. The senate granted the expenses necessary for the procession after the quæstor urbanus had examined and confirmed the commander's claims. Streets and squares through which the procession had to pass were festively adorned. The temples were opened, and incense burnt on the altars. Improvised stands were erected in the street, filled with festive crowds shouting "Io triumphe!" The commander, in the meantime, collected his troops near the temples of Bellona and Apollo, outside the gates of Rome; the *imperium* within the walls being exceptionally granted him during the triumph. The victor was met at the *porta triumphalis* by the senate, the city magistrates, and numerous citizens, who took the lead of the procession, while lictors opened a way through the crowd. After the city dignitaries followed tibicines, after them the booty, consisting of armour, standards arranged as trophies, also models of the cities or ships taken from the enemy, and pictures of battles, tablets with the deeds of the victor inscribed on them, statues personifying the rivers and towns of the subjected country—all these being carried by crowned soldiers at the points of long lances or on portable stands (*furculæ*); we further mention treasures of art, valuable plate and vases, silver and gold coins, and products of the conquered soil. Fettered kings, princes, and nobles followed, doomed to detention in the Mamertine prison. Next came sacrificial oxen with gilt horns, accompanied by priests; and finally, preceded by singers, musicians, and jesters, the triumphal chariot drawn by four horses. Clad in a toga picta and the tunica palmata, temporarily taken from the statue of the Capitoline Jupiter, the triumphator stood in his chariot holding the eagle-crowned ivory sceptre* in his hand, while a servus publicus standing behind him held the corona triumphalis over his head. The army brought up the rear of the procession, which moved from the Campus Martius through the circus of Flaminius to the Porta Carmentalis, and thence, by way of the Velabrum and the Circus Maximus, the Via Sacra and the Forum,

---

* According to a custom introduced by Augustus, the emperors wore a crown and held a branch of laurel taken from a grove which that emperor had planted at the ninth milestone of the Via Flaminia, near the Villa of Livia. After the triumph, the laurel-branch was planted again.

to the Capitol. Here the triumphator deposited his golden crown
in the lap of the Capitoline Jupiter, and sacrificed the usual
suovetaurilia. A festive meal concluded the day. In the last
centuries of the Republic, when the art-treasures of Greece and
the wealth of the East were paraded in these processions, one day

Fig. 534.   Fig. 533.   Fig. 532.

was found insufficient. The triumph of Sulla, for instance, lasted
two; that of Æmilius Paullus, after his victory over Perseus,
three days. The last triumph of a Roman general was that
granted to Octavianus, after his victory over Antonius. After this
the emperors reserved the right of the triumphal entrance to

Fig. 535.

themselves, the *ornamenta triumphalia,* consisting of the toga
picta, the tunica palmata, the Scipio eburneus, the sella curulis, the
currus triumphalis, and the corona laurea being granted to the
generals instead. The emperors immortalised their feats by the

erection of triumphal arches. Our illustrations of the triumphs
are taken from the bas-reliefs of several imperial monuments, being
arranged in the order indicated above. The buglers opening the
procession (Fig. 532) are taken from the arch of Constantine, as

Fig. 536.

are also the soldiers following them, who carry Victories and other
statuettes (Fig. 533). The next following figure of a warrior and
his tropæum (Fig. 534) we have had to compose from various statues
for want of an original suiting our purpose; the soldier himself is

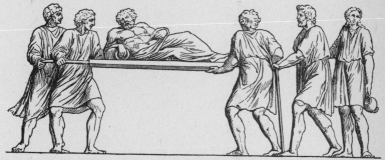

Fig. 537.

from the arch of Severus, the trophy from the theatre of Orange.
Fig. 534, soldiers with carts containing stores, is taken from the
column of Severus: we add it for the sake of completeness.
Fig. 536, from the arch of Titus, shows soldiers carrying the

treasure of the temple of Jerusalem : in front the golden table of
sacrifice, the chalice, the *tubæ* used at the Jewish service, and
further back the seven-branched candlestick.   Magistrates clad in
the toga accompany these valuable pieces of booty.   Fig. 537,

Fig. 538.   Fig. 539.

from the same arch, shows the river-god Jordan in a similar
position to those of Rhenus and Nilus in the Vatican.   The group
of fettered Parthian princes (Fig. 538) is taken from the arch of
the Goldsmiths.   Fig. 539, from the arch of Titus, shows an ox

Fig. 540.

led by a butcher and accompanied by priests.   Fig. 540, lastly,
shows the emperor, with the sceptre in his right, in his triumphal
chariot.   The corona triumphalis is held over his head by the
Goddess of Victory, while Roma leads the horses of the quadriga.

Lictors and senators surround the chariot. Sometimes the chariot was drawn by four elephants, as is proved by monumental (coins) and written evidence. Fig. 541, from the arch of Constantine, shows the sacrifice performed by Trajan in the presence of his army.

The *ovatio* was granted for less important conquests, or to a general for victories not won *suis auspiciis*. The victor, adorned with the toga prætexta and the myrtle crown, originally used to walk; in later times he rode on horseback.

Fig. 541.

110. *Justa facere* or *ferre* was the expression used for doing the last honour to the dead (compare the Greek expressions τὰ δίκαια and τὰ νόμιμα, § 60). The nearest relative used to receive the last breath of the dying person in a kiss (*extremum spiritum ore excipere*); his hand also closed the eyes and the mouth of the deceased, so as to produce a peaceful impression of death. After this, the name of the deceased or a wail was uttered several times by those present, so as to make sure of his death, after which the last farewell (*extremum vale*) was said (*conclamatio*).

The preparation for the burial naturally varied according to the wealth of the owner. The body of a poor person was, after the usual ablutions, put on a bier (*sandapila*) and carried at night by the *vespillones* (carriers of corpses) to the common burial-ground outside the Esquiline gate—a quarter chosen by Horace for the scene of Canidia's conjurings, but transformed by Mæcenas into a park (*horti Mæcenatiani*). Burial-clubs (*collegia tenuiorum*) were formed by the poorer classes, from whose funds, supplied by annual contributions, a certain sum was paid to the surviving families of the members. The burials of the wealthy classes were conducted on a more splendid scale. The death was first announced to the *libitinarius* (an official of the temple of Venus Libitina), who inserted the name in the register of deaths (a

register of births was kept at the temple of Venus Lucina). The
libitinarius furnished for payment the utensils and slaves necessary for the preparation and burial of the corpse. The corpse was
taken from the death-bed and laid on the ground (*deponere*), where
it was washed with hot water and anointed by the *pollinctor*,
partly in order to take away from the terror of death, partly to
stop the decomposition, because amongst well-to-do people it was
kept for seven days. Clad in a toga and adorned with the richest
garments, the body was placed on the *lectus funebris*, a bed entirely
made of ivory, or at least resting on ivory legs, over which purple
blankets embroidered with gold were spread. Flowers and foliage
adorned the bed, but not the body itself, as was the custom
amongst the Greeks; only crowns of honour, earned during their
lifetime, were deposited in the graves of dead persons, and have
repeatedly been discovered there, being made of very thin gold
leaf. The lectus funebris was put in the atrium of the house,
with the foot end turned towards the door, and a pan with
incense was placed by its side. Branches of cypress and fir-trees
were fastened in front of the house as signs of mourning.

After having been exhibited for seven days, the body was buried
in the forenoon, when the streets were filled with the bustle of life,
and when the largest attendance of invited guests and spectators
might be expected. In case the funeral was connected with public
games, a herald solicited the attendance of the people. A public
burial of this kind was called *funus indictivum* or *funus publicum*.
The following is the formula used by the public crier in inviting
the spectators: " *Ollus Quiris leto datus est. Exsequias (L. Titio.
L. filio) ire cui commodum est, iam tempus est. Ollus ex ædibus
effertur.*" The procession was arranged in front of the house of
the deceased by the *dissignator*, with the aid of an *accensus* and of
one or several lictors to keep order. Ten tibicines (this was the
highest number permitted by the law of the twelve tablets)
opened the procession, followed, at least in older times, by female
mourners (*præficæ*) singing plaintive songs (*næniæ, mortualia*) in
honour of the deceased. A band of actors following served to
attract and entertain the crowd; they recited passages from tragic
poets with reference to the deceased, or they acted comic scenes,
one amongst their number sometimes mimicking the peculiarities
of the dead person. In front of the deceased, the wax masks of

his ancestors were worn by persons appointed for the purpose; the historic costume of the dead person, including even his insignia, had to be rendered exactly. The collateral lines of old families used to send their ancestors to the funeral of a relative, while *parvenus* frequently paraded images of fictitious persons. The bier was carried by the nearest relatives, or by the slaves liberated by the last will of the deceased. Other relatives, friends, and freedmen surrounded the bier in black garments without gold ornaments. In imperial times, when the wearing of colours had become customary, white was considered mourning, at least for women. The procession went to the Forum, where the bier was set down in front of the rostra, whereat the wearers of the ancestral masks sat down on the sellæ curules, and one of the relatives mounted the tribune to deliver an oration (*laudatio funebris*) in honour of the deceased and of his ancestors, whose images were present. The expression of Cicero as to the earlier Greek funeral eulogiums, "*nam mentiri nefas habebatur,*" was not strictly acted upon by the Romans, their orators refraining at least from all censure. After the speech was over, the procession proceeded to the burial-place in the order described.

The corpse was either placed in a sarcophagus (*arca, capulus*) and deposited in a grave made of brick or stone, according to the older custom* retained by some patrician families, for instance, by the Cornelii, up to a late period, or it was burnt, and the ashes, collected in an urn, deposited in the grave-chamber (see § 77). Cremation is said to have been introduced by Sulla, who feared that his body would be defiled by the people. Inhumation in coffins (*humatio*), however, by no means ceased; both kinds of burial existed together, no law being made on the subject. Each burial-place had a separate enclosure for burning the bodies (*ustrinum*), private ustrina being attached to large family-graves where there was no law to prevent it. In the ustrinum the pyre (*pyra, rogus*) was erected, the height and decorations of which again depended upon the wealth of the family. It consisted of pieces of wood and other combustible materials, piled up in the shape of an altar, on which the bier with the body was placed, after having

* According to Pliny ("Hist. Nat.," II. 98 ; compare XXXVI. 27), there existed near Assos, in Troas, a kind of stone which, made into coffins, destroyed the corpse in forty days, excepting the teeth, and which therefore was called flesh-eater (*sarcophagos*).

been covered with balsam, incense, utensils, ornaments, or weapons. The pile was ignited by one of the nearest relatives or friends, with face averted, the bystanders raising a *conclamatio*.

After the pile was consumed (*bustum*) the hot ashes were extinguished with wine, and the bones collected by the relatives (amidst acclamations to the manes of the deceased) in the folds of their mourning robes (*ossilegium*) ; a previous washing of the hands was, of course, not forgotten. The remains were sprinkled with milk and wine, then dried with linen, and mixed with scents, after which preparations they were enclosed in an urn (*ossa condere*), to be afterwards deposited in the grave-chamber. The last farewell was spoken by those present in the words : "*Have anima candida,*" or "*Terra tibi levis sit,*" or "*Molliter cubent ossa;* " and after the usual lustrations had been performed the mourners separated. Urns (*urna, olla ossuaria*), frequently in the form of hydriæ, or (in Etruscan graves) of cinerary boxes with covers to them, are found in most of the grave-chambers described in § 77 *et seq.*, as also in the columbaria (Fig. 401 *et seq.*) and sarcophagi : they are generally made of burnt clay, travertine, marble, alabaster, porphyry, or bronze. We also meet with glass urns, mostly protected by leaden cases of a shape similar to that of the urn : three urns of this kind have been found in the above-mentioned grave of Nævoleia Tyche at Pompeii.

The second offering to the manes, and a meal connected with it, took place on the ninth day after the burial (*novemdialia, feriæ novemdiales*), in accordance with the Greek custom. On the steps of the grave-monument a simple meal (*epulæ funebres*), consisting of milk, honey, oil, and blood of the sacrificed animals, was prepared ; larger tombs had a separate *triclinium funebre* attached to them, where the meal was taken. The limited space of the necropolis did not admit of numerous guests, for which reason wealthy people (particularly in cases where games were connected with the funeral) used to distribute meat (*viscerationes*), in later times money, amongst the people. The sacrifices to the manes were repeated by the relatives on the anniversary of the birth or death of the deceased (*parentalia*) : the 21st of February of each year was the day of the dead celebrated by the whole people by sacrifices to the manes (*feralia*).

The funeral of the emperor was arranged in the grandest way,

particularly if his *consecratio* by the senate was connected with
it. Cæsar was the first Roman received amongst the gods as
Divus Julius by decree of the senate : Octavianus instituted a
permanent worship of this divinity. The same honour after
death was awarded to Augustus himself, and after him to many
emperors and empresses down to Constantine the Great ; their
names appear on coins marked as consecration-medals by the
word CONSECRATIO inscribed on them. Herodian (IV. 3)
gives a full account of the ceremony of consecration. " It is the
Roman custom," he says, " to consecrate the emperors who leave
heirs. The mortal remains are buried, according to custom, in a
splendid manner ; but the wax image of the emperor is placed on
an ivory bed covered with gold-embroidered carpets in front of
the palace. The expression of the face is that of one dangerously
ill. To the left side of the bed stand, during greater part of the
day, the members of the senate ; to the right the ladies entitled
by birth or marriage to appear at court, in the usual simple
white mourning dresses, without gold ornaments or necklaces.
This ceremony lasts seven days, during which time the imperial
physicians daily approach the bed as if to examine the patient,
who, of course, is declining rapidly. At last they declare the
emperor dead ; after which the bier is carried by the highest-born
knights and the younger senators through the Via Sacra to the
old Forum, and there deposited on a scaffolding built in the manner
of a terrace. On one side stand young patricians, on the other
noble ladies, intoning hymns and pæans in honour of the deceased
to a solemn, sad tune ; after which the bier is taken up again and
carried to the Campus Martius. A
wooden structure in the form of a house
has been erected on large blocks of wood
on a square base ; the inside has been
filled with dry sticks ; the outside is adorned
with gold - embroidered carpets, ivory
statues, and various sculptures. The bottom story, a little lower than the second,
shows the same form and ornamentation as
this ; it has open doors and windows: above
these two stories rise others, growing

Fig. 542.

narrow towards the top like a pyramid (Fig. 542). The whole

structure might be compared to the lighthouses (φάροι) erected
in harbours. The bier is placed in the second story, spices,
incense, odoriferous fruits, and herbs being heaped round it.
After the whole room has been filled with incense, the knights
move in procession round the whole structure, and perform some
military evolutions; they are followed by chariots filled with
persons wearing masks, and clad in purple robes, who represent
historic characters, such as celebrated generals and kings. After
these ceremonies are over the heir to the throne throws a torch
into the house, into which, at the same time, flames are dashed
from all sides, which, fed by the combustible materials and the
incense, soon begin to devour the whole building. At this juncture an eagle rises into the air from the highest story as from a
lofty battlement, and carries, according to the idea of the Romans,
the soul of the dead emperor to heaven (Fig. 543); from that
moment he partakes of the honours of the gods."

Fig. 543.

LIST OF ILLUSTRATIONS.

INDEX OF TERMS.

THE END.